Selected Readings on Information Technology Management:
Contemporary Issues

George Kelley
University of Massachusetts, Boston, USA

INFORMATION SCIENCE REFERENCE

Hershey · New York

Director of Editorial Content:	Kristin Klinger
Managing Development Editor:	Kristin M. Roth
Senior Managing Editor:	Jennifer Neidig
Managing Editor:	Jamie Snavely
Assistant Managing Editor:	Carole Coulson
Typesetter:	Lindsay Bergman
Cover Design:	Lisa Tosheff
Printed at:	Yurchak Printing Inc.

Published in the United States of America by
Information Science Reference (an imprint of IGI Global)
701 E. Chocolate Avenue, Suite 200
Hershey PA 17033
Tel: 717-533-8845
Fax: 717-533-8661
E-mail: cust@igi-global.com
Web site: http://www.igi-global.com

and in the United Kingdom by
Information Science Reference (an imprint of IGI Global)
3 Henrietta Street
Covent Garden
London WC2E 8LU
Tel: 44 20 7240 0856
Fax: 44 20 7379 0609
Web site: http://www.eurospanbookstore.com

Library of Congress Cataloging-in-Publication Data

Selected readings on information technology management : contemporary issues / George Kelley, editor.

   p. cm.

  Summary: "This book presents quality articles focused on key issues concerning the management and utilization of information technology"--Provided by publisher.

  Includes bibliographical references and index.

  ISBN 978-1-60566-092-9 (hbk.) -- ISBN 978-1-60566-093-6 (ebook)

  1. Information technology--Management. 2. Information resources management. I. Kelley, George, 1960-

  HD30.2.S4545 2008

  658.4'038--dc22

                        2008019460

British Cataloguing in Publication Data
A Cataloguing in Publication record for this book is available from the British Library.

All work contributed to this book set is original material. The views expressed in this book are those of the authors, but not necessarily of the publisher.

Table of Contents

Section II
Development and Design Methodologies

Section III
Tools and Technologies

Detailed Table of Contents

Section I
Fundamental Concepts and Theories

Reference modeling is located in a field of conflict between research and practice. Despite the array of theoretical concepts, there is still a deficit in knowledge about the use and problems inherent in the implementation of reference models. Accordingly, in the past years the supply-sided development of reference models predominant in the science world has distanced itself from their demand-sided use in business and administration. This chapter analyzes the causes of these problems and presents a solution in the form of an integrative approach to computer-supported management of reference models.

Information and knowledge have become a crucial resource in our knowledge-based, computer-mediated economy. But knowledge is primarily a social phenomenon, on which computer processing has had only a limited impact so far, in spite of impressive advances. In this context have recently appeared various collaborative systems that promise to give access to socially situated information. The authors of this chapter argue that a prior analysis of the social context is necessary for a better understanding of the whole domain of collaborative software. They examine the variety and functions of information in modern society, where collaborative information management is now the dominant type of occupation.

E-governance uses Internet and communication technologies to automate governance in innovative ways, so that it becomes more efficient, more cost-effective, and empowers the human race even more.

The emergence of Web-services technologies, the continually proliferating computer networks, and the irreversible migration towards digital information strongly confirm the view that e-governance is here to stay. The eventual success of any e-governance project is intimately linked to the methodology used, and to that complex mesh between men, machines, and mindsets.

Chapter IV

James Courtney, University of Central Florida, USA
Yasmin Merali, Warwick Business School, UK
David Paradice, Florida State University, USA
Eleanor Wynn, Intel Corporation Information Technology, USA

This chapter addresses complexity in information systems. It defines how complexity can be used to inform information systems research, and how some individuals and organizations are using notions of complexity. Some organizations are dealing with technical and physical infrastructure complexity, as well as the application of complexity in specific areas such as supply chain management and network management. The concepts and ideas in this chapter are relevant to the integration of complexity into information systems research.

Section II
Development and Design Methodologies

Chapter V

Murray E. Jennex, San Diego State University, USA
Lorne Olfman, Claremont Graduate University, USA

This chapter describes a knowledge management (KM) success model that is derived from observations generated through a longitudinal study of KM in an engineering organization and KM success factors found in the literature, which were modified by the application of these observations and success factors in various projects. The DeLone and McLean (1992, 2003) IS Success Model was used as a framework for the model, since it was found to fit the observed success criteria and provided an accepted theoretical basis for the proposed model.

Chapter VI

Jakob Holden Iversen, University of Wisconsin Oshkosh, USA
Lars Mathiassen, Georgia State University, USA
Peter Axel Nielsen, Aalborg University, Denmark

This chapter shows how action research can help practitioners develop IT risk management approaches that are tailored to their organization and the specific issues they face. Based on literature and practical experience, the authors present a method for developing risk management approaches to use in real-world innovation projects. The chapter illustrates the method by presenting the results of developing a risk management approach for software process improvement projects in a software organization.

Chapter VII

This chapter introduces a generic modeling approach that explicitly represents the perspectives of stakeholders and their evolution traversing a collaborative process. This approach provides a mechanism to analytically identify the interdependencies among stakeholders and to detect conflicts and reveal their intricate causes and effects. Collaboration is thus improved through efficient knowledge management. This chapter also describes a Web-based information system that uses the perspective model and the social network analysis methodology to support knowledge management within collaboration.

Chapter VIII

This chapter introduces a virtual enterprise architecture for environmental information management, integration and dissemination. On a daily basis, our knowledge related to ecological phenomena, the degradation of the natural environment and the sustainability of human activity impact is growing, and as a consequence, raises the need for effective environmental knowledge exchange and reuse. In this work, a solution among collaborating peers forming a virtual enterprise is investigated. Following an analysis of the main stakeholders, a service-oriented architecture is proposed. Technical implementation options, using Web services or software agents, are considered and issues related to environmental information management, ownership and standardization are discussed.

Section III
Tools and Technologies

Chapter IX

This chapter asserts that almost any public-sector task employing a computer can be accomplished more efficiently with a variety of tools rather than any single one. Basic tools include word processing, spreadsheet, statistics, and database-management programs. Beyond these, Web authoring software, presentation software, graphics, project-planning and -management software, decision analysis, and geographic information systems can be helpful depending upon the job at hand.

Chapter X

This chapter focuses on business process design as a middle point between requirement elicitation and implementation of a Web information system. The authors face the problems of deciding which notation to adopt in order to represent the business process in a simple manner and creating a formal representation of the design in a machine-readable format. The authors adopt Semantic Web technology to represent a business process and explain how this technology has been used to reach their goals.

Within this selection, the reader is introduced to various key ideas in cryptography without exploring technicalities. The chapter discusses the need for use of cryptography in electronic communications, and describes the symmetric key techniques as well as public key cryptosystems. Digital signatures, along with data integrity and data authentication are also discussed.

Chapter XII

Finding the right software is often hindered by different criteria as well as by technology changes. Within this chapter, the authors describes performing an analytic hierarchy process (AHP) analysis using Expert Choice to determine which data mining package was most suitable for their use. Deliberating a dozen alternatives and objectives led them to a series of pair-wise comparisons. When further synthesizing the results, Expert Choice helped them provide a clear rationale for the decision. Data mining technology is changing very rapidly, so the current article focused only on the major suppliers typically available in the market place. The method and the process that the authors used can be easily applied to analyze and compare other data mining software or knowledge management initiatives.

Section IV
Utilization and Application

Chapter XIII

The development of applications by end users has become an integral part of organizational information provision. It has been established that there are both benefits and risks associated with end-user development, particularly in the areas of spreadsheets and databases. Web development tools are enabling a new kind of end-user development. The fact that Web page creation may impact, not only locally but also globally, significantly raises the importance of this type of end-user application development. This chapter reports on the extent of Web page development amongst end users and investigates their perceptions of the benefits and risks of end-user Web development relative to those associated with spreadsheet development and explores approaches to reducing the risks.

Federica Paganelli, University of Florence, Italy
Maria Chiara Pettenati, University of Florence, Italy
Dino Giuli, University of Florence, Italy

Effectively managing documents is a strategic requirement for every organization. Available document management systems (DMSs) often lack effective functions for automatic document management. This chapter proposes a metadata model, the DMSML (Document Management and Sharing Markup Language) to enable and to ease unstructured document management by supporting the design of DMSs. The authors argue that the extensive use of this metadata language will render organizational information explicit, promoting information reuse and interoperability in a more profitable way than what is guaranteed by proprietary DMSs.

Mary C. Jones, University of North Texas, USA
Randall Young, University of North Texas, USA

This chapter presents the results of an exploratory study of Fortune 1000 firms and their enterprise resource planning (ERP) usage, as well as benefits and changes they have realized from ERP. The study empirically examines ERP in these organizations to provide insight into various aspects that firms can use to evaluate how they are managing their ERP systems. Findings provide information about functionality implemented, extent to which benefits are realized, extent of ERP-related organizational changes firms have realized, and the way firms measure ERP success. The study also addresses the extent to which various types of ERP software have been implemented and whether there is a relationship between type of software and benefits.

Murali Raman, Multimedia University, Malaysia
Terry Ryan, Claremont Graduate University, USA
Lorne Olfman, Claremont Graduate University, USA

This chapter concerns the design and implementation of an information system, using Wiki technology to improve the emergency preparedness efforts of the Claremont University Consortium. Managing knowledge across the various entities involved in such efforts is critical. This includes having the right set of information that is timely and relevant and that is governed by an effective communication process. This chapter suggests that Wiki technology might be useful to support knowledge management in the context of emergency preparedness within organizations. However, issues such as training in the use of a system(s), a knowledge-sharing culture among entities involved in emergency preparedness, and a fit between task and technology/system must be there in order to support emergency preparedness activities that are given such structures.

Section V
Critical Issues

Chapter XVII

Aileen Cater-Steel, University of Southern Queensland, Australia
Mark Toleman, University of Southern Queensland, Australia

Service management standards such as the IT Infrastructure Library (ITIL), and now ISO/IEC 20000, provide guidance and tools for the effective management and control of IT service delivery. These standards are of increasing importance to organizations around the globe. Education about these standards and possibilities for training IT staff are, therefore, important. This chapter considers the training offered and the requirement for education related to IT service management. Benefits to universities, graduates, and industry are numerous including increases in student numbers, enhanced employment options for graduates, and improved IT service quality, but there are challenges too, in particular, how to effectively transfer the knowledge to students who have not experienced the IT service environment firsthand.

Chapter XVIII

Lynn Crawford, University of Technology – Sydney, Australia
Julien Pollack, University of Technology – Sydney, Australia

Professional standards are a significant issue for professions such as IT and Project Management, where certification and licensure are either necessary to practice or to demonstrate individual competence and capability. In many professions there is no basis for international reciprocity of professional standards. This chapter documents the development of a standard for global reciprocity between already existing professional standards in the field of Project Management. This discussion addresses different approaches to standardisation, how common issues in the standardisation process have been addressed, and how the hindering influence of the professional associations' proprietorial interest was avoided.

Chapter XIX

Bruce Rocheleau, Northern Illinois University, USA

This chapter provides examples of the politics of managing information in public organizations by studying both its internal and external aspects. Within the organization, politics is involved in structuring decision making, struggles over purchases of hardware and software, interdepartmental sharing of information, and the flow of communications such as e-mail among employees. The chapter analyzes examples of each of these internal aspects of politics. The chapter also discusses evidence concerning whether political appointees or career administrators are more effective as information managers.

The chapter proposes a simple framework termed 'knowledge fusion' to extend the rigor and relevance of knowledge management (KM). It points to some gaps in the current body of knowledge about KM, and provides a parsimonious set of 'partitions' that link to and from traditional knowledge management research and practice.

Knowledge intensive applications rely on the usage of knowledge artifacts, called patterns, to represent in a compact and semantically rich way, huge quantities of heterogeneous raw data. Due to characteristics of patterns, specific systems are required for pattern management in order to model, store, retrieve, and manipulate patterns in an efficient and effective way. Several theoretical and industrial approaches have already been proposed for pattern management. However, no critical comparison of the existing approaches has been proposed so far. The aim of this chapter is to provide such a comparison. In particular, specific issues concerning pattern management systems, pattern models and pattern languages are discussed. Several parameters are also identified that will be used in evaluating the effectiveness of theoretical and industrial proposals.

Section VI
Emerging Trends

The widespread use and expansion of the World Wide Web has revolutionized the discovery, access, and retrieval of information. The Internet has become the doorway to a vast information base and has leveraged the access to information through standard protocols and technologies like HyperText Markup Language (HTML), active server pages (ASP), Java server pages (JSP), Web databases, and Web services. Web services are software applications that are accessible over the World Wide Web through standard communication protocols. A Web service typically has a Web-accessible interface for its clients at the front end, and is connected to a database system and other related application suites at the back end. The true success of this technology largely depends on the efficient management of the various components forming the backbone of a Web service system. This chapter presents an overview and the state of the art of various management approaches, models, and architectures for Web services systems toward achieving quality of service (QoS) in Web data access.

Doing business on the Internet has many opportunities along with many risks. This chapter focuses on a series of risks of legal liability arising from e-mail and Internet activities that are a common part of many e-businesses. E-business not only exposes companies to new types of liability risk, but also increases the potential number of claims and the complexity of dealing with those claims. The international nature of the Internet, together with a lack of uniformity of laws governing the same activities in different countries, means that companies need to proceed with caution.

Chapter XXIV

Knowledge is increasingly being viewed as a critical component for organizations. It is largely people-based and the characteristics of groups of individuals, in the form of organizational cultures, may play a key role in the factors that lead to either the acceptance or rejection of knowledge management systems (KMS). The primary objective of this research is to explore how dimensions of organizational culture influence factors that lead to the acceptance of KMS. The current study examined the effects of three dimensions of organizational culture through a research model that was tested and analyzed utilizing a field survey of corporate knowledge management users. Our results indicated that both process-oriented and open communication system organizational cultures significantly influenced the factors that led to the acceptance of KMS.

This study was conducted to examine the relationships that may exist between IT infrastructure capabilities (ITC), business process improvements (BPI), and IT governance-related constructs such as the reporting relationship between the chief executive officer (CEO) and chief information officer (CIO), and senior management support of IT and BPI projects. Using a sample of multinational and Hong Kong-listed firms operating in Greater China, this study yielded empirical support for the perceived achievement of capabilities in some dimensions of the IT infrastructure in the companies under study.

A large number of tools are available in the software industry to support different aspects of knowledge management (KM). Some comprehensive applications and vendors try to offer global solutions to KM needs; other tools are highly specialized. In this chapter, state-of-the-art KM tools grouped by specific classification areas and functionalities are described. Trends and integration efforts are detailed with a focus on identifying current and future software and market evolution.

Prologue

Sholie iwanded the door open and settled in with eager anticipation. Her iwand celebrated her on time arrival with a reassuring two-tone chime. The immersion displays around her told the story. Dubai in 2030 had much professional appeal to a promising 22 year old. "As if."

The audio receiver behind her left ear chirped a question. Something about googling. The iwand autosynched in beat with the question. The answer came in real time. Sholie's eyes rolled in dismay. "As if."

Sholie learned from her iwand that googling was something you once did with 'keywords'. "Once popular with parents" the iwand added helpfully. Not that Sholie could fathom why from the rest of the explanation. "Old technology" the iwand continued, "built around (*q.v., arch.*) 'SQL database lookups'."

The iwand's ergometric sensors registered Sholie's frustration. And switched to speech, mock derisive: "Googling was a way to generate lists of links ... neatly ordered like a bowl of spaghetti!"

Oh, Sholie laughs enlightened. Like in early versions of my iwand. The ones with the dial-up voice channel and that annoying click-based browser. Nothing like the "I-want" universal remote immediacy of her iwand. "Enough!" she decides.

As the door swooshed shut behind her, Sholie's iwand came to life with an insistent color pattern. Her friends in Lagos and Melbourne wanted to know if she would join them at a virtual party in Cancun. Her eyes lit up too. "As if."

TOOLS OF THE DAY

Every generation is defined by the characteristic tool of its day. From the plow to the loom to the computer took centuries. Computers to iwands, only a few decades. Sholie was born today, the very moment you picked up this book. What part will you play that fateful day in her life in 2030?

Electrification, telephony, radio and TV were all important contributions of the 20th century. So were the motherboard and the CPU, the computer keyboard and the mouse, disk drives and CRT displays, routers and network adapters. They prepared the infrastructure of which you as an IT professional are now the steward.

You must now act to use and expand the Internet to its full potential. Soon every person on the planet will become heavily dependent on your insights, skills and decisions as an IT professional. Your personal contribution as an IT professional will be one of high impact, and so also one of high responsibility. Sure the wheel that gets the credit will be IT. But the axle that will do the real work will be you.

This book addresses some of the important issues you will be asked to act on in the next several years to help make information technology management a better steward of electronic assets and user experiences of the knowledge society.

Spear to plough, potter's wheel to compass, loom to lathe, every new tool of the day defined an age for all centuries to come.

For the knowledge society, the tool of the day is the Internet.

And someone has to manage it, change it, and improve on it.

That someone is you.

YOUR POST-GOOGLE WORLD

You may have heard of a company called Google. Soon out of business. Obsolete. Laughably so. Why?

The first 30 years of the Internet were about porting our physical reality to the electronic world. For example the nytimes.com Web site anachronistically advertises subscriptions to the "real paper," just like it looks in print. PDF documents were created to overcome the limitations of HTML to render business forms "just like they looked on print." University research databases output pdf's "just like they looked in the printed version of the journal." And Google took the key-oriented SQL database index thinking of the 1970s and applied it to word content intended to be displayed by HTML in a browser. Key-words, get it?

You will soon see Google's approach to be a primitive. Manual keyword injection to pull content off the web. A re-invention of the nickel newsreel and Sears catalog, more than one hundred years after their original introduction. And a fundamentally mal-adapted way of interacting with the Internet you will soon be managing as an IT professional. Because SQL keys are storage and record oriented, and words are about things and facts. Closed physical systems. When the Internet 2.0 is flow- and time- oriented, and about people and events. Open cyber systems.

Internet 1.0 was like watching a traffic light: predictable, repetitive, and boring (Wolfram, 2008).

People first marveled at the click-link connectivity of 1.0. You knocked, and was let in. Oh, the ability to read the newspaper without traipsing to their own porch. Send a letter without the need for a stamp. Steal some mp3's. Drag shopping carts down electronic aisles. Watch some video. Just knock. On doors. Links. And ads.

Internet 2.0 however is much more. Much more. Exciting. New. Very new. It's about participation, sharing, contact and discovery.

In 2.0, you don't knock on doors for permission to enter. You live there. Everywhere actually. All the time. With your many yous.

In 2.0, you can bring your own shopping cart, and leave with your own shopping cart after checkout.

In 2.0, like the Wizard's Apprentice, you can have multiple shopping carts trolling for you. All 10 or 20 or 150 of you. But there will be no Google urchin watching you.

Because you won't be online.

We'll explain in a bit.

IT SPEED BUMPS

Your transition to 2.0 in the next several years will run into two little speed bumps. Friendly but for their ugly names, IPv6 and Y2K38.

Much to the delight of hourly IT consultants worldwide, there will be a forced transition from IPv4 to IPv6 sometime around 2015. The changeover is not to support streaming media or bandwidth bottlenecks. Earlier QoS concerns about IPv4 packet latency and jitter have been allayed by backend optimization, lighting dark fiber, and improvements in last mile connectivity.

Between 2010 and 2015, IANA will have run out of unused IPv4 addresses to dole out. The use of NAT and CIDR with IPv4 has delayed but not eliminated the problem of IPv4 address space exhaustion. So the exhaustion of the address space will be the real driver for the introduction of IPv6.

In anticipation of the IPv6 changeover, early in 2008 IANA added IPv6 support to about half of the Internet root name servers. But relax. Automated transition mechanisms based on proxy servers and tunneling will ensure that the overlay of IPv6 will be transparent to the current IPv4 Internet (Hallam-Baker, 2008, pp. 325-326). And IPv4 won't be phased out anywhere near before your retirement. Or that of your grandchildren.

The speed bump that will jostle you a bit is whether it will be necessary or politic to enable the flow QoS field in the IPv6 data packet. The flow field was intended to enable priority routing of different classes of traffic, for example real-time multimedia, asynchronous requests, provisioning or storage replication traffic, and paid traffic. The use of the field for traffic shaping is controversial because its benefit comes at the expense of 'net neutrality. Should the rich ride on better roads than the poor? You decide. At the moment, the flow field is part of the IPv6 data packet, but remains unused.

Next to the IPv6 overlay, another area of discussion for the IT community in coming years will be Y2K38. Son of Sam. Heir to Y2K. The earlier bug caused by the use of 2-digit years instead of 4-digit years in software doing date computations. Y2K38 comes from the use of a 32 bit signed integer to tick off seconds since the arbitrary birth of computer time, Thursday January 1 1970 00:00:00 GMT. The largest possible value for this integer is $2**31 - 1 = 2,147,483,647$ seconds (Y2K38, n.d.).

Oops. On Tuesday, January 19, 2038 03:14:07 GMT the clocks of unpatched 32 bit platforms will tick:

```
Tue Jan 19 03:14:06 2038   OK
Tue Jan 19 03:14:07 2038   OK
Fri Dec 13 20:45:52 1901   !?
Fri Dec 13 20:45:52 1901   !?
```

Y2K38! About 80% of today's Web servers worldwide run on computers that have Y2K38 problems.

Fear not. Y2K38 doomsday scenarios won't happen. But they won't be entirely pre-empted even with the full replacement of the current worldwide stock of 32 bit PCs and embedded processors with 64 bit versions.

Even if little of today's hardware survives to Y2K38, and despite every IT consultant's lucrative efforts at preemptive remediation in the years to come, there will almost certainly still be some of today's unpatched software programs designed for 32 bit OSs running in 2038.

If (and a big if it is) the original source code is still available, such software programs can be fixed by recompiling. With new timestamp libraries which use 64 bit (long long integer) values for tick time.

A good number of today's databases may well survive until 2038. Nearly all use dates in some form, and so will need Y2K38 sanity review. And of course. Billable IT work.

What about the tens of millions of what are today's new portable devices? The smartphones with Web-enabled capabilities which will find their way to poor corners of the world. Mumbai junket anyone? Else, how will these recycled devices be upgraded?

In earnest though. The actuarial drumbeat call for pre-emptive Y2K38 IT remediation, and corporate officer personnel, and general public education in businesses has already sounded. And it will only grow louder and more insistent the next several years.

After January 19, 2008, for example, IT professionals at business organizations who have to process 30 year home mortgages, trade in 30-year Treasury Bonds, track pension or Social Security years of service, or purchase EE/E Savings Bonds, will already begin answering Y2K38 questions.

And so will you. That's your other speedbump.

Security

IPSec, PKI, SSL, and RSA under FCAPS, TMN and ITIL will all be part of your alphabet soup security diet for years to come (Parker, 2005). So will the CIA.

No, not the spooks. We mean the foundational "CIA" tripod concepts of Confidentiality, Integrity, and Assurance (Thomas, Seiferth, & Kelley, 2004). How so? Let's see.

Confidentiality

In the area of confidentiality, you have your work cut out for you. The technologies exist. Yet there are no IT infrastructures in place, or even user-based software, which paint true the secondary colors of Confidentiality (Thomas, Seiferth, & Kelley, 2004):

- **Privacy:** The right not to have disclose what you know about yourself;
- **Quietude:** The right not to be disturbed by outside intrusions when engaged in your activities); and
- **Transparency:** The right to keep your level of activity, or your lack of activity, and contact points invisible to outsiders.

Don't forget. 2.0 is about flow and time, people and events. So new thinking is needed in these areas which emphasizes the right of individuals to retain lifetime control over the use and disclosure of their confidential information.

The current thinking is based on the business record model. It holds that confidential information once included in an organization's database becomes that organization's business record, i.e., property. And as such subject to few and feeble legal constraints. Often just the use and disclosure policies of the business. Themselves shaped by the fiduciary duty of the officers of the organization to use its assets in the manner most advantageous to the business owners.

Read: shaped to the disadvantage of the individual who really owns it.

Alarms have sounded (Hartzband & Groopman, 2008). Heed them. Consider for example "health insurance." In quotes yes. Because the business of health insurance is both immoral and economically unsound. Health insurance is legislated murder. Health is not a good subject to pricing considerations based on the elasticity of supply and demand. Risk management and cost containment in health care must be managed by behavior modification and education. Not financial gerrymandering. Prevent now not to have to cure later. Reward medical outcomes, not procedures. Impose access to care, not barriers (Whittaker, Adkins, Phillips, et al., 2004). Health is an atomic good. Indivisible is health from the human condition. It needs to be treated as a right, like the air you breathe (UN, 1948). Not as a privilege, as is currently the case for the poor in the U.S. and worldwide.

IT plays an enormous role in health care in the United States. You will see for yourself. Repeatedly as your career in IT progresses. As the Baby Boom generation ages, your will find your career in IT time and again ensnared in health care issues. Because laws like HIPAA, SOX, FACTA/FCRA, ERISA and the GLBA have all failed to address the conceptually flawed business-record-oriented storage view of personal information. And of health information in particular. Various DNA protection laws have also stalled in legislative committees.

When in the U.S., your access to care is subject to employer-based or government-based enrollment pools. And constrained by coverage exclusions for so-called "pre-existing conditions."

Now then. Pre-existing conditions are an artificially created coverage exclusion concept. They arise from fractured procedural enrollment and dis-enrollment processes. Book-keeping entries. For example when moving or changing employers. Pre-existing conditions are a legal concoction which criminalizes being sick. They doom many a patient to death for lack of treatment (Nolte & McKee, 2004). When pre-existing conditions do not exist in the physical world.

Life is a pre-existing physical condition. A covered enrollment pool isn't. Hence the problem.

To fix, start by making "pre-existing condition" discrimination illegal. Then you come in. To implement content rights management (CRM). To provide a means in IT to make available cradle-to-grave, and intergenerational datavault services. Personal database access services tied to permission access tokens. Under CRM, the decryption key is only released when specific release constraints satisfactory to the owner of the data are met (Hallam-Baker, 2008).

In such databases, the access token is the only information stored in the third-party business database. The token limits access to a number of accesses within a certain period of time. And only for specific reasons. It also forbids forwarding of the token to third parties, and certainly storage and replication of the read content.

The token issuer retains the right to revoke the token later. With the use of the token, there is no copying of the personal medical information in a business database. So there is no un-necessary duplication of data. Access to data is improved, and errors are reduced. Privacy is preserved. Lifetime. Across generations.

And, importantly, private medical data never becomes a corporate business record.

Ever.

You need to act. The "health insurance" example shows new models of token-friendly and non-business record database storage are urgently needed in IT. Heed the warnings (Hartzband & Groopman, 2008). No satisfactory solutions exist today. You will have to discover and implement them.

Remember. The current SQL approach to databases took form in the early 1970s. It has not been meaningfully updated in nearly forty years now. It tripped up Google.

But not you. You know SQL is a storage-oriented model. Today woefully inadequate to support data not intended to be stored under the business record model.

Medical records are not the only issue. SQL does not adequately support or index multimedia and streaming data, timed-lifetime and time-to-live token based access, role-constrained access, access under digital rights management, or even access of data stored in encrypted form. Let alone access tokens candy-wrapped with CRM instructions.

Do better. Please!

Integrity

Integrity is the property of data which specifies it has not been altered away from its intended value. There are three secondary colors subsumed under the integrity rainbow (Thomas, Seiferth, & Kelley, 2004):

- **Authentication:** You credentials are solid;
- **Authorization:** You were privileged to do it; and
- **Non-Repudiation:** You can't deny it was you who did it.

Much work has been done in IT towards the attainment of data integrity in the secondary colors of authentication and authorization.

In the case of authentication, examples are the development of SQL (for the integrity of business records), the use of VPN-based end-to-end traffic encapsulation and encryption, the widespread use of two-factor authentication (the familiar combination of a credit card magnetic stripe and a pin), and the near-universal adoption of PKI (public/private-key infrastructure) for third-party Web server authentication and traffic encryption.

A needy area of research in IT is how to authenticate the rapidly growing number of small hand-held wireless devices (Corbett, 2008). That's where you come in. For example, it should not be necessary to replace a SIM chip on a cellphone when of intercontinental travel. Fix it!

In the case of authorization, adequate IT mechanisms exist, for example Role-Based Access Control, the Principles of Need To Know, Defense-In-Depth, and Separation of Duties, and the concepts of No-Write-Down and No-Read-Up (Solomon & Chapple, 2005).

However softwares to easily implement them are only realistically attractive to large organizations. New hosted models are needed with pre-implemented software which makes Authorization more attractive and affordable to smaller businesses. Create them!

The weakest link is non-repudiation. Spam e-mail provides daily examples in your mailbox. A new SMTP protocol with encryption and non-repudiation built-in is needed. Patch approaches based on Personal security certificates have been unsuccessful. PGP failed as a company. The need for improved Non-Repudiation will increase as the rapidly growing number of smaller devices provide multiple access points opportunities for the same individual (cell phones, laptops, business computers, PDAs). Don't dally. Invent it now.

Assurance

Assurance addresses the issue of being able to access your data when you want. Assurance has three components (Thomas, Seiferth, & Kelley, 2004):

- **Availability:** It's up-time and running when you need it,
- **Reliability:** It functions as intended, without surprises; and
- **Serviceability:** It performs a meaningful function, meets its purpose well.

Availability and reliability are currently generally satisfactory. If only because of their marked reliance on the wasteful concept of redundancy. Redundancy is achieved for example from a second power supply; RAID hard-disk sharing technologies; fewer moving components, say from the elimination of fans and the introduction of disk-less hard-drives; automated failovers to an alternate site when of flood and fire; the increased reliance by small companies on hosted services, with stronger house expertise and infrastructures, and the self-rerouting capabilities of the Internet. But let these be. Hardware is cheap really. And other issues in IT are more urgent.

Serviceability is the component of assurance in the greatest need of additional IT development. Here you will be busy. Single sign on for example is still notoriously difficult to implement and maintain, dooming us to having to remember multiple passwords for every Web site we visit. Personal-level PKI security certificates, for example PGP for personal e-mail and blogs, failed to gain acceptance because too difficult to use and maintain at the retail level. The result is most personal e-mail is sent unencrypted, the sender retains no control over forwarding rights, and the Internet arteries are clogged with spam e-mail. And serviceable personal datavaults don't exist. That content ends up in business records. But you already promised to fix that, right?

Flaws in serviceability flow already from basic IT architectural design flaws. The most glaring are the many and increasingly inexcusable software bugs. But the issue of software bugs is of course not specific to security. Software development in IT still has much to learn from the construction engineering disciplines. Examples are the need to learn to rely on proper software equivalents of (a) architectural blueprints (itemized bills of materials, and detailed plan-, section-, and elevation-views, all drawn to scale); (b) purpose-built sub-component modules (like windows and doors); (c) conformance to a standardized software building code (akin to the ICC); (d) the definition of a proper IT professional corps body of knowledge and the establishment of a related Duty-Of-Care professional standard; and (e) adequate professional software contractor licensing laws (no different from engineers, attorneys, physicians and nurses, accountants, electricians, plumbers, and barbers). Grab a hard-hat and talk to a licensed engineer. They'll explain.

IT Outsourcing and Offshoring

IT outsourcing is the practice of farming out work that is not a core competency of an organization to a specialist for whom it is. IT offshoring is the specialized variation of outsourcing in which the IT work is farmed out to a specialist organization in a country in which the organization does not otherwise normally do business. Outsourcing is done primarily to improve organizational effectiveness, and offshoring is to reduce costs.

In the U.S. there has been public concern that offshoring exports desirable IT jobs. Given the shortage of IT talent in the U.S., and in most every other country worldwide, this argument does not have merit. No local resource is left idle but for lack of foresight and planning in the education of the high-skill workers sought by today's employers:

Every big employer in the city, it seems, can cite an example of high-paying jobs that had to be relocated to foreign cities [...] Until now, visa restrictions have been seen as a problem that primarily affected technology companies in Silicon Valley and elsewhere in the West. [...] But [...] there is more demand for visas for specialized jobs in New York, New Jersey and Connecticut than in California, and most of the demand comes from small and midsize companies, not the largest corporations. [...] The partnership recommended adjusting the cap on H-1B visas to meet demand and more than doubling the annual limit on employment-based green cards to 290,000 from 140,000. It also suggested exempting workers with advanced degrees in science and math from any cap on H-1B visas and extending the term of visas for workers receiving practical training to 29 months from 12 months. (Mcgeehan & Bernstein, 2008)

Offshoring has always existed. Be it copper, bananas, automobiles, or digital software projects, commodity products always go to the high volume, low cost producers. Let them have them! What many fail to see is that offshoring and outsourcing free up local resources for higher-level functions like:

- Specifications gathering
- Solution design and architecture
- Vendor selection and coordination

- Scheduling and deadline management
- Marshaling and resource allocation
- Digital warehousing and distribution
- Electronic marketing and brand building
- Multi-modal financing and payments clearing
- Electronic branding and trust building
- Multipresence electronic customer support

Why be a bricklayer when you can be an engineer? A bookkeeper when you can be a controller? Or a software programmer when you can be a software architect? Isn't that why you picked IT as a profession? Do good, get paid more, serve others as you move up in life?

By 2030 there will be over 8 billion people on the planet, about half under the age of 25. A billion more by 2050, many in poverty. The need to plan and implement the IT infrastructure needed to support the electronic needs of these new populations exists already today (Corbett, 2008). These population growth pressures will compete with the rocket effect of IT wealth creation: the rich have robopets when the poor lack shoes (Normile, 2008).

In the U.S., the collapse of the economies in say Michigan, Ohio and Pennsylvania was not caused by offshoring of IT jobs to India or manufacturing jobs to China. It was caused by a lack of vision and a grossly short-sighted planning horizon. The failure to educate the young quickly enough as they came out of grade school in the 1970s so as to raise blue-collar job expectations from assembly workers and food servers to high-level and high-paying MBA-level career expectations in product and process design, project management, engineering, and enterprise management.

As IT virtualizes society, there will be a need for highly skilled IT engineers, technical MBAs, and science and technology PhDs by the millions to manage increasingly abstract and variegated projects. Today's tragedy in Ohio, Michigan, and Pennsylvania is that millions for decades have instead dropped out of high-school (Dillon, 2008). Minds abandoned for life.

While local talent works low-paying jobs at the mall or goes to prison, about 30% of the students enrolled in graduate STEM (science, technology, engineering, and mathematics) programs in the U.S. hold foreign student visas, virtually all on paid appointments and free-ride scholarships (NSF, 2008).

Then upon graduation, these students obtain automatic residence and work permits to meet the clamor of employers for their skills and talents (Mcgeehan and Bernstein, 2008). At a time when U.S. employers demand doubling the annual limit on highly-skilled worker visas to 290,000, 32% of black males in the U.S. drop out of school and end up in prison at some point in their lives (Mcgeehan and Bernstein, 2008; USDOJ, 2007).

To adequately support the knowledge society of the 21st century, executive MBA and STEM disciplines today should be enrolling ten times more students than is currently the case. For example, China today has maybe 5,000 MBAs when it will need some 75,000 by 2020 (Lavelle & Rutldege, 2006). Yet even though the MBA degree was invented in the U.S. to combat a dearth of mid-career management depth, it was not the U.S. but tiny Dubai and Qatar which has had the vision to build entire new cities from scratch to house dozens of new university campuses to train the world's leadership of tomorrow (Lewin, 2008).

Shortages of vision seed many of the tragedies of life. But you can help. As an IT professional, you're in the right place, at the right time. Every technological revolution was constrained by a shortage of higher-skilled talent, not a lack of lower-skilled labor: agricultural irrigation and crop rotation; steam mechanization; industrial scale mining, chemicals and refining; power generation and electrification; telecommunications (radio, TV, telephony); and now IT and digitalization.

Entire lines of new Electronic Project Manager professions in IT are needed to provide the people and technology implementation and coordination skills needed to support these new functions. It's unconscionable factories are being emptied of blue collar workers while so many attractive Web mechanic and virtual society architect jobs go unfilled.

The reality is there are not enough people in the collegiate pipeline being trained with the undergraduate technical skills needed to support these Web mechanic functions once implemented. And the education needed to function in the design and management of these new jobs is tragically also not well covered by existing graduate-level MBA or engineering degrees. The situation is sufficiently alarming to warrant the creation of a graduate school GI Bill to make it possible to recruit and train IT professionals in sufficient numbers. In the meantime, yes you can help. Mentor.

IT and Electronic Collaboration

Much in the news is the notion of an IT convergence. Meaning the merging of any number of once separate devices into a single one: remote controls and cell phones, TV and radio, laptops and computers, printers and scanners.

The exciting part about convergence is not convenience. It is the ability to participate. While being selective about the mode and timing of your participation, and the size of you audience.

TV and radio, libraries and art museums, movies and theater, newsprint and newscasts, Web pages and blogs. All were essentially observational opportunities. You watched. Sometimes by appointment. Sometimes at your convenience. Content was broadcast. You did not participate.

Under pincasting, you do. Your thoughts and actions count (Story, 2008). What you are contributes (Hanell, 2007). Your voice is heard (Stone, 2008). Work collaboratively towards a goal (Stelter, 2008). Share ideas, successes, and failures (Goetz, 2008). From any device of your choice. Always at your convenience. Just about everywhere you visit.

When you flip the crate to use it as your dais, your browser is no longer a container. It is a world stage (Jackson, Gharavi, & Klobas, 2006). That's quite a step up from the day in 1872 when an Act of Parliament set aside an end of London's Hyde Park as the Speaker's Corner.

Some forms of pincasting are already familiar to you. When you e-mail, chat online, or send an SMS text message, your dispatch speaks for you when delivered. But pincasting also includes listing your resume on Monster. Posting classified ads on Craigslist. Bidding on eBay. Annotating Yahoo maps. Entering a trouble ticket online with your cable provider. Adding your personal ratings and recommendations to your Amazon purchases. Sharing photos on Flickr. Uploading movies to YouTube. Adding your comments to blogs. Bookmarking newsclips with Digg. Requesting money with Paypal. Chirping your friends on Facebook. And editing articles collaboratively with strangers on Wikipedia (Stvilia, Twidale, Smith et al., 2008).

Social networking is the flipside of pincasting. Under pincasting, you hop from site to site to participate. You take your clicks with you. And you have to know where to visit.

With social networking, you participate from the same place. And the clicks come to you. Examples are MySpace and Facebook.

The combination of pincasting and social networking will transform our understanding and experience with computers. "Compare a modern PC of 2004 to the first Macintosh shipping in 1984 and the major difference you will see is color." (Web 2.0, n.d.)

No longer. You will change this. You know computers are no longer single-user, keyboard, touchscreen, and mouse-driven closed systems anymore. And that content is not limited to disk files and Web pages. You see computers are now gateways open to interaction with any number of immersive metaverses.

External digital worlds in which avatars interact as proxies for humans. To establish a virtual presence for collaboration. Or accomplish an individual goal. But without physical limitations.

For example, teleportation of self between islands, rooms and minihompies is a natural part of Second Life, Habbo Hotel and Cyworld. And with a strong sense of execution time and sustained identity. Every message intended for delivery to an island object specifies the time at which it is to be executed. "These messages are literally the island clock." (Croquet, n.d.) And Second Life, Habbo Hotel, and Cyworld self-entities all know how to display themselves and respond to events, and communicate outcomes back to the exosphere.

Islands, hotels, and cyworlds are metaverses. A complicated word for electronic playgrounds. Metaverses like Second Life, Habbo Hotel, and Cyworld have characteristics not available to closed systems PCs:

1.   **Persistence:** Every act of speech (message) alters the state of the metaverse, and so imprints it for all posterity;
2.   **Receptivity:** State changes are welcomed at any time and can be executed asynchronously;
3.   **Independence:** Message execution is not tethered to the presence of the controlling exosphere;
4.   **Sociability:** Because speech acts are journaled and identity defined by text properties, it is easy to find like-minded objects by property search and discovery by reflection;
5.   **Pervasiveness:** The metaverse accommodates all users in all spaces all the time;
6.   **Adaptability:** Changes and updates can be made to serve new uses;
7.   **Permanence:** Updates can be applied without disruption, while the system is live and running;
8.   **Synchronicity:** All elements are aware of the same clock;
9.   **Schedulability:** Event deadlines exist and are met or diverted;
10.   **Dressability:** The views presented can be shaped by individual preferences and folksonomies (collaborative tagging);
11.   **Extensibility:** New objects and functionality can be added to support new content and sources; and
12.   **Shareability:** Content and functionality can be shared with other metaverses without exosphere mediation.
       (Adapted from Boyd, 2008; Crocket, n.d.; Web 2.0, n.d.)

Not yet available that is. You will add them. Why? Need. And the bane of IT. Change.

VIRTUAL SOCIETIES: THE DEMISE OF THE BROWSER

Pincasting and social networking the creation of an entirely new class of online communities: virtual societies.

It is here in the building of the infrastructure needed to support these new virtual societies that your skills as an IT professional will be most needed.

The scope of work is enormous. The vision needed is that of Peter The Great and Eleanor Roosevelt combined.

India and China combined for all their size still can't put together enough IT personnel to support their own growth, let alone virtualize global trade, support persistent electronic cities, and digitalize reality on the scale to come in the next twenty and forty years as virtual societies aggregate and take shape online.

Blogospheres, wikis and similar Content 2.0 Web sites, and common interest Web sites like LinkedIn, Facebook, eBay, Skype, World of Warcraft, Blackboard, SecondLife and Yahoo annotated maps, these are all examples of early form virtual societies. They are the beginning of something big. Very big.

They all establish persistent virtual presences for their inhabitants, all of whom share a common interest and change state as they live online.

What they have in common is that the share the common interests and goals, and they allow you to maintain a telepresence by means of electronic avatars listening in and cataloging events for you, and acting on threshold and timed trigger commands on your behalf.

You exist. Online. Even when you're not logged in.

You live by multiple clocks, all ticking in their own worlds, awaiting events and triggering actions based on mandates and contingency instructions you have provided.

Physical distance? Vanished. And with that location. You can be two and more places at the same time. Your avatars will speak and listen and act on your behalf. Electronic mini-me goblins watching and acting on your interests everywhere.

You can and do become an inhabitant of multiple virtual societies. Each new individual avatar presence you add helps multiply the worlds' population of Internet users. And because the actions and interactions of your avatars are traceable and rewindable, the diffusion of self into virtual worlds they represent promises to eventually challenge our current ontological understanding of time evolution and consciousness (Jenkins, 2006). You will experience multiple "immersion digital lives." Yes. All 10 or 20 or 150 of you.

You will enjoy multiple sets of experiences on the Internet 2.0. Truly rich. No need to live within a single bubble realm of experience. You will be free to act and choose, in a vast existential virtual playground. One which would please Heidegger and Sartre to no end. Your personal, work, family, and community participation will be real, and simultaneously virtual. For example, soon individual consumers with common needs and preferences will come together. To communicate with each other, and upon reaching a consensus collectively negotiate their market with prospective sellers before disbanding again (Chena, Jeng, Leea, et al., 2008). To share their hopes and tears (Goetz, 2008). Yes. Soon, you won't just watch a movie or ball game. You will act or play in it. Or at least one of your avatars will.

The next 20 years of the Internet will be about the establishment of virtual societies. The scale of electronic sharing and collaboration virtual societies will enable will be staggering. And the transformative role of IT research and the impact of your work as an IT professional immense too. Just think. Internet traffic has been doubling every five years. The same amount of IT work that was done building Internet 1.0 Web sites between 1995 and 2005 will be needed in a geometric multiple as Sholie comes of age.

A glance at the techno-needs imposed by the current digital revolution in IT reveals the urgent need for IT technologies to design, implement, and support advanced and highly abstracted processes:

- Multi-point electronic asset distribution under federated regimes;
- Orchestration, and choreography of events into processes;
- Global electronic timing, coordination, and virtual event scheduling;
- Support for digital neighborhoods, which group by asset, interest and skill instead of physical location;
- Ordinary plumbing services for entire electronic cities populated by multi-presence avatars;
- Distributed mesh computing for resource discovery, marshalling, task allocation, and supply chain assembly;
- Real-time multimedia search, real-time asset tracking, and real-time statistical projections and electronic mining

Every single of the interactions and transactions just listed will have to be enabled secured in some layered fashion by new families of security protocols, inter-venue cooperation agreements, competing target-specific products and services, and of course the people with the high-level know-how, experience, and talent in IT to design, implement and manage them. Where are these bodies? These brains? Without them, how are you ever going to retire?

The primary means of interaction with the Internet will be avatars. Your proxies. Controlled from observation, command, and control centers. The exosphere. Content will not be generated for HTML presentation. It will be generated for API delivery. With tools like Coghead, Project Zero, QEDWiki, the WSO2 Mashup Server, and their descendents. For rendering in gateways to virtual worlds with built-in collaborative capabilities: mashups (Boss & Krauss, 2007; Yee, 2008).

For an early peek, look at Vuze, LinkedIn, Second Life, Habbo, and Cyworld.

Then flip through this book.

By the time you're done reading it, you'll want to help.

And by the time you're done helping, there will be many of you.

But there will be no clicking. No knocking on doors. No need for a browser. Or Google.

George Kelley
June 2008
Boston, MA

REFERENCES

Boss, S. & Krauss, J. (2007, August). Power of the Mashup: Combining Essential Learning with New Technology Tools. *Learning & Leading with Technology*, 35(1), pp. 12-17.

Boyd, D. (2008). Why Youth Love Social Network Sites: The Role of Networked Publics In Teenage Social Life. In *Youth, Identity, and Digital Media,* D. Buckingham (ed.). The John D. and Catherine T. MacArthur Foundation Series on Digital Media and Learning. Cambridge, MA: The MIT Press, 2008, pp. 119-142, doi: 10.1162/dmal.9780262524834.119.

Chena, D.-N. Jeng, B., Leea, W.-P., & Chuang, C.-H. (2008). An Agent-Based Model For Consumer-to-Business Electronic Commerce. *Expert Systems With Applications*, 34(1), 469-481.

Corbett, S. (2008, April 13). Can the Cellphone Help End Global Poverty? Selling To The Other Three Billion. *The New York Times*.

Croquet (n.d.). See http://www.opencroquet.org/index.php/System_Overview

Dillon, S. (2008, March 20). States' Data Obscure How Few Finish High School. *The New York Times*.

Goetz, T. (2008, March 23). Practicing Patients: Patients Like Me. *The New York Times*.

Hallam-Baker, P. (2008). *The DotCom Manifesto: How To Stop Internet Crime*. Reading, MA: Addison-Wesley.

Hanell, S. (2007, November 13). Inbox 2.0: Yahoo and Google to Turn E-Mail Into a Social Network. *The New York Times*.

Hartzband, P., & Groopman, J. (2008). Off the Record — Avoiding the Pitfalls of Going Electronic. *The New England Journal Of Medicine*, 358(16), 1656-1658.

Jackson, P., Gharavi, H., & Klobas, J. (2006). Technologies of the Self: Virtual Work and the Inner Panopticon. *Information Technology & People*, 19(3), 219-243.

Jenkins, P. S. (2006). Historical Simulations: Motivational, Ethical and Legal Issues. *Journal of Futures Studies*, 11(1), 23-42.

Lavelle, L., & Rutledge, S. (2006, January 9). *China's B-School Boom*. Business Week.

Lewin, T. (2008, February 10). Global Classrooms: U.S. Universities Rush to Set Up Outposts Abroad. *The New York Times*.

Mcgeehan, P., & Nina Bernstein, N. (2008, March 24). Businesses Say New York's Clout Is Emigrating, With Visa Policies to Blame. *The New York Times*.

Nolte, E. & McKee, M. (2004). Measuring The Health of Nations: Analysis Of Mortality Amenable To Health Care. *Journal of Epidemiology and Community Health*, 58, p. 326.

Normile, D. (2008, March 9). Trumpets vs. Crumpets In A Robot Duel. *The New York Times*.

NSF (2008, January 28). Foreign Science and Engineering Graduate Students Returning to U.S. Colleges," Division of Science Resources Statistics, National Science Foundation. Available online at http://www.nsf.gov/statistics/infbrief/nsf08302/

Parker, J. (2005). *FCAPS, TMN & ITIL. Three Key Ingredients to Effective IT Management*. OpenWater Solutions. Available online at http://www.openwatersolutions.com/docs/FCAPS_TMN_%20ITIL.pdf

Solomon, M. G., & Chapple, M. (2005). *Information Security Illuminated*. Sudbury, MA: Jones and Bartlett Publishers.

Stelter, B. (2008, March 27). Finding Political News Online, the Young Pass It On. *The New York Times*.

Stone, B. (2008, March 31). Online Chat, as Inspired by Real Chat. *The New York Times*.

Story, L. (2008, March 9). How Do They Track You? Let Us Count the Ways. *The New York Times*.

Stvilia, B., Twidale, M. B., Smith, L. C., & Gasser, L. (2008). Information Quality Work Organization In Wikipedia. *Journal of the American Society for Information Science and Technology*, 59(6), 983-1001.

Thomas, A., Seiferth, J., & Kelley, G. (2004). Security and Virtual Private Networks (VPNs): An Overview of New Business Models for the Small to Medium Enterprise (SME). *Information Systems: Exploring Applications in Business and Government*, The Information Institute, pp. 189-231.

UN (1948). Universal Declaration of Human Rights, *United Nations General Assembly*, Resolution 217A (III). Article 25(1): "Everyone has the right to a standard of living adequate for the health and well-being of himself and of his family, including food, clothing, housing and medical care and necessary social services, and the right to security in the event of unemployment, sickness, disability, widowhood, old age or other lack of livelihood in circumstances beyond his control."

USDOJ (2007, August 8). *Criminal Offender Statistics: Summary Findings*. United States Department Of Justice, Office Of Justice Programs, Bureau Of Justice Statistics. Available online at http://www.ojp.usdoj.gov/bjs/crimoff.htm

Web 2.0 (n.d.). Wikipedia: The Online Encyclopedia. Available online at http://en.wikipedia.org/wiki/Web_2.0

Whittaker S. L., Adkins S., Phillips R., Jones J., Horsley M. A., & Kelley G. (2004). Success Factors In The Long-Term Sustainability Of A Telediabetes Programme. *Journal of Telemedicine and Telecare*, 10(2), pp. 84-88.

Wolfram, D. (2008). Search Characteristics In Different Types Of Web-Based IR Environments: Are They The Same? *Information Processing & Management*, 44, 1279-1292.

Y2K38 (n.d.). Wikipedia: The Online Encyclopedia. Available online at http://en.wikipedia.org/wiki/Year_2038_problem

Yee, R. (2008). *Pro Web 2.0 Mashups: Remixing Data and Web Services*. Berkeley, CA: Apress.

About the Editor

Prof. George Kelley, PhD, has served in the IT industry for more than 25 years as a technical consultant, project manager, and director of IT. He has worked for private and publicly traded companies, with layered staff and capital and operating budget responsibilities. In addition, he has published about 30 peer-refereed papers and contributed to more than two dozen academic and professional conferences as a speaker, editor, and event organizer. Dr. Kelley has also taught technical and professional undergraduate and graduate university courses on IT project management, information security, Web technologies, computer interfacing, messaging and networking, relational databases, and computer programming for more than 10 years. He is currently a member of the editorial board of the *Information Resources Management Journal* and a professor at the University of Massachusetts, Boston. George Kelley attended the University of Göttingen (Germany), Wayne State University, the University of California, San Diego State University, the University of Cincinnati, and Texas A&M University. He did his post-doctoral work at Brookhaven National Laboratories and the California Institute of Technology.

Section I
Fundamental Concepts and Theories

Chapter I
Reference Model Management

Oliver Thomas
*Institute for Information Systems (IWi) at the German Research Center for
Artificial Intelligence (DFKI), Saarbrücken, Germany*

ABSTRACT

Reference modeling is located in a field of conflict between research and practice. Despite the array of theoretical concepts, there is still a deficit in knowledge about the use and problems inherent in the implementation of reference models. Accordingly, in the past years the supply-sided development of reference models predominant in the science world has distanced itself from their demand-sided use in business and administration. This contribution will analyze the causes of these problems and present a solution in the form of an integrative approach to computer-supported management of reference models. The task to be carried out with this solution approach will be concretized using data structures and a system architecture and then prototypically implemented in the form of a reference model management system.

INTRODUCTION

Business Process Modeling and Reference Modeling

The central idea in reference modeling is the re-utilization of the business knowledge contained in reference models for the construction of specific information models (Hars, 1994; Scheer, 1994b; Schütte, 1998; vom Brocke, 2003; Becker & Schütte, 2004; Fettke & Loos, 2004; Thomas, 2006a). Reference models provide companies with an initial solution for the design of organization and application systems. The possibility of orienting oneself with the specialized content in a reference model can, on the one hand, decisively save time and costs for the model user and, on the other, can increase a model's quality because reference models present general recommendations for the subject area under analysis.

Towards the end of the 1990s, a certain "reference modeling euphoria" could be detected which could be attributed to the strong influence of process-oriented paradigms, such as business process reengineering (Hammer & Champy, 1993) or continuous process improvement (Robson, 1991). However, while process consulting and, especially, software tools for business process modeling established themselves as a separate market segment (Gartner Inc., 1996), a development in the opposite direction can be observed for reference modeling—despite the often mentioned close connection to business process modeling.

Today, the systematic development of reference models is seldom seen in practice. Reference models are rarely oriented towards customer segments or enterprise processes. The potential for improvements which result from the enterprise-specific adaptation of reference models is usually not consequently integrated into them. Modeling tool providers are discontinuing modeling projects due to restrictions in time, personnel and finances. Few reference models exist on the basis of a modeling method which offers comprehensive support for model adaptation—the few exceptions here are the reference models from some providers of ERP systems.

Reference modeling as a field of research in the information systems discipline finds itself conflicted between theory and practice. This field of conflict is characterized by the fact that the theoretic foundation of reference modeling propagated by researchers is rarely consistent with the pragmatic simplicity of reference models and the manageability of their enterprise-specific adaptation called for in business practice. This discrepancy can, for the most part, be ascribed to the problems discussed below.

PROBLEMS IN REFERENCE MODELING

Research Diversity

The number of scientific contributions on the topic of reference modeling has multiplied in the last few years. From the contextual perspective, works come to the fore which support the development of reference models for branches of trade not considered up to now, such as public administration, health care systems or credit and insurance business (Fettke & Loos, 2003). Today's literature also provides a multitude of different suggestions from the methodological perspective for the construction and usage of reference models. The number of modeling methods and techniques applied with the corresponding approaches is so diverse, that even their classification has become a subject of reference modeling research (Fettke & Loos, 2002b). Up to now, few recommendations for the case-specific selection of classes of methods or individual techniques of reutilization have been made. The question also remains open, as to whether the technologies examined can be integrated into construction processes. The fact that most of the examined technologies are geared to a certain modeling language (Fettke, et al., 2002b, pp. 18 ff.) should at least make an integrated usage difficult. Reference model developers and users are therefore hardly in the position of deciding which of the methods, techniques and languages suggested in literature are adequate for their use cases. In this connection, it becomes clear why so few "unique" languages in reference modeling (e.g., Lang, 1997; vom Brocke, 2003) or reference modeling-specific extensions of established languages in information modeling (e.g., Remme, 1997; Schütte, 1998; Schwegmann, 1999; Becker, Delfmann, Knackstedt, & Kuropka, 2002) have so far not found great acceptance in practice.

Findings Deficit

There is a considerable degree of unanimity in literature regarding the application possibilities of reference models. Nevertheless, few empirical studies on the topic of "reference modeling" are documented. The only German-language empirical study on the creation and usage of reference models was carried out in the spring of 1997 at the University of Muenster (Schütte, 1998, pp. 75 ff.).

A survey of 390 reference model users in business practice was planned for the questionnaire campaign (planned random sample). The actual sample size (final sample size) however, with only 22 questionnaires filled out (rate of return approx. 5.6%) (Schütte, 1998, p. 371), was so low that no statistically significant statements could be made. Thus, a deficit still exists regarding the benefits and problems inherent in the use of reference models.

Implementation Deficit

The deficit in findings in reference modeling mentioned above is also reflected in the lack of IT implementations. Despite the diversity of the theoretical solutions for sub-problems in reference modeling, only a few of these concepts were implemented technically or tested in practice. Thus, in connection with his approach for using reference process building blocks, Lang (1997, p. 8) explicitly points out the fact that modeling tools are circumstantial, because one can fall back on existing tools. He does not, however, explain how this is to be done. Schwegmann (1999, p. 2) completely differentiates his approach to object-oriented reference modeling from implementation-technical problems, although he sees the information systems represented by reference models in a more or less technical light through the use of the object-oriented paradigm.

One reason for the lack of IT implementations is the low "degree of formalization" in the respective approaches—usually, it is a consequent transfer of the requirements definition to a data-processing concept that is lacking. This would, for example, allow the integration into a professional modeling tool and, in doing so, allow many users to be reached and practical experiences made.

REFERENCE MODEL MANAGEMENT

Objective and Subject Area

In light of the problems shown in reference modeling, the author is of the opinion that the current significance of reference modeling in research does not so much result from the necessity of methodically analyzing it, but is rather much more the realization in operational practice that, in times of dynamic markets, knowledge about application system and organization design has become a critical factor for business success.

The current occupation with reference models focuses on a central question in business information systems: "How can application systems and organizations be designed so that they meet the demands of their environment as best possible?" The analysis of this problem pertains to many interdisciplinary fields of work, such as organizational theory, systems theory, enterprise modeling, business process management, knowledge management, innovation management and software engineering. However, respective theoretical concepts often neglect the competition-relevant role of knowledge about the design of application systems and organizations. Therefore, based upon the theoretical concepts, the following modified question should also be asked regarding the problem discussed above: "How is the knowledge concerning the design of application systems and organizations planned and controlled?" Moreover, if one understands reference models as memories for explicit domain knowledge, then one must interpret reference modeling as an instrument, which aims at the transfer of business and IT knowledge (Scheer, Habermann, Thomas, & Seel, 2002, pp. 209ff.; Fettke et al., 2003, pp. 35ff.), and if one summarizes the terms planning and control in the term "management," then the resulting question can be none other than: "How can reference models be managed?" The author will do his part in answering this question, as expressed in the title of this contribution, in the following.

As touched upon in the previous paragraph, this article understands *reference model management* (RMM) as the planning and control of the development and usage of reference models. The terms "management of reference models" and "reference model management" will be used here as synonyms.

Core Functions

The management of reference models can be conceived as a process. This process is characterized by creativity and is highly complex due to its multifariousness and dependency on human judgment. Procedure models have established themselves in reference modeling—in analogy to software engineering—as being useful in making this complexity controllable. These procedure models which are presented by, among others, Schütte (1998, pp. 184 ff.), Schwegmann (1999, pp. 165 ff.), Schlagheck (2000, pp. 77-91), Fettke and Loos (2002a, pp. 9 ff.) and vom Brocke (2003, pp. 320-344), emphasize the developmental phase of a reference model on the one hand and, on the other, the phase of creation of enterprise-specific models based on a reference model (i.e., the usage of a reference model). In both cases, a process of construction must be gone through and this process can be supported by operationalizable approaches to the creation of models. The processes of development and usage of a reference model are, however, usually chronologically, as well as contextually and organizationally separated from one another (Thomas & Scheer, 2006):

- **Chronological separation:** The chronological separation of the construction process results directly from the definition of a reference model. A model can be referred to as a reference model when used to support the construction of other information models.

Thus, the construction of a reference model always precedes the construction of specific models.

- **Contextual separation:** Usually, the reference model constructor does not know the demands regarding the content of future reference model adaptations. He must therefore try to foresee them. This problem occurs especially when construction techniques, such as the configuration (e.g., Rosemann & van der Aalst, 2003) are used, whereas in dependence of specific conditions, construction results from the reference model are selectively adopted.

- **Organizational separation:** The model provider and customer, respectively constructor and user, are usually different people, departments or companies. An enterprise is, for example, either the provider of the knowledge in the reference model or—through the enterprise-wide introduction of a modeling tool—a customer for the reference model. This organizational separation can lead to the fact that, on the one hand, the customer-requirements on the reference model are not adequately fulfilled by the supplier and on the other, that the customer's experiences using the reference model are not used continuously for the improvement of the model.

This separation of the processes "reference model development" and "reference model usage" as regards time, context and organization is seen here as a problem of integration. In general language use, integration is understood as the recreation of a whole. From the system theoretic perspective, integration means the linking of elements and components to form a complete system. This integration can take place by merging or connecting elements and components which logically belong together. One can refer to integration as either the process of recreating a whole or the result of such a process. For the field of information systems, integration means connecting man, task and technology—the components of an information system—to form a whole.

If we transfer this understanding of the term to the topic dealt with here, then we can identify the development, usage and integration of reference models as the core functions of reference model management (cf. Figure 1):

- **Reference model development:** The planning and realization of reference model construction. The development of reference models encompasses the acquisition of and search for relevant information sources and content, as well as the explication and documentation of an employee's application system knowledge and organizational knowledge. The development of reference models refers to the development of new reference models, as well as the modification and continual improvement of existing ones.

- **Reference model usage:** The planning and realization of the construction of information models using reference models. The usage of reference models comprises the search and navigation of the reference models relevant for the use-case, their selection and distribution to the persons concerned, the presentation of knowledge content, as well as the support of the reference model adaptation. It also comprises the retroactive evaluation of the reference models used and associated information.

- **Reference model integration:** The fusion of the separated processes in the development of reference models and the use of reference models for the construction of enterprise-specific models in the sense of the (re) creation of a whole.

IT-Support

The usage of reference models for the construction of enterprise-specific information models is a fundamental idea resulting from paper-less, tool-supported data-processing consulting (Scheer, 1994a). Thus, this contribution will not deal with the question as to *whether it* makes sense to economically develop a computer-aided information system for the management of reference models from the research perspective, as well as from the practice perspective. This question has long been "answered" by the economic success of modeling and analysis-tool providers (Sinur, 2004). On the contrary, we must investigate the question of *how* an information system should be designed so that it can support reference model management adequately.

Because it is the design-objective of information systems in the sense of the planning, construction and modification of operational reality and supportive information systems that is emphasized in this contribution, the goal to be achieved cannot be found in design alone but rather, also in the creation of an information system which can

Figure 1. Core functions of the management of reference models

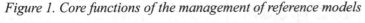

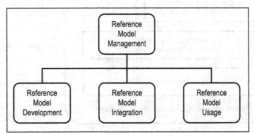

support the management of reference models. This information system will be referred to as a *reference model management system* (RMMS).

Concretion of the Challenge

The framework shown in Figure 2 will be used as a guideline for the challenge to be carried out. Due to its system-theory character, it illustrates the most important components of an RMMS, as well as their functional interaction.

The graphic is oriented on the contextual and technical interface-concepts for modeling tools which allow die retention of various IT-platforms (Scheer, 1994a). This allows the consideration of the underlying networking of conceptual research results, prototypes and professional software developments. The RMMS-framework is also oriented on studies concerning instruments and processes for the access to and usage of information models which, among other things, lead to the conception of a model library (Mili, Mili, & Mittermeir, 1998). In addition, results from the prototypical development of an integrated information system for the documentation, net-working and design of operational measures for business process improvement have been used for its construction (Scheer et al., 2002).

The framework consists of seven components, which are arranged in five layers. The components are represented by rectangles, the relations existing between them by shaded grey connecting lines and the system limits by a rectangle with rounded corners (cf. Figure 2).

In addition to the support in the development and usage of reference models, a third main function was identified for the management of reference models: reference model integration. These functions also form the core functionalities of the information system for the support of reference model management on the *tool layer*. The link between the elements "reference model development" and "reference model usage" is created by the element "reference model integration." This "bracket" is illustrated by the arrangement of the components, as well as by the connections representing the relations between the components in Figure 2.

The information model for reference model management, derived from the *conceptual layer*,

Figure 2. Framework for a reference model management system

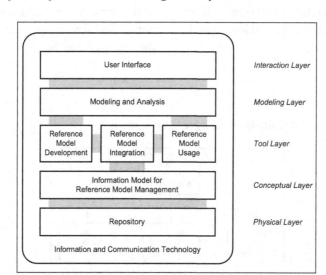

can be seen as the core component for the organizational framework. It identifies and links the most important information objects of the reference model management as well as associated information objects and, at the same time, forms a basis for its physical management. It is a semantic data-model, which—against the background of the research diversity discussed in the first section—is used to clarify relevant terms, as well as to define a uniform terminology.

The RMM-information model forms the technical basis for the functionality "reference model integration" of the RMMS on the tool layer. It is, however, also the basis for the logical database structure of the RMMS on the *physical layer*. It is also referred to as a repository. Both relationships are illustrated in Figure 2 by way of the connections plotted between the components.

Because established products exist in the field of information, and especially business process modeling, the complete new development of an RMMS is not necessary, but rather only the extension of existing systems. Thus, on the *modeling layer* especially, professional tools were used for the design of the component "modeling and analysis." The functionalities necessary for the development and usage of reference models which, for example, require a model modification, have already been implemented in corresponding systems. Functionalities which, however, serve the documentation of a construction process or a certain procedure in the usage of reference models may require a new implementation. Moreover, the deficit in findings discussed above is met through the implementation of the RMMS as an integrated part of a professional tool for business process modeling.

The user-interface of the RMMS is designed on the *interaction layer*. In addition to human judgment, the user interface of the RMMS represents a large bottleneck in the implementation of computer-aided information systems. Great importance must therefore be attributed to its design.

In the following, the design target defined by the RMMS-framework, that is, the description of the individual components of the framework, as well as their interactions, will be pursued. In doing so, the conceptual aspects of the RMM-information model, as well as the technical aspects in the form of an RMMS-system architecture, will be discussed.

REFERENCE MODEL MANAGEMENT SYSTEM

Information Model

The RMM-information model pursues two goals. First, the model, as the core component of the RMMS-framework on the conceptual level, builds the foundation for the design of the RMMS-functionality "reference model integration" on the tool level. This was identified as the "link" between the RMMS-functionalities for the development and usage of reference models before. Thus, the RMM-information model must identify and connect the most important information objects for the development and usage of reference models. In addition to the technical analysis of the field of application, the RMM-information model also pursues another goal. It serves as a starting point for the technical implementation of the information system and forms the foundation for the database-structure of the RMMS on a physical layer (RMMS-repository). The modeling language in which the RMM-information model is explained must therefore allow the representation of the relevant business content and be so formalized that a subsequent transfer of this content to information technology can be accomplished. The class diagram from the unified modeling language (UML) (http://www.uml.org/) was selected as a modeling language.

With the help of an object-oriented model, many classes and associations are constructed in the description of the application field "manage-

Figure 3. Macro-model of the reference model management

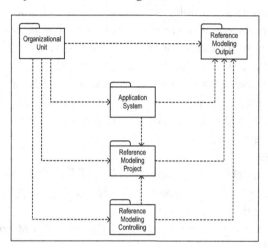

ment of reference models." Due to the resulting complexity of the total model, a structuring approach is required which abstracts from details while at the same time illustrating them, clarifying the underlying "superordinate" structure. The differentiation of information models according to the attribute "degree of aggregation" in macro- and micro-information models is such a structuring approach. While macro-information models represent aggregated and contextually similar objects (of another information model) and can be broken down into finer elements, micro-models contain no aggregated information and cannot be broken down into finer elements. The package diagram performs this task in the UML. It will be used in the following to show the fundamental dependencies between the components of the reference model management on a highly aggregated level (macro-modeling). In the next step, these components will be analyzed more closely and their "inner" structure will be constructed (micro-modeling). The UML-package diagram model presented in Figure 3 identifies the most important components for the management of reference models, as well as their interactions.

Reference models created within the framework of a construction or enterprise-specific information models designed during the adaptation of a reference model by persons, departments or enterprises can generally be interpreted as output. The usefulness of this output can be acknowledged by its recipients (for example, customer or a certain company-internal department). This interrelationship is represented in Figure 3 by the two packages *Organizational Unit* and *Reference Modeling Output*, as well as by their relationship to one another.

During the structuring of the macro-model, the idea was pursued that certain processes must be run through for the development and usage of reference models. These processes generally possess project-character due to their chronological and contextual restrictions. The respective reference modeling projects are therefore realized using concrete measures initiated and carried out by organizational units. The reference modeling projects, in turn, aim at creating reference modeling output. Thus, the package *Reference Modeling Project* is also introduced and is the center of the macro-model in Figure 3. The connection described is illustrated by the relationships between

Figure 4. Micro-model of the reference model management (section)

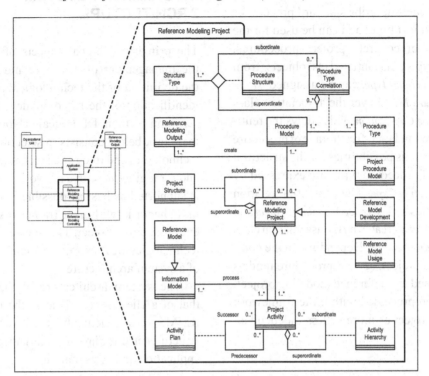

the packages *Organizational Unit*, *Reference Modeling Project* and *Reference Modeling Output*.

Reference models are recorded in electronic form or conventionally on paper. The models stored electronically can be assigned to application systems, such as modeling, and analysis tools as supporting media. The package *Application System* addresses this point.

Reference Model Controlling also carried out by organizational units, plans and controls the costs resulting from the activities in connection with reference modeling output and in addition, evaluates the reference modeling measures carried out according to their economic aspects.

The application field "Reference Model Management" is characterized in a survey-like manner with the UML-package diagram model. We will concentrate in the following on the classes assigned to the individual packages in this macro-

model and the associations existing between them. Due to reasons of space, the description is limited only to the central package Reference Modeling Project (cf. Figure 4).

Reference modeling projects are instantiated from the homonymous class *Reference Modeling Project* which refers to the interface of the corresponding package in the macro-model. A reference modeling project is comprised of the concrete project activities with which a target reference modeling output is to be created. A "network" is constructed here as a general procedure structure for project activities. The association class *Activity Plan* states that an activity can, but must not, have several successors and predecessors. The association class *Activity Hierarchy* suggests the possibility that an activity can consist of several sub-activities and is an element of a superordinate activity. The data structure for describing procedure models is also illustrated in Figure 4. Procedure models describe standard procedures for certain project types and can be used for the specification of concrete project procedures. Procedure types, instantiated as objects from the class *Procedure Type*, can be assigned to the class *Procedure Model* over the association class *Procedure Type Correlation*. This allows the reutilization and redundancy-free storage of procedure types. The various possibilities for the structural connection of procedure types are expressed by the class *Structure Type*. The contextual relation between the classes *Reference Modeling Project* and *Procedure Model* is created by the association class *Project Procedure Model*. Depending on the complexity of the project, several procedure models can be assigned to a reference modeling project. They are then processed within the framework of the total project as more or less independent sub-projects.

INFORMATION SYSTEM ARCHITECTURE

The primary technical aspects of the tool for the management of reference models refer to the definition of the technological platform, the identification of the IT-components and the description of their DP-logical relationships. The main task below consists in selecting individual technologies and integrated technology systems, and arranging these in a network so that the user is supported as best as possible in carrying out his or her tasks within the framework of the reference modeling project. The selected information technologies are illustrated in Figure 5 in the form of a system architecture.

The system architecture of the RMMS is that of a client/server. Due to the multitude of RMMS-system elements, these are "classically" structured in three layers—the data management, application and presentation.

Figure 5. RMMS-system architecture

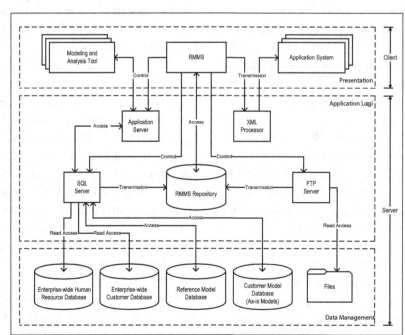

The *data management-layer* of the RMMS-system architecture is divided up into database and file management. While the structured data (human resource and customer data, as well as as-is and reference models) is managed in relational databases, the weakly-structured data (text documents, spreadsheets, presentation graphics, images, video and audio files, as well as links to further documents), is stored in a file system. The database structure is built upon the logically integrated data models developed on the conceptual level.

The data management-layer differentiates between four databases—an enterprise-wide human resource database, an enterprise-wide customer database, an as-is-model database and a reference model database. The reference model database, in particular, is a systematized collection of reference models (reference model library). It stores the reference model constructs, as well as their structural relationships, model attributes such as name, identification number, type of model (for example, EPC or ERM), description, time of creation, originator and last modification or last processor. The customer model database is also a model database, as is the case with the reference model database. It contains documented as-is-models, that is, sections of the customer's enterprise-structure interpreted by the creator of the model at the time of modeling.

The external databases in Figure 5 manage the data needed by the RMMS. Together they form the "minimum configuration" of the external RMMS-database. The individual databases in Figure 5 are represented as logical entities for purposes of simplicity, which, as a rule, consist physically of several distributed databases. For example, the reference model database could consist of several external databases. This is the case, for example, when in modeling projects reference models from different modeling tools are used to manage the models in their own databases.

The *application layer* comprises the server-services and data (RMMS-repository) which are used to carry out the technical tasks. The programs in this layer receive the user's (client's) instructions and carry them out on the relevant data. By using a client/server-architecture, several applications and users can access the same database at the same time and process it.

The RMMS-repository, in the center of the application layer, is completely defined by the data model designed above (cf. Figure 6). It structures the information objects necessary for the development and usage of reference models and can be searched. As already mentioned, textual project documents (for example, offers, commissions, specification sheets and bills) and presentation graphics or multimedia files (for example, audio and video recordings) are not stored in the RMMS-repository. They are managed in the file system of the data management layer and processed with external programs. Nevertheless, the search for and in these files is controlled with the help of links to the repository. It is especially the connection of structured and weakly structured documents via the database and file-server that is of importance here. The repository-data is stored in an XML-structure for internal processing. Through this, the integrated application of the structured data (database), as well as the weakly-structured data (files) are guaranteed, because they can be managed independently of their format. Thus, for the user, the database and file system appear to be one.

The project database is at the center of the RMMS-repository. It manages internal and external reference modeling project commissions between organizational units by storing data such as project name, type, objective, time period and status or progress. The data-structure of the project database corresponds to the UML-class-diagram model in Figure 4. Project documents, such as project commissions, structure plans, schedules, minutes and status reports or specification sheets,

Figure 6. RMMS-repository and databases

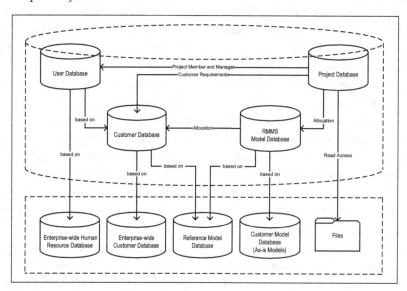

are not directly stored in the RMMS-repository. These documents are created by the users locally and managed in an external file directory. The project database also supports project management by managing the number, type and logical order of all activities with which a reference modeling project is to be realized, as well as by storing model histories. With the help of relations to the user database, each reference modeling project is assigned a project leader and a group of project members. Associations to the customer database take reference modeling-specific customer requirements into consideration. The project-related new development, configuration or reengineering of reference models, as well as the documentation of changes in the knowledge basis, require access to the reference model database.

While read-access to the weakly-structured data is controlled via the FTP-server, the SQL-server controls the read and write-access to the external databases and the data transfer to the repository (cf. Figure 5). The application server gives the RMMS-users access to the modeling and analysis tools. The application-server allows the flexible modification and extension of the RMMS-system architecture. When, for example, a new modeling and analysis tool is added, all that must be done is to adjust the respective software on the application-server.

The components of the RMMS with which the user has contact are assigned to the presentation layer (cf. Figure 5). They make the input and output user-friendlier and are represented by a graphic interface. The operational concept of the RMMS and its graphic user interface should be adapted to the interface design of established modeling and analysis tools. This way, the separate systems appear to be a logical entity for the user—from the technological point of view. This also makes access to the RMMS easier for users familiar with modeling tools.

The central element of the presentation layer is the RMMS-client. This term refers to the graphic user interface for the reference model management system in Figure 5. The access to the repository data, as well as the control of the SQL and FTP-servers, takes place over the interface of the RMMS. In addition, the requirements to the modeling and analysis tool are routed to the application-server and, when necessary, data are transferred to the XML-processor.

While the RMMS-components are used for processing information which is important for the development and usage of reference models, the creation, processing and deletion of information models remains the task of the modeling and analysis tools. Several different modeling and analysis tools may be used here. This is illustrated by the rectangles arranged one after another in Figure 5. In order to not focus on the integration capability of modeling tools (Mendling & Nüttgens, 2004) the use of only *one* modeling and analysis tool will be assumed. Not the interactions between several modeling tools, but rather the general exposure to reference models and associated information objects are the subject here. It is important, thereby, to secure the compatibility of the database of the modeling tool with the model databases in the data management-layer.

A decisive difference exists between the components "modeling and analysis tool" and "application system" (cf. Figure 5) on the technical side. While the modifications of the modeling and analysis tools flow back into the database of the RMMS, the information from the RMMS is only transferred to the application systems. This means that the knowledge won from these systems does not flow back into the RMMS-repository.

The repository-data is stored as XML-documents. Due to the independence of these documents from logical and physical structures, the integration of other application programs which use these documents is facilitated in the RMMS-system architecture. Applied RMMS-interfaces are conceivable in the software categories of office information (for example, word processing, spreadsheets and presentation graphics), computer-aided software engineering, computer-supported cooperative work, document management, enterprise resource planning, knowledge management, organizational memory and project management or workflow management. A simple implementation would be, for example, the inte-

gration of components which help to generate and output HTML-descriptions of process models. This can be especially useful in international reference modeling projects, where separate project groups operate. It allows the discussion of modeling results via Internet and Intranet. Some manufacturers of modeling tools already offer such components.

Prototype

The graphic user interface of the RMMS is illustrated in Figure 7. The prototype, implemented in the platform independent programming language Java (http://java.sun.com/), differentiates between a project and a model view of the tasks associated with the development and usage of reference models.

The project view has been selected in the screenshot in Figure 7. The RMMS workspace is divided up into an explorer and a viewer. These are connected logically with each other—a project selected in the explorer is displayed in detail in the viewer and can be manipulated there. The project active in Figure 7 is called "Reference Model for Event Management" and is used for the development of a reference model for the application domain "event management."

The title, the project's customer segment and information concerning the project period, progress and type were selected by the project manager while setting up the project with the help of the assistant (project wizard). This information can, in addition, be modified using the buttons "Project" and "Subject." A detailed representation of the customer assigned to the activated reference modeling project (i.e., his or her address, branch of business, turnover, number of employees, range of products, etc., can be reached using the button "Customer"). This functionality also allows the user to call up information such as customer description, goals or requirements. While this assignment in the use of reference models pertains more to individual customers, projects in reference model development are usually assigned an entire customer segment, as reference models are constructed for a whole class of use cases.

The Viewer is divided up into index cards, which can be selected using their respective tabs. The index card "Overview" (cf. Figure 7) basically characterizes the modeling projects. The elements in this card form important criteria according to which the projects stored can be sorted or searched.

The index card "Activities" contains the tasks or activities necessary for the realization of the targeted reference modeling project. Furthermore, descriptions of the above, activity plans and hierarchies are also stored here. These tasks are individually assigned to project members (via a link to the index card "Members"), as well as to project documents, such as meeting minutes or

the presentation of results (linked to the index card "History").

The creation of the team, which will work together in realizing the reference modeling project, takes place using the index card "Members." This card also contains the name, position, location, organizational unit and contact information for each member of the team, as well as the respective tasks assigned to them.

In addition to the project activities and employees involved in business engineering projects, one should also document information about the progress of the tasks and the problems met, as well as possible and ultimately selected measures for solving these problems. The history of the reference modeling project is therefore documented in a project history ("History"). This can be used by the project members as a source of information

Figure 7. Graphic user interface of the RMMS

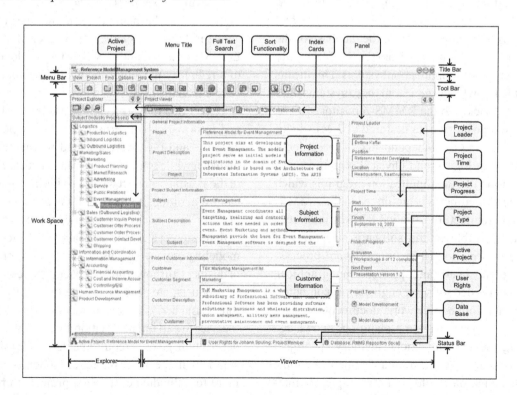

regarding the project history and can support the user in planning future projects.

The collaboration between employees in different departments and at different locations is also customary in the development and usage of reference models (vom Brocke, 2003). The RMMS thus has functionalities which support collaboration during reference modeling projects. To this purpose, an asynchronous communication medium (discussion) is offered on the "Collaboration"-card. One is also given the possibility of reviewing project documents.

The workspace in the RMMS-model view is also divided up into an explorer and a Viewer (cf. Figure 8, screenshot in the background). In the model explorer, all of the information models managed by the RMMS are displayed. This pertains to reference models constructed in development projects, as well as enterprise-specific models created in application projects.

The index card system in the "Model Viewer" is used to manage the most important model-related information for the management of reference models.

The information models managed by the RMMS are characterized on the index card "Overview" of the model view. This is similar to the corresponding card in the project view. The elements of the card "Overview" provide criteria similar to the corresponding information in the project view, according to which the information models stored can be sorted or searched. Potential sorting criteria, which can be selected in the corresponding pulldown menu in the upper part of the "Model Explorer" are: branch-of-trade, model name, application domain, model developer, period of development, modeling progress and modeling language. In the screenshot in Figure 8, the criteria "Economic Activity" is selected,

Figure 8. Interaction-design between the RMMS and the ARIS-Toolset

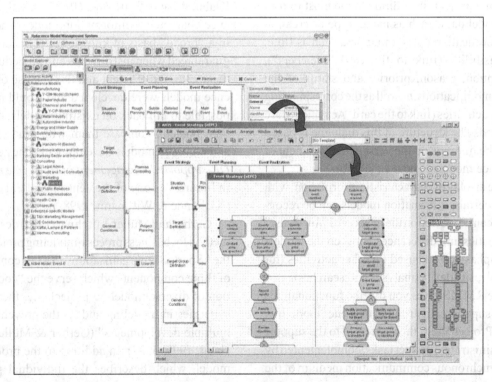

which differentiates between branches of trade at the top level. The reference model selected, which due to its form is referred to as "Event-E," is assigned to the branch "Marketing."

A graphic representation of the model to be constructed in the modeling project is made possible with the card "Graphic." Figure 8 illustrates the connected requirements clearly, as well as the resulting interactive-design between the RMMS and the modeling tool ARIS-Toolset (IDS Scheer AG, 2003). The example illustrates that the user can make modifications on a version of the reference model organizational framework for event management. To do so, he or she must open the ARIS-Toolset by clicking the "Edit" button. In addition to reading, editing or deleting models and model elements, the user is given further functionalities of the modeling tool.

The subject of the dialogue which can be reached using the "Versions" button on the "Graphic"-card (cf. Figure 8) is the management of the models and model element versions (model history) created in the course of the reference modeling project. In addition to the most important model data, such as name, type or creation and modification dates, other data such as time, responsibility (link to the card "Members"), description, reason, priority and status of the model modifications, as well as the corresponding project activities (link to the card "Activities"), are recorded. The structure of this dialogue is based upon the findings on the version management of reference models (Thomas, 2006b).

The display of characteristic information, with which certain information models can be recognized, can be viewed on the index card "Attributes." Similarities and differences between the models are emphasized and used for other activities (for example, similarity analyses and searches).

The RMMS gives you diverse functionalities for the support of distributed reference modeling. In the Project View, these referred to the support of administrative project tasks, complemented by the asynchronous communication medium of the

discussion forum. These functionalities have been extended by way of a synchronous communication medium on the index card "Collaboration," a shared whiteboard for the interactive viewing and annotation of graphic data.

Related Work

"Reference model management" is a term rarely used in science and in practice for the description of the management tasks associated with the development and usage of reference models. Therefore, a few examples for the use of this term will be discussed below.

Within the framework of his approach to the computer-aided use of reference data models HARS (1994, p. 11) sees the purpose of meta-models in creating a more favorable structure for the storage and *management of models*. What he means by this term, however, is not explained.

In a paper within the framework of the research project, "Business Process Design with Integrated Process and Product Models" (GiPP) Klabunde and Wittmann (1998), see the reference character of information models anchored in a "broad" basis of knowledge. This could be guaranteed when instruments and procedures for the access and efficient and flexible use of reference models were developed and would make it possible to fall back on existing models, discuss their content, compare them with other models and continue models development. They see the *DP-supported management of reference models* in libraries as one of the central challenges here (Klabunde & Wittmann, 1998, p. 16).

Gerber and Müller-Luschnat (1999) describe a method for business process-modeling projects for the "Sparkassenorganisation" (SKO), consisting of three components which serve the "coordination of diverse modeling projects, ... the use of synergies in modeling and ... the prevention of multiple developments" (Gerber & Müller-Luschnat, 1999, p. 27). In addition to the procedure model, which describes the individual project phases and the reference process model which serves the reutilization of process templates, they define *process model management* as a third component. This model "describes the processes necessary for the permanent care and further development of a reference model" (Gerber et al., 1999, p. 28). They declare the consistency of the reference process model during the usage of models from different BPR-projects to be the main task in process model management.

The goal of the project "Transformation of Reference Models for Standard Business Software" (TREBES) is the development of a theory for procedure model transformations with special regard to the requirements of business process engineering and reference model-based customizing (Oberweis, 2003). Petri-nets are used as a modeling language. According to existing procedure description methods, business objects are integrated and described using the extensible markup language (XML). The simultaneous transformation of several models during customizing (delta analysis) and the *computer-based management of reference models* are seen as problematic areas.

In addition, the term "model management" is often discussed by consulting firms in connection with the integration of enterprise applications. Model management then refers to the integration and contextual adjustment of models (for example, organization models, process models, data models and object-oriented models) within the same task and is seen as an important medium for increasing quality in software development (Resco GmbH, 2002). While model management deals primarily with instance models with respect to the degree of abstraction from the original, enterprise model management aims at type and cluster models. *Enterprise model management* (EMM) integrates and consolidates models on the project-level and tries to generalize their facts, so that the models can be applied on the department, division or enterprise level. The resulting models are, in turn, adjusted to each other and by adding other areas, further generalized.

CRITICAL DISCUSSION OF THE RESULTS AND FURTHER RESEARCH

The instrument "reference modeling" has not yet established itself extensively in business practice. This is due to the particular field of conflict between research and practice in which reference modeling is at home. Thus, there is still a deficit in knowledge about the use and problems inherent in the implementation of reference models despite the array of theoretical concepts. Accordingly, in the past the supply-sided development of reference models predominant in the science world has distanced itself from their demand-sided use in business and administration. This contribution has been devoted to this problem.

The rationale for the "reference model management" approach selected here is based on an analysis of the state of the art in reference modeling, whereby potentials were seen in two respects. First, we have shown that the contributions at hand comprehensively address the design of construction results but, however, disregard the corresponding construction processes which make the retraceability and, thus the reuse of the results, difficult. On the other hand, results pertaining to the design of the construction processes are available; they concentrate, however, either on the development or the use of the reference models or they do not sufficiently reduce the chronological, contextual and organizational separation between both processes. Reference model management was therefore formulated explicitly with the purpose of recreating the connection between the separated processes in reference model development and usage. Thus, within the framework of a process-oriented interpretation, the integration of both processes has been identified as a third function in reference model management next to the development and usage of reference models. The design and realization of an information system for the management of reference models were concretized as objectives here because, due to the magnitude of the models in modeling projects, the economic construction and use of models is only possible with the help of IT-tools. The development of this information system referred to as a reference model management system was structured by a framework.

The knowledge won in this analysis can be used as a starting point for more detailed research work. Thus, for example, empirical studies could be made to investigate whether the insights won more or less deductively coincide with the reality of business practice. One could also investigate how the use of the RMMS affects efficiency in modeling projects. The investigation of the effects of this prototype in operational business reality is seen as a future challenge for the author in his research activities.

The reasons for further research in the field of reference modeling lie in the fact that up to now no uniform reference modeling language has been established in theory or practice. Even the reference modeling-specific extensions of established languages in information modeling created primarily for research are rarely used in practice. Reference modeling research must carefully weigh formal precision against pragmatic manageability when developing such a modeling language: If modeling languages have formal semantics then they are suited to machine processing, but the interpretation of real-world connections can become more difficult. In this case, studies should be carried out to resolve this conflict. Thus, one of the central tasks in the future of reference modeling researchers should be to not only present the consequences of their results for science, but also for modeling practice.

Obviously, more fundamental research is required in order to understand the effects connected with the creation and usage of reference models in science and practice. However, this topic is dealt with in the future in reference modeling research, the compilation of improved knowledge about application system and organization design remains a central task in the field

of information systems. With the cognition won within the framework of this study, a concept and a prototypical implementation for the management of this knowledge, which is represented by reference models, are to be available.

ACKNOWLEDGMENT

The system presented in this article was developed at the Institute for Information Systems (IWi) at the German Research Center for Artificial Intelligence (DFKI) in Saarbruecken. The development of the system was funded by the "Deutsche Forschungsgemeinschaft" (German Research Foundation) within the research project "Reference Model-Based (Reverse-) Customizing of Service Information Systems" as part of the initiative BRID. The author is also grateful to Johann Spuling for supporting the implementation of the presented prototype.

REFERENCES

Becker, J., Delfmann, P., Knackstedt, R., & Kuropka, D. (2002). Configurative reference modeling. In J. Becker & R. Knackstedt (Eds.), *Wissensmanagement mit Referenzmodellen. Konzepte für die Anwendungssystem- und Organisationsgestaltung* (pp. 25-144). Berlin: Springer. [in German]

Becker, J., & Schütte, R. (2004). *Retail information systems* (2nd ed.) Landsberg/Lech: Moderne Industrie. [in German]

Fettke, P., & Loos, P. (2002a). The reference modeling catalogue as an instrument for knowledge management—methodology and application. In J. Becker & R. Knackstedt (Eds.), *Wissensmanagement mit Referenzmodellen: Konzepte für die Anwendungssystem- und Organisationsgestaltung* (pp. 3-24). Heidelberg: Physica. [in German]

Fettke, P., & Loos, P. (2002b). Methods for reusing reference models: Overview and taxonomy. In J. Becker & R. Knackstedt (Eds.), *Referenzmodellierung 2002: Methoden—Modelle—Erfahrungen* (pp. 9-33). Münster: Westfälische Wilhelms-Universität. [in German]

Fettke, P., & Loos, P. (2003). Classification of reference models: A methodology and its application. *Information Systems and e-Business Management, 1*(1), 35-53.

Fettke, P., & Loos, P. (2004b). Reference models for retail enterprises. *HMD - Praxis der Wirtschaftsinformatik, 235*, 15-25. [in German]

Gartner Inc. (Ed.). (1996, June 20). *BPR-Tool Market* (Gartner's Application Development & Maintenance Research Note M–600–144). Stamford, CT: Gartner Research.

Gerber, S., & Müller-Luschnat, G. (1999). Are reference process models useful in practice? In J. Desel, K. Pohl, & A. Schürr (Eds.), *Modellierung ,99: Workshop der gesellschaft für informatik e. V. (GI), März 1999 in Karlsruhe* (pp. 27-42). Stuttgart: Teubner. [in German]

Hammer, M., & Champy, J. (1993). *Reengineering the corporation: A manifesto for business revolution* (1st ed.). London: Brealey.

Hars, A. (1994). *Reference data models: Foundations for efficient data modeling.* Wiesbaden: Gabler. [in German]

IDS Scheer AG. (Ed.). (2003). *ARIS Toolset, ARIS Version 6.2.1.31203* [Computer software]. Saarbrücken: IDS Scheer AG.

Klabunde, S., & Wittmann, M. (1998). *Reference models and model libraries.* Saarbrücken: Institut für Wirtschaftsinformatik [in German].

Lang, K. (1997). *Business process management with reference model components.* Wiesbaden: DUV. [in German]

Mendling, J., & Nüttgens, M. (2004). XML-based reference modelling: Foundations of an EPC markup language. In J. Becker & P. Delfmann (Eds.), *Referenzmodellierung : Grundlagen, techniken und domänenbezogene Anwendung* (pp. 51-71). Heidelberg: Physica.

Mili, A., Mili, R., & Mittermeir, R. T. (1998). A survey of software reuse libraries. *Annals of Software Engineering, 5*(0), 349-414.

Oberweis, A. (Ed.). (2003). *TREBES: Transformation von Referenzmodellen für betriebswirtschaftliche Standardsoftware.* [in German] [On-line]. Retrieved August 17, 2003, from http://lwi2.wiwi.uni-frankfurt.de/projekte/trebes/

Remme, M. (1997). *Designing business processes.* Wiesbaden: Gabler. [in German]

Resco GmbH (Ed.). (2002). *EMM : Enterprise model management.* Hamburg: Resco.

Robson, G. D. (1991). *Continuous process improvement: Simplifying work flow systems.* New York: Free Press.

Rosemann, M., & van der Aalst, W. M. P. (2003). *A configurable reference modelling language* (Rep. No. FIT-TR-2003-05). Brisbane: Queensland University of Technology.

Scheer, A.-W. (1994a). A software product is born. *Information Systems, 19*(8), 607-624.

Scheer, A.-W. (1994b). *Business process engineering: Reference models for industrial enterprises* (2nd ed.). Berlin: Springer.

Scheer, A.-W., Habermann, F., Thomas, O., & Seel, C. (2002). Cooperative organizational memories for IT-based process knowledge management. In M. Blay-Fornarino, A. M. Pinna-Dery, K. Schmidt, & P. Zaraté (Eds.), *Cooperative systems design: A challenge of the mobility age. Proceedings of the 6th International Conference on the Design of Cooperative Systems (COOP2002)* (pp. 209-225). Amsterdam, The Netherlands: IOS Press.

Schlagheck, B. (2000). *Object-oriented reference models for controlling processes and projects.* Wiesbaden: DUV. [in German]

Schütte, R. (1998). *Guidelines for reference modeling.* Wiesbaden: Gabler. [in German]

Schwegmann, A. (1999). *Object-oriented reference modeling.* Wiesbaden: DUV. [in German]

Sinur, J. (2004). *Magic quadrant for business process analysis, 2004.* Stamford, CT: Gartner Research. Gartner's Application Development & Maintenance Research Note M-22-0651, March 4, 2004.

Thomas, O. (2006a). Understanding the term reference model in information systems research: History, literature analysis and explanation. In C. Bussler & A. Haller (Eds.), *Business process management workshops, BPM 2005 International Workshops, BPI, BPD, ENEI, BPRM, WSCOBPM, BPS,* Nancy, France, September 5, 2005, *Revised Selected Papers* (pp. 484-496). Berlin: Springer.

Thomas, O. (2006b). Version management for reference models: Design and implementation. In *Multikonferenz Wirtschaftsinformatik 2006 (MKWI'06). Universität Passau.* Accepted for presentation and publication in the track "reference modeling."

Thomas, O., & Scheer, A.-W. (2006, January 4-7). Tool support for the collaborative design of reference models—a business engineering perspective. In R. H. Sprague (Ed.), *Proceedings of the 39th Annual Hawaii International Conference on System Sciences,* Kauai, HI. Abstracts and CD-ROM of Full Papers. Los Alamitos, CA: IEEE Computer Society Press.

vom Brocke, J. (2003). *Reference modelling: Towards collaborative arrangements of design processes.* Berlin: Logos. [in German]

Chapter II
The Social Context of Knowledge

Daniel Memmi
Université du Québec à Montréal, Canada

ABSTRACT

Information and knowledge have become a crucial resource in our knowledge-based, computer-mediated economy. But knowledge is primarily a social phenomenon, on which computer processing has had only a limited impact so far, in spite of impressive advances. In this context have recently appeared various collaborative systems that promise to give access to socially situated information. We argue that a prior analysis of the social context is necessary for a better understanding of the whole domain of collaborative software. We will examine the variety and functions of information in modern society, where collaborative information management is now the dominant type of occupation. In fact, real information is much more complex than its usual technical sense: one should distinguish between information and knowledge, as well as between explicit and tacit knowledge. Because of the notable importance of tacit knowledge, social networks are indispensable in practice for locating relevant information. We then propose a typology of collaborative software, distinguishing between explicit communities supported by groupware systems, task-oriented communities organized around a common data structure, and implicit links exploited by collaborative filtering and social information retrieval. The latter approach is usually implemented by virtually grouping similar users, but there exist many possible variants. Yet much remains to be done by extracting, formalizing, and exploiting implicit social links.

INTRODUCTION

The development of computers and electronic networks has considerably advanced our society's capacity for information processing, and the very scale of this global phenomenon raises quite a few questions. Yet electronic data processing is by now so pervasive in advanced societies that it is easy to forget how recent it all is: computer science started about the time of World War II, but personal computers, the Internet, and the Web only go back a couple of decades in spite of their explosive progress.

As a matter of fact, information processing (i.e., the collection, creation, elaboration, and transmission of useful knowledge) has been around for as long as human history, and has become more and more important with the advent of modern bureaucratic industrial states two centuries ago. Recent technological developments take place within this social framework, which determines their shape, usage, and direction. The interaction between pre-existing social practices and new technologies is then an obvious issue to consider.

So how do human beings and organizations process information in today's technological, computer-mediated environment? How do they interact with each other through electronic networks? How can they put recent technical advances to the best possible use? And what future directions can be foreseen? To try and answer such questions, it would be useful to first analyze human information processing in more detail.

The classical approach, prevalent notably in cognitive psychology, has been to focus on individual information processing capabilities (Neisser, 1967; Mandler, 1985). A body of studies on perception, learning, recall, association and inference, and so forth has been performed on individual subjects in laboratory conditions. Much has been learned in this way on human information processing: for example our limited short-term memory, perceptual schemas, associative recall, probabilistic learning, and inference mechanisms are by now fairly well-established findings.

These studies have however been increasingly criticized for dealing mostly with isolated subjects performing artificial tasks in unrealistic ("non-ecological") environments. One has seen in the past 20 years a gradual shift to the study of situated and collective cognition. There has been more emphasis so far on physically situated rather than socially situated behavior, but the general trend is clear (Clark, 1998; Harnad & Dror, 2006).

Researchers in this growing movement try to understand how human beings perform tasks and solve problems in real physical and social situations. What they may lose in precision and experimental control, they hope to gain in scope and realism. Such an approach seems more relevant to the complex socio-technical environment in which human information processing must take place today.

The recent emergence of virtual communities which has been made possible by the Internet and other electronic networks is also a phenomenon worth investigating. These communities constitute a novel, computer-mediated form of social grouping, combining in variable proportion traditional social relations with more functional, goal-oriented features. Virtual communities should be studied as a collective entity rather than a mere collection of individual participants (Kollock & Smith, 1999; Rheingold, 2000; Memmi, 2006).

Understanding the social and technical context of individual information processing is important for several reasons. Beside the inherent interest of this subject, studying the way human beings use their social skills and social networks to acquire relevant information would help develop better information retrieval systems. As a matter of fact, there has recently appeared a variety of collaborative software systems inspired by human task-oriented social interactions.

Even if socially situated knowledge management cannot be totally reproduced with computers, software systems can be designed to borrow from the most pertinent aspects of human collective processing. Such distributed systems will also fit better the manner in which human beings naturally operate and solve tasks within society, and should thus prove easier to use. More generally, we will see how studying the role and use of knowledge in our society may prove useful to software designers and developers.

Our main thesis will be that information retrieval and information management in general should profit greatly from the study of socially situated information processing by human beings. This text intends to survey fundamental issues more than recent technical solutions. Understanding the nature and functions of knowledge in society appears necessary for long-term advances. We thus hope to bring some order to a fairly diverse range of proposals and to point to new research directions.

In this chapter we will therefore describe in turn: (1) the social and economic context of human information processing, (2) the nature and varieties of knowledge as well as its social pathways, and (3) various technical methods that have been devised to make use of the social aspects of human information processing.

We will resort in rather eclectic fashion to several disciplines, notably cognitive psychology, structural sociology, economics, management theory, and of course computer science and software design. But our main goal throughout will be to replace present work in collaborative software systems within the context of socially situated human cognition.

SOCIAL CONTEXT

We will start by showing more precisely how information processing can be seen as socially situated. This point of view will also have concrete technical consequences for the design of software systems.

The Social Import of Information

Far from being a purely individual phenomenon, information is intimately interwoven with the social and economic fabric of human groups. Social life is not possible without a constant exchange of information within groups and organizations. Because the social functions of information are

still largely underestimated, they deserve much more emphasis.

In this respect, one might want to make a distinction between raw information and knowledge acquired by human beings. Whereas information could be formulated objectively, knowledge is inherently a cognitive phenomenon and knowledge acquisition is a complex process. This distinction will prove useful later on, but following common usage, we will use the two terms more or less interchangeably for the time being.

Information can be defined in various ways, notably in probabilistic terms, but its practical function is to reduce uncertainty and to answer questions, allowing us to avoid dangers, fulfill goals, solve problems, and plan for the future. Information obviously has a biological survival function: all life forms, from insects to mammals, need information about their environment in order to find food and mates, avoid predators, and seek appropriate living conditions.

Information comes from the environment, be it physical, biological, or social. But most of our human environment is in fact a social one. Like most primates and many mammals, mankind is a highly social species and social situations are an integral art of our daily life. In modern urban society, moreover, we live in a mostly artificial, man-made environment replete with social functions and meanings.

As I look out of my window while writing this, I can see mostly buildings, whether residential or commercial, cars and traffic, and people walking by, many of them probably to or from work. This physical urban environment is actually a social environment. In my home, radio, television, telephone, fax machine, the Internet, papers, and magazines keep me informed about the larger world. The workplace is also a place of high informational density, where information is constantly exchanged and elaborated upon so as to perform complex social tasks.

As an ordinary member of modern society, I am extremely well connected with my environment, which turns out to be a highly social one. We could indeed be defined as social beings by the rich pattern of informational interactions we regularly maintain with our surroundings. Sociologists and anthropologists have often remarked that social cohesion is both ensured and demonstrated by regular exchanges of goods and services (Mauss, 1923), and information most probably plays a similar role, from office gossip to the Internet.

More concretely, a constant flow of information is obviously necessary for the coordination of social activities. This is true at all levels of social organization, from small business firms to the highest levels of government. The more complex the social and economic organization, the more important coordination activities become (Mintzberg, 1979). At the same time, communication is often highly ritualized and the practical functions of information blend insensibly with its cohesive role. For instance, office memos carry useful information while reaffirming organizational structure.

Another factor to consider is the economic value of information. It is a fact that is not yet sufficiently recognized, that information (or more accurately, human knowledge) has been the dominant source of growth and wealth in advanced societies for more than half a century. Investment in education, research and development, management, and other intangible factors has now overtaken investment in physical assets both in value and contribution to economic productivity and growth (Kendrick, 1994).

It is knowledge, and not physical investment in plants and machines, that is now the driving force in our post-industrial society. Knowledge-based domains such as electronics, computers and data processing, aeronautics, aerospace, biotechnology, and pharmaceutical companies clearly are the most dynamic, productive, wealthiest, and fastest-growing sector of the economy. And this is not a temporary phenomenon, but a solid long-term trend.

In short, most of our information originates from social situations, fulfills social and economic functions, and knowledge has become crucially important in a modern economy. Information must therefore be considered within its social context in order to really understand its functions and uses, and information processing techniques should also be seen in this context.

Toward the Information Society

Information processing is then not only an individual activity, it is the blood flow that keeps our societies running and prospering. Knowledge-intensive occupations and organizations have accordingly become more and more important: research and education, engineering, high-tech companies, consulting activities, law firms, financial services, health care, and so forth. A whole class of "knowledge workers" has emerged whose jobs consist mostly of handling and elaborating information on a daily basis (Drucker, 1992).

Knowledge workers not only handle information, but also create, transform, acquire and store, transmit and exchange, apply, and teach all forms of knowledge. They usually do so in a highly collaborative manner. For various reasons, the management of knowledge in many modern organizations tends to be a collective, distributed activity.

Information being an intangible asset, it is easily duplicated (especially with electronic techniques) and lends itself to cumulative development, a fact that encourages its dissemination and collective production and use. Network effects reinforce this tendency: it is often all the more advantageous to use an informational product (such as software) when it has many more users. Knowledge workers value collaborative work accordingly.

So information and knowledge are used mainly in social situations, even when processed by individuals. Information processing in real life is socially situated, and individual uses are secondary and derived from social goals. Not only most of the information we handle fulfills social functions, it is also managed collectively. As a consequence, useful or necessary information is to be found as much (if not more) in social circles as in libraries or databases.

The growing importance of information in a knowledge-oriented society has also been considerably accelerated by the recent developments in electronic information processing. Social and professional changes have gone hand in hand with technological advances—progress in one area taking place in synergy with evolutions in another. What is striking is not only the enormous increase in computing power available on the job in many professions, but its distributed character and the connectivity between individual computers.

Centralized mainframes have been replaced by cohorts of ubiquitous personal computers, and everybody is now connected to everybody and everything else by the Internet. More than the arrival of computers, the prominent fact of our time is the advent and rapid spread of electronic networks. They have made possible an amazing acceleration in the speed and quantity of information exchanged in our society.

At the same time, and this is of course no coincidence, sociologists have noticed an evolution toward a "network society" of loose, temporary, flexible relationships (Castells, 1996; Wellman, 1999). Instead of staying within closed groups, many social actors tend to shift from one connection to another as required by a different tasks or objectives. Traditional organizations give way to more flexible arrangements, and the Internet has proven to be the obvious tool to switch between diverse social links, regardless of time and distance.

The powerful conjunction between social changes and technological advances makes the information flow ever more important and significant. A network society can only function by constantly exchanging information, and a network structure is the appropriate organization for an information society (Shapiro & Varian, 1999). Computers, electronic networks, urban life, as well as rapid transit systems provide the technical infrastructure for this kind of social life.

The recent movement known as "Web 2.0" is characteristic of this socio-technical evolution (O'Reilly, 2005). This encompasses a loose collection of software tools and applications fostering social relations and collaborative work on the Internet. In this approach, the Web is seen as a platform for various social communication applications. Such tools accelerate even more the present trend toward a network society.

One may speculate about the causes and effects in this global evolution, and whether social changes or technical advances have been the dominant factor. But is clear that changes in different areas have reinforced one another, forming a coherent system that is reshaping our whole society. *Collective, distributed knowledge processing is now the prototypical occupation in today's information society.*

Technical Consequences

Because of these various social, cultural, and technical changes, human information processing is thus becoming more and more a collective, collaborative activity. Information can still be accessed individually in books, libraries, databases, or on the Web, but the sheer volume of accessible information makes social guidance or filtering practically inevitable. And more often than not, pertinent information resides partly in people's heads or expertise, and not in explicit documents, whether physical or electronic.

The constantly increasing complexity of tasks and problems makes it necessary to first locate the right person in order to perform a given task or solve a problem, and this requires a particular kind of social expertise. The diversity and dispersion of information, the fact that various sources of information must be put together and reformulated to become relevant, usually require some human collaboration. And one cannot stay within a small familiar circle of close colleagues or acquaintances to find all the required answers.

The information needed is often to be found somewhere within or by way of a larger social network of professionally related people. These networks may be formal (employees of a firm, professional organizations) or informal (personal address book, casual professional contacts), but they must be searched to locate information or knowledge that could not be found otherwise. Information retrieval thus becomes a social problem.

This means that *the whole domain of information retrieval should be fundamentally rethought in the light of the social nature of human knowledge.* Information has too often been thought of as some kind of objective material, detached from its social environment and use. This simplistic approach has probably made possible the first developments of information retrieval techniques, but one will not advance beyond those techniques without considering the ways in which human beings process knowledge in society.

Classical information retrieval has dealt fairly successfully with how to represent texts, how to evaluate semantic proximity, and how to index and retrieve documents efficiently (Salton & McGill, 1983; Baeza-Yates, 1999; Manning & Schütze, 1999). But new questions should now be considered: Who is the most likely person able to answer a request? How can we find this person quickly and efficiently? How can one represent people and social links? How can one use social expertise and distributed knowledge to recommend or filter documents?

This is the general setting in which must be seen the recent developments of collaborative software, social filtering, recommendation systems, and similar work. The present interest in such systems is no accident, but rather a sign of our times. We will describe below concrete technical approaches, but we must discuss beforehand the variety of knowledge forms involved in social processes.

NATURE OF KNOWLEDGE

We will now analyze in more detail how human beings manage information in real social situations and how they handle different varieties of knowledge.

A Simple Example

To illustrate this discussion, let us start with a concrete example. Let us suppose your organization has asked you to write or prepare a report on free and open source software, a subject you might not know too well. So how would you go about it? The first step might be to visit a library, looking up the computer science section directly, or consulting the catalog. But there just are not many books on the subject, they are still unlikely to be found in a public library, and relevant articles are scattered among so many journals.

Nowadays, your first reflex would probably be to use a search engine instead, to find references on the Web. But you will then be flooded with a profusion of references, of various relevance and quality. Which ones should you read and use? Can you trust these references to reflect a consensus in the domain? Or are they unorthodox divagations? Should you start with this long official report by a reputable organization or does this unassuming Web page offer a decent summary?

At this point, you will probably try to locate a knowledgeable colleague or acquaintance, somebody who could give you a leg up by recommending a few basic references or by inspecting your first list of references. He or she might also explain how to best exploit those sources, and tell you things about the domain that are not easily found in written documents. And if he happens to be a practitioner of open software, the discussion could become quite lively and really interesting...

He might assert, for instance, that popular discussions on the subject tend toward wishful thinking and unsubstantiated ideological claims. He could, however, recommend two or three studies in which one can find the real professional status and economic support of free software developers. This would probably help you write a better, more informed report on the matter.

But how can you be sure your colleague really knows what he is talking about? Well, you can never be totally sure (until you become an expert yourself). But if he has been recommended by close colleagues of yours, if he has been involved in this subject for years, if he belongs to an association dealing with free software, you might be reasonably confident. If he does not belong to your organization, you will probably try to evaluate somehow the competence of his organization and his own standing, before you trust his advice.

And how does one locate the right person? In most cases, this is done simply by asking personal acquaintances deemed to be closer than you to the information required. For instance, if you do not know anybody working on free software, you might ask a software engineer or your system manager to recommend somebody else to consult. By following two or three such links, you will quickly find a knowledgeable expert.

Such a simple strategy has been shown to be fairly efficient. In a well-known experiment, people in the United States were asked to forward a letter through personal acquaintances only, in order to reach a target person whose occupation was mentioned, but not the exact address (Travers & Milgram, 1969). People were instructed to hand over the letter to somebody they thought closer to the target, geographically or professionally, and the process would be repeated from one person to the next. Not all letters reached the final target, but those that arrived at their destinations took no more than five steps on average. This is a good example of the "small-world" phenomenon (Watts, 1999).

We often use a similar strategy when looking for preliminary information on a subject we do not know much about yet. In other words, *we first perform a kind of social look-up in order to access relevant information or knowledge.*

This fairly straightforward example illustrates some of the points we will now elaborate upon: the difficulty for an individual to manage socially distributed information on his own, the need for social guidance, the problem of trust, how help can be found by exploiting social links, the importance of tacit knowledge and personal expertise, the role and structure of social groups, and so forth. The issue will then be how to formalize and exploit these social phenomena.

The well-known Internet bookseller Amazon. com offers prospective buyers a simplified version of such social guidance. When a book on a given subject is found through Amazon's search engine, the system displays a list of ratings and comments on this book by former buyers and users. This is still very crude (the trustworthiness of the ratings is questionable), but this is an effort to help individual online buyers with social advice.

Varieties of Knowledge

Yet to fully understand human information processing, it must be realized that we are actually dealing with different forms of information or knowledge which are managed in different ways. To begin with, one should distinguish between *information* and *knowledge,* a distinction we have glossed over so far. Although usage varies somewhat, information is basically the raw material of information processing, whereas knowledge has been acquired by human beings through a learning process.

Information can be found in physical form, for instance in written documents, databases, images, and recordings. Information may be defined objectively in probabilistic terms according to information theory: the quantity of information contained in a message is inversely proportional to (the logarithm of) its probability of occurrence. This mathematical approach has proven its worth in signal processing and telecommunications, but its application to human cognition is debatable, as it proves hard to separate information from its practical context of use.

Knowledge, for its part, is inherently personal or social: knowledge is information acquired by human beings. Knowledge must be learned in context, individually or collectively, before being put to use to accomplish human goals and functions. The very notion of knowledge is inseparable from cognitive and social processes, while information could be defined more narrowly as a property of the physical world.

The point is that even if information can be objectively quantified for engineering purposes, *only knowledge is of real social and economic importance.* But knowledge is also difficult to acquire. Information may be copied or reproduced mechanically, but knowledge must be assimilated by humans before it can be used. And specialized knowledge can only be acquired by well-prepared specialists, restricting its effective social range of application.

The increasing division of labor, the complexity of technical knowledge, and the pace of innovation make it more and more difficult to ensure the transmission of knowledge within organizations and firms. Training or tutoring mechanisms may be devised, but bringing together the appropriate people remains a problem for learning to succeed. One must find both adequate experts and well-prepared apprentices. This is very much a social problem, which must first be solved for knowledge transmission to take place.

Another important distinction is between *explicit* and *tacit* knowledge, or perhaps more accurately between explicit information and tacit knowledge (usage is unfortunately not coherent here). Explicit knowledge or information is public and formalized, in linguistic or mathematical form

notably. Books, journals, textual documents of all kinds, Web sites, databases, and so forth—all contain explicit knowledge, as long as one knows the linguistic or formal conventions necessary to interpret their content.

Information retrieval and computer science deal mostly with explicit information, so that it is too easy to forget that this is only one kind of knowledge. Real social life, however, makes frequent use of other forms of knowledge as well, which can be grouped together under the general label of tacit or implicit knowledge (Polanyi, 1966; Baumard, 1999). There is in fact a variety of forms of tacit knowledge (such as body language, common sense, work expertise, procedural knowledge, etc.), and one might distinguish further between unformulated and unconscious knowledge, but we will not attempt a more detailed analysis here.

Tacit knowledge is knowledge that has been acquired from practical experience: medical expertise, technical know-how, teaching experience, and management skills are forms of tacit knowledge. This cannot be learned from books alone, as learning by doing is a necessary component. Organized tutoring may help, but transmission will then be from person to person, which proves to be a slow and cumbersome process. *Tacit knowledge remains a serious bottleneck in the information society.*

One should also notice that tacit knowledge is often collective. Many organizations perform (more or less adequately) thanks to collective routines and procedures that are distributed among many actors and are often left unformalized. The knowledge inherent in organizational functions is not expressed publicly, and no single actor knows the whole picture. This lack of clarity may lead to serious inefficiencies.

Tacit or implicit knowledge is thus hard to learn and to pass on, and the computer revolution has so far not helped very much in this respect. As tacit knowledge is unfortunately an essential part of social life and economic performance, this is an area that begs for more consideration from knowledge management in general and information retrieval in particular. We feel that serious advances could be expected in this domain.

Last but not least, *social knowledge* is the (largely implicit) knowledge necessary to make use of social relationships so as to perform tasks and solve problems. It is an important component of most professions, but one that is usually learned by long practice and experience. The social skills and expertise necessary to find information needed for a given task, ensure social cooperation, and negotiate common rules are crucial to task performance in most lines of work.

Social knowledge has not yet been given sufficient recognition, however, and is rarely discussed, described, or formalized. Sociologists have been interested in the social structure of groups and how this constrains individual choices and strategies (e.g., Lazega, 2001). But there has been much less emphasis on individual knowledge of these constraints, on how they might be represented and processed cognitively. This calls for more research in social psychology.

To be able to access or use social knowledge would be quite useful for information retrieval systems. Finding the appropriate expert most likely to answer a technical question, for example, is often a better idea than searching the Web by oneself. Though the issue is usually not presented directly in this way, we will see below that collaborative software systems have started to incorporate elements of social expertise.

Social Networks

It should be obvious by now that an important part of human knowledge management takes place by way of social links and requires appropriate social expertise. Social networks have fortunately been studied and formalized by structural sociology, and there is a sizable body of methods and techniques to draw upon (Wassermann & Faust, 1994).

Social networks are a simplified model of social relationships, schematic enough to be represented and handled mathematically on a computer. The basic data structure is a graph, where nodes stand for social actors (individuals or groups) and links represent social relations. Links are usually not labeled, but may have an associated numerical value (standing for the strength or frequency of the relation). This graph is in turn implemented as a matrix on which various operations can be performed.

If the matrix represents direct links, indirect relations (requiring several steps through the network) can be found by computing successive powers of the basic matrix. For instance the square of the matrix will show two-step relations, the cube of the matrix three-step relations, and so on. Many other operations are also possible, and there are various algorithms for extracting from the social graph densely linked subgroups of nodes.

This approach is obviously a drastic simplification of the complexity of real human relationships, but the formal structure of such models can already be very revealing. In particular, the structural subgroups that can be extracted automatically from the graph correspond to social groupings of actors, working on similar tasks and exchanging information about common concerns. Structural subgroups are usually functional groups as well.

For example, after mapping the network of collaboration relationships between 71 lawyers in an American law firm, it is possible to find 11 dense subgroups corresponding to specific locations or specialties (see Lazega, 2001). As these subgroups also interact with one another, they can be seen as forming a higher-level network with fewer nodes, a kind of summary of the basic network. The whole process requires some human interpretation, but reveals social facts that are simply not obvious to the naked eye.

The position of an actor within the social network is usually significant: it shows the centrality or prominence of the actor, and the resources and information he has immediate access to. The network also shows the nodes and paths an actor would have to follow in order to access more remote information. Sociologists tend to interpret structural positions in terms of power relationships: central positions are strategic while actors located at the margins have to go through others to access various resources (Burt, 1992).

From our point of view, however, the main issue to consider is that *structural networks determine social access to information*. Central actors have quick and easy access to socially embedded knowledge, while marginal actors might have to contend with longer access routes. The social expertise necessary to retrieve socially situated information comprises social skills (such as diplomacy or bargaining tactics), but also the basic ability to perceive and exploit the social structure as such.

Social expertise may remain more or less unconscious, but the deliberate "networking" behavior of the ambitious professional is also quite common. Many professionals know the importance of "weak ties": useful information and opportunities are often obtained through casual relations which thus deserve to be strenuously cultivated (Granovetter, 1973). At the same time, developing and using a network of close contacts in the workplace is often a prerequisite to successful work performance.

Social information retrieval and problem solving by human beings is thus achieved through social networks, which govern information circulation and information flow. Formalizing this structure should be very helpful in order to model human knowledge management skills and capabilities, and possibly to design better collaborative software systems.

Now the development of electronic transmission networks has made it possible to extract automatically many social relations, as they leave electronic traces. For instance one may note the pattern of e-mail messages exchanged within an organization and formalize it as a graph. Of course, not all social interactions are reflected in electronic messaging, but e-mail traffic is obviously significant in many modern organizations. Web browsing is also a more indirect source of social affinities, which can be exploited to retrieve social information.

As a matter of fact, collaborative software systems make use of social links and social information, directly or indirectly. They might have been consciously designed in this way, but this may also be the result of practical attempts to solve an informational problem.

TECHNICAL APPROACHES

After this review of human information processing in social context, it is now time to consider how the insights gained during this study can be used to design social information systems. This should also help us put in perspective recent work in collaborative software.

Typology of Collaborative Software

There is already a variety of collaborative systems, but one can try to regroup various proposals into a few classes. We would like to propose a general typology of these systems, using a few relevant features to differentiate between them.

What collaborative systems have in common is the modeling of a social environment and use of social expertise to access relevant information. They differ, however, in the manner, explicit or implicit, in which they model the social community that serves as context for information purposes. Some systems provide users with an explicit representation of a social group, which may be consciously accessed as such. Other systems use social links implicitly, and the end users do not have to be aware of the underlying social structure (we prefer calling such links *implicit* rather than tacit because they might be totally unconscious).

Another pertinent distinction is whether the focus of operations is on the group itself or on the informational task being performed. Virtual communities tend to be task oriented and more impersonal than real communities, and some collaborative systems will emphasize the task more than the social group. In such a case, representing the task at hand is the central issue, and the explicit or implicit representation of the group structure becomes of secondary importance.

One should also remember that a collaborative information system does not have to reproduce faithfully every aspect of human information processing. There are fruitful lessons to learn from studying socially situated human cognition, but a software system can do things differently (and more efficiently in some ways) than the human mind. For example, social expertise about how to retrieve relevant knowledge may be implicitly built into a computer system, whereas a human being would have to search his social network consciously.

In fact some software systems stick closely to the structure and functioning of real human groups, and exhibit the same limitations in terms of group size or cognitive load. We would contend that virtual communities may well function differently, and that collaborative software should be designed accordingly. On the other hand, present software is still far from the complexity and capabilities of human social processing, so that there remains much to be learned from real human cognition.

Still, collaborative systems may also be classified in different ways, notably by using more technical criteria. The manner in which individual participants, relationships, and communities are represented and the clustering algorithms are used to regroup similar actors, the data structures and implementation techniques could also be used to differentiate between systems. But the emphasis

being here on social issues, a classification based on community type seems more appropriate to this discussion.

To sum up, we think that work on collaborative systems up to now can be roughly classified into three main types: building explicit communities, building task-oriented communities, and using implicit social links.

Building Explicit Communities

This is the most obvious direction, and this research field is often known as *groupware* (Favela & Decouchant, 2003). Such systems try to make as explicit as possible the structure of the group, the biography and interests of participants, their role and status, and the history of interactions. The goals, tasks, common tools, past actions, and current problems can be posted publicly. The rationale is that group awareness and explicit interactions are conducive to better problem solving.

In a hospital setting for instance, there is an intense exchange of information between various medical staff (physicians, nurses, laboratory technicians, etc.), and timely access to correct information is clearly vital. But medical staff is highly mobile, and information is heterogeneous (verbal exchanges, textual records, images, etc.) and rapidly changing. The collective task to be performed (taking care of patients) is therefore highly distributed and in constant evolution.

And the problem is not just information distribution, but rather one of coordination between different actors and collective decision making. Although they often communicate through common objects (such as whiteboards and clipboards), medical personnel must be aware of each other, because the source and time of information may be crucial. A multi-agent architecture can then be used to locate or notify the right person at the right time with the appropriate information (Munoz, Gonzalez, Rodriguez, & Favela, 2003). In this way interactions are made explicit but also kept under tight control.

Yet groupware systems, properly speaking, can only function for small groups of participants. When the number of active members reaches more than 30 or 40 people, personal information and individual interactions may prove overwhelming. On the other hand, high awareness about individual group members may lead to personal relations and allow focusing a search for information on the person most likely to know the answer to a problem.

In this way, groupware systems try to reproduce the functioning of small social groups as we traditionally know them: family and friends, office life, workgroups, neighborhood associations, and so forth. Such systems are often used in a close professional context (e.g., a hospital or a firm) where people already know each other or are likely to meet face to face sooner or later. In this case, groupware will reinforce or assist real or potential social relationships, but will not create unexpected links.

Groupware design presents interesting technical challenges for computer scientists: managing synchronous and asynchronous communication between participants in various and changeable locations, transmission of heterogeneous data (including text files, messages, images, and sound), maintaining the coherence of common data structures, and so on. Sophisticated systems have been developed, notably for healthcare environments and computer-supported collaborative learning. But these systems are not widely used, probably because they are still too cumbersome and not appropriate for many social groups.

Groupware can be useful in professional domains requiring intensive social links with focused interactions dealing with very specific tasks. The density and quality of interactions require fairly elaborate software to update and transmit information in a graceful and readable way, with heterogeneous data and more and more mobile users. But groupware is inadequate and unwieldy for larger groups and casual interactions.

Another possibility is to use the social network that can be inferred from Web pages, social interactions, and common interests to locate experts on a given subject (Kautz, Selman, & Shah, 1987). This might be the only way to find tacit information, which is not publicly available. This approach may also be developed to improve information retrieval by taking advantage of the social links of document authors for instance—well-connected authors are probably more reliable (Kirsch, Gnasa, & Cremers, 2006). But we will see below how to exploit implicit links.

Still another research direction that has not yet been developed much in computer science would be to post an explicit structure for the social network in a given domain. So this would also be an explicit representation, but a more schematic and lighter one.

We have seen that structural sociology has elaborated formal models of social groups considered as networks of relations (Wassermann & Faust, 1994). The complexity of real social interactions is deliberately simplified so as to represent a group by a graph, in which nodes are actors and links are relations. Social interactions are reduced to simple relations, such as collaboration, advice, or influence.

Without going into more detail, the point is that structural sociology is well formalized and sufficiently advanced to offer relevant representation tools for larger communities. Representing groups with hundreds of members is not a problem, and the nature of links (edges in a graph) is simpler and more abstract. For larger communities, these formal methods might be a better source of inspiration than current groupware techniques.

From a practical point of view, structural methods could be used to map the current state of a community and to show participants their position in the network, the coherence of the structure, what the sub-groups are, the dynamic evolution of the network, and so forth. This would be another way to raise group awareness, not in personal terms but from a structural, more abstract perspective.

In a large firm, for example, it might be useful to be able to identify structural subgroups in order to find appropriate contacts on a functional rather than a personal basis. Although this is technically possible and software systems are now available for this purpose, they are not really used in practice, perhaps because they are felt to be too revealing and intrusive.

Still, when participation is only occasional or unique, and when interactions are mostly impersonal, the notion of structural network loses significance. If all interactions take place through a common workspace, the most one could probably hope for is to make it easy for users to enter the system and to deal with common objects. A good data structure and convenient access and modification procedures are then necessary.

Building Task-Oriented Communities

Virtual communities are frequently task oriented. Computer-mediated communities are often quite different from traditional social groups, a fact that is too rarely acknowledged in the literature. By comparison with traditional groups, participation in virtual communities is more impersonal, often temporary or anonymous, with a lower level of emotional involvement. These communities are mostly goal oriented: participants contribute to a common goal or task, but are less interested in personal relationships.

In such a case, group activities revolve around a common data structure (forum, discussion thread, Web site, wiki, database, etc.) that shows the current state of the task in progress and is regularly updated. This is a *blackboard* model, where all interactions go through a central data structure rather than by means of particular links.

Such an architecture was originally proposed for the Hearsay-II speech understanding system as an efficient method to coordinate the operation of various modules: all communication between modules takes place through the blackboard (Lesser & Erman, 1977). In our domain, this can be seen as a form of situated cognition, determined by a common public environment which is represented here by a central blackboard.

Since most of the information necessary for group activities is posted on this blackboard, *information retrieval can be done by accessing the common workspace.* Information management is collective, in the sense that the blackboard somehow summarizes the whole history of group interactions and contains all the information deemed relevant by the group. This is another form of collaborative retrieval, but of an indirect and impersonal kind.

One reason that may explain the prevalence of this type of communication is simply that it minimizes the complexity of interactions. The number of potential point-to-point links between n actors is $n(n-1)/2$, which grows like the square of the number of actors. But the number of interactions with a common data structure only increases linearly with the number of participants, a much more manageable proposition for larger groups.

There is in fact no sharp boundary between explicit communities and blackboard-mediated groups, and the distinction is not always clear. For example, in hospital wards, the "blackboard" (actually a whiteboard) is only one source of information among others. Yet there is a strong tendency in modern life, notably in virtual communities, toward more impersonal, functional, flexible social groups organized around a common task or goal. Such groups have their own informational requirements, which must be served by access to a simple, robust, easily maintained blackboard structure.

The recent *wiki* technique is a good example of user-friendly blackboard management system. A wiki is basically an interactive Web site with simple and easy editing procedures. Registered participants may post text messages on the site, and they can also augment, comment on, or modify previous messages. So everybody can contribute to the site, but interventions must be signed and the history of modifications is kept automatically. In practice, a moderator is useful to check interventions before they are posted.

The well-known online encyclopedia Wikipedia has been (and still is) developed in this way with very good results overall (*www.wikipedia.org*). The quality of entries is not always consistent, and there have been a few problems with inaccuracies or vandalism (hence the importance of competent moderators). But on the whole Wikipedia has proven to be a successful collective, collaborative enterprise and a model of what could be accomplished online.

Although it is in fact a more complex phenomenon, the development of free or open source software may also be seen as a task-oriented activity (Feller, Fitzgerald, Hissam, & Lakhnani, 2005). A software project under development serves as a common object which is repeatedly corrected and improved by a wide community of programmers and testers, many of whom do not interact on a personal basis. This community is strongly structured, however, with a small inner core of project leaders surrounded by concentric circles of contributors and critics, so that this would really be a hybrid example between personal and impersonal relations.

Using Implicit Social Links

Other software systems do not post group structure or common data. This is usually the case with collaborative information retrieval, collaborative filtering, and recommender systems. There exist many variants, but the basic idea consists of exploiting the implicit structure of a group of users in order to find relevant documents, filter search results, or recommend information or products. The grouping may be made public in some systems, but is usually not handled by the users themselves, who might remain totally unaware of this virtual structure.

These collaborative systems work by computing similarities between human users and by taking advantage of the resemblance to share information between similar users (Resnick, Iacovou, Suchak, Bergstrom, & Riedl, 1994; Shardanand & Maes, 1995; Adomavicius & Tuzhilin, 2005). For example one may recommend movies, books, music, or other products to a given user by finding "similar" users and quoting their best choices. Or one may retrieve or filter documents by noting which documents have been retrieved or used by groups of similar users.

To throw some light on the variety of such systems, one may want to make several distinctions between them. Although real systems often blur these distinctions, the following categories of collaborative systems may be useful:

- **Collaborative filtering (recommender systems):** These systems recommend (or rank) products, services, or documents for the benefit of an individual user by collecting the preferences of similar users.
- **Collaborative retrieval systems:** These retrieve (or filter) relevant documents by using the profiles of similar users. Poor initial queries can thus be augmented with more expert information.
- **Active (explicit) rating:** Users explicitly take the time to rate or recommend products. People are amazingly willing to do so (probably as a form of self-expression, in order to promote a product they like, out of sheer sociability, etc.), but their active intervention is required.
- **Passive (implicit) rating:** Information on user preferences is collected by noting significant user actions (buying products, Web browsing, bookmarking, downloading files, etc.). This can be done automatically, but user tastes are inferred, not directly measured.

This general approach requires establishing an interest profile for each end user, and choosing a similarity measure so as to be able to compare users in a coherent way. By analogy with classical information retrieval methods, each user is usually characterized by a vector of relevant features, and users are compared by computing their proximity in vector space. The group profile used as a basis for recommendations can then simply be the average of member profiles.

There have been quite a few variations, such as employing statistical correlation, angle or distance between vectors, or various clustering algorithms to estimate user resemblance, but the determination of a user profile is of course crucial to the operation of the system. One may want to compare different methods, but results depend on the task and the nature of the data (Breese, Heckerman, & Kadie, 1998).

Instead of comparing users to find subgroups of users with similar interests, it is also possible to compare and cluster items with regard to user preferences (this is what Amazon.com does). If you like a particular item, the system can then recommend similar items. But the latter method is in fact a dual representation of the former: one may equivalently represent users in item space or items in user space, but a choice can be made for reasons of implementation.

Collaborative systems unfortunately suffer from a "cold-start" problem: a critical mass of users and user preferences is needed for the system to prove valuable. There is then little incentive for initial users to join the club, and some way must be found to attract them in order to build this critical mass. Symbolic rewards might help in this regard (the pleasure of participating in an innovative experiment for example).

One should also be aware that rankings depend on the particular rating method chosen to evaluate the relevance of documents or products. We have seen that the rating of a particular item could be determined by explicit user evaluations, by semantic proximity to user profiles, or

by recording user actions concerning this item. Evaluations may depend both on user profiles and user actions in variable combinations.

In short, *implicit collaborative systems work by setting up groupings of similar users* and then exploiting these virtual groups to retrieve or recommend socially supported items. Collecting individual ratings (whether explicit or not) about items is a prerequisite to calculating their overall social value in the group of reference.

Another example of the implicit use of social structure is offered by PageRank, Google's ranking algorithm for Web pages (Brin & Page, 1998). This famous search engine retrieves pages in classical fashion (by computing their textual similarity to a user query) but then orders them by exploiting the structure of Web links. The page ranking is meant to solve the frequent problem of information overflow with too many answers to a query.

More precisely, Web pages are ranked by the sum of hyperlinks pointing to them from other Web sites, each link being weighted with the value of the pointing site, determined recursively in the same way by considering its own incoming links. The ranking of a site thus increases with the number and value of sites pointing to it. A careful matrix implementation of the graph of hyperlinks speeds up the recursive value computation.

The hyperlink structure used by the PageRank algorithm is in fact the public trace of an implicit social consensus. Web sites with numerous incoming links are better known (and tend to attract even more new links) as they have been judged more relevant by other Web site publishers. This is a measurable form of hyperspace reputation on the Web, which is presumably a good indicator of the interest and trustworthiness of a Web page. The success of Google is largely due to the clever use of this social indicator.

Peer-to-peer file sharing systems such as Napster, Gnutella, or KaZaA have also been very successful, to the horror of major music companies. They work by distributing requests through a network of participants so as to find users with similar tastes. Music files or other documents can then be exchanged among like-minded participants. Napster employed a central server to store and compare user profiles, but in more recent systems both data and processing are totally distributed throughout the network (Memmi & Nérot, 2003; Wang, Pouwelse, Lagendijk, & Reinders, 2006).

Peer-to-peer architectures can be used for file sharing, information retrieval, and collaborative filtering. But the implicit links between users do not have to be made public for the system to work, thus allowing a minimum of privacy.

In spite of their differences, these various collaborative systems all make use of distributed, implicit, socially situated knowledge by building or revealing virtual communities. Relevant information is accessed through social links, and retrieval algorithms embody social expertise about information handling. But individual systems users are not made directly aware of the underlying group structure.

TRENDS AND PERSPECTIVES

Even though our survey has not been exhaustive, the diversity of approaches and collaborative systems is striking. So the question arises whether one can discern general tendencies among recent research work. It is by no means clear at this time that one approach will predominate over the others, but we would like to venture a few general observations and suggest likely developments.

Following the typology proposed above, explicit communities and task-oriented groups are the most obvious phenomena and have probably attracted more initial attention as a basis for computer-aided communication. But it seems to us that *there remains more to discover about implicit social links,* so that interesting novel techniques may be expected to appear in this direction. Because more and more information

is becoming available in electronic form about human relationships, new ways will be found to exploit such information.

For example, commercial transactions and work connections often leave electronic traces which can used for informational purposes. Profiling people by their commercial or browsing behavior can also be used to put together virtual groups with similar interests and needs. On the other hand, such techniques could also prove very intrusive, posing difficult ethical and social problems about individual privacy.

We believe that more detailed analyses of human social information processing would be a fruitful source of new techniques. We have tried here to show the wealth and complexity of social information processes, but we still do not know enough about such common social mechanisms. Studying and modeling collective information management should bring about new insights and suggest new approaches.

Unfortunately, interest in this area has traditionally been dispersed among very different disciplines, which do not communicate very well with each other. Sociology, economics, and management studies notably have contributed valuable observations about human knowledge management, but this is too rarely a central concern and approaches vary widely. Fundamental research in this domain is then more likely to be a source of inspiration to computer science than to provide a store of directly applicable models.

Accessing and making use of tacit knowledge has hardly started, and usually only indirectly. In spite of the social and economic importance of this type of knowledge, it only becomes accessible online as a by-product of explicit communication links on the Internet. No systematic effort has been made so far to address this question by computer, although the problem is largely recognized in real life (tutoring relationships and training schemes are basically meant to ensure the transmission of implicit or tacit knowledge).

Profiling individuals by their electronic behavior is the most likely route in order to gain access to the tacit knowledge they might possess, but for privacy reasons this is probably feasible only within work situations and inside organizations. And as to collective tacit knowledge (the kind of knowledge that makes a company more or less efficient), one simply knows very little about how to describe or formalize such distributed information.

We would also like to suggest that a generic platform or general toolbox for collaborative software design would be a good idea for experimenting with various methods. It would help build prototypes and new software systems. Such a platform should contain the main representation and processing techniques we have seen so far, with capacities for exchanging information between different approaches. Common data representations would make it possible to share information among various tools.

A recent example of this kind of open toolbox can be found in the Sakai project (*www. sakaiproject.org*). This is a free collaborative environment which contains many of the communication techniques currently available for virtual communities. The emphasis is on education and e-learning, but the software can easily be extended to other areas.

In our view, such a toolbox should include in particular the following methods:

- Current communication tools (e-mail, chat, forums).
- Blackboard facilities (a wiki structure, for example).
- Social network simulation software.
- Social network analysis software.
- Common profiling and clustering algorithms.

Most of these software tools are already available, but in different domains, and they are rarely employed together. For example, elaborate methods have been developed for social network analysis, and software packages are easily obtainable (e.g., Ucinet or Structure), but they have mostly been used by sociologists. Electronic mail is widely used, but communication patterns are rarely collected and studied. Putting together different methods would make data available for analysis, and help investigate a complex and multidisciplinary field of enquiry.

To sum up, socially situated human information management is an intricate, multi-faceted domain, which we still do not understand well enough to reproduce in all its wealth and power. More fundamental studies are needed, as well as more friendly generic research tools. It is time for a global approach and for comprehensive software tools in order to improve our capacity for useful and efficient collaborative software design.

CONCLUSION

We have tried to show here how human information processing takes place in a social context and to what extent human beings use this context to retrieve information and solve problems. Shifting the emphasis from individual to social processes greatly improves our ability to understand and reproduce real human abilities. Studying and modeling socially situated information processing is therefore an important source of inspiration for the design of better collaborative information systems.

Of course, technology does not have to imitate life. It has often been the case in the history of computer science that efficient solutions to practical problems were derived mostly from technical considerations. Computers do not work by duplicating human thought processes faithfully, but by exploiting the speed and accuracy of electronic devices. Technical constraints and possibilities may have their own logic.

For high-level abilities, however, and especially when dealing with new areas to model, analyzing human cognitive processes is often both a prerequisite and a good start for system design. In the domain of information retrieval and knowledge management, studying closely the way human society performs its knowledge tasks by using distributed, collaborative processes has proven to be a fruitful approach. We are convinced that useful design ideas are still to be gained in this manner.

REFERENCES

Adomavicius, G., & Tuzhilin, A. (2005). Toward the next generation of recommender systems: A survey of the state-of-the-art and possible extensions. *IEEE Transactions on Knowledge and Data Engineering, 17*(6).

Baeza-Yates, R. (1999). *Modern information retrieval*. Boston, MA: Addison Wesley.

Baumard, P. (1999). *Tacit knowledge in organizations*. London: Sage.

Breese, J.S., Heckerman, D., & Kadie, C. (1998). Empirical analysis of predictive algorithms for collaborative filtering. *Proceedings of the 14ᵗʰ Conference on Uncertainty in Artificial Intelligence*.

Brin, S., & Page, L. (1998). *The anatomy of a large-scale hypertextual Web search engine*. Computer Science Department, Stanford University, USA.

Burt, R.S. (1992). *Structural holes: The social structure of competition*. Cambridge, MA: Harvard University Press.

Castells, M. (1996). *The rise of the network society*. Oxford: Blackwell.

Clark, A. (1998). *Being there: Putting brain, body, and world together again*. Cambridge, MA: MIT Press.

Drucker, P.F. (1992). *The age of discontinuity*. New York: Harper & Row.

Favela, J., & Decouchant, D. (Eds.). (2003). *Groupware: Design, implementation and use*. Berlin: Springer-Verlag.

Feller, J., Fitzgerald, B., Hissam, S.A., & Lakhnani, K.R. (2005). *Perspectives on free and open source software*. Cambridge, MA: MIT Press.

Granovetter, M.S. (1973). The strength of weak ties. *American Journal of Sociology, 78,* 1360-1380.

Harnad, S., & Dror, I.E. (Eds.). (2006). Distributed cognition—special issue. *Pragmatics and Cognition, 14*(2).

Kautz, H., Selman, B., & Shah, M. (1997). Referral Web: Combining social networks and collaborative filtering. *Communications of the ACM, 40*(3).

Kendrick, J.W. (1994). Total capital and economic growth. *Atlantic Economic Journal, 22*(1).

Kirsch, S., Gnasa, M., & Cremers, A. (2006). Beyond the Web: Retrieval in social information spaces. *Proceedings of the 28ᵗʰ European Conference on Information Retrieval*.

Kollock, P., & Smith, M. (Eds.). (1999). *Communities in cyberspace*. London: Routledge.

Lazega, E. (2001). *The collegial phenomenon*. Oxford: Oxford University Press.

Lesser, V., & Erman, L. (1977). A retrospective view of the Hearsay-II architecture. *Proceedings of the 5th IJCAI* (pp. 790-800).

Mandler, G. (1985). *Cognitive psychology*. Hillsdale, NJ: Lawrence Erlbaum.

Manning, C.D., & Schütze, H. (1999). *Foundations of statistical natural language processing*. Cambridge, MA: MIT Press.

Mauss, M. (1924). Essai sur le don. *Année Sociologique 1923-1924.*

Memmi, D., & Nérot, O (2003). Building virtual communities for information retrieval. In J. Favela & D. Decouchant (Eds.), *Groupware: Design, implementation and use.* Berlin: Springer-Verlag.

Memmi, D. (2006). The nature of virtual communities. *AI and Society, 20*(3).

Mintzberg, H. (1979). *The structuring of organizations.* Englewood Cliffs, NJ: Prentice Hall.

Munoz, M.A, Gonzalez, V.M., Rodriguez, M., & Favela, J. (2003). Supporting context-aware collaboration in a hospital: An ethnographic informed design. In J. Favela & D. Decouchant (Eds.), *Groupware: Design, implementation and use.* Berlin: Springer-Verlag.

Neisser, U. (1967). *Cognitive psychology.* New York: Appleton-Century-Crofts.

O'Reilly, T. (2005) *What is Web 2.0.* Retrieved from *http://www.oreillynet.com/pub/a/oreilly/tim/news/2005/09/30/what-is-web-20.html*

Polanyi, M. (1966). *The tacit dimension.* London: Routledge & Kegan Paul.

Rheingold, H. (2000). *The virtual community.* Cambridge, MA: MIT Press.

Resnick, P., Iacovou, N., Suchak, M., Bergstrom, P., & Riedl, J. (1994). GroupLens: An open architecture for collaborative filtering of Netnews. *Proceedings of the 1994 Conference on Computer-Supported Cooperative Work.*

Salton, G., & McGill, M. (1983). *Introduction to modern information retrieval.* New York: McGraw-Hill.

Shapiro, C., & Varian, H.R. (1999). *Information rules: A strategic guide to the network economy.* Cambridge, MA: Harvard Business School Press.

Shardanand, U., & Maes, P. (1995). Social information filtering: Algorithms for automating "word of mouth." *Proceedings of the 1995 Conference on Human Factors in Computing Systems.*

Travers, J., & Milgram, S. (1969). An experimental study of the small world problem. *Sociometry, 32,* 425-443.

Wang, J., Pouwelse, J., Lagendijk, R., & Reinders, M. (2006). Distributed collaborative filtering for peer-to-peer file sharing systems. *Proceedings of the 21ˢᵗ Annual ACM Symposium on Applied Computing.*

Wasserman, S., & Faust, K. (1994). *Social network analysis: Methods and applications.* Cambridge: Cambridge University Press.

Watts, D.J. (1999). *Small worlds.* Princeton, NJ: Princeton University Press.

Wellman, B. (Ed.). (1999). *Networks in the global village.* Boulder, CO: Westview Press.

This work was previously published in Social Information Retrieval Systems: Emerging Technologies and Applications for Searching the Web Effectively, edited by D. Goh and S. Foo, pp. 189-208, copyright 2008 by Information Science Reference, formerly known as Idea Group Reference (an imprint of IGI Global).

Chapter III
E-Governance

Srinivas Bhogle
National Aerospace Laboratories, India

ABSTRACT

E-governance uses Internet and communication technologies to automate governance in innovative ways, so that it becomes more efficient, more cost-effective, and empowers the human race even more. E-governance exercises are being attempted for more than a decade now, but have so far achieved only mixed success. The long-term prognosis for e-governance, however, remains extremely positive. The emergence of Web-services technologies, the continually proliferating computer networks, and the irreversible migration towards digital information strongly confirm the view that e-governance is here to stay. The eventual success of any e-governance project is intimately linked to the methodology used, and to that complex mesh between men, machines, and mindsets. We explain the "what," "why," and "how" of e-governance. We also talk of e-governance concerns, and discuss a few illustrative case studies.

WHAT IS E-GOVERNANCE?

Definitions

The biggest problem in developing countries is good governance, not poverty. It is, for example, well known that only a miniscule fraction of the money earmarked for development, relief, or rehabilitation eventually filters down to fulfill its mandated objective. There are also numerous instances where the concern is not how to *find* the money, but how to go through the maze of complicated procedures to *spend* the available money before the financial year ends.

Until a decade ago, the sheer logistics of accounting, bookkeeping, correspondence, and approvals was an onerous overhead. But the World Wide Web completely changed things. With e-mail, correspondence across the globe became almost instantaneous, and richer, because mail attachments were possible. The technologies to make Web pages interactive, and connect them to databases, worked wonders on the approval processes: approvals became faster, were based on more intelligent inputs, and could be securely archived. It was now possible, and indeed highly desirable, to use the Web for real governance.

Electronic governance (or e-governance) could therefore be defined as the use of Internet and communication technologies to automate governance in innovative ways, so that it becomes more efficient, more cost-effective, and empowers the human race even more.

Since "governance" is normally associated with a "government," may authors choose to explicitly mention the government while defining e-governance. Backus (2001), for example, defines e-governance as the "application of electronic means in the interaction between government and citizens and government and businesses, as well as in internal government operations to simplify and improve democratic, government and business aspects of governance." The strategic objective of e-governance, as Backus explains, is simply to use electronic means to support and stimulate good governance.

Governance vs. E-Governance

Both governance and e-governance are based on the same principles, and aim to achieve the same end objective. But the means used are widely different. Consider, for example, the requirement of a publicly funded national R&D lab to recruit scientists. A decade ago, the following procedure was probably adopted: (a) advertise widely in national newspapers indicating the job requirement and eligibility, (b) identify the format in which applications must be submitted, (c) receive, sort, and classify the applications sent, (d) shortlist the applicants and invite them for a test or interview, and (e) select the candidates and issue them appointment letters.

This entire process usually took almost a year—so long that the applicants often got tired of waiting and flew away to some other opportunity. The excuse offered for the delay was that pre-scribed government procedures were too complex and tedious. It was ironical that these classical governance procedures were actually sending away the best talent instead of bringing it in.

The e-governance approach would dramatically change things: the job requirement and eligibility would appear as hyperlinked Web pages on the lab's Web site. The application format would be a Web page template, with thoughtful validations to improve data quality. Upon submission, the applicant's data would instantaneously flow into database tables on the lab's server. The shortlisting process would merely involve making lists based on a wide variety of database queries and, finally, the selected candidates would be issued appointment letters via an e-mail attachment.

The advantages offered by this e-governance procedure are abundantly clear, but let us list them for the record. First, the "time-to-recruit" is dramatically reduced: 12 months could be reduced to 1-2 months. Second, the quality of the selected candidates is significantly better because of timely selection and improved data quality and search procedures. Third, the procedure is much less expensive; there are no advertisement or data tabulation costs. Fourth, the e-recruitment procedure reaches a much larger number of applicants right across the globe because of the growing ubiquity of the Web, and because the application window is open 24 × 7. And, finally, the e-governance procedure automatically guarantees data or content in digital form, making them more amenable for future knowledge management or data mining exercises.

On the down side, e-governance procedures frequently raise security concerns, for example, could someone access or modify information? Electronic procedures also require widespread, efficient, and reliable computer networks. But the biggest concern relates to mindsets: officials involved in governance fiercely resist change.

Table 1 summarizes the arguments for and against e-governance. It can be seen that the advantages significantly outweigh the concerns.

Table 1. Advantages and concerns of e-governance

Advantages	Concerns
Significant time saving ("there are no delays")	Mindsets of governance teams
Improved information quality	Security concerns ("can information be tampered or delayed?")
Less expensive (especially after e-governance infrastructure is set up)	Requirement of widespread, efficient and reliable computer networks and software
Wider reach ("can reach the whole world")	
Digital content (data capture is digital)	

Evolution of E-Governance

E-governance became possible only after the appearance of the World Wide Web and the widespread use of browsers like Netscape and Internet Explorer. In the early years (until about 1997), browsers simply displayed "static" Web pages. These pages were attractive, available on different computer platforms, allowed you to "mix" text with multimedia content, and could be hyperlinked.

From an e-governance viewpoint, this still was not good enough. Imagine that the task is to secure admission in a school or college. With Web pages, you could display all kinds of information about the college: its history, its courses, names of teachers on its faculty, pictures of the college buildings and swimming pools, college maps, and so forth. You could also post formats of application forms that must be submitted. But you could not *actually fill up such forms online*. With static Web pages, you could only "inform," but you could not "interact."

The chief reason was that Web pages use the Hypertext Markup Language (HTML), and HTML simply was not meant to be interactive. It was a one-way street: the college could reach its information to you, but you could not get back to the college using the same browser.

One could, of course, still print the application form off the Web page, fill it up off-line, and then mail or fax it to the college. The college could then, if it wished, reenter the details on an electronic database. But this did not seem right. If you could "connect" to the college, why could you not "reach" its database as well?

HTML's inability to directly connect to a database had to be corrected; one had to get HTML to talk to SQL (the structured query language that all databases use). The early efforts (1997-99) to achieve this involved the use of a common gateway interface (CGI) and a programming language like PERL. It worked rather well, although the programming overhead was a little severe. Later, especially after the widespread use of a platform-independent language like Java (by 2001), the database connectivity problem was solved much more elegantly.

From an e-governance perspective, this meant that we had moved from the "inform" to the "interact" phase. Our college applicant was now only required to fill up an online form and "submit." The data would seamlessly flow into the college's backend database. Better still, the student could also obtain an online or e-mail response, for example, to say that the application has been received or accepted.

A typical governance transaction, however, involves much more than filling or submitting a form. The conventional procedure is to put this application form on a file or dossier. The file then travels from one "governance desk" to the next. At each desk, the concerned individual is required to carry out a process involving either "scrutiny and verification" or "decision-making and judgment." Each process therefore involves information addition or manipulation. In the college application example, the process might involve seeking referee reports, administering a test, determining qualification criteria, and eventually reaching a decision.

How would one achieve an electronic adaptation of this governance transaction? We would first of all store the applicant's information and documents into carefully structured databases ("files") or similar digital repositories. Every participant in the governance transaction ("desk") would then access the databases in the prescribed sequence, and either add or manipulate data. As the transaction proceeds, information is continually updated digitally. The eventual verdict is based on the same information inputs, albeit in the digital format.

A transaction therefore involves multiple, and usually richer, interactions. We are therefore moving higher in the e-governance hierarchy: after "inform" and "interact," it is now "transact." In terms of technology, a transaction is considerably more complicated. Basically, transactions involve workflows (a supply chain is an example of a workflow). There are now more participants, and issues relating to security now require greater attention. Even workflow management can get sufficiently complicated, because workflows may not be straightforward. For example, after traveling through desks A -> B -> C -> D, D might suddenly decide to revert the file back to B for a clarification; or, in certain situations, one may be directly required to jump from desk B to desk D.

Technologies relating to such electronic transactions matured by about 2003. In most cases, these were Web-enabled implementations of the enterprise resource planning (ERP) solutions that had been around for many years.

But even as e-governance solutions became more sophisticated technologically, a very different sort of problem was becoming increasingly evident. The technology was "ready," but the people required to use the technology were "not ready"; in fact, often "not willing" to change. This mindset problem was apparent even earlier, when full-blown ERP solutions started being implemented, because such solutions required considerable process reengineering, and established organizations with aging managers simply refused to change.

While developing technologies for e-governance transactions constitutes a very big forward step, it is not the end of the story. These transactions must eventually go on to "transform" businesses; they must change business paradigms. There are still serious problems in migrating from the "transact" stage to the "transform" stage.

Consider again the case of an applicant to College A. If College A rejects the applicant, he would like to be considered for College B, College C ... and so on until he eventually gains admission somewhere. Unfortunately, it is still unlikely that College A and College B can seamlessly exchange the applicant's information. Their information systems would be engineered at least a little differently, making such information exchanges difficult and expensive. Consider another example where Enterprise A takes over Enterprises B. Sadly, the billing procedures in Enterprises A and B are significantly different, although each procedure is, by itself, efficient and streamlined. Exchanging information between Enterprises A and B will therefore become a major handicap. So severe, in fact, that many information managers might find it more convenient (Hagel III, 2002) to adopt a "no tech" solution—backroom boys (perhaps outsourced from India!) would manually "convert" formats and then throw the data back into the system.

This difficulty arises because we do not have standardized information formats and processes. One recalls the electronic data interchange (EDI) initiative of the 1990's that fell through because it was not sufficiently versatile, and because it allowed the business "big brother" to become the "big bully" by "controlling" data formats.

The way out seems to be to evolve universal (and "open") frameworks, and then build supporting frameworks for interoperability so that every enterprise's formats are "reduced" to this universal format. This approach should hopefully usher in true e-governance.

G2B, G2C, G2G

The three principal participants in e-governance are the government, the citizen, and the business entities. So e-governance is essentially about interactions between these participants in which the government plays the pivotal role.

It is customary to classify these interactions. G2C, for instance, refers to interactions between the government (G) and the citizen (C). Obtaining a driving license is an example of such an interaction. The citizen approaches the government for a license with the relevant supporting documentation. The government eventually grants him the license and ensures that the citizen's details enter the government's information repositories. These details can then be used in governance, for example, to fine the citizen after a traffic violation.

G2B refers to the interactions between the government (often as a regulatory authority) and business enterprises. The procedures involved in receipt and payments of taxes are an example of

G2B e-governance. There could be very complex underlying processes such as date management, discounts, payment policies, and so forth, in G2B e-governance.

Finally, G2G refers to interactions between two government departments, for example, between a state and federal government or between government agencies respectively involved in development and funding projects. The real G2G e-governance challenge is to create a monolithic government entity in which the citizen or the business interacts with an apparently single entity (a "single window") for all governance transactions. This is a very formidable task given the wide disparity in governance procedures between two government departments.

An E-Governed Future

E-governance is a very attractive and compelling concept. But the path towards this ideal is exceedingly difficult and complicated.

First of all, we need the *infrastructure*: every enterprise, every government department, and every home must hold electronic devices such as computers, mobile handsets, or wireless sensors that must be "connected" with robust, fast, and reliable networks. The networking technologies could be different (wired, wireless, terrestrial,

Table 2. Different phases in the evolution of e-governance

E-Governance phase	Attributes
'Inform' (<1997)	Web pages containing 'static' information (featuring text, pictures, or even multimedia clips) posted on a Web site. Pages are hyperlinked.
'Interact' (1997-2001)	Web pages with database connectivity. Now possible to submit queries and receive responses.
'Transact' (>2001)	Improved interactivity. Transactions across workflows. Security features. ERP-like formulations
'Transform' (?)	Universal frameworks. Enterprises can seamlessly exchange information over distributed networks.

satellite-based), but this variety need not be a concern.

Second, we need *enabling software* that is compatible across these diverse hardware platforms: ideally, software with open architectures. Software solutions must seamlessly support (a) browsers or other communication devices at the "front-end," (b) the information repositories and databases at the "back-end," and (c) the business logic and intelligence in the "middle-tier."

Third, we need *digitization*. All data or information in the archives, in administrative ledgers, in books, in court proceedings, and so forth, must eventually get digitized. This is an onerous task, but, thankfully, not an urgent prerequisite. A pragmatic approach would be to choose a cutoff date and make sure that at least all future records are digital. We also need supporting instruments such as scanners, document management systems, and so forth, for digitization.

Fourth, we need *security*, operating at different levels: (a) user identification and authentication using smart cards and digital signatures, (b) data protection using encryption and fault-tolerant software, and (c) protection from other external threats such as hackers, viruses, spam mails, and service denial programs.

Finally, we need *universal standards and frameworks* to facilitate data exchange. The eventual success of e-governance would depend on how good these standards are, and how faithful and widespread is the compliance with these standards. Such standards would grow into frameworks, and the emergence of robust Internet technologies like XML, or more generally, Web services, would eventually package these standards and frameworks into successful e-governance implementations.

Thus, in tomorrow's e-governed future, anyone, any time, from anywhere, using any connection device, can ask for any service. This looks like a pipe dream right now … but there is no reason to believe that it cannot happen tomorrow, or the day after, if there is a shared collective will.

WHY E-GOVERNANCE?

Empowerment

In historical narratives, a king was considered virtuous and benign if each of his subjects had the freedom to approach the king's court with a request or a grievance. In many ways, this continues to be the ideal of democratic societies even today. But the governance agencies are getting more "distant" because of growing populations, growing procedures and, sadly, growing indifference.

One of the chief merits of e-governance is that it can again empower the citizen. To take a trivial example, most governance procedures are initiated with an application form. It is common, especially in developing countries, to deny a citizen even access to this form! One has to know an influential contact, or pay a modest bribe, to obtain this form. In an e-governed world, this form would be available almost instantaneously … in fact it could be filled out and submitted almost as easily.

The citizen is also often completely ignorant of procedures, and of his rights. He needs counseling or advice before he can choose his preferred option. Such advice, however, is often denied or only made available at a price. In e-governed societies, the citizen could have access to video films or interactive help routines to permit him to make a better-informed decision. He could also join discussion groups where individuals share their personal experiences in working around procedures.

E-governance offers a 24 × 7 service desk, and this too is a major instrument for empowerment. Government offices worldwide are known to have an abnormally large number of holidays, and, even on working days, service counters are often not manned all the time ("Mr. X still isn't back from lunch").

E-governance will also empower businesses. Every businessman knows how difficult it is to

Table 3. The prerequisites for e-governance

Prerequisite	Attributes
Infrastructure	Participants must have electronic interfaces such as computers or mobile handsets. There must be a robust, reliable, and fast network to connect these participants
Enabling software	Software with open architectures to seamlessly connect the front-end, back-end and middle tiers
Digitization	Data must become digital: new data must be entered in digital formats, legacy data must be digitized using scanners and document management systems
Security	User authentication, data protection, and protection from external threats
Universal standards and frameworks	Development and compliance of universal standards to exchange data and applications.

bid for, and perhaps eventually obtain, a lucrative government contract. The associated paperwork requires him to interact with a large number of different government offices and officials who have no worthwhile information exchange processes between their establishments. This significantly delays the award of the contract and proves to be an unnecessary and expensive overhead.

Finally, e-governance will empower because of its wider reach. It is, for example, well known that a cartel of big vendors often gobbles up most of the big government contracts. Likewise, citizens residing in a country's capital often run away with most of the lucrative international opportunities. When such tenders or announcements are put on easily accessible Web sites, they will reach practically every entrepreneur or citizen.

Profitability

E-governance will make businesses and enterprises more profitable. One route to greater profits will emerge because of reduced lead times. Every business process can be streamlined to a greater degree, parallel activities can be initiated and the project can be completed faster. It is always more profitable if projects are completed on time.

E-governance will offer significant gains because businesses can deploy a reduced, but more skilful, manpower component. All project teams have a team of core technical experts and a second team of "facilitators." These facilitators are not really productive in a business sense; they are needed to cover up the deficiencies in the governance processes. As e-governance implementations improve, we will need fewer facilitators.

E-governance has also opened up the extremely profitable opportunity of outsourcing. Project tasks can be transferred, for example, from Boston in the U.S. to Bangalore in India, because businesses are electronically wired up, and a country like India offers manpower of matching quality at a fraction of the international costs. Starting from about 2003, the outsourcing business is booming; it even easily survived a campaign debate in the 2004 U.S. presidential elections.

Efficiency

Anyone visiting Asia after a gap of about 5 years would be struck by two very visible phenomena: the ubiquity of bank ATM counters and the pervasive use of mobile telephones. This is a strongest possible signal that e-governance is coming.

The example of mobile telephones is most interesting. Starting off as a status symbol that every rich man was supposed to flaunt, it has now made deep inroads into the middle-class income groups and the small business or service segments. Plumbers, electricians, car and scooter mechanics, and even cooks and priests are now just a phone call away! Mobile phones have provided decent livelihood to a significant fraction of the population and made businesses much more efficient.

ATM counters too have dramatically improved efficiency. ATM services have often served as "robots" to reduce the burden on banking clerks, and ensure that fewer citizens crowd bank offices. Best of all, the ATM experiment has made signatures less sacrosanct. Two of the most dreadful requirements of classical governance are (a) to ask that every request be written out on paper, and (b) to insist that every governance agent affixes his signature after even the most trivial transaction. The acceptance of an ATM card with its secret pin code, instead of a printed signature, to disburse money is a step forward.

Flexibility

One often encounters administrative procedures that are extremely tedious, and for no apparent reason. Both the administrators and the customers are aware of this, but seem incapable of changing things. This is largely because the established governance procedures are inflexible. You realize, for example, that A -> D -> C -> E is a better way of going about things than A -> B -> C -> D -> E, but you are told that this cannot be done because it would disturb the existing administrative set-up, and require reprinting of all the stationery and the bound ledgers. An e-governance set-up that would easily permit modification of workflows would solve the problem.

We need flexibility in a wide variety of other situations as well, for example, while changing from summer times to winter times, if we decide to shift a particular business operation from Location A to Location B, or if we wish to transfer a responsibility from Mr. A to Ms. B.

Anticorruption

Corruption is arguably the biggest obstacle to good governance, at least in the poorer states and countries. E-governance can counter corruption in at least two ways: first by introducing *transparency* in all governance processes, and, second, by being a very effective *deterrent*. For example, consider all governance procedures associated with land or property records. These procedures are so seeped in corruption that even a legal owner of land or property can never feel secure. Ownership is normally established based on an appropriate entry in an official governance record—but what if this record is modified for a bribe? Farmers in poorer countries are often the biggest victims; their land can be "grabbed," and their land records "destroyed" by the evil nexus of politicians, lawyers, and the land mafia. Digitizing all land records securely, and educating the local farmer to use electronic procedures to protect his ownership rights, could defeat such corruption. Another example of the transparency of e-governance is the management of examinations by universities: all worries about exam paper leaks, faulty evaluation, and manipulation of results can be banished once the entire process becomes publicly visible, and thus accountable. Even corrupt practices in elections, arguably the greatest scourge of democratic societies, can be countered by e-governance.

The role of e-governance as a corruption deterrent is more subtle, but equally effective. Information about every high value government transaction can be posted on a public Web site for citizens, public interest groups, and the media to peruse. This will ensure that every transaction is publicly watched, and every decision fiercely debated. This simple e-broadcasting ploy can keep every official on his toes, and make him think twice before making a wrong move! Aggressive e-advocacy can also help reverse decisions where corruption has been spotted.

Digital Repositories

In an e-governed world, all records will be entered or sensed into electronic repositories, and will therefore be automatically digital. This "forced digitization" is extremely useful because digital content is easiest to manipulate, and also potentially the most durable (although the rapid obsolescence of the data capture and storage devices is a matter of concern). The ability to easily manipulate or play with data will enable more efficient "knowledge" extraction, or discovery, for example, using data mining or using algorithms based on artificial intelligence (AI) methodologies.

The digital medium also embraces multimedia content. We already see many instances of multimedia in governance: "in-camera" court depositions from geographically distant locations, animated weather forecasts and hurricane alerts on TV, tracking a criminal's movement using GPS/GIS devices, and so forth. Digital multimedia is therefore poised to become a powerful and versatile force in e-governance.

Once Again, Why E-Governance?

It is interesting that while practically everyone advocates e-governance, the reasons cited are widely different, although each is thought provoking. The following one-liners (W'O Okot-Uma, 2001) are in response to the question: "Why good governance?". If we assume that e-governance is the most likely vehicle to deliver good

Table 4. The benefits of e-governance

Benefit	Reasons
Empowerment	Empowers the citizen or business because of unfettered access to governance, education on governance procedures, 24 x 7 service, and wider reach
Profitability	Reduced lead times, better manpower deployment, possibility of outsourcing
Efficiency	Opportunities for mobile connectivity, sophisticated devices to automate mechanical and repetitive tasks, faster transfer of money, encourages digital signatures
Flexibility	Reengineering or reconfiguring business processes, easy transfer of business locations or individual responsibilities
Anticorruption	Introduces transparency in the governance process, acts as a deterrent
Creates digital repositories	Forces data digitization, this allows easier data manipulation and more efficient knowledge retrieval. Supports multimedia content.

Table 5. One-line responses to "Why good governance?"

Respondent	Response
Amartya Sen	Development of freedom
John Paul II	Freedom of a person to live out his/her creative potential
John Rawls	Social justice as fairness
Mahathir Mohamed	Global civilized society
George Soros	Global open society
UNDP	Human development
Atlantic Charter	World free from fear and want

governance, then these are also answers to "why e-governance?"

We therefore see that e-governance is much more than just an implementation of information and communication technologies. It is also intimately linked to a wide variety of social, economic, and political factors such as "freedom," "social justice," "openness," "globalization," "economic liberalization," and "human development." E-governance could, one day, redefine human civilization itself.

HOW E-GOVERNANCE?

Climb the Mountain

How does one actually begin the business of ushering in e-governance? There is really only one way: start climbing the mountain that takes you from the "inform" phase to the "interact" phase, and thereafter, to the "transact" and "transform" phases.

It is also still not completely clear how we will scale the ultimate peak; but if we keep climbing, and equip ourselves with the essential "tools" to trudge upwards, we will surely get there. Better still, the benefits start coming in almost as soon as we harness this resolve to climb; and they grow incrementally as we conquer each intermediate peak.

For the "inform" phase, we need rather modest tools: at the "governance end" we will need a Web server to host the Web site, and at the "citizen end" we will need no more than a networked desktop computer with browser software. As we move to the "interact" phase, the governance end will have to be bolstered: faster servers, and a database server to complement the Web server. At the citizen end, the same desktop computer would still do the job, but it would help if the network connect speed improves, and if the connectivity can be sustained over longer time periods.

The climb up to the "transact" phase is significantly more difficult, and we need more powerful and versatile technology tools. More importantly, we have to steel our human resolve. The inform phase is great fun; no one protests … in fact, everyone says: "hey, I didn't know this was so easy, and so cool!" The honeymoon endures as we enter the "interact" phase … we are now gushing: "I didn't have to wait in long queues to get this done, I applied right from my home, and in the middle of the night!". The "transact" phase brings in the big worries; at the governance end there are concerns about the performance of the servers and fidelity of the processes. Officials are also alarmed by a perceived loss of power, since they no longer physically hold official records and the office hierarchy gets disturbed. At the citizen end, there are widespread concerns especially about security, and confusion about the process workflows. By the time we reach the "transform" phase, the big action has shifted to the backend: the concerns are about how to exchange and manage data seamlessly and share the same processes. At the citizen end, things have now become rather simple: a single, completely configured, and customized desktop provides that ultimate "window to the whole world."

We will now introduce the many underlying e-governance building blocks. It must be mentioned that the real technological challenge is significantly greater than what this narrative might suggest.

Hypertext Markup Language

The Hypertext Markup Language (HTML) is used to create Web pages. The general procedure is to first key in the text, and then add "tags" to (a) embellish the page appearance, (b) insert multimedia content, and (c) hyperlink the Web page to other related Web pages. Internally, HTML identifies the IP address of the server holding the referred Web page, and requests the server to send the page across the Internet.

Table 6. The major steps in e-governance implementation

Phase	"Governance end"	"Citizen or client end"	Technology prerequisites
Inform	Host an attractive and informative Web site on a Web server with hyperlinked Web pages and multimedia content	A desktop computer with browser software; at least a rudimentary network connection	HTML, browsers, devices for content digitization (scanners, optical character recognition software, conversion to pdf) TCP/IP network connectivity
Interact	Database server to complement the Web server. Ability to connect to databases. Design front-end forms with suitable validations. Routines to populate and query back-end databases	A desktop computer with browser software, and an improved network connection. Logins and passwords to identify and authenticate user	HTML, browsers, digitization, improved network connectivity, database design and development, programming for database connectivity (e.g., using Java)
Transact	Cluster of servers for specialized functions such as database management Web hosting, Web application management, security and fault tolerance. Design and coding of process workflows, and of user-friendly and secure front-end interface. Data encryption.	A desktop computer with browser software, and a fast and reliable network connection. Logins, passwords, and digital signatures or security tokens to identify and authenticate user	HTML, browsers, digitization, reliable and secure network connectivity, database design and development, programming for database connectivity (e.g., using Java), software to support workflows, process integration, rights and privileges. Hardware devices and software tools for information security
Transform	Cluster of servers for specialized functions like database management, Web hosting, Web application management, security, and fault tolerance. Design and coding of process workflows, and of user-friendly and secure front-end interface. Data encryption. Standards and frameworks to connect diverse data and application implementations.	A desktop computer with browser software and a fully user-specific configured desktop. Fast, reliable, and persistent network connection. Wide slew of features to authenticate and protect the user.	HTML, browsers, digitization, reliable and secure network connectivity, database design and development, programming for database connectivity (e.g., using Java), software to support workflows, process integration, rights and privileges. Hardware devices and software tools for information security. XML and Web services. Data format standardization. Frameworks for interoperability.

From an e-governance perspective, HTML provides the richest possible machinery to inform. In spite of its apparent simplicity, designing a Web page is still a considerable challenge. The Web pages must be appealing, must contain compelling links to other information sources, and must have an intelligent underlying structure. Web pages must also be frequently updated, with old pages being promptly weeded out.

Internet

There would be no e-governance without the Internet. The Internet is a worldwide computer network created by interconnecting computers. The most popular connecting "topology" uses a switch (earlier, a hub) with multiple ports. Every computer in the local neighborhood connects into this switch. Then the switch itself connects into another switch, and so the network telescopes out. Computers are identified by a unique IP address (that is, quite like a phone number; IP addresses currently are "dotted quads," 202.12.13.14, for example), and there are searching and connecting mechanisms on the Internet to quickly identify computers and then exchange data packets. When a user types in http://www.google.com on his browser, the domain name server on the network (that is like a telephone book) quickly identifies the IP address of the server hosting the Google site, and then attempts to establish the connection. Things happen very fast, and the data packets are delivered at great speed and with uncanny precision.

Networks are now turning "wireless"; instead of cables, networks use radio as the primary carrier. Wireless networks, using associated technologies like WiMAX (Vaughan-Nichols, 2004), will provide a major fillip to e-governance because they allow use of *mobile* devices. So if you want to book an airline ticket, you could use the handset of your mobile telephone instead of a "wired" computer. If you are a soldier patrolling a border area, you could use a palmtop computer to update the army's database on enemy positions. If you are a fisherman on the high seas, you could connect to a database indicating the supply requirement at different points on the coastline to plan and optimize your catch.

Indeed it appears increasingly likely that "full-blown" e-governance will eventually be achieved using wireless networks, and wireless data collection technologies, such as RFID (Want, 2004), that use electronic tags to store data. RFID tags can make any object "visible" to a network—anywhere and at any time. RFID tags are still rather expensive, and so used rather sparingly (to track expensive goods in transit, for example). But their use will proliferate once they

become more affordable. Every book in a library or bookstore, every commodity in a supermarket, every inventory in an engineering or medical establishment, every car on an auto route, and even every child's schoolbag could then be tagged. Indeed, these tags could go on to redefine the very art of governance.

Databases

A lot of governance involves the collection, storage, and retrieval of data. Databases store data intelligently so that it can be retrieved easily and quickly using powerful querying options.

As data gets more complex and interlinked, database design becomes important in e-governance. For example, if a database field seeks a respondent's *age*, instead of his *date of birth*, things will become very awkward a few years down the line.

One of the challenges in database design is to ensure that the data locked in different database tables always remain consistent; this is usually achieved by the normalization technique (Gilfillan, 2000), where the designer works his way through the first, second, and third normal forms.

Another e-governance challenge was to connect "front-end" HTML-based user interfaces to "back-end" SQL-based databases. Such database connectivity initially tended to be specific to the database software product used, and that was obviously not very comfortable. Now the connectivity issue has been resolved more elegantly with the appearance of platform-independent "middle-tier" *Web servers*, for example, using Java.

A related problem arises when the number of "hits" becomes very large. Simple Web servers can no longer cope up with the traffic of users wishing to connect to databases at practically the same instant. One way out is to use the more powerful *Web application servers*. A second option is to move the data out of the database and store it between customized Extensible Markup Language (XML) tags. Since XML pages show up almost instantaneously on browsers, the user receives a much quicker response to his query. In fact, XML is now emerging as the preferred choice for data exchange across disparate networks.

Workflows

Most transactions in e-governance depend on workflows. After an applicant initiates a process, the application normally travels from one official desk to the next, until the process is eventually terminated. For example, an application for a loan will involve a careful scrutiny of the applicant's credit-worthiness before a decision on the loan request is made.

Most of the "bad" governance, especially in developing countries, can be attributed to faulty workflows. To start with, the workflow could be clumsy and tedious, and spread across geographically distant locations. This involves multiple queues and much grief. Then, bad workflows tend to introduce unacceptable lead times in the governance procedures. Finally, and rather sadly, flawed workflows promote corrupt practices. A file containing valuable documents and endorsements might, for example, simply vanish into thin air, and reappear only after a hefty bribe is paid.

"Good" workflows, on the other hand, provide the surest route to good governance. Like all evolutionary processes, good workflows evolve over time. Paths or chains in workflows must be trimmed, elongated, diverted, or concatenated until the optimal procedure evolves. The recent appearance of powerful workflow engines greatly simplifies such business process reengineering exercises.

ERP

Enterprise resource planning (ERP) is about tightly integrating all the business processes, usually *within* the enterprise. Most enterprises have very similar sort of functions: inventory management, manufacture, sales, marketing, human resource

development, payrolls, budgeting, and so forth, and they usually operate in the "project mode," It would obviously be a great advantage if all these functions, and their interdependencies, are continually watched and monitored by a single information system. Successful ERP solutions, therefore, allow the enterprise to be much more alert and responsive, and make more intelligent business decisions.

On the down side, ERP solutions have proved to be expensive and rather difficult to implement. The difficulty in implementation is directly proportional to the extent of process reengineering ("customization") that the ERP solutions demand. But ERP solutions still provide a very valuable platform and facilitate the eventual migration to full-blown e-governance.

Security

As e-governance implementations grow, so too will security concerns. Most enterprises work around a security policy that outlines rules for network access. Security threats can be internal or external, could involve men or machines, be either willful or accidental … or be a combination of some or all of these factors.

To counter internal security threats, users are required to use passwords, or passwords in combination with other devices (smart cards, synchronized tokens, biometric matching) if the perceived threat is greater. All data and information are encrypted, and multiple back ups are maintained on diverse media. Software routines also archive detailed transaction logs so that security breaches can be investigated.

External threats are controlled by firewalls. These threats are largely from hackers or malicious software such as viruses, spasm, worms, or Trojan horses that seek to disrupt or deny service. Firewalls typically try to cut off most of the network access "ports." Because of the ubiquity of the Web, the "80 port," which brings in all the HTTP traffic, has necessarily to be kept open. The effort therefore is to funnel *all* network traffic through this single (well-guarded) port. This partly explains the growing popularity of the Web services framework.

Finally, security threats can be significantly reduced by good user practices. An ongoing training program on correct user behavior is often the first, and vital, step in the wider social engineering that enterprises must undertake.

XML and Web Services

HTML's greatest merit is that it is based on *open* standards. That is why Web pages can show up on any browser sitting on any operating system. But HTML can only *display* data; it cannot *describe* data, or facilitate the *exchange* of data. XML corrects this weakness. XML too is based on open standards, but it can also encode data or information.

XML therefore provides a wonderful opportunity to exchange data across disparate information systems. Suppose Enterprise A, having all its data on the Oracle database, wishes to exchange information with Enterprise B using the SQL Server database. Both Enterprises A and B could encode their data using XML, and the platform-independent XML could then easily facilitate the information exchange via the Web route (Hagel III, 2002).

Indeed, as the Web and Web protocols become ubiquitous, it is now even possible for two different Web-based applications to interact dynamically! A connection can be set up, for example, between an application using Java and another using .Net. Such connection technologies (Web services) will allow e-governance to move up from the "transact" phase to the "transform" phase.

Implementation Strategies

E-governance is not just about technology; the social, political, and economic challenges in its implementation are just as daunting. The citizens and officials must be willing to accept change; the political leadership must have a roadmap and aggressively push it; and the project funding must be committed and available. It also helps if

Table 7. The e-governance building blocks

Technology	Role
HTML	Open standard for displaying Web pages. The first step in e-governance is to build a Web site that is visible to all users
Internet	The information carrier. All users participate in e-governance by using a computer or mobile device connected to the Internet. Networks are built using cable or radio
Databases	All information used in e-governance is usually stored on databases. Databases allow easy and secure storage, and quick and smart data retrieval.
Workflows	Workflows describe the paths of the e-governance processes. Most transactions are modeled using workflow engines
ERP	A tool to tightly couple business processes in an enterprise. Enterprises with ERP solutions are significantly better equipped to implement full-blown e-governance
Security	Software and hardware solutions to protect e-governance implementations from internal and external threats
XML and Web services	Open standards to exchange disparate data and applications across the Web. The recommended model to implement e-governance, especially in the "transform" phase.

good (but not electronic) governance practices are already in place.

To get e-governance off the ground, Andersen Consulting (Backus, 2001) recommends a strategy of "think big, start small and scale fast." At the top end of the e-governance implementation spectrum, John Hagel et al (Hagel, Brown, & Layton-Rodin, 2004) suggest that the secret to creating value from Web services is to "keep it simple, keep it incremental, and learn, learn, learn."

E-GOVERNANCE CONCERNS

The Three Big Worries

To make e-governance a reality, "soft" leadership and management skills must complement "hard" technology skills. There are many instances where the technology development and infrastructure creation has been impeccable, but e-governance implementations have failed because the "soft" concerns were not addressed.

Three worries will be apparent as we take the long road to e-governance, and at different stages in the implementation life cycle. The first barrier, which we face soon after an e-governance project starts, relates to *human mindsets*. We often do not appreciate how radically e-governance will change human interactions and affect the "power" that people feel by physically "holding" information repositories.

Midway through a successful e-governance implementation, we worry about the *digital divide*. E-governance apparently favors "digitally well-connected" governments and enterprises. Imagine a scenario where e-governance causes the trusted postman to disappear, but the e-mail connection, which is supposed to replace the postman, has not been installed, or is unreliable. The fear, therefore, is that, for the less privileged, the old order will change, but a new order will not replace it.

Finally, in full-blown or near full-blown e-governance implementations, there is a real concern that the citizen will lose all his *privacy*: the citizen's bank balance, medical condition, voting preference, physical movements, and even his love life will be visible as e-governance radars relentlessly scan every moment of his life. We already hear protests about mobile phones being unacceptably intrusive. Tomorrow's e-governance processes could blow the privacy lid wide open.

Human Mindsets

Human reaction to an e-governance initiative can be widely different. While many enthusiastically embrace Web connectivity, others strongly resist change. It is important to understand why they respond this way, and see how we can correct that response.

Often, there is a *fear of technology*, or of interacting with "alien" machines instead of familiar humans. The attitude is: "I will submit my form to the office clerk, not a dumb computer." This is also why many callers are not comfortable leaving a message on a voice recorder, or of typing in a credit card number on a Web interface.

In most cases, however, there is the *fear of losing power or authority*. E-governance brings in sweeping process changes that make officials very uncomfortable. Most officials enjoy the power of receiving files, making remarks on files, signing on them with a flourish, and entertaining visitors soliciting favors. E-governance initiatives dilute this power and make their hallowed role rather redundant. And, if indeed this is a corrupt official receiving bribes for a favorable verdict, the pinch is felt even more.

In the early days of e-governance, there was also the very genuine *fear of losing your job* and livelihood. That is why labor unions stoutly resisted electronic initiatives. Now that fear is fading, but this is still no guarantee that an employee or official will change his mental makeup.

These mindsets must be corrected gradually. A continuous and intensive training program will be very useful. Enterprises could also start with e-governance projects of the "win-win' type; for example, showing a clerk how a click of the mouse will generate a report that took him 5 hours to write. Incentive and rewards for the best participants in e-governance projects also help in swinging things.

Digital Divide

A frequently articulated concern is that e-governance will create a digital divide between the technology "haves" and "have not's." One reason cited is the wide divergence in Internet access: while practically every citizen of a developed country would soon have Internet access, the access percentage in an under-developed country could be abysmally low. According to a recent estimate, only 7% of the human race has Internet access.

It is feared (Norris, 2001) that this wide gap between the information rich and poor will actually exacerbate social tensions, not reduce them. It is also feared that this divide, caused by e-governance, will actually weaken democracy, not strengthen it. The counterview is that "the simple binary notion of technology haves and have not's doesn't quite compute" (Warschauer, 2003) and that the "divide is not caused by just physical hardware availability, but also by the ability to engage technologies" (Warschauer, 2004).

It does indeed seem that the early concerns on the digital divide are now receding. Computer hardware and networking costs continue to decline rapidly, and the growing usage of open standards in e-governance is also diminishing software costs. The availability of cheap mobile interfaces, and the growing geographical reach through wireless networking are also encouraging developments. So although the digital divide will not disappear, it does appear that this divide will be no deeper than the other divides that have always plagued human civilizations.

Loss of Privacy

At a recent seminar of Indian CIOs in Bangkok, one of the technology solution vendors surprised the audience by openly declaring that he was not a nice man to know because he did a lot of nasty things: for example, buy up the old laptop computer that the CIO had recently sold after formatting its hard disk. "I can recover every byte on that computer using special software tools … and then threaten to publish all your valuable data," he said only half in jest.

E-governance indeed poses a very serious threat to a citizen's privacy. For example, software for tracking a voter's preference would give a political party the sort of inputs it needs to win the next election. The e-governance tool that uses a sophisticated GIS-based software to track down criminals could just as easily be used to blackmail an innocent citizen—and things would become even easier when RFIDs start flooding the marketplace! The infrastructure created for e-governance implementations can also facilitate serious sexual misconduct on the Web.

We already see minor privacy invasions: mobile phone operators, for instance, cheerfully sell customer databases to banks and market research agencies without the customer's permission! While the menace can be partly countered by better security implementations, and by legislating more punitive legal measures to counter cyber crimes (Sinha & Condon, 2005), it does look as though, with e-governance, citizens are doomed to suffer at least a certain loss of privacy forever.

How to Address E-Governance Concerns

In a very detailed appraisal of e-governance implementations worldwide ("eGovernment for development," 2004), the "eGovernment for

Development Information Exchange" project, coordinated by the University of Manchester's Institute for Development Policy and Management, has identified the "enablers" and "constraints" for every individual case study. In Tables 8 and 9, we summarize the major e-governance enablers and constraints. In Table 10, we run through the major recommendations retrieved from this study.

E-GOVERNANCE CASE STUDIES

We will look at e-governance case studies drawn from different parts of the world. The case studies highlight the many phases in an e-governance implementation. A very large number of case studies are available on the WWW; see, for example, UN Public Administration compilations ("UN-PAN: Virtual Library ..", 2006) or the collection put together by the University of Manchester's Institute for Development Policy and Management ("eGovernment for development," 2004).

Citizen's Web Portal in Estonia

Every citizen in Estonia, as indeed in many other parts of Europe, has the right to know the information stored about him on the government's official databases. Typical queries could be: "give me my data from the population register," or "show me my entries in the motor vehicles register." This service had to be offered to each of Estonia's 1.4 million citizens.

Estonia, therefore, created its special citizens' Web portal (Kalja & Ott, 2004) with standard database services, at a cost of about a million euros. This service, which became fully operational by 2002, offered access to about a hundred government databases. Interactions with some of these databases could be intense and frequent; each of the 10 most popular databases recorded a few thousand hits daily. This portal could be accessed both by the citizens and the authorized civil servants.

Table 8. Enablers of e-governance

Enabler	Remarks
Champion	Someone in the enterprise, preferably the CEO himself or one of his trusted advisers, must aggressively support e-governance and facilitate its implementation
Political will	Things become a lot simpler if the political leadership shows its willingness and keenness to usher in e-governance
Funding	The timely availability of the requisite funds is a big advantage
Frequent awareness and promotion campaigns	Many of the human mindset problems can be overcome this way
Continuous training	Even after the e-governance solution is put in place, training must continue on a regular basis
User acceptance	Start with e-governance applications offering win-win option for both the employee and the enterprise
User pressure	Once a user feels empowered by e-governance, he will ask for more
Correct location	A location with the right mix of resources is a better enabler; for example, Bangalore in India is better than Dhaka in Bangladesh
Government-citizen partnership	If both the government and the citizen perceive a shared stake in e-governance, both cooperate to make it happen. If the government fails to involve the citizen, it is less likely to work.

Table 9. E-governance constraints

Constraint	Remarks
Lack of leadership	An e-governance project without a champion, and without strong government support may not succeed
Scale	A big vision is desirable, but scales must be manageable and grow incrementally. Goals should not be overambitious
Technology availability	Projects launched without sufficient infrastructure, or using the wrong technology, tend to fail
Legislation	Even the best e-governance solution cannot be successful without supporting legislative action, for example, to permit business process reengineering
Political interference	A feud between rival political parties may hurt e-governance plans
Official disinterest	Officials will scuttle e-governance if they fear a loss of power or opportunity; a video conferencing initiative in Africa failed because officials thought it would deny them opportunities for foreign jaunts
Hostile work conditions	Implementations are not likely to succeed if work conditions are inimical
Apathy or resistance	If the participants are not excited by e-governance, or are illiterate, it will not work
Poor research	If the e-governance solution is poorly designed, it will fail far too often.

Table 10. E-governance recommendations

•	Get the technology right	•	Provide intensive training
•	Start small	•	Use a phased approach
•	Match e-governance to organizational reality	•	Look for 'win-win' situations
•	Encourage transparency	•	Undertake risk management

The challenge in this relatively simple e-governance project was to ensure that the data was *secure* and *comprehensive*. To authenticate users, the portal required citizens to either log in using their ID-card, or ride on the authentication service of the country's commercial banks (this ensured access to about 75% of the citizens). Another highlight of this project was the use of open architectures to create the portal.

The project has been quite successful and triggered off other similar citizen friendly services. This project is likely to be replicated in neighboring Latvia and Lithuania.

E-Procurement in Brazil

Brazil's federal government set up an e-procurement system called COMPRASNET around 2000. Two years later, more than 1,000 federal government purchase units used this Web-based system for online quoting and reverse auction commodity purchases.

The procedure was rather simple. Every department of the federal government was required to post the specifications of its required purchase online. If the value of the commodity was relatively low, the federal procurement officer opted for online quoting; for higher value purchases he recommended the reverse auction procedure.

In a review of this system, Marcos Ozorio de Almeida (2002) notes: "COMPRASNET was introduced to automate the procurement process. The aim of the automation was to make the procurement process uniform without centralizing the buying process of the federal organizations. It was also intended to reduce procurement costs and give more transparency to the process. Other aims were to increase the number of government suppliers, reduce participation cost for these suppliers, and increase competition among suppliers to reduce costs and improve the quality of goods or services acquired."

The COMPRASNET system was rated to be "largely successful." In its first 2 years it recovered about 30% of its investment cost, chiefly because it achieved an average reduction of about 20% in the cost of goods or services. Procurement times were substantially reduced; in typical cases, the time came down from 2 months to 15 days. The project was a success because it was backed by "political will inside the government" and the "external pressures" from the suppliers for a fair playing ground. The project also benefited because "it got the technology right," "provided intense training," and "adopted a phased approach." The idea of using the Web for a reverse auction, to

Table 11. Citizen's portal in Estonia

Attribute	Details
Why?	To guarantee the right to information to every Estonian citizen.
Who gains?	The citizen and the civil servant in Estonia, because both can quickly and securely access official records. The State, because its records get digitized.
Technology inputs	Open standards with internationally accepted protocols. The alpha version used XML RPC. The final version uses SOAP.
Lesson	Web technology could be used to offer citizens an information service that was practically free. The quality of data could be improved because citizens e-mailed corrections. There were some problems because suitable legislation did not precede the project implementation.
E-governance phase	"Inform"

Table 12. E-procurement by Brazil's federal government

Attribute	Details
Why?	Automate procurement process, make it more transparent and uniform, reduce procurement costs, speed up procurement, increase pool of suppliers.
Who gains?	The Brazilian federal government because of reduced costs, improved quality, and faster procurement. The suppliers because of better opportunity and a more level playing field.
Technology inputs	Classical client-server architecture with Windows-based servers and clients, Web application services, and application software from Vesta Business Services Suite
Lesson	Even a relatively simple e-governance implementation improves efficiency, increases profits, empowers suppliers, and builds goodwill for the federal government.
E-governance phase	"Inform" and "interact"

whittle down prices, was also sufficiently innovative (Joia & Zamot, 2002).

eChoupal to Empower Indian Farmers

In Indian agriculture, the farmer often benefits the least although he does the most work and takes the biggest risks. The farmer is obliged to sell his produce at the village marketplace for ridiculously low prices to "middlemen"; these middlemen, who have better storage, transport, and marketing resources, often go on to make big profits.

The eChoupal software (Annamalai & Rao, 2003), from ITC, electronically recreates the village meeting place—where farmers meet to discuss crop prospects and selling rates—by positioning computers in the village with Internet connectivity. At these kiosks, often located in the house of the educated village head, farmers can order seeds, fertilizer, and other products at prices lower than those available with the village trader. They also obtain information about new farming techniques.

This e-governance project, which started gathering steam by 2003, has reached thousands of villages and helped millions of farmers. Although it started off as a project to "inform" the farmer,

and help him in his trade "interactions," eChoupal is now acquiring a community center character by also advising farmers on health and creating e-learning portals for farmer education. The project should receive a significant fillip when wireless connectivity becomes more widespread.

Beijing's Business E-Park

The Zhongguancun Science Park was established in Beijing in 1988 following China's decision to open its economy to the outside world. By 2000, there were 6,000 business houses operating out of the Science Park, including international giants such as IBM, Microsoft, and Motorola.

Managing all these business establishments was proving to be very difficult because of diverse administrative procedures and workflows, a large number of approving and monitoring government departments, and long operational lead times. These business establishments contributed $12 billion in revenue and $200 million in foreign investment, so it was essential not to lose goodwill.

In 2000, therefore, the Chinese government set up the Zhongguancun E-Park as a pilot project to improve the efficiency and responsiveness of the Government (Lin, Zhu, & Hachigian, 2006).

Table 13. The eChoupal project for the Indian farmer

Attribute	Details
Why?	Empower the Indian farmer by educating him about good agricultural practices and enabling him to sell his produce at more attractive prices.
Who gains?	The Indian farmer and ITC who run eChoupal. ITC's investments allowed it to replace the old "middlemen" and profit from commercial transactions. It is a win-win for both.
Technology inputs	Computers with Internet connectivity; the best results were achieved using the VSAT technology.
Lesson	E-governance can be successful even in the sparsely networked Indian countryside. The project succeeded because it was visionary and ITC had the financial muscle to push it through. The project illustrates how human mindsets can indeed be changed.
E-governance phase	"Inform" and "interact"

Table 14. Beijing's Zhongguancun E-Park

Attribute	Details
Why?	It was becoming very difficult to manage the operations of the 6,000 business establishments in the Zhongguancun Science Park. These businesses brought in valuable revenue and investments.
Who gains?	The business establishments because of efficient and streamlined governance. The Chinese government because of better trade and positive goodwill.
Technology inputs	A conventional Web-faced solution by Beijing Beauty Beard Ltd. with enhanced security and workflow management systems. Major investments in hardware, fiber, and application software.
Lesson	E-governance brings about a dramatic increase in efficiency, revenue, and goodwill, but it is important to manage mindsets and legal bottlenecks. Legislation must be in step with implementation.
E-governance phase	"Inform," "interact," and "transact."

Over 30 G2B and G2C functions such as "apply for license," "submit tax reports," or "file monthly statements" were introduced in a comprehensive software solution that had modules for e-application, e-registration, e-reporting, e-administration, and e-consulting. The solution also contained "reminder routines" and options to monitor the workflow progress online.

The Zhongguancun E-Park initiative has been very successful. Ninety percent of the application and approval procedures are now performed online, with as many as 4,400 companies actively interacting with the e-governance system. Application filing can now be completed in 3 days, instead of 15 days. The number of visits to complete the application filing is down from a dozen or more to just one. In fact, the Mayor of Beijing has gone on record to say that *all* administrative procedures in Beijing will be converted to this E-Park model by 2010.

The chief difficulty involved in this $1.5 million implementation was the unwillingness of officials to accept this e-governance solution because of a decrease in their power and autonomy. There were also several legal hurdles encountered during the process. Continuous and intensive training was

very useful. An attractive spin-off is that there are now no traffic jams around Beijing's government establishments since most of the activity happens online!

Electronic Reservation in Indian Railways

The Indian Railways use 7,000 passenger trains to carry 5 billion train passengers every year across a network spanning 63,000 km and 7,000 railway stations. Because of overcrowding and long journey times, the recommended procedure is to board an Indian train only after prior reservation.

While software solutions to manage train reservations were implemented over a decade ago, the procedure still required the passenger *to physically visit* a reservation booth to make his booking and payment. From 2003 or so, however, a comprehensive online booking system is now operational.

The new procedure seeks the passenger's travel details, offers an interactive session to verify seat availability online, and eventually prepares a travel bill with the option to connect to the passenger's preferred bank. An electronic

Table 15. Summary of e-governance initiative for Indian Railway ticket reservation

Attribute	Details
Why?	Indian Railways only have about 3,000 automated reservation counters. These counters are always crowded and expensive to manage.
Who gains?	(a) Every passenger using Indian Railways. (b) Indian Railways, because it can manage its business processes much more efficiently, offer its customers a 24x7 service, and eventually downsize its expensive reservation counters to smaller kiosks.
Technology inputs	Conventional interactive Web architecture with the provision to link the disparate railway and bank databases.
Lesson	Political pressure required the Indian Railways to innovate almost 15 years ago. Now user pressure and user acceptance ensures that there is no going back.
E-governance phase	"Inform," "interact," "transact," and fledgling elements of "transform"

payment is made using a secure connection and the passenger either has the option of printing an e-ticket or receiving the ticket by courier.

REFERENCES

Annamalai, K., & Rao, S. (2003). *ITC's eChoupal and profitable rural transformation: Web-based information and procurement tools for the Indian farmer*. World Resources Institute.

Backus, M. (2001). *E-governance and developing countries: Introduction and examples*. Retrieved September 1, 2005, from http://www.ftpiicd.org/files/research/reports/report3.pdf

eGovernment for development. (2004). *Cases of eGovernment success and failure from developing/transitional countries*. Retrieved September 10, 2005, from http://www.egov4dev.org/topic-1cases.htm

Gilfillan, I. (2000, March). Database normalization. *Database Journal*. Retrieved February 13, 2006, from http://www.databasejournal.com/sqletc/article.php/1428511

Hagel III, J. (2002). *Out of the box: Strategies for achieving profits today and growth tomorrow*

through Web services. Boston: Harvard Business School Press.

Hagel, J., Brown, J. S., & Layton-Rodin, D. (2004). *The secret to creating value from Web services today: Start simply*. Retrieved September 17, 2005, from http://www.johnhagel.com/paper_start-simply.pdf

Joia, L. A., & Zamot, F. (2002). Internet-based reverse auctions by the Brazilian government. *The Electronic Journal on Information Systems in Developing Countries, 9*(6), 1-12.

Kalja, A., & Ott, A. (2004). *Special citizens Web portal with standard DB-services (Estonia)*. Retrieved February 8, 2006, from http://unpan1.un.org/intradoc/groups/public/documents/Other/UNPAN022018.pdf

Lin, Zhu, & Hachigian. (2006). *Beijing's buisiness e-park*. Retrieved December 11, 2006 from http://unpan1.un.org/intradoc/groups/public/documents/APCITY/UNPAN002122.pdf

Norris, P. (2001). *Digital divide: Civic engagement, information poverty, and the Internet worldwide*. Cambridge: Cambridge University Press.

Ozorio de Almeida, M. (2002). *eProcurement by Brazil's federal government*. Retrieved February

10, 2006, from http://unpan1.un.org/intradoc/groups/public/documents/Other/UNPAN022347.pdf

Sinha, T., & Condon, B. J. (2005). *Legal liabilities in a brave new cyberworld: Making electronic risk management work*. Retrieved September 8, 2005, from http://ssrn.com/abstract=800890

UNPAN Virtual Library. (2006). *Information by content type*. Retrieved February 13, 2006, from http://www.unpan.org/autoretrieve/content.asp?content=case%20studies

Vaughan-Nichols, S. J. (2004). Achieving wireless broadband using WiMAX. *Computer, 37*(6), 10-13.

Want, R. (2004). RFID: A key to automating everything. *Scientific American, 290*(1), 46-55.

Warschauer, M. (2003). Demystifying the digital divide. *Scientific American, 289*(2), 34-39.

Warschauer, M. (2004). *Technology and social inclusion: Rethinking the digital divide*. Cambridge, MA: The MIT Press

W'O Okot-Uma, R. (2001). *Electronic governance: Re-inventing good governance*. Retrieved September 2, 2005, from http://www1.worldbank.org/publicsector/egov/Okot-Uma.pdf

Chapter IV
On the Study of Complexity in Information Systems

James Courtney
University of Central Florida, USA

Yasmin Merali
Warwick Business School, UK

David Paradice
Florida State University, USA

Eleanor Wynn
Intel Corporation Information Technology, USA

ABSTRACT

This article addresses complexity in information systems. It defines how complexity can be used to inform information systems research, and how some individuals and organizations are using notions of complexity. Some organizations are dealing with technical and physical infrastructure complexity, as well as the application of complexity in specific areas such as supply chain management and network management. Their approaches can be used to address more general organizational issues. The concepts and ideas in this article are relevant to the integration of complexity into information systems research.

However, the ideas and concepts in this article are not a litmus test for complexity. We hope only to provide a starting point for information systems researchers to push the boundaries of our understanding of complexity. The article also contains a number of suggested research questions that could be pursued in this area.

INTRODUCTION

This article reflects some thoughts of the editorial review board for the complexity area of this new journal. We are pleased to see a journal introduced whose mission is to truly emphasize a systems approach in the study of information systems and information technology. Within this area of the journal, we will focus on the issue of complexity. We think it is befitting of the area that this article was a group effort. Complexity has many aspects, and we are eager to receive submissions that are truly informed by a systems approach in general and a complexity perspective in particular.

In the sections that follow, we will outline some thoughts on what complexity is, what it can mean when used to inform information systems research, and how some individuals and organizations are using notions of complexity. We provide some comments on how organizations are dealing with technical and physical infrastructure complexity, as well as the application of complexity in specific areas such as supply chain management and network management to more general organizational issues. We offer these pages as a beginning of a dialog on the topic, not as an exhaustive or restrictive set of criteria. We believe the concepts and ideas in this article are relevant to the integration of complexity into information systems research and that, in most cases, some aspect of these topics will be apparent in future submissions. However, the ideas and concepts in this article are not a litmus test for complexity. We expect, and hope, that information systems researchers will push the boundaries of our understanding of complexity through their efforts, which they report in this journal.

COMPLEXITY CONSIDERED

Human life is frequently described as becoming more and more complex, and rightly so. It seems that the terms "complex" or "complexity" appear everywhere. In some part, this is because life really is complex! But this conclusion is also driven by the fact that over the last few decades, we have learned more about the nature of complexity and the role that complexity plays in our lives. Complexity is a feature of all living and natural

systems. The approach we speak of has permeated the natural sciences as a way of understanding natural order. However, its application to human systems is to date fragmented.

A recent issue of the journal *Complexity* (Complexity at large, 2007) provides a glimpse of this phenomenon. The first seven pages provide an index into complexity studies from a wide range of disciplines. Here we find news about studies in biodiversity, weather prediction, stem cells, learning, gene therapy, battlefield operations, algorithm development, morality, neural activity in primates, topographical issues in anthropology, organ development, consciousness, robotic reasoning, human moods, and, appropriately, complexity measures. Presumably, the common thread in all of the articles referenced is some notion of complexity.

The focus of this area in the *International Journal of Information Technology and the Systems Approach* (IJITSA) cannot, unfortunately, be so broad. We must limit our scope to topics in information technology. That, however, will not be a serious constraint. The application of complexity theory to information system design, implementation, testing, installation, and maintenance is well within the scope of this IJITSA area. Fundamental issues related to definition, measurement, and application of complexity concepts are valid areas of inquiry. In looking at complexity in information technology, however, we cannot overlook the organizational structures that technology supports, in the image of which information technology is designed.

Information technology underlies and supports a huge part of the operations of modern organizations. By extrapolation, therefore, the role of information systems as they support complex organizational processes is well within our scope. Simon (1996) argued that complexity is a necessary feature of organizations and Huber (2004), in a review of management research, underscores the importance of recognizing that organizational decision making in the future will occur in an environment of growing and increasing complexity.

Indeed, information technology underlies a large part of life itself for young people today. Their lives are entwined in online social networks. They may have a "relationship" with hundreds of other people who they have never met. Their identity may be connected to online activities in ways that no other prior generation has ever experienced. Concepts such as "network" and "relationship" are fundamental to complexity. Investigations of information technology supported communities through a complexity theory lens are certainly within the scope of this area of IJITSA. But complexity and interdependency underlie "normal" social science as well. Granovetter's seminal work (1973, 1983) on "weak ties" in social networks remains a model today in social network theory (Watts, 2003). As well, Lansing's study of Balinese farming reflects a complex systems approach to traditional society (Lansing, 2006).

COMPLEXITY EXPLORED AND DESCRIBED

But let us not get ahead of ourselves, for our understanding of complexity is still evolving. A good starting point for this area is to define, to the extent that we can, what our terms mean. A distinction has to be made between a system having many different parts—complexity of detail and a system of dynamic complexity. In the case of complexity of detail, the system may be treated by categorization, classification, ordering, and systemic-algorithmic approach. A system has dynamic complexity when its parts have multiple possible modes of operation, and each part may be connected, according to need, to a different part. Dynamic complexity exists when a certain operation results in a series of local consequences and a totally different series of results in other parts of the system (O'Connor & McDermott, 1997). So we see that even constructing a defini-

tion is no small task when dealing with the topic of complexity. In fact, we will not be surprised to publish papers in the future that clarify or expand the definitions we offer today.

Complexity is a characteristic that emerges from the relationship(s) of parts that are combined. The idea that the "whole is greater than the sum of the parts" is fundamental to considerations of complexity. Complex describes situations where the condition of complexity emerges from that being considered. Complexity cannot be foreseen from an examination of the constituent parts of a thing. It is a characteristic that emerges only after the parts are entwined in a way that subsequent separation of the parts would destroy the whole. We can see hints of this characteristic even in descriptions of situations that are not focused specifically on complexity. For example, Buckland (1991) writes of information systems that support libraries: "By complexity, we do not simply mean the amount of technical engineering detail, but rather the diversity of elements and relationships involved" (p. 27). He further observes that systems that are provided on a noncommercial basis are necessarily more complex than commercial systems due to the political dimension of their provision. Clearly, this notion of complexity goes well beyond the hardware and software and considers a much broader system in use.

One widely accepted definition of a complex adaptive system comes from Holland (1995), as cited in Clippinger (1999). A complex adaptive system is said to be comprised of aggregation, nonlinearity, flows, diversity, tagging, internal models, and building blocks. What these mean in the context of information systems is the subject of an entire paper. The basic principle is that complex systems contain many interaction variables that interact together to create emergent outcomes. Initial conditions may be local and small in scale, but may gain nonlinearity due to aggregation, and so forth.

Thinking in terms of complexity and some of the concepts and metaphors that are emerging in the study of complexity is a departure from some traditional scientific thinking. Many approaches to understanding that are "scientific" have involved decomposing some thing into its parts so that the parts may be better understood. This reductionism in understanding often sacrifices as much as it gains by losing the richness of context in which the object studied exists. Such an approach provides great knowledge about parts, but little about the whole. It assumes that each part has its own trajectory unaffected by other parts. Moreover, this approach is limited by relying entirely on countable "units" as opposed to analog conditions.

The dynamics of interaction between elements gives rise to a number of features that are difficult to reconcile with some of the tenets of the "classical" IS paradigm and its methods for dealing with complexity (see Merali, 2004, for more detail). Schneider and Somers (2006) identify three "building blocks" of complexity theory: nonlinear dynamics, chaos theory, and adaptation and evolution. By nonlinear dynamics, they refer to dissipative structures that exhibit an inherent instability. These structures may be easily affected by a small change in the environment. They do not tend toward equilibrium. Rather, they go through transitions, typically moving into conditions of greater complexity both quantitatively and qualitatively. This is fundamentally different from the General Systems Theory inclination toward equilibrium.

Chaos is a deterministic process that is progressively unpredictable over time. Chaos theory provides a basis for the study of patterns that initially seem random, but upon closer inspection turn out to be nonrandom. Schneider and Somers observe that under chaos, a basis of attraction is formed that brings about the nonrandomness. A "strange attractor" accounts for the system's bounded preferences.

Chaos is critical to the process of adaptation and evolution. Schneider and Somers (2006) observe that complex adaptive systems (CAS)

reflect an ability to adapt through the emergent characteristic of self-organization. Karakatsios (1990) has developed a simple illustration of how order can emerge from chaos or randomness in such systems. First, a matrix is randomly populated with a binary variable, say zeroes and ones. Let a zero value represent the notion of "off" and a one value represent the notion of "on". Next, the following algorithm is iteratively applied to the matrix:

For each cell in the matrix
If 3 or fewer neighboring cells and this cell are on, set this cell to off.
If 6 or more neighboring cells and this cell are on, set this cell to on.
If 4 neighboring cells are on, turn this cell on.
But if 5 neighboring cells are on, turn this cell off.
Repeat until no changes occur.

Some of us have tried it and found that the matrix typically stabilizes in as few as five or six iterations. However, not all systems have the capacity to adapt. Some systems find small changes in the environment too disruptive to ever evolve to another state. Catastrophe theory studies systems that may transition into one of two states, one stable and the other highly chaotic. Whether a system enters a chaotic state or remains stable may be highly sensitive to initial conditions, so sensitive in fact that it may not be possible to know inputs precisely enough to predict which state the system will enter. This may appear to be troublesome to those attempting to manage organizational systems, but work in the area of complex adaptive systems tells us that systems can adapt and learn and information can be fed back to the control mechanism (management) to keep the organization on a relatively stable path. On the other hand, other systems are too stable and do not react to the environment in any meaningful way. These systems are essentially inert. They continue in their current behavior oblivious to the environment around them. Somewhere between these two extremes are systems that are able to react to the environment in a meaningful way. Kauffman (1995) suggests it is the systems "poised" at the edge of chaos, the ones that are not too stable and not too instable, that have the flexibility to evolve. He theorizes a set of variables that affect the degree of chaos/nonchaos in a system, and hence its ability to evolve. The application of chaos theory to information systems design, implementation, testing, installation, and maintenance is well within the scope of IJITSA.

With the impressive growth of the field of complex systems, the lack of a clear and generally accepted definition of a system's complexity has become a difficulty for many. While complexity is an inherent feature of systems (Frank, 2001), a system may be complex for one observer while not for another. This is not due to subjective observation, but due to the observers' scales of observation. A system that is highly complex on one scale may have low complexity on another scale. For example, the planet Earth is a simple dot—a planet moving along its orbit—as observed on one scale, but its complexity is substantial when viewed in terms of another scale, such as its ecosystem. Thus, complexity cannot be thought of as a single quantity or quality describing a system. It is a property of a system that varies with the scale of observation. Complexity, then, can be defined as the amount of information required to describe a system. In this case, it is a function of scale, and thus a system is to be characterized by a complexity profile (see Bar-Yam, 1997, 2002a, 2002b, 2004).

COMPLEXITY AS A LENS FOR INVESTIGATION

Complexity concepts have been deployed to study complex systems and their dynamics in two ways. The first is through the direct use of complexity concepts and language as sense-making and explanatory devices for complex phenomena in diverse application domains. To capture the "unfolding" of the *emergent* dynamics, we need to have methods that can provide a view of the *dynamics* of the *changing* state in continuous time. The complex systems approach to doing this is by describing state cycles using mathematical models or by running simulations.

The second is through agent-based computational modeling to study the dynamics of complex systems interactions and to reveal emergent structures and patterns of behavior. Agent-based computational modeling has characteristics that are particularly useful for studying socially embedded systems. Typically agent-based models deploy a diversity of agents to represent the constituents of the focal system. The modeler defines the environmental parameters that are of interest as the starting conditions for the particular study. Repeated runs of the model reveal collective states or patterns of behavior as they emerge from the interactions of entities over time. Agent-based models are very well-suited for revealing the dynamics of far-from equilibrium complex systems and have been widely used to study the dynamics of a diversity of social and economic systems.

With the escalation of available computational power, it will be possible to build bigger models. The mathematicians and the natural scientists have a powerful battery of technologies for studying dynamical systems. However, for social systems, the specification of the components for the construction of agent based models is a challenging prospect. The challenge of creating entire mini-economies in silicon is not one of processing power, but one of learning how to build sufficiently realistic agents.

The science of complexity allows us to consider the dynamic properties of systems. It allows us to explore how systems emerge and adapt. When viewed as a complex adaptive system, it provides us a mechanism for dealing with both the technical and the social aspects of systems. We have new metaphors for articulating how IS are used and how they evolve. We move from concepts embedded in an assumption of stable hierarchies to ideas embedded in an assumption of networks of dynamic relationships. With this, we move closer to a unified view of IS and management.

Simon (1996) writes: "Roughly, by a complex system I mean one made up of a large number of parts that have many interactions" (p. 183). This simple definition can be readily applied to organizations and their information systems. Thus, an organization is a complex system if it has many units (departments, for example) and there are many interactions among units. A complex information system is one that has many elements (programs, modules, objects, relationships, attributes, databases, etc.) that interact in many ways.

At the most fundamental level, technological developments have the potential to increase connectivity (between people, applications, and devices), capacity for distributed storage and processing of data, and reach and range of information transmission and rate (speed and volume) of information transmission. The realization of these affordances has given rise to the emergence of new network forms of organization embodying complex, distributed network structures, with processes, information, and expertise shared across organizational and national boundaries. The network form of organizing is thus a signature of the Internet-enabled transformation of economics and society. Merali (2004, 2005) suggests conceptualizing the networked world as a kind of global distributed information system.

Yet, this only begins to get at the complexity of complex systems. Systems have boundaries that separate what is in the system from what is outside—in the environment. Environments themselves may be complex, and the system, the organization, or the information system may interact with the environment in many ways. Moreover the interactions themselves may be complex.

An information system that exists with a particular organization (ignoring inter-organizational systems, for the moment) has the organization as its environment. If the organization and its information requirements are stable, then the information system itself has relatively little need to change, other than to keep up with changes in relevant hardware and software technologies (which may be no mean feat in and of itself).

However, it seems to be the norm today for organizations and their environments to be in a state of constant change. Organizations must adapt to environmental changes in order to survive, not to mention thrive. The same can be said for information systems in organizations. Organizations may even rely upon their information systems in order to understand, analyze, and adapt to such changes. Thus, we say that organizations and information systems are one form of complex adaptive systems, a topic of great interest today among those interested in systems theory.

Simon (1996) describes three time periods in which there were bursts of interest in studying complex systems. The first followed World War I and resulted in the definition of "holism" and an interest in Gestalts, and a rejection of reductionism. The second followed World War II and involved the development of general systems theory, cybernetics, and the study of feedback control mechanisms. In one perspective, in the second era, the information system of an organization is viewed as a feedback mechanism that helps managers guide the enterprise towards its goals.

We are now in a third era. The foundation had been laid for the development of the concept of complex adaptive systems, elements of which include emergence, catastrophe theory, chaos theory, genetic algorithms, and cellular automata. Complex adaptive systems receive sensory information, energy, and other inputs from the environment, process it (perhaps using a schema in the form of an updatable rule-base), output actions that affect the environment, and feedback control information to manage system behavior as learning occurs (update the schema).

Complex adaptive systems are reminiscent of the concepts of organizational learning and knowledge management, which have been viewed from the perspectives of Churchman's (1973) inquiring systems which create knowledge or learn and feed that knowledge back into an organizational knowledge base (Courtney, 2001; Courtney, Croasdell, & Paradice, 1998; Hall & Paradice, 2005; Hall, Paradice, & Courtney, 2003). Mason and Mitroff (1973), who studied under Churchman as he was developing the idea of applying general systems theory to the philosophy of inquiry, introduced this work into the IS literature early on, and it has ultimately had great influence on systems thinking in IS research.

Complexity in this context is in the form of "wicked" problems (Churchman, 1967; Rittel & Weber, 1973). In sharp contrast to the well-formulated but erratically behaving deterministic models found in chaos theory, in a wicked situation, "formulating the problem *is* the problem," as Rittel and Weber put it (1973, p. 157, emphasis theirs). The question that arises here is whether problems in management domains that involve human behavior are of such a different character that elements of complexity theory and chaos may not apply. This is clearly an open question and one that can only be addressed through additional research.

WHAT DOES THIS MEAN FOR IS?

There is no question that information systems in organizations, as they have been defined, are complex. The very basis of information systems, the underlying technologies, programs, machine language, and so forth, are inherently ways of dealing with complexities of calculation and the complexity of the use contexts, in this case, the organization. What has not been included in the description of information systems as "systems"

are several key notions from complex adaptive systems and current compute models that directly or indirectly reflect complex systems modeling. These include machine learning, Bayes nets, inferencing algorithms, complex calculations for science applications, visualization, virtualization schemes, network traffic modeling, social networking software, and diverse other areas.

Organizational analysis as we know it, even in its evolution to be inclusive of multiple paradigms of research, has failed to acknowledge that organizations are inherently complex. Organizations defy simplification, and the only way to deal with this fact is to embrace and manage complexity. Structuration theory and actor network theories applied to organizations both begin to cope with this reality that the whole is greater than the sum of the parts and that outcomes are emergent.

While visionary management authors like Wheatley (1992, 2006), Weick and Sutcliffe (2001), Axelrod and Cohen (2000), and others have written directly on the topic, the application of their thinking is not evident in the ordinary management situation. There is some adoption on the edges in areas where complexity is defined by the behavior of objects, like supply chain management, RFID tagging and tracking, and network traffic. However, these applications often occur without recognition of the greater framework they represent. Further, attempts to generalize from these technically specific domains to the overall behavior of the organization have not been accepted easily.

What is missing from the computational paradigms that do use complexity in their mode of operation is simply the recognition that this is so. It is as if connectionists have entered into the world of dealing with complexity as a "natural environment", like air or water, which ceases to be noticed.

At this point in history, the organization and its information systems are inextricable. There is no turning back, as there may have been as late as the 1970s when paper systems were still an option.

Figure 1.

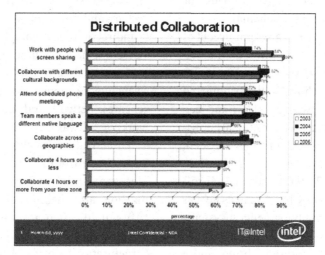

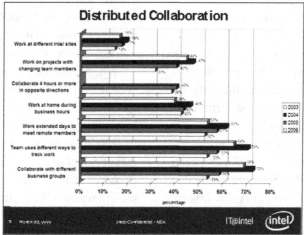

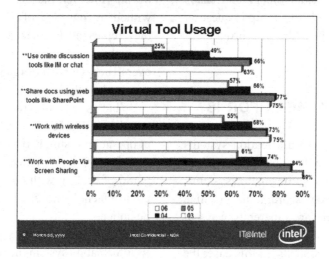

Table 1. Some research questions related to complexity and information systems

Does chaos theory really apply to the IS domain? IS seems to have characteristics more resembling those of wicked problems where formulating the problem is the problem. Chaos consists of well-specified models whose behavior gets less predictable over time because of nonlinearities. The two do not seem to be isomorphic.
How does one go about modeling agents in IS problems? Modeling computer systems may not be so difficult, but modeling human actors seems to be problematic. How, for example, do you model changing schemata as learning occurs? Human agents have almost limitless attributes. What characteristics of human agents are important to model? How do you model the exchange of knowledge among agents?
As organizations and IS become more intertwined, it becomes increasingly important that the IS be reliable. Does chaos theory make sense here, in that the organization's behavior may be unpredictable if the IS fails?
How does management's attitude about importing innovation from the environment affect the IS function? Does sharing or importing innovations help the organization fit the environment?
How do we define and measure organizational and information systems complexity? How do we test complex models of organizations and information systems? We need to measure to be able to test.
Is it possible to organize and manage so that the organization and its information systems co-evolve and emerge together? Can prototyping help support co-evolution?
From Rouse (2007, pp. 16-17): What architectures underlie the physical, behavioral, and social phenomena of interest? How are architectures a means to achieve desired system characteristics? How can architectures enable resilient, adaptive, agile, and evolvable systems? How can and should one analytically and empirically evaluate and assess architectures prior to and subsequent to development and deployment? What is the nature of fundamental limits of information, knowledge, model formulation, observability, controllability, scalability, and so on? How can decision support mechanisms be developed for multistakeholder, multi-objective decisions?

Aside from back-ups for legal purposes, all large organizations are fully committed to their information systems environments as infrastructure. Indeed, technical infrastructure encroaches on physical infrastructure with outsourcing, telecommuting, globalization of work, and other major trends. As information systems facilitate more and more networked operations and distributed work, as enterprise applications emerge that serve one and all, the very functioning of the organization, especially a large one, becomes impossible without an information system. Studies of Intel's workforce find that on six dimensions of time, space, organizational affiliation, software tools, culture, and number of projects, the workforce can be said to be operating approximately 2/3 in "virtual mode"—across time, space, culture,

multiple teams, and so forth (Wynn & Graves, 2007).

This means that the workforce coordinates itself mostly on the network. If the medium of coordination, action, and work production is primarily a network, it more and more resembles a rapidly changing complex system that has the possibility of being self-organizing in a very positive way. Indeed, that is the case. But without the recognition that virtuality equates with greater capacity for self-organization (and that self-organization is adaptive), then this enormous potential will be not only underutilized, but at times interfered with, sub-optimized, and cut off from its latent functionality.

The interesting thing is that the science is there; the systems are there; the computational capacity is there. All that is lacking is the consciousness to apply them. Some notable exceptions exist, however. The Department of Defense Command Control Research Project has a number of publications that apply a self-organizing system concept to hierarchical command and control systems. Boeing PhantomWorks (Wiebe, Compton, & Garvey, 2006) has drawn out the Command and Control Research Program (CCRP) scheme into a large system dynamic model. In short, there is no lack of research and conceptual material.

But getting this across to people responsible for the stock price and cost containment of a very large organization is no simple matter. It seems risky, even though it is likely much less risky than acting as if the world were a stable place and a linear progress model will provide a safe approach to operations. As a defense strategy organization, CCRP recognizes acutely that they are dealing with volatile, rapidly changing, network-based asymmetrical conflicts that also have great potential for reaching critical mass and nonlinear effects so large they could overwhelm conventional forces, or at least those using conventional methods.

The large organization lives in very much the same world as the military organization, only effects are slower to take hold and direct loss of life is not normally a risk. However, there are environmental instabilities in global politics, competition and licensing, labor forces, currency and liquidity, stock market fluctuations, energy costs, supply chains that reach across the globe, transportation, changing demand, and of course, competitors. All of these elements together, and others not noted, comprise a highly complex and turbulent environment. That is the external environment. The internal environment of the organization and its information system can create the adequate response to the external environment. For that to happen, both workforce and information systems need to be seen as comprising an adaptive resource. This is where explicit recognition of complexity can make the difference.

A recent special issue of the journal *Information Technology & People* (Jacucci, Hanseth, & Lyytinen, 2006) took a first step in applying this approach to what we know about information systems research (Benbya & McElvey, 2006; Kim & Kaplan, 2006; Moser & Law, 2006). However, a journal that is regularly dedicated to this theme is needed both to publish available research and to foster further research on this important topic.

We offer a set of possible research questions in Table 1. This list is by no means exhaustive, and we welcome work on these and others that our audience may conceive.

CONCLUSION

Few would argue that complexity is not inherent in living today. As networked information environments become more integrated into both our social and our working lives, the number of relationships with others may grow, and the relationships we have with them may become more complex. We exist, along with our relationships, in an environment of equal or greater complexity.

We strive to understand what complexity means and what it implies for us. We believe that a better understanding of complexity will give us a better ability to function more effectively and achieve our goals, both personal and professional. We welcome research that will broaden our understanding of complexity, help us understand how to embrace a notion such as emergence in complexity, show us how to use complexity to inform our social and our work lives, leverage the self-organizing capabilities of complex adaptive systems to achieve personal and organizational goals, and apply metaphors from chaos and other complexity-oriented theories to better describe and understand our world. We look forward to publishing the best work in these areas and in others that will surely emerge.

REFERENCES

Alberts, D., & Hayes, R. (2005). *Power to the edge: Command and control in the information age* (CCRP Publication Series). CCRP.

Atkinson, S., & Moffat, J. (2005). *The agile organization: From informal networks to complex effects and agility* (CCRP Information Age Transformation Series). CCRP.

Axelrod, R., & Cohen, M. (2000). *Harnessing complexity: Organizational implications of a scientific frontier.* New York: Basic Books.

Bar-Yam, Y. (1997). *Dynamics of complex systems.* Reading, MA: Perseus Press.

Bar-Yam, Y. (2002a). Complexity rising: From human beings to human civilization, a complexity profile. In *Encyclopedia of Life Support Systems (EOLSS).* Oxford, UK: UNESCO, EOLSS Publishers.

Bar-Yam, Y. (2002b). General features of complex systems. In *Encyclopedia of Life Support Systems (EOLSS).* Oxford, UK: UNESCO, EOLSS Publishers.

Bar-Yam, Y. (2004). Multiscale variety in complex systems. *Complexity, 9,* 37-45.

Benbya, H., & McKelvey, H. (2006). Toward a complexity theory of information systems development. *Information Technology & People, 19*(1), 12-34.

Buckland, M. (1991). *Information and information systems.* New York: Praeger Publishers.

Churchman, C.W. (1967). Wicked problems. *Management Science, 4*(14), B141-B142.

Churchman, C.W. (1971). *The design of inquiring systems: Basic concepts of systems and organization.* New York: Basic Books.

Clippinger, J.H. (1999). *The biology of business: Decoding the natural laws of enterprise.* Jossey-Bass.

Complexity at large. (2007). *Complexity, 12*(3), 3-9.

Courtney, J.F. (2001). Decision making and knowledge management in inquiring organizations: A new decision-making paradigm for DSS [Special issue]. *Decision Support Systems, 31*(1), 17-38.

Courtney, J.F., Croasdell, D.T., & Paradice, D.B. (1998). Inquiring organizations. *Australian Journal of Information Systems, 6*(1), 3-15. Retrieved July 10, 2007, from http://www.bus.ucf.edu/jcourtney/FIS/fis.htm

Frank, M. (2001). Engineering systems thinking: A multifunctional definition. *Systemic Practice and Action Research, 14*(3), 361-379.

Granovetter, M. (1973). The strength of weak ties. *American Journal of Sociology, 78,* 6.

Granovetter, M. (1983). The strength of weak ties: A network theory revisited. *Sociological Theory, 1.*

Hall, D.J., & Paradice, D.B. (2005). Philosophical foundations for a learning-oriented knowledge management system for decision support. *Decision Support Systems, 39*(3), 445-461.

Hall, D.J., Paradice, D.B., & Courtney, J.F. (2003). Building a theoretical foundation for a learning-oriented knowledge management system. *Journal of Information Technology Theory and Applications, 5*(2), 63-89.

Holland, J.H. (1995). *Hidden order: How adaptation builds complexity.* Helix Books.

Huber, G. (2004). *The necessary nature of future firms.* Thousand Oaks, CA: Sage Publications.

Jacucci, E., Hanseth, O., & Lyytinen, K. (2006). Introduction: Taking complexity seriously in IS research. *Information Technology & People, 19*(1), 5-11.

Karakatsios, K.Z. (1990). *Casim's user's guide.* Nicosia, CA: Algorithmic Arts.

Kauffman, S. (1995). *At home in the universe: The search for laws of self-organization and complexity.* Oxford University Press.

Kim, R., & Kaplan, S. (2006). Interpreting socio-technical co-evolution: Applying complex adaptive systems to IS engagement. *Information Technology & People, 19*(1), 35-54.

Lansing, S. (2006). *Perfect order: Recognizing complexity in Bali.* Princeton University Press.

Lissack, M.R. (1999). Complexity: The science, its vocabulary, and its relation to organizations. *Emergence, 1*(1), 110-126.

Lissack, M.R., & Roos, J. (2000). *The next common sense: The e-managers guide to mastering complexity.* London: Nicholas Brealey Publishing.

Merali, Y. (2004). Complexity and information systems. In J. Mingers, & L. Willcocks (Eds.), *Social theory and philosophy of information systems* (pp. 407-446). London: Wiley.

Merali, Y. (2005, July). Complexity science and conceptualisation in the Internet enabled world. Paper presented at the *21st Colloquium of the European Group for Organisational Studies,* Berlin, Germany.

Moser, I., & Law, J. (2006). Fluids or flows? Information and qualculation in medical practice. *Information Technology & People, 19*(1), 55-73.

O'Connor, J., & McDermott, I. (1997). *The art of systems thinking.* San Francisco: Thorsons.

Rittel, H.W.J., & Webber, M.M. (1973). Dilemmas in a general theory of planning. *Policy Sciences, 4,* 155-169.

Rouse, W.B. (2007). *Complex engineered, organizational and natural systems: Issues underlying the complexity of systems and fundamental research needed to address these issues* (Report submitted to the Engineering Directorate, National Science Foundation, Washington, DC).

Schneider, M., & Somers, M. (2006). Organizations as complex adaptive systems: Implications of complexity theory for leadership research. *The Leadership Quarterly, 17,* 351-365.

Simon, H.A. (1996). *The sciences of the artificial.* Boston: The MIT Press.

Watts, D. (2003). Six degrees: The science of a connected age. New York: W.W. Norton & Co.

Webster. (1986). *Webster's ninth new collegiate dictionary.* Springfield, MA: Merriam-Webster, Inc.

Weick, K., & Sutcliffe, K. (2001). *Managing the unexpected: Assuring high performance in an age of complexity.* Jossey-Bass Publishers.

Wheatley, M. (1992, 2006). *Leadership and the new science: Discovering order in an age of chaos.* Berrett-Koehler Publishers.

Wiebe, R., Compton, D., & Garvey, D. (2006, June). A system dynamics treatment of the essential tension between C2 and self-synchronization. In *Proceedings of the International Conference on Complex Systems,* New England Complex Systems Institute, Boston, Massachusetts.

Wynn, E., & Graves, S. (2007). *Tracking the virtual organization* (Working paper). Intel Corporation.

This work was previously published in International Journal of Information Technologies and Systems Approach, Vol. 1, Issue 1, edited by D. Paradice and M. More, pp. 37-48, copyright 2008 by IGI Publishing, formerly known as Idea Group Publishing (an imprint of IGI Global)

Section II
Development and Design Methodologies

Chapter V
A Model of Knowledge Management Success

Murray E. Jennex
San Diego State University, USA

Lorne Olfman
Claremont Graduate University, USA

ABSTRACT

This article describes a knowledge management (KM) success model that is derived from observations generated through a longitudinal study of KM in an engineering organization and KM success factors found in the literature, which were modified by the application of these observations and success factors in various projects. The De-Lone and McLean (1992, 2003) IS Success Model was used as a framework for the model, since it was found to fit the observed success criteria and provided an accepted theoretical basis for the proposed model.

INTRODUCTION

Knowledge management (KM) and knowledge management system (KMS) success is an issue that needs to be explored. The Knowledge Management Foundations workshop held at the Hawaii International Conference on System Sciences in January 2006 discussed this issue and reached agreement that it is important for the credibility of the KM discipline that we be able to define KM success. Also, Turban and Aronson (2001) list three reasons for measuring the success of KM and KMS:

- To provide a basis for company valuation
- To stimulate management to focus on what is important
- To justify investments in KM activities.

All are good reasons from an organizational perspective. Additionally, from the perspective of KM academics and practitioners, identifying the factors, constructs, and variables that define KM success is crucial to understanding how these initiatives and systems should be designed and implemented. It is the purpose of this article to present a model that specifies and describes the antecedents of KM and KMS success so that researchers and practitioners can predict if a specific KM and KMS initiative will be successful. The article assumes that KM and KMS success cannot be separated, which is based on a broad, Churchman view of what constitutes KMS and a definition of success that is not reliant solely on technical effectiveness. The other basic assumption for this article is that success and effectiveness, as used in the KM literature, are synonymous terms. The remainder of the article uses the term *KM* to refer to KM and KMS and the term *success* to refer to success and effectiveness. The reasoning for these assumptions is discussed later in the article.

The proposed KM Success Model is an explication of the widely accepted DeLone and McLean (1992, 2003) IS Success Model, which was used since it was able to be modified to fit the observations and data collected in a longitudinal study of Organizational Memory, OM, and KM. It fit success factors found in the KM literature, and the resulting KM Success Model was useful in predicting success when applied to the design and implementation of a KM initiative and/or a KMS. Additionally, the stated purpose of the DeLone and McLean (1992, 2003) IS Success Model is to be a generalized framework that describes success dimensions for which researchers can adapt and define specific contexts of success (DeLone & McLean, 2003). Before presenting the KM Success Model, we will discuss the concepts of knowledge, KM, KMS, and KM/KMS success. We then will discuss briefly the DeLone and McLean (1992, 2003) IS Success Model, present the KM Success Model, and discuss the differences. We will conclude by summarizing studies that support the KM Success Model and will present operationalizations that can be used to evaluate the constructs used to define the KM Success Model dimensions.

KNOWLEDGE, OM, AND KM

Alavi and Leidner (2001) summarize and extend the significant literature relating to knowledge, knowledge management, and knowledge management systems. They view organizational knowledge and OM as synonymous labels, as do Jennex and Olfman (2002). This is useful, as it allows for the combination of research results from OM and KM. It is also born out in the literature. Huber, Davenport, and King (1998) summarize OM as the set of repositories of information and knowledge that the organization has acquired and retains. Stein and Zwass (1995) define OM as the means by which knowledge from the past is brought to bear on present activities, resulting in higher or lower levels of organizational effectiveness, and Walsh and Ungson (1991) define OM as stored information from an organization's history that can be brought to bear on present decisions.

Davenport and Prusak (1998) define knowledge as an evolving mix of framed experience, values, contextual information, and expert insight that provides a framework for evaluating and incorporating new experiences and information. Knowledge often becomes embedded in documents or repositories and in organizational routines, processes, practices, and norms. Knowledge is also about meaning in the sense that it is context-specific (Huber et al., 1998). Jennex (2006) extends the concepts of context also to include associated culture that provides frameworks for understanding and using knowledge. Ultimately, we conclude that knowledge contains information, but information is not necessarily knowledge. Also, we conclude that OM contains knowledge. However, for the sake of simplicity, we will use the term *knowledge* to refer to OM and knowledge throughout this article.

Various knowledge taxonomies exist. Alavi and Leidner (2001) and Jennex and Croasdell (2005) found that the most commonly used taxonomy is Polanyi's (1962, 1967) and Nonaka's (1994) dimensions of tacit and explicit knowledge. This article uses this taxonomy for knowledge. Tacit knowledge is that which is understood within a knower's mind. It consists of cognitive and technical components. Cognitive components are the mental models used by the knower, which cannot be expressed directly by data or knowledge representations. Technical components are concrete concepts that can be expressed readily. Explicit knowledge also consists of these technical components that can be directly expressed by knowledge representations. KM in an organization occurs when members of an organization pass tacit and explicit knowledge to each other. Information Technology (IT) assists KM by providing knowledge repositories and methods for capturing and retrieving knowledge. The extent of the dimension of the knowledge being captured limits the effectiveness of IT in assisting KM. IT works best with knowledge that is primarily in the explicit dimension. Knowledge that is primarily in the tacit dimension requires that more context be captured with the knowledge where context is the information used to explain what the knowledge means and how it is used. Managing tacit knowledge is more difficult to support using IT solutions.

Jennex (2005) looked at what KM is and found no consensus definition. However, using the review board of the *International Journal of Knowledge Management* as an expert panel and soliciting definitions of KM that were used by the board members, the following working definition is used to define KM for this article:

KM *is the practice of selectively applying knowledge from previous experiences of decision making to current and future decision making activities with the express purpose of improving the organization's effectiveness.* (Jennex, 2005, p. iv)

KM is an action discipline; knowledge needs to be used and applied in order for KM to have an impact. We also need measurable impacts from knowledge reuse in order for KM to be successful. Decision making is something that can be measured and judged. Organizations can tell if they are making the same decisions over and over and if they are using past knowledge to make these decisions better and more quickly. Also, decision making is the ultimate application of knowledge. This working definition provides this direction for KM and leads to a description of success for KM as being able to provide the appropriate knowledge for decision making when it is needed to those who need it.

KNOWLEDGE MANAGEMENT SYSTEMS

Alavi and Leidner (2001) defined KMS as "IT (Information Technology)-based systems developed to support and enhance the organizational processes of knowledge creation, storage/retrieval, transfer, and application" (p. 114). They observed that not all KM initiatives will implement an IT solution, but they support IT as an enabler of KM. Maier (2002) expanded on the IT concept for the KMS by calling it an ICT (Information and Communication Technology) system that supported the functions of knowledge creation, construction, identification, capturing, acquisition, selection, valuation, organization, linking, structuring, formalization, visualization, distribution, retention, maintenance, refinement, evolution, accessing, search, and application. Stein and Zwass (1995) define an Organizational Memory Information System (OMS) as the processes and IT components as necessary to capture, store, and apply knowledge created in the past on decisions currently being made. Jennex and Olfman (2002) expanded this definition by incorporating the

OMS into the KMS and by adding strategy and service components to the KMS. We expand the boundaries of a KMS by taking a Churchman view of a system. Churchman (1979) defines a system as "a set of parts coordinated to accomplish a set of goals" (p. 29) and that there are five basic considerations for determining the meaning of a system:

- System objectives, including performance measures
- System environment
- System resources
- System components, their activities, goals, and measures of performance
- System management

Churchman (1979) also noted that systems are always part of a larger system and that the environment surrounding the system is outside the system's control but influences how the system performs. The final view of a KMS is as a system that includes IT/ICT components, repositories, users, processes that use and/or generate knowledge, knowledge, knowledge use culture, and the KM initiative with its associated goals and measures. This final definition is important, as it makes the KMS an embodiment of the KM initiative and makes it possible to associate KM success with KMS success.

KM SUCCESS

The previous paragraphs define KM success as reusing knowledge to improve organizational effectiveness by providing the appropriate knowledge to those that need it when it is needed. KM is expected to have a positive impact on the organization that improves organizational effectiveness. DeLone and McLean (1992, 2003) use the terms *success* and *effectiveness* interchangeably. This article uses KM success and KM effectiveness interchangeably by implying that increasing decision-making effectiveness has a positive impact on the organization, resulting in successful KM. KM and KMS success also is used interchangeably. KMS success can be defined as making KMS components more effective by improving search speed, accuracy, and so forth. For example, a KMS that enhances search and retrieval functions enhances decision-making effectiveness by improving the ability of the decision maker to find and retrieve appropriate knowledge in a more timely manner. The implication is that by increasing KMS effectiveness, KMS success is enhanced, and decision-making capability is enhanced, which leads to positive impacts on the organization. This is how KM success is defined, and it is concluded that enhancing KMS effectiveness makes the KMS more successful as well as being a reflection of KM success.

Figure 1. DeLone and McLean's (1992) IS success model

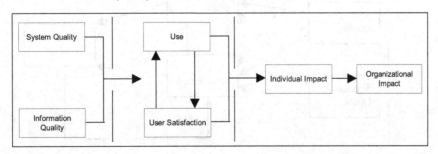

DeLone and McLean IS Success Model

In 1992 DeLone and McLean published their seminal work that proposed a taxonomy and an interactive model for conceptualizing and operationalizing IS success (DeLone & McLean, 1992). The DeLone and McLean (D&M) (1992) IS Success Model is based on a review and integration of 180 research studies that used some form of system success as a dependent variable. The model identifies six interrelated dimensions of success, as shown in Figure 1. Each dimension can have measures for determining their impact on success and on each other. Jennex, Olfman, Pituma, and Yong-Tae (1998) adopted the generic framework of the D&M IS Success Model and customized the dimensions to reflect the System Quality and Use constructs needed for an organizational memory information system (OMS). Jennex and Olfman (2002) expanded this OMS Success Model to include constructs for Information Quality.

DeLone and McLean (2003) revisited the D&M IS Success Model by incorporating subsequent IS success research and by addressing criticisms of the original model. One hundred forty-four articles from refereed journals and 15 papers

from the International Conference on Information Systems (ICIS) that cited the D&M IS Success Model were reviewed, with 14 of these articles reporting on studies that attempted to empirically investigate the model. The result of the article is the modified D&M IS Success Model shown in Figure 2. Major changes include the additions of a Service Quality dimension for the service provided by the IS group, the modification of the Use dimension into a Intent to Use dimension, the combination of the Individual and Organizational Impact dimensions into an overall Net Benefits dimension, and the addition of a feedback loop from Net Benefits to Intent to Use and User Satisfaction. This article modifies the Jennex and Olfman (2002) OMS Success Model into a KM Success Model by applying KM research and the modified D&M IS Success Model.

KM SUCCESS MODEL

The model developed in this article was initially proposed by Jennex, et al. (1998) after an ethnographic case study of KM in an engineering organization. The model was modified by Jennex and Olfman (2002) following a five-year longitudinal

Figure 2. DeLone and McLean's (2003) revisited IS success model

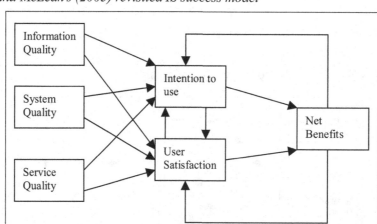

Figure 3. KM success model

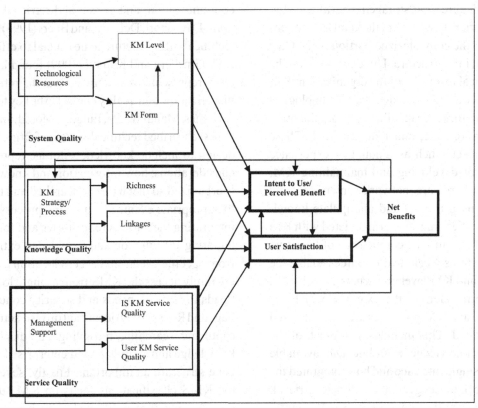

study of knowledge management in an engineering organization and is based on the DeLone and McLean (2003) revised IS Success Model. This final model was developed to incorporate experience in using the model to design KMS and for incorporating other KM/KMS success factor research from the literature. Figure 3 shows the KM Success Model. The KM Success Model is based on DeLone and McLean (2003). Since the KM Success Model is assessing the use of organizational knowledge, the Information Quality dimension is renamed the Knowledge Quality dimension. Also, because use of a KMS is usually voluntary, the KM Success Model expanded the Intention to Use dimension to include a Perceived Benefit dimension based on Thompson, Higgins, and Howell's (1991) Perceived Benefit model used

to predict system usage when usage is voluntary. Finally, since KM strategy/process is key to having the right knowledge, the feedback loop is extended back to this dimension. Dimension descriptions of the model follow.

SYSTEM QUALITY

Jennex and Olfman (2000, 2002) found infrastructure issues such as using a common network structure; adding KM skills to the technology support skill set; and using high-end personal computers, integrated databases; and standardizing hardware and software across the organization to be keys to building KM. The System Quality dimension incorporates these findings and defines system quality by how well KM performs the functions of knowledge creation, storage/retrieval, transfer, and application; how much of the knowledge is represented in the computerized portion of the OM; and the KM infrastructure. Three constructs—the technological resources of the organization, KM form, and KM level—are identified. Technological resources define the capability of an organization to develop, operate, and maintain KM. These include aspects such as amount of experience available for developing and maintaining KM; the type of hardware, networks, interfaces, and databases used to hold and manipulate knowledge, capacities, and speeds associated with KM infrastructure; and the competence of the users to use KM tools. Technical resources enable the KM form and KM level constructs.

KM form refers to the extent to which the knowledge and KM processes are computerized and integrated. This includes how much of the accessible knowledge is online and available through a single interface and how integrated the processes of knowledge creation, storage/retrieval, transfer, and application are automated and integrated into the routine organizational processes. This construct incorporates concerns from the integrative and adaptive effectiveness clusters proposed for KMS effectiveness used by Stein and Zwass (1995). This construct, along with the technological resources construct, influences the KM level construct.

KM level refers to the ability to bring knowledge to bear upon current activities. This refers explicitly to the KM mnemonic functions such as search, retrieval, manipulation, and abstraction, and how well they are implemented. The technological resources and form of the KMS influence this construct in that the stronger the technical resources and the more integrated and computerized knowledge is, the more important this construct is and the more effective it can be.

Additional support for these constructs comes from Alavi and Leidner (1999), who found it important to have an integrated and integrative

technology architecture that supports database, communication, and search and retrieval functions. Davenport, DeLong, and Beers (1998) found technical infrastructure to be crucial to effective KM. Ginsberg and Kambil (1999) found knowledge representation, storage, search, retrieval, visualization, and quality control to be key technical issues. Mandviwalla, Eulgem, Mould, and Rao (1998) described technical issues affecting KMS design to include knowledge storage/repository considerations; how information and knowledge is organized so that it can be searched and linked to appropriate events and use; and processes for integrating the various repositories and for reintegrating information and knowledge extracted from specific events and access locations, as users rarely access the KMS from a single location (leads to network needs and security concerns). Sage and Rouse (1999) identified infrastructure for capturing, searching, retrieving, and displaying knowledge and an understood enterprise knowledge structure as important. Finally, several of the KMS classifications focus on KM support tools, architecture, or life cycle, which all require strong system quality.

Ultimately, given the effectiveness of information technology to rapidly provide search, storage, retrieval, and visualization capabilities, it is expected that a more fully computerized system that utilizes network, semantic Web, and data warehouse technologies will result in the highest levels of system quality.

KNOWLEDGE QUALITY

Jennex and Olfman (2000, 2002) identified that having a KM process and an enterprise-wide knowledge infrastructure, incorporating KM processes into regular work practices, and that knowledge needs were different for users of different levels, were key issues in order to determine and implement what is the right knowledge for KM to capture. Additionally, it was found that

KM users have formal and/or informal drivers that guide them in selecting information and knowledge to be retained by KM and formal and informal processes for reviewing and modifying stored information and knowledge. The Knowledge Quality dimension incorporates this and ensures that the right knowledge with sufficient context is captured and available for the right users at the right time. Three constructs: the KM strategy/process, knowledge richness, and linkages among knowledge components are identified. The KM strategy/process construct looks at the organizational processes for identifying knowledge users and knowledge for capture and reuse, the formality of these processes including process planning, and the format and context of the knowledge to be stored. This construct determines the contents and effectiveness of the other two constructs. Richness reflects the accuracy and timeliness of the stored knowledge as well as having sufficient knowledge context and cultural context to make the knowledge useful. Linkages reflect the knowledge and topic maps and/or listings of expertise available to identify sources of knowledge to users in the organization.

Hansen, Nohria, and Tierney (1999) describe two types of knowledge strategy: personification and codification. They warn of trying to follow both strategies equally at the same time. These strategies refer to how knowledge is captured, represented, retrieved, and used. However, KM strategy/process also needs to reflect that the knowledge needs of the users change over time, as found by the longitudinal study (Jennex & Olfman, 2002) and that new users have a hard time understanding codified tacit knowledge (Koskinen, 2001). For example, new users will follow personification until they understand the context in which knowledge is captured and used, and then they are willing to switch to a codification strategy. Personification corresponds to linkages in the model shown in Figure 3 and refers to the situation in which new users initially feel more comfortable seeking knowledge contexts from recognized human experts on a particular subject. Following this phase, these users tend to switch to codified knowledge; thus, codification corresponds to richness in the model. Additionally, Brown, Dennis, and Gant (2006) found that as the procedural complexity and teachability of knowledge increased, the tendency of users to rely on linkages (person-to-person knowledge transfer) also increased. Jennex (2006) discusses the impact of context and culture on knowledge reuse, and the conclusion is that as knowledge complexity grows, the ability to capture the context and culture information needed to ensure the knowledge is usable and, used correctly, becomes more difficult, and the richness of the stored knowledge is less able to meet this need, which results in users shifting to using linkages and personification. This model disagrees with Hansen, et al.'s (1999) finding that organizations need to select a single strategy on which to concentrate, while using the other strategy in a support role by recognizing that both strategies will exist and that they may be equal in importance.

Additional support for these constructs comes from Barna (2003), who identified creating a standard knowledge submission process, methodologies, and processes for the codification, documentation, and storage of knowledge, processes for capturing and converting individual tacit knowledge into organizational knowledge as important. Cross and Baird (2000) found that in order for KM to improve business performance, it had to increase organizational learning by supporting personal relationships between experts and knowledge users, providing distributed databases to store knowledge and pointers to knowledge, providing work processes for users to convert personal experience into organizational learning, and providing direction to what knowledge the organization needs to capture and from which to learn. Davenport, et al. (1998) identified three key success factors for KM strategy/process: clearly communicated purpose/goals, multiple channels for knowledge transfer, and a standard, flexible knowledge structure. Mandviwalla, et al. (1998) described several strategy issues affecting KM design, which include the KM focus (who are the users); the quantity of knowledge to be captured and in what formats (who filters what is captured); what reliance and/or limitations are placed on the use of individual memories; how long the knowledge is useful; and the work activities and processes that utilize KM. Sage and Rouse (1999) identified modeling processes to identify knowledge needs and sources, KM strategy for the identification of knowledge to capture and use and who will use it, an understood enterprise knowledge structure, and clear KM goals as important.

SERVICE QUALITY

The Service Quality dimension ensures that KM has adequate support in order for users to utilize KM effectively. Three constructs—management support, user KM service quality, and IS KM service quality—are identified. Management support refers to the direction and support an organization needs to provide in order to ensure that adequate resources are allocated to the creation and maintenance of KM; a knowledge sharing and using organizational culture is developed; encouragement, incentives, and direction are provided to the work force to encourage KM use; knowledge reuse; and knowledge sharing; and that sufficient control structures are created in the organization in order to monitor knowledge and KM use. This construct enables the other two constructs. User KM service quality refers to the support provided by user organizations to help their personnel to utilize KM. This support consists of providing training to their users on how to use KM, how to query KM, and guidance and support for making knowledge capture, knowledge reuse, and KM use a part of routine business processes. IS KM service quality refers to the support provided by the IS organization to

KM users and to maintaining KM. This support consists of building and maintaining KM tools and infrastructure; maintaining the knowledge base; building and providing knowledge maps of the databases; and ensuring the reliability, security, and availability of KM.

Our previous KM success model versions included the previous constructs as part of the system quality and knowledge quality dimensions. These constructs were extracted from these dimensions in order to generate the constructs for the service quality dimension and to ensure that the final KM success model was consistent with DeLone and McLean (2003).

Additional support for these constructs comes from Alavi and Leidner (1999), who found organizational and cultural issues associated with user motivation to share and use knowledge to be the most significant. Barna (2003) identified the main managerial success factor as creating and promoting a culture of knowledge sharing within the organization by articulating a corporate KM vision, rewarding employees for knowledge sharing and creating communities of practice. Other managerial success factors include obtaining senior management support, creating a learning organization, providing KM training, precisely defining KM project objectives, and creating relevant and easily accessible knowledge-sharing databases and knowledge maps. Cross and Baird (2000) found that in order for KM to improve business performance, it had to increase organizational learning by supporting personal relationships between experts and knowledge users and by providing incentives to motivate users to learn from experience and to use KM. Davenport, et al. (1998) found senior management support, motivational incentives for KM users, and a knowledge-friendly culture to be critical issues. Ginsberg and Kambil (1999) found incentives to share and use knowledge to be the key organizational issues. Holsapple and Joshi (2000) found leadership and top management commitment/support to be crucial. Resource influences such as having sufficient financial support and skill level of employees were also important. Malhotra and Galletta (2003) identified the critical importance of user commitment and motivation but found that using incentives did not guarantee a successful KMS. Sage and Rouse (1999) identified incentives and motivation to use KM, clear KM goals, and measuring and evaluating the effectiveness of KM as important. Yu, Kim, and Kim (2004) determined that KM drivers such as a learning culture, knowledge-sharing intention, rewards, and KM team activity significantly affected KM performance

USER SATISFACTION

The User Satisfaction dimension is a construct that measures satisfaction with KM by users. It is considered a good complementary measure of KM use, as desire to use KM depends on users being satisfied with KM. User satisfaction is considered a better measure for this dimension than actual KM use, as KM may not be used constantly yet still may be considered effective. Jennex (2005) found that some KM repositories or knowledge processes such as e-mail may be used daily, while others may be used once a year or less. However, it also was found that the importance of the once-a-year use might be greater than that of daily use. This makes actual use a weak measure for this dimension, given that the amount of actual use may have little impact on KM success, as long as KM is used when appropriate and supports DeLone and McLean (2003) in dropping amount of use as a measurement of success.

INTENT TO USE/PERCEIVED BENEFIT

The Intent to Use/Perceived Benefit dimension is a construct that measures perceptions of the benefits of KM by users. It is good for predicting

continued KM use when KM use is voluntary, and amount and/or effectiveness of KM use depend on meeting current and future user needs. Jennex and Olfman (2002) used a perceived benefit instrument adapted from Thompson, et al. (1991) to measure user satisfaction and to predict continued intent to use KM when KM use was voluntary. Thompson, et al.'s (1991) perceived benefit model utilizes Triandis' (1980) theory that perceptions on future consequences predict future actions. This construct adapts the model to measure the relationships among social factors concerning knowledge use, perceived KM complexity, perceived near-term job fit and benefits of knowledge use, perceived long-term benefits of knowledge use, and fear of job loss with respect to willingness to contribute knowledge. Malhotra and Galletta (2003) created an instrument for measuring user commitment and motivation that is similar to Thompson, et al.'s (1991) perceived benefit model but is based on self-determination theory that uses the Perceived Locus of Causality that also may be useful for predicting intent to use. Additionally, Yu, et al. (2004) found that KM drivers such as knowledge-sharing intention significantly affected KM performance.

NET IMPACT

An individual's use of KM will produce an impact on that person's performance in the workplace. In addition, DeLone and McLean (1992) note that an individual impact also could be an indication that an information system has given the user a better understanding of the decision context, has improved his or her decision-making productivity, has produced a change in user activity, or has changed the decision maker's perception of the importance or usefulness of the information system. Each individual impact should have an effect on the performance of the whole organization. Organizational impacts usually are not the summation of individual impacts, so the association between individual and organizational impacts is often difficult to draw. DeLone and McLean (2003) recognized this difficulty and combined all impacts into a single dimension. Davenport, et al. (1998) overcame this by looking for the establishment of linkages to economic performance. Alavi and Leidner (1999) also found it important to measure the benefits of KM, as did Jennex and Olfman (2000).

We agree with combining all impacts into one dimension and the addition of the feedback loop to the User Satisfaction and Intent to Use/Perceived Benefit dimensions but take it a step further and extend the feedback loop to include the KM Strategy/Process construct. Jennex and Olfman (2002) showed this feedback in their model relating KM, OM, organizational learning, and effectiveness, as shown in Figure 4. This model recognizes that the use of knowledge may have good or bad benefits. It is feedback from these benefits that drives the organization either to use more of the same type

of knowledge or to forget the knowledge, which also provides users with feedback on the benefit of the KMS. Alavi and Leidner (2001) also agree that KM should allow for forgetting some knowledge when it has detrimental or no benefits. To ensure that this is done, feedback on the value of stored knowledge needs to be fed into the KM Strategy/Process construct.

OPERATIONALIZATION OF THE SUCCESS MODEL

Jennex and Olfman (2002) performed a longitudinal study of KM in an engineering organization that identified a link between knowledge use and improved organizational effectiveness. Although a great deal of quantitative data were taken, it was not possible to quantify productivity gains as a function of knowledge use. KM was found to be effective and to have improved in effectiveness

Figure 4. The OM/KM model

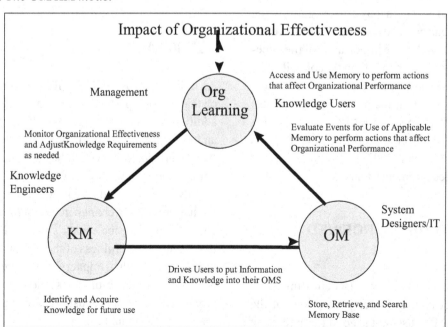

over a five-year period. Additionally, the engineers were found to be more productive.

Jennex (2000) applied an early version of this model to the construction and implementation of a knowledge management Web site for assisting a virtual project team. It was found that applying the model to the design of the site resulted in the project going from lagging to a leading project in just a few months.

Hatami, Galliers, and Huang (2003) used the KM Success Model to analyze knowledge reuse and the effectiveness of decision making. They found the model useful in explaining the effects of culture and knowledge needs on the overall KM success.

Jennex, Olfman, and Addo (2003) investigated the need for having an organizational KM strategy to ensure that knowledge benefits gained from projects are captured for use in the organization. They found that benefits from Y2K projects were not being captured, because the parent organiza-

tions did not have a KM strategy/process. Their conclusion was that KM in projects can exist and can assist projects in utilizing knowledge during the project. However, it also led to the conclusion that the parent organization will not benefit from project-based KM unless the organization has an overall KM strategy/process.

The following discussion combines these studies to provide methods of operationalizing the constructs proposed previously. Table 1 summarizes the various measures applied in these studies.

SYSTEM QUALITY

Three constructs were proposed for the system quality dimension: technical resources, KM form, and KM level. Jennex and Olfman (2002) found that the capabilities of the IS organization and the users can impact the success of KM. IS

Table 1. KMS success model data collection methods

Construct	Data Collection Method
Technical Resources	User competency survey, observation and document research of IS capabilities, interview with IS Manager on infrastructure
Form of KMS	Interviews and survey of knowledge sources and form
Level of KMS	Survey of satisfaction with retrieval times, usability testing on KMS functions
KM Strategy/Process	Survey on drivers for putting knowledge into the KMS and for satisfaction with the knowledge in the KMS, check on if a formal strategy/process exists
Richness	Usability test on adequacy of stored knowledge and associated context, interviews and satisfaction survey on adequacy of knowledge in KMS
Linkages	Usability test on adequacy of stored linkages, interviews and satisfaction surveys on satisfaction with linkages stored in KMS
Management Support	Interviews and Social Factors construct of Thompson, Higgins, and Howell's survey on perceived benefit
IS KM Service Quality	Interview with IS Manager on IS capabilities. Interviews with users on needs and capabilities. Suggest adding user satisfaction survey on service issues
User Organization KM Service Quality	Interview with user organization KM team on capabilities and responsibilities, and needs from IS. Interview with users on needs and capabilities. Suggest adding user satisfaction survey on service issues
User Satisfaction	Doll and. Torkzadeh (1988) End User Satisfaction Measure, any other user satisfaction measure
Intent to Use/ Perceived Benefit	Thompson, Higgins, and Howell's (1991) survey on perceived benefit
Net Impacts	Determine Individual and Organizational productivity models through interviews, observation, tend to be specific to organizations

infrastructure and organizational capabilities that enhanced KM effectiveness included a fast, high-capacity infrastructure, strong application development skills, network skills, and awareness of the user organization's knowledge requirements. Users' capabilities that enhanced KM effectiveness included a high degree of computer literacy and high-end personal computers. Given the importance of these technical resources, operationalization of the technical resources construct can be accomplished by focusing on the overall experience of the development group in building and maintaining networked systems that support KM; the computer capabilities of KM end users; and the quality of hardware, network, application, and operating system capabilities of workstations supporting KM.

KM level was defined as the ability to bring past information to bear upon current activities. This can be measured in terms of Stein and Zwass' (1995) mnemonic functions, including knowledge acquisition, retention, maintenance, search, and retrieval. It is expected that more effective KM will include more sophisticated levels of these functions. For example, more sophisticated KM should contain the ability to do filtering, guided exploration, and to grow memory. Usability testing of these functions can serve as measures of how effective they are implemented.

KM form refers to the extent to which knowledge is computerized and integrated. In essence, the more computerized the memory (personification and codification approaches), the more integrated it can be. That is, if all knowledge sources are available in computer-based form, then it will be possible to search and retrieved knowledge more effectively. Integration also speaks to the external consistency of the various KM tools. Jennex and Olfman (2002) found that although much of the KM used by the engineering organization was computerized, there were many different KMS components, each with varying kinds of storage mechanisms and interfaces. These components were poorly integrated, relying mainly on the copy-and-paste features of the Windows interface and, therefore, limited the ability of workers to utilize KM effectively. It was evident that more sophisticated technical resources could produce a more integrated set of components. Surveys of actual knowledge repositories that are used for KM can determine how much knowledge is stored in computerized forms. It is desired but not practical to have all knowledge in a computer. Assessment of this construct should focus on how much of the knowledge that is practical for computer storage is computerized.

KNOWLEDGE QUALITY

Knowledge quality has three constructs: KM strategy/process, richness, and linkages. Jennex and Olfman (2002) used surveys of users to determine drivers for putting knowledge into KM repositories and user satisfaction with the knowledge that was in these repositories. Jennex, et al. (2003) surveyed organizations to determine if they had a KM strategy and how formal it was. Jennex and Olfman (2002) used interviews of KM users to determine their satisfaction with the accuracy, timeliness, and adequacy of available knowledge. The need for linkages and personification of knowledge was found through interviews with users on where they went to retrieve knowledge. Additionally, it was found that users' KM needs vary, depending on their experience levels in the organization. Context of the knowledge is critical. New members did not have this context, and the knowledge repositories did not store sufficient context in order for a new member to understand and use the stored knowledge. It was found that new members need linkages to the human sources of knowledge. It is not expected that KM will ever be able to do an adequate job of storing context, so it is recommended that KM store linkages to knowledge.

SERVICE QUALITY

Service quality was defined previously as how well the organization supports KM. Three constructs are proposed: management support, IS KM service quality, and user KM service quality. Jennex and Olfman (2002) identified these constructs through interviews that found evidence to show that the service quality of the IS and user organizations can impact KM success and that service quality was determined by the organizations that possess certain capabilities. IS KM service consisted of IS being able to build and maintain KM components and to map the knowledge base. IS organizational capabilities that enhanced this service effectiveness included data integration skills, knowledge representation skills, and awareness of the user organization's knowledge requirements. User organization KM service consisted of incorporating knowledge capture into work processes and being able to identify key knowledge requirements. User organization KM capabilities that enhanced this service effectiveness included understanding and being able to implement KM techniques, such as knowledge taxonomies, ontologies, and knowledge maps, and to process analysis capabilities. Additionally, service was enhanced either by the IS or the user organization providing training on how to construct knowledge searches, where the knowledge was located, and how to use KM.

The key construct—management support—was measured by using interviews and the social factors measure of Thompson, Higgins, and Howell's (1991) survey on perceived benefit. The social factors measure uses a Likert scale survey to determine perceptions of support from peers, supervisors, and managers, and gives a good view of the ability of the organizational culture to support KM and management support for doing KM. Additionally, individual and organizational productivity models were generated by using interviews with managers that provide an assessment of the impact of knowledge use on individuals

and organizations and what incentives are being used to encourage KM participation.

IS organization KM support was measured by determining the overall experience of the development group in building and maintaining networked systems that support KM and the satisfaction of the KM end users with this support. User organization KM support was measured by determining what support was provided and how satisfied the users were with it. Measures assessing specific areas of capability can be used, should less-than-acceptable service satisfaction be found.

USER SATISFACTION

User satisfaction is a construct that measures perceptions of KM by users. This is one of the most frequently measured aspects of IS success, and it is also a construct with a multitude of measurement instruments. User satisfaction can relate to both product and service. As noted, product satisfaction often is used to measure knowledge quality. Product satisfaction can be measured by using the 12-item instrument developed by Doll and Tordzadeh (1988). This measure addresses satisfaction with content, accuracy, format, ease of use, and timeliness. Additionally, measures addressing satisfaction with interfaces should be used. Other user satisfaction measures can be used to assess the specific quality constructs, as discussed in previous paragraphs.

INTENT TO USE/PERCEIVED BENEFIT

Jennex, et al. (1998) used Thompson, Higgins, and Howell's (1991) Perceived Benefit Model to predict continued voluntary usage of KM by the engineering organization. The following four factors from the model plus one added by Jennex and Olfman were in the survey:

- Job fit of KM, near-term consequences of using KM
- Job fit of KM, long-term consequences of using KM
- Social factors in support of using KM
- Complexity of KM tools and processes
- Fear of job loss for contributing knowledge to KM

All five factors were found to support continued KM use during the initial measurements. Jennex and Olfman (2002) found continued KM use throughout the five years of observing KM usage and concluded that the Perceived Benefit model was useful for predicting continued use. Jennex (2000) used these factors to design the site, work processes, and management processes for a virtual project team, using Web-based KM to perform a utility Year 2000 project. Promoting the social factors and providing near-term job fit were critical in ensuring that the virtual project team utilized KM. KM use was considered highly successful, as the project went from performing in the bottom third of utility projects to performing in the top third of all utility projects.

NET BENEFITS

The net benefits dimension looks for any benefits attributed to use of the KMS. We attempted to measure benefits associated with individual and organizational use of KM through the generation of productivity models that identified where knowledge use impacted productivity. KM benefits for an individual are found in their work processes. Jennex and Olfman (2002) queried supervisors and managers in order to determine what they believed was the nature of individual productivity in the context of the station-engineering work process. The interviews revealed a complex set of factors. Those benefiting from KM include the following:

- Timeliness in completing assignments and doing them right the first time
- Number of assignments completed
- Identification and completion of high-priority assignments
- Completeness of solutions
- Quality of solutions (thoroughness and accuracy)
- Complexity of the work that can be assigned to an engineer
- Client satisfaction

While many of these factors are measured quantitatively, it was not possible to directly attribute changes in performance solely to KM use, although improvements in performance were qualitatively attributed to KM use. Additionally, Jennex and Olfman (2002) asked 20 engineers to indicate whether they were more productive now than they were five or 10 years ago, and all but one thought that they were. This improvement was attributed primarily to KM use but also was a qualitative assessment.

Organizational impacts relate to the effectiveness of the organization as a whole. For a nuclear power plant, specific measures of effectiveness were available. These measures relate to assessments performed by external organizations as well as those performed internally. External assessments were found to be the most influenced by KM use. Jennex and Olfman (2002) found measures such as the SALP (Systematic Assessment of Licensee Performance) Reports issued by the Nuclear Regulatory Commission and site evaluations performed by the Institute of Nuclear Power Operations (INPO). Review of SALP scores issued since 1988 showed an increase from a rating of 2 to a rating of 1 in 1996. This rating was maintained through the five years of the study. An INPO evaluation was conducted during the spring of 1996 and resulted in a 1 rating. This rating also was maintained throughout the five years of the study. These assessments identified several strengths directly related to engineer productivity using KM, including decision making, root cause analysis, problem resolution, timeliness, and Operability Assessment documentation. This demonstrates a direct link between engineer productivity and organization productivity. Also, since organization productivity is rated highly, it can be inferred that engineer productivity is high.

Two internal indicators were linked to KM use: unit capacity and unplanned automatic scrams. Unit capacity and unplanned scrams are influenced by how well the engineers evaluate and correct problems. Both indicators improved over time. These two indicators plus unplanned outages and duration of outages became the standard measure during the Jennex and Olfman (2002) study, and reporting and monitoring of these factors significantly improved during the study.

The conclusion is that net benefits should be measured by using measures that are specific to the organization and that are influenced by the use of KM. Suitable measures were found in all the studies used for this article, and it is believed that they can be found for any organization.

CONCLUSION

The DeLone and McLean IS Success Model is a generally accepted model for assessing success of IS. Adapting the model to KM is a viable approach to assessing KM success. The model presented in this article meets the spirit and intent of DeLone and McLean (1992, 2003). Additionally, Jennex (2000) used an earlier version of the KM Success Model to design, build, and implement intranet-based KM that was found to be very effective and successful. The conclusion of this article is that the KM Success Model is a useful model for predicting KM success. It is also useful for designing effective KM.

AREAS FOR FUTURE RESEARCH

DeLone and McLean (1992) stated, "Researchers should systematically combine individual measures from the IS success categories to create a comprehensive measurement instrument" (pp. 87–88). This is the major area for future KM success research. Jennex and Olfman (2002) provided a basis for exploring a quantitative analysis and test of the KM Success Model. To extend this work, it is suggested that a survey instrument to assess the effectiveness of KM within other nuclear power plant engineering organizations in the United States should be developed and administered. Since these organizations have similar characteristics and goals, they provide an opportunity to gain a homogeneous set of data to use for testing the model and, ultimately, to generate a generic set of KM success measures.

Additionally, other measures need to be assessed for applicability to the model. In particular, the Technology Acceptance Model, Perceived Usefulness (Davis, 1989) should be investigated as a possible measure for Intent to Use/Perceived Benefit.

REFERENCES

Alavi, M., & Leidner, D.E. (1999). Knowledge management systems: Emerging views and practices from the field. *Proceedings of the 32ⁿᵈ Hawaii International Conference on System Sciences*, IEEE Computer Society.

Alavi, M. & Leidner, D.E. (2001). Review: Knowledge management and knowledge management systems: Conceptual foundations and research issues. *MIS Quarterly, 25*(1), 107–136.

Barna, Z. (2003). *Knowledge management: A critical e-business strategic factor*. Master's thesis, San Diego State University, San Diego, CA.

Brown, S.A., Dennis, A.R., & Gant, D.B. (2006). Understanding the factors influencing the value of person-to-person knowledge sharing. *Proceedings of the 39ᵗʰ Hawaii International Conference on System Sciences.*

Churchman, C.W. (1979). *The systems approach.* New York: Dell Publishing.

Cross, R., Baird, L. (2000). Technology is not enough: Improving performance by building organizational memory. *Sloan Management Review, 41*(3), 41–54.

Davenport, T.H., DeLong, D.W., & Beers, M.C. (1998). Successful knowledge management projects. *Sloan Management Review, 39*(2), 43–57.

Davenport, T.H., & Prusak, L. (1998). *Working knowledge.* Boston: Harvard Business School Press.

Davis, F.D. (1989). Perceived usefulness, perceived ease of use, and user acceptance of information technology. *MIS Quarterly, 13*, 319–340.

DeLone, W.H., & McLean, E.R. (1992). Information systems success: The quest for the dependent variable. *Information Systems Research, 3*, 60–95.

DeLone, W.H., & McLean, E.R. (2003). The De-Lone and McLean model of information systems success: A ten-year update. *Journal of Management Information Systems, 19*(4), 9–30.

Doll, W.J., & Torkzadeh, G. (1988). The measurement of end-user computing satisfaction. *MIS Quarterly, 12*, 259–275.

Ginsberg, M., & Kambil, A. (1999). Annotate: A Web-based knowledge management support system for document collections. *Proceedings of the 32ⁿᵈ Hawaii International Conference on System Sciences.*

Hansen, M.T., Nohria, N., & Tierney, T. (1999, March-April). What's your strategy for man-

aging knowledge? *Harvard Business Review,* 106–116.

Hatami, A., Galliers, R.D., & Huang, J. (2003). Exploring the impacts of knowledge (re)use and organizational memory on the effectiveness of strategic decisions: A longitudinal case study. *Proceedings of the 36ᵗʰ Hawaii International Conference on System Sciences.*

Holsapple, C.W., & Joshi, K.D. (2000). An investigation of factors that influence the management of knowledge in organizations. *Journal of Strategic Information Systems, 9*, 235–261.

Huber, G.P., Davenport, T.H., & King, D. (1998). Some perspectives on organizational memory (Working Paper for the Task Force on Organizational Memory). *Proceedings of the 31ˢᵗ Annual Hawaii International Conference on System Sciences.*

Jennex, M.E. (2000). Using an intranet to manage knowledge for a virtual project team. In D.G. Schwartz, M. Divitini, & T. Brasethvik (Eds.), *Internet-based organizational memory and knowledge management* (pp. 241–259). Hershey, PA: Idea Group Publishing.

Jennex, M.E. (2005). What is knowledge management? *International Journal of Knowledge Management, 1*(4), i–iv.

Jennex, M.E. (2006). Culture, context, and knowledge management. *International Journal of Knowledge Management, 2*(2), i–iv.

Jennex, M.E., & Croasdell, D. (2005). Knowledge management: Are we a discipline? *International Journal of Knowledge Management, 1*(1), i–v.

Jennex, M.E., & Olfman, L. (2000). Development recommendations for knowledge management/organizational memory systems. *Proceedings of the Information Systems Development Conference.*

Jennex, M.E., & Olfman, L. (2002). Organizational memory/knowledge effects on productivity: A longitudinal study. *Proceedings of the 35th Annual Hawaii International Conference on System Sciences.*

Jennex, M.E., Olfman, L., & Addo, T.B.A. (2003). The need for an organizational knowledge management strategy. *Proceedings of the 36th Hawaii International Conference on System Sciences.*

Jennex, M.E., Olfman, L., Pituma, P., & Yong-Tae, P. (1998). An organizational memory information systems success model: An extension of DeLone and McLean's I/S success model. *Proceedings of the 31st Annual Hawaii International Conference on System Sciences.*

Koskinen, K.U. (2001). Tacit knowledge as a promoter of success in technology firms. *Proceedings of the 34th Hawaii International Conference on System Sciences.*

Maier, R. (2002). *Knowledge management systems: Information and communication technologies for knowledge management.* Berlin: Springer-Verlag.

Malhotra, Y., & Galletta, D. (2003). Role of commitment and motivation as antecedents of knowledge management systems implementation. *Proceedings of the 36th Hawaii International Conference on System Sciences.*

Mandviwalla, M., Eulgem, S., Mould, C., & Rao, S.V. (1998). Organizational memory systems design [working paper for the Task Force on Organizational Memory]. *Proceedings of the 31st Annual Hawaii International Conference on System Sciences.*

Nonaka, I. (1994). A dynamic theory of organizational knowledge creation. *Organization Science, 5*(1), 14–37.

Polanyi, M. (1962). *Personal knowledge: Toward a post-critical philosophy.* New York: Harper Torchbooks.

Polanyi, M. (1967). *The tacit dimension.* London: Routledge and Keoan Paul.

Sage, A.P., & Rouse, W.B. (1999). Information systems frontiers in knowledge management. *Information Systems Frontiers, 1*(3), 205–219.

Stein, E.W., & Zwass, V. (1995). Actualizing organizational memory with information systems. *Information Systems Research, 6*(2), 85–117.

Thompson, R.L., Higgins, C.A., & Howell, J.M. (1991). Personal computing: Toward a conceptual model of utilization. *MIS Quarterly, 15*(1), 125–143.

Triandis, H.C. (1980). *Beliefs, attitudes, and values.* Lincoln, NE: University of Nebraska Press.

Turban, E., & Aronson, J.E. (2001). *Decision support systems and intelligent systems* (6th ed.). Upper Saddle River, NJ: Pearson/Prentice Hall.

Walsh, J.P., & Ungson, G.R. (1991). Organizational memory. *Academy of Management Review, 16*(1), 57–91.

Yu, S.-H., Kim, Y.-G., & Kim, M.-Y. (2004). Linking organizational knowledge management drivers to knowledge management performance: An exploratory study. *Proceedings of the 37th Hawaii International Conference on System Sciences.*

This work was previously published in International Journal of Knowledge Management, Vol. 2, Issue 3, edited by M. E. Jennex, pp. 51-68, copyright 2006 by IGI Publishing, formerly known as Idea Group Publishing (an imprint of IGI Global).

Chapter VI
Building IT Risk Management Approaches:
An Action Research Method

Jakob Holden Iversen
University of Wisconsin Oshkosh, USA

Lars Mathiassen
Georgia State University, USA

Peter Axel Nielsen
Aalborg University, Denmark

ABSTRACT

This chapter shows how action research can help practitioners develop IT risk management approaches that are tailored to their organization and the specific issues they face. Based on literature and practical experience, the authors present a method for developing risk management approaches to use in real-world innovation projects. The chapter illustrates the method by presenting the results of developing a risk management approach for software process improvement projects in a software organization.

INTRODUCTION

Organizations that manage IT innovations have long been accused of having poor project execution and low product quality. These problems are often referred to as "The Software Crisis," in which software projects frequently are delivered late, over budget, with missing features, and with poor quality. Furthermore, it has been very difficult to predict which organization would do a good job on any given project. These issues led to the establishment of the software process improvement (SPI) movement, in which poor processes in organizations are considered a major reason for the software crisis.

Organizations routinely rely on experienced developers to deliver high quality IT systems. However, in the 1990s, organizations realized that by defining and improving the processes these professionals used, it was possible to deliver more consistent results with better quality. SPI projects were established to improve specific aspects of a process, and in many cases to take advantage of standards like the Capability Maturity Model (CMM) (Paulk et al., 1993) and the Capability Maturity Model Integration (CMMI) (Chrissis et al., 2003). For each process that needed improvement, a focused SPI project would design and implement specific improvements into current practices.

However, not only is this hard work, it also is risky business. Much can go wrong in improvement projects, and mistakes can eventually lead to failure. The involved improvement actors might not possess appropriate skills and experiences. The design of a new process might not suit the organization or effectively meet requirements. The improvement project might be organized inappropriately, with unrealistic schedules or insufficient management attention. Also, the actors might pay too little attention to customers, failing to consider the interests, problems, and motivations of the people and groups that are expected to use the new process.

To deal proactively with such issues in SPI projects, the involved actors must manage the involved risks. The need for such risk management was the rationale behind Danske Bank's development of a practical risk management approach to reduce failures in their SPI initiative. Using this approach, improvement actors periodically held disciplined and tightly structured workshops in collaboration with SPI facilitators. The workshops gave each team a better overview and understanding of their project and its organizational context, and helped them address risks proactively.

Organizations face many different and quite diverse activities in which there are strong reasons to manage IT risks. While the literature provides a portfolio of IT risk management approaches that cover many types of activities, organizations often face situations in which they need to develop a risk management approach that is tailored to their particular needs or that addresses issues not covered by the available portfolio of documented risk management approaches. This chapter offers organizations a generic method to develop new and dedicated IT risk management approaches. The method is based on action research into an organization's specific risk management context and needs, and builds on the available literature about IT risk management. It is based on our experiences from developing the tailored approach to risk management in SPI projects at Danske Bank.

RISK MANAGEMENT LITERATURE

A number of different approaches to IT risk management have been proposed. In this section, we provide an overview and categorization of the different approaches (risk list, risk-action list, risk-strategy model, risk-strategy analysis). We offer, in this way, a framework to help select an appropriate risk approach suited to particular organizational contexts and needs. An overview of the framework is shown in Table 1.

Risk List

The first and simplest form of available approaches are risk lists. They contain generic risk items (often prioritized) to help managers focus on possible sources of risk; they do not contain information about appropriate resolution actions. These lists are easy to use in assessing risks; they are easy to build, drawing upon published sources on risks or experiences within a particular context; and they are easy to modify to meet conditions in a particular organization or as new knowledge is captured. While these approaches offer strong support to help managers appreciate risks, they

Table 1. Four types of approaches to IT risk management

Type of Approach	Characteristics	Assessment E	xemplars
Risk list	A list of prioritized risk items +	Easy to use + Easy to build + Easy to modify + Risk appreciation - Risk resolution - Strategic oversight	(Barki et al., 1993; Keil et al., 1998; Moynihan, 1996; Ropponen & Lyytinen, 2000)
Risk-action list	A list of prioritized risk items with related resolution actions	+ Easy to use + Easy to build + Easy to modify + Risk appreciation + Risk resolution - Strategic oversight	(Alter & Ginzberg, 1978; Boehm, 1991; Jones, 1994; Ould, 1999)
Risk-strategy model	A contingency model that relates aggregate risk items to aggregate resolution actions	+ Easy to use - Easy to build - Easy to modify + Risk appreciation + Risk resolution + Strategic oversight	(Donaldson & Siegel, 2001; Keil et al., 1998; McFarlan, 1981)
Risk-strategy analysis	A stepwise process that links a detailed understanding of risks to an overall risk management strategy	- Easy to use - Easy to build + Easy to modify + Risk appreciation + Risk resolution + Strategic oversight	(Davis, 1982; Mathiassen et al., 2000)

do not support identification of relevant resolution actions and they do not provide a strategic oversight of the risk profile and relevant strategies for action. Based on previous research, Barki et al. (1993) offer a detailed and precise definition, a measure of software development risk, and a systematic assessment of the reliability and validity of the instrument. Moynihan (1996) presents a comprehensive list of risk items based on how software project managers construe new projects and their contexts. Keil et al. (1998) offer a list of nearly a dozen risk factors that IT project managers in different parts of the world rated high in terms of their importance. Ropponen and Lyytinen (2000) report six aggregate risk components, for example, scheduling and timing risks, that experienced IT project managers found important in a recent survey.

Risk-Action List

The second, slightly more elaborate, form of approaches are risk-action lists. They contain generic risk items (often prioritized), each with one or more related risk resolution actions. They also are easy to use; they are quite easy to build, but compared to risk lists, they require additional knowledge of the potential effects of different types of actions; finally, they are easy to modify when needed. Risk-action lists offer the same support as the risk lists to appreciate risks. In addition, they adopt a simple heuristic to identify possible relevant actions that might help resolve specific risks. However, by focusing on isolated pairs of risk items and resolution actions, they do not lead to a comprehensive strategy for addressing the risk profile as a whole. Alter and Ginzberg (1978) list eight risk items related to IT system implementation, for example, unpredictable impact; and they offer four to nine actions for each risk, for example, use prototypes. Boehm (1991) offers a top-ten list of software development risks, with three to seven actions per risk. Jones (1994) presents specialized risk profiles for different types of IT projects, together with advice on how to prevent and control each risk. Finally, Ould (1999) suggests maintaining a project risk register for identified risks, assessment of the risks, and risk resolution actions to address them.

Risk-Strategy Model

The third form of approaches are risk-strategy models. These contingency models relate a project's risk profile to an overall strategy for addressing it. They combine comprehensive lists of risk items and resolution actions with abstract categories of risks (to arrive at a risk profile) and abstract categories of actions (to arrive at an overall risk strategy). The risk profile is assessed along the risk categories using a simple scale (e.g., high or low), which makes it possible to classify a project as being in one of a few possible situations. For each situation, the model then offers a dedicated risk strategy composed of several detailed resolution actions. Compared to the other types, risk-strategy models provide detailed as well as aggregate risk items, and resolution actions. The heuristic for linking risk items to resolution actions is a contingency table at the aggregate level. Risk-strategy models are easy to use because of the simplifying contingency model, but they are difficult to build because the model must summarize multiple and complex relationships between risks and actions. They also are difficult to modify except for minor revisions of specific risk items or resolution actions that do not challenge the aggregate concepts and the model. Models like these help appreciate risks and identify relevant actions, and managers can build an overall understanding of the risk profile they face (at the aggregate level) directly related to a strategy for addressing it (in terms of aggregate actions).

The best known of these approaches is McFarlan's (1981) portfolio model linking three aggregate risk items (project size, experience with technology, and project structure) to four aggregate resolution actions (external integration, internal integration, formal planning, and formal control). Keil et al. (1998) present a model that combines the perceived importance of risks with the perceived level of control over risks. The model suggests four different scenarios (customer mandate, scope and requirements, execution, and environment) with distinct risk profiles and action strategies. Donaldson and Siegel (2001) offer a model categorizing projects into a high, medium, or low risk profile. They suggest a different resource distribution between project management, system development, and quality assurance, depending on a project's risk profile.

Risk-Strategy Analysis

The final form of approaches are risk-strategy analyses. These approaches are similar to risk-strategy models in that they offer detailed as well as aggregate risk items and resolution actions, but they apply different heuristics. There is no model linking aggregate risk items to aggregate resolution actions. Instead, these approaches offer a stepwise analysis process through which the involved actors link risks to actions to develop an overall risk strategy. Compared to the risk-strategy models, there is a looser coupling between the aggregate risk items and aggregate resolution actions. In comparison, we find these approaches more difficult to use because they require process facilitation skills. They are as difficult to build as the risk-strategy models, but they are easier to modify because of the loosely defined relationship between aggregate risk items and resolution actions. Davis (1982) provides such a stepwise approach to address information requirements risks where the overall level of risk is assessed and then associated with four different strategies to cope with requirements uncertainty.

Mathiassen et al. (2000) offer a similar approach to develop a risk-based strategy for object-oriented analysis and design.

The comparative strengths and weaknesses of these four risk approaches are summarized in Table 1. Comparing the list approaches and the strategy approaches suggests that the former are easier to use, build, and modify, whereas the latter provide stronger support for risk management. Comparing risk-strategy models and the risk-strategy analysis approaches suggests that the former are easier to use, but they require that a contingency model be developed. The latter are easier to modify because they rely on a looser coupling between aggregate risk items and resolution actions. Organizations can use the insights in Table 1 to choose appropriate forms of IT risk management that are well suited to the particular challenges they want to address.

ACTION RESEARCH

Action research allows practitioners and researchers to interact with a real-world situation gaining deep insights into how an organization functions and how different interventions affect the organization. At the same time, it allows practitioners to reflect on their practice and gives them strong tools to improve their current situation (Checkland, 1991; McKay & Marshall, 2001). Along similar lines, Schön (1983) refers to the reflective practitioner that is informed by research, allowing researchers sometimes to act as practitioners and practitioners sometimes to act as researchers. We propose a modified action research approach, called collaborative practice research (CPR) that is appropriate for developing risk management methods by reflective practitioners or by collaborative groups of practitioners and researchers (Iversen et al., 2004; Mathiassen, 2002).

At Danske Bank, the cyclic nature of action research combined theory and practice as follows. The research interest and practical problems we faced were about SPI and how SPI teams can manage risks. The practical setting in which we addressed risk management was the SPI teams in the IT Department of Danske Bank (the largest Danish bank). The purpose here was to improve the SPI Teams' handling of SPI-related risks. Within this area we applied and combined theories and concepts about SPI and IT risk management. The result of this cyclic process was double: an approach to manage SPI risks in Danske Bank and a generic method for developing risk management approaches. The approach to manage SPI risks is presented in the section *Managing SPI Risks*, while the generic method for developing tailored risk approaches is presented in the rest of this section, based on the cyclic process of action research.

Our method to developing risk management approaches is illustrated in Table 2. It addresses a particular area of concern and is supported by risk management knowledge. The method provides an iterative approach to develop a tailored risk

Table 2. Developing risk management approaches

Initiating

   1. A ppreciate problem situation

   2. S tudy literature

   3. S elect risk approach

Iterating

   4. D evelop risk framework

   5. D esign risk process

   6. A pply approach

   7. E valuate experience

Closing

   8. E xit

   9. A ssess usefulness

   10. Elicit research results

management approach through application to a real-world situation in a specific organizational context, as shown in Table 2.

The proposed method is based on the ten activities of a CPR process (cf. Table 2), and consists of three phases: Initiating (activities 1 to 3), Iterating (activities 4 to 7), and Closing (activities 8 to 10). The sequence between activities 4 and 5 may not hold in practice, and only points to the logical dependencies between the activities. The sequence from 4 to 7 is based on the canonical problem-solving cycle (Susman & Evered, 1978). The iterating phase leads to risk management within the area of concern. The closing phase produces a refined risk management approach, together with an assessment of its usefulness.

The actors in this process enter the problem situation, bringing in prior experience and knowledge of the area of concern (activity 1). The actors should: (1) have experience within the area; (2) perceive the situation as problematic; and (3) find out to what extent and in which way risk management would be beneficial. Part of this activity is to assess whether these prerequisites are met and to establish a project with goals and plans to develop a tailored risk management approach. Activity 1 leads to an appreciation of the risk items and resolution actions perceived to be important within the area of concern (SPI in our case). Activity 2 uses the relevant risk management literature to complement activity 1 and leads to a comprehensive set of risk items and resolution actions that are used in activity 4. The type of risk approach is selected in activity 3 (cf. Table 1), based on the desired features of the approach and the characteristics and needs of the organizational context. This choice defines the basic structure of the risk management approach to be developed.

Activity 4 aggregates the identified risk items and resolution actions into a risk framework of the area of concern (see section *Managing SPI Risks*). Then a risk process is developed in activity 5. The process is based on the framework and

on specific risk items and resolution actions. The risk approach is applied subsequently to specific situations or projects within the area of concern (activity 6). This leads to risks being managed and to experiences using the new approach (activity 7).

The iterating phase ends when the actors agree that the risk management approach is developed sufficiently and the problems in the area of concern are alleviated (activity 8). Whether the applications of the risk management approach were useful in practice is assessed relative to the problem situation at hand (activity 9). A simple way to do this is to ask the participants in the risk assessment if they found the risk management approach useful and to document whether risk management led to actions and improvements. The ways in which the new risk management approach contributes to the discipline in general are assessed relative to the relevant body of knowledge (activity 10).

We suggest that this method can be used in different contexts within information systems and software engineering. In adopting the method, actors are advised to consider specific criteria that will help them achieve satisfactory relevance of the outcome and sufficient rigor in the process. Actors are, as described, advised to use the framework of IT risk management approaches in Table 1 to guide their design.

CASE: RISK MANAGEMENT APPROACH IN SPI

This section presents the action research project that forms the basis for this research. It explains how we used the proposed method to develop a specific risk management approach and how this approach works.

Case Organization

This action research project was conducted at Danske Bank's IT Department, Danske Data,

Table 3. Action research performed by practitioners and researchers

Activities (see Table 2)	Initiating 10.97-12.97	First iteration 01.98-02.98	Second iteration 03.98-08.98	Third iteration 09.98-11.98	Fourth iteration 11.98-02.99	Closing 02.99-02.00
1. Appreciate problem situation	Part of on-going research collaboration [p1-4; r1-4] Brainstorm risk items and actions [p1-4; r1-4]					
2. Study literature	Study SPI [p1-4; r1-4] Study risk management [r1-2]					
3. Select risk approach	Synthesis [r1-3]	Confirmed selection [r1-3]		Appreciation of actors' competence [r1-3]		
4. Develop risk framework		Synthesis [r1-3] Review of framework of risk items and actions [r3] Revised framework [r1-3]				
5. Design risk process		List of risk items and actions [r1-3] Strategy sheets [r1-3]	Additional step and items reformulated [r2-3]	Improved documentation scheme [r1-3]		
6. Apply approaches		Risk assessment of Quality Assurance [p5-7; r2-3]	Risk assessment of Project Management [p3-4; r1-2]	Risk assessment of Metrics Program [p2; p8; r3]	Risk assessment of Diffusion [p9-10; r4; r3]	
7. Evaluate experience		Lessons learned [p5-7; r2-3]	Lessons learned [p3-4; r1-2]	Lessons learned [p2; r3]	Lessons learned [p9-10; r4; r3]	
8. Exit			Delay after 2nd iteration			Action part closed
9. Assess usefulness			Assessment of first two projects [p1-4; p11; r1-4]	Discussion of risk approach at CPR workshop [r1-r3]		Assessment of Metrics and Diffusion projects [p1-4; r1-4]
10. Elicit research results						Result and lesson elicitation [r1-3]

which was spun into an independent company, with Danske Bank as its primary customer. As the IT department began as part of the bank's accounting department, the traditional rigor of banking procedures still pervaded the culture to some extent. This had diminished somewhat in recent years as emerging technologies and the strategic role of IT to the bank's business became increasingly important.

Danske Bank joined a larger CPR (Mathiassen, 2002) project in 1997 (Mathiassen et al., 2002), aimed at implementing SPI projects in the participating organizations. Danske Data established a software engineering process group (Fowler & Rifkin, 1990) to manage and coordinate the SPI effort, which management clearly had articulated was intended to improve productivity (Andersen, Krath et al., 2002). The action researchers joined the SPI effort, along with a dedicated project manager, a consultant from the Methodology Department, and two information systems managers. One of the first activities conducted was a maturity assessment to determine which areas to target for improvement (Iversen et al., 1998). The assessment identified seven improvement areas. Subsequently, action teams were established to address each of these areas. As their work got underway, it became clear that there was a need to manage the inherent risks in conducting these organizational change projects. Danske Data called on the action researchers, who had extensive experience with risk management, to develop an approach to manage the risks faced by each of the SPI action teams. To satisfy the request, the action researchers embarked on the project described here, which eventually led to development of the method described in the previous section as well as the risk management approach for SPI described briefly in the Managing SPI Risks section and more fully in Iversen et al. (2002, 2004).

Action Research Project

The project was structured around four iterations, as described previously in Table 2. This section describes in detail how each iteration was conducted and what was learned. The effort involved 10 practitioners and 4 researchers (3 of whom are the authors). Table 3 illustrates a timeline of the four iterations and the involved actors and activities that took place in each. Most of the activities for this project took place between October 1997 and February 1999. Generally, the project was carried out in an iterative fashion, where risks and actions were identified in a bottom-up fashion and with practitioners and researchers collaborating closely on developing and testing the approach.

The project was initiated with a workshop that identified the risks and resolution actions that practitioners and researchers thought were the most important for SPI. When the workshop was conducted, the SPI project had been on-going for approximately one year, and both researchers and practitioners had significant practical experience with conducting SPI projects. Prior to the workshop, the practitioners worked through an existing SPI risk analysis approach (Statz et al., 1997), but found this approach too unwieldy and not sufficiently relevant to Danske Data. At the workshop, the researchers presented classical approaches to IT risk management (Boehm, 1991; Davis, 1982; McFarlan, 1981), after which the entire group conducted two brainstorms to determine risks and potential resolution actions that were relevant to SPI in Danske Data. Both of the resulting lists were very long and detailed (31 risk items and 21 resolution actions), which made them difficult to use. We obviously needed more structure.

Following the workshop, the authors studied the risk management literature and identified four types of approaches (Table 1). We chose to adopt a risk-strategy analysis approach, inspired by Davis (1982), for several reasons: We chose a strategy approach over a list approach because the practitioners explicitly stated that they wanted an approach that could help them obtain an overall, strategic understanding of each SPI project. We chose the risk-strategy analysis approach over the risk-strategy model approach for two reasons. First, the stepwise analysis approach would help each SPI team obtain a shared, detailed understanding of risks and possible actions. Second, we were not confident that we would be able to develop a contingency model that would summarize the many different sources of risks and ways to address them in SPI. The action research subsequently went through four full iterations before closing.

First Iteration

Based on the lists of risk items and resolution actions from the workshop and insights from the SPI literature, the authors synthesized the brainstorms and developed a prototype of the risk management approach. A key challenge was developing a framework to understand risks and actions (see Figure 1 and Table 4). We further developed our initial classifications through a detailed examination of risk items and resolution actions mentioned in the SPI literature (Grady, 1997; Humphrey, 1989; McFeeley, 1996; Statz et al., 1997). The resulting risk management process

was based on detailed lists of risk items and resolution actions for each of the four categories in the framework, and designed similarly to Davis' (1982) risk management approach (Iversen et al., 2004). Finally, we designed strategy sheets and simple scoring mechanisms to encourage a group of actors to engage in detailed risk and action assessments as a means to arrive at an informed, strategic understanding of how to address risks.

To test the approach, we arranged a workshop with the three practitioners responsible for improving quality assurance. We presented the risk framework and the process, but let the practitioners themselves apply the process, assisting only when they got stuck. The main experience was that the basic idea and structure of the approach was useful. However, during this first trial session, we only had time to cover half of the risk areas. The practitioners suggested that the process needed to be facilitated and managed by someone trained in the process, for example, the researchers. The practitioners found it especially difficult to interpret the questions in the risk tables in the context of their specific project. Some of the risk items needed to be reworded. Finally, to ease the interpretation of the risk items, the session should have started with an interpretation of the general terms in Figure 1 in the particular SPI context.

Figure 1. Risk areas for SPI teams

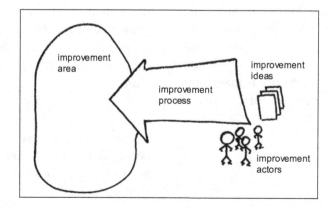

Table 4. Risk resolution strategies for SPI teams

Type of action	Concern
1. Adjust Mission	What are the goals of the initiative? Goals may be adjusted to be more or less ambitious, e.g., targeting only projects developing software for a specific platform.
2. Modify Strategy	What strategy is the initiative going to follow? Covers the approach to develop the process as well as to roll it out in the organization. Roll-out may, for instance, follow a pilot, big bang, or phased approach.
3. Mobilize	From what alliances and energies can the initiative benefit? The likelihood of success of an improvement initiative can be improved significantly by adjusting which organizational units and actors are involved and by increasing their commitment.
4. Increase Knowledge	On which knowledge of software processes and improvement is the initiative based? Knowledge can be increased by educating team members, by including additional expertise into the team, or by hiring consultants.
5. Reorganize	How is the initiative organized, conducted, and managed? Covers organizing, planning, monitoring, and evaluating of the initiative.

Second Iteration

In the second iteration, we reworded the risk items and introduced a first step in which the SPI team should interpret the risk model in Figure 1 in their particular context. Then we performed a risk analysis with the two SPI practitioners responsible for improving project management. Both practitioners were skilled project managers with experience in risk management. The session included a complete risk analysis with identification of key risks and resolution strategies. The participating practitioners and researchers agreed upon the major lessons. First, the framework and the process assisted even skilled project managers through a more disciplined analysis than they usually would do on their own. Second, it would be advantageous to document the interpretations of specific risk items and resolution actions continuously throughout the workshop.

At subsequent meetings in the local research group, the two risk management workshops were discussed and assessed in terms of which actions were taken later by the two SPI teams. Present at the meetings were the four SPI practitioners, the three authors, and the fourth researcher. Both SPI teams found that the suggested framework

provided a comprehensive overview of risk items and resolution actions. Many comments about the detailed lists of risk items and resolution actions led to subsequent modifications and rewording, but the aggregate structure that we had created based on the initial brainstorm and a study of the SPI literature was not changed.

The quality assurance improvement project was not very active during that period. The manager of the quality assurance project was not present at the risk analysis session and had not yet devoted full attention to quality assurance. The other project members were, therefore, mainly in a reactive mode, and little had happened. Risks surfaced during the analysis, but none of the practitioners were able to resolve these risks in practice. From this, we learned that realizing a risk and identifying a set of resolving actions do not ensure that actions are or will be taken. The practitioners that need to commit to the results of a risk analysis session should be present and involved in the session. After 7 months, there was no agreed-upon plan for the organizational implementation of quality assurance procedures. After 10 months, the quality assurance project had rolled out its procedures, but the identified risks never were managed effectively and consequently impacted the initiative.

The project management improvement project, in contrast, had considerable activity. The main risk was that project managers would not find the improvement attractive and worth their effort. The strategy was, therefore, directed at creating incentives for the project managers. After 1 month, an appropriate incentive structure was in place. After 5 months, the project manager education was a huge success, and all project managers wanted to participate (Andersen, Arent et al., 2002).

Third Iteration

We started the third iteration by appreciating the lesson learned from the first two iterations: successful application of the risk management approach required participation of practitioners with sufficient authority to address key risks. By including these actors in the workshop, we ensure that they agree with the outcome of the workshop, and thereby increase the chances that the agreed-upon actions actually will be implemented. We also introduced a new way to document the process directly onto transparencies and paper versions of the templates.

In the third iteration, we tested the changes on a project that was responsible for establishing an organization-wide metrics program (Iversen & Mathiassen, 2003). The new documentation scheme made it easier for the participants to relate risk questions to their particular situation. We documented each risk in more detail by answering the following question: "What are the specific issues that make this risk particularly important?" As we progressed through the risk assessment, this made it easier to determine why something had been given a specific characterization. The session included a complete risk analysis. The practitioners found the identified actions useful and relevant, and they emphasized the benefit of having reached a shared, overall understanding of risks and actions. The practitioners suggested

including the traditional distinction between consequences and probability of a risk into the process. To keep the approach as simple as possible, we decided not to implement this idea.

Fourth Iteration

For the fourth iteration, we made no changes, and applied the approach to an improvement project responsible for improving diffusion and adoption practices (Tryde et al., 2002). The session had three participants: two practitioners from Danske Bank's IT Department and the fourth action researcher involved in this project. All three found the approach generally useful. They found the analysis of the risk areas and the specific actions particularly useful, but they did not find summarizing the strategies particularly helpful. The participants emphasized the importance of not merely following the suggested lists of risk items and resolution actions, but also of supplementing this with a more open-minded exploration. "We haven't asked ourselves, 'what can go wrong?'" said one participant. They merely had considered each risk separately as it was presented to them.

Closing

We discussed and assessed the third and fourth risk analysis sessions with the four SPI practitioners and the fourth researcher at a later meeting of the local research group. The metrics program had suffered several setbacks due to political turmoil when previously hidden data about software projects' performance were publicized (Iversen & Mathiassen, 2003). Nevertheless, the risk analysis session led to actions that the project took later. The two main actions decided at the risk management session were: (1) develop and maintain top management's support and commitment and (2) create immediate results that are perceived useful by software projects. At a meeting 3 months later, it was reported that the project successfully had convinced top management that the collected metrics results should be publicized in all of Danske Bank's IT Department, which later happened (Iversen & Mathiassen, 2003). The diffusion and adoption project was successful (Tryde et al., 2002). Many of the performed activities came out of the risk analysis. It was decided to exit the iterations at this point because the experiences from the four iterations suggested that the risk management approach was in a stable and useful form. Our final activity was eliciting lessons for the overall action research endeavor (Iversen et al., 2004).

Managing SPI Risks

This section outlines the resulting risk analysis approach. The method has been described in more detail in other published works (Iversen et al., 2002, 2004).

The approach to managing SPI risks is based on a framework that aggregates risk items into areas and risk resolution actions into strategies. The first part of the framework describes the relevant SPI risk areas; the second part outlines the potential SPI risk resolution strategies. The approach is intended to be applied to the risks faced by individual SPI action teams. Figure 1 illustrates the four different areas in which SPI action teams might identify risks:

- **The improvement area:** those parts of the software organization that are affected by the specific SPI initiative.
- **The improvement ideas:** the set of processes, tools, and techniques that the SPI initiative seeks to bring into use in the improvement area.
- **The improvement process:** the SPI initiative itself and the way in which it is organized, conducted, and managed.
- **The improvement actors:** those involved in carrying out the SPI initiative.

As an example, consider an SPI team concerned with introducing configuration management in software engineering projects. Here the *improvement area* includes the software development projects that will use configuration management and the people supporting the process after institutionalization. The *improvement ideas* include the configuration management principles relied upon by the SPI team and the tools and methods that are developed to support these principles. The *improvement process* is the improvement itself, the way it is organized, and the involved stakeholders. The *improvement actors* are the members of the SPI team.

The risk resolution actions that SPI teams can apply are aggregated into five different types of strategies, as shown in Table 4. The strategies are listed according to the degree of change we suggest the SPI team's risk-based intervention will cause. *Adjust Mission, Modify Strategy,* and *Reorganize* target the improvement project's orientation and organization; *Increase Knowledge* targets the involved actors' level of expertise and knowledge; and *Mobilize* targets alliances and energies that will increase the project's chance of success.

The mission of an SPI team on configuration management may be to introduce configuration management on all documents (including documentation, code, etc.) in all software engineering projects in the company. This mission could be *adjusted* to include fewer projects (perhaps only large projects, critical projects, or projects in a specific department) or to exclude certain types of documents. The SPI team's strategy might be to involve a few key developers to give input to the process and, based on this, select a standard configuration management tool that every project then has to use. *Modifying the strategy* may entail involving more (or fewer) developers or implementing the chosen tool gradually in each project. *Mobilizing* may involve establishing agreements with an existing method department, a production department, or other departments or persons that have a vested interest in the results of the team's effort. The SPI team could *increase its knowledge* by attending courses on configuration management or SPI, or by hiring knowledgeable consultants. If the project is not organized optimally for the task at hand, the effort could be *reorganized*, e.g., by establishing a formal project, negotiating a project contract with management and the software engineering projects, or developing a new project plan.

To help SPI practitioners determine a strategy based on current risks facing the project, the approach offers a four-step process based on Davis (1982):

1. **Characterize Situation** by interpreting the profile and scope of the elements of Figure 1.
2. **Analyze Risks** to assess where the most serious risks are. This involves rating each of the detailed risk items in the risk lists for the four areas, and then determining which area carries the highest risk exposure.
3. **Prioritize Actions** to decide on a strategy that will deal effectively with the identified risks. Here, actors use a process that alternates between individual and group judgments to determine which strategy is the most sensible given the current assessment of risks facing the project.
4. **Take Action** by revising project plans to reflect resolution actions.

CONCLUSION

IT managers see risk management as a key to success (Barki et al., 1993). Such approaches help appreciate many aspects of a project: they emphasize potential causes of failure, they help identify possible actions, and they facilitate a shared perception of the project among its participants (Lyytinen et al., 1996, 1998). This indicates that organizations can benefit from adopting IT risk management to their particular needs. The method we have presented can be used for that purpose, and thereby adds to the portfolio of approaches that are available to adapt generic insights to specific organizations. Similar methods are, for example, available to tailor knowledge on software estimation to specific organizational contexts (Bailey & Basili, 1981).

The method builds on action research experiences that can help organizations address IT-related problems effectively in line with scientific insights. Our own experiences using the method indicate that a number of competencies are required to adopt the method effectively. First, we had intensive domain (SPI) and risk management knowledge. Second, we had general competence in modeling organizational phenomena that we used to identify and classify risk items and resolution actions. Third, we had experimental competence that we used to collect feedback from the test situations to iteratively arrive at the resulting approach. Each of these competencies is required to apply the proposed CPR method in other contexts. It is also important to stress that the method, like most action research processes, is a template that needs to be adapted and supplemented in action, depending on the conditions under which it is applied.

In addition to being useful in a specific organizational context, the CPR method can help tailor risk management approaches to new domains within information systems and software engineering, for example, business process innovation, integration of information services, and ERP implementation. Any form of organizational change enabled by IT is complex and difficult. Risk management, as illustrated well in relation to software development and SPI, is a highly effective way to bring relevant knowledge within a particular organization or domain into a form in which it can support and improve professional practices. We, therefore, encourage researchers and practitioners within information systems and software engineering to adopt action research to tailor risk management to specific organizations and new domains.

We conclude this chapter with good advice to those who wish to create a risk management approach for their organization:

- Make sure practitioners are able to relate wording of risks and resolutions to their project.
- Be aware of whether the approach needs to be facilitated. For practitioners to apply the approach on their own, it must be simple or well documented and supplemented by training.
- Build in documentation of rationales along the way (what was it about a certain risk that made it particularly evident in this project?).
- Include mechanisms to ensure action. It is not enough to create a risk resolution plan — the project also needs to carry it out.
- Iterate until the approach is stable. Then keep updating risks and actions to stay current with changes in the context as well as in the literature.

REFERENCES

Alter, S., & Ginzberg, M. (1978). Managing uncertainty in mis implementation. *Sloan Management Review, 20*(1), 23-31.

Andersen, C. V., Arent, J., Bang, S., & Iversen, J. H. (2002). Project assessments. In L. Mathiassen, J. Pries-Heje, & O. Ngwenyama (Eds.), *Improving software organizations: From principles to practice* (pp. 167-184). Upper Saddle River, NJ: Addison-Wesley.

Andersen, C. V., Krath, F., Krukow, L., Mathiassen, L., & Pries-Heje, J. (2002). The grassroots effort. In L. Mathiassen, J. Pries-Heje, & O. Ngwenyama (Eds.), *Improving software organizations:*

From principles to practice (pp. 83-98). Upper Saddle River, NJ: Addison-Wesley.

Bailey, W., & Basili, V. R. (1981, March 9-12). Meta-model for software development expenditures. *Proceedings of the 5th International Conference on Software Engineering*, San Diego, CA.

Barki, H., Rivard, S., & Talbot, J. (1993). Toward an assessment of software development risk. *Journal of Management Information Systems, 10*(2), 203-225.

Boehm, B. W. (1991). Software risk management: Principles and practices. *IEEE Software, 8*(1), 32-41.

Checkland, P. (1991). From framework through experience to learning: The essential nature of action research. In H.-E. Nissen, H. K. Klein, & R. A. Hirschheim (Eds.), *Information systems research: Contemporary approaches and emergent traditions* (pp. 397-403). North-Holland: Elsevier.

Chrissis, M. B., Konrad, M., & Shrum, S. (2003). *CMMI: Guidelines for process integration and product improvement.* Boston: Addison-Wesley Professional.

Davis, G. B. (1982). Strategies for information requirements determination. *IBM Systems Journal, 21*(1), 4-30.

Donaldson, S. E., & Siegel, S. G. (2001). *Successful software development.* Upper Saddle River, NJ: Prentice Hall.

Grady, R. B. (1997). *Successful software process improvement.* Upper Saddle River, NJ: Prentice Hall PTR.

Humphrey, W. S. (1989). *Managing the software process.* Pittsburgh, PA: Addison-Wesley.

Iversen, J., Johansen, J., Nielsen, P. A., & Pries-Heje, J. (1998, June 4-6). Combining quantitative and qualitative assessment methods in software process improvement. *Proceedings of the European Conference on Information Systems (ECIS 98)*, Aix-en-Provence, France.

Iversen, J. H., & Mathiassen, L. (2003). Cultivation and engineering of a software metrics program. *Information Systems Journal, 13*(1), 3-20.

Iversen, J. H., Mathiassen, L., & Nielsen, P. A. (2002). Risk management in process action teams. In L. Mathiassen, J. Pries-Heje, & O. Ngwenyama (Eds.), *Improving software organizations: From principles to practice* (pp. 273-286). Upper Saddle River, NJ: Addison-Wesley.

Iversen, J. H., Mathiassen, L., & Nielsen, P. A. (2004). Managing risks in software process improvement: An action research approach. *MIS Quarterly, 28*(3), 395-433.

Jones, C. (1994). *Assessment and control of software risks.* Upper Saddle River, NJ: Yourdon Press, Prentice Hall.

Keil, M., Cule, P. E., Lyytinen, K., & Schmidt, R. C. (1998). A framework for identifying software project risks. *Communications of the ACM, 41*(11), 76-83.

Lyytinen, K., Mathiassen, L., & Ropponen, J. (1996). A framework for software risk management. *Scandinavian Journal of Information Systems, 8*(1), 53-68.

Lyytinen, K., Mathiassen, L., & Ropponen, J. (1998). Attention shaping and software risk: A categorical analysis of four classical risk management approaches. *Information System Research, 9*(3), 233-255.

Mathiassen, L. (2002). Collaborative practice research. *Information Technology and People, 15*(4), 321-345.

Mathiassen, L., Munk-Madsen, A., Nielsen, P. A., & Stage, J. (2000). *Object-oriented analysis and design.* Aalborg, Denmark: Marko.

Mathiassen, L., Pries-Heje, J., & Ngwenyama, O. (Eds.). (2002). *Improving software organizations: From principles to practice.* Upper Saddle River, NJ: Addison-Wesley.

McFarlan, F. W. (1981). Portfolio approach to information systems. *Harvard Business Review, 59*(5), 142-150.

McFeeley, B. (1996). *Ideal: A user's guide for software process improvement* (Tech. Rep. No. CMU/SEI-96-HB-001). Pittsburgh, PA: Software Engineering Institute.

McKay, J., & Marshall, P. (2001). The dual imperatives of action research. *Information Technology and People, 14*(1), 46-59.

Moynihan, T. (1996). An inventory of personal constructs for information systems project risk researchers. *Journal of Information Technology, 11*, 359-371.

Ould, M. (1999). *Managing software quality and business risk.* Chichester, UK: Wiley.

Paulk, M. C., Weber, C. V., Garcia, S. M., & Chrissis, M. B. (1993). *The capability maturity model: Guidelines for improving the software process.* Upper Saddle River, NJ: Addison-Wesley.

Ropponen, J., & Lyytinen, K. (2000). Components of software development risk: How to address them? A project manager survey. *IEEE Transactions on Software Development, 26*(2), 98-112.

Schön, D. A. (1983). *The reflective practitioner. How professionals think in action.* New York: Basic Books.

Statz, J., Oxley, D., & O'Toole, P. (1997). Identifying and managing risks for software process improvement. *Crosstalk - The Journal of Defense Software Engineering, 10*(4), 13-18.

Susman, G. I., & Evered, R. D. (1978). An assessment of the scientific merits of action research. *Administrative Science Quarterly, 23*, 582-603.

Tryde, S., Nielsen, A.-D., & Pries-Heje, J. (2002). Implementing SPI: An organizational approach. In L. Mathiassen, J. Pries-Heje, & O. Ngwenyama (Eds.), *Improving software organizations: From principles to practice* (pp. 257-271). Upper Saddle River, NJ: Addison-Wesley.

Chapter VII
Modeling and Analyzing Perspectives to Support Knowledge Management

Jian Cai
Peking University, China

ABSTRACT

This chapter introduces a generic modeling approach that explicitly represents the perspectives of stakeholders and their evolution traversing a collaborative process. This approach provides a mechanism to analytically identify the interdependencies among stakeholders and to detect conflicts and reveal their intricate causes and effects. Collaboration is thus improved through efficient knowledge management. This chapter also describes a Web-based information system that uses the perspective model and the social network analysis methodology to support knowledge management within collaboration.

INTRODUCTION

The ability to effectively manage distributed knowledge and business processes is becoming an essential core competence of today's organizations. Various knowledge management theories and approaches have been proposed and adopted (Earl, 2001). These include ways to align knowledge processes with strategies (Spender, 1996), to leverage organizational learning abilities (Nonaka & Takeuchi, 1995), and to build IT infrastructures to support knowledge activities (Lu, 2000; Zack, 1999). Knowledge management systems (KMSs) can be viewed as the implementation of the KM strategy. KMS improves the knowledge processes through IT infrastructures and information-processing methodologies (Tanriverdi, 2005). Although the importance of knowledge management has been well recognized, organizations are still facing the problems of how to successfully implement knowledge management. In order to effectively utilize these theories and technologies to support teamwork, it is necessary to gain more fundamental understandings of the characteristics of knowledge management within collaboration processes.

BACKGROUND

Previous knowledge management approaches can be generally classified into two categories (Hanson, Nohira, & Tierney, 1999). The strategies supporting knowledge replication provide high-quality, fast, and reliable information systems implementation by reusing codified knowledge. The strategies supporting knowledge customization provide creative, analytically rigorous advice on high-level strategic problems by channeling individual expertise. The codification approaches view information technology as the central infrastructure of knowledge-based organizations. KMSs are thus treated as system-integration solutions or applications that retain employees' know-how. The major concern of these approaches is how to help organizations monitor the trends of rapidly changing technologies and inventions in order to recognize new applications that may provide competitive advantage (Kwan & Balasubramanian, 2003). However, IT is just one of the elements of KMS. As knowledge management involves various social and technical enablers, the scope, nature, and purpose of KMS vary during the collaboration processes. Researches from the knowledge-customization perspective focus on understanding knowledge and its relationships with organizations (Becerra-Fernanaez & Sabherwal, 2001; Nonaka & Takeuchi, 1995). A typology of knowledge creation and conversion of tacit and explicit knowledge was proposed (Nonaka, Reinmoeller, & Senoo, 1998). The conversion involves transcending the self of individuals, teams, or organizations and reveals the importance of organizational architecture and organizational dynamics to capitalize on knowledge. Recent research on knowledge management has been focusing on developing models that interconnect knowledge management factors, such as collaboration, learning, organizational structure, process, and IT support (Lee & Choi, 2003). These research works have been mainly addressing understanding the nature of knowledge

and knowledge management. Both approaches provide workable models and methods for implementing knowledge management.

In fact, knowledge replication is interlaced with knowledge customization within a collaborative process. In collaborative projects, it is important to systematically integrate these two groups of KM approaches to build methodologies and systems to facilitate the teamwork. First, KM methodologies should be coupled with process management in collaborative projects. An organization and its members can be involved in multiple knowledge management process chains. The tangible tasks are accompanied by the implicit knowledge-integration activities. As such, knowledge management is not a monolithic but a dynamic and continuous organizational phenomenon (Alavi & Leidner, 2001). Second, KM and KMS have to take account of various social factors within collaboration processes. Collaborative projects involve various stakeholders (i.e., all of the human participants and organizations who influence the collaboration process and the results) from different disciplines to work cooperatively over distance and time boundaries. When many heterogeneous groups work together on large projects over a long period of time, their knowledge of the system, the product, and other people will keep on evolving (Dym & Levitt, 1991; O'Leary, 1998). The professional expertise in particular is framed by a person's conceptualization of multiple, ongoing activities, which are essentially identities, comprising intentions, norms, and choreographies (Carley & Prietula, 1994; Erickson & Kellogg, 2000; Siau, 1999; Sowa & Zachman, 1992). Although the collaboration process might appear relatively technical, it is essentially a social construction process when different persons perform their tasks within various adaptive situations (Berger & Luckman, 1966; Clancey, 1993, 1997). The situations will eventually impact the evolution of participants' roles and form a shared understanding (Arias, Eden, Fischer, Gorman, & Scharff, 2000). Even within well-defined technical roles, every stakeholder makes the role his or her own by adapting or executing the role based on his or her conceptions and circumstances. It is the social interaction that determines the variation or adaptability of these roles in a particular application context. As their roles evolve, stakeholders' learning customs and attitudes will vary, which will directly or indirectly affect their internal knowledge and the knowledge creation and conversion processes. Therefore, to manage the distributed knowledge within the complicated collaborative process, it is necessary to have well-developed methodologies for describing and analyzing the social interactions in collaborative contexts of the emerging practice.

This chapter presents a methodology for supporting knowledge management within collaboration by modeling and analyzing the stakeholders' perspectives. The methods to depict and control the evolution of distributed knowledge are introduced. This chapter also describes a prototype knowledge management system developed for a U.S. government research institute. It implements the methodology and uses the advanced network computing techniques to facilitate stakeholders' interaction within their work practice.

MODELING PERSPECTIVES TO SUPPORT KNOWLEDGE MANAGEMENT

The previous approaches and methodologies for supporting KM in collaborative work have been mainly concentrating on either modeling the explicit knowledge or supporting communication of implicit knowledge. The knowledge management systems built upon these approaches included three types of functions: (a) the coding and sharing of best practices, (b) the creation of corporate knowledge directories, and (c) the creation of knowledge networks (Alavi & Leidner, 2001). Recent research has proposed systems to support information and knowledge seeking and

use within the decision or problem-solving process (Kwan & Balasubramanian, 2003; Rouse, 2002; Shaw, Ackermann, & Eden, 2003). Modeling approaches are widely used for developing such methodologies and systems. For instance, the activity modeling approach was used to develop a knowledge management system to provide a computer-based guidance and interactive support for office workers (Reimer, Margelisch, & Staudt, 2000). Knowledge-engineering processes were modeled to capture, store, and deploy company knowledge (Preece, Flett, & Sleeman, 2001). However, most of the existing approaches still view stakeholders as homogeneous and do not emphasize their intricate needs at various stages of the processes. Nevertheless, a lack of understanding of stakeholders' needs—and the provision of support systems accordingly—is precisely the missing link in the success of many information and knowledge management systems (Rouse). This requires understanding multiple aspects of stakeholders' needs in seeking and using information and knowledge within the collaboration.

Recent published studies have shown that besides technologies, the social aspects are essential to the success of collaboration (Briggs, Vreede, & Nunamaker, 2003; Easley, Sarv, & Crant, 2003; Erickson & Kellogg, 2000; Hardjono & van Marrewijk, 2001). Technologies are part of a social network and a KM system is likely to include not only technology, but also social and cultural infrastructures and human agents (Chae, Koch, Paradice, & Huy, 2005). One of the key social factors is the cognitive interaction process. As stakeholders' preferences, environments, and knowledge are dynamically changing during their interactions, collaborative activity over the Internet is more than an online data-accessing and information-sharing process. Accordingly, frequently occurred conflicts influence the project schedule and team performance. Team coordination has to be achieved through not only the sharing of data and information, but also the realization of the decision contexts of each other (Chung,

Kim, & Dao, 1999; Kannapan & Taylor, 1994). The decision context consists of at least two parts: the circumstances of the decision makers and the stages of the process. When people exchange information, they should understand under what circumstances this information is generated and in which situation it can be potentially used. Otherwise, it is difficult for them to interpret the purposes and implications of each other during the activity coordination. Therefore, to represent and organize the situated knowledge (i.e., the context) is essential to support the coordination among different groups. It is also of immense importance to understand how to design knowledge management systems so that they mesh with human behavior at the individual and collective levels. By allowing users to "see" one another and to make inferences about the activities of others, online collaboration platforms can become environments in which new social forms can be invented, adopted, adapted, and propagated—eventually supporting the same sort of social innovation and diversity that can be observed in physically based cultures (Erickson & Kellogg, 2000).

To address these issues, our research uses a sociotechnical framework to model the interactions within collaborations (Lu & Cai, 2001). The framework addresses that one cannot utilize information to map from "what to do" to "how to do" in the collaboration process without knowing the perspective of the "who" that generates the information. A collaborative project is modeled as a coconstruction process among a group of stakeholders. The key feature is to explicitly model the who (i.e., the stakeholders' perspectives) within the process (i.e., the what, how, and when). During collaboration, each individual has a perspective that evolves over time and acts like a lens through which she or he understands and collects information external to her or him. Each individual builds over a lifetime an evolving base of information that is internal. The information that each individual produces, or exchanges through any medium (e.g., computers, speech, and writing), is the external manifestation of internal information, appropriately filtered through "perspective lens." Based on the sociotechnical framework, knowledge management systems require the

Figure 1. The perspective modeling approach of knowledge management in collaboration

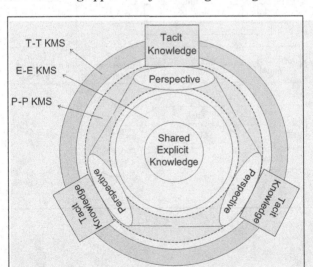

explicit modeling of stakeholders' perspectives within their social interactions. The perspective modeling and analyzing methodology focuses on representing and handling the interactions among the heterogeneous stakeholders. It provides associations with other knowledge management and decision-support models. It also provides ways to build and integrate various processes with the realization of sharing knowledge and managing conflict. Different from traditional KMS, which either focuses on the codification of explicit knowledge (E-E KMS) or communication of tacit knowledge (T-T KMS), the perspective modeling approach will realize a new way of building KMS (P-P KMS) through controlling the interfaces between the explicit and tacit knowledge (i.e., stakeholders' perspectives; Figure 1).

PERSPECTIVE MODELING AND SOCIOTECHNICAL ANALYSIS

Methodology Overview

The central function of the research framework is the sociotechnical analysis to model and analyze the perspectives of stakeholders at each step of the collaboration process. The sociotechnical analysis methodology takes three input parameters (i.e., the concept model, the perspective model, and the process model; Figure 2). The concept model is a structure that organizes the ontology models representing the shared or private notions of the stakeholders. The process model is a feasible computational model that represents the interactions of individual tasks. It specifies the sequences

Figure 2. The sociotechnical analysis methodology for knowledge management

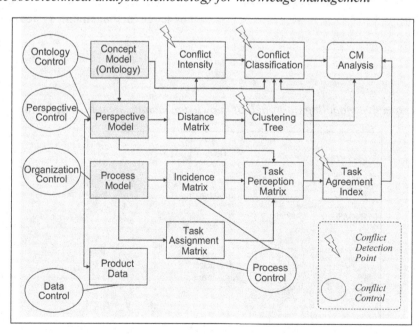

and dependencies of decisions and actions to be jointly performed. The perspective model provides a generic means to formally capture, represent, and analyze stakeholders' perspectives and their interactions with each other. The concept model and perspective models represent the shared knowledge and social characteristics of various stakeholders during the collaboration process. They are derived from the surveys of stakeholders' attitudes toward the ontology models at a point of time.

The dependencies among these models are represented as matrices for mathematical analysis. Conflict analysis applies systematic strategies to analyze inconsistencies among these matrices. At a certain stage within the process, conflicts can be detected by tracking and comparing the perspective states of different stakeholders associated with a certain task. This analysis will derive three major outputs (i.e., process feasibil-

ity, conflict possibility, and perspective network). Then, based on these outputs, the systems can apply various control strategies so that the quality of the collaboration is enhanced. Control mechanisms adaptively handle the interplay among the three factors by systematically reconciling various perspectives, improving the processes, and controlling the product data and organizational structure.

Perspective Modeling

The perspective modeling mainly consists of building the concept model and the perspective model. While the process model depicts the tangible activities of the project, the concept model and perspective model track the knowledge evolution and changes of social behaviors.

The first step is to generate the concept structure hierarchy. A concept model is a hierarchi-

Figure 3. A concept structure built by stakeholders in a collaborative design project

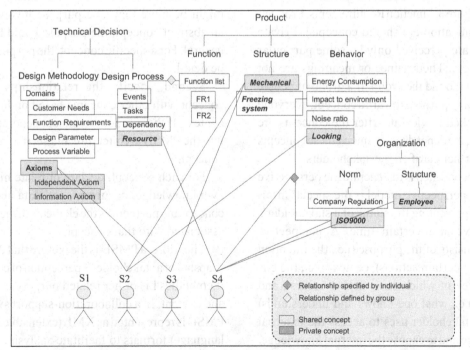

cal structure that represents the organization of the ontology (Huhns & Stephens, 1999; Staab, Schnurr, Studer, & Sure, 2001) that stakeholders propose and use in their collaboration. Figure 3 shows a concept structure example of a product development team. Stakeholders may use both top-down and bottom-up construction methods (Vet & Mars, 1999) to build the concept structure. It is possible to apply some templates (e.g., product function template, organizational template, conflict types template, etc.) to clarify the concepts. These templates act as the contend-based skeletons for organizing the external information that stakeholders may share with others.

When stakeholders propose new concepts, the concept structure is updated and is used to systematically organize these concepts and their relationships. Since a stakeholder should first consider whether there are same or similar concepts in the structure, only the novel concepts can be specified and added. The concepts involved within the collaboration are classified into two types. Shared concepts are those that have been well defined from previous projects. They have widely accepted meaning shared among the stakeholders (e.g., in Figure 3, Function Requirements, Product, and Organization are shared concepts). Private concepts are perceived only by some particular stakeholders. Their names or meanings are not expressed around the group. If a group of people have a shared purpose toward a concept, everyone will be asked to view it. After the concepts are identified, the dependencies among these concepts can be further clarified by stakeholders.

The second step is to generate the perspective model. A perspective model is the special information representing the status of a stakeholder's perspective at a certain time. A perspective model consists of the purpose (i.e., the intention to conduct certain actions), context (i.e., the circumstances in which one's action occurs), and content (i.e., what one knows and understands) that the stakeholder uses to access the external knowledge and to expose the internal knowledge.

In information systems, the perspective model can be depicted as a data format relating to other information entities.

Our research develops a format for representing perspectives and a procedure to capture, generate, and analyze perspective models. Given the well-organized structure of concepts, it is feasible to ask the stakeholders to build the perspective-model state diagrams (PMSDs) at a certain time. A stakeholder's PMSD attempts to depict the explicit relationships among his or her concepts (including the shared concepts and private concepts) and purpose, content, and context information. The concepts listed in the PMSD are categories of perspective contents. Using the concept structure to generate the PMSD provides a structured way for us to systematically compare and examine the perspective differences among stakeholders.

Each concept of the concept model can be associated with a stakeholder by a set of purposes, contexts, and contents. The operation is to ask the stakeholders to do the following.

First, relate this concept to their purposes. A stakeholder is able to specify his or her purpose within the project for a given concept. There might be more than one purpose involved. For an abstract concept, the purpose could be more general. For a specific concept, the purpose could be detail.

Second, specify the relationships of this concept with other concepts based on his or her context. If there is a new concept generated, add it to the PMSD architecture and set it as a private concept.

For each concept, declare or relate his or her own knowledge, document, and data about that concept and put them as the elements of the content associated with that concept.

Therefore, a PMSD is the picture that depicts a snapshot of a stakeholder's perception of concepts. It embodies his or her related purposes, context, and content. In a collaboration-support system, a PMSD is represented as XML (extensible markup language) formats to facilitate analysis.

Figure 4. The perspective analysis procedure

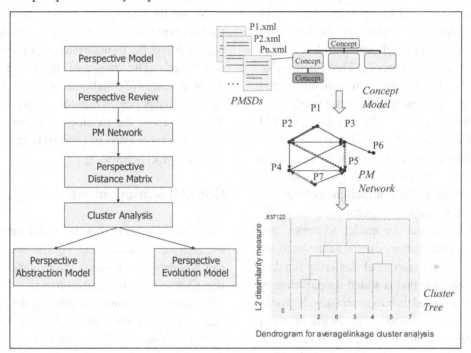

The third step is to conduct the perspective analysis. By comparing and analyzing stakeholders' perspective models, it is possible to determine the degree of agreement among their opinions during their interaction. As shown in Figure 4, given the PMSDs for certain stakeholders, we can ask them to review others' perspective models. The review information is used to compare the perspective models and determine the similarity of two stakeholders' perspectives toward a shared concept. We can also aggregate multiple stakeholders' perspective models and compare their general attitudes at different levels of abstraction. Furthermore, we can track the evolution of the perspective model based on the clustering analysis results. The procedure is called perspective analysis (Figure 4).

The first step is to determine the inconsistency (i.e., the distance) among a group of perspective models. There are two approaches: the intuitive approach and the analytical approach. The intuitive approach relies on the insights of the stakeholders. The analytical approach uses mathematical algorithms to derive the distance through positional analysis, which is based on a formal method used in social network analysis (Wasserman & Faust, 1994). This approach views the perspective models of a group of stakeholders toward a single concept as a network of opinions associated with each other. In this network, a stakeholder, who possesses a perspective model, has relationships with others' perspective models. We define these relationships as their perceptional attitudes toward each other. A group of perspective models toward a given concept are placed as a graph (i.e., a PM network). Two perspective models are compatible (or similar) if they are in the same position in the network structure. In social network analysis, position refers to a collection of individuals who are similarly embedded in networks of relations. If two perspective models are structurally equivalent (i.e., their relationships with other perspective models are the same), we assume that they are purely compatible and there are no detectable differences. That implies that they have the same perception toward others, and others have same perception toward them.

A distance matrix is derived for each PM network. It represents the situation of perspective compatibility among a group of stakeholders for a given concept. We can also compare stakeholders' perspective models for multiple concepts by measuring the structural equivalence across the collection of perspective model networks. Perspective distance matrices serve as the basis for cluster analysis. Hierarchical clustering is a data analysis technique that is suited for partitioning the perspective models into subclasses. It groups entities into subsets so that entities within a subset are relatively similar to each other. Hierarchical clustering generates a tree structure (or a dendrogram), which shows the grouping of the perspective models. It illustrates that the perspective models are grouped together at different levels of abstraction (Figure 4).

The cluster tree exposes interesting characteristics of the social interactions. Within a collaborative project, the participants of the organization cooperate and build the shared reality (i.e., the common understanding of the stakeholders toward certain concepts) in the social interaction process (Berger & Luckman, 1966). Understanding the process of building shared realities is the key to managing social interactions. The shared reality can be represented by the abstraction of close perspective models among a group of stakeholders. As a matter of fact, the cluster tree depicts the structures of the shared reality since a branch of the clustering tree at a certain level implies an abstract perspective model with certain granularity. The height of the branch indicates the compatibility of the leaf perspective models. A cluster tree with simple structure and fewer levels implies that all of the perspective models have similar attitudes

(or positions) toward others.

While the perspective models are changing, the clustering analysis can be used as a systematic way to depict the transformation of the perspective models. The change of the cluster trees at different stages of collaboration reveals the characteristics of perspective evolution. Investigating the changes of the topological patterns of the clustering trees leads to ways to interfere in the perspective evolutions.

Conflict Management

Given the condition that the social interactions are analytically measured, control mechanisms can be derived to manage the evolutions of the perspective models and therefore to support collaboration. Theses mechanisms could be selected and used by the group managers or coordinators to control conflicts. They can be classified into the following strategies.

Process Control

The perspective analysis can be performed for all of the stakeholders who might act on or influence a task. By evaluating their perspective compatibility and the execution feasibility of future tasks, which are in the plan but have not been conducted yet, we can prevent some conflicts by noticing their potential existence earlier. By providing certain information to stakeholders, it is possible to change the perception matrix and therefore to increase the perspective consistency of a task. It is possible to directly adjust the sequences and dependencies among the tasks to maintain the integrity of the opinions of stakeholders.

Perspective Control and Ontology Control

First, it is possible to directly influence stakeholders' perspectives (their content, purpose, and context) to maintain the integrity and compatibility of the opinions toward a certain concept or task. Analyzing social interactions will identify the perspective models with low similarities and reveal the conflicts clearly. Thus, we can focus on the stakeholders who have singular perspectives and understand their rationale. Second, communication channels can be built to increase the interaction opportunities among stakeholders with different perspective models. The group can manipulate the concept structure through clarifying the meanings and definitions of critical concepts so that people have shared understanding. It is also feasible to serve stakeholders with different concepts to isolate their perspectives. An opposite way is to use conflicting perspectives as means to enhancing brainstorming and innovation. Third, strategies can be derived to manage the conflicts through influencing stakeholders' information access and comprehension. Possible solutions include providing suitable trainings based on their perspectives and the job requirements, assisting the critical stakeholder to review the relevant information during certain conflicting tasks, and recording the discussions about the shared concept for future reuse.

Organization Control

The clustering tree shows the grouping features of stakeholders' perspectives. Using different organizational structures will change the communication channels and the perception distances. If two stakeholders are separated into different groups, the possibility of interaction will decrease. We can change the task assignment or modify stakeholder' roles to affect their contexts. It is even possible to add or remove stakeholders associated with a certain task to avoid the conflicting situation or to move the stakeholders with similar perspectives together.

Data and Information Control

This control mechanism is to affect the conflicts through appropriately providing and handling external data and information that will be accessed by the stakeholders. Examples are to use consistent checking and version-control mechanisms to maintain the product data integrity, to track the changes of shared data and information by referencing to the perspective changing, and to map the shared data and information to perspective models so that the system realizes the specific impact of the conflicts toward the working results.

Building Electronic Collaboration Support Systems Using the Perspective Modeling Approach

The perspective modeling and analyzing methodology provides a theoretical basis for building new knowledge management systems. The STARS system is a prototype system to support collaboration over the Internet. It is also developed as an experimental apparatus for testing the research. The system implements the process modeling, perspective modeling, and sociotechnical analysis methodologies. On the other hand, it collects process and perspective data once stakeholders use it as a collaboration tool. By investigating the collected experimental data, we can determine the effectiveness of the approach and therefore improve it.

The STARS system provides a Web-based environment that supports the collaboration process representation, conflict management, and knowledge integration within a project team. Stakeholders declare, share, and modify their perspective models on the Web. The perspectives models are analyzed in the system and stakeholders' roles in the collaboration tasks are depicted. The system implements the functional modules (e.g., perspective management, process management, conflict management, etc.) by using J2EE1.4 and Web services technologies (Figure 5).

It provides methods to detect, analyze, and track the conflicts during collaboration. It also supports the business-to-business process communications through SOAP and UDDI.

Figure 6 shows the knowledge perspective management module that allows stakeholders to declare and review their perspective information according to a concept structure tree. The system can analyze the perspective models, detect and predict conflicts, and suggest possible control strategies. The process management system of STARS uses an XML-based process modeling tool for process planning, scheduling, simulation, and execution. It helps the stakeholders notice what is happening and who is doing what at any time. Stakeholders declare their perspectives during each step of the process. The system determines the conflict ratio of each task based on the perspective analysis.

Groups of designers, business analysts, and consultants working in a U.S. national construc-

tion research institute have been using STARS in their small projects. Feasibility and computability of the analysis algorithms were proved. Figure 7 depicts an example of using STARS to solve a conflict problem through perspective analysis. Before using STARS, similar cases as described below often happened in one design team:

Within a design project, at the first meeting, the client's design consultant stated that the building was to be placed at a location on the site. The architect listened to the client's reasoning but noted that this location is not ideal from either an aesthetic or a functional point of view, since it would be too close to a major road intersection.

The STARS perspective analyzing functions helped users notice the dependencies and differences of views among the stakeholders. The conflict was detected by tracking and mapping the perspective models of the three stakeholders.

Figure 5. STARS system architecture

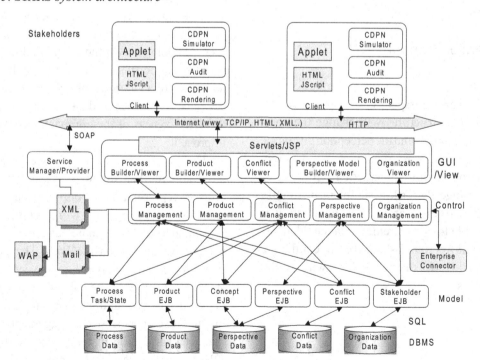

Figure 6. The perspective-management and conflict-management modules of STARS

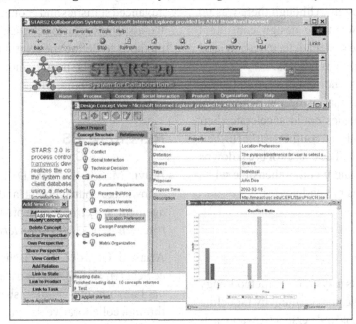

Figure 7. An example of detecting conflicts from perspective analysis

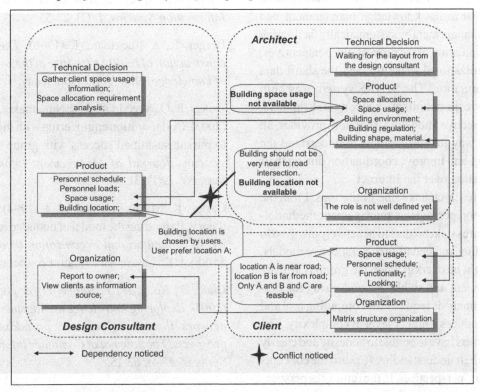

STARS compared the perspective models at an early stage of the design. Although there was no direct meeting between the design consultant and the architect, the system detected a potential conflict during the design process.

The stakeholders who participated in the experiment considered that using the perspective modeling methodologies could accelerate their learning process and detect conflicts earlier in their collaborative projects. The causes of breakdowns of collaboration are more comprehensible when applying the analysis methodologies.

CONCLUSION

This chapter presents a systematic methodology to support knowledge management by modeling and analyzing stakeholders' perspectives and their social interactions within collaborative processes. This approach provides methods for capturing perspectives and understanding their relationships to facilitate the control of the evolution of the shared insights. It avails knowledge management and conflict management by systematically facilitating the manipulation of the process, the perspectives, the organizational structure, and the shard data and information. The STARS system was built to improve the coordination among stakeholders. Its perspective modeling function provides an efficient way for stakeholders to understand the meanings and improve coordination during their collaboration over the Internet.

This research has some limitations. First, the closed-loop perspective management methodology requires stakeholders to be actively involved in the building and updating of perspective models. This might be overkill when the group is already very efficient and stable. Second, using the perspective analysis requires the computing tool and thus introduces a higher level of complexity. The system users have to be able to honestly and clearly specify their understandings toward the concepts and others' perspectives. In the future, the perspec-

tive analysis model can be improved by applying advanced statistics and econometrics techniques. It is also important to generate dynamic modeling methods to define the relationships between the evolution of perspective models and the quality of online collaboration.

REFERENCES

Alavi, M., & Leidner, D. E. (2001). Review: Knowledge management and knowledge management systems: Conceptual foundations and research issues. *MIS Quarterly, 25*(1), 105-136.

Arias, E. G., Eden, H., Fischer, G., Gorman, A., & Scharff, E. (2000). Transcending the individual human mind-creating shared understanding through collaborative design. *ACM Transactions on Computer-Human Interaction, 7*(1), 84-113.

Becerra-Fernanaez, I., & Sabherwal, R. (2001). Organizational knowledge management: A contingency perspective. *Journal of Management Information Systems, 18*(1), 23-55.

Berger, P., & Luckman, T. (1966). *The social construction of reality a treatise in the sociology of knowledge.* New York: Doubleday.

Briggs, R. O., Vreede, G.-J., & Nunamaker, J. F., Jr. (2003). Collaboration engineering with thinkLets to pursue sustained success with group support systems. *Journal of Management Information Systems, 19*(1), 31-64.

Carley, K. M., & Prietula, M. J. (1994). ACTS theory: Extending the model of bounded rationality. In *Computational organization theory* (pp. 55-88). UK: Lawrence Erlbaum Associates.

Chae, B., Koch, H., Paradice, D., & Huy, V. V. (2005). Exploring knowledge management using network theories: Questions, paradoxes, and prospects. The Journal of Computer Information Systems, 45(4), 62-15.

Chung, C.-W., Kim, C.-R., & Dao, S. (1999). Knowledge and object-oriented approach for interoperability of heterogeneous information management systems. *Journal of Database Management, 10*(3), 13-25.

Clancey, W. J. (1993). Guidon-manage revisited: A socio-technical systems approach. *Journal of Artificial Intelligence in Education, 4*(1), 5-34.

Clancey, W. J. (1997). The conceptual nature of knowledge, situations, and activity. In P. Feltovich, R. Hoffman, & K. Ford (Eds.), *Human and machine expertise in context* (pp. 247-291). CA: AAAI Press.

Dym, C. L., & Levitt, R. E. (1991). Toward the integration of knowledge for engineering modeling and computation. *Engineering with Computers, 7*(1), 209-224.

Earl, M. J. (2001). Knowledge management strategies: Toward a taxonomy. *Journal of Management Information Systems, 18*(1), 215-233.

Easley, R. F., Sarv, D., & Crant, J. M. (2003). Relating collaborative technology use to teamwork quality and performance: An empirical analysis. *Journal of Management Information Systems, 19*(4), 247-268.

Erickson, T., & Kellogg, W. A. (2000). Social translucence: An approach to designing systems that support social processes. *ACM Transactions on Computer-Human Interactions, 7*(1), 59-83.

Hanson, M., Nohira, N., & Tierney, T. (1999). What is your strategy for managing knowledge? *Harvard Business Review*, 106-116.

Hardjono, T. W., & van Marrewijk, M. (2001). The social dimensions of business excellence. *Corporate Environmental Strategy, 8*(3), 223-233.

Huhns, M. N., & Stephens, L. M. (1999). Personal ontologies. *IEEE Internet Computing, 3*(5), 85-87.

Kannapan, S., & Taylor, D. (1994). The interplay of context, process, and conflict in concurrent engineering, *Journal of Concurrent Engineering Research and Applications, 2*(1), 183-196.

Kwan, M. M., & Balasubramanian, P. (2003). Process-oriented knowledge management: A case study. *Journal of Operational Research Society, 54*(1), 204-211.

Lee, H., & Choi, B. (2003). Knowledge management enablers, processes, and organizational performance: An integrative view and empirical examination. *Journal of Management Information Systems, 20*(1), 179-228.

Lu, S. C.-Y., & Cai, J. (2001). A collaborative design process model in the sociotechnical engineering design framework. *Artificial Intelligence for Engineering Design, Analysis and Manufacturing, 15*(1), 3-20.

Nonaka, I., Reinmoeller, P., & Senoo, D. (1998). The "ART" of knowledge: Systems to capitalize on market knowledge. *European Management Journal, 16*(6), 673-684.

Nonaka, I., & Takeuchi, H. (1995). *The knowledge-creating company*. New York: Oxford University Press.

O'Leary, D. E. (1998). Enterprise knowledge management. *IEEE Computer*, 54-61.

Preece, A., Flett, A., & Sleeman, D. (2001). Better knowledge management through knowledge engineering. *IEEE Intelligent Systems*, 36-43.

Reimer, U., Margelisch, A., & Staudt, M. (2000). EULE: A knowledge-based system to support business processes. *Knowledge-Based Systems, 13*, 261-269.

Rouse, W. B. (2001). Need to know: Information, knowledge, and decision making. *IEEE Transactions on Systems, Man, and Cybernetics. Part C: Applications and Reviews, 32*(4), 282-292.

Shaw, D., Ackermann, F., & Eden, C. (2003). Approaches to sharing knowledge in group problem structuring. *Journal of the Operational Research Society, 54*, 936-948.

Siau, K. (1999). Information modeling and method engineering: A psychological perspective. *Journal of Database Management, 10*(4), 44-50.

Sowa, J. F., & Zachman, J. A. (1992). Extending and formalizing the framework for information systems architecture. *IBM System Journal, 31*(3), 590-616.

Spender, J. C. (1996). Making knowledge the basis of a dynamic theory of the firm. *Strategic Management Journal, 17*, 45-62.

Staab, S., Schnurr, H.-P., Studer, R., & Sure, Y. (2001). Knowledge processes and ontologies. *IEEE Intelligent Systems*, 26-34.

Tanriverdi, H. (2005). Information technology relatedness, knowledge management capability, and performance of multibusiness firms. *MIS Quarterly, 29*(2), 311-335.

Vet, P. E., & Mars, N. J. (1998). Bottom-up construction of ontologies. *IEEE Transaction on Knowledge and Data Engineering, 10*(4), 513-526.

Wasserman, S., & Faust, K. (1994). *Social network analysis: Methods and applications*. New York: Cambridge University Press.

Zack, M. H. (1999). Managing codified knowledge. *Sloan Management Review, 40*(4), 45-58.

This work was previously published in Research Issues in Systems Analysis and Design, Databases and Software Development (Advances in Database Research Series), edited by K. Siau, pp. 185-205, copyright 2007 by IGI Publishing, formerly known as Idea Group Publishing (an imprint of IGI Global).

Chapter VIII
Towards a Virtual Enterprise Architecture for the Environmental Sector

Ioannis N. Athanasiadis
Dalle Molle Institute for Artificial Intelligence (IDSIA), Switzerland

ABSTRACT

This chapter introduces a virtual enterprise architecture for environmental information management, integration and dissemination. On a daily basis, our knowledge related to ecological phenomena, the degradation of the natural environment and the sustainability of human activity impact, is growing and as a consequence raises the need for effective environmental knowledge exchange and reuse. In this work, a solution among collaborating peers forming a virtual enterprise is investigated. Following an analysis of the main stakeholders, a service-oriented architecture is proposed. Technical implementation options, using Web services or software agents, are considered and issues related to environmental information management, ownership and standardization are discussed.

INTRODUCTION

On Service-Orientation

Service oriented approaches attract the broad interest of the scientific community, investing on the added value for the digital world of tomorrow. The promising point of service orientation is the synergy of computer science with artificial intelligence theories and computer networks practices. The primitives of distributed computing, the semantic Web, human-computer interaction, software engineering and agent computing are put together in order to design and deploy open, complex yet intelligent and adaptive computer systems that are based on simple agents of fine granularity, which, in turn, provide services in virtual enterprise (VE) environments.

Virtual enterprise architectures could be valuable for efficient information processing and open, loosely coupled service integration, not only in business-related sectors, from where they originate, but also in non-for-profit sectors. For example, consider these sectors related with public domain data and citizen-centered services in the context of e-government, e-health, e-agriculture, e-environment, e-science and so forth. In such a setting, the notion of a virtual enterprise is rather decoupled from its narrow business context, and extended to a broader scheme that accommodates constellations of cooperating service-providers. Service orientation became quite fashionable lately in several implementation variations, as those of software agents, Web services or grid computing. Each one of the technical solutions has advantages and disadvantages that make it more suited in some types of applications. For example, software agents are considered to be active entities, able to take initiatives, in contrast with Web services, which are required to be invoked, that is, operate in a passive way. In this respect, agents are well suited in competitive environments, as those of knowledge brokering and auction-like environments, while Web services are typically used for integrating heterogeneous components in open environments. Finally, grid computing seems more appropriate for computationally-intense applications. Whatever the application case or the suitable technical approach might be, unarguably, service orientation and virtualization remain a critical characteristic that aims in extending sytem capabilities through the composition of fine-granularity service elements with the ultimate goal of providing added-value services in dynamic environments.

This chapter explores the potential of formulating virtual enterprises for the environmental sector. Firstly, the background is set by introducing concepts related to environmental management information systems (EMIS) and the major challenges for environmental information processing and dissemination. Next, a virtual enterprise architecture for environmental information management is introduced and specifies the operational fashion of such a virtual enterprise. Finally, it summarizes latest developments on the field, and discusses the potential for wide-range adoption of virtual enterprises in the environmental sector.

ENVIRONMENTAL INFORMATION AND CHALLENGES

Environmental Data

Environmental data, although considered as public domain, have not been treated as such so far. Environmental information, either collected by public institutes, private industries or generated as a result of scientific computations in academia, has been kept for long in nonreusable, legacy systems and reports. Therefore the vision for enabling access to information and the provision of value-added services that will benefit from the information society initiatives, technologies and tools, often referred as e-environment, or e-agriculture applications, is still in infancy. Nowadays, there are ongoing efforts on defining standards for sharing data about the natural environment, including these published by the US Environmental Data Standards Council in January 2006 (EDSC, 2006) along with the standards developed gradually since 1994 by the european environment information and observation network (EIONET, 1994) and the guidelines (on vegetation plots and classifications) of the Ecological Society of America (VEGBANK, 2006). Also, Food and Agriculture Organization (FAO) of the United Nations has recently made its thesaurus of food and agricultural terms, publicly available through the AGROVOC Web services (AGROVOC, 2006). This task is part of FAO's activities for establishing agricultural information management standards. Significant is the contribution of the OpenGIS specifications by the Open Geospatial Consortium (OGC, 1994) for the standardization of geo-referenced data, which are very common in environmental applications.

However, it is still a long way to go for disseminating effectively environmental information, as there still are problems of data availability and quality that need to be addressed. As Dave Swayne underlined:

the problems of data quality and availability in environmental systems are areas of research that continue to require support" and that "the advances in database technology are not uniformly available in the environmental domain. (Swayne, 2003)

Common practice has proven that environmental data are usually stored in nonreusable raw formats, situated in sparse locations and managed by different authorities, which ultimately raise obstacles in making environmental information accessible. With the growing concern of the public for the sustainability of the planet and the degradation of the natural environment, environmental information, data acquisition management and processing and dissemination, becomes a key element for the sound justification of environmental studies, integrated assessment and policy making. A second issue related to environmental studies has to do with the scaling complexity and reuse of prior studies and models in new application areas. Open services for both data and model access and reuse are one of the important components that can boost future developments in the field. This chapter argues that service orientation and the formulation of virtual enterprises can be utilized for overcoming both of these two obstacles.

Environmental Management Information Systems

Environmental management information systems (EMIS) is a broad term that we use as an umbrella for a range of IT systems related to natural resources data management, varying from environ-

mental databases, simulation packages, reporting tools or visualization applications, geographical information systems (GIS), to extremely complex systems such as environmental decision support systems, or integrated assessment toolkits. An environmental management information system can be considered as an enterprise information system that provides efficient and accurate access to knowledge elements related to information about the natural environment. Collections of data sources and databases, simulation algorithms and environmental models, or decision support modules can be parts of an environmental management information system, which packages them together for addressing complex problems.

Among the challenges that modern environmental management information systems have to face is the documentation and dissemination of their results, ultimately via the provision of information services. Significant efforts are required for providing environmental information services to broad audiences, through the exploitation of digital technologies. Modern environmental management information systems are required to broaden their system goals and core requirements for encapsulating open dissemination e-services. Traditionally, environmental management information systems were developed for specific case studies, therefore the generalization of the approach and the potential reuse of the tools was a very seldom situation. This is partially an intrinsic characteristic of environmental systems, as model configuration and adaptation to local conditions is required. However, the disadvantages of EMIS development that do not confront to (any) common specifications become evident to the environmental community. Knowledge sharing, in any forms from raw data to sophisticated environmental model implementations, has become an increasingly important aspect of sound environmental management. As a consequence, the need for modular, service-oriented approaches rises to prominence.

This chapter investigates the potential of creating virtual enterprises for managing and disseminating environmental information, and summarizes recent developments towards this direction. Given the diversity of standards, formats and practices in collecting, managing and storing environmental data, alongside with the emerging need for sharing and disseminating environmental information to wide-ranging audiences, modular service-centered approaches, which form loosely-coupled synergies in open environments, can be the medium for overcoming the existing problems and meeting the requirements.

VIRTUAL ENTERPRISES FOR ENVIRONMENTAL INFORMATION

The Main Users

Day by day natural resources, the physical environment, and sustainability attain the interest of our society. As a result, the community of stakeholders asking for environmental information, from raw measurements to model simulation results or other kind of studies, is growing rapidly.

In this respect, there is an emergent need for sharing environmental information, among diverse and cross-disciplinary audiences. This is one of the major challenges that environmental management information systems are facing today: disseminating environmental information across a broad spectrum of potential end–users.

The major stakeholders involved in the life-cycle of environmental information are illustrated in Figure 1. They consist of the scientific community, governmental bodies and institutions, industry and the business sector, nongovernmental organizations and the wide public. Obviously, each one of them has its own perceptions, goals, objectives and interests on the environment and natural resources, which signifies the conflicting perspectives on environmental data interpretations. The main stakeholders and their involvement in the lifecycle of environmental information are summarized as follows:

a. **Environmental institutes:** Mainly occupied with the collection and the analysis of environmental data

b. **Scientific community:** Responsible for the study of the natural phenomena involved;

Figure 1. Main stakeholders to environmental information

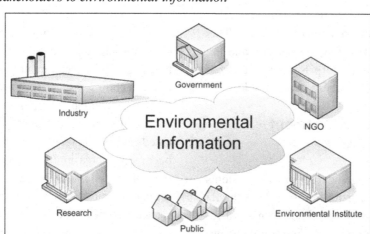

note that both environmental institutes and the scientific community are proposing policy options (alternatives) to the governmental bodies.

c. **Industry and the business sector:** Required to monitor the environmental effects of their activities, as a result of legal obligations, or even of their marketing strategies (as for example the ISO19000 family standards (ISO TC 211, 2004), the Eco-label products (ECO-LABEL, 1994), EMAS certifications (EMAS, 1995-2001), green technology campaigns, etc.)

d. **Government and governmental bodies:** Have the main responsibility of decision making and enforcing regulatory policies.

e. **Nongovernmental organizations:** Exist for a variety of purposes related to the preservation of the natural environment, and have very strong interests in accessing environmental information; NGO's participate in consultation procedures for policy-making and influence policy-makers to adopt environmental-friendly options.

f. **Public:** Generally interested in the preservation of the physical environment, natural resources and biodiversity, as a significant factor of every-day quality of life

From the description above, it becomes quite evident that there are significant disagreements among stakeholders' interests, which result to clashing interpretations of environmental data, as the basis for justifying policies, business-activity orientation and the expenditure of natural resources. Even if the various interpretations of environmental data are subjective, conflicting or overlapping, and raw environmental measurements often suffer from low reliability, there is a common, emergent need for *sharing environmental data*. In Figure 1, we illustrate the main stakeholders involved in environmental information management, as players around a cloud of environmental information, which they want to contribute in its creation, have effective access to it, and ultimately share.

On Virtualization of Environmental Information

In a collaborative setting that involves all the abovementioned users, environmental data need to be shared and re-used in different contexts and for divergent purposes. The virtualization of a collaborative environment is essential for treating environmental information as a common asset that is shared among peers, instead as a resource in scarcity that peers strive for. Environmental information is required to become a *virtual resource* that is manipulated by all virtual organization peers. In such a setting, the members of a virtual enterprise are enabled to construct scientific workflows for combining original data sources, with environmental models, reporting tools and consequently achieve their own goals.

The virtualization of environmental information, though, raises two very important issues: one is data standardization, and the second is related to data ownership and rights of disclosure. Related to the first one, XML documents associated with ontologies defining scientific data observations and measurements could be the way for resolving issues related to standardization. The success stories from several business sectors (i.e., in e-publishing, or in business-to-business services) are showing the way for similar development in environmental data management. Consider for example the contribution of ISBN/ISSN numbering system in the development of publishing business in a global scale, or the ebXML business standards. (See related the Organization for the Advancement of Structured Information Standards (OASIS) specifications available at: www.ebxml.org). Similar approaches for standardization of environmental data are required to be established, as those initiatives discussed earlier. A second aspect relates to issues of ownership and disclosure. On this front, the digital rights management frame could be followed. Although free access to environmental data is still mandated by the public's right to know about human health and environmental issues, there are often conflicts with other interests. For example, industrial patent protection, intellectual property rights or private information and privacy issues often conflict with the amount of information available. Also, note that even if in many countries there is a legal obligation for environmental reporting and dissemination, the frequency and scale of reporting is an issue of dispute among peers. Such issues of scale and access rights need to be handled effectively within a virtual enterprise for environmental data processing.

A FUNCTIONAL VIRTUAL ENTERPRISE FRAMEWORK ARCHITECTURE

Abstract Agent Roles in a Virtual Enterprise

To realize the requirements for making environmental data as commonly available as virtual resources, an abstract virtual enterprise architecture is presented which accommodates common stakeholders' needs and the requirements of sharing public domain data. Within the virtual enterprise, stakeholders can be represented, as agents that could potentially realize three roles (also discussed in Athanasiadis, 2006).

a. **Contribution agents:** These agents act as data fountains of the system and implement the appropriate interfaces to grant access to raw collections of environmental information. Contribution agents could be located in geographically remote locations. Contribution agents provide data gathering, and preprocessing services, including activities like filtering, standardization and normalization.

b. **Data management agents:** These agents are responsible for data fusion and processing. Data management agents operate as knowledge brokers, and are occupied with orchestration, and synthesis and querying activities and the calculation of environmental indicators.

c. **Distribution agents (DA):** These agents are the marketplace of environmental information, as they are occupied with publishing data to the final audiences. Distribution agents deliver the final data implement custom interfaces to the end-user applications.

These three roles are considered as agents to underline their proactive behavior within a virtual organization. To shed some light on this argument, contribution agents are not considered simply as a Web service or portal-like function that can retrieve environmental information upon request, that is, in a passive way, rather they have the responsibility to make available online resources. In this way, contribution agents take the initiative and make environmental information available to the virtual enterprise. In a similar fashion, data management agents capture information as it becomes available and exploit it appropriately. This could mean that, for example, that they run simulation models or execute environmental assessment toolkits as soon as the required inputs become available. Consequently, distribution agents are constantly updating end-user applications as environmental data and indicators are offered. In such a situation, a virtual enterprise for environmental information management and processing operates as a vigorous virtual organization that intentionally delivers tasks, instead of responding to final-audience requests. Agency of the three roles has the meaning of purposive action and proactiveness, as opposed to passive invocation of available services, rather than implying a technical restriction on the implementation side.

Integration and Demonstration

The integration of the previously discussed agent roles in a generic service-oriented architecture is presented in Figure 2. The main stakeholders involved in environmental data processing can engage services of three agent roles, based on their needs, interests or priorities. However, it must be pointed out that such an architecture requires that all agents in the virtual enterprise should adhere common semantics and standards in environmental data representation, as for example the ISO19100 family of spatial information standards. Ontologies could play a vital role in the definition of a general cognition within the virtual enterprise, that is, for specifying shared terms, vocabularies and data constructs. They could also be used for the integration/mediation of data with dissimilar semantics.

In Figure 2, an example virtual enterprise architecture is presented: we assume that industry, research, NGO and environmental institutes employ (several) contribution agents for "registering" their data and making them available within the virtual enterprise. Similarly, government, NGO, research and the public employ their distribution agents for granting access to the environmental information services available. Knowledge brokering and mediation is performed through the management agents which fuse data coming from contribution agents, process and combine services and ultimately make them available to distribution agents. Note that in this example the roles employed by each stakeholder are indicative. A detailed design of such a virtual enterprise may vary, depending on the technical solutions selected for deployment. Nevertheless it should include functionalities that support an open architecture, where agents of generic types may register and operate. In this respect, the requirements for extensibility and reusability are achieved, along with main objective for service composition and orchestration. Also, it should be pointed that each stakeholder could employ more than one agent, of the same or dissimilar types, according to their needs. Agent communication and service composition is an intrinsic characteristic of the proposed system.

Figure 2. An example virtual enterprise for environmental information management

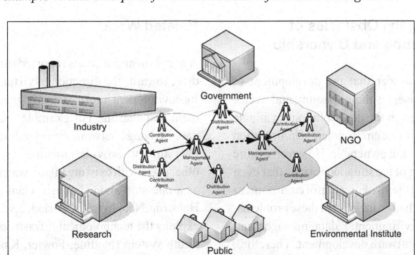

Implementation Considerations

The implementation of the system could rely either on Web services or software agent implementations, acting as service providers in an open, virtual, collaborative environment, which undertakes environmental information management tasks. In this way, a virtual enterprise is formulated that can both tackle the obstacles of legacy systems, data noise and redundancy, lack of data standardization and variety of data formatting and aggregation, and to (semi) automate the environmental data review processes by incorporating decision support capabilities (i.e., see Athanasiadis & Mitkas, 2004). Virtual enterprises for managing environmental data can ultimately come out with solutions for providing advanced information services to a wider user group. The need for conducting scientific workflows and the integration of environmental models, integrated assessment tools or raw environmental datasets can be also achieved within a virtual enterprise. In this way, future environmental studies could be built using existing components that are available as services from the peers of the virtual enterprise. Data sources, simulation or optimization models, and dissemination platforms are made available within the enterprise and can be reused for building up new services.

Overcoming the Obstacles of Standardization and Ownership

Some could consider that the development of virtual enterprises in the environmental sector is unrealistic, given the poor solutions available related to problems of environmental information standardization and ownership. However, a more positive reading of the situation reveals that even by investigating the virtualization of environmental information had brought forth these problems, essential to environmental data management, modeling and software development. Therefore, the virtualization of environmental information

should be considered as a motivation to tackle such problems, and as a part of their remedy. The adoption of service-orientation in environmental software, along with the virtualization of environmental information will eventually lead to solutions of these data-related problems. In the presented architecture, we consider environmental information to be provided in the virtual enterprise through the contribution agents. Let a contribution agent a be responsible for providing access to some data source. Through its proactive behavior, Agent a can require from the potential "consumers" that request portions of the date, to show credentials of their rights for accessing the data. Agent a may contact other services of the systems for verifying the credentials. A procedure for digital rights certification will essentially mandate the decision of agent a, whether to respond to a request or not, and in case it will, to decide how detailed this response should be (in terms of resolution, frequency, scale, units, etc). Such kind of negotiation among the peers within a virtual enterprise can resolve issues of data ownership, so that dissemination can be modularized, follow some rules, instead of the common situation of obscuring environmental data.

DISCUSSION

Related Work

A couple of applications reported in the literature drive towards the direction of virtual enterprises for environment information integration, management and sharing. For example, environmental data exchange network for inland water (EDEN-IW) aims to provide citizens, researchers and other users with existing inland water data, acting as a one-stop-shop (Felluga, Gauthier, Genesh, Haastrup, Neophytou, & Poslad, 2003). EDEN-IW exploits the technological infrastructure of Infosleuth system (Nodine, Fowler, Ksiezyk, Perry, Taylor, & Unruh, 2000; Pitts & Fowler, 2001), in which software agents execute data management activities and interpret user queries on a set of distributed and heterogeneous databases. Also, InfoSleuth agents collaborate for retrieving data and homogenizing queries, using a common ontology that describes the application field.

A quite analogous system that uses software agents for accessing environmental data is New Zealand distributed information system (NZDIS). NZDIS (Cranefield & Purvis, 2001, Purvis, Cranefield, Ward, Nowostawski, Carter, & Bush, 2003) has been designed for managing environmental metadata in order to service queries to heterogeneous data sources.

The Australian Bureau of Meteorology reports (Dance, Gorman, Padgham, & Winikoff, 2003) the development of forecast streamlining and enhancement project (FSEP), where agents are utilized for detecting and using data and services available in open, distributed environment. In FSEP agents manage weather monitoring and forecasts data.

Efforts towards the use of distributed architectures for environmental data integration and service provision have been given in the followings work also:

- **The Bremen University semantic translator for enhanced retrieval (BUSTER):** Utilizes ontologies for retrieving information sources and semantic translation into the desired format (Neumann, Schuster, Stuckenschmidt, Visser, & Vögele, 2001); BUSTER prototype is to be redesigned using software agents

- **The multi-agents-based diagnostic data acquisition and management in complex systems (MAGIC):** Even if it does not target only environmental applications, its objective is to develop a flexible multi-agent architecture for the diagnosis of progressively created faults in complex systems, by adopting different diagnostic methods in parallel. MAGIC has been demonstrated in

an automatic industrial control application (Köppen-Seliger, Ding, & Frank, 2001). A similar application, developed by the same team is the DIstributed Architecture for MONitoring and Diagnosis (DIAMOND) architecture, which adopts an agent-based architecture for distributed monitoring and diagnosis (Albert, Laengle, Woern, Capobianco, & Brighenti, 2003). DIAMOND will be demonstrated for monitoring of the water-steam cycle of a coal fire power plant.

- **The Rilevamento dati Ambientali con Interfaccia DECT (RAID):** This system deals with pollution monitoring and control in indoors environments. *RAID* exploits the general architecture of *Kaleidoscope* that uses "entities" for the dynamic integration of sensor (Micucci, 2002).

Towards the direction of virtual enterprises for the environmental sector fall our prior experiences in developing environmental information management systems in distributed agent-based architectures. The O$_3$RTAA system (Athanasiadis & Mitkas, 2004) utilizes a community of intelligent software agents for assessing urban air quality. O$_3$RTAA agents share a domain-ontology for capturing information from air quality monitoring sensors, assess air quality and ultimately disseminate alarms to the public. A follow-up generic middleware system called AMEIM (Athanasiadis, Solsbach, Mitkas, & Gómez, 2005) has been developed that enables a configurable community of software agents to adjust dynamically behavior by introducing new services dynamically, based on already existing ones.

Future Trends

Previous experiences in the above-mentioned applications give a clear indication that the technological infrastructure for realizing complex, distributed architectures that manage environmental data, are available. Building upon these experiences, this chapter proposed a virtual enterprise formulation that exploits a distributed, service-oriented architecture for efficient environmental data fusion. A new paradigm for future EMIS design and development is established. However, inborn properties of environmental information make things much harder in real world, large-scale implementations. The lack of standardization in environmental data management, or to rephrase it more precisely: the poor penetration of standards in the every day environmental data collection and management practices has already led to a Babel of environmental information. Sound and semantically consistent integration of these data is a critical requirement for knowledge sharing. Virtualization of environmental information is the mean for overcoming problems (as those mentioned previously), but also for maximizing reusability, open access and easy integration of environmental software services. Finally, the role of ontologies for environmental data annotation and modeling is essential in future work in virtual enterprises for the environmental sector.

REFERENCES

AGROVOC (2006). The AGROVOC multilingual dictionary of the United Nations Food and Agriculture Organization. Retrieved February 18, 2007, from www.fao.org/agrovoc/

Athanasiadis, I. N., & Mitkas, P. A. (2004). An agent-based intelligent environmental monitoring system. *Management of Environmental Quality, 15*(3), 238-249.

Athanasiadis, I. N., Solsbach, A. A., Mitkas, P., & Gómez, J. M. (2005). An agent-based middleware for environmental information management. In L. Filho, et al. (Eds.), *Second international ICSC symposium on information technologies in environmental engineering* (pp. 253-267). Osnabrück, Germany: Shaker-Verlag.

Athanasiadis, I. N. (2006). An intelligent service layer upgrades environmental information management. *IEEE IT Professional, 8*(3), 34-39.

Albert, M., Laengle, T., & Woern, H. (2002). Development tool for distributed monitoring and diagnosis systems. In M. Stumptner & F. Wotawa (Eds.), In *Proceedings of the 13th International Workshop on Principles of Diagnosis*, Semmering, Austria.

Albert, M., Laengle, T., Woern, H., Capobianco, M., & Brighenti, A. (2003). Multi-agent systems for industrial diagnostics. In *Proceedings of 5th IFAC Symposium on Fault Detection, Supervision and Safety of Technical Processes*, Washington DC.

Cranefield, S., & Purvis, M. (2001). Integrating environmental information: Incorporating metadata in a distributed information systems architecture. *Advances in Environmental Research, 5*, 319-325.

Dance, S., Gorman, M., Padgham, L., & Winikoff, M. (2003). An evolving multi agent system for meteorological alerts. In *Proceedings of the 2nd international joint conference on Autonomous Agents and Multiagent Systems, AAMAS-03*.

ECO-Label. (1994). The European ECO-label certification scheme for distinguished environmental friendly products. Retrieved February 18, 2007, from www.eco-label.com

EDSC (2006). Environmental data standards council data standards. Retrieved February 18, 2007, from www.envdatastandards.net

EIONET (1994). European environment information and observation network. Retrieved February 18, 2007, from www.eionet.europa.eu

EMAS (1995-2001). The eco-management and audit scheme (EMAS) registry of acknowledged organizations that improve their environmental performance on a continuous basis. Retrieved

February 18, 2007, from http://ec.europa.eu/environment/emas

Felluga, B., Gauthier, T., Genesh, A., Haastrup, P., Neophytou, C., Poslad, S., Preux, D., Plini, P., Santouridis, I., Stjernholm, M., & Würtz, J. (2003). *Environmental data exchange for inland waters using independent software agents* (Report 20549 EN). Institute for Environment and Sustainability, European Joint Research Centre, Ispra, Italy.

ISO TC 211 (2004). The ISO technical committee 211 ISO19000 standards series on geographic information/geomatics. Retrieved February 18, 2007, from www.iso.org

Köppen-Seliger, B., Ding, S. X., & Frank, P. M. (2001). European research projects on multi-agents-based fault diagnosis and intelligent fault tolerant control. *Plenary Lecture IAR Annual Meeting*, Strasbourg.

Micucci, D. (2002). Exploiting the kaleidoscope architecture in an industrial environmental monitoring system with heterogeneous devices and a knowledge-based supervisor. In *Proceedings of the 14th international conference on Software Engineering and Knowledge Engineering*.

Neumann, H., Schuster, G., Stuckenschmidt, H., Visser, U., & Vögele, T. (2001). Intelligent brokering of environmental information with the BUSTER system. In L. M. Hilty & P. W. Gilgen (Eds.), *International symposium informatics for environmental protection* (Vol. 30) (pp. 505-512). Metropolis, Zurich, Switzerland.

Nodine, M. H., Fowler, J., Ksiezyk, T., Perry, B., Taylor, M., & Unruh, A. (2000). Active information gathering in InfoSleuth. *International Journal of Cooperative Information Systems, 9*(1-2), 3-28.

OGC (1994). The open geospatial consortium. Retrieved February 18, 2007, from http://www.opengeospatial.org

Pitts, G., & Fowler, J. (2001). InfoSleuth: An emerging technology for sharing distributed environmental information. *Information systems and the environment* (pp. 159-172). National Academy Press.

Purvis, M., Cranefield, S., Ward, R., Nowostawski, M., Carter, D., & Bush, G. (2003). A multi-agent system for the integration of distributed environmental information. *Environmental Modelling & Software, 18*, 565-572.

VEGBANK (2006). The vegetation plot database of the Ecological Society of America. Retrieved February 18, 2007, from www.vegbank.org

This work was previously published in Agent and Web Service Technologies in Virtual Enterprises, edited by N. Protogeros, pp. 256-266, copyright 2008 by Information Science Reference, formerly known as Idea Group Reference (an imprint of IGI Global).

Section III
Tools and Technologies

Chapter IX
Computer Tools for Public–Sector Management

Carl Grafton
Auburn University Montgomery, USA

Anne Permaloff
Auburn University Montgomery, USA

ABSTRACT

Almost any public-sector task employing a computer can be accomplished more efficiently with a variety of tools rather than any single one. Basic tools include word processing, spreadsheet, statistics, and database-management programs. Beyond these, Web authoring software, presentation software, graphics, project-planning and -management software, decision analysis, and geographic information systems can be helpful depending upon the job at hand.

INTRODUCTION

The use of computer technology in government taps into three sometimes incompatible concepts: government responsiveness to the public, bureaucracy, and technocracy. The tensions between the first two have long been a staple of textbooks and scholarly work in public administration and organization theory (Blau & Meyer, 1971; Borgmann, 1988; Gullick, 1996; Rosenbloom & Kravchuk, 2002). At first, when all computers were mainframes, the technocratic perspective (rule by experts) appeared to bolster Weberian bureaucracies (Ellul, 1964; Freeman, 1974). Even today, computers are often used by bureaucrats to perform routine tasks efficiently or analysts to rationalize policy, and most of this chapter is taken up by descriptions of some of the tools available to them. However, today's computers are employed in far more ways and by many more members of all parts of government than they were a few years ago. The bureaucracy is less centralized just by virtue of the widespread access of government personnel to information and their ability to process that information.

Changes wrought by computers may go beyond bureaucratic decentralization. Eugene J. Akers (2006) speculates that government organized along Weberian bureaucratic lines is increasingly out of step with public expectations of a transparent and responsive service-oriented government. Similarly, Carl Grafton and Anne Permaloff (2005) depict what they call Jeffersonian budgeting: understandable government budgets available on the Internet with which the news media and the public can hold public officials accountable. In addition, Christa Slaton and Jeremy Arthur (2004) describe ways to facilitate public participation in government administration using computer technology.

This chapter concerns computer applications and information technology in government other than financial accounting software, which deserves a chapter of its own. Topics covered include Web publishing, spreadsheets, statistics packages, database management, presentation software, project-planning and -management software, decision analysis, graphics for illustrations, and geographic information systems. Since most readers are likely to have substantial word-processing experience, it would be unproductive to devote much space to this topic.

A VARIETY OF TOOLS

To make the most of their time and talents, computer users in the public sector or virtually any other setting should have access to more than one tool for nearly any task that extends much beyond typing a short memo. Access to a variety of tools is usually more productive than having the latest version of a single one.

Word-Processing and Web Authoring Software

Word-processing programs are designed primarily for generating print and graphic images on paper; Web authoring programs do the same thing for the Internet. Web pages are generated using HTML (hypertext markup language) sometimes in conjunction with supplemental tools such as Java, a programming language.

When a browser such as Microsoft Explorer reads a file containing HTML code (called tags) and text, it displays the file on the computer monitor according to formatting information in the tags (e.g., whether text is centered or in bold face or whether a separate file containing a graphic image is to be merged with the text). The marketplace offers a variety of text editors primarily designed to generate text with HTML tags (see Kent, 2000, for a list). Ordinary word-processing software can do so as well, but specialized HTML editors contain more features that ease the process of Web-page creation or maintenance.

Most government agencies have adopted particular HTML editors that employees are expected to use. Government agencies often appoint individuals responsible for Web-page work partly to preserve consistency in appearance and also out of concerns for security. The majority of employees will submit text generated with an ordinary word processor along with graphic images to accompany the text to these specialists who will then convert these files into Web pages.

The authors' experience in using government Web sites suggests that they are of three basic types: marketing, informational, and interactive. Marketing sites are designed for such purposes as to attract students to universities and visitors to cities. Marketing sites usually contain photographs scanned from prints or downloaded from a digital camera together with attractively arranged text and various decorative graphics. A certain amount of taste is required to make the marketing part of a Web site attractive, and the assistance of someone with a background in art might be helpful. Peter Kent (2000) lists Web sites that collect badly designed Web sites including one called *Web Pages That Suck: Learn Good Design by Looking at Bad Design*. While the bad Web-site collections dramatize how Web designs can go horribly wrong, fledgling designers will also want to visit sites of organizations similar to theirs to see what works.

Most Web pages presented by government agencies are meant to be entirely informational. Beyond basic neatness, the only significant design considerations are clarity and consistency. For example, the Web sites of most states and cities describe tax structures. These sites typically provide an overview and links that lead to more detailed information such as how taxes can be calculated and paid. These pages are usually quite informative, but sometimes a variety of fonts and formats are employed. For example, in one state, some pages contained buttons while others used simple lists, giving the whole enterprise a somewhat unprofessional appearance. Sometimes information is simply difficult to find, and built-in Web-site search engines require overly precise wording.

Interactive Web sites are the most difficult to build (Kent, 2000). Interactive sites gather information from users. They may take orders for goods or services, maintain an inventory of goods and services available, and accept credit-card information, among other tasks. An example is an online university class-registration system. Interactive sites require specialized programming skills beyond the reach of most public administrators. It is critical that potential users test all Web sites, especially interactive ones. Information and procedures that seem clear to programmers may be sources of confusion and irritation to those unfamiliar with a Web site's logic.

Richard Heeks (2006) observes that failed or flawed Web sites and other IT applications may be found at all levels of government. The central cause of failure is that the planning, construction, implementation, and maintenance of IT systems are important to many actors including agencies with differing responsibilities and agendas, elected members of the executive and legislative branches, and competing vendors, but participation is often limited to engineers, programmers,

and high-level management (Coursey & Killingsworth, 2005). Most government employees lack IT backgrounds and tend to surrender Web-site and IT-system development and maintenance to technical personnel. If a system is to serve the needs of all stakeholders including government agency clients, participation in system design must be widespread.

Spreadsheets

No desktop computer tool is more widely used for numerical data storage and analysis than the spreadsheet family of programs. Desktop computers are ubiquitous in homes and workplaces, and spreadsheet programs such as Excel reside on many hard disks as part of a suite of programs; however, a large percentage of public managers know little about spreadsheet operations beyond basic budgeting uses.

Programs such as Excel present the user with a series of worksheets grouped as a book of related information. Each worksheet is a grid of columns and rows. The rectangular intersection of a column and row is a cell. Three major kinds of information may be entered into a cell: text, numbers, and formulas that perform calculations on the numbers or on other formulas. Excel, by far the most widely used spreadsheet program, is also able to utilize Visual Basic, the program language common to the products that make up the Microsoft Office Suite. In addition to performing calculations based on user-inputted formulas, spreadsheet programs can produce graphics such as pie charts, bar charts, and time-series graphs, and they can be used to query a database stored in the spreadsheet. They can also perform statistical analysis with a variety of built-in tools and add-ins (defined below). In addition, the spreadsheet program's basic worksheet is one of the formats used for inputting data into a variety of other programs. It is also used as a format for downloading information (e.g., budget information and election results) from public Web sites.

Benefit-Cost Analysis

Benefit-cost analysis compares the benefits and costs of various choices and selects the choice that yields the highest net benefit (Ammons, 2002; Boardman, Greenberg, Vining, & Weimer, 2001; Stokey & Zeckhauser, 1978). In practice, most benefit-cost problems involve capital expenditures where benefits and costs are received and spent over a period of years.

The first step in performing a benefit-cost analysis is to list sources of benefits and costs associated with a project (Panayotou, n.d.). In this initial phase, the focus is on categories, not dollar amounts. For example, a benefit-cost analysis of a proposed monorail in Seattle listed the following benefits to monorail riders: travel-time savings, parking savings, automobile cost savings, and reliability. Those who continued to drive would enjoy the benefit of lessened traffic congestion (DJM Consulting, 2002; Slack, n.d.).

The second step is to evaluate the relationship between costs and benefits. The analyst is studying the causal relationship (or lack thereof) between expenditures and the benefits they yield (Panayotou, n.d.; Schmid, 1989). For example, the Seattle monorail benefit-cost analysis included an estimate of ridership partly based on comparisons with rail systems in other cities (People for Modern Transit [PMT], n.d.). The three largest benefits (travel-time savings, parking savings, automobile cost savings), which constituted more than 86% of claimed benefits, were heavily dependent on a ridership estimate that could only have been an approximation, a point ignored in a PowerPoint briefing presented by a consulting firm employed by advocates of the monorail. A benefit-cost analysis that fails to provide a range of estimates of critical parameters should be regarded with deep suspicion.

The next step is to establish direct effects of a project: the dollar benefits to project users and costs to build the project. When the market is functioning, project costs are simply off-the-shelf costs (e.g., concrete for highway construction; Levin, 1983; Nas, 1996). If market failure exists (e.g., leading-edge technology provided by a small number of competitors), cost valuation becomes more difficult (Panayotou, n.d.).

In some cases, project benefits are comparable to products or services sold in the private sector. An example is public housing. The value of a public-housing apartment will be close to that of a similar apartment offered by the private sector. If the government decides to offer units at a discount, the benefit to the renter will be the difference between the private-sector value of the apartment and the rent actually being charged. However, project benefits are often not directly comparable to private-sector market values. Thus, for example, a monorail may offer a faster and safer route. The problem is how to value time saved and deaths averted. In the case of the Seattle monorail, travel time was valued at $10.10 per hour, an amount that was half the mean wage rate in that area in 2002 (Slack, n.d.). The value of a life saved is more problematic, and the benefit-cost analysis literature offers many ways of doing so, most of which produce widely varying results (Fuguitt & Wilcox, 1999; Nas, 1996). Advocates of the Seattle monorail claimed $6.3 million in savings from reduced motor-vehicle accidents, but apparently these figures were confined to property damage and not loss of life.

The indirect effects of a project impact individuals or groups who are not users of project output (Schmid, 1989). With the monorail, those who can avoid driving automobiles through Seattle's crowded streets and parking them at high cost are direct beneficiaries. Those whose property values are increased or decreased or who experience other economic impacts because of the monorail are experiencing indirect benefits or costs (Marsden Jacob Associates, 2005; Tindall, 2005). Note that a single individual can enjoy both direct and indirect benefits or pay both direct and indirect costs. The distinction between direct and indirect effects is useful for organizing a benefit-cost study, but whether a given effect is placed in one or the other category should not have an impact on the results.

The two most common numerical indicators used in benefit-cost analysis are net benefits and the benefit-cost ratio. Net benefits are the difference between benefits and costs calculated on a present-value basis. The benefit-cost ratio is benefits divided by costs also on a present-value basis. The present value is the present-day equivalent of a stream of costs or benefits over time. The Seattle monorail net-benefit figure claimed by DJM Consulting in its 2002 briefing was $67 million. However, the benefit-cost ratio was only 1.04. In other words, the project would yield only $1.04 for every $1.00 spent. The 1.04 ratio represents a very thin margin. With slight cost overruns and tiny mistakes in ridership estimates, a 1.04 ratio could easily have flipped to less than the 1.00 breakeven point, and net benefits would have been negative tens of millions of dollars instead of positive. Again, the failure of this briefing to present ranges of estimates should have raised red flags. In fact, Seattle voters ultimately defeated the project.

The basic perspective of benefit-cost analysis is that of society as a whole (Fuguitt & Wilcox, 1999). So, for example, in a project's planning and construction phase, planners and engineers are benefiting in the form of fees and salaries, but from society's perspective, their benefits are costs. Society does not begin to benefit from a project until it is complete.

Large projects often affect geographical, racial, and other groups differently (Boardman et al., 2001; Nas, 1996; Schmid, 1989). Indeed, benefit-cost analysis' common society-wide perspective not only ignores such differential effects, but it may be biased against the disadvantaged. For example, other things being equal, benefit-cost analyses of alternative routes for a highway will favor a route plowing through economically depressed neighborhoods because property acquisition costs will be relatively low. For that

reason, the federal government discourages the use of benefit-cost analysis by states in making routing decisions (Clinton, 1994; Federal Highway Administration, 1998).

The formula for calculating present value for any benefit or cost stream is:

$$PV = S_0/(1+r)^0 + S_1/(1+r)^1 + S_2/(1+r)^2 + \dots + S_n/(1+r)^n,$$

where S_n represents any sum of money (benefit or cost) in year n, and r is the discount rate. The value of n may be the physical life of a project or its technologically useful life.

Performed on a hand calculator, the benefit-cost analysis of one or two streams of figures using the above formula is of no difficulty, but an actual benefit-cost analysis performed to aid decision making (as opposed to providing decorative support for decisions already made) typically involves sensitivity or "what if" analysis applied to combinations of benefits, costs, and discount rates. The basic question being posed by any kind of sensitivity analysis is how the result will be affected by change in inputs—in this case, benefits, costs, and the discount rate. If the estimates for each of these are all performed using a hand calculator, one is facing a considerable amount of work. With a spreadsheet such a prospect represents no problem.

Figure 1 shows a typical benefit-cost situation. In the first 2 years, benefits are zero because the project in question (e.g., a building) is under design and construction. The design and construction costs are relatively high compared to annual benefits. Because high design and construction costs are incurred in the first few years, they are discounted relatively little by the present value formula. The smaller benefit figures are more and more heavily discounted as they extend further into the future. Thus, the higher the discount rate, which governs the severity of the discounting, the worse the project will look as calculated either by net benefits (benefit minus cost) or the benefit-cost

Figure 1. Benefit-cost analysis using a spreadsheet

	A	B	C	D	E	F	G	H	I	J
1					Benefit-Cost Estimates					
2					(millions of dollars)					
3										
4										
5					Year					
6			0	1	2	3	4	5	6	
7	Pessimistic benefits		0	0	3	3	3	3	3	
8	Most likely benefits		0	0	3.5	3.5	3.5	3.5	3.5	
9	Optimistic benefits		0	0	3.8	3.8	3.8	3.8	3.8	
10	Pessimistic costs		1.5	14	0.2	0.2	0.2	0.2	0.2	
11	Most likely costs		1	12	0.1	0.1	0.1	0.1	0.1	
12	Optimistic costs		0.9	10	0.08	0.08	0.08	0.08	0.08	
13										
14										
15			=NPV(C19,$D$7:$I$7)+$C$7							
16						=NPV(C19,$D$10:$I$10)+$C$10				
17					Present Value					
18	Benefits	Costs	Rate	Benefits	Costs	Net				
19	Pessimistic	Pessimistic	0.03	$13.34	$15.98	($2.64)	=D19-E19			
20	Most likely	Pessimistic	0.03	$15.56	$15.98	($0.42)				
21	Optimistic	Pessimistic	0.03	$16.90	$15.98	$0.91				
22	Pessimistic	Most likely	0.03	$13.34	$13.10	$0.24				
23	Most likely	Most likely	0.03	$15.56	$13.10	$2.47				
24	Optimistic	Most likely	0.03	$16.90	$13.10	$3.80				
25	Pessimistic	Optimistic	0.03	$13.34	$10.96	$2.37				
26	Most likely	Optimistic	0.03	$15.56	$10.96	$4.60				
27	Optimistic	Optimistic	0.03	$16.90	$10.96	$5.93				

Figure 2. Pivot table output

		Present Value Net Benefits				
				Rate		
Benefits	Costs	0.03	0.035	0.04	0.045	0.05
Most likely	Most likely	2.47	2.24	2.02	1.80	1.59
	Optimistic	4.60	4.36	4.12	3.90	3.68
	Pessimistic	-0.42	-0.63	-0.84	-1.03	-1.23
Optimistic	Most likely	3.80	3.55	3.30	3.06	2.83
	Optimistic	5.93	5.67	5.41	5.16	4.91
	Pessimistic	0.91	0.68	0.45	0.23	0.01
Pessimistic	Most likely	0.24	0.06	-0.12	-0.30	-0.47
	Optimistic	2.37	2.18	1.98	1.80	1.62
	Pessimistic	-2.64	-2.81	-2.98	-3.13	-3.29

ratio (benefit divided by cost). Obviously, results also depend on cost and benefit estimates.

The table at the top of Figure 1 contains six sets of pessimistic, most likely, and optimistic benefits and costs. We are assuming a range of discount rates from 3 to 5% increasing in one half of 1% increments. The table below the top table contains all possible combinations of benefits, costs, and discount rates; it is used to build a pivot table (see below) to display the results in a readable fashion. The formulas in the present value columns for benefits and costs all resemble

the ones in cells D19 and E19. The formulas in Column F all resemble the one in cell F19.

The syntax of the present value (NPV) function is =NPV(rate,range), where rate is the discount rate and range is a range of cells. Column C contains the discount rates. As the Excel's help utility notes, the NPV function begins discounting with the first cell in the range specified in the formula. Thus, if the block D10:I10 was replaced with C10:I10, the NPV function would begin the discounting 1 year too early. The cell address of the cost for year 0 is subtracted separately (cell C10). There is at least one way to enter the benefit-cost data that would make keying in the formulas more efficient than what we show in Figure 1, but our presentation demonstrates the basic principles more clearly.

The pivot table in Figure 2 summarizes all the combinations of benefits, costs, and discount rates within the specified ranges. Note that along each row, the present value figures decline with increasing discount rates, as they must. This distinctive pattern does not guarantee that the functions in Figure 2 were entered correctly, but it suggests that they were. This table would give decision makers a sense that optimistic or most likely assumptions would produce positive results even at the highest calculated discount rate, but that some inclusion of pessimistic benefit or cost assumptions can generate negative results.

Pivot Tables

We saw that Figure 1 displays part of a worksheet containing four dimensions: benefits characterized as pessimistic, most likely, and optimistic; costs with the same labels; discount rates; and net benefits. There is no way to display all of these data on a single two-dimensional worksheet. It would be even worse if there were an additional dimension such as geographical area. The pivot table in Figure 2 allows us to see benefit and cost categories in rows and rates in columns. Had it been necessary to include geographical categories, they could have been added as well. Potential reader confusion limits the number of variables that can be included in a single pivot table, but it is an efficient way to lay out multidimensional data sets. We lack the space to explain the steps required to build a pivot table, but many reference works (e.g., Berk & Carey, 2004) and Excel help screens explain it clearly. The pivot-table procedure allows us to include and exclude whatever data we want.

The data filter function offers another way to suppress or include data. The data filter function is invoked in Excel by clicking in succession on Data, Filter, and Autofilter. This choice automatically generates menus at the top of a worksheet—one menu for each column. For example, in Figure 1, the menu for the benefits column (beginning in cell A18 and going downward) contains the three benefits categories (pessimistic, most likely, and optimistic). By selecting, for example, pessimistic benefits and in the next column pessimistic costs, the worksheet would seem to eliminate all other benefits and costs, giving the decision maker a quick look at the worst-case scenarios at various discount rates for this project.

Spreadsheets and Statistics

Spreadsheets possess statistical computing capabilities adequate for many public-administration tasks. Excel can perform basic descriptive statistics, curve smoothing, analysis of variance, multiple regression, random number generation, sampling, *t*-test, and others. These capabilities are part of the Analysis ToolPak, an add-in that comes with all versions of Excel that are likely still to be in use. An add-in is a computer program that when installed merges with a base program (Excel in this case) making the add-in an integral part of the base program. Excel's Analysis ToolPak can be supplemented by another add-in called StatPlus, available with *Data Analysis with Microsoft Excel* (Berk & Carey, 2004). Various editions of this reasonably priced text contain versions of StatPlus designed to work with specific versions of Excel and Windows. This book is perhaps the most clearly written and informative introduction to spreadsheet usage and introduction to statistics on the market. Relatively advanced statistical analysis cannot be done readily or at all with Excel, but for many administrative jobs, it may be adequate. Advanced work is more conveniently performed using statistics packages to be discussed later.

Spreadsheets are better tools than statistics packages for data entry, data editing, data storage, and printing. A statistics package is a computer program optimized for statistical analysis. Generally speaking, the best statistics packages (e.g., SYSTAT, SPSS, and NCSS) are more suitable for statistical analysis than are spreadsheets, but spreadsheets are superior for printing raw data as well as performing a wide variety of nonstatistical quantitative chores. If spreadsheet data entry follows simple rules specified by all leading statistics package manufacturers, the data may be exported to the statistics package; leading statistics packages can read spreadsheet files almost as easily as they can their native format.

Data to be read by a statistics package should be arranged so that the top row is devoted to variable names and each subsequent row is an observation. For example, if the analyst is examining U.S. coal-mine fatalities over time, data would be arranged as seen in Table 1.

Elsewhere on the worksheet, the definitions of the variables can be entered along with data sources and other information. It is especially convenient to enter such information in the form of comments in cells containing variable names. Some statistics packages allow such comments to be added to a data set, but many do not.

Note that the FATLPERMINER variable in Column D was calculated with a formula that reads =C2/B2. This formula (entered in D2) was copied downward to the last row of data. Someone new to spreadsheet work might think that the copied versions of this formula would all generate the

result 0.002197, but spreadsheet formulas should not be read literally in terms of specific cell locations, but in terms of the relationship among cells. So, for example, the formula in D2 is correctly interpreted to mean to take the number in the Cell One to the left of D2, divide it by the number in Cell Two to the left of D2, and display the result in D2. This is called a relative cell reference formula. When this formula is copied, it maintains this relationship wherever it is put unless the user writes an absolute cell reference formula.

If it is determined that a variable (column) is no longer needed, it can be easily eliminated in a spreadsheet. If a transposition of variables (columns) can aid readability, this is much more easily accomplished with a spreadsheet than a statistics package.

Data sets can easily number 50, 100, 200, or more variables. To avoid mistakes while inputting data, it is important that a key variable, such as YEAR in this example, remain in view. With many statistics-package data-entry screens, when more than approximately five variables have been added, the first column (variable) scrolls to the left out of sight. The invisibility of the YEAR variable could easily result in the user entering data for 1999 when it should be in the 2000 row. With a spreadsheet, the YEAR column may be frozen so that it is always in view. Similarly, with some statistics packages, once data have been entered for roughly the first 20 years, variable names scroll away upward. In a spreadsheet, variable names

Table 1. Example of data arrangement to be read by a statistics package

	A	B	C	D
1	YEAR	MINERS	FATALTIES	FATLPERMIN-ER
2	1935	56,5316	1,242	0.002197
3	1936	58,4494	1,342	0.002296
4	.	.	.	.
5	.	.	.	.

can also be frozen in place. One can also view two entirely different parts of the worksheet with a split window, a feature we have not seen in any statistics-package data-input screen.

Many statistics packages lack even elementary print formatting capabilities producing crude-looking or confusing raw-data printouts. The statistics package output may be saved in a format readable by a word-processing program (or a spreadsheet) where the cleanup of layout and fonts may be accomplished. A spreadsheet allows complete control over what appears on which printout page. It is far superior to a statistics package in terms of the appearance of the printout.

Curve Smoothing and Forecasting

A time-series data set is "a sequence of observations taken at evenly spaced time intervals" (Berk & Carey, 2004, p. 408). Although it is characterized by serious theoretical weaknesses, the single moving average is one of the most common tools of applied time-series analysis, especially among financial securities analysts. The single moving average is easily calculated and plotted using a spreadsheet.

The time-series data in Figure 3 represent fatalities per coal miner in the years 1935 to 2005. The data are relatively noisy. To highlight trends obscured by year-to-year fluctuations and to perform rudimentary forecasting, it can be smoothed by calculating the mean of data over a number of time periods, in this case 10 years (see Berk & Carey, 2004, pp. 424-426). The first moving average data point (cell F11) is the mean of the first 10 years of raw data; the second moving average data point omits the first year of raw data and includes the 11th, and so forth.

The distance between the moving average curve and the raw-data curve is sensitive to changes in trend. Because each point on the moving average curve represents the past, each point on the moving average will be above raw data when the trend is down as it is in most of the years shown in Figure 3. Note the sharp spike in 1968. This data point might have reflected a

Figure 3. Curve smoothing with spreadsheets

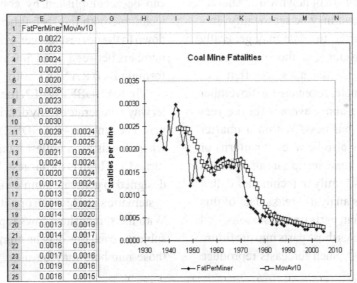

data-entry mistake, but in fact it was due to an increase in fatalities (222 miners in 1967 and 311 in 1968) combined with a decrease in miners (139,312 in 1967 and 134,467 in 1968; Mine Safety and Health Administration, n.d.). The moving average can easily be calculated by entering the formula and copying it or by using the Excel trend line dialog box.

In financial forecasting (e.g., the Dow Jones Industrial Average), moving averages of 30, 60, or even 90 days are common. In such calculations, each day is treated as being equally important; that is, data from a day 30, 60, or 90 days ago is accorded as much weight as yesterday's data. It seems likely that yesterday's data are somewhat more important than data from a day before that, which in turn is more important than data from 3 days ago, and so forth. A family of curve-smoothing techniques known as exponential smoothing takes this likely truth into account by systematically weighting more recent time periods more heavily than earlier ones (Fosback, 1987). Excel also contains a number of exponential smoothing techniques (see Berk & Carey, 2004, pp. 427-429).

Many time-series data sets contain several components. As we have already seen, one such component may be a trend, a relatively long-term tendency to move upward or downward. Another time-series component may be seasonality: In a given month or quarter, the data may generally be average, below average, or above average for the year. City sales-tax revenues are often seasonal with, for example, revenues for November and December being above average for the year because of holiday business. Within a quarter or month, there may also be weekly patterns or other cycles. Finally, time-series data also contain random variation. A family of techniques called complex time-series analysis breaks data of this sort into its component parts (trend, seasons, and cycles) and reassembles those parts into the future generating a forecast. Such forecasts reproduce

the long-term trend of the data set and the ups and downs of seasons and cycles to produce impressive-looking graphs. Of course, the accuracy of such forecasts depends on whether past trends, seasonal patterns, and cycles are maintained. Excel and StatPlus can almost automatically perform complex time-series analysis using trend and season but not cycle. The statistics package NCSS contains one of the most sophisticated time-series analysis modules that we have seen among general-purpose statistics packages (see as follows).

Sampling

Spreadsheets contain functions that can be used to generate random numbers convenient for sampling. In Excel, the function RAND() generates a random number greater than or equal to 0 and less than 1. For example, entering =RAND() into three cells yielded 0.917547614, 0.364495084, and 0.209362913. The numbers are evenly distributed. In other words, there is an equal likelihood that any digit will appear in any of the decimal places.

The Excel help utility advises the following: "To generate a random real number between a and b, use: RAND()*(b-a)+a." The generation of integers (whole numbers) instead of decimals can be accomplished by combining the above technique with the INT function, which rounds down to the nearest integer. For example, random numbers between 1 and 500 are generated by the formula INT(RAND()*500)+1.

The RANDBETWEEN function is an even easier way to generate evenly distributed random integers. The syntax is =RANDBETWEEN(low,high), where low is the smallest integer that will be returned and high is the largest. Worksheets can be designed to generate simple random samples and systematic samples with or without stratification. With the spreadsheet rows representing cases or subjects, each row may be numbered quickly, and those numbers may be used with a formula to generate a simple random sample. The stratified systematic sample is first developed by sorting the data on one or more variables (for example, sex). Using a formula to generate a skip interval (population size divided by sample size), it is easy to generate another formula for sampling the list once simple random sampling within the first interval generates a random start number. If the data were sorted by sex, the resulting sample will have numbers of males and females proportionate to their numbers on the list.

Spreadsheets contain a calendar with dates represented by integers that can be used to generate random dates between desired limits. The number 1 represents January 1, 1900, something that the reader can confirm by keying 1 into any cell and formatting it as a date (Format, Cell, Number, Date). The generation of random dates is accomplished by determining what integers represent the desired dates and setting up the correct INT(RAND()) or RANDBETWEEN formula.

Linear Programming

Linear programming is a technique for minimizing or maximizing a variable in the face of constraints. We might, for example, be attempting to minimize cost in a government cartography shop by making the most efficient use of equipment and personnel or to maximize the use of city garbage trucks by minimizing travel time between where they start in the morning, pickup locations, and dump locations (both examples are actual applications). Spreadsheets can perform such calculations. Explaining how data for a particular situation are arranged for linear programming solution in a spreadsheet requires far more space than is available here, but many texts on advanced spreadsheet usage provide guidance (Albright, Winston, & Zappe, 2006; Gips, 2002; Weida, Richardson, & Vazsonyi, 2001).

Database Applications

Everything regarding spreadsheet usage up to this point has concerned databases, but there are specific data-storage and -manipulation operations known collectively as database management. The traditional database structure is identical to the column (variable) and row (observation) arrangement discussed above except that in database management, columns are known as fields and rows as records. Inventories, mailing lists, and room assignments in buildings are examples of the kind of information stored and processed as part of database-management operations.

Spreadsheets can be used for this purpose if the number of records does not exceed the maximum number of rows in the spreadsheet. This amount varies depending on spreadsheet manufacturer and version, and it also may be limited by the amount of memory (RAM) in the computer. The practical maximum number of records is also governed by how the user plans to manipulate data; many operations can take additional space. With the spreadsheet software found on most computers of average memory capacity, a database larger than 5,000 records is probably better processed using a database-management program such as Microsoft Access or the easier to use and more reasonably priced Alpha-Five. Database-management programs are better suited to manipulating large data sets than spreadsheets. Database-management programs are also better suited for creating customized data-entry screens.

Statistics Packages

As noted previously, spreadsheets can perform statistical calculations and database-management programs can as well, but if those operations are many in number, involve relatively sophisticated techniques, and/or involve large data sets, statistics packages such as SYSTAT, SPSS, or NCSS are far superior to spreadsheets and database-management programs. For some calculations, statistics packages are the only tool that can be used by the nonprogrammer.

In public-administration applications, a statistics package might be used for elementary operations such as descriptive statistics. Even for this purpose, a statistics package is more convenient than a spreadsheet if work is to be done on more than a few dozen variables. Some policy analysis work requires more advanced techniques.

Regression Analysis

Regression analysis can be employed to explain the relationships between and among variables, and it can be used alone or in concert with other techniques for forecasting. Regression analysis is one of the most commonly described techniques in the statistics literature, and there is no point in our duplicating the many fine treatments of this subject (Berk, 1998; Berk & Carey, 2004; Garson, 2002; Schroeder, Sjoquist, & Stephan, 1986; Wilkinson, Blank, & Gruber, 1996). An example of one application of regression analysis concerns the relationship between the change in per-capita income and the change in university enrollment for the states. This example is part of a university lobbyist's claim that a state's economic well being was directly proportional to the number of people enrolled in universities. Using the language of statistics, a state's economic health was the dependent variable being acted on by the independent variable, higher education enrollment. Regression analysis allows the user to determine how much, if any, variation in a state's economic health is explained by variation in higher education enrollment.

Regression analysis is used in the fields of human-resource administration and justice and public safety to analyze whether discrimination based on race, sex, or other illegal factors is statistically likely. In this instance, regression

analysis with several independent variables (multiple regression) is often the tool of choice (Berk & Carey, 2004). Regression analysis also can be used for forecasting time-series data, with time serving as the independent variable (horizontal axis). The resulting regression line or the regression equation can be used to forecast the dependent variable, which can be anything from tax revenues to jail inmate populations.

Interrupted Time-Series Analysis

Interrupted time-series analysis, an application of regression analysis, is an especially helpful analytical tool for policy analysis (Welch & Comer, 1988). For example, the authors (Permaloff & Grafton, 1995) used it to test the claim that George Wallace's first term as governor had a positive effect on education spending in Alabama, and Bloom (1999) estimated educational program impacts on student achievement.

With interrupted time-series analysis, data must be available for a number of time periods before and after an event such as the election of a new governor or the enactment of a coal-mine safety law. This extremely useful technique measures whether the event has made a statistically significant difference and the nature of that difference. There are two basic kinds of statistically significant differences that an event can produce: an abrupt increase or reduction and a long-term increase or reduction. In addition, an event may produce no abrupt change and/or no long-term change. These alternatives yield nine possible combinations: no immediate change but a long-term increase, no immediate change but a long-term reduction, and so forth.

As an example, we can apply this technique to the data in Figure 3. Figure 3 shows a sharp spike in fatalities per coal miner that occurred in 1968 followed by a dramatic reduction after passage of the Coal Mine Safety Act of 1969 (CMSA). The question is whether the CMSA improved coal-mine safety. The analysis begins by adding two variables to the data set. One variable (CV) is a counter variable that begins at zero in 1935 and remains zero for each successive year until 1970 when it becomes one and remains one for the remaining years of the data set. A multiple regression analysis including CV will result in an indication of statistical significance connected with CV if there is an immediate or abrupt shift in fatalities per miner. The second variable is a post-policy intervention counter variable (PPICV). Like CV, it begins at zero in 1935 and remains zero for each successive year until 1970 when it becomes one and, unlike CV, it then increases by one in each successive year. There will be an indication of statistical significance for PPICV if continuing change occurs after CMSA.

Figure 4 shows SYSTAT output for the multiple regression analysis interrupted time series. The P(2 Tail) column shows that the CV variable is statistically significant beyond the 0.001 level, indicating that the drop after 1968 is statistically significant. On the other hand, the PPICV variable is not statistically significant showing that the long-term reduction in fatalities after 1968 is not statistically significant. However, this is only a first cut at the analysis. Many questions

remain. One concerns the 1968 spike. It alone could be the origin of statistical significance for CV. We eliminated the impact of the 1968 spike by replacing it with the mean of fatalities per miner for 1967 and 1969. The resulting analysis still showed CV to be statistically significant but this time at the 0.001 level. Nevertheless, the hypothesis that CMSA resulted in a one-time drop in fatalities is supported. (PPICV remains not statistically significant.)

The lack of statistical significance for PPICV may be in part due to the 1935 starting point that we selected. Soon after 1935, a sharp drop in fatalities began that continued until roughly 1950. The period of 1950 to 1970 was marked by a gradual increase in fatalities. After 1970, fatalities resumed their downward path. What would happen if we began the analysis with 1950 instead of 1935? The result is that both CV and PPICV were statistically significant beyond the 0.001 level suggesting that CMSA had both a short term and long term effect.

Questions regarding how to treat data spikes (or drops) and at what year the data series should be said to begin are very common in interrupted time-series analysis. Answers are matters of

Figure 4. Interrupted time series data output from SYSTAT

```
Dep Var: FATPERMINER   N: 71   Multiple R: 0.929   Squared multiple R: 0.863

Adjusted squared multiple R: 0.857   Standard error of estimate: 0.000

Effect        Coefficient   Std Error    Std Coef Tolerance     t    P(2 Tail)

CONSTANT         0.053        0.010        0.0        .        5.203    0.000
YEAR            -0.000        0.000       -0.654     0.120    -5.013    0.000
CV              -0.001        0.000       -0.343     0.250    -3.797    0.000
PPICV            0.000        0.000        0.042     0.187     0.405    0.686

                          Analysis of Variance

Source         Sum-of-Squares   df   Mean-Square    F-ratio      P

Regression         0.000         3      0.000       141.127     0.000
Residual           0.000        67      0.000
---------------------------------------------------------------------

*** WARNING ***
Case        36 is an outlier      (Studentized Residual =        3.280)

Durbin-Watson D Statistic    0.814
First Order Autocorrelation  0.590
```

judgment. The 1968 spike was real and certainly had to be included in a regression run, but it was an unusual figure that invited another run with the spike deleted. Similarly, the original data set from which we took these data began in 1900. We assume that it would not be appropriate to run the analysis that far back; presumably, coal-mine technology improved considerably since 1900, making data of that era meaningless. But at what time point should the analysis begin? If the authors possessed greater knowledge of mining technology, we could have selected a starting point that marked what might be termed contemporary technology. The only certainty is that this data set required multiple analyses and required that they be reported.

It should be noted that we omitted another factor that should be covered in a serious analysis of coal-mine safety: Surface mining is inherently safer than deep mining, and surface mining has increased over the years. A serious analysis would treat them separately. Again, this is the kind of judgment that must be made in analysis of this sort.

Curve Smoothing and Forecasting

SYSTAT, NCSS, SPSS, and other statistics packages contain a wide variety of curve-smoothing and forecasting techniques, some of which have already been discussed in connection with spreadsheets. Generally speaking, this kind of analysis is more conveniently done in a statistics package than a spreadsheet, and statistics packages offer a greater variety of analysis techniques.

Complex Time-Series Analysis

The topic of complex time-series analysis was introduced earlier in the section on spreadsheets. The NCSS statistics package contains one of the easiest to use and most sophisticated complex time-series analysis modules on the market as well as possibly the clearest documentation available

(Armstrong, Collopy, & Yokum, 2005; Jarrett, 1987; NCSS, 2004).

Database Management

Database-management software such as Micro-soft Access or Alpha-Five from Alpha Software Corporation is commonly used for personnel records, inventory management, or whenever large numbers of records will be stored. Database-management software is also ideal when data are to be entered by a computer novice. Data-input screens can be designed that include instructions for the user to help ensure that the correct types of information are keyed into particular fields. To some degree, each field can also be designed so that incorrect types of information cannot be entered. A spreadsheet can be modified in a similar fashion, but the expertise required to accomplish this is somewhat greater than is needed with a database-management program, especially one intended for ease of use such as Alpha-Five.

With database-management software, large numbers of records can be sorted and queried and particular records and particular fields can be printed or exported to other software (e.g., statistics, spreadsheet) for further processing. Database-management programs also are ideal for the generation of large numbers of mailing labels and form letters (Schmalz, 2006).

Access, Alpha-Five, and many other database-management programs are relational; they can link and draw information from two or more differently structured databases (as long as the databases have a common field) as if those databases were one (Grafton & Permaloff, 1993). This powerful feature is not shared with the other categories of software represented here.

On a recent project for a state government agency, we received two data files in Excel for each of 19 counties. The files had no common col-umn or field. We used Excel's LEFT and RIGHT functions to extract portions of one column in one data file to create a variable or field common to one found in the second data file. We then created one merged data file for each county using Alpha-Five. The Alpha-Five file is in dBASE format and readable by Excel and the statistics packages we use most often. We employed Excel pivot tables and sorting commands to generate descriptive data required for the project by the federal government. The databases were exported into SYSTAT for multiple regression and other analysis, including cross-tabulation with control variables and associated statistics. The extraction option in SYSTAT allowed us to create specialized subsets of the data files quickly and easily. Portions of the SYSTAT analysis output were saved in text format and read into WordPerfect for final report writing.

Large organizations sometimes buy specialized relational database-management programs set up for their specific applications. Such programs may cost thousands, if not hundreds of thousands, of dollars to buy, install, and maintain. Often a training component is included in the installation fee. Database-management programs are frequently used to store personnel records. Another function is the processing of government regulatory agency records. For example, a state regulatory board may have multiple responsibilities: licensing applicants to a profession, disciplinary functions including the receipt of complaints and their investigations, monitoring of continuing-education providers, and oversight of educational training programs. Each area would be served by different staff personnel with differing record-keeping needs. As long as each area has at least one common field such as Social Security number as an identifier linking the databases, one set of records could be queried for information needed by another area of the organization. For example, the licensing section may need to know the current status of disciplinary actions to determine if a renewal should be granted. With relationally linked databases, licensing personnel can query the separate components of the database as if they were a single database. At the same time, access to specific fields can be granted or blocked on a need-to-know basis.

We have observed three pitfalls with database management in government. If standard database software is adapted by a government agency employee for use by the agency (all such software is designed to be tailored to fit specific needs), it is important that at least one other employee be taught how the customization was implemented and backups be made of the complete system, and, of course, all data. If the employee who performs the customization leaves the agency and the computer on which it is running crashes, an agency can be left without access to its records or worse yet the records may disappear. In fact, this has happened. Events of this sort are less likely to occur if the program is sold and maintained by a commercial developer assuming that the developer remains in business.

Another database-management pitfall is the mutation of the database over a period of years with no records kept of changes made. The original database structure may be clearly described by paper or online documentation, but incremental modifications over a period of years with no accompanying editing of the documentation can produce a database difficult for newcomers to use.

A third pitfall is a database that does not reject grossly incorrect data entries. No software can detect slight numerical mistakes in a field intended to hold numbers such as a 1 instead of a 2, for example, but any modern database-management system ought to reject such mistakes as two-digit numbers entered where there should be three or letters entered where numbers are needed. Also, a database-management program should force input of data into a field containing mandatory information before allowing the user to complete follow-on fields. Database-management systems that permit gross mistakes will produce a database full of inaccuracies, especially when hundreds of people are keying in data.

Data Mining

Data mining is a collection of techniques primarily intended to handle extremely large secondary data sets. A secondary data set is by definition not collected with analysis as the primary objective, so the way this transactional information is gathered and structured may not be ideal for traditional statistical analysis. The Transportation Security Administration (TSA) provides an example of a large secondary data set. This agency uses credit reports and more than 100 commercial and government databases to identify potential terrorists among airline passengers (Rotenberg & Hoofnagle, 2003). Other examples of governmental use of data mining come from law enforcement, higher education, and tax administration (SPSS, n.d.).

Large data sets require enormous computer capacity and they sometimes are in the form of multiple related files (the TSA example above fits this characteristic). These factors mean that traditional statistical techniques cannot be applied without complicated sampling (Hand, 1998). Another problem with large secondary data sets is that they almost certainly contain contaminated data requiring mechanized (because they are so large) data cleaning.

The secondary nature of the data sets also means that they may be characterized by selection bias (some geographical regions may be over-represented) and nonstationarity (the population may be changing in subtle ways). These problems can also arise in smaller data sets, but they are more difficult to detect and correct in large data sets (Hand 1998).

Another complication with data mining is that it is often exploratory in nature (Statsoft, 2003). Analysts are often not testing relationships derived from theory as they do (or should) in academic research. Instead, they are frequently searching for unknown clues that lead to answers to vaguely defined questions (Hand, 1998). The sheer size of data-mining data sets combined with the frequent lack of theory also makes analysts vulnerable to discovering spurious relationships.

Data mining requires data-mining software, large computers, and specialists. Our sense is that an army of particularly hungry dealers and consultants awaits any government agency venturing into this field.

Project Planning and Management

Project planning and management programs are designed to assist in planning and managing complex projects in terms of time schedules as well as budgets, personnel, and other resources. This category of software can be used to schedule and estimate personnel requirements and budgets for construction jobs, landscape projects, conference planning, scheduling activities in a complex lawsuit, or any other enterprise with a clearly defined beginning and end. Over the years, the widely used Primavera Project Planner (P3) has received some of the most positive reviews, but Microsoft Project is easier to use. A Google search on "project planning software" will yield many other products, some of which offer free trial downloads.

Project planning requires that a project be broken down into building blocks called activities or tasks. An activity or task is the responsibility of one person, involves one kind of work, can be scheduled, and uses the same resources from beginning to end.

Gantt charts are one of two major graphical devices used by this family of programs. A Gantt chart is a bar graph with a horizontal bar representing each task in a project. Each bar's length is proportional to the time the task requires. The beginning of a bar is located at the start date of a task, and the end of the last bar is located at the date the last task should be complete.

The PERT (Project Evaluation Review Technique) chart is the other major graphical tool used by project-planning and -management programs. It is a better tool for highlighting relationships

Figure 5. A decision tree

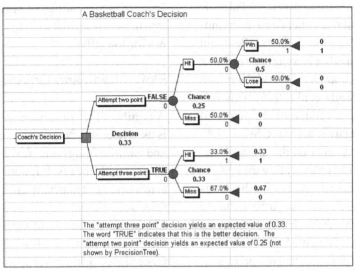

among tasks, but the Gantt chart is more space efficient, allowing more tasks to be displayed on screen or on a single sheet of paper. Programs of this sort can also display bar charts and tables showing personnel plans and budgets.

Information is entered in these programs in forms. The user keys in task names, duration, personnel, and other resources used to complete the task. The software calculates start and finish dates, personnel plans, budgets, and so forth.

Frequently, the first draft of a project plan results in an end date that is too late. These programs automatically highlight the longest path (the critical path) in a plan where a number of tasks are being executed simultaneously. In concentrating changes on the critical path, an administrator can reduce the completion time of the overall project by focusing attention where it will do the most good. Project planning and management programs are also used to monitor progress once a project is under way. Project-wide implications of early or late task completions are quickly observed.

Decision Analysis

Decision analysis is a graphical form of applied probability theory useful for analyzing situations in which uncertainty plays a part. The most common situation to which this technique is applicable has a decision maker trying to choose between two or more policies, each of which is associated with a variety of benefits and costs and probabilities that those benefits and costs will occur. In decision-analysis terminology, a benefit is a positive payoff and a cost is a negative payoff.

As an example, imagine that a basketball team is behind by two points, and it has time for only one shot. Assume that there is a 50% chance of hitting a two-point shot that would tie the game and a 33% chance of hitting a three-point shot that would produce a victory. Also, assume that the team has a 50% chance of winning in overtime. Which shot should the coach call (Clements, 2006)?

Figure 5 shows a decision tree that represents all possible futures in this situation. This decision tree was entered and calculated in an Excel add-in called PrecisionTree, manufactured by Palisade Corporation. It is available either from the manufacturer or in a trial version in an excellent and reasonably priced (for what it contains) textbook called *Data Analysis and Decision Making with Microsoft Excel* (Albright et al., 2006). This volume also comes with a version of the powerful and easy-to-use simulation tool @RISK.

The decision tree begins on the left with the rectangle (a choice node) representing the coach's choice. The choice to take the two-point shot leads to a chance node (a circle) offering a 50% chance of hitting the shot and a 50% chance of missing. We use 0 as the value of a game loss and 1 as the value of a victory. A miss at the two-point shot produces a payoff of zero. If the two-point shot is made, there follows another chance node offering a 50:50 chance of a win and a loss. If the coach's basic two-point choice could be made repeatedly as an experiment or simulation, the game would be won only 25% of the time. Instead of running this choice as an experiment or simulation, PrecisionTree can calculate the probabilities and payoffs. In this case, the coach should go for the three-point shot, which offers a 33% chance of victory.

Data such as the names of the branches, probabilities, and pay-offs are entered in the Precision-Tree program one form at a time. PrecisionTree draws the tree and calculates the result. The program also allows the user to conduct sensitivity analyses (with some difficulty at first) to determine the effect on the result of differing pay-off values (which would not arise in this case) and probabilities. Although this example is extremely simple, decision trees can be quite complex.

Graphics for Illustrations

Illustrations often play an important part in reports, presentations, budgets, and other docu-ments. Specialized software can be of great assistance, augmenting the graphics features built into the software discussed previously (Permaloff & Grafton, 1996).

Flow Charts and Organization Charts

A family of programs such as RFFlow and Visio is used to create flow charts, organization charts, and similar diagrams featuring boxes (of all shapes) and lines (solid, dotted, with or without arrowheads). Diagrams are created by the user selecting box shapes from menus, keying in labels (the boxes expand to fit labels), and connecting the boxes with lines also selected from menus. Once placed on the screen, boxes and lines can be rearranged as aesthetics and logic dictate.

The choice of programs depends on features needed, budget, and time available for learning. For example, comparing RFFlow and Visio, the former is the least expensive ($49 vs. $199) and by far easier to learn, but it is limited to creating flow charts and organization charts. Visio can render a greater variety of shapes, and it can be tied to powerful Visual Basic programs. Visio, like all Microsoft products, subjects the user to an intrusive online product-registration process lacking in RFFlow. As with most other products discussed in this chapter, a Web search yields many other flow-chart and organization-chart generation programs, many of which can be downloaded.

We do not recommend that most public administrators attempt to employ a computer-aided design (CAD) program for occasional diagram work unless the individual is already trained in its use. CAD programs can do far more than specialized flow-chart programs, but they exact an even higher price than Visio in terms of learning time, and they require many steps and much more time to complete tasks (see Permaloff & Grafton, 1996.)

Scanned Graphics

Documents can sometimes be improved with the inclusion of scanned material such as photographs. Scanners range in price from $50 to approximately $650, but even the least expensive are sufficient for many applications. Flatbed scanners are probably the easiest to use. The flatbed scanner resembles a small photocopy machine. The original image is placed in the scanner that generates a digitized version of the image that can be saved on disk and inserted into application programs including word processing, spreadsheet, database management, and project planning. In some cases, the image can be dragged directly from the scanning program into an application program without the need to save on disk.

Presentation Programs

The use of computers and computer projection hardware or large monitors for presentations is gaining in popularity as the cost of projection equipment declines. Although 35mm slides, the old mainstay of presentations, are virtually gone, computer presentations are built on what might be termed virtual slides. Transparencies, another kind of slide, are still used, but they appear to be regarded as passé despite their continued practicality, readability on a large screen, and low cost.

A computer slide may contain any combination of text and graphics, including sound and motion. A single slide may contain elements from several sources. Menu choices or built-in templates determine the background on which text and/or graphics will appear. That background can be any color or texture. Similarly, each slide's basic layout (whether there is a centered heading, bulleted text, a graphic, columns, etc.) is chosen from menus or templates.

It is easy to include so many clever graphics and sound effects in a computer presentation that the audience is distracted from content or even irritated by excesses. Indeed, a former chairman of the Joint Chiefs of Staff became so annoyed with elaborate PowerPoint presentations he reportedly attempted to ban the program's use in the military.

Another drawback of slide presentations is audience boredom, a major reason some presenters employ what they hope are entertaining effects. One clever and subtle solution to the boredom problem is the use of two projectors and two screens. Image 1 appears on Screen A and then Image 2 on Screen B (with Image 1 still seen on Screen A). Image 3 then replaces Image 1 on Screen A, and so forth. This idea's effectiveness must literally be seen to be believed. It reduces boredom and eliminates the need for gimmicky dissolves from slide to slide.

Geographic Information Systems

Geographic (or geographical) information system (GIS) programs assemble, store, and display data that are specific to geographical areas such as countries, states, counties, or zip codes. Data might include information regarding population, economics, numbers of users of government agency services, and crime rates. Data are typically displayed in the form of maps in which geographical areas are colored or patterned to represent various levels of whatever is being measured (Garson & Vann, 2001; Orford, Harris, & Dorling, 1999; Vann & Garson, 2001; Vann & Garson, 2003).

Some GIS programs such as MapInfo and BusinessMAP are free standing while others are attached to software such as Excel or Visio. GIS packages vary widely in terms of file formats that they can read, data-manipulation features, display capabilities, and price, so considerable research is required to make an informed purchasing decision. A list of resources including GIS programs, boundary files, and data files is available at the Web site of the Department of Geography, University of Edinburgh (http://www.geo.ed.ac.uk/home/agidict/welcome.html).

LONG-TERM STORAGE

Editable data files (e.g., word processing or work-sheets) and scanned images of printed pages can be stored digitally for archival purposes. But on what medium should archived documents be stored? One convenient but unsafe possibility is CD-R (compact disk-recordable) or CD-RW (compact disk-rewritable) disks. Unfortunately, these media may not be suitable for long-term storage. CD-R and CD-RW disks are not the same as CD-ROMs (compact disk–read only memory), which are commonly used for commercial software and music. CD-ROMs are manufactured by molding polycarbonate with pits that constitute digital information. The pits are then coated with a reflecting layer of metal. That layer is then coated with protective plastic. Even these relatively tough disks can be rendered unreadable by scratches, but with careful handling, they can probably last for decades.

Recordable or rewritable disks probably have a much shorter life span because they are physically more delicate. CD-Rs use transparent dye, not pits, as their data-storage method. When the disks are "burned," the computer's laser darkens the dye. CD-RWs use an alloy that changes state when the recording process occurs (Ancestry.com, 2000). CD manufacturers claim that recordable and rewritable disks can last for decades, but Kurt Gerecke, an IBM storage specialist, estimates that inexpensive and high-quality disks only last approximately 2 to 5 years, respectively (Blau, 2006). Gerecke also cautions against relying on a hard drive for archival purposes. Here the problem is not surface degradation, but the longevity of the disk bearings. Gerecke recommends magnetic tapes for long-term storage. Tape life spans range from 30 to 100 years depending on their quality (Blau; Practical PC, n.d.).

Storage media formats represent another and different kind of problem for archiving. Consider how difficult it would be to locate a disk drive that can read a $5\frac{1}{4}$-inch floppy disk much less the larger format that preceded it. The safest materials for long-term storage may still be paper and microfilm or microfiche.

CONCLUSION

Most tasks in government employing a computer can be accomplished more efficiently with a variety of tools. Happily, most of those tools are under $500. Of the software discussed here, only customized database-management programs, data-mining software (which often require highly trained staff or hired consultants), and high-end geographic information systems go past the $1,000 mark.

REFERENCES

Akers, E. J. (2006). *A study of the adoption of digital government technology as public policy innovation in the American states.* Unpublished doctoral dissertation, Auburn University, Auburn, AL.

Albright, S. C., Winston, W. L., & Zappe, C. J. (2006). *Data analysis and decision making with Microsoft Excel* (3rd ed.). Stamford, CT: Duxbury, Thomson Learning.

Alpha-Five [Computer software]. (n.d.). Burlington, MA: Alpha Software Corporation. Retrieved from http://www.alphasoftware.com

Ammons, D. N. (2002). *Tools for decision making.* Washington, DC: CQ Press.

Ancestry.com. (2000). *The life span of compact disks.* Retrieved March 26, 2006, from http://www.ancestry.com/learn/library/article.aspx?article=2131

Armstrong, J.S., Collopy, F., & Yokum, J.T. (2005). Decomposition by causal forces: A produce for forecasting complex time series. *International Journal of Forecasting, 12* (pp. 25-36).

Berk, K. N. (1998). *Introductory statistics with SYSTAT.* Upper Saddle River, NJ: Prentice-Hall.

Berk, K. N., & Carey, P. (2004). *Data analysis with Microsoft Excel: Updated for Windows XP.* Belmont, CA: Brooks/Cole–Thomson Learning.

Blau, J. (2006, January 10). Storage expert warns of short life span for burned CDs: And don't count on hard disk drives for long-term storage, either. *Computerworld.* Retrieved March 20, 2006, from http://computerworld.com/hardwaretopics/ storage/story/ 0,10801,107607,00.html

Blau, P. M., & Meyer, M. (1971). *Bureaucracy in modern society.* New York: Random House.

Boardman, A. E., Greenberg, D. H., Vining, A. R., & Weimer, D. L. (2001). *Cost-benefit analysis: Concepts and practice.* Upper Saddle River, NJ: Prentice-Hall.

Borgmann, A. (1988). Technology and democracy. In M. E. Kraft & N. J. Vig (Eds.), *Technology and politics* (pp. 54-74). Durham, NC: Duke University Press.

BusinessMAP 4 [Computer software]. (n.d.). Dallas, TX: CMC International. Retrieved from http://www.businessmap4.com

Clementine [Computer software]. (n.d.). *Chicago: SPSS.* Retrieved March 26, 2006, from http:// www.spss.com/downloads/Papers.cfm?Product ID=Clementine&DLT

Clements, J. (2006, March 15). Net gains: How watching basketball can improve your approach to investing. *Wall Street Journal,* p. D1.

Clinton, W. J. (1994). *Executive Order 12898: Federal actions to address environmental justice in minority populations and low-income populations.* Retrieved March 19, 2006, from

http://www.fhwa.dot.gov/legsregs/directives/orders/6640_23.htm

Coursey, D. H., & Killingsworth, J. (2005). Managing e-government in Florida: Further lessons from transition and maturity. In G. D. Garson (Ed.), *Handbook of public information systems* (2nd ed., pp. 331-343). Boca Raton, FL: CRC Press, Taylor & Francis Group.

DJM Consulting. (2002). *Benefit-cost analysis of Seattle monorail proposal: Elevated Transportation Company Board PowerPoint briefing.* Retrieved March 20, 2006, from http://archives. elevated.org/documents/Cost_Benefit_Analysis_DJM.pdf

Ellul, J. (1964). *The technological society.* New York: Vintage.

Federal Highway Administration. (1998). *FHWA actions to address environmental justice in minority populations and low-income populations* (Directive 6640.23). Retrieved March 19, 2006, from http://www.fhwa.dot.gov/legsregs/directives/orders/ 6640_23.htm

Fosback, N. (1987). *Stock market logic.* Fort Lauderdale, FL: Institute for Econometric Research.

Freeman, D. M. (1974). *Technology and society.* Chicago: Markham.

Fuguitt, D., & Wilcox, S. J. (1999). *Cost-benefit analysis for public sector decision makers.* Westport, CT: Quorum Books, Greenwood Publishing Group, Inc.

Garson, G. D., & Vann, I. B. (2001). Resources for computerized crime mapping. *Social Science Computer Review, 19,* 357-361.

Gips, J. (2002). *Mastering Excel: A problem-solving approach* (2nd ed.). New York: John Wiley.

Grafton, C., & Permaloff, A. (1993). Statistical analysis and data graphics. In G. D. Garson & S. S. Nagel (Eds.), *Advances in social science and computers* (Vol. 3, pp. 267-284). Greenwich, CT: JAI Press.

Grafton, C., & Permaloff, A. (2005). Analysis and communication in public budgeting. In G. D. Garson (Ed.), *Handbook of public information systems* (2nd ed., pp. 463-488). Boca Raton, FL: CRC Press, Taylor & Francis Group.

Gullick, L. (1996). Notes on the theory of organization. In J. M. Shafritz & J. S. Ott (Eds.), *Classics of organization theory* (pp. 86-95). Fort Worth, TX: Harcourt Brace College Publishers.

Hand, D. J. (1998). Data mining: Statistics and more? *American Statistician, 52*, 112-118. Retrieved March 26, 2006, from http://www.amstat. org/publications/ tax/hand.pdf

Heeks, R. (2006). *Implementing and managing eGovernment*. London: Sage.

Jarrett, J. (1987). *Business forecasting methods*. Oxford, England: Basil Blackwell.

Levin, H. (1983). *Cost-effectiveness: A primer*. London: Sage.

Marsden Jacob Associates. (2005). *Frameworks for economic impact analysis and benefit-cost analysis*. Retrieved March 20, 2006.

MapInfo [Computer software]. (n.d.). Troy, NY: MapInfo Corporation. Retrieved from http://www. mapinfo.com

Mine Safety and Health Administration. (n.d.). *Coal fatalities from 1900 through 2005*. Retrieved March 23, 2006, from http://www.msha.gov/stats/ centurystats/ coalstats.htm

Nas, T. F. (1996). *Cost-benefit analysis*. London: Sage.

NCSS [Computer software]. (n.d.). Kaysville, UT: Number Cruncher Statistical Systems. Retrieved from http://www.ncss.com

Orford, S., Harris, R., & Dorling, D. (1999). Geography information visualization in the social sciences: A state of the art review. *Social Science Computer Review, 17*, 289-304.

Panayotou, T. (n.d.). *Basic concepts and common valuation errors in cost-benefit analysis*. Cambridge, MA: Harvard University, Institute for International Development. Retrieved August 14, 2001, from http://www.eepsea.org/publications/specialp2/ACF2DB.html

Permaloff, A., & Grafton, C. (1995). *Political power in Alabama: The more things change*. Athens, GA: University of Georgia Press.

Permaloff, A., & Grafton, C. (1996). Computer tools for crafting clear and attractive diagrams in social science. *Social Science Computer Review, 14*, 293-304.

People for Modern Transit. (n.d.). *Break-even on operations: A myth*. Retrieved April 24, 2006, from http://www.peopleformoderntransit.org/pmtadmin/home.nsf/e93bad-dc3ba8bf0a88256d42000f7a73/58502

Practical PC. (n.d.). *CD-R media lifespan*. Retrieved March 26, 2006, from http://www.practicalpc.co.uk/computing/storage/cdrlifespan.htm

Primavera Project Planner (P3) [Computer software]. (n.d.). Bala Cynwyd, PA: Primavera Systems, Inc. Retrieved from http://www.primavera.com

RFFlow [Computer software]. (n.d.). Loveland, CO: RFF Electronics. Retrieved from http://www. rff.com

Rosenbloom, D. H., & Kravchuk, R. S. (2002). *Public administration*. Boston: McGraw Hill.

Rotenberg, M., & Hoofnagle, J. (2003). *Memo to representatives Adam Putnam and William Clay, House Government Reform Subcommittee on*

Technology, Information Policy, Intergovernmental Relations, and the Census, March 25, 2003. Retrieved March 10, 2006, from http://www.epic. org/ privacy/profiling/datamining3.25.03.html

Schmalz, M. (2005). *Integrating Excel and Access.* Cambridge, UK: O'Reilly Media.

Schmid, A. A. (1989). *Benefit-cost analysis.* Boulder, CO: Westview.

Schroeder, L. D., Sjoquist, D. L., & Stephan, P. E. (1986). *Understanding regression analysis: An introductory guide.* Beverly Hills, CA: Sage.

Slack, B. (n.d.). *Cost/benefit analysis in practice.* Retrieved March 20, 2006, from http://people. hofstra.edu/geotrans/eng/ch9en/appl9en/ch9a3en. html

Slaton, C. D., & Arthur, J. L. (2004). Public administration for a democratic society: Instilling public trust through greater collaboration with citizens. In M. Malkia, A. Anttiroiko, & R. Savolainen (Eds.), *eTransformation in governance* (pp. 110-130). Hershey, PA: Idea Group.

SPSS. (n.d.). Chicago: Author. Retrieved from http://www.spss.com

Statsoft. (2003). *Data mining techniques.* Retrieved March 27, 2006, from http://www.statsoft. com/textbook/stdatmin.html

Stokey, E., & Zeckhauser, R. (1978). *A primer for policy analysis.* New York: W. W. Norton & Company.

SYSTAT [Computer software]. (n.d.). Richmond, CA: Systat Software, Inc. Retrieved from http:// www.systat.com

Tindall, C. (2005). *The monorail episode redux.* Retrieved March 20, 2006, from http://uchicagolaw.typepad.com/faculty/2005/11/the_monorail_ep.html

Vann, I. B., & Garson, G. D. (2001). Crime mapping and its extension to social science analysis. *Social Science Computer Review, 19*, 417-479.

Vann, I. B., & Garson, G. D. (2003). *Crime mapping: New tools for law enforcement.* New York: Peter Lang.

Weida, N. C., Richardson, R., & Vazsonyi, A. (2001). *Operations analysis using Microsoft Excel.* Pacifica Grove, CA: Duxbury.

Welch, S., & Comer, J. (1988). *Quantitative methods for public administration: Techniques and applications.* Pacific Grove, CA: Brooks/Cole.

Wilkinson, L., Blank, G., & Gruber, C. (1996). *Desktop data analysis with SYSTAT.* Upper Saddle River, NJ: Prentice-Hall.

This work was previously published in Modern Public Information Technology Systems: Issues and Challenges, edited by G. Garson, pp. 239-264, copyright 2007 by IGI Publishing, formerly known as Idea Group Publishing (an imprint of IGI Global).

Chapter X
A Design Tool for Business Process Design and Representation

Roberto Paiano
Università di Lecce, Italy

Anna Lisa Guido
Università di Lecce, Italy

ABSTRACT

In this chapter the focus is on business process design as middle point between requirement elicitation and implementation of a Web information system. We face both the problem of the notation to adopt in order to represent in a simple way the business process and the problem of a formal representation, in a machine-readable format, of the design. We adopt Semantic Web technology to represent process and we explain how this technology has been used to reach our goals.

INTRODUCTION

Today, the impact of business processes within companies gains more and more importance and provides tools to the managers, and methodologies useful to understand and manage them are a must. It is important to integrate business processes in the overall information system (IS) architecture with the goal to provide, to the managers, the right flexibility, to avoid the reimplementation of the applications in order to follow the business process changes, and to adapt the existing applications to a different management of the existing business logic. As a consequence the process-oriented management requires both the ability to define processes and the ability to map them in the underlying system taking into consideration the existence of heterogeneous systems.

It is clear that business and information technology (IT) experts must work together to provide the right flexibility to the IS and thus to improve the overall management. The semantic gap between business and IT experts is a problem in the development of an overall system oriented to the improvement of the business process. The first thing to do to solve this problem is to study a common language between these two classes of users with very different requirements:

- Business experts will focus on the processes and on the direct management of them in order to modify the company work without giving many technical details: A change to the process must be immediately translated in a change to the applications that implement it.
- IT experts require more details about processes and require simplicity in order to understand the process flow and thus application requirements.

Business process design is the middle point between requirement elicitation and Web IS implementation that is between business and IT experts. The tool that supports business process design must be the same for both business and IT users and must answer to two different key aspects:

- Easy to use with a notation easy to understand and allows to gives all technical details but, at the same time, hiding the complexity to the final user.
- Supports the export of the process design in a formal way in order to give to the IT experts all the process detail that they need. The process description must be machine readable.

In our research work we consider these two aspects by two approaches:

- The use of a standard notation for business process representation.
- The use of an ontological language that, thanks to its flexibility and machine-read-

able feature, is able to express all process complexity in a formal way.

In the next section of this chapter we explain the background about the concept of business process management (BPM) and the analysis of several BPM suites, and then we explain the open issue and the possible solutions related to the BPM suites. Next, we present our approach to the business process representation and we provide an overview about business process management notation (BPMN), Semantic Web languages, and about the concept of the metamodel. In the next section we explain what metamodel means and what the main problems are in the meta object facility (MOF) approach. In the section: *BPMN Ontological Metamodel: Our Approach to Solve MOF Problems* we explain how to solve problems about the classical metamodel approach with the use of the Web Ontology Language (OWL) and then, in the next section, we explain the steps followed to develop the ontological metamodel. Finally, we highlight the future trends about our research work and the conclusions.

BACKGROUND

Since the 1990s, process management has gained more and more importance in companies. Process management began to affirm with the *business process reengineering (BPR) theory* (Hammer, 1990) that allows us to improve company management thanks to the analysis and redefinition of the company's processes. BPR theory does not give a structured approach to the introduction of the process in the overall IS architecture but the process logic was in the mind of IT experts that were free to implement them.

Starting from BPR, the evolution was workflow idea (proposed and supported by Workflow Management Coalition [http://www.wfmc.org]), which is the automation of some companies' processes where only people performed process steps.

BPR theory and workflow idea allow to take into consideration vertical processes involving a single company department, but process, usually, covers several departments (a process may involve also several companies), so BPR and workflow do not cover the overall company complexity.

The traditional vertical vision of the company that locates business logic in functional areas is not the best way to provide the overall vision of the company and to improve process management, so this vision is today abandoned: Managers need a horizontal vision with the goal to manage the overall flow and to understand and correct—in the most rapid way possible—managements errors. Obviously, we speak about administrative business processes extended throughout the entire organization where they take place.

Actually, the attention is turned to the BPM with an innovative idea that allows us to have a horizontal (rather than vertical) vision of the company and to consider processes where steps are performed both from people and systems. The goal of BPM is to make explicit the process management in the IS architecture. Process logic is, today, hidden in the application level and, often, the way with which this is made is in the mind of the IT experts of the company, and it is not well documented. The IS obtained is difficult to maintain. A change to the process logic needs a revision to the business logic, and this requires a lot of time and incurs high costs. The processes are not explicit and thus it is very difficult to monitor and manage them.

There are a lot of BPM suites on the market that try to make explicit the definition and management of the processes. A recent study (Miers, Harmon, & Hall 2005) compares different BPM suites (http://www.Fuego.com; http://www.ilog.com; http://www.popkin.com; http://www.w4global.com; http://www.filenet.com) from different points of view such as cost, platform, user interface, and so forth. These BPM suites allow us to represent processes and to manage their execution; and they provide administration tools that

allow us to manage processes and users involved in the system. Several suites focus on document management and thus on the possibility to manage, with a high degree of security, documents that are involved in the process, versioning, and so forth. BPM suites also provide a Web application that allows different actors in the process to load their task and to work with it. In the Web application a single user can view and work with the process and, despite this being visible in the Web, each user has access to only one page and thus information, navigation, and transactional aspects of Web application are not taken into consideration. An important aspect of the BPM suites is the application program interface (API) that allows us to develop a custom application but does not supply any information about design.

BPM SUITES: OPEN ISSUE AND POSSIBLE SOLUTIONS

The main problems highlighted in the study of these suites are:

- The high cost of suites are difficult to apply in small- to medium-sized companies, and they require high investments both to purchase hardware and to train people in the company that will use these frameworks.
- Ad hoc notation to represent processes that are often hard to read and to understand both from business experts and from IT experts and thus the semantic gap problem is not solved.
- There is a lack of methodology that helps in the transition from process design to the final Web application.

In this study we focus on two of these main problems: high costs and process representation.

Small- to medium-sized companies may have several advantages from BPM suite because it helps to control all the company activities in a simple and easy way. Small- to medium-sized companies have several economic problems in acquiring these suites, a part from hardware and software costs there is the necessity to reach skilled people able to work with these complex suites. The difficulty to acquire hardware, software, and people make it impossible for these companies to adopt the BPM suite and, of consequence, to improve their overall management.

In regards to a low-cost BPM suite, there is another important problem: BPM suite may be used both from IT and from business people but business people have a technical experience about management and they do not understand IT technical aspects; IT experts do not know management aspects. The semantic gap is very large and hard to cover, so it is important to take into consideration only notations that are easy to learn both by IT and business experts. The business process notation must be, of consequence, simple, easy to use, and easy to understand both by business experts and by IT experts, in a few words, the notation to represent processes must cover the semantic gap between business and IT experts.

There is a different way to represent business process. Unified modeling language (UML) activity diagram, for example, allows a defining process but it is not simple to understand: As an example, the actor of the processes is not immediately visible. The same problem is true for the traditional workflow representation, that is, it is not intuitive and allows defining only the process flow without taking into consideration human and/or system interaction. UML, standard de facto in the software analysis, may be useful for IT experts but hard to learn, to use, and to understand for business experts; workflow may be, instead, useful for business experts but hard to understand for IT experts.

Exploring several notations, we study a recent notation (White, 2004) proposed by the business process management initiative (BPMI) that,

thanks to its simplicity and completeness, seems the best way to represent a process.

BPMN, today, is not a standard but it is supported by several companies, and it does not allow designing information, strategies, or business rules.

The design obtained through BPMN is clear and it is easy to understand which actors (human or system) are involved in the process and what the relationships are between them.

To complete a BPM suite the graphical process representation is not enough to automate the business process so we need a formal representation of the process.

Starting from BPMN notation (and from its complexity) we observe that there is not a well-defined, machine-readable standard to represent a process (business process execution language [BPEL]; business process execution language for Web services [BPEL4WS], and so forth). From these considerations, the final goal of our study is to develop a light framework to manage processes. This framework will be efficient, easy to use, and low cost. In this phase of our study we focus on the design and implementation of a business process editor and we face two main problems: (1) the choice of the notation to adopt in the business process design, and (2) the choice of the formal language to adopt in order to make the design machine readable.

BUSINESS PROCESS REPRESENTATION: OUR APPROACH

The first and most important problem to solve to reach the goal to define a low cost framework that supports process definition and management is to select the notation to adopt. The notation must cover the semantic gap between business and IT experts and must answer to two main requirements: completeness and simplicity. These aspects may be found in the BPMN notation: Its main goal is to cover the gap between IT and business experts, which is the gap between process design and process implementation. BPMN notation is, also, very easy to learn and to understand, so we select it as the notation to represent processes.

As we saw in the previous section, BPMN notation is not tied to a specific machine-readable format but there are several machine-readable formats not yet standard. In our research work, we explored several alternatives before choosing a language to represent processes; finally, we chose to use ontology *in an innovative way*: Our use of ontology is different from the traditional Semantic Web where ontology describes, in general, a domain of knowledge. We adopt both the ontology and the concept of metamodel: Ontology is, in our research work, the language to represent both the BPMN metamodel (that we develop) and the process model starting from the metamodel. The ontological language used in our research work is OWL (World Wide Web Consortium, 2004a): a text language without graphical notation.

To understand the following part of our study we introduce an overview about BPMN notation, next a brief definition of ontology and of the semantic languages, and finally, we present the concept of metamodel.

BPMN Notation Overview

In daily BPM, business experts start their analysis with the design in the large of the process: Details are given to the design in the following steps. Implementation details, that are details needed in the implementation phase, are given in the last step of the analysis and are obviously given by IT experts and not by business experts. To follow this natural evolution from design in the large to design in the small, BPMN notation is made up of two different levels of details:

- A core object (business process diagram modeling objects) made up of base elements that allow us to define a process in the large.
- An extension mechanism that allows us to extend core objects and to add properties to obtain a detail level near to the detail needed in the implementation phase.

These different detail levels make the final design easy to understand not only by experts of the notation but also by nonexperts of the notation and thus by IT experts that may operate directly in the design by adding their details. So, in the

Figure 1. Main primitives of BPMN notation

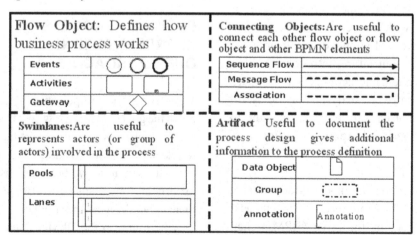

design phase both IT and business experts may provide all the details needed.

Business process diagram modeling objects are made up of four different groups of primitives: Flow Object, Connecting Object, Swimlanes, and Artifact (Figure 1).

Flow objects have three types: *Events* that represent something that occurs during the normal process execution; events have a cause (trigger) or an impact (result). Different icons allow us to define start, intermediate, or end an event. Internal market (and this is another detail level) represents triggers that define the cause of the events. For example, start event may be a circle without any icon or may have an envelope icon to represent that the process starts when a message is arriving. A complete set of events and icons are shown in Figure 2.

Another type of Flow Object is *activities,* which is generic work that a company performs. Activities may be of two different types: *task* and *sub-process.* Task is an atomic activity, that is, the work not broken down to a finer level of process model detail; sub-process is an activity made up of several subactivities.

The third type of Flow Object is the *gateway* used to control the divergence and convergence of multiple sequence flow. Gateway represented with a diamond has, as events, different icons to represents different possible flow control behavior.

Flow objects may be connected to each other or may be connected to Artifact by three different types of connecting objects: *sequence flow* is used to connect a Flow Object with the next Flow Object that will be performed in the process. The second Connecting Object is the *message flow* used to show the flow of messages between two participants (participants are represented by Swimlanes); finally *associations* are used to connect information (Artifact) with Flow Object.

Swimlanes are used to group Flow Object, Connecting Object, and Artifact. Swimlanes are made up of Pools that represents a participant in a process. A Pool may be subpartitioned by lanes used to organize and categorize activities. For example if the designer wants to represent the activity in an office and to highlight the role of each person in the process, it is possible to use a Pool to represent the office and, within the Pool, lanes will be used to represent each person.

Artifact may be used for documentation purposes and does not have direct effect on the normal process flow. Artifact may be of three different types: (1) *data object* that is often used to represent a document required and/or produced by an activity; (2) *group* is often used to identify activities in different Pools, and finally (3) *text*

Figure 2. Events icon defined in BPMN notation

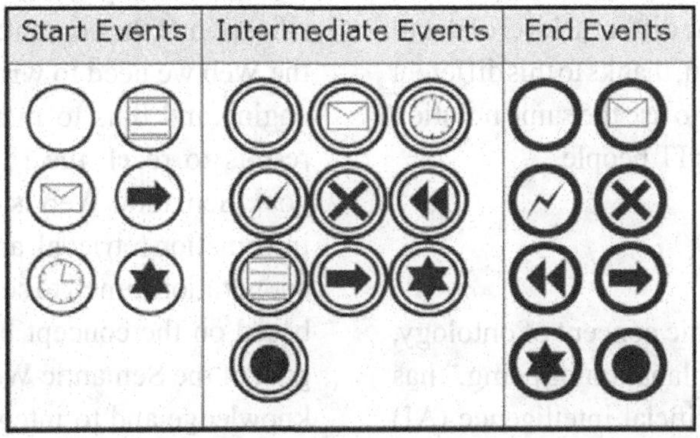

Start Events	Intermediate Events	End Events

annotation helps designers to give additional (textual) information to the reader of the design.

In order to have a final diagram easy to understand, BPMN notation defines connection rules for both sequence flow and for message flow. Connection rules are useful to understand how Flow Object, Swimlane, and Artifact may be connected to each other, and what condition is required to connect them together. As an example, message flow cannot connect objects in the same Lane but only objects in two different Lanes; similarly sequence flow cannot connect an object in two different Lanes but only objects in the same Lane.

At this point we can observe that with four different types of objects (and relative subtypes) and following simple connecting rules, business users are able to design the process in all its complexity, but implementation details are needed.

BPMN defines another detail level: each BPMN elements has its own properties. Suppose, for example, that the designer defines a start event of type "message." In the implementation phase IT experts need to know what message is required and what technology is used to send/receive the message. Start event has among its property the attribute message that allows us to supply the message to send/receive and the attribute implementation to define the technology used to receive the message (Web services or other technology).

Other details about property are out of the scope of this work but will be found in the BPMN specification. Here we want to underline all the BPMN complexity and the different level of detail that composes this notation; thanks to this different details level it is possible to use the same notation both for business and for IT people.

What is Ontology?

The traditional philosophic concept of ontology, that is, "a systematic explanation of being," has been inherited in the artificial intelligence (AI) with several definitions. In the AI idea, ontology is the study of something that exists or may exist in some domain; ontology may be defined as terms linked together to define a structure in a well-defined application domain.

The definition of ontology near to the IT aspect is given by Gruber (1993, pp. 199-220): "ontology is a formal, explicit specification of a shared conceptualization." The concept of conceptualization is the abstraction of some concept through the definition of some peculiar characteristic; the term *explicit* is related to the fact that constraints about the concept must be defined in an explicit way; finally, *formal* means that ontology must be defined in a machine-readable format.

Ontology is a collection of terms and related definitions or a map of concepts where we can forward or backward from one concept to another in a well-defined domain.

The application of the ontology in the Semantic Web was defined by Berners-Lee, Hendler, and Lassila (2001) as "the semantic web is not a separate web but an extension of the current one in which information is given well-defined meaning, better enabling computers and people to work in cooperation." The necessity to go over traditional Web and to go into the Semantic Web is due to the fact that the Web contains a tremendous amount of data, information, and knowledge freely available but poorly organized: A large amount of information is in textual format, thus it is difficult to filter and to extract content.

Traditional Web works on information retrieval are based on keyword search and on manual classification of the content: To reach information on the Web we need to write a keyword on a search engine and thus to manually filter between all results to reach the right result nearest to our goal. Semantic Web is oriented to the semantic information retrieval, and on a machine-machine cooperation aimed to select the right information based on the concept behind the keyword. The goal of the Semantic Web is to make explicit the knowledge and to integrate different sources of knowledge with the goal to extract knowledge from knowledge.

Semantic Web Languages

Behind the idea of Semantic Web, the World Wide Consortium (W3C) works around languages for knowledge representation. One of the main goals of the ontology is the interoperability of both syntactic and semantic. Semantic interoperability means that ontology must be machine readable, that is, it must be interpreted by a machine in a well-defined format. Syntactic interoperability is the ability to provide support to a reason that is to learn from the data. Languages born to support ontology are different: The first ontology language is resource description language (RDF) (W3C, 2004c) and RDF schema (RDFS) (W3C, 2004b).

RDF has a model similar to the entity-relationship model which allows us to give interoperability through applications that interact with each other in order to exchange information on the Web in a machine-readable format. RDF does not give reasoning support but has the basis to achieve this. The three main concepts of RDF are:

- **Resource.** Anything that will be defined in RDF is named Resource. Resource is named by a uniform resource identifier (URI) and can be a Web page or part of it; a resource can be an object in the real word not directly accessible on the Web.
- **Property.** Property allows us to define a characteristic of a resource through a binary relationship between two resources or between a resource and a well-defined data type.
- **Statement.** It is a sentence with a fixed structure: subject, predicate, and object. Subject and predicate must be a resource while an object may be a literal. Statement

allows us to represent complex situations if the object is used as a subject on a new statement.

Successors of RDF (and RDF schema) are Darpa Agent Markup Language (DAML) and Ontology Interchange Language (OIL); these two languages are antecedent to the Ontology Web Language (OWL) used today.

OWL allows us to provide more machine readability than extensible markup language (XML), RDF, and RDF schema. In the Semantic Web, OWL is used when information must be processed from application (and not only presented to human). OWL allows us to provide a detailed description of any domain.

OWL added new vocabulary (compared to RDF and DAML+OIL) to describe classes and relationships; it supports a useful mechanism to integrate different ontologies. OWL is made up of three different languages each of them is the extension of its ancestor:

- OWL lite allows us to give simply a taxonomy without complex constraint.
- OWL description logic (OWL DL) gives high complexity, completeness, and decidability.
- OWL full gives expressiveness but does not give decidability.

The OWL main primitives are:

- **Classes.** Classes allow the abstraction of some concepts. Each class has a set of properties (each one for specific concept characteristics). A class would be composed by subclasses.
- **Properties.** There are two types of properties: DataType specific to each class and ObjectProperty used to create a link between classes. ObjectProperty has both domains:

Figure 3. MOF and ontological approaches compared

Approach / Level	MOF	Ontological
Meta-meta model (M3)	MOF-language	OWL-language
Meta-model (M2)	Classes, associations, packages	Ontological classes and properties
Model (M1)	Derived classes, associations, packages	Instances of classes and properties
Data (M0)	Data	Data

class (to which the property is connected) and range (the possible values of the property). In each class we can indicate "restrictions" that define constraints.

- **Individuals.** Individuals are objects with the characteristics defined by classes and properties. Both classes and properties may have individuals.

What is Metamodel?

The metamodel idea was born about 10 years ago and the interest around it is increasing. A metamodel can be defined as a language to describe a model, so, to create a metamodel it is important to work in an abstract level. Metamodel allows us to describe a well-defined methodology, so, starting from the metamodel, it will be possible to define a model: metamodel provide, in a few words, guidelines for model definition.

The introduction of the metamodel idea has brought forth the introduction of metacase tools. Standard case tools support a fixed notation hard coded in tools: A change in the methodology requires a change in the code of the tool and this fact requires high costs and a lot of time. Metacase tools, based on the metamodel, allow us to separate notation from the methodology

definition, so a change in the methodology will reflect in the tool with a few changes (or without change) in the code. To be included in the metacase tool a metamodel must be well defined so it must answer to three important requirements: a metamodel must be:

- **Complete.** It must cover all the primitives of the methodology that represent.
- **Extensible.** Metamodel must follow the methodology evolution so it will be possible to adapt the metamodel in a simple way without redefining it from scratch.
- **Semantic.** Metamodel must express all the semantics of the methodology primitives in order to give the right meaning to each element.

To avoid confusion between metamodel and model, we explain the meta-object facility (MOF) approach to meta-model proposed by the Object Management Group (OMG) (http://www.omg.org). MOF architecture is very helpful because it allows us to separate, in a simple way, the concept of the meta-model from the concept of the model: A model will be an instantiation of the meta-model.

MOF approach is based on a 4-level architecture. It allows us to define a language for the methodology representation and to use this language for model definition. The 4-level architecture proposed by OMG is very helpful to separate different levels of abstraction.

As show in Figure 3 in the M3 level (the meta-meta model level) the MOF language, that is, the abstract language used to describe MOF metamodel, is defined. In the M2 level MOF approach allows us to define the metamodel. MOF is object oriented and strictly connected to UML: UML notation is used to express MOF metamodel. The main MOF elements are classes, associations, and packages; moreover, to express model rules it is necessary to define constraints. MOF does not force the use of a particular language but suggests the object constraint language (OCL) (OMG, 1997). Starting from the metamodel defined in the M2 level, the designer of a particular methodology using metamodel (guidelines for methodology) designs its model. Finally M0 level represents data of a specific model.

MOF METAMODEL: OPEN ISSUE

The architecture proposed by OMG is very helpful to obtain a meta-model of BPMN notation, but in our study we highlight some problems related to the language in the M3 level strictly related to UML that impose some limits when used to define metamodel.

The first problem is about the *metamodel semantics*: It is very important to assign a meaning to every metamodel concept in order to have the meaning of each methodology primitive. In MOF approach the use of stereotypes to define primitives which are not directly supported by UML is intensive: A lot of primitives are not directly supported by UML and, thus, all primitives are represented by stereotypes. Metamodel semantics, consequently, coincide with stereotype semantics. Furthermore, the *lack of semantics* creates

confusion to the unskilled designer during the practical applications of modeling concepts. The explicit presence of semantics helps the designer to understand how the modeling concepts should be used.

Another problem strictly connected to semantics concerns *semantic relationships among classes*: MOF allows us to use only two relationships: aggregation and association. In the definition of a metamodel methodology it is necessary to define specific methodology relationships (different from association and aggregation) with its relative semantics.

Another problem is that *relationships among classes* are lost in the transition from metamodel to model. Supposing that in the metamodel we have a relationship among classes: When we define the model, relationships among classes must be redefined because relationships are not inherited by the model. This problem could be solved creating intermediate classes to represent the relationships; the disadvantage of this solution is that it will make the model unreadable for the large number of intermediate classes.

Finally, in the MOF approach, each class has specific primitive attributes. If an attribute is the same for two different concepts, in MOF approach it is defined once for each class because each attribute is strictly connected to each class. This MOF limit creates confusion letting designers think that semantics are different for each attribute, while semantics are the same.

Another problem is the metamodel *flexibility,* that is, the possibility to enrich the model with new primitives defined in methodology or to add new characteristics to the primitives already defined. The solution proposed by UML (both 1.x and 2.0 [OMG, 2001; OMG, 2003]) is to enrich the UML metamodel with the extension mechanism. The *extension mechanism approach* is based on a good knowledge of UML. Another problem related to the language evolution concerns the unique name assumption principle: In the UML approach different words must refer to different objects. In order to meet methodology evolution, it is often necessary to define new versions of concepts (defined before) and to use the same name. The unique name assumption makes it impossible. The UML and MOF do not support the *dynamic classification of classes*. It is possible that, when metamodel is extended to include the methodology evolution, two classes must be replaced by their intersection: The instance of the new class contains both previous classes. This is not possible in UML, since every instance can be only the instance of a class and not the instance of two classes at the same time.

It is important to have a machine-readable description of the model. In MOF approach we use XML metadata interchange (XMI) as a model representation language (but we are free to use any XML description). XMI is an OMG standard and there are different formats according to the graphic editors that produce it. A model description must be understandable in an easy and univocal way by the software agent and preferably should be a W3C standard.

Finally, classes, attributes, and relationships are insufficient to express all the methodology primitives and so, in the MOF approach there is an external language, OCL, to describe the methodology constraints.

THE ONTOLOGY LAYER: ONTOLOGY REPRESENTATION OF BPMN NOTATION

It is clear that to define all business process design details it is a hard task and cooperation between business and IT experts is a must. These two types of users must work on the same project and each of them must add the right detail to the design based on their point of view. To insert the process design in the overall IS architecture, that is, to make explicit and tangible the knowledge embedded in the mind of IT and business experts, it is important to represent in a machine-readable format the overall business process design with all details.

The project of BPMI is to define standards in order to cover the overall chain starting from the business process design (through BPMN notation) to a business process execution language, and finally, the efforts will be focused on a business process query language that allows us to reach, through the right questions, information about processes. The choice of BPMN notation to design business process does not tie to a particular machine-readable format because, although there are big efforts in this direction, there is not a standard machine-readable format to represent

Figure 4. The ontology layer

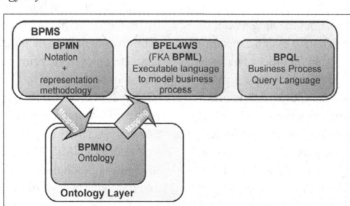

business processes. Starting from these problems in our research work, our idea (Figure 4) is to add an ontology layer. The choice of ontology (in our approach we adopt Semantic Web technologies different from the Semantic Web idea) helps us to provide, immediately, a process representation in a machine-readable format and, thanks to its flexibility, ontology will help, when necessary, to translate in any formal language the model obtained when this formal language will be defined and will be standard.

BPMN ONTOLOGICAL METAMODEL: OUR APPROACH TO SOLVE MOF PROBLEMS

In order to solve the MOF problems highlighted, we look to other languages different from MOF. In our research work we adopt an innovative language more expressive than MOF: we choose OWL.

The architecture that we adopt in our work is the MOF 4-level architecture but the language in the M3 level is OWL, instead of MOF language thus, the metamodel in M2 level is made up of ontological classes and ontological properties linked together. Finally in the M1 level we obtain the model through instantiation of classes and property previously defined. The M0 level represents, also in our approach, the data of a specific model.

Ontology and OWL as metamodel definition languages help us to obtain several advantages such as:

- **Metamodel semantic:** OWL allows us to define a semantic to what we represent through classes and properties that allow us to express characteristics of classes.
- **Semantic relationship:** OWL and ontology allow us to define ad hoc relationships different from UML where there are only two types of relationships: aggregation and association.

- **Standard description of the model:** By using OWL it is possible to obtain a machine-readable description of the model that a software agent may read in univocal way. OWL is supported by W3C differently from other formats such as XMI (XMI is the export format starting from UML model). XMI is an OMG standard (and not W3C) but there are different formats based on the graphical editor that allow us to define the model.
- **Graphical representation:** Ontological languages are based on text and not on a specific notation so it is possible to provide to the metamodel and to the model a specific graphical representation based on a methodology and not on a general representation.

Our research contribution is oriented to use ontology in a different way from the Semantic Web technologies, which is the traditional one. Following the 4-layer architecture proposed by MOF, we focus on the M3 and M2 levels. In the M3 level (metamodel level) we define all BPMN primitives through classes and properties. Classes and properties are, in some cases, not sufficient to express all BPMN primitives so we also adopt instances of some classes and properties to define the metamodel. The M2 level is made up only by instances of classes and properties that have already been defined. Classes and properties (the metamodel) are the guidelines for the design in order to define the model, that is, to insert the instance of the model.

We develop an ontological metamodel where classes and properties are defined in order to express all BPMN primitives. In our ontological BPMN metamodel we define not only the main primitives but also properties of each of them.

In our approach we develop BPMN metamodel following different steps:

- Analysis of BPMN specification in order to extract the main concept: each concept is defined as ontological class.
- Analysis of BPMN in order to extract details of each concept defined in the previous step: each concept is modeled as ontological subclasses tied to the main classes.
- Analysis of BPMN in order to extract concepts that support the concept defined in the previous steps. Each concept is defined as ontological class.
- Analysis of BPMN in order to extract properties that allow us to provide a semantic to concepts previously defined. It is important to define both Object properties that allow us to link together concept and Data Type properties, that is, simple type.
- Analysis of BPMN in order to reach some concept that is not modeled by classes and properties but as an instance of classes and properties.

In the following section we explain in detail the BPMN ontological metamodel.

DEVELOPMENT OF BPMN ONTOLOGICAL METAMODEL

In the development of the BPMN ontological metamodel we follow the BPMN specification and we try to translate in ontological classes the main concepts defined in BPMN specification.

In the BPMN ontological metamodel we define two main types of classes: Concrete and Abstract classes. Concrete classes are classes that may contain instances when we define a specific model starting from the metamodel. Abstract classes are used only to define BPMN concepts but these classes cannot contain instances of a specific model. Each Abstract class has at least one Concrete class where it is possible to define instances.

In the BPMN metamodel we define both the four different groups of primitives defined in BPMN specification and two other concepts: the concept of the business process diagram and the concept of process.

- **Business process diagram.** It is a Concrete class; it contains general information about design such as author, creation date, and so on. Following the BPMN specification a business process diagram is made up of several Pools.
- **Process.** This concept has been defined to contain the process design that is all the BPMN elements that allow us to define different steps in the process execution design. Process is a Concrete ontological class and has three ontological subclasses of type "Specialization."[1]**AbstractProcess, PrivateProcess, and CollaborativeProcess.** in order to meet the BPMN definition of Process.
- **Swimlane:** This concept has been defined in order to make a generalization of Pool and Lane. *Pool* and *Lane* are concrete subclasses (of type "specialization") of the abstract class Swimlane. The concept of Pool, following the BPMN definition, allows us to define an actor (a person or/and a machine) of the process. A Pool may contain a Lane, Flow Object (defined below) or nothing. The ontological class Lane meets the concept of Lane defined by BPMN and is defined in order to allow the definition of a Lane within a Pool.
- **FlowObject.** With regards to following the BPMN specification, the ontological Abstract class FlowObject is defined as a superclass that contains three subclasses: Activity, Events, and Gateway. The abstract class FlowObject is linked to the concrete classes Activity, Events and Gateway with a "Specialization" relationship. Both Activity, Task, and Event have a subclass that allows us

to define the specific characteristics defined in BPMN specification. As an example to define three different type of Event (Start, Intermediate, End) we define three different subclasses of the class Event.

- **Artifact.** With regards to following the BPMN specification, the ontological class Artifact allows us to define information not tied to the process flow. Ontological class Artifact (an Abstract class) contains three Concrete subclasses Annotation, Data Object, and Group.
- **ConnectingObject.** With regards to following BPMN notation, Connecting Object is defined as a superclass that contains three different subclasses SequenceFlow, MessageFlow, and Association Flow.

The abstract class GenericBusinessProcessObject is the generalization of the last four concrete classes in the bullet item (SwimLane, FlowObject, Artifact and ConncetingObject). In the GenericBusinessProcessObject class we define the datatype property shared by these four classes. The datatype property are:

- **Categories.** In BPMN specification it has documentation purpose; in the metamodel it is a datatype property of type "text."
- **Documentation.** As categories, it is a datatype property of type "text."
- **Name.** It is a text data type property that allows us to define a unique name in the

business process diagram for each Generic Business Process Object.

Properties defined in the Abstract classes cannot contain instances but, thanks to the class-subclass the relationship property will be inherited by subclasses until the subclasses will be concrete.

At this point the main concepts of BPMN are represented as ontological classes. In order to link together the main concepts we define the Object Property in the proper classes.

The use of Object Property in the BPMN ontology is a little different from the traditional Semantic Web. An example is useful in understanding this interesting aspect. Each process may be composed by different GenericBusinessProcessObject, and it is not a must to define in each process all the GenericBusinessProcessObject defined in the BPMN specification. If each GenericBusinessProcessObject is defined only by its name a solution may be to define in the class Process several properties (datatype properties) each of one of the generic business process. The generic business process is a more complicated concept: It has several subclasses and each of them has its own properties. To solve this problem in the metamodel that we developed, we adopt an Object Property "hasGenericBusinessProcessObject," which has the class Process as domain and the class GenericBusinessProcessObject as range. The OWL code is in Figure 5.

Figure 5. OWL code of hasGenericBusinessProcessDiagramGraphical Object

```
<owl:InverseFunctionalProperty
rdf: ID="hasGenericBusinessProcessObject">
    <rdfs:range rdf:resource="#BusinessProcessObject">
    <rdfs:domain rdf:resource="#Process"/>
    <rdf:type
  rdf:resource="http://www.w3.org/2002/07/owl#ObjectProperty"/>
    </owl:InverseFunctionalProperty>
```

In this way it is possible, when defining the model starting from the metamodel, to define several instances of the property "hasGeneric-BusinessProcessObject" each of them define a specific business process object with its own properties. Starting from this example, we define, in the same way, the property "hasSwimlane." This property has the ontological class Business-ProcessDiagram as domain and the ontological class Swimlane as range. Finally, we define the property "isMadeOfLane" to state that each Pool (class Pool is the domain of this property) may contain one or more Lane (range of property).

Starting from previous consideration the core classes and main relationship of the ontology metamodel are represented in Figure 6.

Some special cases have been faced during the development of the BPMN ontology metamodel.

A Pool, following BPMN specification, may contain both a Lane and a GenericBusinessProcessObject (different from Swimlane) (Figure7). The problem is how to model this concept: make two different Object Properties or the same? The best solution, following the ontology idea, is to provide the same Object Property because the semantics of the relationship are the same. We define the Object Property "belongsToPool" with only one class as range (the ontological class Pool) and the domain as the union of the other classes: Flow Object, Artifact, and Connecting Object. In this way the same property, depending on the context, is used to express both the fact that a Lane belongs to Pool and to lay Flow Object, Artifact, and Connecting Object to the specific Pool.

In the same way, the Object Property "belongsToLane" (Figure 8) is used both to model the fact that one Lane can contain another Lane and to define which Flow Object and/or Artifact are defined in the same Lane.

Additional Classes

In order to cover all the BPMN complexity, during the BPMN metamodel development, we define concepts modeled as ontological classes, not clearly defined in the BPMN specification. As an example we consider the class Trigger. We observe that a trigger is the mechanism that allows an event to start, so a trigger is what allows the events to start. BPMN specification defines some properties for a trigger; for example, if a trigger is of type Timer, it has the property timeCycle that defines the duration of the event and timeDate that define when the event starts. We link the Ontological class Trigger with the Event by the property "hasTrigger." The class Trigger is made up of several subclasses each of them, following BPMN specification, expressing a special type of trigger (Figure 9).

Finally, to define all the BPMN properties of each BPMN primitives we define, where appropriate, ontological properties to meet the BPMN specification.

From the BPMN Metamodel to the Ontological Business Process Model

Starting from the metamodel, previously defined, it is possible to define a business process model defining instances of ontological classes and properties (we talk about concrete ontological classes). Suppose that we want to define a simple business process made up of one Pool and of a star event, one task and the end event. The task is linked to the start and end event with sequence flow.

We define an instance of the class Process and we define the instances of all (of some of them) properties defined by BPMN specification and in the metamodel. Following the property "isDefinedInPool" we define a Pool (and all its properties). Following the property "hasGeneric-BusinessProcessDiagramObject" (starting from the class process) we define the Start Event, the task, the End Event and two sequence flow: one

Figure 6. Core classes and relationship

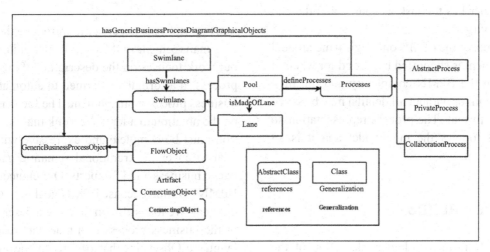

Figure 7. Ontological property belongsToLane and belongsToPool

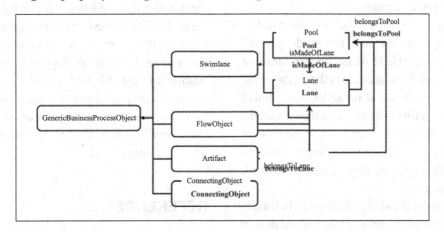

Figure 8. OWL code of the "belongsToPool" properties

```
<owl: ObjectProperty rdf:ID="belongsToLane">
    <rdfs:range rdf:resource="#Lane"/>
    <rdfs:domain>
    <owl:Class>
        <owl:unionOf rdf:parseType="Collection">
            <owl:Class rdf:about="#FlowObject"/>
            <owl:Class rdf:about="#Lane"/>
            <owl:Class rdf:about="#Artifact"/>
        </owl:unionOf>
    </owl:Class>
    </rdfs:domain>
```

has the start event as source and the task as target and another has the task as source and the end event as target.

Obviously, the BPMN ontological metamodel development is supported by our editor where it is hidden the BPMN complexity and the final design (with or without all details) may be saved in OWL format. The process representation so obtained follows the metamodel and it is an instance of it.

FUTURE TRENDS

Starting from an ontological definition of the BPMN metamodel and thus from an ontological definition of the model, our next step is oriented to two different directions.

One way is to understand the possible key performance indicator and thus to design and implement a tool able to make the *simulation* of the process in order to provide to the manager the possibility to understand possible management and/or design errors and to correct them immediately. The ontology representation of the process may help in this work thanks to the possibility to associate rules to the ontology and thus to think on a reasoning tool.

Starting from the idea to define a light framework to manage processes and to help in the design and implementation of Web application based on a process design, we look to the *guidelines* that support the steps from process design to Web application design. Guidelines will be, as soon as possible, a *Web application design methodology* that supports the process definition: This design methodology will cover the gap in the traditional Web application design methodology based on a "user experience" paradigm but not focused on a process.

CONCLUSION

Starting from the necessity to introduce the process management in the overall IS architecture, our work focuses on the description of business process in a formal way aimed to automate the business process management. The focus is first on the notation to adopt: We think that the notation must be complete and expressive with the goal to cover the traditional semantic gap between business and IT experts. Our choice is the BPMN notation because BPMN goal is nearer to our goal. We focus also on the formal description of the business process in a machine–readable language. Observing that to represent the process we need a metamodel that is a guideline in the model definition, the focus on the 4-layer MOF metamodel is very helpful for our purpose but we highlight that the UML language used is poor for several reasons. So we introduce an innovative way to think on ontology different from the traditional Semantic Web use. OWL provides us several advantages both in the description of the metamodel and in the description of the model. OWL and Semantic Web technologies will help us in our future works.

REFERENCES

Berners-Lee, T., Hendler, J., & Lassila, O. (2001, May). The Semantic Web. *Scientific American, 284*(5), 34-43.

Gruber, T. R. (1993). A translation approach to portable ontology specifications. *Knowledge Acquisition, 5,* 199-220.

Hammer, M. (1990). *Reengineering work: Don't automate, obliterate. Harward Business Review, 68,* 104-112.

Miers, D., Harmon, P., & Hall, C. (2006). *The 2006 BPM suites report Realise 2.0.* Retrieved

September 30, 2006, from http://www.bptrends.com/reports_toc_01.cfm

Retrieved March 15, 2005, from http://www.bptrends.com

Object Management Group (OMG). (1997, September). *Object constraint language specification* (Version 1.1).

Object Management Group (OMG). (2001, September). *Unified modeling language specification* (Version 1.4).

Object Management Group (OMG). (2003, September 8). *UML 2.0 superstructure specification* (Version 2.0).

White, S. A. (2004, May 3). *Business process modeling notation (BPMN)* (Version 1.0). Retrieved May, 2004, from http://www.bpmn.org

World Wide Web Consortium (W3C). (2004a, February 10). OWL *Web ontology language reference.*

World Wide Web Consortium (W3C) (2004b, February 10). *RDF vocabulary description language 1.0: RDF Schema.*

World Wide Web Consortium (W3C) (2004c, February 10). *RDF/XML syntax specification.*

ENDNOTE

[1] Specialization subclass is also called IS-A, and it allows us to connect a general concept with a more specific concept. In our example an AbstractProcess IS-A Process.

This work was previously published in Semantic Web Technologies and E-Business: Toward the Integrated Virtual Organization and Business Process Automation, edited by A. Salam and J. Stevens, pp. 77-100, copyright 2007 by IGI Publishing, formerly known as Idea Group Publishing (an imprint of IGI Global).

Chapter XI
Introduction to Cryptography

Rajeeva Laxman Karandikar
Indian Statistical Institute, India

ABSTRACT

The chapter introduces the reader to various key ideas in cryptography without going into technicalities. It brings out the need for use of cryptography in electronic communications, and describes the symmetric key techniques as well as public key cryptosystems. Digital signatures are also discussed. Data integrity and data authentication are also discussed.

INTRODUCTION

With a many-fold increase in digital communication in the recent past, cryptography has become important not only for the armed forces, who have been using it for a long time, but for all the aspects of life where Internet and digital communications have entered. *Secure and authenticated communications* are needed not only by the defense forces but, for example, in banking, in communicating with customers over the phone, automated teller machines (ATM), or the Internet.

Cryptography has a very long history. Kahn (1967) describes early use of cryptography by the Egyptians some 4,000 years ago. Military historians generally agree that the outcomes of the two world wars critically depended on breaking the codes of secret messages. In World War II, the breaking of the Enigma code turned the tide of the war against Germany. The term cryptography comes from the Greek words kryptós, meaning "hidden," and gráphein, meaning "to write." The first recorded usage of the word "cryptography" appears in Sir Thomas Browne's Discourse of 1658 entitled "The Garden of Cyrus," where he describes "the strange Cryptography of Gaffarel in his Starrie Booke of Heaven."

This chapter provides an introduction to the basic elements of cryptography. In the next section, we discuss the need for cryptography. The following four sections describe the four pillars of cryptology: confidentiality, digital signature, data integrity, and authentication. The final section concludes the chapter.

WHY WE NEED CRYPTOLOGY

First, if a company that has offices in different locations (perhaps around the globe) would like to set up a link between its offices that guarantees secure communications, they could also need it. It would be very expensive to set up a separate secure communication link. It would be preferable if secure communication can be achieved even when using public (phone/Internet) links.

Second, e-commerce depends crucially on secure and authenticated transactions–after all the customers and the vendors only communicate electronically, so here too secure and secret communication is a must (customers may send their credit card numbers or bank account numbers). The vendor (for example, a bank or a merchant), while dealing with a customer, also needs to be convinced of the identity of the customer before it can carry out instructions received (say the purchase of goods to be shipped or transfer of funds). Thus, authenticated transactions are required. Moreover, if necessary, it should be able to prove to a third party (say a court of law) that the instructions were indeed given by said customer. This would require what has come to be called a *digital signature*. Several countries have enacted laws that recognize digital signatures. An excellent source for definitions, description of algorithms, and other issues on cryptography is the book by Menezes, van Oorschot, & Vanstone (1996). Different accounts can be found in Schneier (1996), and Davies and Price (1989).

Thus, the objectives of cryptography are:

1. **Confidentiality-secrecy-privacy:** To devise a scheme that will keep the content of a transaction secret from all but those authorized to have it (even if others intercept the transcript of the communication, which is often sent over an insecure medium).
2. **Digital signature:** Requires a mechanism whereby a person can sign a communication. It should be such that at a later date, the person cannot deny that it (a communication signed by him) was indeed sent by him.
3. **Data integrity:** Requires a method that will be able to detect insertion, substitution, or deletion of data (other than by the owner). (Say on a Web server or in a bank's database containing the information such as the balance in various accounts.)
4. **Authentication:** Two parties entering into a communication identify each other. This requires a mechanism whereby both parties can be assured of the identity of the other.

CONFIDENTIALITY-SECRECY-PRIVACY: ENCRYPTION

Encryption is necessary to secure confidentiality or secrecy or privacy. This requires an understanding of the encryption process. Most of such encryption in the past involved linguistic processes.

Consider the following example. Suppose two persons, A and B, would like to exchange information that may be intercepted by someone else. Yet A and B desire that even if a transmitted message is intercepted, anyone (other than A and B) should not be able to read it or make out what it says. Two friends may be gossiping or two senior executives in a large company may be exchanging commercially sensitive information about their company. This may be executed via e-mail (which can be intercepted rather easily). The most widespread use of secure communication is in the armed forces, where strategic commands are exchanged between various officers in such a fashion that the adversary should not be able to understand the meaning, even if they intercept the entire transcript of communication.

Let us first see how this objective could be achieved. Consider a *permutation* of the 26 letters of the Roman alphabet:

abcdefghijklmnopqrstuvwxyz
sqwtynbhgzkopcrvxdfjazeilm

Suppose that A and B both have this permutation (generated randomly). Now when A would like to send a message to B, he/she replaces every occurrence of the letter a by the letter s, letter b by q, and so on (a letter is replaced by the letter occurring just below it in the list given). Since B knows this scheme and also has this permutation, he can replace every letter by the letter occurring just above it in the list, and he can recover the message. This scheme has the disadvantage that word lengths remain the same and thus could be a starting point for *breaking the code*. This could be done using the same techniques that linguists have used to decode ancient scripts based on a few sentences written on stone. The word length remaining the same could be rectified by adding a *space* to the character set used (for ease of understanding we will denote a space by &). We will also add the punctuations , . and ?. Let us also add the 10 digits 0,1,2,3,4,5,6,7,8,9. Thus, our character set now has 40 elements. Let us write the character set and its permutation (randomly generated) as follows:

abcdefghijklmnopqrstuvwxyz0123456789&.,?
s&q69w5ty.n,b4hg0zk7opc8r?vxd1fjaze2ilm3

Now the coding scheme is a goes to s, b goes to & (space) and so on. Now even the word lengths would not be preserved, and so the attack based on word lengths would not be a threat. However, if a rather long message is sent using this scheme, say 15 pages of English text, then the scheme is not safe. A statistical analysis of the coded message would be a giveaway. It is based on the observation that frequencies of characters are different: vowels, in particular the letter e, occur most frequently in any large chunk of English text. Thus, word frequencies in the encoded text are a starting point for an attack in an attempt to recover an original message.

These are naive examples of encoding schemes. We can construct more complicated schemes, thereby making it more difficult for an attacker to recover an original message. For example, instead of one character at a time, we can form words of two characters, and have a permutation of two character words that could act as an encoding scheme. Perhaps too difficult to encode or decode manually, machines or computers could be used for these operations. For schemes that have these characters as the basic alphabet, linguists, along with mathematicians, could attempt to break the code, as was done for the Wehrmacht Enigma cipher used by Nazis during World War II. Different Enigma machines have been in commercial use since the 1920s. However, the German armed forces refined it during the 1930s. The breaking of the Werhmacht version was considered so sensitive that it was not even officially acknowledged until the 1970s.

Today, the information to be communicated is typically stored on a computer, and is thus represented using a binary code (as a string of 0s and 1s). So coding and decoding is of strings of 0s and 1s and in such a scheme, linguists have a minimal role, if any.

BASIC NUTS AND BOLTS OF CRYPTOLOGY

Let us now introduce terminology that we will use in the rest of the article. The message to be sent secretly is called *plaintext* (though it could be say a music file, or a photograph). We will assume that the text or the music file or photograph has been stored as a file on a storage device (using a commonly used format such as ASCII, mp3, or jpg). We will regard the plaintext as a string of 0s and 1s. The scheme, which transforms the plaintext to a secret message that can be safely transmitted, is called an *encryption algorithm,* while the encrypted message (secret message) is called the *ciphertext.* The shared secret, which is required for recovery of original plaintext from the ciphertext, is called the *key.* The scheme that recovers the ciphertext from plaintext using the key is called *decryption algorithm.*

The encryption/decryption algorithms that require a common key to be shared are known as the *symmetric key ciphers*. In this framework, there is an algorithm, Encrypt, that takes a plaintext M_0 and a key K_0 as input and outputs ciphertext C_0:

$$\text{Encrypt: } (M_0, K_0) \longrightarrow C_0$$

and an algorithm, Decrypt, that takes a ciphertext C_1 and a key K_1 as input and outputs plaintext M_1:

$$\text{Decrypt: } (C_1, K_1) \longrightarrow M_1.$$

The two algorithms, Encrypt and Decrypt, are related as follows: If the input to Decrypt is C_0, the output of Encrypt, and the key is K_0, the same as the key used in Encrypt, then the output of Decrypt is the plaintext M_0 that had been used as input to Encrypt. Thus, if A and B share a key K, A can take a plaintext M, use Encrypt with input (M,K) to obtain ciphertext C, and transmit it to B. Since B knows K, using (C,K) as input to Decrypt, B gets back the original message M that A had encrypted. The important point is that even if an interceptor obtains C, unless he has the original key K that was used as input to Encrypt, the message M cannot be recovered.

An adversary will try to systematically recover plaintext from ciphertext, or even better, to deduce the key (so that future communications encrypted using this key can also be recovered). It is usually assumed that the adversary knows the algorithm being used (i.e., the functions Encrypt and Decrypt), and he has intercepted the communication channel and has access to the ciphertext, but he does not know the true key that was used. This is the worst-case scenario. The algorithm has to be such that the adversary cannot recover the plaintext, or even a part of it in this worst-case scenario. The task of recovering the message without knowing the key or recovering the key itself is called cryptanalysis.

Here are different situations against which we need to guard the algorithm depending upon the usage:

- A *ciphertext-only attack* is one where the adversary (or cryptanalyst) tries to deduce the decryption key or plaintext by only observing ciphertext.
- A *chosen-plaintext attack* is one where the adversary chooses plaintext and is then given corresponding ciphertext in addition to the ciphertext of interest that he has intercepted. One way to mount such an attack is for the adversary to gain access to the equipment used for encryption (but not the encryption key, which may be securely embedded in the equipment).
- An *adaptive chosen-plaintext attack* is a chosen plaintext attack wherein the choice of plaintext may depend on the ciphertext received from previous requests.
- A *chosen-ciphertext attack* is one where the adversary selects the ciphertext and is then given the corresponding plaintext. One scenario where such an attack is relevant is if the adversary had past access to the equipment used for decryption (but not the decryption key, which may be securely embedded in the equipment), and has built a library of ciphertext-plaintext pairs. At a later time without access to such equipment, he will try to deduce the plaintext from (different) ciphertext that he may intercept.

One kind of attack that an adversary can always mount (once he knows the algorithm being used) is to sequentially try all possible keys one by one, and then the message will be one of the outputs of the decryption function. It is assumed that based on the context, the adversary has the capability to decide which of the decrypted outputs is the message. Thus, the total number of possible keys has to be large enough in order to rule out exhaustive search. Note that if all keys of p-bits are allowed, then p = 128 would suffice for this purpose, for now, as there will be 2^{128} possible keys. Let us examine why.

Suppose we have a machine that runs at 4GHz clock speed, and we have an excellent algorithm that decides in one cycle if a given p-bit string is the key or not. Then in 1 second, we will be able to scan through $4 \times 1024 \times 1024 \times 1024 = 2^{32}$ keys. In 1 year, there are approximately 2^{25} seconds, and thus in 1 year, we can scan 2^{57} keys. Even if we use 1,000 computers in parallel, we would still have covered only 2^{67} keys. Thus, the fact that there are 2^{128} possible keys assures us that exhaustive search will not be feasible or *exhaustive search is computationally infeasible*. While designing crypto algorithms, the designer tries to ensure that the total number of possible keys is so large that exhaustive search will take a very long time (given the present computing power), and at the same time ensuring that no other cryptanalytic attacks can be mounted.

We will now describe a commonly used family of ciphers, known as *stream ciphers*.

Many of the readers may be aware of *pseudo random number generators*. These are algorithms that start from a seed (or an initial value, typically an integer) that generates a sequence of 0s and 1s that appear to be random or generated by tossing of fair coin, where 0 corresponds to tails and 1 corresponds to heads. Another way to put it is the output is indistinguishable from the output of a sequence of fair coin tosses. For any integer N, this algorithm, with the seed as input, produces x_1, $x_2, \ldots, x_N$, where each x_i is 0 or 1. Such algorithms are part of every unix/Linux distribution, and also of most C/C++ implementations.

Suppose A wants to send plaintext (message) $m_1, m_2, \ldots, m_N$ (each m_i is either 0 or 1) to B. Let the shared secret key be an integer K. Using K as the seed, it generates random bits $x_1, x_2, \ldots, x_N$ and defines:

$$c_i = x_i \oplus m_i$$

(Here $\oplus$ is the addition modulo 2, $0 \oplus 0=0$, $0 \oplus 1=1$, $1 \oplus 0=1$, $1 \oplus 1=0$).

Now $c_1, c_2, \ldots, c_N$ is the ciphertext that can be transmitted by A to B. On receiving it, B uses the shared key K as the seed, generates the bits $x_1, x_2, \ldots, x_N$ and computes:

$$d_i = c_i \oplus x_i.$$

It can be verified easily that for all a, b in $\{0,1\}$, $(a \oplus b) \oplus b=a$, and thus $d_i = (x_i \oplus m_i) \oplus m_i$ for all i.

Thus, having access to the same random number generator algorithm and the same seed enables B to generate the same random bit-sequence x_1, $x_2, \ldots, x_n$ and thereby recover the message m_1, $m_2, \ldots, m_N$ from the ciphertext $c_1, c_2, \ldots, c_N$.

It should be noted that even if an adversary knew the algorithm or the scheme being used including the random number generator, as long as she does not know the secret shared K, the generation of $\{m_i\}$ would not be possible, and hence recovery of $\{x_i\}$ will not be possible.

So the strength of this algorithm is in the pseudorandom number generator. There are algorithms that are very good for simulation (for example, the Mersenne Twister algorithm), but are not good for using in a stream cipher in the manner described, since the entire sequence can be computed if we know a few of the previous bits. This can be utilized to mount an attack on a stream cipher based on the Mersenne Twister random number generation algorithm. There are other methods to generate pseudorandom numbers for cryptographic purposes that yield good stream ciphers. Most commonly used stream ciphers are based on linear feedback shift registers (LFSR). Several LFSRs are combined via a nonlinear combining function to yield a good random bit generator. The stream cipher encrypts the binary digits of the plaintext one by one using an encryption transformation that varies with time or the position of the bit to be encrypted in the sequence (Golomb, 1967).

Another type of symmetric key (or shared key) cipher that is commonly used is a *block cipher*. This divides the plaintext into blocks of fixed size (m-bits, say), and transforms each block into another block (preferably of the same size) in such a way that the operation can be inverted (necessary for decryption). This transformation is dependent on the key, and thus decryption is possible only when we know the key that was used for encryption. The encryption transformation that operates on a block does not vary with the position of the block (in contrast with the stream cipher). Also, if the ciphertext encrypted using a block cipher is transmitted over a noisy channel, a single transmission error would lead to erroneous decryption of the entire block. Thus, errors propagate over an entire block. When ciphertext encrypted using a stream cipher is transmitted over a noisy channel, errors do not propagate. Apart from this advantage that errors do not propagate, stream ciphers are faster than block ciphers when implemented in hardware. However, as of now, no single algorithm is accepted as a standard. Lots of algorithms that are in use are proprietary.

In the early 1970s, IBM established a set of standards for encryption. It culminated in 1977 with the adoption as a U.S. Federal Information Processing Standard for encrypting unclassified information. The data encryption standard (DES) thus became the most well-known cryptographic mechanism in history. It remains the standard means for securing electronic commerce for many financial institutions around the world. (see, Menezes et al., 1996, chapter I). Block ciphers have been extensively studied from the point of view of cryptanalysis. Two techniques, called differential cryptanalysis and linear cryptanalysis, are used in cryptanalysis. In differential cryptanalysis, two plaintexts are chosen with specific differences, and each is encrypted with the same key. The resulting ciphertexts are then studied for possible mathematical relationships. If a relationship can be found that, in turn, can be used to mount an attack, it is thus a chosen plaintext attack. It is widely believed that designers of DES were aware of this technique and thus ensured that DES is secure against differential cryptanalysis. Linear cryptanalysis consists of studying the relationship between specific bits of plaintext, key, and ciphertext. If it can be established that such a linear relationship exists with high probability, it can be used to recover (a part of) the plaintext.

With increasing computing power, experts realized in the nineties that they need a new standard. Several proposals were considered and finally, in 2000, an algorithm named, *Rijndael* had been chosen by experts as a standard, now known as *dvanced Encryption Standard* or AES (see Daemen & Rijmen, 2002, also see AES1, AES2, AES3). It is used extensively in many communication devises. This uses a 128-bit key, and is considered secure for commercial transactions.

While symmetric key ciphers (stream-ciphers and block-ciphers) require that the encryption and decryption is done using the *same* key, thus requiring the sender and receiver to share the key, another framework, called *public key encryption*, does away with this requirement. Originally proposed by Diffie and Hellman (1976), this scheme consists of two algorithms, encryption algorithm and decryption algorithm, and uses a pair of (distinct) keys, one for encryption and one for decryption. The scheme works as follows: each person (or entity) in a group generates a pair of keys; one key, called the *public key,* is available in a directory of all members (or stored with a trusted third party), and the other key, called the *private key,* is kept secret by each member. A public key E_0 and the corresponding private key D_0 are related as follows: a message encrypted with the key E_0 can be decrypted using the key D_0.

Let us denote the public keys of A, B by E_A and E_B, and private keys by D_A and D_B respectively. When A wants to send a message M to B, A obtains the public key E_B of B from the directory of members, and then encrypts the message M using this key- E_B and sends the ciphertext (encrypted message) to B. Now since B knows his/her private key D_B, he/she can decrypt the ciphertext using D_B and recover the message. Also, since D_B is known only to B, only B can recover the message.

Thus, public key encryption also has two algorithms, Encrypt and Decrypt. In this framework Encrypt that takes a plaintext M_0 and a key K_0 as input and outputs ciphertext C_0:

$$pubEncrypt: (M_0, K_0) \longrightarrow C_0$$

and an algorithm, Decrypt that takes a ciphertext C_1 and a key K_1 as input and outputs plaintext M_1:

$$pubDecrypt: (C_1, K_1) \longrightarrow M_1$$

The two algorithms, pubEncrypt and pubDecrypt, are related as follows: Let K_0 be the public key of an individual and K_1 be the corresponding private key (of the same entity). If the ciphertext input to pubDecrypt is C_0 (the output of pubEncrypt) and the key is K_1, then the output of pubDecrypt is the plaintext M_0 that had been used as input to Encrypt. Note that in symmetric key encryption, the requirement was that K_0 is the same as K_1, whereas in public key encryption, the requirement is that the pair (K_0, K_1) are respectively the public and private keys of the same entity.

Thus, A and B no longer need to share a key K, A only needs to know the public key K_0 of B and then he/she can take a plaintext M, use Encrypt with input (M, K_0) to obtain ciphertext C, and transmit it to B. Since B has the corresponding private key K_1, using (C, K_1) as input to Decrypt, B gets back the original message M that A had encrypted. The important point is that even if an interceptor obtains C, (and knows K_0, which is usually the case since the public key of all entities can be obtained) unless he/she has the corresponding private K_1, the message M cannot be recovered.

It is of course required that it should not be possible to compute the private key from the public key. Here, the phrase "not possible" is to be interpreted as computationally difficult in the sense that even several computers working in parallel would take years to compute the same. A commonly used algorithm used for public key cryptography is known as the RSA (The name RSA comes from the initials of the last names of authors Ron Rivest, Adi Shamir, and Len Adleman, who first described it). Yet another algorithm is ElGamal. The ElGamal algorithm is an asymmetric key encryption algorithm for public key cryptography, which is based on the Diffie-key agreement. Taher Elgamal discovered it in 1984.

The RSA was proposed in 1977. Initially, the computational requirements were thought to be so large, that it remained a mathematical curiosity. In fact, Clifford Cocks, in the British Intelligence Agency, proposed the same algorithm in 1973. MIT took out a patent in 1983 (which expired in 2000). Had Cocks' work been made public, it would not have been possible for MIT to patent it.

RSA is based on the widely accepted belief among experts that if p and q are two *large* prime numbers and n is their product, then given n is computationally difficult to factorize n (i.e., given n to determine p,q). What is large depends on the computational power available. Even in the late nineties, 24-bit primes, (prime numbers which in binary would require 24 bits to represent, roughly 8 digits in the decimal system) were considered very safe (p, q have to satisfy some additional restrictions). In this case n is about 48 bits. Currently, 64-bit primes are considered large enough for commercial applications, though for military and defense application, 512- or 1024-bit primes are used.

Why not use only public key cryptography and forget about symmetric key cryptography, since the former does not require sharing of a common secret key? Moreover, why not use 1024-bit primes even for commercial applications? The answer to both of these questions lies in the fact that the computational power required to encrypt or decrypt a message using public key cryptography is high, and it grows with the size of n. So public key cryptography has its limitations. Also, for a commercial communication involving a few thousand dollars, the adversary is not going to spend huge sums on breaking the code, whereas when it comes to a nation's security, the adversary can (and probably will) have a lot more resources (in terms of computing power) to try and break the code. Thus, we see that we can increase the *cost* of breaking the code for the adversary, but in turn we have to put in more resources for encryption and decryption. So like many other things in life, we have to strike a balance between costs and benefits.

So if a small piece of plaintext is to be sent, it can be encrypted using RSA. But if a long plaintext (say several pages of text along with some data files) is to be sent, it would be too time (and resource) consuming to encrypt it using RSA and we have to use a symmetric key cipher. An interesting solution is to use a combination of both. First a (random) key K of required size (for the chosen symmetric key cipher) is generated by the sender, and then this key K is encrypted using RSA and sent to the receiver, who retrieves K. Subsequently, the plaintext is encrypted using the agreed symmetric key algorithm and the key K and the ciphertext so generated is sent. The receiver already has K, and so she can decrypt it to get the plaintext.

In the evolution of the Internet, secrecy and authentication were not built into the design. Thus, unless otherwise instructed, the information is exchanged as it is and can be retrieved easily as other users also have access to the "packets" of information that are being exchanged. To be specific, say a student or a professor at a university accesses the server at her university via Telnet. After typing the login id, she types her password, which on her terminal shows as ******** so that someone looking at her screen cannot see it. However, it is very easy for someone at a university with access to another terminal on the same local area network (LAN) to capture the entire transcript of her session (all communications between her terminal and the server) including her password. The same is the story when someone accesses his or her Web-mail account through the "http" protocol from a browser. Thus, if someone gives her credit card number to a vendor while she has connected over a connection that is not "secure," the same information can be trapped by anyone who is monitoring the traffic.

To work around this is to build a secure layer over the Internet. Let us explain this with ssh, namely "secure shell" (which replaces Telnet), and **sftp**, "secure FTP" (which replaces FTP). Both **ssh** and **sftp** are built in most Linux distributions and are also available for Windows/Mac operating systems. At installation, the ssh client as well as the **ssh** server both generate a public key/private key pair. When an **ssh** client seeks a connection to an ssh server, they agree on one symmetric key algorithm and one public key algorithm to be used that are supported by both the server and client, then exchange their public keys. The **ssh** client then generates a session key for the agreed symmetric key cipher, encrypts it with the server's public key using the agreed public key algorithm, and transmits the resulting ciphertext. The **ssh** server now decrypts this and has the session key for a symmetric key cipher. Once this is done (all this is over in fraction of a second), all further communications are encrypted (and on receiving decrypted) using the session key. The same protocol applies when we use the **sftp**.

When a user accesses a Web site with an **https** protocol, the same steps as are carried out (provided the Web site is running the **https** server and the browser at the client end has the capability). So over a secure https connection, secret information can be transmitted safely. The user still has to ensure that others do not have access to his/her computer for the private key; (in principle) the session key as well as the information transmitted can be recovered from the user computer unless special precautions are taken. This now brings us to an important question. When a user accesses a Web site that he/she believes to be his/her bank and receives (or in the background, the browser receives) what is supposed to be his/her banks public key, how can he/she protect against the possibility that someone has intervened and replaced the bank's public key with another key? If indeed this happens, the user will send the session key to the imposter and subsequently, the information sent (could be his/her PIN or credit card number or other identification information) may be compromised. Thus there should be a way for the user to verify that the public key indeed belongs to the bank. This can be achieved via *digital signatures,* which we now discuss. This was introduced by Diffie and Hillman (1976).

DIGITAL SIGNATURE

When two persons/entities enter into a contract over the Internet (an e-contract), it is necessary that they put their *signature* on the contract so that, at a later date, either party cannot repudiate the fact that they had agreed to the terms of the contract. Of course this cannot be achieved by appending a signature at the end of the e-contract as in the paper contract since, in the e-form, parts can be changed, leaving the rest intact.

A digital signature will have to be something that binds the identity of signatory and the contents of the document being signed. The framework discussed earlier about public key cryptography can be used as a framework for the digital signature.

Once again we assume that various individuals (and entities) generate a public key and a private key pair for an agreed algorithm, say RSA. A trusted third party stores identities of individuals, along with their public keys. Suppose A wants to send a digitally signed document to B. Now A encrypts the document using his/her private key, and then the resulting ciphertext is now taken as the digitally signed document and sent

to B. On receiving the document, B can obtain A's public key and recover the document and, at the same time, be assured that it was signed by A. Moreover, in case of a dispute later, B can prove to a third party, say a court, that indeed A had signed the document; all he/she has to do is to preserve the ciphertext received and produce that as evidence.

Let us closely examine the last statement. The argument goes as follows: The ciphertext received is such that when decrypted using the public key of A it yields a meaningful text. Thus, it could only have been generated by someone who has access to A's private key. Since it is assumed that only A knows his/her private key, it must have been signed by A.

At the outset it looks to be a weak argument. The probability that someone can produce a bit stream that, when decrypted with A's public key, would yield meaningful text is very small, therefore, it must have been generated by A. It may still seem a rather weak argument, but it is accepted and indeed recognized by law in several countries. Indeed, this is the backbone of all e-commerce and e-transactions.

Let us assume that all individuals or entities that may exchange signed messages store their public key with a trusted third party. This trusted third party (TTP) itself generates a private key/public key pair, and its public key is available with each user. For each user, the TTP generates a digital certificate, it generates a document giving the identity of the user and the users public key, and signs it with its own private key. When A sends a digitally signed document to B, A also sends the digital certificate issued by TTP. Then B first decrypts the certificate using TTP's public key, thus recovering the identity as well as the public key (authenticated) of the sender, and can proceed to decrypt the ciphertext using the public key of the sender to recover the signed message.

Note that this system requires that there exists a trusted third party whose public key is known to all users; each user gets a digital certificate from TTP that binds his/her identity with his/her public key. Beyond this, the system does not require anything else. The individual users communicating with each other may be total strangers to each other.

In the scenario described, anyone who intercepts the communication can recover the document since all it needs is the public key of the sender. However, the same infrastructure can be used to have secret authenticated communication as follows: let KA1, KA2 be the public key and the private key of A ,and KB1 and KB2 be the public key and the private key of B. Suppose A wishes to send B a secret document, say M, signed by A. He/she follows the following steps.

Sign the document (using his/her private key) to generate C1, which is the signed document as described:

pubEncrypt: $(M, KA2) \longrightarrow C1.$

Encrypt C1 using public key of B to generate signed ciphertext C2:
pubEncrypt: $(C1, KB1) \longrightarrow C2.$

Transmit C2 to B:
B can now decrypt the transmitted message C2 using his/her private key:
pubDecrypt: $(C2, KB2) \longrightarrow C3.$

C3 is the same as C1. Thus, B has the digitally signed document C1. Now B can get the document (message) M by decrypting it using the public key of A. Moreover, B can retain the signed document C1 as proof that, indeed, A has signed the document M. Even if an adversary intercepts the transmission C2, (and knows or can find out the public keys of both A and B, but does not know the private key of B), he/she cannot recover C1 from C2, and so he/she cannot decrypt to get M.

Thus, the infrastructure for public key cryptography, a TTP, with a registry of users' identities and their public keys (while the users keep their private keys to themselves), suffices for digital signatures.

We had earlier remarked that if a large document is to be encrypted using a public key cryptoprotocol, say RSA, it needs a huge computational effort for encryption as well as decryption. Instead, it is common to exchange a session key for a symmetric key algorithm via public key algorithm, and then encrypt the message using this session key and symmetric key algorithm.

This does not work for a digital signature. The signature has to be something that depends on the full document and the identity of the person signing the document. However, there is one way to avoid signing the full document; it uses the notion of *hash function,* which we will discuss next.

DATA INTEGRITY

One way to ensure data integrity is to use hash functions. A hash function, or more precisely cryptographic hash function, h, is a function that takes as an input a message M (or a file) of arbitrary length and produces an output h(M) of fixed length, say n bits. The output h(M) is often referred to as the hash or hash value of M. Of course this would mean that there are bound to be collisions, that is, two distinct messages M_1, M_2 can lead to identical hash values ($h(M_1)=h(M_2)$). However, if the size of the output n is large, say 1,024, then the chance that two messages M_1, M_2 (chosen independently) could lead to the same hash value is very small – $2^{\{-1024\}}$. This is smaller than the probability that two randomly chosen persons have the same DNA!

Uses of the hash function: Suppose two users have downloaded a large file from the Web and, at a later date, would like to know if the two files are identical? Suppose they are in two locations far away from each other and can communicate over the Internet. Can this be done without the whole file being transferred from one location to the other? Yes, the two users can compute the hash value of their files and then compare the hash values. If they are identical, the chances are very high that the two files are the same. Another usage is in the distribution of public domain software, say *FileUtilities,* that is downloadable from several Web sites. How does the distributor and the buyer ensure that someone else is not passing off a malicious software in the name of *FileUtilities* name that has a virus embedded in it? One way to do this is (that along with the executable file) the creator publishes its hash value and before installing the software, the buyer cross-checks the hash value of the downloaded version with the value published by the creator.

In order that a hash function be useful for this purpose given, it is necessary that a change in the input leads to an unpredictable change in the hash value. If not, a malicious person can first change the file and then make other changes that have no effect on the virus, but lead to the same hash value as the original.

Desirable properties of a hash function:

- **Pre-image resistance:** given any y for which a corresponding input is not known, it is computationally infeasible to find any pre-image M such that h(M) =y.
- **2ⁿᵈ-pre-image resistance:** given M, it is computationally infeasible to find a 2nd-pre-image M* different from M such that h(M) = h(M*).
- **Collision resistance:** It is computationally infeasible to find any two distinct inputs M_1, M_2 that hash to the same output, that is, such that $h(M_1) = h(M_2)$. (Note that here there is free choice of both inputs.)

If h is a hash function with these properties, then for a message (or file) M, its hash value h(M) can be taken as a representative for the purposes described. Thus, if we are presented a copy M* of a message M (M* may be sent over an insecure channel, which is subject to tampering) and the hash value y=h(M) (say sent over a secure channel), we can compute the hash value h(M*), and if this equals y, we can conclude that M* is indeed a copy of the message M. This would follow from the 2nd pre-image resistance property.

Hash functions can be used for data integrity checks as follows: as soon as an authorized modification of a database (or some other data source) is carried out, the administrator can generate its hash value and store it securely. Now any modification (addition, deletion) would change the database and would disturb the hash value. Thus, the administrator can periodically compute the hash value and compare it with the value stored with him. If the hash values match, the administrator can be (almost) certain that the data has not been altered.

Hash functions can also be used in the context of a digital signature, where we wish to avoid huge computations involved in digitally signing a large document. Given a hash function h with the properties of pre-image resistance, 2ⁿᵈ-pre-image resistance, and collision resistance, in order to digitally sign a message M, first the hash value y of M is computed (h(M) = y) and y is digitally signed using RSA. Note that irrespective of the size of M, y has a fixed predetermined size. Of course M cannot be recovered from y, but M is sent along with the digitally signed copy of y. Now y is recovered from its signature and the hash value of M is computed. If these two quantities coincide, we can conclude that M was signed by the person who signed y.

We will now see the reasons for demanding the listed properties of the hash function. Here h should be 2ⁿᵈ-pre-image resistance, otherwise, an adversary may observe the signature of A on h(M), then find an M# such that h(M) = h(M#), and claim that A has signed M#. If the adversary is able to actually choose the message that A signs, then C need only find a collision pair (M, M#) rather than the harder task of finding a second pre-image of y=h(M#), thus collision resistance is also required. This forgery may be of concern if the attacker can find a pair (M, M#) with same hash such that M seems harmless and so the person agrees to sign it, while M# is something that the adversary could use (say a promise to pay $10,000!).

Number theory has played an important role in development and analysis of various algorithms described. As the computing power increases, there is need to develop new algorithms that need a lot more computing power to break, especially in defense applications. Elliptic curves are playing an increasing role in developments on the cryptography front. These days, the computing power available on desktops (and other low-cost computing environments such as Linux clusters) is large and is increasing. Thus, elliptic curve-based algorithms would become essential even for commercial algorithms.

AUTHENTICATION

All users of e-mail are used to logging into their accounts, where they choose a user name (or user_id) and then a password at the time of account set up and then, subsequently, when they wish to access their account, they have to identify themselves to the system by providing the user_id and password. The system checks this combination with the stored records and if it matches, then the user is allowed to access the account. In Unix/Linux systems, the password is not stored directly, but its hash value is stored (in some implementations, the password and user_id are concatenated to produce a string whose hash is stored). The same operation is done when a user tries to access the account and if hash values match, the access is allowed. A disadvantage of this system is that once a user has given password, someone having access to his/her system can trap it and, thereafter, impersonate him/her.

There are alternatives to this scheme; these are interactive and are based on challenge-response, Here when a user is trying to identify and authenticate himself, the system sends one or more challenges (a different set each time) and the user is to give an appropriate response. One such protocol, Feige-Fiat-Shamir (FFS) protocol (Feige, Fiat, & Shamir, 1988) relies on the computational difficulty of the problem of finding the square root modulo composite integers n that are the product of two large "RSA like" primes p,q (n=pq). This, and some other identification protocols, are known as *zerokKnowledgepProtocols(ZK)*.

They have a property that, at the end of the identification, they have passed on no other information than the identification itself. Thus, anyone having the full transcript of the communications by one user A over a period of time would still not be able to impersonate A.

We will discuss a simpler version of FFS called Fiat-Shamir protocol (Fiat & Shamir, 1987).

Setup time:

- A trusted third party generates RSA-like modulus n=pq and publishes n, but keeps p, q secret.
- Each user generates a random number s, $0<s<n$ (not equal to p,q) and computes $v=s^2$ modulo n and registers v (the users signature) with the trusted third party. The users signature is public knowledge.

Identification protocol: A user (prover) identifies himself/herself to the trusted party (verifier) and the verifier retrieves the prover's registered signature v. The following steps 1-4 are carried out say 20 times.

1. The user (prover) generates a random number r, $0<r<n$ and computes $x=r^2$ and sends x (called a witness) to the trusted party.
2. The trusted party (verifier) generates e=0 or e=1 with probability ½ each and sends e to the prover. (e is called challenge).
3. If e=0, the prover sends y=r and if e=1 sends y=rs to the verifier.
4. If e=0 and $y^2=x$ or if e=1 and $y^2=xv$ then accept the prover's claim.

If the prover's claim is accepted in all the rounds, then the prover's identity is accepted. At first glance, it would appear strange that in step 2, the verifier may select e=0 and would require the user to send only the random number r. This step is required to prevent forgery: suppose the prover always generates e=1 and a malicious person knows this (and also v, which is public knowledge), then the user can generate a number t, compute $x=t^2/v$ (modulo n) and send as witness and in step 3, send y=t. Without knowing s, the malicious person would have satisfied the condition $y^2=xv$. In this case, if e=0 is allowed, then the malicious person will not be able to send the square root of $x=t^2/v$ (modulo n) in step 3.

This protocol can be thought of as follows: in step 1, the prover sends a witness x and claims to have answers to the questions "what is r?" and "what is y=rs?", but in one instance would answer any of the two questions but not both (as it would reveal his/her secret).

CONCLUDING COMMENTS

In this chapter, we have four pillars of cryptology: confidentiality, data signature, data integrity, and authentication. Thus, we have discussed the problems that can occur when data is transmitted over *insecure* lines.

There are other dangers as well. Starting from someone observing the keystrokes when a person enters a key or password via a keyboard, to someone running a simple program on a person's computer that traps (and record) all keystrokes, an adversary can recover a key or password that was typed. Likewise, unless one is careful, one can recover files that were deleted (even after the recycle bin on Windows operating system has been emptied!). Garfinkel and Shelat (2003) analyzed 158 second-hand hard drives. They found that less than 10% had been sufficiently cleaned, and a wide variety of personal and confidential information was found in the rest. Thus, there

are simple measures that most people ignore to secure information. No amount of cryptographic safeguards can save us from human follies.

REFERENCES

Advanced Encryption Standard 1. (n.d.). Retrieved August 16, 2006 from http://csrc.nist.gov/publications/fips/fips197/fips-197.pdf

Advanced Encryption Standard 2. (n.d.). Retrieved August 16, 2006 from http://csrc.nist.gov/CryptoToolkit/aes/round1/conf2/papers/biham2.pdf

Advanced Encryption Standard 3. (n.d.). Retrieved August 16, 2006 from http://csrc.ncsl.nist.gov/CryptoToolkit/aes/rijndael/misc/nissc2.pdf

Daemen, J. & Rijmen, V. (2002). *The design of Rijndael: AES—the advanced encryption standard.* Berlin: Springer-Verlag.

Davies, D. W., & Price, W.L. (1989). *Security for computer networks* (2nd ed.). New York: John Wiley & Sons.

Diffie, W., & Hellman, M. E. (1976). New directions in cryptography. *IEEE Transactions on Information Theory, IT-22*(6), 644-654.

Feige, U., Fiat, A., & Shamir, A. (1988). Zero-knowledge proofs of identity. *Journal of Cryptography, 1,* 66-94.

Fiat, A., & Shamir, A. (1987). How to prove yourself: Practical solutions to identification and signature problems. *Advances in Cryptology—Crypto '86* (pp.186-194). Berlin: Springer-Verlag.

Garfinkel, S. L., & Shelat, A. (2003). Remembrance of data passed: A study of disk sanitation practise. *IEEE Security and Privacy, 1*(1), 17-27.

Golomb, S. W. (1982). *Shift register aequences.* San Francisco: Holden-Day. Walnut Creek: Aegean Park Press.

Kahn, D. (1967). *The codebreakers.* New York: Macmillan Publishing Company.

Menezes, A., van Oorschot, P., & Vanstone, S. (1996). *Handbook of applied cryptography.* Boca Raton: CRC Press.

Rivest, R. L., Shamir, A., & Adleman, L. (1978). A method for obtaining digital signatures and public-key cryptosystems. *Communications of the ACM, 21*(2), 120-126.

Schneier, B. (1996). *Applied cryptography: Protocols, algorithms, and source code in C* (2nd ed.). New York: John Wiley & Sons.

Chapter XII
A Comparison and Scenario Analysis of Leading Data Mining Software

John Wang
Montclair State University, USA

Xiaohua Hu
Drexel University, USA

Kimberly Hollister
Montclair State University, USA

Dan Zhu
Iowa State University, USA

ABSTRACT

Finding the right software is often hindered by different criteria as well as by technology changes. We performed an analytic hierarchy process (AHP) analysis using Expert Choice to determine which data mining package was best suitable for us. Deliberating a dozen alternatives and objectives led us to a series of pair-wise comparisons. When further synthesizing the results, Expert Choice helped us provide a clear rationale for the decision. The issue is that data mining technology is changing very rapidly. Our article focused only on the major suppliers typically available in the market place. The method and the process that we have used can be easily applied to analyze and compare other data mining software or knowledge management initiatives.

INTRODUCTION

Based on the *knowledge life cycle* model, four stages of knowledge creation, knowledge storage/retrieval, knowledge transfer, and knowledge application have been proposed by Alavi and Leidner

(2001) and confirmed by Jennex (2006). "To be effective knowledge management systems, KMS, must support the various knowledge management functions of knowledge capture, storage, search, retrieval, and use" (Jennex, 2006, p.3). Knowledge discovery is generally one of the important stages or phases of KM. And while this incorporates identifying critical knowledge (this may also be what this stage is called), using data mining to aid in knowledge discovery is appropriate as being a useful KM tool.

Data mining is a promising tool that assists companies to uncover patterns hidden in their data. These patterns may be further used to forecast customer behavior, products and processes. It is important that managers who understand the business, the data, and the general nature of the analytical methods are involved. Realistic expectation can yield rewarding results across a wide range of applications, from improving revenues to reducing costs (Davenport & Harris, 2007; Porter & Miller, 2001). It is crucial to properly collect and prepare the data, and to check the models against the real figures. The best model is often found after managers build models of several different types or by trying different technologies or algorithms. This alone demonstrates the active role managers play in the data mining or other knowledge management processes.

Selecting software is a practical yet very important problem for a company (James, Hakim, Chandras, King, & Variar, 2004). However, not enough attention is given to this critical task. Current literature is quite limited because selecting software is such a complex problem, due to many criteria and frequent technology changes (Elder IV & Abbott, 1998; Giraud-Carrier & Povel, 2003). Haughton, Deichmann, Eshghi, Sayek, Teebagy, and Topi (2003) generally reviewed several computer *software packages* for *data mining, including* SPSS Clementine, XLMiner, Quadstone, GhostMiner, and SAS Enterprise Miner. Corral, Griffin, and Jennex (2005) exam-

ined the potential of knowledge management in data warehousing from an expert's perspective. Jennex (2006) introduced technologies in support of knowledge management systems.

Firstly, this article will take a brief look at data mining today, through describing some of the opportunities, applications and available technologies. We will then discuss and analyze several of the most powerful data mining software tools available on the market today. Ultimately, we will also attempt to provide an analytical analysis and comparison among the brands we have selected. Our selection is based, in part, on our own experience using data mining software as well as writing data mining code, SQL code and our work as relational database administrators. For our analytical comparison we will be using *Expert Choice* (Version 11) advanced decision support software.

DATA MINING SOFTWARE

Data mining software analyzes- based on open-ended user queries- relationships and patterns that are stored in transaction data. Available are several types of analytical software: statistical, machine learning and neural networks, decision trees, Naive-Bayes, K-Nearest Neighbor, rule induction, clustering, rules based, linear and logistical regression time sequence, and so forth. Along the lines of Mena (1998) and Martin (2005), the basic steps of data mining for knowledge discoveries are:

1. Define business problem
2. Build data mining data base
3. Explore data
4. Prepare data for modeling
5. Build model
6. Evaluate model
7. Deploy model
8. Results

Note: Each of these steps contains managerial issues which must be addressed.

The key to knowledge discovery is a true understanding of your data and your business. Without this understanding, no algorithm is going to provide you with a result in which you should confide. Moreover, without this background you will not be able to identify the problems you are trying to solve, prepare the data for mining, or correctly interpret the results. There are many tasks involved in the construction of a database: data collection, data description, selection, data quality assessment and data cleansing, consolidation and integration, metadata construction, and maintaining the database. In exploring the data, the manager must choose the appropriate hardware to accomplish this feat. The goal is to identify the most important fields in predicting an outcome, and determine which derived values may be useful. According to O Chan (2005), a good interface and fast computer response are very important in this phase because the very nature of your exploration is changed when you often have to wait up to 30 minutes for some graphs to be created.

Preparing data for modeling consists of four main parts: selecting variables, selecting rows, constructing new variables and transforming variables. The managerial decision in this case focuses on identifying key variables to examine, nonfully functional variables inclusive. The time it takes to build a model increases with the number of variables while blindly including extraneous columns can lead to incorrect models. The most important thing to remember about data model building is that it is an interactive process. Many alternative models may have to be examined to find one that is most appropriate in solving your business problem. A manager searching for a good model may go back and amend the data he or she is using or even modify his or her problem statement. In the evaluation and interpretation process, the accuracy rate found during testing applies only to the data on which the model was built. The accuracy may vary if the data to which the model is applied differ in important and unpredictable ways from the original data set.

Once a data mining model is built and validated, it can be used in two main ways. First, the manager may recommend actions based on simply viewing the model and its results. For example, the manager may look at the clusters the model has identified, the rules that define the model or the lift and ROI charts that depict the effect of the model. The second process involves applying the model to different datasets. The manager may use the model to flag records based on their classification or assign a score such as the probability of an action.

Data Mining Software Alternatives

As stated earlier in our introduction, there are numerous data mining software alternatives that vary in the number of modeling and visualization nodes as well as in price. We have elected the following eight software vendors for comparison due to a limitation of trial version of *Expert Choice* (Version 11):

- Clementine from SPSS
- DB2 Intelligent Miner from IBM
- Enterprise Miner from SAS
- GhostMiner by Fujitsu
- Insightful Miner V5.2 for Insightful
- Megaputer PolyAnalyst
- Microsoft SQL Server 2005 Enterprise Edition
- Oracle Data Miner

Although there are various other comparable programs available, we were limited in our selection. One of the limiting factors was the inadequacy of alternatives in our decision tools' evaluation copy.

Decision Tool

To aid in comparing our software choices, we used an evaluation copy of *Expert Choice* version 11, a leading software solution construed to analyze, categorize, prioritize, select, allocate and choose a selection based on relevant criteria (Expert Choice Inc, 2007). *Expert Choice* incorporates a process known as *Analytical Hierarchical Process* (AHP) into its software (Saaty & Vargas, 2006; Saaty, 1980, 1996, 2001, 2005). Research has demonstrated that AHP is a powerful decision-making tool that can help organizations avoid making costly mistakes caused by bad decisions (Hemaida & Schmits, 2006). AHP was developed by Saaty and Kearns and consists of four stages (Roper-Lowe & Sharp, 1990). The first stage is to construct a hierarchy where the primary objective, or goal, is at the highest level. Criteria, which can also be subdivided, follow in decreasing order. At the bottom of the hierarchy are the alternatives to be evaluated. The second stage calculates weights for the criteria using pair-wise comparisons. In the next stage, the alternatives are also compared to each other in respect to each criterion. Finally, all weighted scores are tallied to yield a final score. The alternative with the highest score is considered the best alternative.

SAMPLE PRODUCTS

In this section, we will analyze the various features and benefits offered by each of our software alternatives that are to be considered, as well as researching product reviews and professional opinions. The information gathered from this analysis will serve as the basis for the pair-wise comparisons of the software alternatives with respect to each of our criteria In other words, we will investigate how important one choice is over the other alternative given a specific criterion, when comparing any two software alternatives,

CART by Salford Systems

CART is an easy to use decision tree tool that uses the CART algorithm and boosting. Its main objective is to rifle through databases, identifying significant patterns and relationships, which are then used to generate predictive models. CART uses an exhaustive, recursive partitioning routine to generate binary splits by posing a series of yes-no questions. It searches for questions that split nodes into relatively homogenous child nodes. As the tree evolves, the nodes become more homogenous, identifying segments. CART supports more than 80 file formats, including SAP, SPSS databases such as Oracle and Informix, Excel spreadsheets, and Lotus 1-2-3 spreadsheets.

CART was formulated from the original CART code developed by Stanford University and University of California at Berkeley statisticians. The frequent addition of new features and capabilities continually enhances the procedure, strengthening the accuracy and reliability of the results. CART has a no-stopping rule, which makes it unique. This means that more data are read and compared, and it ensures that important data are not overlooked by stopping too soon. It produces an over-grown tree, and immediately prunes it back for the most optimal results. CART also uses a powerful binary split search approach. This means the trees are more sparing with data and detect more structure before too little data are left for learning. Next, CART uses automatic self-validation procedures, which are essential in avoiding the trap of finding patterns that apply only to the training data.

CART was designed for both technical and nontechnical users. It can quickly identify important data relationships. It offers users some flexibility, with the choice of how to split criteria. It also offers different models for scalability. The results are easy to read and understand, with decision tree diagrams drawn out. Salford Systems understands that expert and timely technical support is a critical part of the business, which is why they offer many means of customer training and support. The company offers both public and private on-site instruction, user seminars, hand-on training courses, consultation services, and e-mail, NetMeeting, and phone support from offices worldwide.

SPSS—Clementine

Clementine data mining software by SPSS is useful for organizations using SPSS infrastructure as well as those with mixed platforms. This program supports both client and server platforms, including the Windows family of products and Sun Solaris, HP-UX11i, IBM AIX, and OS/400 server platforms.

With regard to reliability, Clementine by SPSS supports decision trees, neural networks, regression, self-organizing maps, clustering, and association rules (Lampe & Garcia, 2004). However, the author states that Clementine implements "a broad set of statistical algorithms, but fewer than in the SAS and IBM packages" (Lampe & Garcia, 2004, p. 18).

In the area of efficiency, Clementine works with SPSS, SAS and SQL and can export to C code and Predictive Model Markup Language (PPML) (Angus, 2006). It can also handle critical data preparation, rapid modeling, and model scoring tasks. These tasks are all performed using GUI graphical layouts, workflow diagrams, scatterplots, distribution, histogram, multiplot and Web charts (which are unique to Clementine (Haughton et al., 2003)).

Training and support for Clementine are available from SPSS in the form of online tutorials, downloadable overview and demos of the program, along with online technical support and excellent help screens. The price of Clementine starts at $75,000 (Angus, 2006).

Enterprise Miner by SAS

Enterprise Miner was developed by SAS Corporation, which was originally called Statistical Analysis System. Enterprise Miner is an integrated software product that provides widespread business solutions for data mining based on SEMMA (Sample, Explore, Modify, Model, Assess) methodology. It has many different statistical tools including decision trees, clustering, linear and logistic regression and neural networks. Data preparation tools include outlier detection, variable transformations, random sampling, and the partitioning of data sets into training, test, and validation data sets. Its advanced GUI allows you to review large amounts of data in multidimensional histograms with ease, as well as compare modeling results graphically.

Enterprise Miner includes several procedures that automate traditional analysis tasks, such as choosing the variables to include in a model and applying the appropriate transformations. The system also provides extensive visualization to help users explore the data to decide on additional manipulations that the system itself does not recommend. Enterprise Miners' graphical user interface and automated framework indicate that the user does not have to know how the tools work to use them. Release 8.2 provides cross-platform national language support that is especially important to international customers.

GhostMiner by Fujitsu

GhostMiner is a data mining software product from Fujitsu that not only supports common databases (or spreadsheets) and mature machine learning algorithms, but also assists with data preparation and selection, model validation, multimodels (like committees or k-classifiers), and visualization. GhostMiner provides a large range of **data preparation** techniques and a broad scope of **selection of featured** methods. Choice of data mining algorithms and v**isualization techniques** are integrated.

GhostMiner offers several project features unique to their platform, which enables users to create simple interfaces for their specific needs. GhostMiner has a human machine interface (HMI) that is fairly user friendly and easy to start up right out of the box. The system is so easy to use that it actually has a feel of being too user friendly and may be missing some of the power of the larger server based data mining software tool such as Darwin IBM and Oracle. GhostMiner can be loaded directly onto a Windows based PC and is equally adept at data mining a system database as it is a series of spreadsheets, text or ASCII files.

GhostMiner contains both data preprocessing capabilities as well as data visualization capabilities. Data preprocessing includes data normalization, standardization and many preliminary statistical analysis functions, such as variance, standard deviation, mean and median across the entire database. GhostMiner does not have the inherent flexibility of some of the larger, more robust products, and also does not offer the same levels of support as the products offered by Oracle and IBM. GhostMiner is a product marketed to small to mid size users who are looking for a simple to use product at a lower price than some of its larger, well known counterparts.

Insightful-Insightful Miner

Insightful Miner is a cost effective data mining software program. The software has numerous model types, algorithms and visualizers, including decision trees, *Block Model Averaging*, linear and logistic regression, neural networks, Naïve Bayes, Cox proportional hazard models, K-means clustering and others. Insightful Miner offers highly scalable algorithms, which train models on very large data sets without the need for sampling or

aggregation. Insightful also offers data preprocessing and data cleansing as well as exploratory data analysis and visualization. Insightful Miner's cost is typically $12,000.

According to a product review in *DM Review* (Lurie, 2004) the main strength of Insightful Miner is its ability to scale large data sets in an accessible manner. It provides the analytic tools required to transform fragmented raw data into "actionable knowledge" (Lurie, 2004, p. 88). Insightful Miner provides cutting edge analytics and reporting tools to identify patterns, trends and relationships in data. Insightfuls' simplicity allows users to quickly aggregate, clean and analyze data. Its powerful reporting and modeling capabilities allow users to deliver clear, usable analytics to designers and producers. Simple visual work maps make it easy for users to become productive relatively quickly. Insightful Miner provides excellent product support and its documentation is complete and easy to understand.

In another product review of Insightful Miner (Deal, 2004), the software was found to be a comprehensive data mining application that includes extensive data input, data manipulation, and analysis capabilities. Insightful Miner can efficiently process large amounts of data by using a chunking and processing algorithm that is intended to be scalable to the mass of data used for each analysis. Insightfuls' ability to integrate S-Plus strengthens and extends its functionality. Deal (2004) stated that Insightful Miner "is a very simple and intuitive process" (p. 46).

IBM-Intelligent Miner

IBM Intelligent Miner V7R1 is very user friendly software. It is an essential e-commerce tool, as it can aid in handling transactions as they come in. It has business intelligence applications, which allow it to make decisions that would be good for any business, large or small. The intelligence part of the software could cut costs and increase profits. The data screens help with decision making and improvement on processes that are out of date. It also maximizes the business to customer relationship, because of the personalization the software can provide for each client. This software package is also compatible with Windows, AIX, Solaris and Linux servers.

IBM Intelligent Miner V7R1 has IM Scoring, in which the user has an advantage, because scores and ranks are done in real time. This means that as a new transaction takes place, it would then reorganize the scores/ranks of the customers' information. For example, when a customer buys an item off the Internet, the software would update for the payment due and when it should be posted. The same would apply for a dentist visit: after 6 months it would indicate that it is time for another checkup for the particular patient. As the appointment would approach, the higher the person would be on the list, that is, moving up the ranks. Another advantage with the IM Scoring is the high performance and scalability of mining functions, thus making sampling obsolete.

The best aspect of this product is its user friendliness. The whole staff would be content with it. It can also be updated easily, without any disruption to the business. IBM is currently promoting the DB2 Query Management Facility version 8.1, because in March 2006, IBM withdrew Intelligent Miner from all marketing and ended all its support for Intelligent Miner tools.

Megaputer-PolyAnalyst

Another data mining software package is Poly-Analyst (the newest version is 4.6) made by the Megaputer Company. This company is quite small, especially compared to some of the other companies we have profiled. Megaputer Intelligence Inc. is a leading developer and distributor of advanced software tools for data mining, text mining, and intelligent e-commerce personalization. The tools help reveal knowledge hidden in data. They add intelligence and insight to every step of the business decision-making process.

Because the Megaputer Company focuses primarily on data mining programs, they can offer a more comprehensive program than other companies who simply have a data mining component to existing products. They offer a vast array of algorithms from which a consumer can choose the ones they need specifically, making the product ready to be customized. The price for an older version of PolyAnalyst (the most recent pricing data found) is an affordable $2,300 for the base version and can go up to $14,900 with all the algorithms. Also, the developer kit for PolyAnalyst is available for $16,000.

PolyAnalyst can be run either on a stand-alone system or in a client/server configuration, where the server would handle the data processing. It only works with the Microsoft Windows O/S, which shows that it is not as portable as some other products analyzed. Also, Megaputer offers possible users a free evaluation version to decide if this is the software right for them. The program offers a rich set of features. PolyAnalyst by Megaputer seems to be a feature rich data mining software package. The price and ala carte feature set seem more suited for a smaller company that cannot afford to use a more expensive data mining solution that would require the use of highly trained employees.

Oracle–Oracle Data Mining

Oracle Data Miner is the graphical user interface for Oracle Data Mining (Release 10.1 and above) that helps data analysts mine their Oracle data to find valuable hidden information, patterns, and new insights. Oracle Data Mining is a powerful data mining software embedded in the Oracle Database that enables you to discover new information hidden in your data and helps businesses target their best customers and find and prevent fraud.

Oracle provides unique portability across all major platforms including Windows, Solaris, HP-UX, IBM AIX, Compaq Tru64, and Linux and ensures that applications run without modification after changing platforms. There are two common ways to architect a database: client/server or multitier. Two basic memory structures are associated with Oracle software: the system global area and the program global area.

Oracle Data Miner facilitates interactive data preparation, data mining model creation, evaluation, refinement and model scoring. Oracle Data Mining provides the following supervised data mining algorithms: Naïve Bayes, Adaptive Bayes Network, decision trees, Support Vector Machines, and attribute importance. Unsupervised algorithms are: clustering, association rules, feature selection, anomaly detection, text mining and unstructured data, and life sciences algorithm. Mining Activity Guides provide structured templates for all users to explore and mine their data.

Oracle Data Mining (ODM) enables companies to extract information efficiently from the very largest databases, and build integrated business intelligence applications and support data mining problems such as: classification, prediction, regression, clustering, associations, attribute importance, feature extraction and sequence similarity searches and analysis. When the capabilities of Oracle Data Mining are combined with the ability of the RDBMS to access, preprocess, retrieve and analyze data, they create a very powerful platform for data analysis.

Oracle Data Mining can generate valuable new insights and reports that can help proactively manage your business, according to the Oracle Discoverer report. Oracle Data Miner models can be visualized graphically and can be display in tables, histograms, line graphs and pie graphs. Data may be in either Excel or the Database. Significant productivity enhancements are achieved by eliminating the extraction of data from the database to special-purpose data mining tools (Berger & Haberstroh, 2005).

Data size is unlimited. The expert analyst can adjust some or all of the parameters manu-ally, but the option to allow the algorithms to optimize the parameters intelligently, with no intervention, is available. There are free demos available: Oracle Data Mining, Integration with Oracle BI EE, Spreadsheet Add-in for Predictive Analytics, and Text Mining. The tutorial Oracle by Example series and online training provides valuable hands-on experience, step-by-step instructions on how to implement various technology solutions to business problems. Oracle Data Mining significantly reduces the cost of data mining. Savings are realized in the avoidance of additional hardware purchases for computing and storage environments, redundant copies and multiple versions of the data and duplication of personnel who perform similar functions. Database analytics includes: engine, basic statistics (free), data mining, and text mining.

SQL Server 2005

SQL server 2005 is Microsoft's solution to database management and data mining. SQL Server database platform provides enterprise-class data management with integrated business intelligence (BI) tools. SQL Server 2005 combines analysis, reporting, integration, and notification. SQL server is closely integrated with Microsoft Visual Studio, the Microsoft Office System, and a suite of new development tools, including the Business Intelligence Development Studio (Bednarz, 2005).

Microsoft SQL Server series utilizes the Windows operating system and features four discrete algorithms. HMI features include a Windows' interface, as well as complete integration with the Microsoft Office suite. Reports that are served by the Report Server in Reporting Services can run in the context of Microsoft SharePoint Portal Server and Microsoft Office System applications such as Microsoft Word and Microsoft Excel (Fontana, 2005). SharePoint can be used to subscribe to reports, create new versions of reports, and distribute reports. SQL Server 2005 also supports rich, full-text search applications. Query performance and scalability have been improved dramatically, and new management tools will provide greater insight into the full-text implementation.

SQL Server also features an online restore function, database encryption and a fast recovery option. It also has a system with built-in scalability features such as parallel partition processing, creation of *remote relational online analytical processing* (ROLAP) or *hybrid online analytical processing* (HOLAP) partitions, distributed partitioned cubes, persisted calculations, and proactive caching.

COMPARISON

We use *Expert Choice* in the evaluation process and will attempt to analytically quantify the aspects of data mining software that best define overall product quality. Before we describe the decision making process, we would like to present several assumptions on which our decision will be based:

1. In addition to our experience, we will rely on manufacture specifications, descriptions and described attributes, along with third party reviews where available.
2. We will base our needs on fundamental business goals such as business-related decision making and business-driven information analysis. Although this definition may seem overly broad, we will attempt to further limit our scope by eliminating research and development, educational and political as well as most human resource applications.
3. Because we are using a trial version of *Expert Choice* advanced decision making software, there will be limits with respect to importing and exporting data as well as with printing and possibly some advanced analytical tools. Therefore, we will utilize screen captures embedded into this document, and will manually write any necessary

data as opposed to systematic imports or exports.

Criteria Revisited

Our selection process will be centered on the below mentioned software quality criteria. We will attempt to compare all of our selections based on the specified criteria. Using *Expert Choice*, we will make objective ratings of each product, comparing in a pair-wise manner, attributes that define each element.

*   **Portability:** the amount of platform independence; the number of support platforms and supported software architectures as well as any software requirements needed to run the software.
*   **Reliability:** the degree of completeness, accuracy and consistency, any stated warranty and support provided by the vendor. The number of data models and algorithms available with the software as well as any templates or custom models available for creation of projects.
*   **Efficiency:** the degree of efficiency and accessibility; the degree in which the product supports the general business goal assumptions and the number of tools available for data preprocessing.
*   **Human engineering:** how well the software interfaces and communicates with the outside world, plus the quality of the human machine interface (HMI). Testability – how well the software is structured; how results are displayed and how results are reintroduced into the process if applicable.
*   **Understanding:** degree of self-descriptiveness; the degree of simplicity of the machine interface, the use of graphical user interfaces, visual programming ability, summary reports, and data model visualization.
*   **Modifiability:** the degree of augmentation ability and the ability to change over time

and expand; the use of batch processing and any expert options as well as data size limitations.

- **Price, training and support:** price of product, availability of evaluation or demo versions, and the amount of post purchase support included in the package.

Evaluation Model

Our evaluation criteria, as entered in the Expert Choice, are as follows:

- Portability: evaluated in terms of:
  - ○ Hardware platform (PC, Unix/Solaris workstation, etc.).

- ○ Software Architecture (standalone, client/server, thin client).
- ○ Software requirements (DB2, SAS, Base, Java/JRE, Oracle, and so forth.
- Reliability - evaluated in terms of:
  - ○ What model classes does the tool support?
  - ○ How many algorithms does the tool use?
  - ○ Does the tool allow custom model creation or simply uses templates?
  - ○ What is the reputation of the vendor supplying the tool?
- Efficiency evaluated in terms of:
  - ○ How well does the product support our general business goal assumption?
  - ○ Ability to perform data preprocessing.
- Human Engineering evaluated in terms of:
  - ○ Simplicity of HMI (human machine interface)
  - ○ Graphical layout
  - ○ Visual programming ability
- Testability evaluated in terms of dissemination and deployment:
  - ○ How well the results are reintroduced into the process "closing the loop"
  - ○ How results are displayed
- Understanding in terms of evaluation and interpretation of data:

Table 1. Weights assigned to criteria

Category	Priorities
Human Engineering	0.22
Training and Support	0.193
Understandability	0.19
Reliability	0.142
Portability	0.128
Modifiability	0.051
Efficiency	0.039
Testability	0.022
Price	0.016

Table 2. Pair-wise comparison grid WRT hardware platform

	CART by Salford Systems	SAS Enterprise Miner	Oracle 8i	GhostMiner	SQL Server 2005
CART by Salford Systems		3.0	3.0	3.0	7.0
SAS Enterprise Miner			2.0	3.0	4.0
Oracle 8i				3.0	3.0
GhostMiner					4.0
SQL Server 2005					
Inconsistency: 0.73					

Table 3. Class weightings for overall hardware platform independence

Vendor	Class Weighting
CART by Salford Systems	0.268
SAS Enterprise Miner	0.223
Oracle 8i	0.215
GhostMiner	0.141
SQP Server 2005	0.152
Overall inconsistency: 0.28	

Table 4. Results from "Choosing a data mining software vendor"

Vendor	Overall Weight
CART by Salford Systems	0.191
SAS Enterprise Miner	0.215
Oracle 8i	0.222
GhostMiner	0.109
SQP Server 2005	0.263
Inconsistency: 0.73	

- Are summary reports available?
- Can the model be visualized graphically?
- Modifiability in terms of scalability and upgrades:
  - What is the data set size limit?
  - Are there expert options or batch processing?
- Training and support evaluated in terms of:
  - Is a free demo available?
  - Is any free training or support available with the purchase?
- Price (where available) – if pricing is not available we will note our evaluation as price neutral.

PROCEDURE OF EXPERT CHOICE

Let's use five products to demonstrate the whole process of *Expert Choice* on a small scale. We commence with pair-wise comparisons for each of our criteria. Figure 1 is a screen capture of

Table 5. Dynamic sensitivity analysis

Category	Category Weight	Vendor	Vendor Preference Weight
Portability	12.8%	CART by Salford Systems	26.8%
Reliability	14.2%	SAS Enterprise Miner	22.3%
Efficiency	3.9%	Oracle 8i	21.5%
Human Engineering	22.0%	GhostMiner	14.1%
Testability	2.2%	SQL Server 2005	15.2%
Understandability	19.0%		
Modifiability	5.1%		
Training and Support	19.3%		
Price	1.6%		

Table 6. Dynamic sensitivity analysis with different constraints

Category	Category Weight	Vendor	Vendor Preference Weight
Portability	0.1%	CART by Salford Systems	24.0%
Reliability	2.6%	SAS Enterprise Miner	18.5%
Efficiency	3.2%	Oracle 8i	17.1%
Human Engineering	5.8%	GhostMiner	20.8%
Testability	3.3%	SQL Server 2005	19.6%
Understandability	21.5%		
Modifiability	4.1%		
Training and Support	15.7%		
Price	33.5%		

our initial results of priorities. As can be seen in Table 1, we placed a great deal of importance on Human Engineering (weight of .220), slightly less on Training and Support (w=. 193) and then on Understanding (w=. 190). Our main driver was that for the software to be successful, people had to know and understand it. Our next highest priority was Reliability, with a relative weight of .142, followed by Portability, which is platform and hardware independence, with a relative weight of .128.

Next, we perform a pair-wise comparison of each software tool for each criterion; that is, we compare the components of each criterion on a case-by-case basis, assigning relative strengths and weaknesses to each product. Although this process is quite tedious, it provides an accurate measurement for each product. Table 2 shows an example of a pair-wise comparison for the contribution of hardware platform independence to overall platform independence, which is a contributor to overall portability within our quality structure.

Table 3 shows a graphical representation from the pair-wise comparison between all products for the hardware contribution, to overall portability. The screen capture shows a weight for each prod-

uct with SQL Server as the best in class (with a weight of .269) and GhostMiner as last in class (with a weight of .109). These criteria are also weighted individually so as to roll up into the overall contribution toward portability.

Overall Results

Table 4 shows the overall results from *Expert Choice* advanced decision support software. From the first iteration of our selection process, the best solution for our chosen attributes and assigned priorities is the CART product, with an overall weight of .268, followed by SAS Enterprise with an overall weight of .223. We also performed several iterations, changing the weights of our criteria.

Table 5 shows the assigned weights of each category along with the overall score for all of the objects. This tool allows dynamic sensitivity analysis with respect to changing priorities. We used this tool to look at how much a change in one weight changes the overall goal. Using this tool is similar to the sensitivity analysis performed in Excel Solver; however, instead of listed ranges the Expert Choice tool allows for dynamic manipulation. From the chart, we can see our weighted emphasis on Human Engineering (22%), Training and Support (19.3%) and Understandability. The window on the right shows which system best fits our stated criteria.

In Table 6 we change our requirements in order to verify the strength of our decision. We increase the importance of Price from 1.6% all the way up to 33.5%. We also change our Human Engineering requirement from 22% down to 5.8%, and also reduce Training and Technical Support, Portability, Reliability, Efficiency and Modifiability (flexibility) substantially and still came up with CART systems as our best overall choice (24% weight).

SCENARIO ANALYSIS

We now start to compare eight leading data mining packages based on seven criteria. Determining the best software is a multiple objective decision-making process because different companies may have completely different needs. An array of software may each be the best choice because their design and performance are defined within a certain type of institution. Usually, one data mining software cannot be the best for every scenario. This is because specific software cannot meet the expectations of every type of institution; therefore, the creation of scenarios is a very important tool in term of decision-making process.

Table 7. Weights assigned to each alternative for both a small and large-sized company

Synthesized Weights - with respect to criteria	Efficiency		Human Engineering\ Understandability		Modifiability		Portability	
	Large	Small	Large	Small	Large	Small	Large	Small
Clementine	0.213	0.153	0.154	0.154	0.159	0.159	0.200	0.059
Enterprise Miner	0.176	0.174	0.155	0.155	0.151	0.151	0.221	0.059
GhostMiner	0.110	0.102	0.124	0.124	0.069	0.069	0.069	0.235
Insightful Miner	0.142	0.168	0.135	0.135	0.108	0.108	0.097	0.235
Intelligent Miner	0.106	0.130	0.112	0.112	0.155	0.155	0.097	0.059
Megaputer	0.086	0.091	0.090	0.090	0.060	0.060	0.067	0.235
Oracle Data Miner	0.102	0.103	0.104	0.104	0.151	0.151	0.148	0.059
SQL Server 2005	0.066	0.078	0.126	0.126	0.147	0.147	0.079	0.059

Synthesized Weights – continued	Reliability		Training and Support\Price		Testability	
	Large	Small	Large	Small	Large	Small
Clementine	0.194	0.194	0.040	0.036	0.156	0.156
Enterprise Miner	0.206	0.206	0.027	0.025	0.149	0.149
GhostMiner	0.069	0.069	0.170	0.194	0.116	0.116
Insightful Miner	0.107	0.107	0.261	0.266	0.147	0.147
Intelligent Miner	0.110	0.110	0.029	0.024	0.099	0.099
Megaputer	0.147	0.147	0.261	0.349	0.151	0.151
Oracle Data Miner	0.101	0.101	0.108	0.051	0.096	0.096
SQL Server 2005	0.066	0.066	0.104	0.054	0.086	0.086

In order to make this project more accurate and realistic, we have combined different scenarios. Factors, such as size, budget, type of business, and the type of data we have to manipulate, can affect the software we attempt to choose and the reasons why we choose it. Having simulated many scenarios, we found that size is a decisive factor. For instance, if we choose two companies with different sizes and follow a traditional reasoning, the tentative result may contradict with our intuition.

After researching all the alternatives, we used our decision tool, *Expert Choice*, to make pair-wise comparisons for each of them. A total of 392 pair-wise comparisons were required to compare each of the alternatives with respect to each of the criteria (196 comparisons for each scenario). This was in addition to the 42 pair-wise comparisons required to assign weights to each criterion with respect to the goal (21 comparisons for each scenario). After completing all of the pair-wise comparisons the software synthesized all of the weights of the alternatives with the weights of the criteria and selected the best alternative of each of the two scenarios. Table 7 below summarizes the weights of the pair-wise comparisons for each of the alternatives with respect to each criterion. As with the weights of the criteria, there is also a direct relationship between the calculated weights in each column and the respective criterion. In other words, the higher a number is in a given column the more important that sized company views that particular software for that specific criterion.

Based on our research of all the alternatives and the weighted criteria calculated by our decision tool, the software has determined that for a small-sized company the top three alternatives are Insightful Miner, Megaputer PolyAnalyst, and SAS Enterprise Miner. These results were somewhat unexpected. We had anticipated that Insightful, Megaputer, and GhostMiner would be among the top three or four alternatives for a small-sized company, primarily because each of these vendors offer stand-alone versions of their software and are also the least expensive among all the alternatives. However, GhostMiner ranked lower than expected while SAS Enterprise Miner ranked higher. A closer analysis of the pair-wise comparisons shows that SAS was more efficient and had better human engineering than Ghost-Miner. Because of the weights given to these two criteria, SAS Enterprise Miner was able to beat all of the other alternatives despite its cost.

According to our decision tool, the top three alternatives for a large company are SPSS Clementine, followed by SAS Enterprise Miner and Insightful Miner. There was not one overwhelming choice for a large company. The differences in weight among the top three alternatives were relatively small (16.7%, 15.9%, and 13.5%, respectively). These results were also a little unanticipated. All of the software reviews that we have read rated SPSS and SAS among the top leading data mining software that are commercially available. We had not expected Insightful Miner to rank among the top three alternatives for a large company. We anticipated that Microsoft, IBM, or Oracle would round out the top three alternatives because these vendors offer enterprise class DBMS. Upon closer examination of the software analysis, Insightful Miner's visualization and modeling nodes were comparable to those of an enterprise class data mining software program such as Enterprise Miner and Clementine. In addition, a closer review of the pair-wise comparisons showed that Insightful Miner ranked higher than the other alternatives (with the exception of SAS and SPSS) in human engineering and efficiency. It also tied for top weight for Training and Support/Price. Table 8 below summarizes the results of the Expert Choice software.

Certainly, different companies may have different priorities, preferences, and prerequisites. We have explored a few individual scenarios.

Special Case 1: This is a large international company, with thousands of employees, doing business between U.S., Mexico and other countries in Latin America. It is an import and export company. The main goal of using data mining software is to determine the best distribution methods in order to maximize profits. Keeping costs down so it can compete with other companies is always a concern. The three main criteria this company is looking for in a software package are: Training and Support with multilingual support because of the language difference between the countries, Human Engineering to assure that employees in different countries with possibly different computer skill levels, will be able to adapt and use the software, and Portability because it is an established company with an IT department and different platforms that include Microsoft, IBM and Sun Microsystems, as well as a range of desktop operating systems that includes Windows 2000 and XP, Linux, and old legacy equipment. They must be certain that the software is compatible with all existing platforms. Because large amounts of data are processed, software must be robust and reliable as well.

- **Our goal is:** To find the best data mining software.
- **Our criteria are:** Listed seven factors. The three most important criteria are Training and Support, Human engineering, and Portability.
- **Our alternatives are:** Clementine, Enterprise Miner, Oracle, Microsoft SQL, IBM DB2, Salford CART, Megaputer, and Insightful Miner.

Criteria	Weights
Portability	.215
Modifiability	.181
Training and Support	.147
Human Engineering/Testability	.130
Understandability	.119
Reliability	.109
Efficiency	.100

Software	Ranking
Clementine	.136
Enterprise Miner	.126
Oracle	.162
Microsoft SQL	.109
IBM DB2	.117
Salford CART	.123
Megaputer	.111
Insightful Miner	.117

Special Case 2: This is a large national corporation, between 500 and 1,000 employees, in the retail industry with many branches throughout the country. They already have an IT department and different types of platforms, including Unix Servers and Microsoft 2000 and 2003, as well as XP and 2000 Workstations. Portability is very important to make sure that the software is able to run with the platforms already in place. This company already has a well-established customer base, so the goal of choosing data mining software is to find the best way to maximize customer retention, while lowering costs. The three most important criteria that this company is looking for in a software package are: Portability, Efficiency to assure it supports the general business goal assumption, and Modifiability because it is a growing business, and they want to be sure that they can go back and customize the software if necessary.

- **Our goal is:** To find the best data mining software.
- **Our criteria are:** Listed seven factors. The three most important criteria are portability, efficiency, and modifiability.
- **Our alternatives are:** Clementine, Enterprise Miner, Oracle, Microsoft SQL, IBM DB2, Salford CART, Megaputer, and Insightful Miner.

Criteria	Weights
Modifiability	.217
Portability	.171
Efficiency	.153
Reliability	.132
Training and Support	.126
Human Engineering/Testability	.123
Understandability	.078

Software	Ranking
Clementine	.134
Enterprise Miner	.127
Oracle	.163
Microsoft SQL	.110
IBM DB2	.115
Salford CART	.125
Megaputer	.108
Insightful Miner	.117

Special Case 3: This is a small start-up landscaping and construction company with less than 50 employees. The employees have limited knowledge of computers and software. The goal of using data mining software is to find the best way to attract new customers.

- **Our goal is:** To find the best data mining software.
- **Our: criteria are:** Listed seven factors. The three most important criteria we are looking for are Human engineering, Training and Support, and Understandability.

- **Our alternatives are:** Clementine, Enterprise Miner, Oracle, Microsoft SQL, IBM DB2, Salford CART, Megaputer, and Insightful Miner.

Criteria	Weights
Training and Support	.226
Human Engineering/Testability	.201
Understandability	.166
Reliability	.145
Efficiency	.130
Modifiability	.076
Portability	.055

Software	Ranking
Clementine	.132
Enterprise Miner	.124
Oracle	.150
Microsoft SQL	.124
IBM DB2	.117
Salford CART	.122
Megaputer	.114
Insightful Miner	.118

Other Cases

Online Company/E-commerce

An online/e-commerce company in the recently growing industry: First of all, because an Internet company has both actual and potential customers, it needs a tool that can hold and analyze

Ideal mode / Alternative	PAIRWISE Portability (L: .055)	PAIRWISE Reliability (L: .145)	PAIRWISE Efficiency (L: .130)	PAIRWISE Human Engineering/ Testability (L: .201)	PAIRWISE Understandability (L: .166)	PAIRWISE Modifiability (L: .076)	PAIRWISE Training and Support (L: .226)
☑ Clementine	.793	.819	.806	.974	.988	.671	.861
☑ Enterprise Miner	.684	.725	1.000	.920	.944	.625	.677
☑ Oracle	1.000	1.000	.993	.984	.946	1.000	1.000
☑ Microsoft SQL	.236	.763	.862	.857	.951	.444	.968
☑ IBM DB2	.727	.806	.796	.714	.923	.389	.814
☑ Salford CART	.527	.738	.855	.783	1.000	.777	.767
☑ Megaputer	.360	.529	.268	1.000	.925	.826	.898
☑ Insightful Miner	.371	.607	.473	.858	.974	.923	.999

large amounts of data. Secondly, it might have engineers or a technical department, so it may not put weight on human engineering and training and support. Consequently, we put more weight on modifiability and less weight on engineering and support. As a result, Oracle would be the best tool for an online/e-commerce company because it scores the highest among eight tools. If Oracle is not available, IBM would be the second choice.

Educational Institutions

Data mining software is used worldwide in the educational industry. One of Megaputer's data mining software called PolyAnalyst gets a majority of its business from educational industry. Microsoft SQL came in first place with Ghost-Miner as the runner up.

Even though these scenarios can be used as references, they did not apply to every type of institution. Thus, it will be interesting to see what other choices are available in term of the best data mining software. What would be the best data mining software for a medical institution?

CONCLUSION

With the use of *Expert Choice* we were able to analytically evaluate eight products within a complex yet controlled environment. The detailed analysis included prioritizing our constraints, evaluating the contributing criteria, entering comparative data and performing relevant sensitivity analysis. The software, *Expert Choice,* performed the analysis, based on our definition, priorities and data.

Data mining technology is changing very rapidly. Our article focused only on the major suppliers typically available in the market place. There is no definite and explicit answer as to which tool is better suited to potential clients, mainly due to their unique priorities. As there

are so many variables to quantify, the problem needs to be defined. Based on what approach the problem requires, then and only then can tools start being quantified. Certainly, the method and the process that we have used can be easily applied to analyze and compare other data mining software for each potential user. Although there is no pattern for pairing the correct software with the proper institution, with the use of this process, every institution should be able to determine which data mining software is the best for their operations.

ACKNOWLEDGMENT

We would like to thank Dr. Jennex, the *Edit-in-Chief of IJKM,* for his tremendous help and guidance during the period of revising our manuscript for more than one year. Dr. Jennex has suggested *Scenario Analysis,* a practical and wonderful idea, and offered many other specific suggestions.

REFERENCES

Alavi, M., & Leidner, D.E. (2001). Knowledge management systems: Emerging views and practices from the field. In *Proceedings of the 32nd Hawaii International Conference on Systems Sciences. IEEE Computer Society.*

Angus, J. (2006). Clementine 8.1 melds BA with BI. *InfoWorld, 26*(19), 28-29.

Bednarz, A. (2005). Microsoft beefs up SQL Server database. *Network World, 22*(13), 12.

Berger, C., & Haberstroh, B. (2005). *Oracle data mining 10g release 2: Know more, do more, spend less.* Oracle White Papers. Retrieved November 8, 2007 from http://www.oracle.com/technology/products/bi/odm/pdf/bwp_db_odm_10gr2_0905.pdf

Corral, K., Griffin, J., & Jennex, M.E. (2005). Expert's perspective: The potential of knowledge management in Data Warehousing. *Business Intelligence Journal, 10*(1), 36-40.

Davenport, T., & Harris, J. G. (2007). *Competing on analytics: The new science of winning.* Harvard Business School Press.

Deal, K. (2004). The quest for prediction. *Marketing Research, 16*(4), 45-47.

Elder IV, J.F., & Abbott, D.W. (1998, August 28). A comparison of leading data mining tools. In *Proceedings of the Fourth International Conference on Knowledge Discovery & Data 5Mining,* New York.

Expert Choice Inc. (2007). *Expert Choice 11.* Retrieved November 8, 2007, from http://www.expertchoice.com/software/

Fontana, J. (2005). Microsoft's future in BI market unclear. *Network World, 22*(43), 9-14.

Giraud-Carrier, C., & Povel, O. (2003). Characterizing data mining software. *Intelligent Data Analysis, 7*(3), 181-192.

Haughton, D., Deichmann, J., Eshghi, A., Sayek, S., Teebagy, N., & Topi, A. (2003). A review of software packages for data mining. *The American Statistician, 57*(4), 290-309.

Hemaida, R., & Schmits, J. (2006). An analytical approach to vendor selection. *Industrial Management, 48*(3), 18-24.

James, G., Hakim, J., Chandras, R., King, N., & Variar, G. (2004). Reviewers' choice: Only the best survive. *Intelligent Enterprise, 7*(1), 34-38.

Jennex, M.E. (2006, April). Technologies in support of knowledge management systems. In *Proceedings of the 6th International Forum on Knowledge Management,* Tunis.

Lampe, J. C., & Garcia, A. (2004). Data mining: An in-depth look. *Internal Auditing, 19*(2), 4-20.

Lurie, I. (2004). Product Review: Insightful Miner. *DM Review, 14*(6), 88.

Martin, W. E. (2005). *Managing information technology* (5th ed.). Saddle River, NJ: Prentice Hall.

Mena, J. (1998). Data mining FAQ's. *DM Review.*

O Chan, J. (2000). Enterprise information system strategy and planning. *Journal of American Business, Cambridge, 6*(2), 148-154.

Porter, M. E., & Miller, V. (2001). Strategy and the Internet. *Harvard Business Review, 72*(3), 62-68.

Roper-Lowe, G. C., & Sharp, J. A. (1990). The analytic hierarchy process and its application to an information technology decision. *The Journal of the Operational Research Society, 41*(1), 49-59.

Saaty, T.L. (1980). *Multicriteria decision making: The analytic hierarchy process.* RWS Publications.

Saaty, T.L. (1996). *Decision making with dependence and feedback: The analytic network process.* Pittsburgh, PA: RWS Publications.

Saaty, T.L. (2001). *The analytic network process* (2nd version). Pittsburgh, PA: RWS Publications.

Saaty, T.L. (2005). *Theory and applications of the analytic network process.* Pittsburgh. PA: RWS Publications.

Saaty, T.L., & Vargas, L.G. (2006). *Decision making with the analytic network process: Economic, political, social and technological applications with benefits, opportunities, costs and risks.* New York: Springer-Verlag.

This work was previously published in International Journal of Knowledge Management, Vol. 4, Issue 2, edited by M. E. Jennex, pp. 17-34, copyright 2008 by IGI Publishing, formerly known as Idea Group Publishing (an imprint of IGI Global).

Section IV
Utilization and Application

Chapter XIII
End-User Perceptions of the Benefits and Risks of End-User Web Development

Tanya McGill
Murdoch University, Australia

Chris Klisc
Murdoch University, Australia

ABSTRACT

The development of applications by end users has become an integral part of organizational information provision. It has been established that there are both benefits and risks associated with end-user development, particularly in the areas of spreadsheets and databases. Web development tools are enabling a new kind of end-user development. The fact that Web page creation may impact, not only locally but also globally, significantly raises the importance of this type of end-user application development. This article reports on the extent of Web page development amongst end users and investigates their perceptions of the benefits and risks of end-user Web development relative to those associated with spreadsheet development and explores approaches to reducing the risks.

INTRODUCTION

End-user computing now dominates organizational use of information technology worldwide. Its growth has been driven by increasingly inexpensive hardware, increasingly powerful and easy to use software, and user demand for control of information resources (McLean, Kappelman & Thompson, 1993; Shayo, Guthrie & Igbaria, 1999). Organizations also rely heavily on applications developed by end users. These applications support a wide range of information provision and decision making activities and contribute to business processing in a wide range of tasks (Rittenberg, Senn & Bariff, 1990). Increasingly, the ability to develop small applications forms part of the job requirements for many positions (Jawahar & Elango, 2001). The study reported on in this article explores the expansion end-user developers are experiencing as they add the role of Web page developer to their repertoire of end-user development skills, and investigates end-user perceptions of the benefits and risks of end-user Web development relative to those of end-user spreadsheet development.

Although a wide range of tools is available for use by end-user developers, the most commonly used software tools have been spreadsheets (Rittenberg et al., 1990). The majority (88%) of the 34 organizations participating in Taylor, Moynihan, and Wood-Harper's (1998) study used spreadsheets for end-user development whereas only 35% used query languages and 12% used databases. Recently Web development tools have started to be used by end-user developers (Govindarajulu, 2003; Nelson & Todd, 1999; O'Brien, 2002; Ouellette, 1999), and it is anticipated that this use will increase rapidly in years to come (Goupil, 2000). Very little is known, however, about how end users acquire the skills necessary for successful development or about how and why they develop Web applications.

A substantial body of research has investigated the benefits and risks of development by end users and explored the factors that influence them (e.g., Alavi & Weiss, 1985-1986; Amoroso & Cheney, 1992; Benson, 1983; Brancheau & Brown, 1993; Davis, 1988; O'Donnell & March, 1987; Rivard & Huff, 1984, 1985). The benefits that have been claimed include improved decision making, improved productivity, and increased satisfaction of end users (Amoroso & Cheney, 1992). The risks that have been identified include mismatches between tools and applications (Alavi & Weiss, 1985-1986; Davis, 1988; O'Donnell & March, 1987), lack of testing (Alavi & Weiss, 1985-1986; Davis, 1988; O'Donnell & March, 1987), inability to identify correct and complete information requirements (Davis, 1988) and failure to back up data (Benson, 1983). The proposed benefits of user development of applications can be attributed to users having a better understanding of the

problem to be solved by the application, and the proposed risks to users having less understanding of the process of system development than do information technology professionals.

While problems with traditional end-user developed applications can have a large impact on organizational decision making, it has largely been believed that the possible negative impacts are limited to local effects, for example, workgroup or department (Nelson & Todd, 1999). Web development tools, however, are now enabling end users to develop applications that are accessible to vast numbers of people from all over the world (Nelson & Todd, 1999). This brings with it greater potential benefits and risks. These benefits and risks may affect business processes, customers, suppliers, and other organizations more than ever before. The study reported on in this article considers end-user perceptions of both the benefits and risks of end-user Web development and compares them to their perceptions of the benefits and risks of end-user spreadsheet development. This comparison will provide insight into areas where end-user developers are gaining new advantages due to their Web development practices, and into areas of risk that may require future attention from those responsible for end-user Web development.

Strategies for reducing the risks associated with end-user development have been presented in the literature and there is some evidence to suggest that employing them is effective. For example, Alavi, Nelson, and Weiss (1987-1988) presented a comprehensive framework of controls for addressing risks at different stages of the application life cycle, and several studies have demonstrated the value of introducing controls during the design and development of spreadsheets (Alavi, Phillips & Freedman, 1990; Janvrin & Morrison, 2000). End-user training has also been shown to positively influence attitudes to technology (Igbaria, Guimaraes & Davis, 1995; Simmers & Anandarajan, 2001) and to improve the quality of end-user developed applications (Kreie, Cronan, Pendley & Renwick, 2000; Kruck, Maher & Barkhi, 2003).

However, despite this evidence, organizations have done little to address the risks of end-user development (Panko & Halverson, 1996; Taylor et al., 1998). Nelson and Todd (1999) investigated what strategies organizations are using to reduce the risks of end-user development on the Web. They followed up on 18 risk reduction activities identified by Alavi, Nelson, and Weiss (1987-1988). Each of these activities was classified as being in one of three categories: standards setting, resource allocation, or management and support of application development. They found that organizations placed most emphasis on setting standards, followed by resource allocation, and that support of development was the least used type of approach. They also noted that there were large gaps between the perceived importance of some approaches to reducing the risks of end-user Web development and the degree to which they were currently being used.

RESEARCH AIMS

Despite the various largely anecdotal reports of the popularity of end-user Web development (e.g., O'Brien, 2002; Ouellette, 1999), there has been little empirical research on end-user Web development. In a recent survey of end-user development, Govindarajulu (2003) found that approximately 40% of his sample of end-user developers had created static Web pages and 25% had created dynamic Web pages; however, information about the levels of experience of these end-user Web developers or the training they had received was not available. Given the potential importance of end-user Web development, more needs to be known about end-user Web developers and the preparation they receive. The first two aims of this study were therefore to:

1. Explore the extent of end-user Web development among current end-user developers
2. Explore the training end users receive to prepare them to undertake end-user Web development

As discussed, Web development tools facilitate the development of applications that are more widely accessible than end-user developed applications have traditionally been (Nelson & Todd, 1999). End-user Web development has the potential to bring greater benefits to end users and their organizations, but also has the potential for increasing risks. The benefits and risks of end-user Web development may affect the various stakeholders more than ever before. As spreadsheet development has been the most common form of end-user development to date, the benefits and risks of Web development relative to spreadsheet development are of interest. The next aim of the study was therefore to:

3. Compare end-user developers' perceptions of the relative benefits and risks of end-user spreadsheet development and end-user Web development

Despite research highlighting the risks of end-user development, organizations have done little to counter them (Panko & Halverson, 1996; Taylor et al., 1998). Given the potential for greater risks to be associated with end-user Web development, more research is required on approaches to addressing these risks. The only significant research to date on the risks of end-user Web development is the study by Nelson and Todd (1999) that surveyed predominantly information technology staff (28 out of 34) with the remainder being senior management. Given that end users themselves have a large degree of control over the success or otherwise of their applications, there is also a need to consider end users' perceptions of the various approaches to reducing risks. The final aim of this study was therefore to:

4. Investigate the perceptions of end-user developers as to the importance of various approaches to reducing the risks of end-user Web development

THE PROJECT

This study was conducted via survey. The participants were a group of end users who were known to have developed spreadsheet applications, but whose experience with Web development was unknown. This group was targeted as it provided an opportunity to explore the uptake of end-user Web development among experienced end-user developers, and also to compare perceptions of the benefits and risks of the two types of development.

Participants

The sample for this study consists of 60 end-user developers who had previously participated in a study on end-user spreadsheet development. The participants in the previous study were active end-user developers from a wide range of business organizations. They had a wide range of experience and training (details of the original study can be found in McGill, 2004). Thirty-five percent of the participants in the current study were males, and 65% were females. Ages ranged from 20 to 67 years with an average of 45 years.

Procedure

A summary of the results of the earlier spreadsheet study was mailed to all participants, along with a request to participate in the current study by completing an enclosed questionnaire. Some participants, for whom no postal address details were recorded, were initially contacted via e-mail and asked to participate in the current study before being mailed the questionnaire. Those who failed to return the questionnaire and for whom e-mail addresses were recorded were sent a reminder by e-mail after approximately three weeks. One hundred and sixty-seven questionnaires were mailed out and 60 completed questionnaires were received, giving a response rate of 36%.

The Questionnaire

The questionnaire consisted of several sections. The first section asked questions about the background and previous computing experience of participants. The second section asked specifically about Web page development experience and training, and where relevant, explored reasons for nondevelopment. The third and fourth sections included questions to be answered by all respondents about the potential benefits and risks of both spreadsheet development and Web page development. The final section addressed approaches to reducing the risks of end-user Web development. The draft questionnaire was pilot tested by four end users and slight changes made to clarify the questions.

Section 1: Background Information

The first section asked questions about the participants and their previous training and experience with computers, spreadsheets, and the Internet. Experience was measured in years. Questions relating to spreadsheet and Internet training asked about formal courses and self study separately using measures that were adapted from Igbaria (1990) and are similar to those used by Simmers and Anandarajan (2001) in their study of Internet user satisfaction in the workplace. The items had a 5-point scale where (1) was labelled "none" and (5) was labelled "very intensive."

Section 2: Web Development Experience

Levels of Web development training were also obtained for formal courses and self study separately, using items similar to those described earlier in this section. In order to determine which Web development tools end users had used, a list of nine popular tools (see Table 4) was created based on information from a review of authoring tools (Moore, 2002). Respondents were asked whether they had used each of them and also given provision to name any other tools used. Reasons for nondevelopment were explored via three items that were developed for this study. Respondents were asked to rate the importance of each reason for nondevelopment on a 5-point scale where (1) was labelled "not important" and (5) was labelled "very important" (see Table 5 for the items).

Sections 3 and 4: Benefits and Risks

A list of the major benefits and a list of the major risks were developed from the literature on benefits and risks of development by end users (Alavi & Weiss, 1985-1986; Amoroso & Cheney, 1992; Benson, 1983; Brancheau & Brown, 1993; Davis, 1988; O'Donnell & March, 1987; Rivard & Huff, 1984, 1985). Each potential benefit and risk was rated for importance on a 5-point scale measured from (1) "not important" to (5) "very important." Twelve questions addressed potential benefits and 12 questions addressed potential risks (see Table 6 and Table 7 respectively for lists of the potential benefits and risks).

Section 5: Approaches to Reducing the Risks of End-user Web Development

The questionnaire included 14 items to measure the perceived importance of the major activities that can be undertaken to reduce the risks of end-user development on the Web. These items are from the Nelson and Todd (1999) instrument. Each approach was rated for importance on a 5-point scale measured from (1) "not important" to (5) "very important."

RESULTS AND DISCUSSION

Spreadsheet, Internet, and Web Development Experience

Table 1 summarizes how long the respondents had been using computers, spreadsheets, and the Internet. On average, they had been using computers for 14 years (ranging from 4 years to 30 years). Some participants had considerable experience, as 30 years of use indicates adoption very early in the personal computing revolution. The average length of spreadsheet use was just under 8 years (with a range of a few months through to 21 years). Respondents had been using the Internet for an average of around 6 years (ranging from not having used it at all to 12 years). Considering

Table 1. Background characteristics of respondents

	Mean	Minimum	Maximum	Standard Deviation
Age (years)	44.68	20	67	10.32
Computing experience (years)	14.22	4	30	6.66
Spreadsheet experience (years)	7.85	0	21	5.40
Internet experience (years)	6.19	0	12	2.79

the WWW came into practical existence around 1994, some of the respondents were obviously at the forefront of online communications, having used the Internet prior to the emergence of the WWW. However, most respondents appear to have used the Internet for between 3 and 9 years, indicating Internet use as being dependent upon the emergence of the WWW. Internet use appears to have coincided largely with spreadsheet use, with respondents having used spreadsheets for only about a year and a half longer on average than they have been using the Internet.

Reasons for spreadsheet and Internet use were also investigated and the results are reported in Table 2. Ninety percent of the respondents used

spreadsheets for work purposes and 73% used them at home. The Internet was used even more heavily for both work and personal tasks (91.7% and 93.3% respectively). It is worth noting that of the 60 respondents, only 1 reported not having used the Internet at all. These figures suggest a rapid increase in Internet usage in the workplace. In an Internet demographics survey in 1998, only 50% of Internet users were found to use the Internet at work (Commercenet, 1999).

Web page development was not as common. Just under half (27 or 45%) of the total sample of 60 spreadsheet end-user developers surveyed had engaged in Web page development. Of these 27 end users, 55.5% (15 people) had created

Table 2. Reasons for use

	Number	Percentage*
Spreadsheet		
Work purposes	54	90.0
Personal purposes	44	73.4
Internet		
Work purposes	55	91.7
Personal purposes	56	93.3
Web page development		
Any Web page development	27	45.0
Work purposes	15	25.0
Personal purposes	18	30.0

* *Of total sample of 60 respondents*

Table 3. Levels of previous training

	Number	Mean	Minimum	Maximum	Standard Deviation
Spreadsheet					
Formal	60	1.98	1	5	1.05
Self study	59	2.69	1	5	1.21
Internet					
Formal	60	1.63	1	4	0.80
Self study	59	2.61	1	5	1.08
Web development					
Formal	27	1.96	1	4	0.98
Self study	26	2.58	1	5	1.03

Table 4. Web development tools used

	Number	Percentage
Microsoft Frontpage	15	55.6
Microsoft Word	13	48.1
Notepad	12	46.2
Macromedia Dreamweaver	11	40.7
HotDog Pro	2	7.4
Adobe GoLive	1	3.7
Macromedia Homesite	1	3.7
CoffeeCup HTML Editor	1	3.7
HotMetal Pro	0	0.0

Web pages for work use and 66.7% (18 people) had done so for personal interests. It would be useful to further explore the nature of the Web development that the participants had undertaken. Simmer and Anandarajan's (2001) index of Web page experience would provide a starting point for future research on the nature of development undertaken.

Previous Training

Respondents had had little formal training in spreadsheets, Internet use, or Web page development. The average level of formal spreadsheet training was 1.98 (out of 5) and the average level of self study training was 2.69, so self study was the main source of spreadsheet training. This is consistent with previous research on spreadsheet users, which has reported that spreadsheet users generally receive little training (Taylor et al., 1998) and that the major means of training is self study (Chan & Storey, 1996; Hall, 1996).

The average level of formal Internet training was 1.63, and the average level of self study training was 2.61, so self study was again the main source of training. This is consistent with the findings of Simmer and Anandarajan (2001) in their study of Internet use in the workplace; however, it is unclear whether the relatively high level of self training is because end-user developers prefer self training or because other forms of training are not available. Over half (55%) had received no formal training and almost half (47%) indicated that they had either not undertaken any self study or had done very little. No respondents rated their formal Internet training as extremely intensive and only two (3.3%) rated their self study as extremely intensive.

Those respondents who had developed Web pages were asked to indicate their prior Web page development training. As can be seen from Table 3, levels of Web development training were relatively low but consistent with levels of spreadsheet training, with an average of 1.96 out of 5 for formal training and 2.58 out of 5 for self study. Self study was again the predominant method of training. Forty percent of those who had developed Web pages had received no formal training. Again, the emphasis on self training is consistent with other forms of end-user development such as spreadsheet development (Chan & Storey, 1996; Hall, 1996), but may also indicate the "fun" aspect of engaging in what is currently seen as "hot" (Atkinson & Kydd, 1997). The role of self training in end-user Web page development should be investigated in further research.

Table 5. Reasons for not developing Web pages

	Mean	Minimum	Maximum	Standard Deviation
No professional need (/5)	1.45	1	5	1.00
No personal need (/5)	1.58	1	4	0.89
Would like to, but do not know how (/5)	2.50	1	5	1.42

Table 6. Perceived importance of benefits

Benefits	Web Development		Spreadsheet Development		Sign.
	Mean Impt.	SD	Mean Impt.	SD	
Improved accessibility of information	4.25	1.07	4.27	0.96	0.922
Improved communication of information	4.12	1.08	4.05	1.02	0.759
Faster response to information requests	3.82	1.15	4.00	1.06	0.216
Direct control over information and applications	3.66	1.28	3.77	1.27	0.153
Better use of limited resources	3.54	1.24	3.62	1.08	0.262
Improved user computer literacy	3.30	1.25	3.07	1.31	0.151
Encourages experimentation and innovation	3.27	1.10	3.18	1.32	0.910
Reduction in development backlog	3.20	1.24	3.10	1.41	0.825
Increased user satisfaction	3.18	1.10	3.31	1.28	0.345
Improved productivity	3.12	1.31	3.97	0.94	<0.001***
Improved decision making effectiveness	3.02	1.26	3.90	1.12	<0.001***
Improved relationships with IT staff	2.46	1.19	2.55	1.94	0.416

It appears that a substantial proportion of Internet and Web development learning may be achieved via activities and interactions that are not perceived as training. This reinforces the popular image that "people enjoy surfing the Web" (Atkinson & Kydd, 1997) and raises the issue of the role of communities of practice, where learning occurs by end-user developers doing and sharing with their peers (Stamps, 2000). The role of communities of practice in end-user Web development should be explored in future research.

Web Development Tools Used

As can been seen in Table 4, the most common tool used by the 27 respondents who had developed Web pages was Microsoft FrontPage (55.6%).

This is consistent with the case study discussed in Ouellette (1999), where Microsoft Frontpage was used by 108 end users who contribute to an intranet. The second most commonly used tool was Microsoft Word (48.1%). The third most frequently used tool was Notepad (46.2%), which suggests some measure of familiarity with HTML code, and may indicate a desire on the part of users to "understand" and have more control over Web page development, not just create the pages. The final tool of significance is Macromedia Dreamweaver, which had been used by 40.7% of users. As Dreamweaver is a rather expensive program for home use, perhaps it would be fair to say that this tool was primarily used in the workplace. No other tools were used by more than two respondents.

Nondevelopment

The reasons why almost one half of the sample of spreadsheet developers had not yet developed Web pages were also explored. Thirty-three respondents (55.0%) reported not having created a Web page and their reasons are listed in Table 5. The most important reason for not creating Web pages was lack of knowledge despite wishing to do so (with an average importance of 2.50 out of 5), while lack of professional need and lack of personal need were rated as less important on average (1.45 and 1.58 respectively out of 5). It is worth noting that not one person strongly disagreed with "no personal need for creating a Web page," indicating a recognition of the role that Web page development plays in many people's personal lives and possibly acknowledging the potential for it to enter their own. This subset of respondents was also asked if they anticipated developing Web pages in the future. Eleven people (33%) indicated that they did not anticipate developing Web pages in the future, 5 (15%) indicated that they would create a Web page in the future, while 19 (58%) acknowledged the possibility of doing so. As it is very difficult to predict future needs, the high percentage in the "possibly" category reflects acceptance of the rate of change that is associated with the Internet (Burn & Loch, 2001).

Benefits of End-User Web Page Development and Spreadsheet Development

Table 6 presents the average perceived importance of each potential benefit for both Web development and spreadsheet development. The ratings of benefits are ranked by perceived importance for Web page development. The average importance of each potential benefit was compared between Web development and spreadsheet development using paired t-tests and the results are also reported in Table 6.

The most important perceived benefits of Web development relate to accessing and disseminating information. Improved accessibility of information was ranked most highly and was followed closely by improved communication of information. Faster response to information requests and direct control over information and applications were ranked third and fourth respectively. End users recognize that Web page development gives them a unique opportunity to both provide and access information. While increasing access to the Internet and the availability of user-friendly browsers has made accessing sites developed by information technology professionals a valuable information gathering approach, the development of user-friendly Web development tools has enabled end users to participate in information dissemination to a degree never before possible. These first four benefits were also rated highly as benefits of spreadsheet development, and no significant differences were found between their importance for Web development and their importance for spreadsheet development. Presumably Web development allows access to, and dissemination of, information over a wider domain, but spreadsheet development allows more focused specific addressing of information needs.

The middle ranked benefits appear to reflect personal benefits from end-user development. Better use of limited resources was ranked fifth followed by improved user computer literacy and encouragement of experimentation and innovation. End-user developers appear to place moderate value on what they learn and gain from development beyond their specific task oriented information needs. These results for end-user Web development are consistent with the literature on other kinds of end-user computing (Agarwal, 2000; Amoroso & Cheney, 1992; Davis, 1988; Pentland, 1989) and no significant differences were found between perceptions of their importance as benefits of Web development and spreadsheet development.

Table 7. Comparison of risks

Risks	Web Development		Spreadsheet Development		Sign.
	Mean Impt.	SD	Mean Impt.	SD	
Unreliable systems	4.24	1.03	3.61	1.21	<0.001***
Lack of data security	4.19	1.10	3.84	1.36	0.057^m
Incompatible end-usertools preventing sharing of applications and information	4.19	0.93	3.93	1.14	0.332
Inability to identify correct and complete information requirements	4.00	1.08	4.02	0.94	0.371
Lack of testing	3.96	1.04	3.77	1.13	0.455
Lack of documentation for applications	3.93	1.11	3.86	1.16	0.672
Mismatch between development tools and applications	3.87	1.10	3.68	1.18	0.667
Use of private systems when organizational systems would be more appropriate	3.83	1.10	3.60	1.12	0.411
Failure to back up data	3.81	1.16	4.16	1.15	<0.001***
Inefficient use of personnel time	3.79	1.04	3.44	1.16	0.225
Solving the wrong problem	3.51	1.28	3.68	1.09	0.044*
Redundant development effort	3.41	1.17	3.70	1.08	0.014*

*** < 0.01; * < 0.05; ^{m} < 0.1

Reduction in development backlog was ranked fairly lowly at eighth in importance among the Web development potential benefits. This implies that end users are not developing applications that would otherwise be developed by information technology professionals. Their Web pages are in addition to those deemed necessary by their organizations and hence their development effort may not impact significantly on development backlogs. This is consistent with the perception of reduction of development backlog as a benefit of spreadsheet development as no significant difference was found between the ratings.

The ninth most important perceived benefit of end-user development was user satisfaction and its relatively low ranking suggests that while Web development tools have become more user-friendly, Web development is not yet a straightforward and satisfying experience. End users perceived the experience as one of learning and self-improvement rather than one that satisfies or results in

applications that improve user satisfaction. The user satisfaction resulting from spreadsheet development was not significantly different from that resulting from Web development, suggesting that spreadsheet development is also not yet a straightforward and satisfying experience.

The tenth and eleventh ranked benefits of Web page development were improved productivity and improved decision making effectiveness. Thus, Web page development was not perceived as a particularly important source of productivity or decision making effectiveness. Web page development leads to information dissemination for the developer, but the participants in this study did not see this as improving their own productivity or decision making effectiveness, nor that accessing information provided from Web pages developed by other end users would play an important role in improving their own productivity. This raises questions about the purposes of user developed Web pages. Future research should explore more closely the reasons for which Web pages are developed by end users. Spreadsheet development was considered to be a significantly more important source of productivity benefits (t(55) = 4.97, p < 0.001) and of benefits resulting from improved decision making (t(55) = 6.46, p < 0.001).

The lowest ranked potential benefit for both Web development and spreadsheet development was improved relationships with information technology staff. The low ranking reinforces the idea that end-user Web development is an activity that is removed from organizational system development. End users do not perceive it as supporting organizational development. The low ranking may possibly reflect the introduction of additional tensions in relationships with information technology staff, brought about by the risks of end-user development.

No significant differences were found in the importance ratings of any benefits between those who had and those who had not previously developed Web pages.

Potential Risks

Table 7 presents the average perceived importance of each potential risk for both Web development and spreadsheet development. The ratings of risks are ranked by perceived importance for Web page development. The average importance of each potential risk was compared between Web development and spreadsheet development using paired t-tests.

All potential risks of Web development were rated fairly highly with averages above the midpoint of the scale, which implies a good awareness of the problems that can plague end-user development. Unreliable systems were perceived as the most important risk, with lack of data security ranked closely behind. The potential for development of unreliable and insecure systems has long been recognized as one of the major problems with end-user development (Benson, 1983; Brancheau & Brown, 1993). Despite this

recognition, organizations have done little to protect against it (Panko & Halverson, 1996). The high ranking of this risk with respect to end-user Web development reflects the increased level of importance of the problem due to the global accessibility of Web-based systems. The potential for damage to the reputation of an organization has increased as applications have become accessible by vast numbers of people from all over the world (Nelson & Todd, 1999). Unreliable systems was perceived to be a significantly less important risk for spreadsheet development (t(53) = -3.60, p = 0.001) and lack of data security was also rated a less important risk for spreadsheet development (t(53) = -1.95, p = 0.057). This suggests that end-user developers are very aware of the increases in risk associated with Web development.

Incompatible end-user tools preventing sharing was ranked equal second in terms of importance as a risk of Web development. The last decade has been marked by great improvements in the compatibility of end-user software; hence this result was unanticipated and requires further research.

The midranked group of risks all focus on the ability of the end-user developer to undertake specific necessary development tasks such as identifying requirements, testing, documenting, and choosing appropriate development tools. The respondents appeared to recognize the importance of each of the activities and the risks that can result from lack of skills in these areas. No significant differences were found between the perceived importance of these risks between Web development and spreadsheet development.

Use of private systems when organizational systems would be more appropriate was ranked the eighth most important risk of Web development, and failure to back up data as the ninth. Both of these risks normally relate to use of user developed Web applications rather than the actual development process and their lower ranking suggests that the respondents recognize that the major risks result from development practices rather than from use of applications. Failure to back up data was rated as significantly less important a risk for Web development than for spreadsheet development (t(52) = 4.43, p < 0.001). In fact, failure to back up data was perceived as the most important of all the potential risks of spreadsheet development. This may be because the types of Web applications developed by end users are likely to involve static data, whereas the data in end-user developed spreadsheet applications is likely to be updated more often, and hence is more vulnerable and reliant on regular backup in case of problems. Further research on the types of Web applications developed by end users is required to understand the perceptions of these risks.

The lowest ranked risks of Web development were inefficient use of personnel time, followed by solving the wrong problem and lastly redundant development effort. However, none of these risks was discounted, with averages that indicate that the majority of respondents recognized them as risks of relative importance. Not one respondent rated inefficient use of personnel time as "not important"; 5 (9.4%) rated solving the wrong problem as "not important," and 1 (1.9%) rated redundant development effort as "not important." The participants considered solving the wrong problem and redundant development effort to be greater risks when undertaking spreadsheet development (t(52) = 2.06, p = 0.044; t(52) = 2.55, p = 0.014). This may reflect an increased sophistication of end-user developed spreadsheet applications compared to end-user developed Web applications.

It was interesting to note that the average importance of each risk was lower for the group who had previously developed Web pages than for the group who had not, although the differences were only significant for four risks (inability to identify correct and complete requirements (t(52) = 2.36, p = 0.022), use of private systems when organizational systems would be more appropriate (t(52) = 2.19, p = 0.033), solving the wrong problem

(t(51) = 2.54, p = 0.014), and redundant development effort (t(52) = 2.70, p = 0.009)). A reason for this difference could be that the development process has given them insight that allows them to discount the risks; however this seems unlikely given the prevalence of problems with end-user developed applications. It would seem more likely that the satisfaction they derive from their own Web development allows an overshadowing of the perceptions of risks. This should be explored further in future studies.

Future research should also differentiate between different types of Web applications that might have different risks and benefits. For example, the risks associated with end-user developed Web pages that merely display information could be considered substantially less than those associated with applications that process information.

Approaches to Reducing the Risks of End-User Web Development

The approaches to reducing the risks of end-user Web page development are ranked by perceived importance in Table 8, which also includes the average importance of each of the approaches reported for the predominantly information technology staff in the Nelson and Todd (1999) study. The importance of each approach as perceived by the end-user developers in the current study is compared with the average obtained in Nelson and Todd's study using one sample t-tests and the results are also presented in Table 8. All of the approaches were rated fairly high by the end-user developers with averages above the midpoint of the scale. The highest ranked approach was training. As discussed earlier, previous studies have found that end-user developers receive very little training and what they do get tends to be self-training rather than formal training (Chan & Storey, 1996; Hall, 1996). The results in this study regarding training for Web development are consistent with other forms of end-user development such as

Table 8. Approaches to reducing the risks of end-user Web development

Rank	Approaches to Reducing the Risks of End-User Web Page Development	This Study Mean SD		N & T Study Mean	Sign.
1	Training	4.39	0.81	3.48	<0.001***
2	Policies on data management	4.39	0.71	4.25	0.157
3	Coordination across organizational boundaries	4.31	0.75	4.00	0.003***
4	Assignment of roles and responsibilities	4.28	0.81	3.61	<0.001***
5	Standards for purchases of hardware and software	4.19	0.83	3.76	<0.001***
6	Data access	4.17	0.86	3.85	0.009***
7	Planning for equipment, capacity, and manpower	4.17	0.77	3.97	0.066^{m}
8	Scope of Web-related activities	4.15	1.02	3.03	<0.001***
9	Systems integration	4.11	0.86	3.36	<0.001***
10	Consulting	4.06	0.90	3.58	<0.001***
11	Audit and review	3.98	1.04	3.47	0.001***
12	Standards for end-userdevelopment	3.98	0.84	3.73	0.031*
13	Setting priorities	3.89	0.90	3.88	0.943
14	Documentation	3.83	1.00	3.18	<0.001***

*** < 0.01; * < 0.05; ^{m} < 0.1

spreadsheet development. The acknowledgment of the importance of training is quite interesting; despite having received little training themselves, the respondents considered training to be the most important approach to reducing the risks of end-user Web development. Nelson (1991) suggested that training is perhaps the most effective tool for minimizing the risks associated with end-user development and the results of this study suggest that end users agree.

Policies for data management were considered to be the second most important approach. This was unexpected because end-user developers have traditionally been dissatisfied with approaches to the management of end-user computing that involved control rather than support (Bergeron & Berube, 1988; Bowman, 1988). However, this ranking is promising as it suggests that end-user Web developers recognize that Internet applications are particularly vulnerable to data

security risks and that therefore these must be addressed.

The middle grouping consisted of a number of approaches of similar importance that include assignment of roles and responsibilities, standards for purchases of hardware and software, and scope of Web-related activities (i.e., clear distinctions between applications that are developed by end users and by information technology professionals) among others. The very consistent levels of importance given to these suggest that end users recognize that a variety of approaches is necessary, all of which are complementary.

Audit and review standards for end-user development and a requirement for documentation of Web applications were ranked towards the bottom of the possible approaches. This is consistent with previous research that suggests that users are less satisfied when subject to greater application development control (Bergeron & Berube, 1988;

Bowman, 1988). Nevertheless, a need for setting and enforcing organizational development standards for end users has been widely recognized (Cragg & King, 1993; Guimaraes, Gupta & Rainer, 1999). Setting priorities was also not given a high importance ranking. This suggests that, as might be expected, end-user developers consider the Web development they do as an individual activity designed to support their own work rather than part of an organizational information technology strategy.

As can be seen in Table 8, the end-user developers who responded to this survey rated every approach to reducing the risks of end-user Web development more highly than did the information technology professionals and senior management who participated in Nelson and Todd's (1999) study. These differences were significant for all except two of the approaches (policies on data management and setting priorities). The approaches on which opinion differed the most were training (t(53) = 8.24, p < 0.001) and scope of Web-related activities (t(53) = 8.08, p < 0.001). Information technology staff involved in managing end-user development should recognize the importance to end users of appropriate training to support their development activities and of the need for clear distinctions to be made to enable the confidence of end users in determining which projects are appropriate for them.

There have been previous calls for increased provision of training to Internet users (Aggarwal, 2003). The results of this study reinforce the importance of this. However, given the relative prevalence of self training in end-user Web development training, the role of self training should be further explored. It has been suggested that, when end users are self taught, the emphasis is predominantly on how to use software rather than broader analysis and design considerations (Benham, Delaney, & Luzi, 1993). The many books that cover introductory Web development typically give a detailed step-by-step coverage of examples that illustrate product features. Ex-

amples are presented as solutions to requirements without the design stages being made explicit. Thus end users may have a narrow knowledge focused on software features but lacking in techniques for developing Web applications that are user-friendly, reliable, and maintainable. Taylor, Moynihan and Wood-Harper (1998) found that few, if any, quality principles are applied in end-user development. Therefore, organizations that rely on self training must ensure that end users have materials available that will help provide all of the skills necessary for developing good quality Web applications. This is consistent with Shaw, DeLone, and Niederman's (2002) finding that documentation to support training was perceived as one of the most important information technology support factors in terms of user satisfaction. Given the current heavy reliance on end-user developed applications and the increased risks associated with end-user development in the Internet domain, it is essential that organizations support end users as they strive to become proficient Web developers.

Guidelines on the kinds of applications that are suitable for end-user Web development should also be provided (Goupil, 2000). Several authors have proposed guidelines recommending what kinds of applications are appropriate for end-user development (Salchenberger, 1993), and what kinds are not (Bowman, 1990). These types of guidelines need to be researched further so that more detailed assistance can be provided to prospective end-user developers. In particular, the ability to tailor recommendations on what types of applications are appropriate to individual end users' backgrounds would be very valuable. Given the current heavy reliance on end-user developed applications and the increased risks associated with end-user development in the Internet domain, it is essential that organizations support end users as they strive to become proficient Web developers.

As discussed in the Introduction, each of the approaches to risk reduction was classified as relating to standards setting, resource allocation, or management and support of application development (Nelson & Todd, 1999). Nelson and Todd (1999) found that organizations in their study placed most emphasis on setting standards, followed by resource allocation, and that support of development was the least used type of approach. They noted that most firms in their study appeared to be relying on a monopolistic control strategy (as described by Gerrity and Rockart, 1986, and Alavi et al., 1987-1988) and then concluded that while such a strategy may be the best approach given the relative infancy of Web technology, it could prove to be an unstable strategy in the future. The results of the study reported in this article suggest that end-user developers would support a change to the strategies used to manage end-user Web development with greater emphasis placed on support of development via such mechanisms as training and clear definition of roles and responsibilities.

Those who had and those who had not previously developed Web pages were compared with respect to their perceptions of the importance of the approaches to reducing the risks of Web development. As with perceptions of risks, those who had previously developed Web pages tended to rate the importance of the approaches lower than did the end users who had not, although the differences were only significant for two approaches: standards for purchases of hardware and software activities ($t(52) = 2.80$, $p = 0.007$) and scope of Web-related activities ($t(52) = 2.22$, $p = 0.031$).

Main End-User Web Development Issues

The study reported on in this article explored the nature of the emerging area of end-user Web development. A range of areas were investigated and Table 9 below summarizes some of the main issues that emerged. The study highlighted that Web development is becoming popular among end users both as part of work responsibilities and in pursuing personal interests. This popularity is likely to increase. Yet, consistent with other kinds of end-user development, end users receive little formal training to prepare them for it. The

Table 9. Summary of main issues

Issue	The study found …
Extent of Web development	Over half of the spreadsheet developers surveyed also develop Web pages.
End users receive little formal training	40% of end users who had developed Web pages had received no formal training.
End users consider training to be the most important strategy for reducing the risks of end-user Web development	The average importance rating for training was 4.39 (out of 5).
End users have a good awareness of the risks of end-user Web development	All potential risks of Web development had averages above the midpoint of the scale (i.e., were considered important).
End users recognize the need for complementary approaches to risk reduction	All strategies for risk reduction had averages above the midpoint of the scale (i.e., were considered important).
End users appear to be becoming more sophisticated in matching tools to applications	Web development was rated very highly for improving accessibility of information, but was significantly less important than spreadsheets for improving decision making effectiveness.

end users surveyed recognized the importance of training and considered it to be the most important strategy for reducing the risks associated with end-user development of Web applications. This finding was not however mirrored in the Nelson and Todd (1999) study. The information technology staff in that study considered training to be one of the less important strategies. Given the potential impacts of end-user developed Web applications, organizations increase the risks by not adequately preparing end users.

The end users surveyed showed a good awareness of the risks of end-user Web development. All potential risks of Web development were rated fairly high with averages above the midpoint of the scale, which implies a good awareness of the problems that can plague end-user development. It is reassuring that end users do not discount the risks. This is also reflected in their recognition of the need for complementary approaches to risk reduction.

There has been concern expressed in the literature about the ability of end users to recognize what kinds of development tools are appropriate for different sorts of applications (Alavi & Weiss, 1985-1986; Davis, 1988; O'Donnell & March, 1987). The comparative rankings of the perceived benefits of Web development and spreadsheet development suggest that end users are becoming more sophisticated in matching tools to applications. For example, Web development was rated very highly for improving accessibility of information, but significantly less important than spreadsheets for improving decision making effectiveness.

CONCLUSION

Despite early concerns about its risks (e.g., Alavi & Weiss, 1985-1986; Davis, 1988), end-user development has become an integral part of organizational information provision (McLean et al., 1993; Shayo et al., 1999). End-user developers

may now take advantage of user-friendly Web development tools to create Web applications and the prevalence of these applications will only increase (Ouellette, 1999). The study reported on in this article investigated the extent of Web page development among end users and compared end-user perceptions of the benefits and risks of end-user Web development with their perceptions of those associated with spreadsheet development. Almost half of the sample of spreadsheet users studied had created Web pages, yet they had received little prior training in Web development. Microsoft Frontpage was the most common tool used for Web development; however almost half had previously used Notepad indicating some familiarity with HTML code. This suggests a desire to "understand" and have more control over Web page development. The most important reason for not creating Web pages was lack of knowledge, and the majority of those who had not yet created Web pages acknowledged the possibility of doing so in the near future.

As can be seen from the discussion of the risks and benefits of end-user development, although end-user Web page development has many characteristics in common with traditional end-user development, there are many areas in which Web page development differs and it is important that research into these areas continues. It seems that end-user Web development is here to stay and will have far-reaching consequences. Management of its risks will therefore be of increasing importance to organizations. The results of this study have practical implications for the management of end-user Web development in organizations. End-user developers are aware of both the benefits and risks of end-user Web development and it will be essential to ensure their involvement in the development of approaches to control risks.

Previous research suggests that end-user developers respond better to approaches that emphasize support for development of high quality and appropriate applications rather than control of development (Bergeron & Berube, 1988;

Bowman, 1988). The results of this study support this, with training seen as the most important approach to the reduction of the risks of end-user Web development. Self training was found to be the most prevalent type of training but it is unclear from this study whether this is because end-user developers prefer self training or because other forms of training are not available. Simmers and Anandarajan (2001, p. 55) recommended that "formal training should be planned and implemented so that the positive attributes of self-training (flexibility, moving at one's own pace, freedom and autonomy) can be blended with organizational requirements, creating a better training experience for both the individual and the organization." This advice appears sound and meshes with the need to explore the role of communities of practice in end-user Web development.

Finally, the current study raises several potential areas for further study. As end-user Web development is likely to increase in the future, better guidelines are needed to help identify applications that are particularly suited for end users with a particular background. The different types of Web applications developed by end users carry different risks, so future studies should differentiate between types of applications in order to further clarify the associated risks. The participants of the present study identified training as one of the most significant factors in reducing the risk associated with end-user developed Web pages, yet users appear to be gaining their knowledge from self training rather than formal training. This role of self training should be further investigated. Additional studies are also needed to further examine the reasons for Web page development, as it appears that the satisfaction derived from end-user Web development may overshadow the risks associated with these applications that are accessible to vast numbers of people from all over the world.

REFERENCES

Agarwal, R. (2000). Individual acceptance of information technologies. In R.W. Zmud (Ed.), *Framing the domains of IT management: Projecting the future ... through the past* (pp. 85-104). Cincinnati, OH: Pinnaflex Educational Resources, Inc.

Aggarwal, A.K. (2003). Internetalization of end-users. *Journal of End User Computing, 15*(1), 54-56.

Alavi, M., Nelson, R.R., & Weiss, I.R. (1987-1988). Strategies for end user computing: An integrative framework. *Journal of Management Information Systems, 4*(3), 28-49.

Alavi, M., Phillips, J.S., & Freedman, S.M. (1990). An empirical investigation of two alternative approaches to control of end-user application development process. *Data Base, 20*(4), 11-19.

Alavi, M., & Weiss, I.R. (1985-1986). Managing the risks associated with end-user computing. *Journal of Management Information Systems, 2*(3), 5-20.

Amoroso, D.L., & Cheney, P.H. (1992). Quality end user-developed applications: Some essential ingredients. *Data Base, 23*(1), 1-11.

Atkinson, M., & Kydd, C. (1997). Individual characteristics associated with World Wide Web use: An empirical study of playfulness and motivation. *The DATA BASE for Advances in Information Systems, 28*(2), 53-62.

Benham, H., Delaney, M., & Luzi, A. (1993). Structured techniques for successful end user spreadsheets. *Journal of End User Computing, 5*(2), 18-25.

Benson, D.H. (1983). A field study of end user computing: Findings and issues. *MIS Quarterly, 7*(4), 35-45.

Bergeron, F., & Berube, C. (1988). The management of the end-user environment: An empirical investigation. *Information & Management, 14,* 107-113.

Bowman, B. (1988). *An investigation of application development process controls.* Unpublished doctoral dissertation, University of Houston.

Bowman, B. (1990). Controlling application development by end-users in a PC environment: A survey of techniques. *Information Executive, 32*(2), pp. 70-74.

Brancheau, J.C., & Brown, C.V. (1993). The management of end-user computing: Status and directions. *ACM Computing Surveys, 25*(4), 450-482.

Burn, J.M., & Loch, K.D. (2001). The societal impact of the world wide Web: Key challenges for the 21st century. *Information Resources Management Journal, 14*(4), 4-14.

Chan, Y.E., & Storey, V.C. (1996). The use of spreadsheets in organizations: Determinants and consequences. *Information & Management, 31,* 119-134.

Commercenet, N.M.R. (1999). *Nielsen Media Research and NetRating to measure at-work Internet use.* Retrieved May 16, 2006, from http://www.nielsenmedia.com/newsreleases/releases/1999/netratings3.html

Cragg, P.G., & King, M. (1993). Spreadsheet modelling abuse: An opportunity for OR? *Journal of the Operational Research Society, 44*(8), 743-752.

Davis, G.B. (1988). The hidden costs of end-user computing. *Accounting Horizons, 2*(4), 103-106.

Gerrity, T.P., & Rockart, J.F. (1986). End-user computing: Are you a leader or a laggard? *Sloan Management Review, 27*(4), 25-34.

Goupil, D. (2000, June). End-user application development: Relief for IT. *Computing Channels,* pp. 2-4.

Govindarajulu, C. (2003). End users: Who are they? *Communications of the ACM, 46*(9), 152-159.

Guimaraes, T., Gupta, Y., & Rainer, K. (1999). Empirically testing the relationship between end-user computing problems and information center success factors. *Decision Sciences, 30*(2), 393-413.

Hall, M.J.J. (1996). A risk and control oriented study of the practices of spreadsheet application developers. In *Proceedings of the Twenty-Ninth Hawaii International Conference on System Sciences* (pp. 364-373).

Igbaria, M. (1990). End-user computing effectiveness: A structural equation model. *OMEGA, 18*(6), 637-652.

Igbaria, M., Guimaraes, T., & Davis, G.B. (1995). Testing the determinants of microcomputer usage via a structural equation model. *Journal of Management Information Systems, 11*(4), 87-114.

Janvrin, D., & Morrison, J. (2000). Using a structured design approach to reduce risks in end user spreadsheet development. *Information & Management, 37*(1), 1-12.

Jawahar, I.M., & Elango, B. (2001). The effect of attitudes, goal setting and self-efficacy on end user performance. *Journal of End User Computing, 13*(3), 40-45.

Kreie, J., Cronan, T.P., Pendley, J., & Renwick, J.S. (2000). Applications development by end-users: Can quality be improved? *Decision Support Systems, 29*(2), 143-152.

Kruck, S.E., Maher, J.J., & Barkhi, R. (2003). Framework for cognitive skill acquisition and spreadsheet training. *Journal of End User Computing, 15*(1), 20-37.

McGill, T. (2004). The effect of end user development on end user success. *Journal of Organizational and End User Computing, 16*(1), 41-58.

McLean, E.R., Kappelman, L.A., & Thompson, J.P. (1993). Converging end-user and corporate computing. *Communications of the ACM, 36*(12), 79-92.

Moore, P. (2002, June). Software test bench mega guide. *Australian PC User,* pp. 54-55.

Nelson, R.R. (1991). Educational needs as perceived by IS and end-user personnel: A survey of knowledge and skill requirements. *MIS Quarterly, 15*(4), 503-525.

Nelson, R.R., & Todd, P. (1999). Strategies for managing EUC on the Web. *Journal of End User Computing, 11*(1), 24-31.

O'Brien, J.A. (2002). *Management information systems: Managing information technology in the e-business enterprise* (5th ed.). New York: McGraw-Hill.

O'Donnell, D., & March, S. (1987). End user computing environments: Finding a balance between productivity and control. *Information & Management, 13*(1), 77-84.

Ouellette, T. (1999, July 26). Giving users the keys to their Web content. *Computerworld,* pp. 66-67.

Panko, R.R., & Halverson, R.P. (1996). Spreadsheets on trial: A survey of research on spreadsheet risks. In *Proceedings of the Twenty-Ninth Hawaii International Conference on System Sciences, 2,* 326-335.

Pentland, B.T. (1989). Use and productivity in personal computing: An empirical test. In *Proceedings of the 10th International Conference on Information Systems* (pp. 211-222).

Rittenberg, L.E., Senn, A., & Bariff, M. (1990). *Audit and control of end-user computing.* Altamonte Springs, FL: The Institute of Internal Auditors Research Foundation.

Rivard, S., & Huff, S.L. (1984). User developed applications: Evaluation of success from the DP department perspective. *MIS Quarterly, 8*(1), 39-49.

Rivard, S., & Huff, S.L. (1985). An empirical study of users as application developers. *Information & Management, 8,* 89-102.

Salchenberger, L. (1993). Structured development techniques for user-developed systems. *Information & Management, 24,* 41-50.

Shaw, N.C., DeLone, W.H., & Niederman, F. (2002). Sources of dissatisfaction in end-user support: An empirical study. *The DATA BASE for Advances in Information Systems, 33*(2), 41-55.

Shayo, C., Guthrie, R., & Igbaria, M. (1999). Exploring the measurement of end user computing success. *Journal of End User Computing, 11*(1), 5-14.

Simmers, C.A., & Anandarajan, M. (2001). User satisfaction in the Internet-anchored workplace: An exploratory study. *Journal of Information Technology Theory and Application, 3*(5), 39-61.

Stamps, D. (2000). Communities of practice: Learning is social. Training is irrelevant? In E.L. Lesser, M.A. Fontaine, & J.A. Slusher (Eds.), *Knowledge and communities* (pp. 53-64). Boston: Butterworth-Heinemann.

Taylor, M.J., Moynihan, E.P., & Wood-Harper, A.T. (1998). End-user computing and information systems methodologies. *Information Systems Journal, 8,* 85-96.

This work was previously published in Journal of Organizational and End User Computing, Vol. 18, Issue 4, edited by M. Adam Mahmood, pp. 22-42, copyright 2006 by IGI Publishing, formerly known as Idea Group Publishing (an imprint of IGI Global).

Chapter XIV
A Metadata–Based Approach for Unstructured Document Management in Organizations

Federica Paganelli
University of Florence, Italy

Maria Chiara Pettenati
University of Florence, Italy

Dino Giuli
University of Florence, Italy

ABSTRACT

Effectively managing documents is a strategic requirement for every organization. Available document management systems (DMSs) often lack effective functions for automatic document management. One reason is that relevant information frequently is conveyed by unstructured documents, whose content cannot be easily accessed and processed by applications. This article proposes a metadata model, the DMSML (Document Management and Sharing Markup Language) to enable and to ease unstructured document management by supporting the design of DMSs. We argue that the extensive use of this metadata language will render organizational information explicit, promoting information reuse and interoperability in a more profitable way than what is guaranteed by proprietary DMSs. We also briefly depict the design and deployment phases of a Web-based DMS prototype based on DMSML. Our overall intent is to increase the awareness of what managers should account for when considering the possibility of adopting a DMS.

INTRODUCTION

Document Management (DM) is the scientific domain dealing with the use of ICTs for the effective "storage, organization, transmission, retrieval, manipulation, update, and eventual disposition of documents to fulfill an organizational purpose" (Sprague, 1995, p. 32). Existing ICT-based DM solutions, hereafter called document management systems (DMSs), do not completely fulfill the expectations of providing enough effective tools for information creation, sharing, and retrieval inside an organization, often causing user frustration, dissatisfaction, and inefficiencies (Ginsburg, 2001).

A typical situation that creates problems in many organizations is the management of unstructured documents that often convey important information and knowledge (the451, 2002); due to their lack of structure, these documents cannot be easily and effectively accessed and processed by applications, thus limiting effective document management. As a consequence, members of organizations have difficulty retrieving the information contained in these documents. Moreover, existing DMSs seldom are designed according to a general and/or standard methodological approach and are built around open data and process models. Thus, related disadvantages are vendor dependence, difficult maintenance, and poor interoperability with other information systems (Stickler, 2001).

In order to deal with these issues, we propose in this article a metadata model, enabling the design of DMSs and aiming at combining the benefits of metadata for document description with the use of Web standards. The metadata language described in this work has been named DMSML (Document Management and Sharing Markup Language). DMSML offers a solution to representing a set of document properties that are relevant to document management and to rendering business and organizational information explicit in a way that promotes reuse, user-driven extensibility, and interoperability with heterogeneous systems. A Web-based prototype developed according to DMSML specifications will help make the theoretical arguments presented throughout this article concrete.

This article is organized as follows: initially, some considerations on the management of unstructured documents are made in order to point out which relevant characteristics of an unstructured document are worth being described in order to improve its efficient management (its *content* and *context of use*). Then, an example of a typical document frequently managed in many types of organizations, the *project proposal*, will sustain what is said from a general perspective. The following paragraphs will be devoted to the analytical description of the requirements for high-quality DMSs. The fulfillment of these requirements will be taken as the basis for the design of the metadata language (DMSML) as well as for the development of the Web-based DMS prototype presented in this work. Examples and comparative evaluation of available products—both commercial and open source—will show that meeting all of the aforementioned requirements is a characteristic satisfied by none of the presented products, to the best of our knowledge.

The central part of this article is aimed at describing (from a general point of view) the use of metadata for document management, illustrating the benefits of their usage in this domain. Existing metadata languages related to document management at the state of the art also will be recalled in this part of the article.

In the sequel, the DMSML metadata specification will be described, highlighting its fulfillment of high-level requirements. DMSML will be proposed as a declarative language for the specification of DMSs, based on existing standards and on a rigorous modeling approach. Metadata modeling, using proper formal representation techniques, then will be illustrated. The advantage of using DMSML for DMS design and development will be described in the related paragraph.

Finally, the Web-based prototype using DMSML metadata specifications will be described in its functional components and implementative details. Using these arguments, we demonstrate that the extensive use of this metadata language in document management systems will help to exploit business and organizational information in a more profitable way than what is guaranteed by proprietary document management applications, because the knowledge (properly codified through a metadata language) will allow both human and machine readability and, consequently, more effective reusability.

MANAGEMENT OF UNSTRUCTURED DOCUMENTS

Unstructured documents are text and multimedia documents such as e-mails, reports, and so forth, stored in various formats that do not provide an explicit, formal, and separate representation of either content structure (also called logical structure) or presentation structure (physical structure). Often, these are encoded in proprietary and binary formats. For instance, a project proposal has a logical structure, because it is organized in a specific set of fields: project title, objectives, activity plan, business plan, and so forth. It also has a physical structure related to presentation instructions; for instance, a project title should be rendered in bold, centered, font size 14.

In unstructured formats, this information usually is blended and cannot be easily and/or automatically extracted and processed by applications. As a consequence, applications do not have explicit references to specific elements of the content, thus preventing automatic document processing and leading to poor interoperability among applications. Currently, effective indexing, retrieval, and processing would require the system to access document content with a degree of granularity, which cannot be provided by unstructured document formats.

As a matter of fact, collaboration among colleagues can be slowed down dramatically by factors such as the use of different word processing applications and graphical and CAD tools.

This dramatically compromises the quality of information reuse and sharing in organizations. It is important to highlight that organizational information not only refers to document content but also to its context of use. With the term *context of use* of a document, we hence refer to by whom, where, how, under which constraints, and for which purpose a document is being accessed, transmitted, and modified (Gilliland-Swetland, 2000; Päivärinta, 2001). For instance, a project proposal document contains a set of information that is strategic in the accomplishment of organizational goals (e.g., objectives and planned activities for innovation in terms of products, processes, and/or services), but it also refers to a set of organizational information that describes its context of use. This kind of information is related strictly to organizational processes, roles, and responsibilities. Usually, business information, such as access right policies and document lifecycle descriptions, is encoded in the application logic of a DMS. In most commercial products, this information is specified in proprietary formats and cannot be reused by other systems. On the other hand, many open source solutions are based on open standards, but the organizational information is encoded in a technology-dependent way. As a consequence, the reuse or extension of this business information and the migration to new technologies can be a difficult process requiring high technical expertise, time, and resources.

EXAMPLE OF A TYPICAL DOCUMENT TO BE MANAGED: A PROJECT PROPOSAL

To clarify the benefits of metadata usage for document management, we describe through this example the characteristics of a common type of document, which is relevant in private as well as academic domains—the project proposal.

In a generic organization, a typical process of project proposal editing can envisage different steps toward the completion of the document. A heterogeneous group of persons can participate in this process, including administrative staff, technical experts, marketing staff, external consultants, and so forth. Different responsibilities then will be assigned to each person according to his or her skills and organizational role.

Possible steps in project proposal editing are:

- Editing an abstract, describing the main objectives of the future project.
- Editing of the project proposal, usually according to a predefined document template; in this phase, actors can collaboratively edit the document.

While undergoing these phases, the project proposal passes through different states, such as draft document, document under review, document under revision, final proposal, and submitted document. The transition between states is regulated by actions operated by persons with specified roles; for instance, the transition from *document under review* to *final* is conditioned by the approval of the person in charge of the project (e.g., a project manager).

According to what is illustrated in this example, it becomes evident that a lot of strategic information needs to be codified and shared among the actors in order to execute the overall process. The organizational information related to the documents' context of use usually refers to the definition of roles in the organizational schema, access control policies, and lifecycle of documents. In order to speed up the process of project proposal editing, this information should be formalized conveniently and made available to the involved actors. Moreover, it should be available after the process is completed in order to formalize the practice and to make this experience available to other colleagues for future activities, such as editing another project proposal.

REQUIREMENTS FOR DOCUMENT MANAGEMENT SYSTEMS

The main critical issues concerning unstructured document management thus can be summarized in terms of poor reuse of content and context of use of business information. These considerations provide hints for the definition of the following general requirements that DMS should fulfill in order to enable effective document management:

- **Standard compliance.** The adoption of international widely accepted standards promotes interoperability among heterogeneous information systems and data sources. Standard compliance includes technological as well as business standards. Examples of technological standards are the eXtensible Markup Language (XML) (Sall, 2002) and J2EE (Java 2 Enterprise Edition) (Sun Microsystems, 2003). With the term *business standard*, we refer to the specifications related to business information describing documents' context of use. Examples of business standards are business process definition languages, such as the XML Process Definition Language (XPDL) (Workflow Management Coalition, 2002), the Petri Net Markup Language (PNML) (Weber & Kindler, 2002), and access right policy languages, such as the eXtensible Access Control Markup Language (XACML) (OASIS, 2003).
- **Multi-platform compatibility and support** (Stickler, 2001). A DMS solution should be deployable on different platforms in order to avoid monolithic and vendor-dependent solutions. Moreover, support of several platforms enables interoperability among heterogeneous information systems and facilitates the integration with existing legacy systems in the organization (e.g., http server, mail server, etc.).

- **Metadata-based approach for the representation of document properties** (Karjalainen et al., 2000; Murphy, 1998; Päivärinta, 2001; Salminen et al., 2000). Metadata are data about data. They provide an explicit representation in a human- and machine-understandable format of document properties. Traditionally, metadata are used in order to represent descriptive properties (i.e., title, author, keywords, etc.) of information resources in order to support document classification, search, and retrieval (Gilliland-Swetland, 2000). An example of descriptive metadata is the Dublin Core (DC) specification (Dublin Core Metadata Initiative, 2003). Moreover, metadata could be conveniently used to describe the document's context of use. In this way, business information, such as document lifecycle and access policies, can be specified by abstracting it from implementation details. For instance, the previously mentioned business standards (e.g., XPDL, PNML, and XACML) provide a meta-language, making it possible to describe organizational processes by means of standardized labels (e.g., activity, task, actor).

- **A standard methodological approach.** It should be followed for the design and development of a DMS rather than a tool-oriented approach (Stickler, 2001). In fact, a methodological approach based on standard models and methods for DMS design and development can facilitate the formalization of user requirements, fast prototyping, and deployment of a high-quality product, accomplishing the formalized requirements. Moreover, a standard methodological approach for the design of an effective DMS should conveniently promote the accomplishment of the previous requirements (i.e., standard compliance, multi-platform compatibility and support, metadata-based

approach) by including proper design and development methods and techniques.

The fulfillment of these requirements can lead to an effective, easily maintainable, flexible, and cost-effective solution for document management.

Existing Document Management Systems

At present, several commercial and open-source DMSs are available. Among the commercial products, the most important solutions in terms of market diffusion in the domain of document management are Documentum, FatWire, IBM, Interwoven, and Microsoft[1] (Moore & Markham, 2002). Among the open-source products, Zope Content Management Framework, OpenCMS, Apache Lenya, and open-source solutions for digital libraries, such as DSpace, and Marian[2], deserve to be mentioned. A comparison of some of these products with respect to their provided features is provided by Moore and Markham (2002). For the purpose of this article, we will evaluate some of these products according to their compliance with the previously mentioned requirements for DMS: standard compliance, multi-platform compatibility and support, metadata-based approach, and use of a standard methodological approach. The analysis synthesized in Table 1 refers to two commercial products—FatWire Content Server and Documentum—and three open-source products—Apache Lenya, Dspace, and Marian.

The analysis of these products highlights that the compliance with technical standards and multiplatform compatibility are requirements commonly understood and addressed by means of wide adoption of industrial standards, such as XML and related standards (Sall, 2002), LDAP (Lightweight Directory Access Protocol) (Yeong et al., 1993), SOAP (Simple Object Access Protocol) (Mitra, 2003), J2EE, and Internet protocols

*Table 1. DMS's evaluation results (***= good; ** = sufficient; * = insufficient compliance level with requirements for document management systems; - = no publicly available information)*

Requirements Products	Open standards compliance		Multi-platform support	Metadata-based approach		Open and standard methodological approach	
	Technical standards	Business standards		Content	Context of use	Data model	Method
FatWire	*** LDAP, XML, SOAP and Internet protocols	-	*** J2EE compliant	-	-	* Object model	-
Documentum	*** LDAP, XML, SOAP and Internet protocols	-	*** J2EE compliant	-	-	* Object - relational model	-
Lenya	*** LDAP, XML and Internet protocols	* No standards for lifecycle and access policy	*** J2EE compliant	*** Dublin Core compliant	* Dublin Core compliant	** Open data model	-
DSpace	** Internet protocols	* No standards for lifecycle and access policy	** It runs only on UNIX and Linux OSs	*** Dublin Core compliant	* Partial compliance with Dublin Core	** Open relational data model	-
MARIAN	*** Internet protocols and XML	* No standards for lifecycle and access policy	*** Thanks to Java code portability	*** It is compliant to USMARC and DC	* It is compliant to USMARC and Dublin Core	** Open data model	*** The study of a standard method is in progress

such as HTTP (Hypertext Transfer Protocol) and FTP (File Transfer Protocol). On the other hand, compliance with business standards is partially accomplished. In fact, while descriptive metadata standards often are used in open source solutions (e.g., Dublin Core), metadata standards for lifecycle and access policy descriptions rarely are used. Moreover, only MARIAN is associated with an open and standard methodological approach for the design and development of the product tailored to the requirements of a specific organization (Gonçalves et al., 2004). The discussion on commercial products is limited by the lack of documentation about some requirements (business standard compliance and metadata-based approach). The overall remark of this analysis is that these products do not address completely the previously mentioned high-level requirements for DMSs.

Research Directions in Document Management

The research in document management as a discipline that encompasses social and organizational issues and user needs and potentially utilizes several technologies in an organizational context is still in its infancy. The work of Sprague (1995) paves the way for a systemic view of electronic document management, which should integrate three perspectives of analysis of document management: *technologies* for document management, *benefits* for the application areas for which documents are mission-critical, and *roles and responsibilities* of the organization's departments and functions for which EDM will be strategic. Based on this seminal contribution, Päivärinta (2001) proposes a method for the requirements analysis for DMS design, based on the use of metadata and the genre theory of organizational communication (Yates & Orlikowski, 1992).

The use of metadata, together with markup languages and formal information models, is recognized widely as a basic mechanism for DMS design (Murphy, 1998; Murray, 1996; Salminen et al., 2000). A more implementation-oriented approach is discussed in Ginsburg (2000, 2001), providing practical guidelines for the design of DMS, such as the use of metadata, mechanisms of coordination between authors and readers, and ontology building. However, this contribution does not aim to define a methodological approach for design, development, and deployment of DMSs supported by standard modeling methods and techniques.

METADATA FOR DOCUMENT MANAGEMENT

Metadata Benefits in Document Management

As mentioned in previous sections, metadata allow the representation of information resource relevant properties in a human- and machine-understandable way. Especially in the case of unstructured document management, metadata are the mechanisms that enable the representation of document content and context of use properties in an explicit and formal way. Metadata can provide a solution to the opacity of unstructured documents (Ginsburg, 2001), allowing a machine-processable representation of document-relevant information.

At present, metadata are used in organizations to describe unstructured documents beyond those used for highly structured information (e.g., databases); for instance, the properties for word-processed documents, the metadata contained in the header records of e-mail messages, and directories of reusable software objects, and the indexes of digital image management and manual record retention systems (Murphy, 1998). Murphy (1998) states that metadata in organizations generally lack the centralized or controlled aspect that metadata have in application domains such as digital libraries or Web communities, and, consequently, they are not exploitable enough in information sharing, organizational learning, or knowledge management. As far as we know, this situation has not changed for many years. Moreover, while several standardization efforts exist for digital libraries, Web communities and other application domains, standard metadata models in document management are still lacking.

State of the Art

Several metadata sets have been proposed by research communities and/or industrial consortia in order to provide a standard way to describe and manage information resources. Most metadata standards belong to the following categories:

- **Description of information resources.** These standards provide metadata for the description and identification of information resources. Examples are Dublin Core (Dublin Core Metadata Initiative, 2003), which is a standard for library information items and also suitable for application to generic information objects; and MPEG-7 (Manjunathn et al., 2002) for multimedia content.

- **Specific functions of information management.** Some of the following metadata standards cover specific issues related to the management of information resources: XPDL and PNML standards for business process description, Extensible Access Control Markup Language (XACML) for the description of access right policies, Common Warehouse MetaModel, CWM (Object Management Group, 2001) for data warehouses, ISO 15489 (International Organization for Standardization, 2001) for record management, just to mention a few.
- **Specific application domains.** There are several standard propositions for specific application domains: USMARC for digital libraries (Crawford, 1989), IMS (IMS Global Learning Consortium, 2003) for e-learning, and IEC 82045 (International Electrotechnical Commission, 2001) for management of technical documents.

From this classification, no existing metadata specifications are focused purposely on document management. The single exception is represented by the IEC 82045 specification, which, however, is a restraint to technical documents.

Some existing standard specifications could be conveniently adapted and integrated in order to represent document properties in organizations (Päivärinta et al., 2002). For instance, Dublin Core (DC), one of the most widely adopted metadata standards for information item description, offers generic descriptive labels that could be used to describe content-related properties of documents in organizations. The DC element set provides 15 labels: *Coverage, Creator, Date, Description, Format, Language, Other Contributors, Publisher, Relation, Resource Identifier, Resource Type, Rights Management, Source, Subject, Title*. Most of them are meaningful in an organizational

context. An exception is certainly provided by the label *Publisher*, which is tied to the author-title-publisher model that traditionally is applicable to documentation that is made publicly available (e.g., books, journals, etc.). This model is not always applicable to organizational documents, as the volume of internal use documents largely exceeds documents from external sources (Murphy, 1998). Obviously, a special case is provided by those kinds of organizations (e.g., publishing companies) that produce material that should be made available for public distribution. In general, a document is described more usefully through its states, such as *draft, authorized, signed*, declaring the evolution of the document during its lifecycle but not necessarily by condition of public distribution of the resource. The example of the document *project proposal*, illustrated in a previous paragraph, clearly highlights what was stated before. As already mentioned, a metadata model that is useful for document management should include the description of the organizational context (i.e., the lifecycle model of the documents) and its relation with organizational processes, roles, and responsibilities (Salminen et al., 2000).

Many standardization efforts exist in the domain of record management, such as the ISO 15849 international standard (International Organization for Standardization, 2001). A Record "is evidence of an activity or decision and demonstrates accountability" (Public Record Office, 2001, p.7). Records are documents (structured and unstructured), whose management requires a rigorous process (Emery, 2003). While a Document Management System is focused on knowledge sharing and collaboration capabilities that can be promoted by using a document repository, a Record Management System is focused more on maintaining a repository of evidence that can be used to document events related to statutory, regulatory, fiscal, or historical activities within an organization (Emery, 2003).

DOCUMENT MANAGEMENT AND SHARING MARKUP LANGUAGE

This article aims to propose a metadata model named Document Management and Sharing Markup Language (DMSML) that represents document properties that are relevant to document management and enable the design of Web-based DMSs in a way that promotes the reuse of content and context of use information, which is conveyed by unstructured documents for organizational purposes. In the following section, we describe the high-level requirements for DMSML metadata specification and the modeling approach that we have adopted.

DMSML Metadata Specification

Specification of metadata elements should guarantee that metadata are representative and relevant properties of documents. In order to decide which properties are representative and relevant for our needs, some high-level requirements are defined. Although these guidelines drove the specification process of DMSML, they are generally applicable to metadata specification in other application domains.

High-Level Requirements for DMSML Specification

The high-level requirements that we identified for the specification of DMSML are: generality, extensibility, and interoperability.

Generality. The metadata model should be applicable to document management for organizations in any application domain (e.g., public administration, construction, software, services businesses, etc.). General commonly sharable and widely adopted labels should be selected. An example of fulfillment of generality is the choice to label as *creator* the person who created a document, instead of *journalist* or *writer*, which

carries the significance of a specific application domain.

Extensibility. Since DMSML cannot contain specific labels tailored to any application domain, it will allow the extension of its element set. Refinement of existing elements (e.g., substitution of the element *creator* with the element *journalist*) or the introduction of new elements should be allowed in order to deal with the requirements of specific application domains. Moreover, the extension of the metadata set should be driven by business requirements rather than technological choices.

Interoperability. Interoperability is defined as "the ability of two or more systems or components to exchange information and to use the information that has been exchanged" (Institute of Electrical and Electronics Engineers, 1990). Two applications that are both DMSML-aware can exchange just the metadata or the metadata with the related document and be able to access and meaningfully process them.

DMSML is not a standard proposition, and interoperability based on DMSML-awareness may be limited, as long as the metadata set is not widely adopted. Furthermore, as mentioned previously, some specific issues that are encompassed in the discipline of document management (e.g., information resource description, access management, and business process) are addressed by existing standards. The adoption of some of these standards in the DMSML specification is an effective way to promote interoperability and to create a comprehensive framework of document management metadata, which takes advantages of existing contributions.

Metadata Modeling

The use of proper formal representation techniques enables the unambiguous understanding of the concepts conveyed by the metadata elements in heterogeneous communities and promotes the metadata exchange across heterogeneous systems (Duval et al, 2002; Murray, 1996). Most metadata standards lack an accounting for underlying data modeling principles, thus not providing a clear exposition of entities and relationships represented in metadata specification (Lagoze & Hunter, 2001). As suggested by several sources (Duval et al., 2002; Melnik & Decker, 2000), it is important to express in a formal and abstract way concepts and relationships embedded in the specification (i.e., the meaning or semantics) and to share strategies and rules for metadata encoding and implementation (syntax) for computer-supported serialization, exchange, access, and manipulation of the metadata set.

Meaning and syntax should be kept as separate as possible in order to allow agreement and adoption of the metadata set independently from technological and implementation choices, which can vary over time.

In order to provide a rigorous formalization of the DMSML metadata model, we refer to two layers of data modeling, usually adopted in the traditional database design approach (Elmasri & Navathe, 2003).

1. **Conceptual layer.** This layer provides an abstract representation of concepts and relations among concepts, independent from implementation details and often by means of standard graphical notations. Conceptual models enable people with low technical expertise to understand the meaning of data and to manipulate the data model and participate in the extension of DMSML for the specific purposes of their own organization; it thus encourages the transfer of business knowledge detained by the organization members to the DMSML metadata set. Conceptual UML class diagrams (Booch et al., 1998) are used in order to represent concepts and relationships underlying the DMSML metadata model.

2. **Logical layer.** The logical layer translates domain-related concepts and relationships in data constructs, which are expressed in a rigorous and standard logical data modeling paradigm. Logical models are used by database designers to translate concepts into database constructs. The traditional paradigms for logical data modeling are the relational and object-oriented models (Elmasri & Navathe, 2003). Our approach aims to benefit from the use of XML, which at present is the standard for data serialization and exchange. XML defines a generic syntax used to mark up data in a text document, using simple and flexible tags. The grammar of XML documents can be defined by means of the XML schema language, as proposed by the W3C in its March 2001 XML Schema Recommendation (Sall, 2002). An XML document that respects the grammar rules of its XML schema is called a valid instance of that XML schema. In our case, DMSML is an XML schema that defines rules in order to represent document metadata and their values in an XML document.

DMSML BUILDING BLOCKS

After analyzing the role of documents in organizations, the content as well as the context of use are relevant properties of documents. DMSML is made of three building blocks: content-related properties are included in the Descriptive Information model, while context of use properties are expressed in the Collaboration and Lifecycle models:

1. **Descriptive Information model.** Contains the set of metadata that describes and identifies the document, such as title, author, and subject.

2. **Collaboration model.** Formalizes how human resources are structured (the organi-

Figure 1. DMSML—Descriptive Information model, conceptual layer

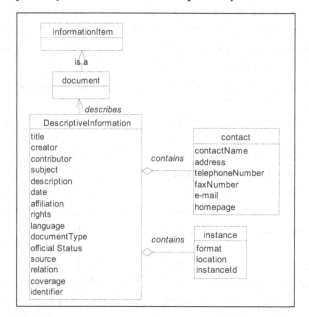

zational model) and how access to information resources is regulated (the access right policy) on the basis of organizational roles or responsibilities of individuals.

3. **Lifecycle model.** Specifies the lifecycle of the document. The document lifecycle usually consists of the following stages: creation, review, publication, access, archive, and deletion. A specific lifecycle may not implement all these stages or implement others. This depends on the characteristics of the document types in use in the organizations. For instance, a project proposal lifecycle is different from the lifecycle of an official communication, which should be conveyed to the personnel of the organization at the final stage of its life cycle (the document passes through the states of draft, revised, final, and published).

DMSML also includes other concepts that represent the entities relevant for document management, such as the *Document*, which is the atomic unit of information that we consider; the *Folder*, which is a collection of documents; and the *Workspace*, which models the working environment and contains documents and folders. Each entity type may be described by specific labels of the DMSML model. In the following paragraphs we will show the conceptual views of the Descriptive Information, Collaboration, and Lifecycle models (Figures 1, 2, and 3), together with an example of metadata specification for our case study (a Project Proposal). Due to limitation of space, we provide an extract of the logical layer for the Descriptive Information model (Figure 2). For more details, the DMSML model is fully presented in Paganelli (2004).

Descriptive Information Model

The Descriptive Information model includes labels that provide descriptions of information resources. It mostly includes static properties, which gener-

Figure 2. DMSML—Part of Descriptive Information model, logical layer

```
<?xml version="1.0" encoding="UTF-8"?>
    ...
    <xs:element name="document" type="DocumentType"/>
      <xs:complexType name="DocumentType">
        <xs:sequence>
          <xs:element name="description" type="DescriptionType"/>
        </xs:sequence>
      </xs:complexType>
      <xs:complexType name="DocumentDescriptionType">
        <xs:sequence>
          <xs:element ref="dc:title"/>
          <xs:element ref="dc:creator"/>              Compliance with
          <xs:element ref="dc:contributor"/>      → the Dublin Core (DC)
          <xs:element ref="dc:subject"/>              metadata standard
          <xs:element ref="dc:description"/>
          <xs:element ref="dc:date"/>
          <xs:element ref="dc:rights"/>
          <xs:element ref="dc:language"/>
          <xs:element name="documentType" type="xs:string"/>
          <xs:element name="affiliation" type="xs:string"/>
          <xs:element name="contact" type="contactType"/>
          <xs:element name="identifier" type="xs:string"/>
                          .....
        </xs:sequence>
      </xs:complexType>
</xs:schema>
```

Figure 3. DMSML specification for a project proposal—Descriptive Information model

```
<document>
        <title> Mobile Commerce Project Proposal </title>
        <creator> John Smith </creator>
        <contributor> Mark Johnson </contributor>
        <subject> wireless technologies, e-commerce </subject>
        <description> Proposal for Mobile Commerce services
                                        architecture</description>
        <date> 10/07/2004 </date>
        <rights> confidential</rights>
        <language> english</language>
        <documentType> Project Proposal</documentType>
        <affiliation> R&D Department </affiliation>
        <identifier> 0012223456</identifier>
        <contact>
        <contactName>John Smith</contactName>
        <address> my address  </address>
        <telephoneNumber> my telephone number </telephoneNumber>
        <faxNumber> my fax number </faxNumber>
        <e-mail> john.smith@mycompany.com </e-mail>
        <homepage> www.mycompany.com/johnsmith/ <homepage>
        </contact>
            .....
</document>
```

Figure 4. DMSML—Collaboration model, conceptual layer

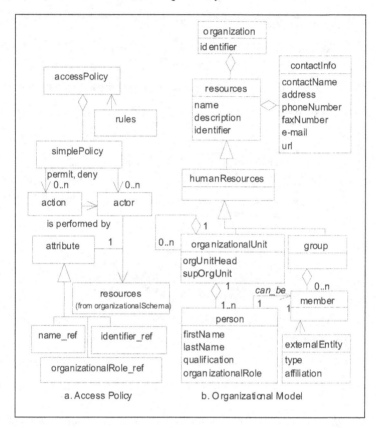

ally are used for search and indexing purposes (e.g., Title, Creator, Date, Description, Document Type, Subject, Contact, Affiliation), as described in Figure 1. These labels are general enough to be applied to any document type and any organization. A subset of these labels also can be used to describe the workspace and folder entities (e.g., Title, Creator, and Description). DMSML can be extended in order to address the requirements of a specific organization by including descriptive elements that are tailored according to the specificities of a document type, organization, or organizational unit. For instance, a scientific paper can be characterized by further elements, such as Abstract, Journal and Publisher, while a document of type *Contract* should be associated

with descriptive elements such as Contract Type, Customer and Product. We chose to integrate the Dublin Core (DC) (Dublin Core Metadata Initiative, 2003) metadata set in the Descriptive Information model, as it provides generic description labels, and it is a widely adopted standard. In addition to the DC elements, DMSML provides labels that are specific to the organizational environment; for instance, *Contact* (e.g., mail, telephone number, etc.) and *Affiliation* (e.g., project, department, organizational unit, etc.).

This conceptual view is mapped into the XML schema modeling primitives (see Figure 2) to provide the logical view of the model. Recalling the example of the project proposal mentioned previously, Figure 3 shows an instance of descriptive DMSML metadata for a specific project proposal document.

Collaboration Model

Document sharing can be considered a specific instance of collaborative activities. During the stages of document lifecycle, the participants collaborate for the accomplishment of organizational purposes. In this context, the DMSML Collaboration model is defined in terms of access policies assigned to the members of the organizational model, as shown in Figure 4. Access policies define the access rights to resources (Figure 4a). There are two dimensions related to permission assignment: a permission can be assigned to a specific employee or user (e.g., by

means of a specific attribute, such as the name or an identifier), or the policy can be specified in terms of organizational entities and roles rather than to specific participants (e.g., by means of the organizational role, attribute), according to the Role-Based Access Control (RBAC) strategy (Sandhu et al., 1996). We adopted the eXtensible Access Control Markup Language (XACML) (OASIS, 2003), allowing the description of access policies to information resources in an extensible and standard way.

Organizational models then map roles and organizational functions and units to individuals or groups (Figure 4b). DMSML includes an organization model that specifies the organizational units, individuals and related organizational roles. In order to satisfy changing requirements (e.g.,

Figure 5. DMSML specification for a project proposal—Collaboration model

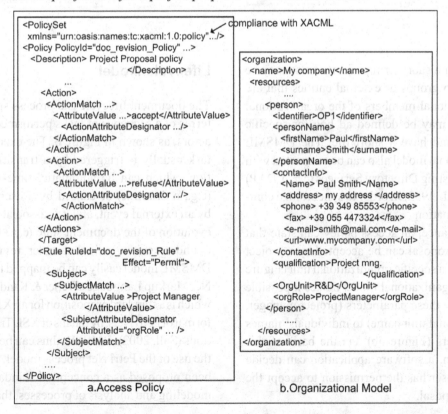

Figure 6. DMSML—Lifecycle model, conceptual layer

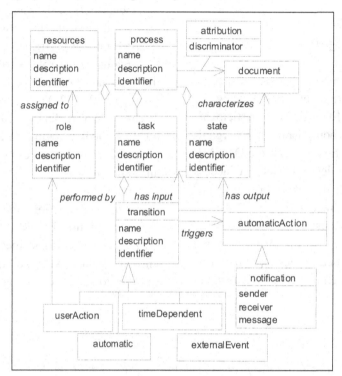

the setup of a short-term project), it also may be extended to groups or external entities that are not institutional members of the organizational model but may be defined ad hoc for specific purposes and have a short life. The DMSML organizational model also can be connected with already existing Directory Services (e.g., LDAP) (Yeong et al., 1993) in order to synchronize common information.

For instance, an access policy can state that a project proposal can be accepted by a project manager of a specific organizational unit (Figure 5a). The organizational model makes it possible to associate these parameters (project manager, organizational unit name) to individuals' names or identifiers (Figure 5b). On the basis of this information, a software application can decide if an end user has the permission to accept the project proposal.

Lifecycle Model

The document lifecycle is a process specified in terms of a sequence of tasks performed by some actors, as shown in Figure 6. The execution of a task usually is triggered by a transition condition, which can be automatic, time-dependent (e.g., a deadline) or caused by a user action or by an external event, and it is associated with an evolution of the document state (e.g., from draft to under_review, to final or under_revision). The DMSML model easily can be mapped to the Petri Net Markup Language (Weber & Kindler, 2002), which is a standard proposition for an XML-based format of Petri Nets, by means of XSL Transformations (Sall, 2002). DMSML thus can benefit from the use of the Petri Net process model, which has been proposed as a conceptual standard for the modeling and analysis of processes, thanks to its

Figure 7. DMSML specification for a project proposal—Lifecycle model

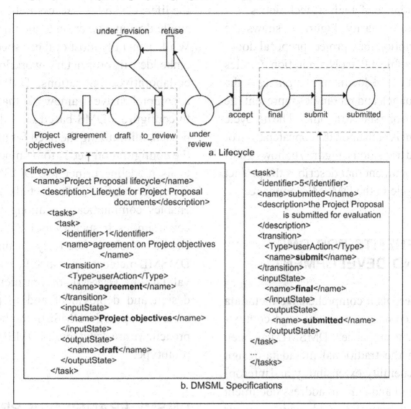

b. DMSML Specifications

Figure 8. DMSML framework prototype architecture

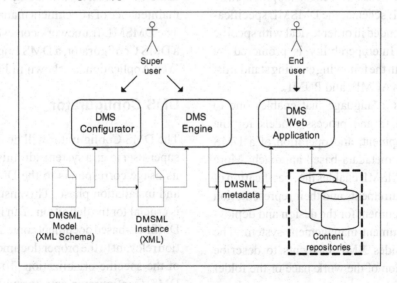

formal semantics, graphic notation, expressiveness, and abundance of analysis techniques.

For the sake of clarity, Figure 7a shows the lifecycle description for a project proposal document in the graphical Petri Net notation. Circles represent the states of documents (or *places* in the Petri Net language), and rectangles represent the transitions from one state to another. The lifecycle of the document is built upon the concatenation of these states and transitions. Figure 7b shows a part of the XML document that describes the project proposal lifecycle in the DMSML language.

DMSML BENEFITS FOR DMS DESIGN AND DEVELOPMENT

DMSML represents a comprehensive metadata model that encompasses content- and context-of-use document properties. DMSML has been designed with the traditional metadata-design principles of generality, extensibility, and interoperability in mind and aims to address document management requirements with which, to our knowledge, existing metadata standards do not deal. As a matter of fact, DMSML contains labels that are applicable to any document type. Thanks to the standard extension mechanisms provided by XML and XML schema, the DMSML specification can be extended in order to deal with specific requirements. Interoperability is promoted by compliance with the following existing standards: Dublin Core, XACML, and PNML.

DMSML is a language that enables one to define open data and process models for the design, development, and operation of a DMS by means of a metadata-based approach. More specifically, DMSML enables the specification of functional requirements and their representation in an XML document for the design and deployment of a document management system. The DMSML provides XML elements to describe the configuration of the workspace or the folder structure in order to create or import a docu-

ment resource classification schema, to specify the lifecycle and the access policies assigned to single documents, or on a document type basis. While generally most of these specifications are embedded in proprietary workflow engines or collaborative applications, DMSML provides a comprehensive framework that enables one to configure a DMS based on a declarative approach, minimizing the need for new code when the configuration needs to be modified. Thanks to its modeling principles, DMSML facilitates the understanding of the metadata meaning and enables communication among heterogeneous communities. In such a way, business knowledge can be exploited effectively for the extension of DMSML metadata in a specific case. In order to validate the DMSML-driven method for DMS design and deployment and to provide some tools to support the DMSML methodological approach, we are developing a DMSML framework prototype.

DMSML FRAMEWORK PROTOTYPE

The DMSML framework prototype provides the user with automated support for adaptation and use of the metadata set and the design, deployment, and maintenance of a document management system. The DMSML framework consists of three parts: a DMS Configurator, a DMS Engine, and a DMS Web Application, as shown in Figure 8.

DMS Configurator

The DMS Configurator will be used by a sort of super-user (e.g., a system administrator), because its usage corresponds to the DMS specification and installation phase. This installation process is crucial for the definition of an instantiation of a DMSML-based document containing all information relevant to the proper document management of the specific organization. To this extent, the DMS Configurator acts through a wizard that will guide the user through the configuration of a DMS Web application according to organization requirements. The configurator application provides a sequence of interfaces that progressively guides the user through the definition of the workspace, the organizational schema, and the structure of folders. The end user can specify a set of lifecycle templates and access policies to be assigned to documents or document types.

The DMSML instance thus created—DMSML specifications—containing business and organizational information, such as organizational schemas and access policies, then will be processed by the DMS Engine.

DMS Engine

The DMS Engine is a Web-based application that enables the user accessing a standard Web browser to deploy a DMS that is customized according to the specifications encoded in the DMSML instance document. Again, the end user of this component of the prototype is a technical person or a system administrator.

Based on the features of the DMSML model, the DMS Engine enables a completely declarative approach for the design and deployment of an ad hoc document management system based on the specifications expressed in the DMSML instance. As shown in Figure 8, the declarative specifications in DMSML then are fed into the DMS Engine to produce tailored document management systems. These are built upon a collection of configurable components (Java classes) that provide the infrastructure for the new DMS. This infrastructure includes core libraries providing document management features.

DMS Web Application

The DMS Web Application provides basic document management features that can be accessed by a generic end user (a member of the organiza-

tion) through a standard Web browser. The DMS Web Application can be automatically configured and deployed, thanks to the facilities offered by the DMS Configurator and the DMS Engine applications.

The functions provided by the DMS Web Application include:

- Facilities for navigation, document upload, version control, and so forth. The interface provides end users with some information about the documents organized in the workspace folders, not only in terms of descriptive properties (e.g., title, creator, etc.) but also of lifecycle and sharing constraints.
- Document lifecycle management.
- Access control (ruling the execution of permitted actions according to the organizational access policies).
- Search functions enabling a metadata-based and full-text document search.
- Log files recording.

Based on the following formal foundations of DMSML, the DMS Web Application aims to provide a solution for document management that is capable of addressing the aforementioned high-level requirements:

- **Open standards Compliance.** The application is based on technical standards (e.g., J2EE and XML) and on business metadata standards as well (e.g., Dublin Core, XACML, and PNML).
- **Multiplatform compatibility.** As it is based on J2EE standard specifications.
- **Metadata-based approach.** Thanks to its extensive use of DMSML metadata.
- **Open and standard methodological approach.** For DMS design and development, thanks to the instrumental support provided by the DMSML framework prototype.

PROTOTYPE IMPLEMENTATION DETAILS

The DMS Configurator is a Java application. Its architecture consists of an *Interface*, which uses the JavaSwing Graphic Toolkit and other graphic utilities (e.g., images, etc.), and the *DMS Configurator Core* built on top of the *Java Virtual Machine*, as shown in Figure 9a. The DMS Configurator Core is composed of five main components:

- An XML Schema Parser, which verifies the validity of the XML document against the DMSML model. The XML Schema Parser also contains an XML parser.
- JDOM API, used to create, access and manipulate XML documents.
- An XPath Engine, enabling one to validate XPath expressions.

- A Rule Manager, which interprets and enforces the rules associated with the user actions.
- A set of Basic Services, such as logging and data storage facilities.

DMS Engine and DMS Web Application are both Web applications designed according to the standard J2EE specifications. They are characterized by a multi-tier architecture consisting of a Client, an Application Logic (composed of an Interaction and a Business Logic side), and a Data tier, as shown in Figures 9b and 9c, respectively. The Client side is a standard Web browser, and the Interaction side is realized by means of JSPs (Java Server Pages).

Regarding the DMS Engine, the Business Logic contains a template of a DMS Web Application and a set of APIs (DMSEngine API). The DMSEngine APIs are a set of Java classes

Figure 9. DMSML framework prototype: a. DMS configurator; b. DMS engine; c. DMS Web application

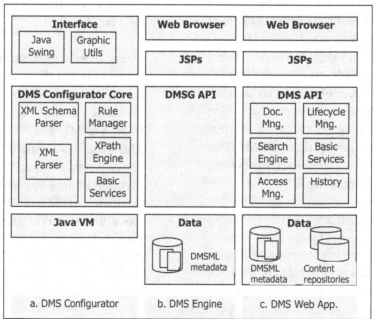

that customize the template according to the DMSML specifications. The Business Logic of the DMS Web Application is composed of a set of DMS APIs implemented by Java classes, which provide basic functions for the management of workspaces, folders, and documents. The DMS APIs consist of several components:

- A Document Management component providing facilities for navigation, document upload, version control, and so forth.
- A Lifecycle Management component that enforces the evolution of the document across the lifecycle steps.
- An Access Manager, which should guarantee that users execute permitted actions according to the organizational access policies.
- A Search Engine, enabling a metadata-based and a full-text document search.
- A History component that records log files.
- Basic Services, such as monitoring and connection to database services.

CONCLUSION AND FUTURE WORK

This article has highlighted some critical issues concerning unstructured document management in organizations, giving sound arguments to increase the awareness of what managers should account for when considering the possibility of adopting a document management system in order to fulfill their organizational needs. In particular, we defended the idea that metadata are the basis for novel strategies and solutions for effective document management. However, since existing metadata specifications are too generic or focused on application domains other than document management, we have proposed in this article a metadata model for the management of unstructured documents in organizations, enabling the design and deployment of DMSs.

The DMSML metadata includes descriptive, collaboration- and process-related properties of unstructured documents. The DMSML modeling approach presented here enables the representation of the metadata set in a way that promotes human and machine understanding by separating and properly representing metadata semantics and syntax.

We also described the DMSML Framework Prototype. The prototype includes a Web-based DMS (based on the DMSML Descriptive Information, Collaboration, and Lifecycle models), a DMS Configurator, and a DMS Engine, enabling end users to specify business requirements to properly configure and customize the DMS for the needs of a specific organization by exploiting the features of the DMSML model.

At the moment, testing activities of the prototype in real application scenarios are undergoing. The evaluation activity aims to verify the capability of the DMSML-based solution, based on the DMSML model and the DMSML Framework Prototype, to address critical factors related to the management of unstructured documents in an organization. We expect that the results of the evaluation provide a measure of the impact of a DMSML-based approach in an application scenario and suggestions for the refinement of the DMSML labels. The testing phase aims also at evaluating the degree of usability and user satisfaction provided by the DMSML Framework Prototype. The evaluation should focus conveniently on those organizations that already have adopted process optimization and re-engineering strategies (i.e., organizations with quality certifications). In this case, the DMSML-based DMS configuration could support predefined organizational processes and document lifecycles. At present, first stages of evaluation are being carried out in an Italian SME (Small Medium Enterprise).

During the evaluation phase, the cost of using metadata also will be analyzed. As illustrated throughout this work, the use of metadata has several benefits, but its cost has to be evaluated in terms of resources needed for metadata creation and management (Duval et al., 2002; Gilliland-Swetland, 2000). Metadata creation and insertion in the system can require a manual or automatic procedure, or a hybrid approach, according to the type of metadata (i.e., *creator* and *date* values can be automatically inserted by the system). The optimal strategy should be found in order to obtain the best compromise of accuracy and efficiency.

At the current stage of the prototypal development of the DMS Web Application, the end user should manually insert most descriptive metadata. Further work is needed in order to investigate strategies and mechanisms in order to automate this stage as much as possible (i.e., using content analysis tools for the automatic extraction of metadata from texts).

REFERENCES

Booch, G., Jacobson, I., & Rumbaugh, J. (1998). *Unified modeling language user's guide*. Boston, MA: Addison-Wesley.

Crawford, W. (1989). *MARC for library use: Understanding USMARC*. Boston, MA: G.K. Hall.

Dublin Core Metadata Initiative. (2003). Dublin core metadata element set, Version 1.1: Reference description. Retrieved May 20, 2003, from http://www.dublincore.org

Duval, E., Hodgins, H., Sutton, S., & Weibel, S. (2002). Metadata principles and practicalities. *D-Lib Magazine, 8*(4). Retrieved June 20, 2003, from http://www.dlib.org/dlib/april02/weibel/04weibel.html

Elmasri, R., & Navathe, S. B. (2003). *Fundamentals of database systems*. Addison Wesley.

Emery, P. (2003). *Documents and records management: Understanding the differences and embracing integration*. Retrieved September 16, 2004, from http://www.zylab.com

Gilliland-Swetland, A. J. (2000). *Setting the stage. Introduction to metadata: pathways to digital information*. Retrieved March 18, 2003, from http://www.getty.edu

Ginsburg, M. (2000). Intranet document management systems as knowledge ecologies. In *Proceedings of the 33rd Annual Hawaii International Conference on System Sciences (HICSS-33)*. IEEE Computer Society Press.

Ginsburg, M. (2001). Openness: The key to effective intranet document management. In *Proceedings of International Symposium on Information Systems and Engineering ISE'2001*. Las Vegas, Nevada.

Gonçalves, M. A., Fox, E. A., Watson, L. T., & Kipp, N. A. (2004). Streams, structures, spaces, scenarios, societies (5s): A formal model for digital libraries. *ACM Transactions on Information Systems, 22*(2), 270-312.

IMS Global Learning Consortium. (2003). IMS learning design v1.0 final specification. Retrieved December 15, 2003, from http://www.imsglobal.org/learningdesign/index.cfm

Institute of Electrical and Electronics Engineers. (1990). *IEEE standard computer dictionary: A compilation of IEEE standard computer glossaries*. New York: Institute of Electrical and Electronics Engineers.

International Electrotechnical Commission. (2001). *Document management. Part 1: Principles and methods* (IEC 82045-1:2001). Retrieved July 15, 2004, from http://www.iso.org

International Organization for Standardization. (2001). *Information and documentation. Records management. Part 1: General* (ISO 15489-1). Retrieved October 22, 2003, from http://www.iso.ch

Karjalainen, A., Päivärinta, T., Tyrväiinen, P., & Rajala, J. (2000). Genre-based metadata for enterprise document management. In *Proceedings of the 33rd Hawaii's Conference on System Sciences, HICSS* (pp. 3013-3023). Los Alamitos CA: IEEE Computer Society.

Lagoze, C., & Hunter, G. (2001). The abc ontology and model. In *Proceedings of the International Conference on Dublin Core and Metadata Applications* (pp. 160-176). Retrieved July 15, 2003, from http://www.nii.ac.jp/dc2001/proceedings/abst-26.htm

Manjunathn, B. S., Salembier, P., & Sikora, T. (2002). *Introduction to MPEG-7 multimedia content description interface.* New York: John Wiley & Sons.

Melnik, S., Decker, S. (2000). A layered approach to information modeling and interoperability on the Web. In *Proceedings of the ECDL'00 Workshop on the Semantic Web*, Lisbon, Portugal.

Mitra, N. (2003). *SOAP Version 1.2 Part 0: Primer* (W3C Recommendation). Retrieved October 2003, from http://www.w3.org/TR/soap12-part0/

Moore, C., & Markham, R. (2002). *Enterprise content management: A comprehensive approach for managing unstructured content.* Giga Information Group, Inc. Retrieved February 2003, from http://www.msiinet.com/html/pdfs/essecm3.pdf

Murphy, L. D. (1998). Digital document metadata in organizations: Roles, analytical approaches, and future research directions. In *Proceedings of the 31st Hawaii International Conference on System Sciences* (Digital Documents) (pp. 267-276).

Murray, P. C. (1996). Information, knowledge and document management technology. *KM Metazine.* Retrieved July 10, 2003, from http://www.ktic.com/topic6/12-INFKM.HTM

OASIS. (2003). *Extensible access control markup language (XACML), v. 1.0.* Retrieved August 10, 2003, from http://www.oasis-open.org

Object Management Group. (2001). *Common warehouse metamodel specification, v 1.0.* Retrieved March 15, 2003, from http://www.omg.org/cgi-bin/doc?formal/01-10-01

Paganelli, F. (2004). *A metadata model for unstructured document management in organizations.* Doctoral dissertation, University of Florence, Department of Electronics and Telecommunications, Florence, Italy.

Päivärinta, T. (2001). *A genre-based approach to developing electronic document management in the organization.* Doctoral dissertation, University of Jyvaskyla, Finland.

Päivärinta, T., Tyrväiinen, P., & Ylimäki, T. (2002). Defining organizational document metadata: A case beyond standards. In *Proceedings of the Xth European Conference on Information Systems (ECIS).*

Public Record Office. (2001). *E-government policy framework for electronic records management.* Retrieved September 2004, from http://www.pro.gov.uk/recordsmanagement/

Sall, K. B. (2002). *XML family of specifications: A practical guide.* Boston, MA: Addison-Wesley Professional.

Salminen, A., Lyytikäinen, V., & Tiitinen, P. (2000). Putting documents into their work context in document analysis. *Information Processing and Management, 36*(4), 623-641.

Sandhu, R. S., Coyne, E. J., Feinstein, H. L., & Youman, C. E. (1996). Role-based access control models. *IEEE Computer, 29*(2), 38-47.

Sprague, R. H., Jr. (1995). Electronic document management: Challenges and opportunities for information systems managers. *MIS Quarterly, 19*(1), 29-50. Retrieved September 20, 2003, from http://www.cba.hawaii.edu/sprague/MISQ/MISQfina.htm

Stickler, P. (2001). Metia—A generalized metadata driven framework for the management and distribution of electronic media. In *Proceedings of the Dublin Core Conference 2001* (pp. 235-241).

Sun Microsystems. (2003). *J2EE 1.4 specification: Final release*. Retrieved November 2003, from http://java.sun.com/docs/index.html

the451. (2002). *Unstructured data management: The elephant in the corner*. Retrieved March 20, 2003, from http://www.the451.com

Weber, M., & Kindler, E. (2002). The Petri Net markup language. Advances in Petri Nets. *LNCS series*. Springer Verlag.

Workflow Management Coalition (2002). *Workflow process definition interface: XML process definition language, v. 1.0*. Retrieved March 16, 2003, from http://www.wfmc.org

Yates, J., & Orlikowski, W. J. (1992). Genres of organizational communication: A structurational approach to studying communication and media. *Academy of Management Review, 17*(2), 299-326.

Yeong, W., Howes, T., & Kille, S. (1993). *X.500 lightweight directory access protocol* (IETF RFC 1487). Retrieved October 15, 2002, from http://www.ietf.org/rfc/rfc1487.txt

ENDNOTES

[1]   www.documentum.com, www.fatwire.com, www.ibm.com, www.interwoven.com, www.microsoft.com

[2]   www.zope.org, www.opencms.org, cocoon.apache.org/lenya, www.dspace.org, www.dlib.vt.edu

This work was previously published in Information Resources Management Journal, Vol. 19, Issue 1, edited by M. Khosrow-Pour, pp. 1-22, copyright 2006 by IGI Publishing, formerly known as Idea Group Publishing (an imprint of IGI Global).

Chapter XV
ERP Usage in Practice:
An Empirical Investigation

Mary C. Jones
University of North Texas, USA

Randall Young
University of North Texas, USA

ABSTRACT

This study presents the results of an exploratory study of Fortune 1000 firms and their enterprise resource planning (ERP) usage, as well as benefits and changes they have realized from ERP. The study empirically examines ERP in these organizations to provide insight into various aspects that firms can use to evaluate how they are managing their ERP systems. Findings provide information about functionality implemented, extent to which benefits are realized, extent of ERP-related organizational changes firms have realized, and the way firms measure ERP success. The study also addresses the extent to which various types of ERP software have been implemented and whether there is a relationship between type of software and benefits. Finally, it examines ERP-enabled change in light of organizational configuration.

INTRODUCTION

Enterprise resource planning (ERP) is a tool that enables organizations to streamline operations, leverage common business processes, and manage multiple operations, and is implemented through an integrated suite of software modules and a centralized database (Jacoby & Bendoly, 2003; Scott & Kaindl, 2000). Although the term ERP may be used to represent a variety of concepts, in this article, the term is used to constitute the seamless integration of processes across functional areas with the standardization and integration of various business practices in order to manage operations more effectively and to gain an overall view of the business (Boudreau & Robey, 1999; Jacobs & Bendoly, 2003; Mabert et al., 2000).

The transition to an enterprise resource planning framework is often a long, difficult, and costly process due to the nature and complexity of ERP systems. Many firms are grappling with the tradeoff between the costs of implementing an ERP system and not having one (Stedman, 1999). For example, some have come to believe that "competitively and technically it's a must-do, but economically there is conflicting evidence, suggesting it is difficult to justify the associated costs, and difficult to implement to achieve a lasting business advantage" (Willcocks & Sykes, 2000, p. 32). However, in spite of many failures reported (Davenport, 1998; Kransner, 2000), there are many success stories, suggesting that if properly managed, organizations can and do realize significant benefits from ERP (Davenport, Harris, DeLong & Jacobson, 2001).

With the abundance of conflicting information and the seeming propensity to report failures rather than successes in the literature, many firms that have not implemented may still be wondering whether ERP is right for them and whether the benefits touted by ERP vendors exist. Others that have implemented may be wondering if the benefits and changes they have achieved are consistent with that of other implementers and whether ERP was worth the effort. The purpose of this study is to examine empirically the organizational usage of ERP in order to provide insight into various aspects of usage that firms can use to evaluate their own ERP usage and what they are gaining from ERP. Although there is much empirical and descriptive work about ERP, there is little that assesses ERP after implementation is complete (Sarkis & Sundarraj, 2001). Although the former research provides valuable insights, it often overlooks the final and longest stage of ERP life in which firms begin to realize the impact of ERP. Much of what is known about ERP may only be a reflection of the state of ERP at or immediately after implementation. However, senior IT and business managers believe that the integration and usage of enterprise systems is one of the most important issues that they are now facing (Luftman & McLean, 2004). Much post-

implementation ERP research provides mixed evidence about ERP's impact on overall organizational performance (Hitt et al., 2002; Hunton et al., 2003; Poston & Grabski, 2001). However, there is a need to explore the impact of ERP at various organizational levels, at the individual level, and at the ERP functionality level (Gattiker & Goodhue, 2002, Hitt et al., 2002). Thus, additional research that extends knowledge about post-implementation ERP is valuable.

The fundamental research question underlying this study is what is the state of post-implementation ERP in terms of benefits and changes organizations are able to realize? In answering this question, this study provides information about the extent to which benefits are realized, the extent of ERP-related organizational changes that firms have realized, and the way firms measure ERP success. It also addresses the extent to which various types of ERP software have been implemented and the relationship between the type of software and benefits. Finally, it examines ERP-enabled change and benefits in light of organizational configuration.

The rest of the article is organized in six sections. One is a discussion of the background for issues and questions examined followed by a brief discussion of the methodology for the study. A profile of respondents is presented in the fourth section, and data analysis and results are presented in the fifth section. The sixth section presents conclusions, implications of findings for practitioners, and directions for future research.

BACKGROUND

Firms implement ERP to help them integrate business processes and to share common resources across the organization (Zheng, Yen, & Tarn, 2000). ERP helps to do this through sets of integrated modules that allow companies to manage multiple operations from a standardized platform (Boudreau & Robey, 1999). At the time of this study, SAP AG® held the largest market share in ERP software, with PeopleSoft®, JDEdwards®, Oracle®, and Baan® following[1]. ERP software provides modules to support all or most functional areas in an organization, including financial operations, purchasing, materials management, project scheduling, human resources management, production planning, and plant maintenance. Some software packages provide a comprehensive set of modules, whereas others provide a more limited set designed for optimizing the management of particular aspects of the organization (Scott & Kaindl, 2000). As a result, some organizations adopt functionality from various ERP software vendors in an effort to put together the best overall set of functionality, sometimes referred to as a best-of-breed strategy (Krumwiede & Jordan, 2000). However, this strategy can lead to integration problems and may result in lack of benefits if the software from various vendors is not compatible (Menezes, 1999; Palitza, 2001). There also seems to be conflicting evidence as to the extent to which firms adopt best of breed. Thus, we wondered both what functionality and what software packages firms are adopting and the extent to which they are following a best-of-breed approach. It is difficult to get a good picture of this aspect of the state of ERP implementation today because there are few, if any, articles that provide all this information in one study. Issues about software in use could become particularly relevant as ERP vendors begin to merge and as firms are forced to fewer sources for new software, upgrades to existing software, and support.

Regardless of the ERP software, firms implement them in order to achieve benefits, the most common being overall cost savings and, specifically, reduced cost of operations (Bingi et al., 1999; Hitt et al., 2002). ERP offers the potential for many beneficial organizational changes across many areas of the firm, including strategy, technology, culture, and organizational structure (Al-Mashari & Zairi, 2000; Murphy & Simon, 2002). Specific changes include reduction in silo behavior, integration of processes, greater collaboration and teamwork, and broader knowledge of employees about tasks and processes (Baskerville et al., 2000; Palaniswamy & Frank, 2000). However, it is difficult to determine the extent to which these benefits are realized, because even when success stories are reported, there is little evidence about the extent to which investments in ERP are paying off (Shang & Seddon, 2002).

Research indicates that far less than one-half of firms that have implemented ERP use metrics to assess their investment (Bradford & Roberts, 2001). More recent research indicates that the number of firms using standard financial metrics to assess ERP, such as return on investment (ROI), is larger than this (Mabert et al., 2003). However, approximately 30% of firms do not perform any type of capital investment analysis on their ERP systems beyond those performed for the initial justification of ERP at the time the system is purchased (Mabert et al., 2003). Because there are widely varying reports of ERP success and failure, and because financial metrics are the standard way that firms evaluate other investments, we believe that it is important for firms to understand the extent to which this is applied to ERP and to think through whether they should apply them to their own ERP investments. Thus, we examine not only the extent to which benefits are realized but also the extent to which firms measure ERP benefits and the types of metrics they are using in order to provide a clearer picture of how and whether firms are assessing ERP investments.

It is also important to understand what impacts the extent to which firms realize benefits. This study examines two key factors that may impact the benefits of ERP implementation: software type and organizational configuration. The ERP packages on the market today evolved out of responses to specific market or organizational needs (Welti, 1999). Some firms have sometimes found it difficult to adapt the products to their own specific needs, even though vendors have revised and expanded the scope of their offerings

(Jones, 2001). A recent anecdotal experience of the authors is an adaptation of an ERP product originally targeted for human resource management in a university environment to support everything from human resource management to student enrollment and admissions. Although the product works well, there were a number of configuration and training issues that had to be resolved in the adaptation of the product to another environment that may or may not have been present if it was adapted to only the human resource facet of the university.

Given that the software products represented in this study are the most widely adopted across industries, it is reasonable to assume that some firms may find differences in their abilities to realize benefits because of differences in the match between their business structures and the ERP software. In spite of the fact that ERP requires organizations to adapt their business processes to the practices embedded in the software, it seems that not everything will port equally well. Therefore, we explore the following proposition about the relationship between software type and a firm's ability to achieve expected benefits:

P1: ERP software type influences the extent to which a firm achieves ERP benefits.

Organizational configuration also may influence the extent to which a firm realizes ERP benefits (Hanseth, Ciborra, & Braa, 2001; Mezenes, 1999). Firms that do not consider fully the impact of their organizational configuration when they implement ERP may implement systems that do not adequately integrate their data and processes (Markus, Tanis, & van Fenema, 2000; Soh et al., 2000). Some organizational configurations are not suited for organization-wide deployment of a single ERP instance (Gattiker & Goodhue, 2004). Other configurations do not facilitate significant enough changes for firms to realize ERP benefits. In addition, firms often implement ERP

with changes to their organizational configuration in mind (Gattiker & Goodhue, 2000). Thus, we explore the following propositions:

P2a: Organizational configuration influences the extent to which ERP benefits, in general, are realized.

P2b: Organizational configuration influences the extent to which organizations are able to make changes after ERP implementation.

METHODOLOGY

The data for this study were collected using a mail survey in a field study during the summer of 2003. Fortune 1000 firms comprised the sampling frame. Because there are few published validated scales that specifically address ERP issues, the survey questions were derived from findings about the constructs of interest in the ERP literature (Jones & Price 2001, 2004; Shang & Seddon, 2002). Questions 1 through 8 and question 26 were checklist questions, where respondents were asked to check which response(s) best applied to them. Questions 9 through 25 were measured with a five-point Likert scale ranging from strongly disagree with the statement (response = 1) to strongly agree with the statement (response = 5). See Appendix A for questions used to measure constructs and demographics in this study.

Surveys were mailed to upper-level managers responsible for the information technology function of their organization, as indicated in a database obtained from Fortune. These respondents were chosen because these individuals have been shown to be appropriate respondents about organization-wide change efforts that depend on information technology (Terziovski et al., 2003). However, in some cases, this executive might not have direct knowledge about their firm's ERP. We asked them in the survey cover letter that if this were the case to forward the survey to the individual who was most directly involved in ERP management at the senior level.

Fortune 1000 was selected as the sampling frame for several reasons. This study examines a variety of ERP issues. Thus, one criterion for a sampling frame was one that contained firms that have completed large-scale implementations, where a variety of functionalities was implemented across divisions of the organization. Both the scope and cost of this type of implementation suggests that the study should draw upon large firms. The Fortune 1000 database is a listing of information for the 1000 largest companies in the U.S., which is compiled and maintained by the publishers of the business magazine, *Fortune*. It includes companies with yearly revenues in excess of $1 billion U.S., and thus fits this criterion. In addition, we were interested in gathering data about a variety of software types. Because some software is more suited to one or more given industries, another criterion was to choose a sampling frame that is representative of a variety of industries. Fortune 1000 also meets this criterion. Finally, we wanted to select a group in which a large percentage of firms are using ERP. It is estimated that more than 70% of Fortune 1000 companies have implemented ERP systems (Barker & Frolick, 2003), thus meeting this criterion.

Of the 1000 surveys mailed, 70 were returned, representing a 7% response rate. Of the 70 returned surveys 20 were discarded because the contact person was no longer there, and either the company returned the survey unopened or the organization has a policy of not responding to surveys. Extrapolating the 20 out of 70 unusable surveys to the population indicates that 285 of the 1000 firms surveyed may fall into one of these categories. Using the remaining 715 as the population, the 50 usable surveys still represent a 7% response rate. Several companies telephoned the authors to indicate that they did not respond to surveys, and others returned the surveys unopened with a stamp on the envelope indicating the contact

person was no longer there. One telephoned to say that they were filing for bankruptcy protection and would not be responding.

One explanation for the low responses rate is the general difficulty of getting responses from executives at that level of the organization and a decline in the response rate of surveys, in general (Hambrick, Gelekanycz, & Frederickson, 1993). This response rate is consistent with those in other exploratory studies of post implementation ERP (Mabert et al., 2003). In the last several years, there has been more demand on executive time for information from academia, industry analysts, external stakeholders, and internal surveyors (Eisenhardt, 1989). Although there are a number of techniques for improving response rates, such as offering incentives, follow-ups, and telephone calls, these techniques have been shown to be relatively ineffective in mail surveys of executives at this level (Cycyota & Harrison, 2002). Thus, we did not use these techniques. Although a higher response rate is desirable, this sample does provide a set of response on which we can base an exploratory assessment of the constructs of interest.

However, assessment of non-response bias indicates that these respondents represent a cross-section of ERP adopters in this sampling frame (the Fortune 1000 companies). Non-response bias was assessed on the basis of two indicators: number of ERP users in an organization and the number of ERP modules implemented. Research suggests that these may be better indicators of the size of an ERP implementation than more traditional organizational size measures (Francalanci, 2001). Very large organizations that implement a broad scope of ERP functions may do so only for one or two business units that represent a smaller percentage of the total company size (Jones & Price, 2004). For example, a firm might have several thousand employees yet only implement in one division that have just several hundred employees. Furthermore, research indicates that ERP implementations are not substantively different among large firms that are defined as having over $1 billion U.S. in annual revenue (Mabert et al., 2003). This is the size of all the firms in our study. Although there may be a variety of reasons for this finding, one is that organizational size may not be sufficient to capture differences. Other findings that there are differences in the ERP implementation experiences of large firms lends support for this (Hebert & Oppenheim, 2004; Songini, 2003; Swanton, 2003). These respondents represent a broad range of size of implementations in terms of number of users (Table 1). Roughly, they are equally distributed across five categories of size, although there is a somewhat larger percentage in the *less than or equal to 500 users* category (27%) than in the others.

Another indicator of ERP size is the number of modules (functionality) implemented (Francalanci, 2001). Because we are comparing across ERP packages and because ERP packages achieve functionality in varying degrees of submodules, we confine our assessment of functionality to the general modules (e.g., financial accounting, materials management, etc.) rather than drilling down into submodules such as master data, general ledger, or inventory control (Francalanci, 2001). The majority of our respondents (69%) have implemented between four and nine modules of functionality (Table 1). Another 21% has implemented 10 or more modules. Therefore, it appears that they represent a broad range of implemented functionalities. Because the sampling frame is comprised of large firms, it is not surprising that few have implemented only one, two, or three modules. Given the range of ERP users and modules implemented that are represented here, this distribution of respondents is believed to be representative of the sampling frame.

PROFILE OF RESPONDENT FIRMS

Because the unit of analysis is the organization, a profile of respondent firms is provided in order to help clarify the lens through which findings are interpreted (Table 1).

Not surprisingly, almost all respondents have implemented the financial accounting and purchasing functions. This is consistent with evidence that accounting and purchasing are the two areas over which firms desire to gain the greatest control. Other functions that have been implemented widely include controlling, asset management, materials management, human resource management, and data warehousing. To achieve this functionality, a larger percentage of respondents (40%) use a combination of software types than individual packages. However, only 18% indicated that they chose the functionality in their packages based on best-of-breed criteria. Among respondents who do use a single software type, SAP is the one used most (30%), followed by PeopleSoft at 18%.

The majority of respondents had implemented ERP at least two years prior to the study. Years of use is roughly equally distributed between two to three years, three to five years, and more than five years. Furthermore, approximately 30% have done one upgrade, 23% have done two upgrades, and 21% have done three upgrades since the initial implementation. This is not unexpected, given the length of time that ERP has been in use in these firms and the relative frequency with which some software companies add new features to their product. These demographics indicate that respondents are from firms with moderate to substantial experience with ERP and that it has been in place long enough for them to have realized benefits and made ERP-related changes.

DATA ANALYSIS

General Benefits and Software Package

Respondents indicated that benefits of ERP have met but not exceeded original expectations (Table

Table 1. Profile of respondent firms

Number of ERP Users in the Organization	Percent of Respondents
Less than or equal to 500	27
Between 500 and 1000	17
Between 1000 and 2500	23
Between 2500 and 5000	15
More than 5000	18

Number of Modules Implemented	
1 to 3	10
4 to 6	31
7 to 9	38
10 +	21

Functionality*	
Financial Accounting (e.g., general ledger, accounts receivable, etc.)	98
Controlling (e.g., profitability analysis, product costing, etc.)	52
Asset Management (e.g., depreciation, planning/acquisition of capital assets, etc.)	76
Project Management (e.g., project planning, project tracking, etc.)	36
Sales and Distribution (e.g., customer order management, product pricing data, etc.)	48
Production Planning (e.g., master scheduling, bill of materials, etc.)	42
Materials Management (e.g., master inventory data, materials tracking, etc.)	64
Purchasing (e.g., requisitions, purchase orders, goods receipt, etc.)	98
Plant Maintenance (e.g., maintenance schedules, equipment histories, etc.)	34
Service Management (e.g., service contracts, warranty coverage, etc.)	16
Human Resources Management (e.g., time accounting, payroll, etc.)	70
Strategic Management (e.g., strategic planning and simulation, balanced scorecard, etc.)	14
Data Warehousing (e.g., central storage of business data, data retrieval, etc.)	50
Other (including Enterprise Portal, Warehouse Management, Trade Management, CRM)	10

* *categories not mutually exclusive*

Software Packages Used	
SAP only	30
PeopleSoft only	18
Oracle only	12
Baan only	0
JDEdwards only	2
Other only (Lawson, Adage, SSA/CT)	6
Combination (any combination of the above packages)	32

Amount of Time Since Implementation *	
Less than 12 months	14
Between 1 year and 18 months	8
Between 18 months and 2 years	4
Between 2 and 3 years	20
Between 3 and 5 years	22
More than 5 years	22

* *numbers do not add up to 100% due to missing values*

continued on next page

Table 1. Profile of respondent firms (cont.)

Number of Upgrades Since Original Implementation*	
0	18
1	26
2	20
3	18
5	2
10	2

* numbers do not add up to 100% due to missing values

Table 2a. Extent to which companies realize ERP benefits

Benefit Realization	μ*	σ
Benefits met original expectations	3.73 0	.92
Benefits exceeded original expectations	2.75 1	.00
Benefits revised downward after implementation	2.54 1	.45
Realized significant cost savings overall	3.54 0	.99
Realized reduced cost of operations 3	.67	0.85

Sample size = 50
* All responses measured on a scale of 1 to 5 where 1 = strongly disagree and 5 = strongly agree

Table 2b. Methods organizations use to evaluate ERP success

Method Used	Respondents*
Return on Investment (ROI) 5	8
Net Present Value (NPV)	24
Change in Return on Assets (ROA)	8
Other**	
Balance Sheets and Income Statement	2
Impact	2
Internal Rate of Return (IRR)	2
Getting Decision Support Information	4
Faster	2
Impact on Strategic Objectives	
Strategic Necessity	

Sample size = 50
* categories not mutually exclusive 24% reported using 2 or 3 measures
** listed by respondents

2a). Extent to which benefits are realized was measured using a five-point Likert scale, where 1 is strongly disagree that they have realized the benefit and 5 is strongly agree that they have realized the benefit. These benefits have been realized in the form of cost savings overall, particularly in terms of reduced cost of operations. Furthermore, it does not appear that respondents simply are reporting their perceptions of whether benefits

and savings are there. Table 2b provides insight into the extent to which respondents report using various tools to evaluate ERP success. Note that these questions address benefits in general. More specific benefits/changes that firms realized from ERP are addressed in detail in the following sections.

Well over one-half of the respondents (58%) indicated that they use ROI, and another 24% use

Table 3a. Analysis of variance results for assessment of relationship between realization of benefits and type of ERP software used*

Dependent Variable	F-value	p
Benefits met original expectations	0.35	0.7904
Benefits exceeded original expectations	1.90 0	.1429
Benefits revised downward after implementation	2.20 0	.1016
Realized significant cost savings overall	2.36 0	.0848
Realized reduced cost of operations** 7	.42	0.0004

Sample size = 50
* Wilks' Lambda for overall effect = 0.43, F = 2.62, p = 0.0021
** significant at α = 0.01

Table 3b. Mean and standard deviations of reduced cost of operations for each category of software type

Software Type	μ **	σ
SAP only 4	.00	0.76
PeopleSoft only	2.63 0	.74
Oracle only	3.50 0	.55
Combination* 3	.84	0.69

Sample size = 50
* As defined in Table 1
** Tukey's HSD test for differences of means indicates that the mean for reduced cost of operations is significantly greater for SAP only than for PeopleSoft only and that the mean for any combination of Software Type is greater than for PeopleSoft only at α = 0.05.

NPV to assess ERP success[2]. These are not mutually exclusive categories, because respondents may use more than one financial measure. In fact, 24% report that they use two or three measures. Again, this paints a somewhat different picture than reports that indicate that few firms have formal financial evaluations of their ERP system results after their initial justification for purchasing the package (Mabert et al., 2003).

Closer examination of benefits indicates that the type of software package used may play a role in the extent to which firms realize ERP benefits, particularly with regard to cost savings. A one-way analysis of variance (ANOVA) was used to examine the relationship between the software package and benefits. Results are shown in Tables 3a and 3b. Because of the small number of respondents in the JDEdwards only (n = 2), Baan only (n = 0), and other only (n = 4) categories, these were removed from analysis. The remaining categories

were SAP only, PeopleSoft only, Oracle only, and any combination of software types. Because the sample sizes are unequal among categories, violation of the assumption of homogeneity of variance necessary for interpreting ANOVA results was a concern. Brown and Forsythe's test of homogeneity of variance was used because it has been shown to be best at providing power to detect variance differences (Conover, Johnson & Johnson, 1981; Olejnik & Algina, 1987). Results indicated that the assumption of homogeneity of variance held at α = 0.05 for all benefits variables except Benefits Greater than Expected (p = 0.00089). However, Welch's ANOVA, which is more robust to violations of the homogeneity of variance assumption than the standard ANOVA (Welch, 1951), provided results consistent with the standard ANOVA at α = 0.01 and α = 0.05. The standard ANOVA results are reported next and in Table 3a.

Table 4. Changes after ERP implementation

ERP Change	μ*	σ
Greater collaboration among functional areas in divisions	3.94 0	.63
Reorganization of processes	3.88 1	.11
Greater integration of processes across the organization	3.69 1	.08
Reduced silo behavior within divisions of the organization	3.67 1	.14
Reduced cost of operations 3	.67	0.85
Reduced silo behavior across the organization 3	.65	1.07
Greater collaboration across divisions of the organization 3	.63	1.05
Greater integration of processes within divisions 3	.50	1.29
People have a better view of the big picture	3.43 0	.89
More teamwork in the organization	3.41 0	.86
More projects that cut across divisions/functional areas 3	.22	0.96
Organization more receptive to change 3	.12	0.95
Easier to access resources in other areas for cross-cutting projects	3.00 0	.84

Sample size = 50
* All responses measured on a scale of 1 to 5 where 1 = strongly disagree and 5 = strongly agree

Wilks' Lambda for overall effect is significant at $F = 2.62$, $p = 0.0021$. This indicates that benefits differ among types of software used. Reduced cost of operations is the only benefit that varies significantly with software type at the $\alpha = 0.01$ level. Overall cost savings were not significant nor were the extent to which benefits were realized, exceeded, or revised downward. Thus, proposition P1 is somewhat supported. Note, however, that P1 addresses benefits in general. A more in-depth examination of specific ERP-related changes is provided in the section to follow. Tukey's Honestly Significant Difference (HSD) test for differences of means indicates that the mean for reduced cost of operations is significantly greater for firms using SAP only than for firms using PeopleSoft only, and that the mean for any combination of software type is greater than for firms using PeopleSoft only at the $\alpha = 0.05$ level (Table 3b). One explanation may be the discrepancy in the extent of functionality implemented across firms that chose different packages. Although it may be tempting to conclude that one software package is better than another, further assessment of our findings does not support that conclusion.

In this study, organizations that had only SAP implemented an average of 9.27 modules/functions, whereas those that had only PeopleSoft implemented an average of 4.67 modules/functions. The average was 4.83 for those using only Oracle and 7.17 for those using a combination. Firms that are using only PeopleSoft may not be realizing as significant a reduction in cost of operations because they have not implemented across a wide enough range of functions to do so. Therefore, rather than serving as an advertisement for a given vendor, these findings suggest that the extent of functionality implemented may be a key indicator of the benefits an organization realizes from its ERP implementation. Although at first this may appear to be tautological, many firms choose not to implement the majority of ERP modules available in a package. While their decisions may be based on a variety of factors, including resources, financial constraints, and current needs, the underlying philosophy of ERP is that it provides the capability to integrate the majority of processes organization-wide (Welti, 1999). ERP was not meant to be implemented piecemeal, and these findings suggest that ERP

Table 5. Factor analysis of changes after ERP implementation

	Factor 1	Factor 2	Factor 3	Factor 4
Factor Stats:				
Eigenvalue	2.97	2.42	1.69	1.63
% variance explained	22.86%	18.62%	13.00%	12.50%
Cronbach's alpha	0.84	0.73	0.41*	0.45*
ERP Change (factor scores in columns)				
Reorganization of Processes	0.84			
Greater Collaboration Among Functional Areas	0.78			
Better View of Big Picture	0.78			
Greater Integration of Processes Across the Organization	0.77			
Reduced Silo Behavior Across the Organization	0.51			
Easier Access to Resources in Other Areas for Cross-Cutting Projects		0.78		
More Projects that Cut Across Divisions/Functional Areas		0.76		
Reduced Cost of Operations		0.66		
Greater Collaboration Among Functional Areas in Divisions		0.61		
Reduced Silo Behavior Within Divisions of the Organization			0.81	
Greater Integration of Processes Within Divisions			0.75	
Organization More Receptive to Change				0.87
More Teamwork in the Organization				0.75

* Pearson product moment correlations were used for these two factors rather than Cronbach's alpha because they only had two items each. The correlations were each significant at a = 0.01. For factor 3, p = 0.0038 and for factor 4, p = 0.0013.

benefits are best realized when a greater number of modules are implemented. Further research is needed to compare the impacts of packages across equivalent scope of functionality implemented.

Specific ERP-Related Changes

In order to examine benefits more closely, we included questions on the survey that tapped respondents' perceptions of specific ERP-related changes in the organization (Table 4). The greatest changes include greater collaboration among functional areas within divisions and reorganization of processes. The least realized change is easier access to resources in other areas for cross-cutting projects. Thus, it appears that even though firms

are doing more integration of processes across the organization and reducing silo behavior, there still may be hoarding or guarding of resources within units. One explanation for this is that the collaboration and reorganization that firms have experienced have not been in place long enough to alter this type of behavior. Another explanation is that the reorganization has not been managed so that it impacts the deeper structure of organizational behavior. Thus, things may have appeared to change, but fundamentally they did not.

A closer inspection of these specific changes indicates that they may be grouped into distinct categories of change. For example, some relate to the organization as a whole (e.g., greater integration of processes across the organization), whereas others relate more to divisions within the organization (e.g., reduced silo behavior within divisions). Much research about ERP-enabled change addresses the changes in terms of the impact of each change item or in terms of somewhat arbitrary groupings of items (Shang & Seddon, 2002). Although identifying specific items may provide useful guidance to managers, any given item or combination of items may not apply to every organization. A list of individual items also is not likely to be comprehensive, so that information about specific ERP enabled change may not inform our understanding of the impact of ERP as much as a validated grouping of items. Therefore, it seems best to examine individual items in terms of where they might fit in terms of larger groupings.

With this in mind, exploratory principle components factor analysis using Varimax rotation was used to determine whether and where these grouped together (Table 5). Factor analysis enables the reduction of a larger number of items to a smaller, more manageable, and perhaps more informative set (Hair et al., 1998). Factor analysis is a powerful tool for this, because it facilitates better assessment of the properties of sets of measures than simpler tools such as correlations. It not only allows assessment of the correlation among items but also uses the correlation matrix to derive factor loadings that represent the correlation between an item and the construct it is thought to measure. Although factor analysis does not directly constitute a test of construct validity, it does offer a way to construct an interrelated set of indicators meeting one of the conditions for construct validity—dimensionality. If one or more indicators measures more than one construct (i.e., the measure is multidimensional), then it is difficult to establish reliability, which is also a necessary component of construct validity. Thus, factor analysis provides a stronger basis on which to group items than either simple correlations or arbitrary groupings (Hair et al., 1998).

Although the sample size in this study is somewhat small, factor analysis can be conducted reliably when the number of items multiplied by four or five is equal to the sample size (Hair et al., 1998). Our set of 13 roughly meets these criteria. However, findings should be interpreted in light of this potential limitation.

Using a standard criterion of Eigenvalue $>= 1$, there appear to be four distinct factors that explain 66.98% of the variance. A factor solution that explains at least 60% of the variance is considered sound when the underlying data are drawn from or are based on human perceptions, as they are in this study (Hair et al., 1998). Cronbach's alpha is a commonly used measure of reliability. This measure addresses reliability through the internal consistency, or homogeneity, of the items (Kerlinger, 1986). Using Nunnally's criteria of 0.70, Cronbach's alpha indicates that the first two factors have adequate internal consistency (Nunnally, 1978). Their Cronbach's alphas are 0.84 and 0.73, respectively. The next two factors have only two items each; thus, Cronbach's alpha could not be used. However, the Pearson product moment correlations for these indicate that the items are correlated significantly within each of the two factors (0.41 and 0.45, respectively). Items were grouped into factors based on having factor scores of 0.50 and above within the factor and not having factor scores of 0.40 or above on any other factor (Hair et al., 1998). All of the items in each factor had factor scores above 0.50 for that factor and less than 0.40 for the other three factors. Furthermore, the items that load together seemed to be logically consistent. In other words, it seems to make sense that the items that loaded together did so. For example, the items that loaded on Factor 1 all seem to address issues at a broader scope of the organization than other factors. Thus, there is both statistical support and logical support for the strength of each of the four factors.

Factor 1 appears to measure items related to the organizational level, such as reducing silo behavior across the organization and integrating processes across the organization. Factor 2 appears to measure items related the operational or functional level of the organization, such as *more projects that cut across functional areas* and *greater collaboration among functional areas*. Factor 3 is related more to the divisional level of the organization with the items *reduce silo behavior within divisions* and *greater integration of processes within divisions*. Factor 4 seems to be related more to the individual (e.g., reception to change and teamwork).

Relationship Between Organizational Configuration and Benefits/Changes

Organizational configuration refers to whether the firm is organized by centralized headquarters control, lateral control by divisions, headquarters coordination of operations, headquarters control of financials only, or total divisional autonomy (Markus et al., 2000). A profile of the organizational configuration at the time of ERP implementation is shown in Table 6.

The relationship between organizational configuration and realization of benefits is examined to assess whether a given configuration(s) is better suited to realize ERP benefits (P2a). In addition, the relationship between organizational configura-

tion and specific ERP-related changes is examined to assess the link between configuration and type of change (P2b).

A one-way analysis of variance (ANOVA) was used to assess the relationship between the five levels of organizational configuration and benefits. Again, unequal sample sizes among categories indicated a concern for violation of the assumption of homogeneity of variance necessary for interpreting ANOVA results. Brown and Forsythe's test of homogeneity of variance indicated that this assumption held at $\alpha = 0.05$ for all variables. Therefore, standard ANOVA tests were used to assess the relationships. However, Wilks' lambda for overall effect is not significant (F=1.32, p=0.1784). Therefore, organizational configuration is not related directly to the extent to which firms realize ERP benefits in general, and P2a is not supported.

Next, we assess whether organizational configuration is related to the specific type of ERP-related change that firms achieve. Brown and Forsythe's test indicates that the homogeneity of variance assumption holds for all variables except operational-level change (p = 0.0063). However, the Welch's ANOVA provided results consistent with the standard ANOVA at $\alpha = 0.01$ and $\alpha = 0.05$. Therefore, the standard ANOVA results are reported below and in Table 7a.

Table 6. Profile of implementations

Organizational Configuration at time of ERP Implementation*	Percent of Respondents
Almost all decisions made centrally by headquarters	26.53
Lateral coordination among divisions without a high degree of control from headquarters	22.45
Headquarter coordination of operations with high degree of autonomy at the division level	40.82
Headquarter control only at the financial level	6.12
Total divisional autonomy 4	.08

Sample size = 50
* 20% indicated they implemented ERP to achieve a different organizational configuration; of these, 80% indicated that the new configuration had been achieved, and 20% indicated that they were still working on the new configuration.

Table 7a. Overall analysis of variance results for assessment of relationship between ERP changes and organizational configuration*

Dependent Variable F	-value (overall)	P (overall)	Significant Difference on Individual ANOVAs
Organization-Level Changes 5	.04	0.0069 S	ignificant (F = 5.04, p = 0.0020)
Operational-Level Changes	0.56 0	.6901 N	ot significant
Division-Level Changes 0	.46	0.7624 N	ot significant
Individual-Level Changes 0	.30	0.8783 N	ot significant

Sample size = 50
* Wilks' Lambda for overall effect of organizational configuration = 0.57, F = 1.59, p = 0.0819

Table 7b. Mean and standard deviations of organization-level changes for each category of organizational configuration

Organizational Configuration	μ *	σ
Almost all decisions made centrally by HQ	4.00 0	.71
Lateral coordination among divisions without a high degree of control from HQ	4.07 0	.83
HQ coordination of operations with a high degree of autonomy at the division level	3.29	0.69
HQ control only at the financial level	4.00 0	.20
Total divisional autonomy 2	.30	0.14

* Tukey's HSD test for differences of means indicates that the mean for organizational-level changes is significantly greater lateral coordination among divisions without a high degree of control from HQ than either HQ coordination of operations with a high degree of autonomy at the division level and total divisional autonomy at a = 0.05.
The mean for organizational-level changes is also significantly greater for firms where almost all decisions are made centrally by headquarters than total divisional autonomy at a = 0.05.

Wilks' Lambda for overall effect is significant at F = 1.59, p = 0.0818. This indicates that change does differ among organizational configurations. Organizational-level change is the only change that varies significantly with organizational configuration (Table 7a). Tukey's HSD test for differences of means indicates that the mean for organizational-level change is significantly greater for firms that have lateral coordination among divisions without a high degree of control from HQ than either those with HQ coordination of operations with a high degree of autonomy at the division level and total divisional autonomy at α = 0.05 (Table 7b). Tukey's HSD test also indicates that the mean for organizational-level change is greater for firms that have almost all decisions made centrally by HQ than for those that have total divisional autonomy. Thus, P2b is supported. This is not surprising, because it is expected that highly centralized firms are focused on organizational-level change, whereas autonomous divisions are expected to be focused on change at the divisional level. Another explanation for this may be that some organizational configurations do not benefit necessarily from ERP at the organizational level. None of the firms in the HQ control only of financials or in the total divisional autonomy configurations indicated that they had plans to change their configurations. Thus, it is not surprising that these highly decentralized, autonomous firms are less focused on organizational-level changes than ones with more centralized or integrated configurations. However, this does not mean that the former do not benefit from ERP, just because they are not changing and integrating their entire organization around a single package. This is partly supported by the findings that there was no difference among configurations on either the organizations' abilities to realize benefits in general or on the realization of change at the operational, divisional, and individual levels.

CONCLUSION, FUTURE RESEARCH, AND IMPLICATIONS FOR PRACTICE

This study provides an exploratory assessment of ERP usage in large organizations from a cross section of implementation size. Factors examined include both the extent to which overall benefits are realized and the types of changes firms are realizing from ERP, as well as the relationship among benefits/changes and organizational configuration. Findings provide several implications that both support and extend what is known about ERP. However, one caveat in interpreting these findings is that they should be interpreted in light of a small sample size. Another caveat is that this was an exploratory study; therefore, the findings should be interpreted as starting points, or thought provoking ideas, for future exploration.

Limitations and Directions for Future Research

One limitation of this study is that it provides only one perspective in each organization—that of either the CIO or the senior ERP manager. One avenue for future research is to examine the issues raised in this study from multiple perspectives.

For example, an examination of the perspectives of users from a cross section of functional areas or business units in addition to that of managers may be useful. Another avenue for future research is to assess the various types of changes (as illustrated in Table 5) across industries or perspectives in order to determine both the antecedents of them and the conditions under which they are influenced most. Another limitation is that the organization is the unit of analysis. Our findings suggest that there are differences in ERP-enabled changes among various levels of the organization. Therefore, an examination of the constructs in this study using either the levels suggested in this study or others, such as business units or processes, may provide deeper insight into ERP usage. Furthermore, a cross section of users, line managers, and executives could be surveyed within each level of analysis. Another avenue for future research is to do a cross-industry comparison of ERP usage with an emphasis on whether there are differences among organizations based on software packages and the extent to which the package was implemented.

Implications for Practice

However, regardless of the limitations, this study does extend our current knowledge of ERP usage. It confirms some intuitive and/or widely accepted knowledge about ERP, and it provides some non-intuitive or surprising insights. One of the more widely held conclusions that is supported by these findings is that the largest percentage of functionality implemented is for financial activities and for purchasing. Although this finding may seem trivial at first, it does have implications for practice. The information we hold largely about the functionality implemented is based on the early days of ERP implementation before it became as widely used as it is today and when reports of ERP focused largely on what was being done rather than on the long-term impacts. One might expect that as ERP has matured as a technology, and as more and more firms have adopted it, they might be using it more for management activities such as strategic management or to integrate project management across the organization. The implication for practice is that although the breadth of ERP usage has increased, perhaps it is not being used as deeply as it could be to attain even greater benefits.

Another finding that is consistent with current knowledge about ERP is the extent to which various packages are used. However, although some ERP packages are used more widely than others, they are not necessarily better in terms of the benefits a firm is able to realize with them. The number of modules implemented may be a better indicator of the ability to attain ERP benefits. One lesson for practitioners from this is that the extent to which they are able to integrate and leverage key processes may impact the success of the ERP more than choosing a popular package. An implication is that if they are not realizing the benefits they expected, then they may need to assess their benefits in light of the extent of the integration that their implementation allows.

One finding that does not support widely held beliefs about ERP is that a substantial number of firms are using traditional financial metrics such as ROI or NPV to assess the investment they have made in ERP. One lesson for practitioners that arises out of this finding is that organizations find these metrics important. An implication from this is that if other firms are assessing their ERP investments in this way, then they may have a different, perhaps more measurable, view of ERP that could give them an advantage in managing it.

Another finding is that realization of benefits is not tied to organizational configuration; any configuration can realize benefits from ERP. However, organizational configuration may influence the types of changes that an organization can affect with ERP, if those changes are viewed at different levels of the organization. One level that seems particularly impacted by configuration is the or-

ganizational level. One lesson for practitioners is that ERP may not be a one-size-fits-all solution. An implication of this is that if a firm is not able to bring about the changes it believed it would, it may do well to examine these changes in light of its organizational configuration. Another implication is that firms may need to look more closely at where ERP is affecting change and benefits. Perhaps some failures are not necessarily failures at all but simply an indication that the changes and benefits that ERP enables are at lower levels or in different pockets of the firm.

REFERENCES

Al-Mashari, M., & Zairi, M. (2000). The effective application of SAP R/3: A proposed model of best practice. *Logistics Information Management, 13*(3), 156-166.

Barker, T., & Frolick, M. N. (2003, Fall). ERP implementation failure: A case study. *Information Systems Management*, 43-49.

Baskerville, R., Pawlowski, S., & McLean, E. (2000). Enterprise resource planning and organizational knowledge: Patterns of convergence and divergence. In *Proceedings of the 21st ICIS Conference* (pp. 396-406), Brisbane, Australia.

Bingi, P., Sharma, M. K., & Godla, J. K. (1999). Critical issues affecting an ERP implementation. *Information Systems Management, 16*(3), 7-14.

Boudreau, M. C., & Robey, D. (1999, December 13-15). Organizational transition to enterprise resource planning systems: Theoretical choices for process research. In *Proceedings of the 20th Annual International Conference on Information Systems* (pp. 291-299), Charlotte, North Carolina.

Bradford, M., & Roberts, D. (2001). Does your ERP system measure up? *Strategic Finance, 83*(3), 30-34.

Brehm, L., Heinzl, A., & Markus, M. L. (2001). Tailoring ERP systems: A spectrum of choices and their implications. In *Proceedings of the 34th Annual Hawaii International Conference on System Sciences.*

Conover, W. J., Johnson, M. E., & Johnson, M. M. (1981). A comparative study of tests for homogeneity of variances, with applications to the outer continental shelf bidding data. *Technometrics, 23,* 351-361.

Cycyota, C. S., & Harrison, D. A. (2002). Enhancing survey response rates at the executive level: Are employee- or consumer-level techniques effective? *Journal of Management, 28*(2), 163-189.

Davenport, T. H. (1998, July-August). Putting the enterprise in the enterprise system. *Harvard Business Review,* 121-131.

Davenport, T. H., Harris, J. G., DeLong, D. W., & Jacobson, A. L. (2001). Data to knowledge to results: Building and analytic capability. *California Management Review, 43*(2), 117-138.

Eisenhardt, K. (1989). Building theories from case study research. *Academy of Management Review, 14*(4), 532-550.

Francalanci, C. (2001). Predicting the implementation effort of ERP projects: Empirical evidence on SAP/R3. *Journal of Information Technology, 16,* 33-48.

Gattiker, T. F., & Goodhue, D. L. (2000). Understanding the plant level costs and benefits of ERP: Will the ugly duckling always turn into a swan? In *Proceedings of the 33rd Hawaii International Conference on System Science.*

Gattiker, T. F., & Goodhue, D. L. (2004). Understanding the local-level costs and benefits of ERP through organizational information processing theory. *Information and Management, 41*(4), 431-443.

Hair J. F., Anderson, R. E., Tatham, R. L., & Black, W. C. (1998). *Multivariate data analysis* (5th ed.). Upper Saddle River, NJ: Prentice Hall.

Hambrick, D. C., Geletkanycz, M. A., & Frederickson, J. W. (1993). Top executive commitment to the status quo: Some tests of its determinants. *Strategic Management Journal, 14,* 401-418.

Hanseth, O., Ciborra, C. U., & Braa, K. (2001). The control devolution: ERP and the side effects of globalization. *The DATA BASE for Advances in Information Systems, 32*(4), 34.

Hebert, D., & Oppenheim, D. (2004, April 13). Conflicts between ERP systems and shared services can inhibit ROI. *ComputerWorld.* Retrieved October 20, 2004, from http://www.computerworld.com/managementtopics/roi/story/0,10801,92194,00.html

Hitt, L. M., Wu, D. J., & Zhou, X. (2002). Investment in enterprise resource planning: Business impact and productivity measures. *Journal of Management Information Systems, 19*(1), 71-98.

Hong, K. K., & Kim, Y. G. (2002). The critical success factors for ERP implementation: An organizational fit perspective. *Information and Management, 40,* 25-40.

Hunton, J. E., Lippincott, B., & Reck, J. L. (2003). Enterprise resource planning systems: Comparing firm performance of adopters and nonadopters. *International Journal of Accounting Information Systems, 4,* 165-184.

Jones, M. C. (2001). *The role of organizational knowledge sharing in ERP implementation* (Final Report to the National Science Foundation Grant SES 0001998).

Jones, M. C., & Price, R. L. (2001, December 16-18). Organizational knowledge sharing in ERP implementation: A multiple case study analysis. In *Proceedings of the 22nd International Conference on Information Systems (ICIS),* New Orleans, Louisiana.

Jones, M. C., & Price, R. L. (2004). Organizational knowledge sharing in ERP implementation: Lessons for industry. *Journal of End User Computing, 16*(1), 21-40.

Kerlinger, F. N. (1986). *Foundations of behavioral research* (3rd ed.). New York: Holt, Reinhart, and Winston.

Krasner, H. (2000, January-February). Ensuring e-business success by learning from ERP failures. *IT Pro*, 22-27.

Krumwiede, K. R., & Jordan, W. G. (2000). Reaping the promise of enterprise resource systems. *Strategic Finance, 82*(4), 48-52.

Luftman, J., & McLean, E. R. (2004). Key issues for IT executives. *MIS Quarterly Executive, 3*(2), 89-104.

Mabert, V. A., Soni, A., & Venkatramanan, M. A. (2000). Enterprise resource planning survey of US manufacturing firms. *Production and Inventory Management, 41*(2), 52-58.

Mabert, V. A., Soni, A., & Venkatramanan, M. A. (2003). The impact of organization size on enterprise resource planning (ERP) implementations in the US manufacturing sector. *Omega, 31*, 235-246.

Markus, L. M., Tanis, C., & van Fenema, P. C. (2000). Multisite ERP implementations. *Communications of the ACM, 43*(4), 42-46.

Menezes, J. (1999, June 25). Companies urged to reexamine ERP models. *Computer Reseller News*, 16.

Murphy, K. E., & Simon, J. S. (2002). Intangible benefits valuation in ERP projects. *Information Systems Journal, 12*, 301-320.

Nunnally, J. C. (1978). *Psychometric theory* (2nd ed.). New York: McGraw-Hill.

Olejnik, S. F., & Algina, J. (1987). Type I error rates and power estimates of selected parametric and non-parametric tests of scale. *Journal of Educational Statistics, 12*, 45-61.

Palaniswamy, R., & Frank, T. (2000, Summer). Enhancing manufacturing performance with ERP systems. *Information Systems Management*, 43-55.

Palitza, K. (2001, April 24). SAP changes strategy from "one-for-all" to "pick-and-choose." *Computergram Weekly*.

Poston, R., & Grabski, S. (2001). Financial impacts of enterprise resource planning implementations. *International Journal of Accounting Information Systems, 2*, 271-294.

Sarkis, J., & Sundarraj, R. P. (2001). A decision model for strategic evaluation of enterprise information technologies. *Information Systems Management, 18*(3), 62-72.

Scott, J. E., & Kaindl, L. (2000). Enhancing functionality in an enterprise software package. *Information and Management, 37*, 111-122.

Shang, S., & Seddon, P. B. (2002). Assessing and managing the benefits of enterprise systems: The business manager's perspective. *Information Systems Journal, 12*, 271-299.

Soh, C., Kien, S. S., & Tay-Yap, J. (2000). Cultural fits and misfits: Is ERP a universal solution? *Communications of the ACM, 43*(4), 47-51.

Songini, M. L. (2003, November 3). Goodyear hits $100M bump with ERP system. *ComputerWorld*. Retrieved October 20, 2004, from http://www.computerworld.com/industrytopics/manufacturing/story/0,10801,86744,00.html

Stedman, C. (1999, October 29). Update: Failed ERP gamble haunts Hershey. *Computerworld*. Retrieved October 20, 2004, from http://www.computerworld.com/news/1999/story/0,11280,37464,00.html

Swanton, B. (2003, June 18). Consistent process execution yields millions in ERP benefits. *AMR Research Outlook*. Retrieved October 20, 2004, from http://www.amrresearch.com/content/view.asp?pmillid=17344&docid=11711&bhcp=1

Terziovski, M., Fitzpatrick, P., & O'Neill, P. (2003). Successful predictors of business process reengineering (BPR) in financial services. *International Journal of Production Economics, 84*, 35-50.

Zheng, S., Yen, D. C., & Tarn, J. M. (2000). The new spectrum of the cross-enterprise solution: The integration of supply chain management and enterprise resources planning systems. *Journal of Computer Information Systems*, 84-93.

ENDNOTES

[1] SAP AG is a registered trademark of SAP AG in Germany and several other countries. Peoplesoft is a registered trademark of Peoplesoft, Inc., Pleasanton, California. JDEdwards is a registered trademark of J.D. Edwards World Source Company, Denver, Colorado. Oracle is a registered trademark of Oracle Corporation, Redwood, California. Baan is a registered trademark of Baan Company, Barneveld, the Netherlands.

[2] Return on investment (ROI) and Net present value (NPV) are commonly used financial ratios that allow for evaluation of investments in terms of the current value of future cash flows from the investment. NPV uses a rate of return determined by the company's actual cost of capital. ROI is the ratio of the net cash receipts of the investment divided by the cash outlays of the investment.

APPENDIX A

Questions to Measure Study Variables

---

1. Which of the following Enterprise Resource Planning (ERP) packages does your organization currently use?

❏ SAP ❏ PeopleSoft ❏ Baan ❏ Oracle ❏ JDEdwards
❏ Other (please specify) _____

If you checked more than one option above, please answer the following questions; otherwise, skip to Question 2.

1a. Did your organization choose functionality based on "best of breed"? ❏ yes ❏ no

1b. Is there one package that is predominant in your organization? ❏ yes ❏ no

1c. If you answered *yes* to 1b, please specify which one and answer the rest of the survey about that package _____

If you answered *no* to 1b, please answer the rest of survey about your overall use of ERP.

2. Which ERP functionality has your firm implemented?

❏ financial accounting (e.g., general ledger, accounts receivable, etc…)
❏ controlling (e.g., profitability analysis, product costing, etc…)
❏ asset management (e.g., depreciation, planning and acquisition of capital assets, etc…)
❏ project management (e.g., project planning, project tracking, etc…)
❏ sales and distribution (e.g., customer order management, product/service pricing data, etc…)
❏ production planning (e.g., master scheduling, bill-of-materials, etc…)
❏ materials management (e.g., master inventory data, materials tracking, etc…)
❏ purchasing (e.g., requisitions, purchase orders, goods receipt, etc…)
❏ plant maintenance (e.g., maintenance schedules, equipment histories, etc…)
❏ service management (e.g., service contracts, warranty coverage, etc…)
❏ human resources management (e.g., time accounting, payroll, employee evaluation, etc…)
❏ strategic management (e.g., strategic planning & simulation, balance scorecard, etc…)
❏ data warehousing (e.g., central storage of business data, etc…)
❏ other (please specify) _____

3. How long ago did you complete implementation of your ERP package?
❏ < 12 months ago
❏ 1 year to 18 months ago
❏ > 18 months ago, but < 2 years ago
❏ > 2 years ago, but < 3 years ago
❏ > 3 years ago, but < 5 years ago
❏ > 5 years ago

4. How many upgrades have you completed since the original implementation? _____

5. Approximately how many ERP users does your organization have? _____

---

continued on next page

APPENDIX A.

Questions to Measure Study Variables (cont.)

---

6. Which of the following best describes the configuration of your organization?

❑ almost all decisions made centrally by headquarters
❑ lateral coordination among divisions without a high degree of control from headquarters
❑ headquarter coordination of operations with high degree of autonomy at the division level
❑ headquarter control only at the financial level
❑ total divisional autonomy

7. Was ERP implemented to achieve a different organizational configuration?
If you answered *yes* to question 7, please answer the following question; otherwise, skip to question 9.
8. Has this been achieved?
❑ yes, for the most part
❑ no, we're still working on this
❑ no, we've decided either to postpone this or not to do at all

   Please mark the choice that most closely describes your organization with regard to the following:
   9. Benefits of ERP have lived up to original expectations
   10. Benefits of ERP have been greater than we originally expected
   11. We have revised our projected ERP benefits downward since implementation
   12. ERP has enabled us to realize significant cost savings

Our organization has used ERP to
13. more tightly integrate processes across the entire organization
14. more tightly integrate processes within one or more divisions
15. reduce silo behavior across the organization
16. reduce silo behavior in pockets of the organization
17. reorganize processes (e.g., movement to purchasing by family of items)
18. reduce cost of operations
19. have greater collaboration across units
20. have greater collaboration across functions
21. place more emphasis on team efforts
22. be more receptive to change
23. make it easier to get access to people or resources in other units for projects that may overlap departments/functions
24. place more emphasis on projects that cut across functions/departments
25. place more emphasis on making sure everyone understands the big picture rather than just their own tasks

26. Which of the following do you use to evaluate ERP success?
❑ return on investment ❑ change in return on assets ❑ net present value ❑ not applicable
❑ other (please specify) _____

This work was previously published in Information Resources Management Journal, Vol. 19, Issue 1, edited by M. Khosrow-Pour, pp. 23-42, copyright 2006 by IGI Publishing, formerly known as Idea Group Publishing (an imprint of IGI Global).

Chapter XVI
Knowledge Management Systems for Emergency Preparedness:
The Claremont University Consortium Experience

Murali Raman
Multimedia University, Malaysia

Terry Ryan
Claremont Graduate University, USA

Lorne Olfman
Claremont Graduate University, USA

ABSTRACT

This article is about the design and implementation of an information system, using Wiki technology to improve the emergency preparedness efforts of the Claremont University Consortium. For some organizations, as in this case, responding to a crisis situation is done within a consortium environment. Managing knowledge across the various entities involved in such efforts is critical. This includes having the right set of information that is timely and relevant and that is governed by an effective communication process. This study suggests that Wiki technology might be useful to support knowledge management in the context of emergency preparedness within organizations. However, issues such as training in the use of a system(s), a knowledge-sharing culture among entities involved in emergency preparedness, and a fit between task and technology/system must be there in order to support emergency preparedness activities that are given such structures.

INTRODUCTION

Research about emergency management information systems has accelerated since the September 11, 2001 events (Campbell, Van DeWalle, Turoff, & Deek, 2004). However, researchers do not use a common terminology to describe emergency management information systems. Jennex (2004, 2005), for instance, calls these systems emergency information systems (EIS). Campbell et al. (2004) use the term emergency response systems. Turoff (2002) uses the term emergency response management information systems (ERMIS) and extends this idea to the notion of a dynamic emergency response management information system (DERMIS) (Turoff, Chumer, Van De Walle & Yao, 2004). Nevertheless, the majority of the researchers in this area seem to agree that, despite different naming conventions, emergency management information systems should be designed to support emergency preparedness and to guide effective response during an actual crisis situation. In addition, although researchers explicitly do not link the idea of emergency management information systems to knowledge management, the influence of the latter on emergency management systems is evident in the literature.

This article presents a case study about the implementation of a Web-based knowledge management system to support the Claremont University Consortium (CUC) and the Claremont Colleges, in general, in emergency preparedness. The academic nature of this study centers on how an information system (specifically, a knowledge management system) can improve emergency preparedness within a consortium environment. The practical nature of the research concerns how CUC was made more ready to respond to and recover from emergencies that it might experience.

This study suggests that Wiki technology might be useful to support knowledge management in the context of emergency preparedness within organizations. However, issues such as training in the use of a system(s), a knowledge-sharing culture between entities involved in emergency preparedness, and a fit between task and technology/system must be there in order to support emergency preparedness activities given such structures.

Turoff et al. (2004) take a design stance in discussing emergency management systems. We suggest that design of any emergency management system can be tied to knowledge management principles. In addition, our findings suggest that, in addition to design, issues such as training with technology fit between tasks and technology and the existence of a knowledge-sharing culture are crucial when an organization intends to implement a knowledge management system to support emergency preparedness efforts.

The article proceeds as follows. Section two provides a snapshot of literature relevant to our study. Section three presents the methodology used, with emphasis on the case setting and the problem domain therein. Section four discusses how Wiki technology was used as an instantiation of a knowledge management system to overcome some of the emergency preparedness issues within the Claremont Colleges. Section five presents an evaluation of the system, which is presented in the form of qualitative data. The article ends with a discussion of how our findings might impact knowledge management theory and practice in the context of emergency preparedness.

RELEVANT LITERATURE

A knowledge management system in this study refers to any information technology (IT) based system that is "developed to support and enhance the organizational knowledge processes of knowledge creation, storage, retrieval, transfer and application" (Alavi & Leidner, 2001, p. 114). Gupta and Sharma (2004) divide knowledge management systems into several major categories, as follows: groupware, including e-mail, e-logs, and wikis; decision support systems; expert systems; document management systems; semantic networks; relational and object oriented databases; simulation tools; and artificial intelligence.

Jennex (2004) defines an EIS as any system that is used "by organizations to assist in responding to a crisis or disaster situation" (p. 2148). He further adds that an EIS should be designed to (1) support communication during emergency response, (2) enable data gathering and analysis, and (3) assist emergency responders in making decisions.

Lee and Bui (2000) document vital observations about the use of EIS during the massive earthquake that hit the city of Kobe, Japan, several years ago. Key lessons for emergency management systems designers that are based on Lee and Bui's (2000) work are as follows:

- Relevant information should be included in the emergency response system prior to the actual disaster situation. This is to ensure that emergency responders have sufficient information to guide decision-making processes when responding to an emergency. The authors imply that the task of gathering relevant information to support emergency response should be incorporated as part of the emergency preparedness strategic initiative.

- Information from prior experiences should become part of the emergency management system. The system somehow should be able to capture both tacit and explicit knowledge about how prior crisis situations were handled. Lessons learned can be used to guide future action. The authors in this regard imply that the design of any emergency preparedness system should support some form of organizational memory component.

In addition to designing relevant systems features to support emergency planning and

response, researchers suggest that successful implementation of any emergency management system is contingent on how well people are trained to use such systems (Lee & Bui, 2000; Patton & Flin, 1999; Turoff, 1972). Turoff et al. (2004) state that emergency management systems that normally are not used will not be used when an actual emergency situation occurs.

In summary, researchers indicate that emergency management information systems should support the following features inherent in any knowledge management system: (1) enable individuals and groups to create, share, disseminate, and store knowledge (Turoff, 1972; Turoff et al., 2004); (2) offer the ability to document experiences and lessons that have been learned to form the overall organizational memory for dealing with crisis situations (Lee & Bui, 2000); (3) support asynchronous and collaborative work (Campbell et al., 2004); (4) provide emergency response-related information that is relevant, accurate, and presented in a timely manner (Jennex, 2004; Turoff, 1972; Turoff et al., 2004); and (5) enhance the overall communication process among people involved in emergency preparedness and response by inserting more structure into the manner in which information is organized and documented (Turoff, 1972; Turoff et al., 2004).

METHODOLOGY

This article uses canonical action research to conduct this study (Davidson & Martinsons, 2002; Lindgren, Henfridsson & Shultze, 2004; Susman & Evered, 1978). Both qualitative and quantitative data were collected and analyzed throughout the research process.

One of the authors worked for CUC for three years as the Emergency Management Assistant. The research process in canonical action research starts with the involvement of the researcher with an identified organization. This is followed by the problem diagnosis by the researcher to determine issues and challenges faced by the organization.

The diagnosis leads to action planning; that is, a formal proposal is made to the client/organization in terms of a proposed solution/system. Upon approval by the client, the proposed solution is implemented. Action or intervention then occurs. Evaluation and reflection of the solution/system that is implemented then is conducted.

The Case Setting

The Claremont University Consortium (CUC) provides services to the seven members of the Claremont Colleges[1] by operating programs and central facilities on their behalf. Each college maintains its own emergency preparedness plan. Every plan calls for the activation of a college-level emergency operations center (EOC) in the event of an emergency. The Multi Agency Coordination Center (MACC) exists to coordinate responses among the seven colleges and CUC. MACC's action plan is guided by the Claremont Colleges Emergency Preparedness Plan. This plan defines an emergency as preparing for and responding to any situation "associated with, but not limited to, disasters such as earthquakes, life threatening incidents, terrorist attacks, bio-terrorism threats and other incidents of a similar capacity" (p. 1).

MACC is a group that becomes active whenever emergencies occur at any of the colleges and at CUC that could impact any one or more of the consortium members. It is intended to (1) coordinate among the colleges and external agencies, (2) prioritize and fill requests for assistance from central resources, and (3) assist the colleges in returning to normalcy as soon as possible.

The Problem

Prior to embarking on the systems design and implementation initiatives, interviews were conducted with nine representatives from five colleges and CUC who were involved in emergency preparedness. Through these interviews, it was found that the top three issues pertaining to emergency preparedness at CUC (and within the Claremont Colleges at large) are (1) communication between college level EOCs and the MACC, both before and during an emergency can be improved; (2) coordination between CUC and college-level EOCs, in terms of activities and overall efforts in preparing for an emergency, can be enhanced; and (3) emergency related information/knowledge could be shared seamlessly. This includes access to information about drills; policy documentation; emergency notification protocols; access to college level emergency plans; and status and availability of emergency resources such as debris removal equipment, housing, and medical expertise. The following statements offer several examples:

Communication issues across the colleges in terms of who knows what, when they know it is vital, but I don't think that we are there yet. For example, in a recent incident, I was informed after five hours only. So communication is an issue. My struggle with that was, if we are indeed mobilized, we need to know and be contacted earlier. The communication of when there is an incident, when a contact is made, this is a concern for all of us.

Communication between colleges can be improved. We need a load of practice in this area to ensure better informational flow. Mutual aid agreement, sharing of resources to handle localized incidents needs to be shared and communicated. Training, and this would include training conducted in a jointly organized fashion. Use of technology during drills that are simulated can help the above.

We rely on written plans and rely on documentation when we need information. This can take time and cost. When we need to update some document we need to make sure that everyone has updated their respective documents. Again, time and cost is involved. The documents that we have are easy to read, but knowing exactly what to do when something happens, remains a challenge.

We at this college do have some of the information available online, on the Web [pdfs] which is used by the building managers. These are secured and restricted to those involved in emergency preparedness. Again, the information may not be easy to retrieve, even in Web format. We need more quick links, shortcuts, and need to know what is new when it comes to emergency preparedness.

Extended Problem Diagnosis

In stage two of the problem diagnosis, interviews were conducted with an additional 25 CUC personnel involved in emergency preparedness. The objective was to focus on the knowledge management issues in the context of emergency preparedness within the Claremont Colleges. A 15-question questionnaire was developed in order to ascertain the critical success factors for implementing a knowledge management system for CUC. These questions were based on the KMS

Table 1. Linking the KMS success model to emergency preparedness at the Claremont Colleges

	Concept (From the KMS Success Model)	Constructs (From the KMS Success Model)	Min	Max	Mean	Std. Deviation
CUC has the necessary resources to develop a KMS to support emergency planning/preparedness	System Quality	Technological Resources	1.00	5.00	3.16	1.07
CUC has the necessary resources to update a KMS to support emergency planning/preparedness	System Quality	Technological Resources	1.00	5.00	3.16	1.03
CUC has the necessary resources to maintain a KMS to support emergency planning/preparedness	System Quality	Technological Resources	1.00	5.00	3.12	1.01
More information about emergency preparedness at CUC can be converted to Web format	System Quality	KMS form	2.00	5.00	4.04	0.79
Knowledge about emergency preparedness from individuals can be made available online	System Quality	Level of KMS	2.00	5.00	4.12	0.83
Knowledge about emergency preparedness from relevant groups can be made available online	System Quality	Level of KMS	2.00	5.00	4.24	0.72
Information about emergency preparedness could be automated, shared, and retrieved from a single Web interface	Knowledge/ Information Quality	Richness	2.00	5.00	4.16	0.90

continued on next page

Table 1. continued

Concept (From the KMS Success Model)	Constructs (From the KMS Success Model)	Min	Max	Mean	Std. Deviation
A KMS for emergency preparedness should simplify searching and retrieving of information	Knowledge/ Information Quality	Richness	2.00	5.00	4.24	0.72
A KMS can enhance the strategic planning process for teams involved in emergency preparedness	Knowledge/ Information Quality	Knowledge Strategy/Process	3.00	5.00	4.32	0.69
A KMS should provide timely information for staff involved in emergency preparedness to support emergency planning	Knowledge/ Information Quality	Richness	3.00	5.00	4.32	0.69
A KMS should provide accurate/up-to-date information for staff involved in emergency preparedness to support emergency planning	Knowledge/ Information Quality	Richness	3.00	5.00	4.40	0.58
A KMS should provide relevant information for staff involved in emergency preparedness to support emergency planning	Knowledge/ Information Quality	Richness	3.00	5.00	4.36	0.57
A KMS to support emergency planning should provide linkages to external and internal information sources	Knowledge/ Information Quality	Linkages	3.00	5.00	4.56	0.58
Top management support is needed in implementation of a KMS to support emergency preparedness	Service Quality	Management Support	3.00	5.00	4.40	0.71
I welcome the idea of being trained in using a KMS to support emergency preparedness activities at CUC	Service Quality	Management Support	1.00	5.00	4.28	1.02

Success Model (Jennex & Olfman, 2005). The KMS Success Model is based on three main constructs: System Quality, Knowledge/Information Quality, and Service Quality (Jennex & Olfman, 2005). The respondents were asked to rank the extent to which they either agreed or disagreed with the statements on a five-point Likert scale.

Table 1 lists the statements and how these map to the KMS Success Model constructs. Table 1 also provides a summary of the data analyzed using SPSS.[2]

The average scores for the statements ranged from 3.12 to 4.56. The high average scores for most of the statements that relate to the key success factors of implementing a Web-based knowledge management system suggest the following:

- The system should provide key features of managing emergency related knowledge, such as being able to provide timely and relevant information.
- The system should provide links to both internal and external sources of knowledge about emergency preparedness.
- The top management within CUC must support the system implementation.
- The system must support committees involved in emergency preparedness to make strategic decisions.

The first three statements relate to post-implementation resource issues. The average scores for these statements (from 3.12 to 3.16) are relatively lower than the other statements. The majority of the respondents feel that CUC may not have the necessary resources to develop, update, and maintain a knowledge management system to support emergency preparedness. This is due to the fact that involvement in emergency preparedness activities, for the majority of the staff, is not part of their main job function. In addition, CUC has a limited budget for emergency preparedness activities.

PROPOSED SYSTEM

The potential use of Wiki technology as an instantiation of a knowledge management system to support emergency preparedness within the Claremont Colleges was discussed with the CEO and key IT personnel. Three criteria guided the selection of a suitable Web-based knowledge management system to support CUC's emergency preparedness efforts.

- **Cost.** During the initial discussion with the CEO, she made it clear that for the time be-

ing, any system developed to support CUC's emergency-related activities had to rely on open source solutions. This is due to the fact that CUC does not have a sufficient budget to implement any commercially available knowledge management system.
- **Our Experience.** We were allowed to develop any system with which we were familiar, so long as it was in the best interest of the organization in the context of its emergency preparedness initiatives.
- **Issues Faced.** The system that is developed has to address the key emergency preparedness issues/concerns faced by the Claremont Colleges, as described earlier.

These criteria then were used to examine the list of options available to CUC. Gupta and Sharma's (2004) categorization of knowledge management systems was used to examine if a particular category met the three system selection criteria discussed previously. It was decided to implement an instantiation of a knowledge management system using Wiki technology, given budgetary and resource constraints, with regard to emergency preparedness faced by CUC. The technology also was selected because of our familiarity with using Wikis for teaching and learning (Raman & Ryan, 2004).

Why Wikis?

Wiki is a Hawaiian word that refers to being quick. Leuf and Cunningham (2001) define a Wiki as "a freely expandable collection of interlinked Web pages, a hypertext system for storing and modifying information—a database where each page is easily editable by any user with a forms-capable Web browser client" (p. 14).

Leuf and Cunningham (2001) suggest that Wiki technology can support knowledge management initiatives for organizations. The authors state that three collaborative models are available over the network today: e-mail exchanges, shared

Table 2. Knowledge management system tasks and sources of knowledge3

Knowledge management system type	Knowledge source	Task
Conversational technologies	Distributed	Ad hoc
FAQ C	entralized R	epetitive
Search engine	Distributed	Repetitive
Portals	Distributed-Centralized	Ad hoc-Repetitive

folders/file access, and interactive content update and access. They suggest that use of e-mail systems solely may not enable effective management of knowledge for an organization, based on the following reasons: (1) e-mail postings cannot be edited easily; (2) a central archiving system might be necessary to support effective documentation of information, which implies that using some form of database that hosts various postings directly might be a more effective manner of managing information flow for the organization; and (3) e-mail systems necessarily may not support shared access to a particular information base.

The second model to support collaborative work and knowledge sharing is the shared access system (Leuf & Cunningham, 2001). The main difference between a shared file system and an e-mail system is that the former enables users to access a common information base. In this regard, different users could be allowed to edit/update, "based on varying degrees of freedom" a particular information base (Leuf & Cunningham, 2001, p. 6). Nevertheless, this system is still similar to an e-mail system in that discussions and knowledge sharing is contingent upon threaded postings or, in a worst case, governed as a regular e-mail system (Leuf & Cunningham, 2001).

Wiki technology is an example of the interactive server model that offers users a newer avenue to share knowledge and to participate in online collaborative work (Leuf & Cunningham, 2001). The main components of an interactive server model are the database, the Web server, and user access to a common front end. The authors suggest that the main benefits of using collaborative server models include, among others: (1) allowing more effective organization of information by individuals and groups and (2) enabling ad hoc groups to collaborate on specific projects.

Wagner (2004) examines the use of different knowledge management systems that can be categorized based on two dimensions: (1) how knowledge is distributed in organizations and (2) the nature of the task involved. He asserts that in an organizational context, the source of knowledge is either centralized or distributed. The nature of the task is either ad hoc or repetitive. Based on these two dimensions, he proposes a particular form of knowledge management system to support a particular organizational need to manage knowledge. Table 2 summarizes the "knowledge management system fit based on knowledge distribution and task repetitiveness" in an organizational context (Wagner, 2004, p. 267).

Wagner's (2004) framework suggests that an organization's need for a knowledge management system is contingent upon the nature of the task involved and where knowledge resides in the organization. Use of FAQs, for instance, is suitable when knowledge is centralized and when tasks are repetitive in nature. Conversational knowledge management systems, in contrast, are more suitable when the source of knowledge is distributed. Wagner's classification of knowledge management systems implies that conversational technologies might be relevant to support emergency preparedness activities at CUC, because emergency preparedness at CUC involves tasks that are ad hoc and dependent upon knowledge that is distributed across the different EOCs and among the MACC members. Wiki technology can support numerous knowledge management requirements for organizations, including filtering knowledge from noise, ensuring knowledge quality, providing search functions, tracing the source of knowledge, building/enhancing knowledge continuously, and supporting the need for dynamically changing information content in a given system (Wagner, 2004). The system selection criteria, our prior experience with Wikis, and support from relevant literature led us to choose Wiki technology.

TikiWiki: Emergency Management System for the Claremont Colleges

The first step during the intervention stage of the project was to install and test a prototype Wiki clone. In December 2004, TikiWiki version 1.7.4 was installed on a test server. TikiWiki is only one instance of Wiki technology. TikiWiki bundles the requirements for a Web server (Apache), a database server (mySQL), and the front-end Web pages (written using Python).

Components of the TikiWiki that were viewed as relevant to the requirements specified by the users then were selected for activation. Only two features have been enabled in the current prototype of the system: the TikiWiki module and linking features. The module feature (administered by the system administrator) was used to create particu-

lar groupings of quick links to information about emergency preparedness. For the purpose of the prototype, the following modules were created:

- **CUC Links:** Provides links to key information sources about emergency preparedness for CUC. This module is based on CUC EOC's organizational structure. It has links to the information requirements for each of the EOC members, based on her or his respective job functions. The planning and intelligence coordinator, for instance, has access to weather information, notification protocols, phone trees, hazardous material information, lessons learned from tabletop sessions, and online maps of the Claremont Colleges.

- **MACC Information:** A quick link and reference to emergency resources and supplies available thorough CUC's Central Services/ Physical Plant. The MACC module now is extended to include other key elements relevant to the MACC.

- **Calendar of Events:** Information about meetings, meeting summaries, drills, training events, and other related activities. The objective of this module is to assist all EOCs and the MACC in coordinating their respective activities.

- **Knowledge Base:** This module has links to local weather conditions, transcripts from tabletop (drill) sessions, and links to federal and local emergency response agencies.

- **Maps:** Online maps for the Claremont Colleges and CUC.

- **Linking:** Permits users to create multiple links within the system, which can be done through the use of the back link function. For example, through a back link, the CUC overview page is linked to the system's home page. TikiWiki also permits users to create links to external sources.

The focus of systems design and implementation in Stage 2 was to improve the communication issues related to emergency planning at CUC. When a crisis of a particular magnitude occurs within the Claremont Colleges, the MACC is activated. The MACC consists of members from CUC and a representative from all the Claremont Colleges. The MACC members provide input to the MACC Chair and Operations Co-coordinator, based on information received from the respective college EOCs. Based on the current protocol, the information flow between MACC and the colleges is facilitated through the use of telephones and information that is documented on a 6 x 8 foot white board located inside the MACC room.

The CUC was aware that during a crisis, the flow of information between the MACC and the college EOCs, was subject to noise and inaccuracy. The CUC also was aware, based on participation in drills, that the MACC does not have sufficient information about actual crisis situations within the respective colleges. This makes response efforts rather difficult during certain incidents. In order to overcome the communicational issues, an additional module in the system called the MACC Situation Board was developed. This module consists of the following four main elements:

- **Situation:** This section enables the MACC representatives to document real-time information about a particular situation at their respective colleges.
- **Action:** This section is used to document specific actions that a college/CUC has taken to address a particular emergency situation.
- **Need:** Links to another page that consolidates the emergency resources (i.e., debris removal equipment, temporary housing, search-and-rescue teams, food, and first-aid supplies) needed by all colleges and CUC in order to respond to an emergency. The MACC Chair and Operations Coordinator were given access to the consolidated

resource needs page, which can be used to guide the decision on resource allocation between CUC and the colleges. The consolidated information about resources needed is expected to improve the communication between MACC and the respective college EOCs.

- **Sharing:** Links to another page that consolidates all information about resources that each college and CUC is willing to share to support a particular emergency response initiative. The type/category, quantity, and status of emergency related resources within the Claremont Colleges will be made known to all MACC members through the system in the near future.

The purpose of this module is twofold. First, as mentioned, it is designed to facilitate documentation of resources required by respective colleges during an emergency. Through this module, member institutions can record a particular type of resource that they need and are willing to share with other colleges when a particular emergency situation occurs. This information, unlike before, is now available via the Web, easily accessible to every EOC and MACC member. Second, the information can be used by the MACC Operations Coordinator to facilitate resource allocation among the colleges when an emergency occurs.

EVALUATION

Effectiveness of the system was evaluated through a series of one-on-one interviews with the MACC members who had participated in two separate training sessions in February 2005, where the system was used. Thirteen individuals were interviewed. The instrument used to facilitate the process had 10 open-ended questions that were divided into two categories: (1) general feedback/overall impression of the system and (2) extent of goal achievement, or the ability of the system to facilitate the knowledge management requirements within the context of emergency preparedness.

Findings

The following subsections list several of the respondents' answers to the open-ended questions. The responses are organized according to the two categories mentioned earlier. Given the action-oriented nature of this study, we acknowledge the potential bias of our involvement in the project and the findings, particularly with reference to the use of Wiki technology.

Category 1: General Feedback/Impression

Overall, the respondents were pleased with the system. The feedback was largely positive. The majority of the respondents felt that the system was simple to use. One of them said the following:

My immediate reaction was very good. I thought that the ease of use of the system was there and that the visual layout was very clear. That's not how I often feel when I am exposed to new systems. It was logical too. Visually it made sense to me. I don't always react very positively to new systems. My immediate reaction was very positive. In prior cases, I have had the experience of feeling "Oh My God," what do we have here? This was not the case this time.

However, not everyone was totally comfortable using the system. One respondent mentioned the following:

It is a key step but it is a little daunting in some ways. One must be a computer savvy person to really play with the system. I look at it from an end user standpoint, particularly how it can be used better. But it sure seems like we are moving in the right direction especially after the last drill

at the MACC when there was chaos in there—that was really wild. This is a good start, but there are issues that we need to address.

Another respondent suggested that the system could improve the overall communication process. Specifically, she said:

It seemed like it would be a very useful tool and could eliminate many of the previous problems with communication. I was excited to hear there would be a standard protocol for us to transfer information from our campus EOCs to the MACC.

Assisting Emergency Preparedness Efforts

On balance, the majority of the respondents felt that the system could assist CUC and the colleges in emergency preparedness efforts. However, this is contingent upon continuous training, access control, and willingness of emergency planners to update the system with relevant information. The following statements offer evidence:

I do think that the system can assist emergency preparedness. Specifically, the system can provide better and quicker access to information. However, before this works, people need to populate the system and be diligent in updating the information base in the system. I am not sure about controlled access through with the Wiki technology. Anyone can update or delete the information. People can go in and mess around even though we can assume that they would not.

The system provides for an additional method of communication between all entities involved in emergency preparedness. The system facilitates a more effective written communication process. This can reduce any misunderstanding between the emergency responders. After all, visual aids are better to process and faster to comprehend, as well. By providing a place where various human and material resources can be listed prior to being needed, enables more common space and a means of documenting what happens during a response.

Aspect of Emergency Preparedness Supported

The general consensus from the respondents was that the system might support the following aspects within emergency preparedness: (1) co-ordinating planning efforts; (2) offering a better mechanism to document processes; (3) assisting in communication efforts; and (4) sharing emergency related information. The following statements offer evidence:

I am tempted to say that the system helps emergency planning, but I don't think the system supports planning solely. If used well, the system can save us all a lot of time in terms of communication. It provides us with an overview of what is happening across the colleges when an emergency occurs, through the MACC Situation Board Module. The campus status for every college is right there. This is why I say that it will help us in all future emergency planning efforts.

I think the system supports both information stor-ing and the emergency response communication process. In terms of communication, the informa-tion that is available readily to the users can help them communicate more effectively. The right word might be information that is immediately viewable or accessible can support the communication process. Also, the system provides a quick way of getting information. The system surely helps to capture knowledge as well. As I mentioned, you have everyone from the respective colleges who report to MACC there, and they post their

knowledge and information into the system. This seems like a very organized way of capturing information.

Category 2: Goal Achievement

Improving Communications

The majority of the users felt that the system can enhance emergency-related communication both before and during an actual emergency. One respondent even suggested that the system might benefit recovery communication with external agencies such as FEMA. However, before this happens, issues such as training, willingness to share information, and trust among one another must be resolved. The following statements offer examples:

The system can improve the overall communica-tion process. This is due to the fact that all the schools have access to the system, and all the schools should be posting information relevant to emergency response. And one can access the system from anywhere. It does not matter which part of the world you are from, you can get to it, as it is Web-based.

The system helps us to communicate better even after an emergency has ended, as the information will be at everyone's fingertips, which could later be served as data for any report or justification in an inquiry, such as FEMA and other agencies that may need that information.

The system can facilitate communication during an emergency. However, before this works, we need to make sure that people are willing to trust each other. For example, under the resources-to-share and resources-needed pages, people need to be aware that just resources available as they have been posted pre-crisis may not necessarily be available when an actual crisis occurs.

Emergency Preparedness Knowledge Capture

The users also generally felt that the system can facilitate some aspects of knowledge management. Specifically, benefits such as being able to archive information, capture knowledge and information about emergency preparedness, and offer a more structured way to manage information were noted. The following statements offer evidence:

I think that it will help us create an archive of every drill, actual emergency, and also any other related activities that we conduct. This tells me that the system might serve as a useful knowledge book or "book of knowledge," so to speak. People must be willing to contribute to this book, though.

The system can help us capture information/knowledge about emergency planning and response. The scribe could copy and paste information into any Microsoft program such as Excel or Microsoft Word for later usage.

The system allows us to better manage emergency related information, because now we have a written record of everything that is done and by whom. This is useful for future references, too. The system also provides a common platform/space, structuring of information.

Knowledge-Sharing

The users were also optimistic about the ability of the system to facilitate knowledge and information sharing among individuals and entities involved in emergency preparedness. However, this is contingent upon the willingness of people to share information and trust the source of informa-

tion/knowledge that resides in the system. Some of the responses to this issue are as follows:

Frankly, I don't think all the members from the various colleges have a knowledge-sharing culture. Based on my experience here, my guess is that people need to share more information about emergency planning with each other. It seems easier to share with some relative to others. I guess we are comfortable with speaking directly with people and may not be willing to share information in an open platform. This needs to change though. People must be willing to share information with each other.

As mentioned, easy access to the system and a fairly direct way to input ideas will allow people to share knowledge about emergency preparedness with each other. It will allow them to populate the database or to fill in the blanks. But people must be willing to do this.

The system has useful refreshing abilities and allows users to share information and knowledge with each other instantaneously. It provides timely information and, therefore, can help better communication between the EOCs and the MACC.

General Concerns

Several issues must be addressed before the value of the system to support emergency preparedness within CUC and the Claremont Colleges is maximized. The respondents mentioned the following general concerns:

I think for the system to work, training is key. People at MACC need to be trained to use the system. But, as you know, the people that report to MACC either don't show up for training sessions or keep changing. Then, there is this issue of the information sharing culture that I spoke to you about. This must change for the system to be used effectively. People should put personality differences aside and be willing to share and communicate with each other. The technology itself seems powerful and is a great idea. It can handle different and very dynamic sets of information when an actual crisis occurs. But at the heart of all of this is the willingness to be trained and share information. For this to happen, emergency preparedness must become part of peoples' job function. With the exception of a few people on MACC, for the majority of us, emergency preparedness is not of a primary concern. We prepare only when we think about drills; otherwise, it seems to be lost in our daily primary functions.

I would be concerned if we don't have Internet connectivity. I think we need a paper-based system as a backup. This is really my only concern. And I saw during our drill, some people are not too Web savvy. There might be issues with training; people who are not familiar with a Web-based system need to be trained. Also the colleges keep sending new people to the MACC. If we have new people who don't know how to use the system or have not been trained to do so, this could cause some problems as well. In the event of an emergency there might not be any IT staff to support the use of the system. This again could become an issue. Ongoing training for staff involved in emergency preparedness is necessary.

I think the challenge is keeping everyone constantly abreast of the system. I think the idea of playing with the system every month when the MACC meets is welcomed. Your relearning time or startup time will become longer if this is not done. We need to make sure that people know where to fill information and not do this inaccurately. Also, people should not edit other people's information.

I think people need to be trained continuously. In addition, it only makes sense if the EOCs for all colleges use this system, too; after all they

need to provide MACC representatives with the information needed.

If it is used properly, updated, and maintained, then this will work. However, this is subject to some budget being approved for a system-resource or admin staff that helps in this task. Also, we need to make sure that people do not mess up due to poor access control.

DISCUSSION AND LESSONS LEARNED

Feedback from the evaluation phase suggests that the system that has been implemented can impact emergency preparedness activities for CUC and the Claremont Colleges in two ways: (1) improve communication and (2) assist in emergency preparedness knowledge/information sharing.

Communication

Key staff members involved in emergency preparedness now realize that, through the project, the Web-based system can assist the overall emergency preparedness communication process as follows:

- Provide a centralized information base about emergency situations, campus action, resource status, and MACC action, which are now accessible to all relevant groups and individuals involved in emergency planning.
- Minimize the overflow of information within MACC and thereby reduce the possibility of communication chaos.
- Empower staff members involved in emergency preparedness to update information as and when it is received, without the need for relying on the MACC scribe to do so.

- Provide a structured way to document emergency-related information, which can support external communication and recovery efforts (e.g., claiming reimbursement from FEMA and other federal agencies). Wiki technology has a function called history, which documents exactly what was entered into the Wiki, by whom, and when.

Knowledge Sharing

Anyone can contribute to a Wiki page in a given Wiki community (Leuf & Cunnigham, 2001). Wiki technology thrives on the principle of being open (Wagner, 2004). Emergency preparedness and response within the Claremont Colleges involves both knowledge and experience from a diverse set of individuals. Within CUC alone, there are staff members that have been trained in particular emergency preparedness areas. Examples are people who are trained in search and rescue, earthquake evacuation procedures, hazardous material handling, CPR, and first aid response.

Critical Success Factors

Our findings suggest that the positive outcomes of the system can materialize fully only if the following factors are taken into consideration by the CUC's top management involved in emergency preparedness:

- People involved in emergency preparedness are willing to share information with one another. The MACC Situation Board module, for instance, can support the Operations Coordinator to plan for and allocate resources during an actual crisis, only if the resource-available template is filled a priori by the respective college EOCs. As one respondent mentioned, "I am not sure if people will be willing to share information with one another, particularly about the status of their resources."
- The technology is designed to support a knowledge-sharing culture. However, we are uncertain if this culture exists among every EOC and individuals involved in emergency preparedness in this case.
- The system must play a vital role in every emergency response drill and training session. Unless the system is used during drills and such events, it will not be used during an actual emergency.
- The technology must support and not hinder the existing emergency response protocol. In this context the CEO indicated the following concern, "Everyone [with reference to the EOCs] can act prematurely and go talk directly to one another without going thorough the central body (MACC) to coordinate efforts. The system should support existing protocols that we have. People should be trained to use it to ensure that the technology supports MACC's role. This can be done."

THEORETICAL IMPLICATIONS

Figure 1 illustrates how the project findings might further inform theory about emergency management information systems. This study suggests that the environment faced by emergency responders is complex, dynamic, and unstructured (Burnell, Priest & Durrett, 2004; Kostman, 2004; Van Kirk, 2004). The majority of literature about emergency management information systems does not state clearly that systems designed to support emergency preparedness are associated with knowledge management. This study suggests that the environment faced by emergency responders forces them to deal with the following characteristics of knowledge:

Figure 1. Theoretical framework

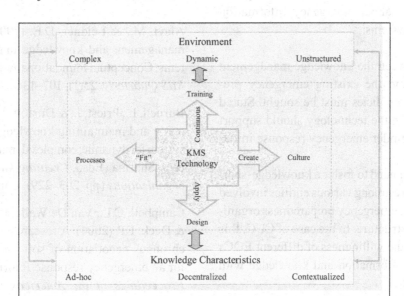

- **Ad Hoc:** Knowledge within emergency responders at the Claremont Colleges is largely tacit and utilized as and when an emergency occurs. Individuals and groups involved in emergency preparedness may not necessarily think about responding to a particular situation beforehand. This implies that the knowledge that they need to respond to an emergency is ad hoc in that it is required as and when a crisis occurs.
- **Decentralized:** The knowledge repository to respond to a particular crisis in a consortium environment is predominantly decentralized. In the case of the Claremont Colleges, this knowledge resides within eight EOCs and the MACC.
- **Contextualized:** Emergency preparedness requires responders to deal with knowledge that is highly contextualized. Every crisis is unique and requires a different set of ideas and response initiatives (Burnell et al., 2004).

Given these characteristics, the findings of this study suggest that any system designed to support emergency preparedness should be linked closely to ideas inherent within the domain of knowledge management. A particular technology selected to support emergency preparedness should cater to knowledge that might be decentralized, ad hoc, and highly contextualized.

We suggest that Wiki technology might be a simple yet cost-effective option for organizations that intend to use or design any information system to manage information and knowledge related to emergency preparedness. Wiki technology is appropriate for knowledge that is dynamic and decentralized (Wagner, 2004). Nevertheless, technology alone is not sufficient to foster effective emergency preparedness initiatives. The system should be designed to cater to the requirements of emergency responders and must be used in every drill and emergency training activities (Turoff et al., 2004). Figure 1 suggests that, in addition to effective design and training considerations, the following two additional factors are required when thinking about emergency information management systems:

- A fit between the knowledge management system and the existing emergency preparedness policies must be sought. Stated differently, the technology should support and not hinder emergency response initiatives.
- There is a need to foster a knowledge-sharing culture among various entities involved in a given emergency preparedness organizational structure. In the case of CUC, this refers to the willingness of different EOCs to share information and knowledge with one another.

CONCLUSION

An organization's emergency preparedness activities might involve collaborative efforts among various entities. A vital activity is responding to an actual crisis situation that hits one or more of the member organizations or entities. For some organizations, as in this case, responding to a crisis situation is done within a consortium environment. Managing knowledge across the various entities involved in such efforts is critical. This includes having the right set of information that is timely, relevant, and governed by an effective communication process. Given such organizational structures and a need to manage knowledge in these environments, IT, which manifests itself in the form of knowledge management systems, might play a crucial role. However, before this occurs, the following issues must be considered: (1) sufficient training in the use of a system(s) must take place; (2) a knowledge-sharing culture among entities involved in emergency preparedness should exist; and (3) a fit between task and technology/system must be guaranteed.

REFERENCES

Alavi, M., & Leidner, D.E. (2001). Knowledge management and knowledge management systems: Conceptual foundations and research issue. *MIS Quarterly, 25*(1), 107–136.

Burnell, L., Priest, J., & Durrett, J. (2004). Developing and maintaining knowledge management system for dynamic, complex domains. In J. Gupta, & S. Sharma (Eds.), *Creating knowledge based organizations* (pp. 203–229). London: IGP.

Campbell, C.L., Van De Walle, B.V., Turoff, M., & Deek, F.P. (2004). A research design for asynchronous negotiation of software requirements for an emergency response information system. *Proceedings of the Americas Conference on Information Systems*, New York.

Claremont University Consortium. (2006). *The Claremont Colleges emergency preparedness plan*. Retrieved February 20, 2006, from http://www.cuc.claremont.edu/emergency/emergplan.pdf

Davidson, R., & Martinsons, M. (2002). Empowerment or enslavement? A case of process-based organizational change in Hong Kong. *Information Technology and People, 15*(1), 42–59.

Gupta, J.D., & Sharma, S.K. (2004). *Creating knowledge based organizations*: Hershey, PA: Idea Group.

Jennex, M. (2004). Emergency response systems: Lessons from utilities and Y2K. *Proceedings of the Americas Conference on Information Systems*, New York.

Jennex, M.E. (2005). Emergency response systems: The utility Y2K experience. *Journal of Information Technology Theory and Application, 6*(3), 85–102.

Jennex, M., & Olfman, L. (2005). Assessing knowledge management success. *International*

Journal of Knowledge Management, 1(2), 33–49.

Kostman, J.T. (2004). 20 rules for effective communication in a crisis. *Disaster Recovery Journal, 17*(2), 20.

Lee, J., & Bui, T. (2000). A template-based methodology for disaster management information systems. *Proceedings of the Hawaii International Conference on Systems Science*, Hawaii.

Leuf, B., & Cunningham, W. (2001). *The WIKI way: Quick collaboration of the Web*. Boston: Addison-Wesley.

Lindgren, R., Henfridsson, O., & Shultze, U. (2004). Design principles for competence management systems: A synthesis of an action research study. *MIS Quarterly, 28*(3), 435–472.

Patton, D., & Flin, R. (1999). Disaster stress: An emergency management perspective. *Disaster Prevention and Management, 8*(4), 261–267.

Raman, M., & Ryan, T. (2004). Designing online discussion support systems for academic setting—"the Wiki way." *Proceedings of the Americas Conferences on Information Systems*, New York.

Susman, G., & Evered, R. (1978). An assessment of the scientific merits of action research. *Administrative Science Quarterly, 23*, 583–603.

Turoff, M. (1972). Delphi conferencing: Computer based conferencing with anonymity. *Journal of*

Technological Forecasting and Social Change, 3(2), 159–204.

Turoff, M. (2002). Past and future emergency response emergency response information systems. *Communications of the ACM, 45*(4), 38–43.

Turoff, M., Chumer, M., Van De Walle, B., & Yao, X. (2004). The design of a dynamic emergency response management information systems (DERMIS). *Journal of Information Technology Theory and Application, 5*(4), 1–35.

Van Kirk, M. (2004). Collaboration in BCP skill development. *Disaster Recovery Journal, 17*(2), 40.

Wagner, C. (2004). WIKI: A technology for conversational knowledge management and group collaboration. *Communications of the Association for Information Systems, 13*, 265–289.

ENDNOTES

[1] There are seven colleges within the Claremont Colleges: Claremont Graduate University, Harvey Mudd College, Scripps College, Pomona College, Keck Graduate Institute, Pitzer College, and Claremont McKenna College (http://www.claremont.edu).

[2] N=25.

[3] Adapted from Wagner (2004), Figure 1, p. 267.

This work was previously published in International Journal of Knowledge Management, Vol. 2, Issue 3, edited by M. E. Jennex, pp. 33-50, copyright 2006 by IGI Publishing, formerly known as Idea Group Publishing (an imprint of IGI Global).

Section V
Critical Issues

Chapter XVII
Education for IT Service Management Standards

Aileen Cater-Steel
University of Southern Queensland, Australia

Mark Toleman
University of Southern Queensland, Australia

ABSTRACT

Service management standards such as the IT Infrastructure Library (ITIL), and now ISO/IEC 20000, provide guidance and tools for the effective management and control of IT service delivery. These standards are of increasing importance to organizations around the globe. Education about these standards and possibilities for training IT staff are, therefore, important. Universities have a place in this education process; however, academics have not embraced these standards in either research or education about them. Regardless, demand grows for IT staff qualified at various levels, particularly on basic or foundational levels, in these standards. This article considers the training offered and the requirement for education related to IT service management. Benefits to universities, graduates, and industry are numerous including increases in student numbers, enhanced employment options for graduates, and improved IT service quality, but there are challenges too, in particular, how to effectively transfer the knowledge to students who have not experienced the IT service environment firsthand.

INTRODUCTION

IT service managers are responsible for an increasingly diverse and crucial infrastructure. They are under pressure to reduce costs while helping the organization generate revenue, and to provide fast, cost-effective service to their customers. Over the last few years, many organizations have adopted the IT Infrastructure Library (ITIL) to provide the effective management and control of IT service delivery and support. The ITIL best-practice framework enables managers to document, audit, and improve their IT service management processes in response to business requirements.

In recent years, a quiet revolution has occurred in IT service management as the ITIL phenomenon has spread from the U.K. government data centers to the IT departments of organizations around the world. With the evolution of ITIL from a company standard to its ratification in December 2005 by the International Organization for Standardization (ISO) as an international standard (ISO/IEC [International Electrotechnical Commission] 20000), growth in its adoption is guaranteed to accelerate.

An important feature of ITIL that has facilitated its acceptance is the internationally recognized certification of ITIL training courses. Today, many consulting firms offer ITIL training in response to the demand for ITIL certified staff. Despite this sweeping adoption by industry, most academic institutions appear to be reticent in including IT service management in their IT curriculum (Watson, Pitt, & Kavan, 1998). In fact, there is very little academic research related to ITIL adoption, the exceptions being Hochstein, Tamm, and Brenner (2005), Potgieter, Botha, and Lew (2005), Niessink and van Vliet (1998, 2000), and Praeg and Schnabel (2006). It is not surprising that little academic research exists as it has been noted that company standards have been neglected in standardization research (Vries, Slob, & Zuid-Holland, 2006). Furthermore, the only academic research related to ITIL education is that published by Bentley (2006) and Jovanovic, Bentley, Stein, and Nikakis (2006).

The objective of this article is to describe the evolution of ITIL from a company standard to international standard, and to consider the growing need for training and the possible role of universities in providing education to assist students in gaining certification related to IT service management.

The article is structured as follows. First, the methodology used to gather evidence is described. Then a detailed explanation is provided of the ITIL framework, its origins, its evolution to an international standard, and its growth in adoption. The current ITIL training schemes are evaluated and the role of universities in improving education related to IT service management is then discussed. In the final conclusions section, suggestions are made for further research.

METHODOLOGY

As well as reviewing recent literature on ITIL adoption and training, the authors have conducted two surveys and six case studies of ITIL adoption with IT service managers. The analysis is based on the data gained from these sources. The case studies used structured interviews based on an instrument developed by Hochstein et al. (2005). Structured interviews were conducted with the managers of ITIL implementation projects in six large organizations between March and September 2006. The organizations were selected on the basis of their response to a survey that was conducted at the IT Service Management Forum (itSMF) Australian national conferences in 2005 and 2006. These six case studies complement the survey data and enable both a broad view of the phenomenon as a whole and a richer, more detailed picture of a few organizations. The interviews were recorded and transcribed, checked by the researchers, and confirmed by the interviewees as a valid record of the interviews.

IT SERVICE MANAGEMENT STANDARDS

Evolution of ITIL to International Standard

In response to the serious economic downturn in the late 1980s, the Central Computer and Telecommunications Agency (CCTA) in the United Kingdom developed the Government Information Technology Infrastructure Management framework to reduce costs and better manage

IT service delivery (Sallé, 2004). Since 2000, the ITIL framework has been administered by the Office of Government Commerce (OGC), an independent office of the U.K. Treasury.

As shown in Table 1, the core of ITIL Version 2 as released in 2001 comprises five service delivery processes, five service support processes, and one service support function (service desk). Service support processes apply to the operational level of the organization whereas the service delivery processes are tactical in nature.

In the 1990s, ITIL gained the support of the British Standards Institution and was extended and adopted as BS 15000 (code of practice for IT service management) in 1995. The second edition of BS 15000, incorporating certification, was launched in June 2003. The development of an international standard based on BS 15000 was fast tracked by the ISO/IEC Joint Technical Committee 1 (JTC1) Sub-Committee 7 (SC7). In December 2005, ISO member countries agreed to adopt ISO/IEC 20000 based on BS 15000. ISO/IEC 20000 integrates the process-based approach of ISO's quality management system (ISO 9001:2000) by including the "plan, do, check, act" cycle and requirements for continual improvement. The IT service management standard comprises two parts.

Table 1. Description of core ITIL components (adapted from OGC, 2005)

Service Delivery: Tactical Level	
Service-Level Management	Negotiates service-level agreements and ensures that these are met. Responsible for ensuring that all IT service management processes, operational-level agreements, and underpinning contracts are appropriate for the agreed service-level targets.
Financial Management	Manages an IT service provider's budgeting, accounting, and charging requirements.
Capacity Management	Ensures that the capacity of IT services and the IT infrastructure is able to deliver agreed service-level targets in a cost-effective and timely manner.
IT Service Continuity Management	Manages risks that could seriously impact IT services. Ensures that the IT service provider can always provide minimum agreed service levels by reducing the risk to an acceptable level and planning for the recovery of IT services.
Availability Management	Defines, analyses, plans, measures, and improves all aspects of the availability of IT services. Ensures that all IT infrastructure, processes, tools, and roles are appropriate for the agreed service-level targets for availability.
Service Support: Operational Level	
Service Desk	The single point of contact between the service provider and the users. Manages incidents and service requests, and also handles communication with the users.
Incident Management	Manages the life cycle of all incidents. The primary objective is to return the IT service to customers as quickly as possible.
Problem Management	Manages the life cycle of all problems. The primary objectives are to prevent incidents from happening, and to minimize the impact of incidents that cannot be prevented.
Change Management	Controls the life cycle of all changes. The objective is to enable beneficial changes to be made with minimum disruption to IT services.
Release Management	A collection of hardware, software, documentation, processes, or other components required to implement approved changes to IT services.
Configuration Management	Responsible for maintaining information about configuration items required to deliver an IT service, including their relationships.

Figure 1. Core components of ISO/IEC 20000 (ISO/IEC, 2005a, p. 1)

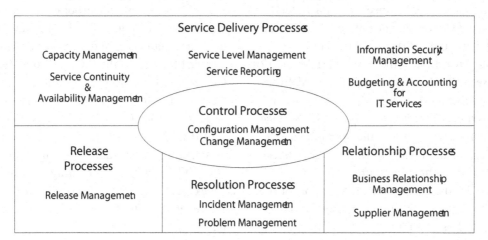

- *Part 1: Specification* promotes the adoption of an integrated process approach to effectively deliver managed services to meet the business and customer requirements (ISO/IEC, 2005a).
- *Part 2: Code of Practice* provides guidance and recommendations based on industry consensus to auditors, and to service providers planning service improvements and/or seeking to be audited against ISO/IEC 20000-1:2005(ISO/IEC, 2005b).

The core components of ISO/IEC 20000 (shown in Figure 1) are similar to those of ITIL with a few exceptions: Two relationship processes have been added (business relationship management and supplier management), service continuity management and availability management are combined into one process, and the service-desk function is not included in ISO/IEC 20000.

To achieve ISO/IEC 20000 certification, companies must successfully undergo a third-party audit by an accredited conformity assessment body. The terms *accreditation* and *certification* have specific meanings in relation to international standards, and are in fact defined in ISO/IEC

17000. Accreditation refers to third-party attestation related to a conformity assessment body conveying formal demonstration of its competence to carry out specific conformity assessment tasks, while certification infers third-party attestation related to products, processes, systems, or persons (ISO/IEC, 2004).

A successful compliance audit is the culmination of months of planning, training, documentation, and review. The qualified auditor seeks objective evidence (records, documents, etc.) to confirm that the activities of the organization are in accordance with the documentation and the requirements of the relevant standard. The process to attain ISO/IEC 20000 certification varies depending on the size of the organization, the breadth of its operation, and the prior and existing level of standardization and documentation.

There is a critical difference between ITIL certification and certification to ISO/IEC 20000: ITIL certification is awarded to individuals after successfully completing assessment from an examination institute, whereas ISO/IEC 20000 certification results from an audit of an organizational unit.

Table 2. Summary of key aspects of six case-study organizations

Case	Organization Type	# of Screens Supported	ITIL Start Date	Processes Implemented	Training Approach
A	Government Department	600+	Mid-2002	Incident, problem, change, service-level, configuration, availability mgmt	Self-study foundation course and external consultants' foundation course
B	Government Department	25,200	2003	Change, configuration, incident, problem, release mgmt	Consultant firm provides foundation course for 350 staff
C	Government Department	12,500	Mid-2001	Financial, service-level, change, configuration, incident, problem mgmt	80 staff completed foundation course of external provider
D	Government Department	35,000	Mid-2001	Change, release, incident, problem mgmt	All IT staff completed foundation course provided by two external providers
E	University	11,000	2003	Incident, problem, change mgmt	Mandated foundation training course for 200 staff (delivered by external consultants)
F	International Finance Company	70,000	2003	Incident, problem, change mgmt, BS 15000, ISO/IEC 20000	Training provider contracted to provide foundation course for 800 staff

Adoption of ITIL

ITIL has a strong following in Europe, especially in the government sector, and adoption is growing in North America and other countries (Barton, 2004). Recent surveys and case studies have reported an upsurge in awareness and adoption of ITIL (Hochstein et al., 2005).

In this section, the salient points from the interviews of the six organizations are presented and illustrated with quotations from the managers interviewed. Due to the commercial sensitivity of the information and comments, the actual names of the organizations cannot be disclosed. The six cases are referred to as Case A to F with the interviewees referred to as Manager A to F and the corresponding organizations as Organization A to F.

The following quotations demonstrate the motivation of each organization regarding the decision to adopt the ITIL framework.

We had built our practices and processes formerly on the ISO 9000 series of standards and we could see that the ITIL framework was much more aligned with an IT service management business. So when we started, it was clear to see that there would be an evolving standard around IT service management that we would be able to adopt. [We wanted] really to align ourselves with an industry reference framework or an industry reference model that made more sense to us than trying to adopt an esoteric principle within 9001 (Manager A).

The major objective was to improve our services. And obviously ITIL was tried and tested and a lot of the IP was there. So, it was an obvious choice (Manager B).

[Previously] you had maverick and cowboy practices whereby every so often somebody would run off and do something and the whole thing would come crashing down and nobody would know who had done what (Manager C).

We had these feral groups doing their own thing, and we had ourselves doing our own thing, and we had IT operations. We didn't have anything related to really best practices. There were good people and I think people were doing best practices as they knew, but in terms of process, no. There was no formal process in place (Manager D).

Standardization makes us more efficient, and using common language, you get benefits out of using the same tools…Our ways of dealing with issues and our ways of responding to critical and noncritical things is the same all across the university: a standard process for service (Manager E).

The director of service delivery ultimately made the decision 'we're going to use ITIL because it's an industry standard' (Manager F).

To summarize the motivation of the cases investigated in this study, all managers support the view that ITIL enables the standardization of IT service management processes and terminology throughout the organization and that such standardization is vital to ensure a consistent and reliable level of service to the business. These benefits are consistent with the incentives mentioned by Hurd and Isaak (2005) in respect to adopting IT standards: clear communication about capabilities, confidence in functional capabilities, and minimization of investment in retraining.

As shown in Table 2, although the sequence of the implementation of processes varied, there

was consistency in the approach to ITIL training. All organizations invested significantly in contracting external training providers for the ITIL foundation certificate course.

ITIL Certification Training

Currently there are three levels of professional qualifications available in ITIL-based IT service management. The ITIL foundation certificate is an entry-level qualification gained by successfully completing a 1-hour multiple-choice examination. The exam focuses on foundational knowledge with regard to the ITIL service-support and service-delivery sets, generic ITIL philosophy, and background.

At the next level, the practitioner certificate can be gained either for a single specific discipline within the ITIL service-support or service-delivery set, or for one of two clusters (release and control, or support and restore). The focus of this qualification is on practical knowledge and skills to implement, manage, improve, and execute the specific discipline. To receive the certificate, students need to complete in-course assessments as well as a 1-hour case-based multiple-choice examination.

The highest level certificate is the manager's certificate in IT service management for experienced IT professionals who intend to implement and/or manage service management functions. The focus of this qualification is on comprehensive knowledge and skills to implement, manage, improve, and execute processes in the ITIL service-support and service-delivery sets. Candidates are assessed based on two 3-hour written examinations as well as in-course assessments (itSMF Australia, 2003).

Of the three levels of certificates offered, the foundation course is by far the most popular. For example, of the 79 respondents to the survey conducted at the 2006 itSMF Australian conference, 85% had received the foundation certificate, 9% had completed the foundation course but did not receive the certificate, 10% held practitioner certificates, and 24% had completed the ITIL manager certificate training.

Training is available from many accredited training providers with the exams developed and administered by two examination institutes: the Information Systems Examination Board (ISEB, a subsidiary of the British Computer Society), and EXIN (Netherlands Examination Institute). As shown in Figure 2, the number of ITIL certification examinations administered by EXIN International has grown exponentially since 2000 to a total worldwide of 100,000 in 2005.

Recently, training courses for ISO/IEC 20000 have been announced,; for example, ISEB and itSMF have accredited ISO/IEC 20000 auditor training courses and both ISEB and EXEN have developed courses for ISO/IEC 20000 consultants.

Demand from Employers for ITIL Trained Staff

To examine the demand for ITIL certification from employers, in September 2006, the authors queried the 20,400 IT jobs at it.seek.com.au, Australia's

top job site, and found 550 Australian job ads requesting ITIL skills posted within that month. These positions were in the areas of help desk and support, project management, business analysis, software engineering, networking, and training. This is a marked increase since May 2004 when Seek.com listed only 25 job ads asking for ITIL skills (Wilson, 2004). These statistics confirm reports in industry that certification has become a recruiting filter in Australia as well as in Europe (Schuller & Wheeler, 2006; Wilson). The demand by employers was confirmed by Manager D who reported that ITIL skills have been included in the position descriptions of IT service staff and are required of IT contractors.

Although ISO/IEC 20000 was only released in December 2005, the standard ranks in ISO's top-10 best-selling standards list for the first half of 2006. Consequently, there has been interest from auditors seeking auditor certification for ISO/IEC 20000. Due to the conformance between ITIL and ISO/IEC 20000, it is expected that ITIL certification will continue to be in demand as an industry qualification for IT service management staff. Therefore, based on reports in industry and comments from the managers interviewed, it ap-

Figure 2. EXIN ITIL examinations delivered worldwide from 2000 to 2005 (Cross, 2006)

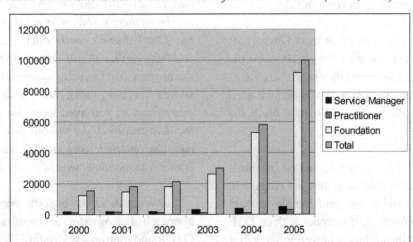

pears that there is growing demand for training in IT service management.

EVALUATION OF CURRENT TRAINING

From the interviews with the managers (as summarized in Table 2), it became evident that they were convinced of the advantages of using external consultants to provide ITIL foundation courses to staff.

At Organization A, initially the IT service managers used a self-study approach to achieve ITIL foundation certification. However, Manager A says:

but in the end, we've had more serendipitous benefits from getting 16 people from across the organization in a room to talk about ITIL foundations than it was worth in the savings that we had by not putting that group through. The serendipitous benefits far outweigh whatever cost savings you might get. That's why I'm really not in favor of online training for foundation. It's about people and organizational change, and about relationships.

Manager D also reported that the ITIL foundation training contributed to change management by effectively getting everyone on side:

There was a lot of opposition from Operations and it wasn't until we actually got them on the course and they saw it and they said, "Yes, okay, I guess we can cooperate with this and we need these things in place," so we started to break the barriers down.

As the ITIL courses are regulated by third-party examination institutes, they are consistent in their content and assessment. Employers can be confident that any staff member with an ITIL foundation certificate has achieved a particular

standard, regardless of who conducted the training. Around the world there are many firms that offer ITIL foundation training. This proved advantageous for Organization F as training was required in seven different cities. Furthermore, the foundation course is suitable for staff from all levels of the organization hierarchy, and staff from business units as well as IT.

Most, if not all, training providers include a simulation exercise in the ITIL foundation course. The exercise is based on a shipping port, airport, or railway and involves the students in various roles as managers, engineers, and service-support personnel. Manager F described the value of the exercise:

[There are] 10 to 15 people at a time and it's based on a shipping port: The idea is you're running a company and you earn money for every ship that comes in and out.....They throw an incident in so your lighthouse goes out, and then you're not making money, and they just teach you by reactive learning. You fail and therefore you learn how to do it better the next time. Eventually you learn you must manage incidents very quickly because if you've got an incident your business isn't making money. You give all the information to your help desk; your help desk knows how to close the incident. I was in some of these training sessions and you can almost hear the penny drop. These people have worked for years and years in IT and know there's a business out there somewhere, but [that] doesn't really affect them, and they suddenly realize that if there's an incident, then the business isn't making money. That affects the share price, our profits, their bonus—that affects everything, so you must work flat out to get the incident resolved, get the business back up and running, and then work on the underlying cause. It was a tremendous way of doing it.

However, there may be some weaknesses to the approach of using external consultants to provide ITIL foundation courses to staff. By relying solely on external consultants, technology transfer is not effective. Internal staff are not encouraged to develop expertise to provide ongoing training to new staff. Another related problem involves the expense: External providers charge between Aus$800 and Aus$1,400 per person for the 3-day ITIL foundation course plus another $150 is required for each examination.

The only form of assessment included in the foundation certificate course is a 1-hour exam comprising 40 multiple-choice questions. Consequently, the objective of course designers and trainers tends to focus on covering the necessary material in such a way that students have a good chance to achieve the necessary 70% correct in the examination. A popular model to evaluate educational objectives is that proposed by Bloom (1956). Bloom's taxonomy presented in Figure 3 comprises six major categories ascending from knowledge through comprehension, application, analysis, and synthesis to evaluation.

The ITIL foundation examination would map onto the lower levels of Bloom's (1956)

taxonomy as it assesses knowledge of specifics including terminology, specific facts, ways of dealing with specifics, and categories. Although it has been claimed that multiple-choice tests can be designed to test higher levels of cognition (Higgins & Tatham, 2003), the ITIL foundation examination does not test anything deeper than a superficial memorizing of facts. Students are given their examination results but are not given any feedback regarding which questions were correctly answered. Therefore, the assessment is not formative as it does not provide opportunities for students to learn from their mistakes.

ROLE OF UNIVERSITIES

The increasing number of private-sector companies providing training, assessment of competencies, and provision of credentials has put increased competition on traditional education providers (Flynn, 2001). The concern raised by Jovanovic et al. (2006) is that industry certification programs

Figure 3. Categories of cognition (Bloom, 1956)

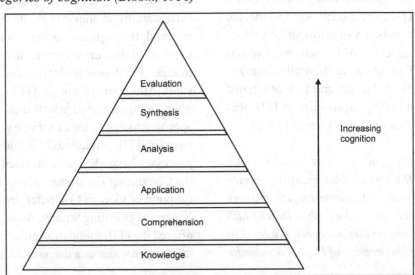

are perceived as training and are therefore not educative. However, to survive, universities need to respond to survey evidence that demonstrates that the "primary reason students attend university is to either find employment or improve their employment prospects" (Sutharshan, Torres, & Maj, 2001). Universities are now expected to provide training, defined as "the development of knowledge and skills to be used immediately, or in the very near future, and deals with developing people who already have, or who are just about to enter, a job" (Tovey & Lawlor, 2004, p. 24).

Professional bodies also influence university programs by emphasizing training rather than education to ensure graduates have the required skills to be admitted as members. For example, the Australian Computer Society (ACS) considers the curriculum content, academic leadership, and staff qualifications when accrediting courses as prerequisites for membership for graduates. This follows the trend of the "professionalization" of university education where science, engineering, business, and law have overtaken the traditional disciplines of arts and humanities (Tadmor, 2006).

Although there are myriad accredited commercial providers offering ITIL training courses, after consulting colleagues and searching the Internet, the authors found that few universities are teaching ITIL; the exceptions include the program for the master's of information science in Norway's University of Bergen, and two undergraduate IT programs in Australia (Bentley, 2006; Rossi, 2006). The general lack of interest by information systems academics in ITIL was noted by Venkataraman and Conger (2006):

The best practice processes and principles that are part of ITIL: Service Management, Service Delivery, Applications Management, etc. are very much in-line with the teaching objectives of MIS departments. Despite this, however, the level of understanding and interest of ITIL in academia,

both on the research and teaching dimensions, significantly lags industry activity.

CURRICULUM INTEGRATION OF IT SERVICE MANAGEMENT

Although most universities have not included ITIL in their curricula to date, many have included other vendor-certified training in IT programs; for example Oracle, SAP, and Microsoft have facilitated the inclusion of their products by developing alliances with universities. However, Jovanovic et al. (2006) believe that the approach has been ad hoc and reactionary and "little has been done to investigate the implementation of IT certification programs within tertiary IT/IS programs" (p. 4).

Prior to including IT service management topics, academic staff are advised to evaluate their existing curriculum and undertake industry research to determine the skills in demand. Then, after identifying gaps, changes can be designed and implemented, and regularly evaluated and reviewed.

Three varieties of implementation models are being tested at Victoria University (Australia): the course-mapping, curriculum-inclusive, and end-on models for SAP, ITIL, i-Net+, and Microsoft certification (Jovanovic et al., 2006). For the ITIL material, the implementation model uses a combination of the curriculum-inclusive and end-on models. Final-year undergraduate students can study in the course Managing IT Service Support, giving a "theoretical, practical and best practice approach to managing IT service support directly based on ITIL guidelines" (Bentley, 2006). ITIL processes have also been included in Managing the Computing Environment, and from a practical point of view in Computer Project and Work Integrated Learning Studies. As well, students are offered the ITIL foundation online course from a training provider at a discounted price.

The approach recently taken by University of Southern Queensland is similar. First, the ISO/IEC 20000 processes are covered in Systems Planning and Management within the IT-management major. This course identifies the objectives and activities of each of the core processes that underpin the ITIL and ISO/IEC 20000 best-practice frameworks. In addition, the associated roles and responsibilities of IT service providers, management, staff, and clients are discussed. The course is underpinned by the principles of service management and IT governance and emphasizes the planning and management aspects of IT service management and the need to align IT service with the organization's strategy and objectives.

The content covered is adequate to prepare students for the ITIL foundation certificate. Additionally, existing courses are being revised to include ISO/IEC 20000 processes and terminology: Principles of Information Security includes service continuity and availability management, information-security management, configuration management, change management, and release management; and Systems Analysis and Design introduces business relationship management, supplier management, and budgeting and accounting for IT services. These courses include formative assessment with feedback to students on written and oral assignments, and also provide opportunities for group discussions, assignments, and peer feedback.

Universities should be preparing graduates for a career, not just a job. For students, there are advantages to learning about IT service management at a university rather than obtaining industry training. More time can be spent on the content as the course is not restricted to 2.5 days, guest speakers from industry can provide real-world insights, the assessment can be more varied and thorough, there are opportunities to include prior rigorous research relating to core processes, and by integrating the concepts into several courses, students are given a broader understanding of IT service management. Consequently, by use of scenario-based tasks, case studies, and comparisons to other related frameworks (such as CobiT, ISO/IEC 17799, CMMI [capability maturity model integration]), courses and assessments can support the achievement of higher educational objectives such as comprehension, application, and analysis.

BENEFITS AND CHALLENGES OF UNIVERSITY-BASED IT SERVICE MANAGEMENT EDUCATION

For any university prepared to provide basic training for the foundation certificate or broader education related to IT service management, there are many possible benefits. As well as the promise of an increase in the number of student enrollments and subsequent income, the reputation of the university could be enhanced as it would be seen as providing internationally recognized qualifications in response to demands from the business community. To ease the education path of students, the possibility would exist for the recognition of prior learning by offering course credit to students who have achieved the ITIL foundation certificate. Furthermore, as demonstrated by the research partnership between the University of Southern Queensland and itSMF Australia, opportunities for research would enhance the relationship of the university and local business community (Rossi, 2006). Such benefits could be ascribed to any curriculum improvement.

As far as benefits specific to IT service management education, currently undergraduate courses tend to focus on the early stage of the information systems life cycle, systems analysis, and development. There is little emphasis on the implementation of new or changed IT services or the ongoing management of IT infrastructure to ensure service quality. An important benefit is that students would have a broader understanding of the importance of IT investment and infrastructure in organizations. It is important for students to understand the essential ongoing role of information systems and the management of service in response to business demands.

These benefits support a positive response to the question of whether or not universities should provide education in relation to IT service management.

However, there are challenges to universities that consider including education on IT service management in their academic curricula. Many of the challenges apply to the inclusion of any new courses: the identification of a suitable textbook and the development of teaching materials; the availability of staff with appropriate expertise, or the provision of funds and time for training IS academics in IT service management; the continual upgrading of standards such as ITIL and ISO/IEC 20000, which makes it difficult to keep course materials and academic skills up to date; difficulties in overcoming the "cumbersome course curriculum approval systems" mentioned by Flynn (2001, p. 5) to change the existing curriculum, and in squeezing the new course into an existing crowded curriculum; the cost of the ITIL foundation exam (currently $150), which would probably not be borne by the university and may be prohibitive for students; and the approval that needs to be sought from accrediting bodies such as ACS.

In addition, there are specific challenges for including IT service management in the curriculum. As the concepts apply to organizations with complex IT infrastructure, it may be difficult to effectively transfer the knowledge to students who have not experienced the IT service environment firsthand. Also, organizations rely on sophisticated tool sets to support processes such as incident and configuration management. Additional cost and training of academic staff would be required to provide access to these tools for students.

Although this might appear to be a daunting list of challenges, some academic IS departments have overcome similar obstacles in providing courses related to other standards such as ISO/IEC 17799 (IT security techniques, code of practice for information security management) and facilitate certification for SAP and Microsoft qualifications. Many universities teach the Project Management Body of Knowledge (PMBOK) in IT project management courses. In the case of PMBOK, students have the option of taking the Project Management Institute exam for the certified project manager professional (PMP) qualification.

SUMMARY AND CONCLUSION

In summary, the ITIL phenomenon has radically changed the discipline of IT service management. There is growing demand for IT staff to understand ITIL concepts and processes. With the recognition of ITIL as the basis for the international standard for IT service management, it is important for universities to include ITIL concepts in programs to ensure graduates are prepared for the workplace. Curricula should include these concepts at least up to the foundation level. Armed with this level of knowledge, graduates will be valuable ambassadors for this standard and standards generally, and may even sway their employers toward higher levels of participation in standards development activities. The benefits to students, academics, universities, and industry are numerous, but so are the challenges.

This research has provided a comprehensive account of the content and evolution of ITIL from a company framework to an international standard. The structure of ITIL certification education is described, with accounts of increasing demand for ITIL certified staff confirmed by industry research.

A clear requirement of future research is to consider how ITIL concepts can effectively be integrated into IT curricula. A starting point would be to follow the lead of the software engineering discipline in its mapping of the Software Engineering Body of Knowledge (SWEBOK) topics to Bloom's (1956) taxonomy (Abran, Moore, Bourque, & Dupuis, 2004). Detailed analysis of the underlying concepts of ITIL from an educational perspective is the first step to enable academics to design effective curricula to address the challenges posed of educating students about ITIL and ISO/IEC 20000.

REFERENCES

Abran, A., Moore, J. W., Bourque, P., & Dupuis, R. (2004). *Guide to the Software Engineering Body of Knowledge SWEBOK*. Los Alamitos, CA: IEEE Computer Society.

Barton, N. (2004, July 8). This year's model: Performance improvement complements IT best practices frameworks. *CIO*, 2005.

Bentley, J. (2006, December). *Integration of ITIL into the IS curriculum*. Paper presented at the 17th Australasian Conference on Information Systems, Adelaide, South Australia.

Bloom, B. S. (Ed.). (1956). *Taxonomy of educational objectives: Handbook 1. Cognitive domain.* New York: Longman, Green & Co.

Cross, P. (2006, November). *EXIN & service quality management.* Paper presented at the Service Quality Management Foundation Examination Launch Workshop, Sydney, New South Wales.

Flynn, W. J. (2001). *More than a matter of degree: Credentialing, certification and community colleges.* Carisbad, CA: National Council for Continuing Education and Training.

Higgins, E., & Tatham, L. (2003). Exploring the potential of multiple-choice questions in assessment. *Learning and Teaching in Action, 2*(1).

Hochstein, A., Tamm, G., & Brenner, W. (2005, May). *Service-oriented IT management: Benefit, cost and success factors.* Paper presented at the 15th European Conference on Information Systems, Regensburg, Germany.

Hurd, J., & Isaak, J. (2005). IT standardization: The billion dollar strategy. *International Journal of IT Standards & Standardization Research, 3*(1), 68-74.

International Organization for Standardization/International Electrotechnical Commission (ISO/IEC). (2004). *ISO/IEC 17000:2004 conformity assessment: Vocabulary and general principles.* Geneva, Switzerland: International Organization for Standardization.

International Organization for Standardization/International Electrotechnical Commission (ISO/IEC). (2005a). *ISO/IEC 20000:2005 information technology: Service management. Part 1: Specification.* Geneva, Switzerland: International Organization for Standardization.

International Organization for Standardization/International Electrotechnical Commission (ISO/IEC). (2005b). *ISO/IEC 20000:2005 information technology: Service management. Part 2: Code of practice.* Geneva, Switzerland: International Organization for Standardization.

IT Service Management Forum (itSMF) Australia. (2003). *Best practice: Professional qualifications.* Retrieved September 23, 2006, from http://www.itsmf.org.au/aboutbestpractice_pro.asp

Jovanovic, R., Bentley, J., Stein, A., & Nikakis, C. (2006). Implementing industry certification in an IS curriculum: An Australian experience. *Information Systems Education Journal, 4*(59), 3-8.

Niessink, F., & van Vliet, H. (1998). Towards mature IT services. *Software Process: Improvement and Practice, 4*(2), 55-71.

Niessink, F., & van Vliet, H. (2000). Software maintenance from a service perspective. *Journal of Software Maintenance: Research and Practice, 12*(2), 103-120.

Office of Government Commerce (OGC). (2005). *Introduction to ITIL*. London: Stationery Office.

Potgieter, B. C., Botha, J. H., & Lew, C. (2005, July). *Evidence that use of the ITIL framework is effective*. Paper presented at the 18th Annual Conference of the National Advisory Committee on Computing Qualifications, Tauranga, New Zealand.

Praeg, C.-P., & Schnabel, U. (2006, January). *IT-service cachet: Managing IT-service performance and IT-service quality*. Paper presented at the 39th Annual Hawaii International Conference on System Sciences (HICSS'06), HI.

Rossi, S. (2006, July 12). University begins local ITIL adoption research. *Computerworld*.

Sallé, M. (2004). *IT service management and IT governance: Review, comparative analysis and their impact on utility computing* (No. HPL-2004-98). Palo Alto, CA: Hewlett-Packard Company.

Schuller, H., & Wheeler, G. (2006, May 31). An ITIL bit of knowledge. *Computerworld*.

Sutharshan, A., Torres, M., & Maj, S. P. (2001, February). *Education or training: Meeting student and employer expectations*. Paper presented

at the 10th Annual Teaching Learning Forum: Expanding Horizons in Teaching and Learning, Perth, WA.

Tadmor, Z. (2006). The Triad Research University or a post 20th century research university model. *Higher Education Policy, 19*, 287-298.

Tovey, M., & Lawlor, D. (2004). *Training in Australia: Design, delivery, evaluation, management* (2nd ed.). Sydney, New South Wales: Pearson Education.

Venkataraman, R., & Conger, S. (2006, August 28). Open invitation to itSMF Academic Forum. In AISWORLD Information Systems World Network (Ed.).

Vries, H. J. D., Slob, F. J. C., & Zuid-Holland, V. G. (2006). Best practice in company standardization. *International Journal of IT Standards and Standardization Research, 4*(1), 62-85.

Watson, R., Pitt, L., & Kavan, C. (1998). Measuring information systems service quality: Lessons from two longitudinal case studies. *MIS Quarterly, 22*(1), 61-79.

Wilson, E. (2004, May 11). Opening the book on ITIL. *Sydney Morning Herald*.

This work was previously published in International Journal of IT Standards and Standardization Research, Vol. 5, Issue 2, edited by K. Jakobs, pp. 27-41, copyright 2007 by IGI Publishing, formerly known as Idea Group Publishing (an imprint of IGI Global).

Chapter XVIII
Developing a Basis for Global Reciprocity:
Negotiating Between the Many Standards for Project Management

Lynn Crawford
University of Technology - Sydney, Australia

Julien Pollack
University of Technology - Sydney, Australia

ABSTRACT

Professional standards are a significant issue for professions such as IT and project management, where certification and licensure are either necessary to practice or to demonstrate individual competence and capability. In many professions there is no basis for international reciprocity of professional standards. This paper documents the development of a standard for global reciprocity between already existing professional standards in the field of project management. Data are based on personal involvement by the authors and interviews with participants. This discussion addresses different approaches to standardisation, how common issues in the standardisation process have been addressed, and how the hindering influence of the professional associations' proprietorial interest was avoided. Significantly different standards of development processes have been used compared to those typical in Project Management standards development, including: an emphasis on negotiation and joint modification rather than market dominance, and an open access approach, rather than one based on exclusion and gate-keeping.

INTRODUCTION

The role of standards in professional licensure and certification has been an important issue for many years. As early as 1953, Carey wrote that the "… medical profession, the dental profession and the certified public accountants have all used standard examinations for many years and with outstanding success ..." (Carey, 1953, p. 36). In 1962 Milton Friedman commented that occupational licensure was then very widespread (Friedman, 1962, p. 139). Researchers have found continuing agitation to extend standardisation to more professions (Leland, 1980, p. 265), and this does not seem to be reducing, with Blind and Thumm (2004, p. 61) recently finding that the number of standards has "... risen tremendously." In the IT industry, certification has been raised from a hiring tool to a screening tool, with high-level certification being necessary for consideration in many jobs (George, 2002, p. 76).

Standards development should be pursued critically and with care, with some industries needing to revisit the role that standards play within the community. For instance, in the IT industry, certification is often viewed as a vital way to indicate competence. However, studies have found that professional IT certification is not a robust predictor of ability (Cegielski, 2004, p. 105). One study found that "... no statistically significant difference exists between the capabilities of certified network professionals and non-certified network professionals ..." (Cegielski, et al., 2003, p. 97). IT standards of certification and accreditation may even mask a lack of the very qualities that employers are looking for (Schrage, 2004, p. 1).

Over the last decade, the profession of Project Management has moved from one typified by isolated national standards to one struggling with the process of creating global professional standards for knowledge, education, and workplace performance. The profession has developed from clusters of professionals sharing knowledge at a company or industry level, to commonly accepted national frameworks for Project Management, and is now moving towards globally accepted and transferable qualifications in the profession. This paper examines recent efforts to create a framework for global reciprocity between Project

Management standards. This is discussed in relation to professional licensure and certification in general, different approaches to standardisation, and recent failures to create globally applicable standards for Project Management.

Project Management Standards: From Community to Profession

Modern Project Management may be considered to have had its genesis in the international arena when, in the 1950s (Stretton, 1994; Morris, 1994), companies such as Bechtel began to use the term "project manager" in their international work, primarily on remote sites. Before long, local communities of Project Management practice developed, becoming formalized in national Project Management professional associations. The development of standards in Project Management began with recognition of shared interests, resulting in fairly informal community gatherings. Through regular meetings and recognition of shared experience, practitioners began to think of themselves as a community and a profession. This led to attempts to define and delineate that profession in order to make it visible and acceptable to those outside the community (Crawford, 2004b, pp. 1389-90).

Dean (1997) identifies seven building blocks of a profession, characteristics that distinguish it from a community. These are: a store or body of knowledge that is more than ordinarily complex; a theoretical understanding of the area of practice; ability to apply theoretical and complex knowledge to a practice; a desire to add to and improve the body of knowledge; a formal process for transferring the body of knowledge and associated practices; established criteria for admission, legitimate practice, and proper conduct (standards and certification); and an altruistic spirit.

Of these building blocks, bodies of knowledge, standards, and certification programs have been of particular significance to Project Management. Before an industry attains a certain maturity, standardisation is of little value. It is less likely to have an interest in standards, or to accept them as valuable. For an immature industry, where new ideas and technologies are in the process of being developed, there is little benefit to investing energy in standardisation, due to the rate of change in the industry (Steele, 2004, p. 42). An interest in standards can then be seen as an indicator of a certain level of maturity within the profession.

A variety of benefits have been identified which accrue from standardisation. General benefits which apply to both technological and professional standardisation include encouragement of technological innovation, guaranteeing marketplace choice, competition, and convenience (JEDEC, 2004, p. 11). Standardisation can also be used as a strategy for fostering economic growth via the broad diffusion of technology and technical rules, and shaping foreign markets according to the specification of local technologies and products (Blind & Thumm, 2004).

At a professional level, standardisation delineates clear professional boundaries, and can be seen as a way of increasing the esteem of a profession. For instance, recent arguments have been made for certification and licensure of HR professionals as a way of increasing respect (Brown, 2005, p. 5). Professional standards are also described as being of benefit to organisations, through acting as "... enablers of more efficient and effective use of resources delivering economic sustainable development" (Bredillet, 2003, p. 464). Furthermore, standardisation can be used as a competitive strategy for new entrants opposing the dominance of existing firms (Baskin, Krechmer, & Sherif, 1998, p. 55).

Project Management Standards: From Local to Global Profession

In the early stages of the development of Project Management as a profession, bodies of knowledge, standards, and certification programs were predominantly developed by independent profes-

sional associations, usually taking a proprietary view of the products they developed. This resulted in the proliferation of competing Project Management standards and certification programs, the majority of which were largely local in their origin, and limited in their application to a narrow range of project types within a single culture.

However, by the second half of the 1990s, it was becoming clear that Project Management practitioners and application areas were becoming increasingly global. It is now often the case that projects are shared across multiple international organisations. The application of Project Management had extended beyond international projects, managed offshore by nationally-based companies, to use by global corporations through globally distributed operations and projects (Crawford, 2004b, pp. 1390-1).

Further incentive to develop globally applicable Project Management standards came from outside the profession. The North American Free Trade Agreement, 1993 and the World Trade Organization's General Agreement on Trade in Services, 1994, required the "... development of policies that evaluate professional competence based on fair, objective criteria and transparent (publicly known) procedures" (Lenn, 1997, p. 2). These agreements put pressure on established professions and their professional associations to consider mutually acceptable standards in cooperation with other countries and to actively plan for reciprocal recognition at a minimum.

Unlike the majority of IT standards, Project Management standards are not technical documents. IT standards often describe the characteristics of physical artefacts, algorithms, or processes, that although complex, are unambiguous once understood and can easily transcend cultural and language boundaries. By contrast, professional standards, such as those that apply to certification in the IT industry and Project Management, describe human practice, knowledge, and skills. Such concepts are open to considerable interpretation. This is especially true in the context of an industry that is still defining professional boundaries, and where practitioners from different cultures potentially have inconsistent appreciations of what the profession actually is.

Creating new standards by consensus is a difficult process. Even for technical standards, it "… may not be clear what the best technical solution actually is" (Warner, 2003, p. 7). This ambiguity is exacerbated in the development of Project Management standards, where it is arguable whether there is any such thing as a "best" solution. Rather, standards which reach the marketplace are often the product of lengthy political negotiation and act as accommodated positions between the different professional associations.

Dramatis Personae: Project Management Professional Associations

The Project Management Institute (PMI) is the largest of the Project Management professional associations. PMI originated in North America in 1969, and now has a significant membership. Membership grew at 37.9 percent in 2005, resulting in a total of 212,000 individual members (PMI, 2006). The Institute itself claims that as

…a steward of the project management profession, PMI has the distinction of being one of the fastest growing professional organizations in the world. (PMI, 2005a)

The PMI has developed arguably the most significant Project Management standard, the *PMBOK® Guide* (PMI, 2004), currently in its third edition. The *PMBOK® Guide* is approved as an American National Standard by ANSI and is recognised by the Institute of Electrical and Electronics Engineers as an IEEE standard (PMI, 2005b). However, it has been developed in North America for a predominantly North American audience, and found to describe a form of Project Management that is not culturally suited to some

application areas (Muriithi & Crawford, 2003). Nonetheless, the *PMBOK® Guide* has become a de facto international standard for Project Management knowledge.

The Australian Institute of Project Management (AIPM), is the Australian national project management association, and had over 6,000 members distributed over eight state and territory chapters by 2006. The AIPM remained unopposed as the national Project Management association until 1996, when the first of a number of PMI chapters was chartered in Australia. By 2003, there were PMI chapters in most Australian capital cities (PMI, 2003a), with a total membership of 1,500 (PMI, 2003b). Relationships between the AIPM and the Australian PMI chapters varies from friendly cooperation to active competition (Crawford, 2004b, p. 1395).

By contrast, project managers in South Africa were for many years represented by a PMI Chapter, first formed in 1982. The PMI South Africa Chapter continues to exist, but Project Management South Africa (PMSA), a separate national association, was established in 1997 to satisfy local economic and regulatory requirements. Unlike Australia, because PMSA was essentially formed by members of the PMI South Africa Chapter, there is a far closer and more consistently cooperative relationship between PMSA and PMI. Membership of PMSA increased from 400 at formation in 1997 to over 1,200 in 2003.

In the UK, the Association for Project Management (APM) was formed in 1972, and currently has more than 13,500 individual and 300 corporate members (APM, 2005). APM has developed an independent knowledge standard, the *APM Body of Knowledge* (2006), currently in its fifth edition. This document takes a significantly different perspective on project management than that presented by the *PMBOK® Guide* (PMI, 2004) in terms of both what is considered to be of relevance and how this information is conveyed.

The Japan Project Management Forum (JPMF) is a division of the Engineering Advancement Association (ENAA), which was founded in 1978 as a non-profit organisation based on corporate rather than individual membership. ENAA addresses the needs of industry and corporations, with membership encompassing 250 engineering and project-based companies. JPMF acts as the professional association for individual practitioners. ENAA has published *P2M: A Guidebook of Project & Program Management for Enterprise Innovation* (2002), including an English translation.

Established in 1991 in China, the Project Management Research Council (PMRC) supports over 100 universities and companies and 3,500 active individual members from universities, industries, and government. In 1994 the PMRC initiated, with support from the China Natural Science Fund, the development of a *Chinese Project Management Body of Knowledge* (C-PMBOK), which was published together with the *China-National Competence Baseline* (C-NCB) in 2001.

The International Project Management Association (IPMA), was initiated in 1965 (IPMA 2003; Stretton, 1994). The IPMA has evolved into a network, or federation, comprising 30 national Project Management associations representing approximately 20,000 members, primarily in Europe but also in Africa and Asia (IPMA, 2003). The largest member of the IPMA is the UK APM, which has had considerable influence on the development of the IPMA. An earlier version of the *APM Body of Knowledge* (APM, 2006) was one of the key documents referenced in writing of the *ICB: IPMA Competence Baseline* (IPMA, 1999). So far, the successes of the IPMA has been hampered by its federated structure, by the differing priorities of its national association members, and by lack of funds available for international and global development (Crawford, 2004b, p. 1393).

Blum (2005) divides standards generation processes into public and industrial standardisation. Public standardisation can be managed through national or sector-specific approaches, while industrial standardisation processes can be

company based or managed through consortia. In the IT industry "...the competition between public standardization and consortium-based standardization had been won and lost around the turn of the millennium, in favour of the latter ..." (Blum, 2005, p. 3).

Nonetheless, in the Project Management community, a variety of public qualifications bodies have ongoing significant influence over the development of Project Management standards. Innovation and Business Skills Australia (IBSA), the South African Qualifications Association (SAQA), and the UK Engineering and Construction Industry Training Board (ECITB) all have their own standards for Project Management qualification, while the New Zealand Qualifications Association has a cooperative agreement with Australia.

Established PM Standards

Project Management standards development has so far relied on a market-based approach. Many of the challenges facing the globalisation of Project Management as a profession and community of practice relate to competition between the various professional associations, which have tended to remain locally focused and exclusionary about the knowledge created by their communities. Qualifications gained under one professional association are not usually recognised for equivalence by other professional associations, although the performance of practitioners qualified by different professional associations may still be equivalent.

There are currently a wide variety of guides and standards, focusing on different aspects of the profession. These have been classified by Duncan (1998) as belonging to one of three categories:

• **Projects:** Focusing on the knowledge and practices for management of individual projects.

Table 1. Project Management standards focusing on people, projects and organisations

People	Projects	Organisations
Engineering Construction Industry Training Board (ECITB)	A Guide to the Project Management Body of Knowledge (PMBOK ® Guide)	Guidebook for Project and Program Management for Enterprise Innovation (P2M)
South African Qualification Authority (SAQA)	International Project Management Association Competence Baseline (ICB)	Organizational Project Management Maturity Model (OPM3)
National Competency Standards for Project Management (NCSPM)	The Association for Project Management Body of Knowledge (APM BoK)	Office of Government Commerce Managing Successful Programmes (OGC MSP)
	British Standards (BS 6079)	Office of Government Commerce Project Management Maturity Model (OGC PMMM)
	International Standards Organization (ISO 10006)	Projects in Controlled Environments (PRINCE 2)

- **Organisations:** Focusing on enterprise project management knowledge and practices.
- **People:** Focusing on the development, assessment, and registration/certification of people.

Existing Project Management standards can be grouped according to these categories (see Table 1). Only some of these standards are discussed here. For a comprehensive review, refer to Crawford (2004b).

Most Project Management standards have been developed through industrial coalitions and consortia, many of which later go on to receive Government endorsement. By far the most popular standards in Project Management are those which focus on projects, the most popular of which have been developed by industry consortia. ISO 10006 and BS 6079 occupy relatively small market shares, compared to the PMBOK ® Guide and APM BoK.

Standards focusing on organisations have also been predominantly created by industry consortia, but their emergence is more recent, and are subsequently less prevalent. By contrast,

the Project Management standards which focus on people have all been developed publicly, and are generally in the form of performance-based competency standards. The majority of these have been specifically designed for assessment purposes, and provide the basis for the award of qualifications within national qualifications frameworks.

Warner (2003) has distinguished between market-based standards and formal processes for creating standards. "In market-based battles, the standard follows success in the market by definition" (p. 2). The standard is recognised as such because it is the strongest survivor, and success may be based on a pre-existing market or good marketing, rather than inherent value. By contrast, standards created through formal processes are products of negotiation, anticipatory and often pre-competitive. Their development may be the result of a perceived need within the industry, and may have little to do with the existing support, or generation, of a market. This is similar to a distinction made by Baskin, Krechmer, and Sherif (1998, p. 59), who use this approach to categorise standards as either anticipatory, participatory, or

Figure 1. Standards in the product development life cycle (based on Baskin, Krechmer, & Sherif, 1998, p. 59).

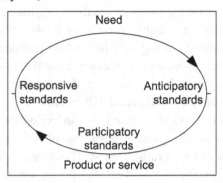

responsive (see Figure 1). Project Management standards, whether they focus on projects, people, or organisations, are consistently participatory or responsive standards, describing or helping to define existing practice.

The current distribution of market share has worked as a hindrance to the process of creating global Project Management standards. "Very often, large companies possessing large market shares will try to establish proprietary *de facto* industry standard ..." (Blind & Thumm, 2004, p. 69). Although the *PMBOK® Guide* only focuses on projects, not people or organisations, it is often considered a de facto standard for the profession as a whole, based on its overall market dominance.

Despite the global presence of the Project Management Institute, over 70 percent of its membership remain located in North America (PMI, 2006). There is considerable reluctance on the part of Project Management professionals in some countries outside the United States to relinquish their independence and genuinely national representation. Furthermore, practitioners in many countries cannot afford the professional membership fees that are acceptable in the United States. In many cases, such as in South Africa, it has been necessary to establish fully national

associations in order to meet the needs of local jurisdictions and/or to provide a more affordable alternative.

Previous authors have identified cultural differences between how standards are created in North America and Europe, which may help to explain the reluctance in some countries to adopt the *PMBOK® Guide* as the standard. Bredillet (2003, p. 465-9) identifies that the American standards development favours a market-based approach, where one standard grows to dominance, excluding others from the market. By contrast, a European approach favours negotiation and joint modification of standards. Krechmer (2004) has identified similar differences in the ways that standards have been developed in North America and Europe, providing an example based on the mobile phone industry. He suggests that in North America, a laissez-faire policy was used in the development of mobile phone technologies, where the commercial organisations did as they wished, and it was expected that market forces would result in a clear de facto standard. This policy has resulted in three competing cellular standards. By contrast, a single unified standard was pursued in Europe. "In Europe two equipment developers, Nokia and Ericsson, pulled far ahead of their largest competitor, Motorola, headquartered in North America" (Krechmer, 2004, p. 50).

Minimum Quality Certification

Project Management standards usually take the form of minimum quality certification, instead of licensure. The distinction between these two forms of professional standards is that in situations where licensure is required, the professional may not legally practice without a license, while in situations where professional certification is used the "...governmental agency may certify that an individual has certain skills but may not prevent, in any way, the practice of an occupation using these skills by people who do not have such a certificate" (Friedman, 1962, p. 144). Standards of certification can be considered to be minimum quality standards, used to identify those who have met the standard, but not to prohibit those who have not.

One of the most common arguments for professional standardisation relates to the protection of public welfare. However, markets using minimum quality standards tend to be typified by information asymmetry, where sellers know the quality of their goods, but buyers do not (Leland, 1979, p. 1329). Over the last few years, certification has proved particularly popular in the IT industry, as a way for personnel to advertise their capabilities. The public is then, in theory, more informed and, as a consequence, buyers have a greater choice, as "... they can buy low-quality goods if they wish" (Leland, 1980, p. 283).

However, just as buyers have to attempt to identify quality, sellers must also communicate this information to buyers. This latter step may be costly or impossible to achieve in some circumstances (Leland, 1980, p. 283). In the case with Project Management certification, where there are multiple levels of certification offered by competing certification organisations, the differences in certifications may be unclear to buyers of services. What follows is that in many cases, if a consumer does not trust their own ability to differentiate between the quality of certified and uncertified products, certification is often treated in much the same ways that licensure is (Leffler, 1980, p. 290).

In such cases, it could be argued that licensure would be more appropriate than certification, as licensure is government imposed over an industry, and so may enforce a level of consistency that may not emerge if an industry is left to its own competing standards for certification. Licensure of professions also allows for government-enforced requirements to be placed on professions, such as the need for continuing professional education, while competing professional associations offering only certification may not be prepared to enforce this requirement on their members.

However, Friedman (1962) found it difficult to see reasons how any argument for licensure instead of certification could be justified. This is because the usual paternalistic arguments for licensure regarding protecting public welfare are almost entirely satisfied, while certification without licensure provides a good deal of protection against the development of monopolies. The "... elasticity of demand will be fairly large, and the limits within which they can exploit the rest of the public by taking advantage of their special position will be rather narrow" (Friedman, 1962, p. 149). In other words, if certified professionals start charging too much and overly restricting access to certification, then the buying public will simply use uncertified professionals. Certification then seems less open to abuse than does licensure.

Arguments for occupational licensure are often based on issues of public welfare, on the basis of preventing people who are not competent from practicing or on improving the level of competence within the profession. However, many question the assumption of a link between licensure and professional quality (e.g., Clarkson & Muirs, 1980, p. 108). It is not necessarily clear that licensure does raise the standards of professional practice (Friedman, 1962, p. 155), and in many cases "...the considerations taken into account in determining who shall get a license often involve matters that, so far as any layman can see, have no relation whatsoever to professional competence" (Friedman, 1962, p. 141).

It is also not clear whether minimum quality standards maintain the quality within a profession. Sobel (2001) provides an interesting analysis of minimum quality standards for entry into a club, examining the conditions under which standards change over time. He finds that this can be related to variation in judging criteria and the proportion of judges' support necessary to grant entry. Unfortunately, Sobel explicitly makes several assumptions which do not hold for Project Management standards, such as a stable total membership and assessment based on direct comparison between potential and existing members. However, Sobel's general finding that standards have the potential to drop is interesting. Indeed, research has shown that "'Minimum competency' examinations … fall short of what is needed, as the 'minimum' tends to become the 'maximum,' thus lowering educational standards for all" (National Commission on Excellence in Education, 1983). Sobel (2001, p. 620) relates dropping quality back to the increase in variety of standards, commenting that "[O]ne is tempted to speculate that the proliferation of new qualifications is a reaction to the degradation of existing qualifications."

If the most common argument for professional standards, namely protection of public welfare, is not met, the question remains why standardisation is so popular. The pressure to regulate professions through licensing or certification usually comes from within the profession to be regulated, instead of consumers of their services (Friedman, 1962, p. 140; Wolfson, Trebilcock, & Tuohy, 1980, p. 182). Indeed, such standards are often written more to protect members of the profession from competition, than to protect the public from incompetent practitioners (Leland, 1980, p. 265). Minimum quality standards in general (Leland, 1979, p. 1329) and professional regulation through licensure, certification, and registration (Friedman, 1962, p. 148) have been linked to the efforts of industry representatives or special producer groups to capture monopoly profits.

Research has also shown that professional incomes can be directly related to degrees of regulations. For instance, it has been found that "… television repair prices are higher in areas (Louisiana) with occupational licensure than in those with mere registration systems (California) or no regulation at all (the District of Colombia)" (Clarkson & Muirs, 1980, p. 108). Furthermore, the bodies which administer admission to the profession tend to accrue rents, which can provide an important impetus for licensure (Benham, 1980, p. 14).

In the case of Project Management, the various Project Management professional associations do have commercial interest in that they accrue rents through the certification of professionals, with maintenance of market share potentially providing a motivator to exclude competitors from the market. However, in many countries, certification is available from more than one professional association, with clear monopolies only occurring in some regions. Certification is also seen by many project managers as a way of overcoming the information asymmetry, by providing a way of advertising their capabilities. Certification clearly provides benefit to those who provide the certifications and to those who gain them, while also providing assurance to employers, who in the face of multiple similar candidates for a position, need some way of making a distinction.

Performance-Based Competency Standards

Glassie (2003, p. 17) argues that conclusions about individual professional competence cannot be reached based on certification status, as certification only measures factors that tend to indicate competence, instead of measuring competence directly. This may be true for some kinds of standards. However, performance-based competency standards are specifically designed for assessment and recognition of current competence. This is assessed independent of how that competence has been achieved. They describe what people can be expected to do in their working roles, as well as the knowledge and understanding of their occupation that is needed to underpin these roles at a specific level of competence. Performance-based inference of competence is concerned with demonstration of the ability to do something at a standard considered acceptable in the workplace, with an emphasis on threshold rather than high performance or differentiating competencies. Threshold competencies are units of behaviour that are essential to do a job but that are not causally related to superior job performance (Boyatzis, 1982).

Models and standards which are based on performance are concerned with outcomes or results in the workplace, as opposed to potential competence, which might be assessed by tests of attributes. In these models, underlying competence in areas which are not easily observed, such as the ability to solve problems, can readily be inferred through performance and results in the workplace. "Performance based models of competence should specify what people have to be able to do, the level of performance required and the circumstances in which that level of performance is to be demonstrated" (Heywood, et al., 1992, p. 23).

Global Standards for Project Management

Work towards the creation of global standards for Project Management first became an issue in 1994, where, at the annual PMI Symposium in Vancouver, Canada, there was a meeting of representatives of PMI, IPMA, APM, and the AIPM, at which "… formal cooperation on several global issues, including standards, certification and formation of a global project management organisation or confederation' were discussed" (Pells, 1996, p. ix). A series of Global Project Management Forums followed.

However, standards-setting organisations must "…remain vigilant to make sure that all its participants are working in the spirit of collaboration" (JEDEC, 2004, p. 11), as "… standard setting is a conflicted, political process" (van Wegberg, 2004, p. 21). Meaningful cooperation between the Project Management professional associations was far from being realised. Informal participation and lip service to cooperation were possible at the Global Project Management Forums. Real progress in the interests of a unified Project Management profession were hampered by political issues and vested

proprietary interests. By the thirteenth Global Project Management Forum in June 2003, little real progress had been achieved.

A lack of progress is not surprising, given the open format and range of topics discussed at the Global Project Management Forums. Lack of a tightly defined purpose and scope increases opportunities for those who would subvert the standards-setting process for personal economic gain. The "…standard-setting process is not perfect nor is it foolproof. It can be subverted by participants intent on bolstering their economic advantage over competitors through manipulation, deception and anticompetitive acts" (JEDEC, 2004, p. 11), as JEDEC would well be aware, given their recent complications with Rambus (Stern, 2001).

As an alternative to the Global Project Management Forums, the Global Performance Based Standards for Project Management Personnel (GPBSPMP) Working Group was initiated. The first meeting was in August 2002, set in the UK, hosted by the South African Government. A great deal of lobbying was initially involved to ensure the attendance of qualifications organisations, professional associations, and industry. At that meeting it was decided that a standards framework would be created that would provide a basis for mutual recognition of Project Management standards and certification. The GPBSPMP chose to take a different approach to standards creation than that taken by the Global Project Management Forums, PMI's market-based approach, or the IPMA's federated structure. It was decided that work on the development of global standards for project management practice "…should remain informal, independent of established professional associations" (Crawford, 2004b, p. 1399).

The typical approach to standards development in Project Management has been based on market dominance. However, as "… involvement in standardisation processes is accompanied by the danger that the other participants could use the disclosed and unprotected technological knowledge for their own purposes, R&D intensive companies whose knowledge is either insufficiently protected by IPR or extremely valuable may be reluctant to join standardisation processes" (Blind & Thumm, 2004, p. 62).

Companies which want a market lead ahead of competitors are often reluctant to join standardisation processes (Blind & Thumm, 2004, p. 69). Given that a market dominance approach to standards development was common in Project Management, it was necessary that the professional associations not feel that they were contributing to a standard which may compete with their own products.

The focus of the GPBSPMP was carefully selected. The most widely accepted of the Project Management standards focus on projects or organisations, not people (Crawford, 2004a, p. 1152). In the interests of achieving market dominance, the professional associations have had proprietary interest in restricting reciprocity between their standards and similar standards produced by other associations. By contrast, the standards which focus on people are part of national qualification frameworks, and governments, unlike the professional associations, have shown consistent interest in reciprocity between Project Management qualifications.

Project Management associations have proven to be very willing to share information regarding enabling processes and educational standards, while Project Management knowledge has been consistently regarded as more political. The different Project Management associations also tend to take proprietary positions concerning their bodies of knowledge, which are their primary "products." These observations influenced the approach taken by the GPBSPMP. It was decided that standards development would focus on people, rather than projects or organisations, and would focus on practice rather than knowledge. This provided the opportunity to harness national Governments' interest in reciprocity, while not appearing as a direct competitor to any of the products provided by the various professional associations.

Defining a standard and choosing the words with which it is to be described is a particularly significant political act. Defining appropriate categories and names in a situation is a process of "… deciding what will be visible or invisible within the system" (Bowker & Star, 1999, p. 44). In this case, effort was taken to define the GPBSPMP as outside the area of competitive concern of the established professional associations, as not running in the same race. Careful naming can be used as a deliberate tool of forgetting and for delegating attention (Bowker & Star, 1999, p. 280). By focusing on people and practice, the GPBSPMP could be classified as an outsider, and therefore thought of as harmless. As a result, the professional association could participate in the process without it being considered a potential threat.

The GPBSPMP decided to focus on performance-based standards. Standards already existed for the assessment of performance, with the UK, Australian, New Zealand, and South African governments having contributed considerable work to their development since the 1980s. Performance-based competency standards involve more' than a test of knowledge. Rather, the Competency standards approach assumes that competence can best be inferred from actual demonstrated performance at a pre-defined acceptable standard (Gonczi, et al., 1993). Such standards are arguably therefore more indicative of practical competence than typical knowledge-based minimum quality standards. Performancebased standards are a way of demonstrating competence gained through practice, such as on-the-job expertise. They provide a way for people who have not had the option to gain qualifications to demonstrate ability and have it formally recognised. As such, this has been a popular approach for governments concerned with equity.

Learning from previous attempts to create global Project Management standards which had been subverted by internal politics, a monetary fee was used as a constraint for entry to the GPBSPMP. Different fees were applicable to organisations and to individuals. Fees were structured to make participation substantially more costly for individuals not representing a subscribing organisation, and subscribing organisations generally were very careful about whom they would allow to represent them. This helped to create a pool of personnel dedicated to, and experienced in, standards development. Participation fees also provided funding, which meant that the process could remain independent of existing associations.

A series of working sessions was initiated, typically involving from 15 to 20 individuals. Organisations who have subscribed and/or sent representatives, excluding those who have specifically requested not to be mentioned, are summarised in Table 2. Table 2 was composed based on internal documentation, after the eighth working session.

All labour on the project was voluntary, excluding secretarial support. It quickly became clear that most progress was achieved while participants were together, so to maximise this,

working sessions typically lasted for three days, occurring at least biannually. The process used by the GPBSPMP was as close as possible to ANSI processes and those of the various participating qualifications bodies, in order to facilitate acceptance. This process started with a complete review of existing project management standards.

Primarily the same groups and individuals were involved throughout the development process. Early on the group established a very strong culture focused on cooperation and work. New people were very quickly absorbed into this culture. Political issues were consciously, vocally, and explicitly put aside. Often there was compromise to make the group happy. The focus was on cooperation and producing a good product. The group would be dedicated to the work for three days at a time, with the social aspect of the meeting providing an important focus for creating a strong culture within the group. As many issues were resolved over the dinner table as at a whiteboard.

One of the few areas of political contention related to nomenclature. This can again be related

Table 2. Organisations which subscribed and/or sent representatives

Standards and qualifications organisations	Professional associations	Academic/training institutions	Industry
• Innovation and Business Skills Australia • New Zealand Qualifications Authority • Project Management Standards Generating Body • Services SETA	• American Society for the Advancement of Project Management • Association for Project Management • China Project Management Association • International Project Management Association • Japan Project Management Association • Project Management Institute • Project Management South Africa • Society of Project Managers, Singapore	• Athabasca University • Cambridge International Examinations • Cranfield University • ESC Lille • Middlesex University • University of Southern Queensland • University of Technology, Sydney	• American Express • Living Planit • Motorola • Project Performance Group • Project Services Queensland

back to the importance of an awareness of classification, and its effect on perceived boundaries, as mentioned earlier. In the UK, performance-based standards are referred to as occupational standards, but the use of the term "occupation" was thought by some to be lowering the image of the profession to that of a trade. "Competency" was rejected as a possible descriptor, due to the fears of participants from one country that the standards would imply behaviour and provide grounds for litigation. An interim result was "Global Performance Based Standards for Project Management," but it was thought that this would encompass the organisational and project levels, so "Personnel" was added, resulting in the unwieldy acronym which persisted for the majority of the development process.

Two years, and six working sessions after the work by the GPBSPMP was started, a draft standard was released for public review. At this point, the larger professional associations who already had their own standards and qualifications processes started to withdraw from the development process. Common excuses were that they were "Reviewing their strategy," "Did not have sufficient volunteer labour," and were worried that "Participation sent mixed messages to their membership." At about the same time, one of the professional associations raised concerns regarding the last three letters of the GPBSPMP acronym, which were reminiscent of the name of one of their existing products. This provided the opportunity to adopt a simpler and preferable name—GAPPS (Global Alliance for Project Performance Standards).

Over 100 reviews for the draft standard were received from members of the public. Comments were sorted by the various sections to which they pertained. An adjudication panel was convened to review and decide upon actions in response to comments, on the understanding that unanimous agreement by the panel on actions to be taken was necessary. Reviewers were notified of actions taken in response to their comments. A process to handle appeals to actions was initiated, with all public reviewers given a right to appeal decisions.

After three years and eight working sessions the GAPPS Global Project Management Framework has been released, and is currently being piloted by a major global corporation. Standards and qualifications bodies involved are addressing their respective local approval processes, with a view towards general adoption as a basis for reciprocity. Similarly, national or other professional associations who don't have their own standards products are currently in the process of examining its suitability and the possibility of adopting it.

CONCLUSION

Two significant differences stand out when comparing the development of the GAPPS standard with more common Project Management standards. First, the standard has been developed as a process of negotiation and joint modification, as opposed to the usual market dominance approach used in Project Management standards development.

Second, minimum quality standards have often been used as a way of ensuring profits for the standards-setting organisation, which then has the opportunity to act as a gatekeeper to those who wish to obtain the professional certification or licensure. Many of the Project Management professional associations could be accused of trying to use such a position to secure a monopoly. A different approach has been adopted in the creation of the GAPPS standard, which, if anything, has been designed to counter any emerging monopoly by focusing on being a basis for reciprocity between existing Project Management standards.

Permission is granted in the standard for distribution, use, modification, publication, and translation of the standard free of charge, although copyright is maintained by GAPPS. GAPPS is making no attempt to act as gatekeepers to the standard. The main benefits to those involved in the production process have been access to developing knowledge and potential increase in reputation through association with the project.

The standard can be seen as an attempt to further the profession, by providing opportunities for countries without existing standards to have a basis for creation of their own and by creating a global basis for professional reciprocity. Open source software has so far had a considerable influence on the software development community. Only time will tell what influence the first open access standard for Project Management will have on its community.

REFERENCES

APM. (2006). *Body of knowledge: Version 5.* High Wycombe, UK: Association of Project Managers.

APM. (2005). Association for project management overview. Retrieved August 24, 2005 from, http://www.apm.org.uk/page.asp?categoryID=3&subCategoryID=21&pageID=0

Baskin, E., Krechmer, K., & Sherif, M. (1998). The six dimensions of standards: Contributions towards a theory of standardization. In L. Lefebvre, R. Mason, , & T. Khalil (Eds.), *Management of technology, sustainable developments and eco-efficiency.* Amsterdam: Elsevier, pp. 53-62.

Benham, L. (1980). The demand for occupational licensure. In S. Rottenberg (Ed.), *Occupational licensure and regulation.* US: American Enterprise Institute for Public and Policy Research, pp. 13-25.

Blind, K., & Thumm, N. (2004). Intellectual property protection and standardization. *International Journal of IT Standards & Standardization Research, 2*(2), 61-75.

Blum, U. (2005). Lessons from the past: Public standardization in the spotlight. *International Journal of IT Standards & Standardization Research, 3*(1), 1-20.

Bowker, G., & Star, S. (1999). *Sorting things out: Classification and its consequences.* London: MIT Press.

Boyatzis, R.E. (1982). *The competent manager: A model for effective performance.* New York: Wiley.

Bredillet, C. (2003). Genesis and role of standards: Theoretical foundations and socio-economical model for the construction and use of standards. *International journal of Project Management, 21*(6), 463-470.

Brown, D. (2005). Raise HR's stature by raising the bar for qualification. *Canadian HR Reporter, 18*(6), 5-8.

Carey, J. (1953). Uniform standards for professional qualifications. *Journal of Accountancy, 95,* 36-37.

Cegielski, C. (2004). Who values technology certification? *Communications of the ACM, 47*(10), 103-105.

Cegielski, C., Rebman, C., & Reithel, B. (2003). The value of certification: An empirical assessment of the perceptions of end-users of local area networks. *Information Systems Journal, 13,* 97-107.

Clarkson, K., & Muris, T. (1980). The federal trade commission and occupational regulation. In S. Rottenberg (Ed.), *Occupational licensure and regulation. .* US: American Enterprise Institute for Public and Policy Research, pp. 107-141.

Crawford, L. (2004a). Global body of project management knowledge and standards. J. Pinto,

& G. Morris (Eds.), *The wiley guide to managing projects*. New York: Wiley, 1150-1196.

Crawford, L. (2004b). Professional associations and global initiatives. J. Pinto, & G. Morris (Eds.), *The wiley guide to managing projects*. New York: Wiley, 1389-1402.

Dean, P.J. (1997). Examining the profession and the practice of business ethics. .*Journal of Business Ethics, 16*, 1637-1649.

Duncan, W.R. (1998). Presentation to council of chapter presidents. *PMI Annual Symposium*. October 10, Long Beach, CA, USA.

ECITB. (2002). *National occupational standards for project management: Pre-launch version*. Kings Langley: Engineering Construction Industry Training Board.

ENAA. (2002). *P2M: A guidebook of project & program management for enterprise innovation: Summary translation. Revision 1*. Tokyo, Japan: Project Management Professionals Certification Center (PMCC).

Friedman, M. (1962). Capitalism & freedom. Chicago: University of Chicago Press.

George, T. (2002). Employees raise the bar on certification. *Information Week, 896*, 76-77.

Glassie, J. (2003). Certification programs as a reflection of competency. *Association Management, 55*(6), 17-18.

Gonczi, A., Hager, P., & Athanasou, J. (1993). *The development of competency-based assessment strategies for the professions*. Canberra, Australia: Australian Government Publishing Service.

Heywood, L., Gonczi, A., & Hager, P. (1992). *A guide to development of competency standards for professions*. Canberra, Australia: Australian Government Publishing Service.

IPMA. (1999). G. Caupin, H. Knopfel, P. Morris, E. Motzel, & O. Pannenbacker (Eds.). *ICB:*

IPMA competence baseline, Version 2. Germany: International Project Management Association.

IPMA. (2003). *Research and development*. www.ipma.ch/

ISO. (1997). *ISO 10006: 1997: Quality management: Guidelines to quality in project management*. Geneva: International Organization for Standardization.

JEDEC. (2004). White paper: The vital role of standard-setting organizations and the necessity of good faith and fair play among participants. *JEDEC 2004 Symposium: The Future of Standards Setting, Legal, Marketplace and Consumer Implications*. Available at: http://www.standardsconference.org/docs/WhitePaper_1-14-05.pdf

Krechmer, K. (2004). Standardization and innovation policies in the information age. *International Journal of IT Standards & Standardization Research, 2*(2), 49-60.

Leffler, K. (1980). Commentary. In S. Rottenberg (Ed.), *Occupational licensure and regulation*. USA: American Enterprise Institute for Public and Policy Research, 287-295.

Leland, H. (1979). Quacks, lemons, and licensing: A theory of minimum quality standards. *Journal of Political Economy, 87*(6), 1328-1346.

Leland, H. (1980). Minimum-quality standards and licensing in markets with asymetric information. In S. Rottenberg (Ed.), *Occupational licensure and regulation*. USA: American Enterprise Institute for Public and Policy Research, 265-284.

Lenn, M.P. (1997). Introduction. In M.P. Lenn, & L. Campos (Eds.), *Globalization of the professions and the quality imperative: Professional accreditation, certification and licensure*. Madison WI: Magna Publications, Inc.

Morris, P.W.G. (1994). *The management of projects*. London: Thomas Telford.

Muriithi, N., & Crawford, L. (2003). Approaches to project management in Africa: Implications for international development projects. *International Journal of Project Management, 21,* 309-319.

National Commission on Excellence in Education. (1983). A nation at risk: The imperative for educational reform. Washington, US: Government Printing Office (Accessed online at: http://www.ed.gov/pubs/NatAtRisk/findings.html).

Pells, D.L. (1996). Introduction. In J.S. Pennypacker (Ed.), *The global status of the project management profession.* Sylva, NC: PMI Communications, , ix–xii.

PMI. (2003a). *PMI chapters outside the United States.* Retrieved June 26, 2003 from, www.pmi.org/info/GMC ChapterListingOutsideUS.asp#P128 1923

PMI. (2003b). PMI Sydney chapter. Retrieved June 26, 2003 from, http://sydney.pmichapters-australia.org.au/

PMI. (2004). A guide to the project management body of knowledge. PA, US: Project Management Institute.

PMI. (2005a). *PMI chapters.* Retrieved August 24, 2005 from, http://www.pmi.org/prod/groups/public/documents/info/gmc_chaptersoverview.asp

PMI. (2005b). *PMI project management standards program.* Retrieved August 24, 2005 from, http://www.pmi.org/prod/groups/public/documents/info/pp_pmstandardsprogram.asp

PMI. (2006). Project management institute fact sheet. Retrieved March 9, 2006 from, http://www.pmi.org/info/GMC_MemberFACTSheetJan06.pdf

Schrage, M. (2004). Hiding behind certification: An over-reliance on IT sheepskins is a recipe for disaster. *CIO, 17*(17), 1.

Sobel, J. (2001). On the dynamics of standards. *RAND Journal of Economics, 32*(4), 606-623.

Steele, R. (2004). Standards as an indicator of maturity? ... and an opportunity for customer and industry advantage? *International Journal of IT Standards & Standardization Research, 2*(1), 42-45.

Stern, R. (2001). More standardization skullduggery. *IEEE Micro, 21*(4), 12-15,69.

Stretton, A. (1994). A short history of project management: Part one: the 1950s and 60s. *Australian Project Manager, 14*(1), 36-7.

van Wegberg, M. (2004). Standardization and competing consortia: The trade-off between speed and compatibility. *International Journal of IT Standards & Standardization Research, 2*(2), 18-33.

Warner, A. (2003). Block alliances in formal standard setting environments. *International Journal of IT Standards & Standardization Research, 1*(1), 1-18.

Wolfson, A., Trebilcock, M., & Tuohy, C. (1980). Regulating the professions: A theoretical framework. In S. Rottenberg (Ed.), *Occupational licensure and regulation. US: American Enterprise Institute for Public and Policy Research,* pp. 180-214.

This work was previously published in International Journal of IT Standards and Standardization Research, Vol. 6, Issue 1, edited by K. Jakobs, pp. 70-95, copyright 2008 by IGI Publishing, formerly known as Idea Group Publishing (an imprint of IGI Global).

Chapter XIX
Politics, Accountability, and Information Management

Bruce Rocheleau
Northern Illinois University, USA

ABSTRACT

This chapter provides examples of the politics of managing information in public organizations by studying both its internal and external aspects. Within the organization, politics is involved in structuring decision making, struggles over purchases of hardware and software, interdepartmental sharing of information, and the flow of communications such as e-mail among employees. The chapter analyzes examples of each of these internal aspects of politics. The chapter also discusses evidence concerning whether political appointees or career administrators are more effective as information managers. Externally, the chapter discusses how information management has been used to attempt to achieve greater political accountability through e-reporting and examples of cases where purchasing problems spill over into the realm of external politics such as through attempts to privatize governmental information management function. Certain topics such as municipal broadband systems and information management disasters are highly likely to involve information managers in politics. The attempts to use governmental Web sites as mechanisms to achieve e-governance and greater citizen participation in the political process also make it impossible for information managers to insulate themselves against politics.

INTRODUCTION

The message of this chapter is that information management has always been political and will become increasingly political due to several important trends that are occurring. First of all, information technology has become a central aspect of organizations, so more people care about it. This high interest can lead to struggles over strategic and operational issues. Second, there are emerging issues that push technology into areas that are potentially fraught with politics. For example, many local governments are interested in establishing governmentally supported broadband and wireless areas and these efforts have already resulted in major political battles with more likely to come. Also, information management is viewed as a method of obtaining increased citizen participation in the political process through various electronic mechanisms such as governmentally supported online e-governance mechanisms such as online rule-making dockets, public Listservs, public blogs, and other forms of computer-mediated communication (CMC). Each of these mechanisms has the potential to achieve positive goals, but they are also fraught with potential for generating political conflict. The underlying premise of this chapter is that information is power and consequently information management is inherently political. Information asymmetries give an advantage of one actor over others (Bellamy, 2000). Maintaining control over information can allow individuals, departments, and organizations to control how successful they appear to others and thus may protect autonomy, job security, and funding. Therefore, in order to provide effective leadership for IT, the generalist and head IT manager will need to actively engage themselves in both internal and external politics. An excellent case illustrating the importance of political issues in managing IT occurred in California. The California Department of Information Technology (DOIT) was eliminated in June of 2002 (Peterson, 2002). The department had been created in 1995 in order to solve the problem of several disastrous contracts in the IT area including a Department of Motor Vehicles (DMV) project that cost over $50 million but never functioned as planned (Peterson). Peterson cites accounts from observers to support the argument that a major reason for the failure was due to the other major agencies that viewed the new department as a threat to their power and lobbied to reduce the authority of the agency in the legislation creating it. In particular, the opponents lobbied to deny the new DOIT control over operations in the legislation creating DOIT. Those with interests opposed to the new DOIT included existing departments that had major authority in the IT field and/or those with large

data centers. The opposition was successful so that the legislation limited DOIT's role mainly to authority over the budget. Consequently, the DOIT did not have control over data centers and was not able to achieve one of its major goals to centralize and consolidate these data centers (Peterson). This lack of operational authority limited its ability to influence other departments as Peterson summarizes:

Without controlling data centers or California's telecommunications network, DOIT simply had no juice, some sources argued. Because DOIT didn't add value to other state agencies, it couldn't exert any leverage on those agencies. DOIT could present ideas, but it couldn't make any real contribution to making those ideas happen. In other words, with the Department of Finance controlling IT budget processes, the Department of General Services controlling IT procurement and the state data centers handling computing needs, what was the DOIT's responsibility?

Also, according to observers, the head of DOIT was not allowed to sit in on cabinet meetings and there were reported cases of other departments doing "end arounds" concerning the formal requirement for DOIT to approve all major new projects. Another symbol of the weakness of the DOIT was that the governor appointed a new head of e-government who was independent of the DOIT, again lending credence to the perception that the DOIT lacked respect and power. The precipitating event in the death of DOIT was the quick approval by DOIT of a controversial project with the Oracle Corporation that resulted in an investigation and the resignation of several of the state's top IT officials. The California case illustrates how IT can become enmeshed in both internal and external political issues that I will analyze in this chapter.

In some cases such as those above, politics appears to refer to actions that tend to be viewed by outside observers as narrow-minded and self-serving. However, it is important to note that I use the term politics in a nonjudgmental manner. Politics can be about money and the "mobilization of bias" as Schattschneider (1983) described it as different forces struggle to prevail. However, politics can also be thought of as the attempt to mobilize resources to achieve public objectives and thus a necessary part of implementing any major project. I agree with Dickerson (2002, p. 52) that politics need not be a "lot of nasty back-stabbing and infighting" but is most often about "working and negotiating with others ... to get things done." It can be as simple as practicing good communication skills to keep others informed.

Although information management involves many technical issues, it is important to understand that it involves major political challenges. A large portion of governmental information managers come from technical backgrounds such as computer science and business. They usually have excellent technical skills and they can quickly rise to leadership positions such as chief information officer (CIO). However, decision making concerning the management of information technology requires more than technical knowledge as Towns (2004) notes: "There's increasing talk that CIO's don't need to be technologists because the position's nature is changing. Project management skills and people skills now mean more to a CIO than IT skills, the argument goes ..."

The most important critical success factors involve organizational and political skills that the technologically skilled often lack; however, these skills can be learned. In this chapter, I identify some of the key political problems that are likely to be faced. Many technical staff dislike politics and try to avoid dealing with political dilemmas. Molta (1999, p. 23) says, "engineers and programmers frequently appear oblivious to the strategic issues that keep management awake at night." He goes on to state that managing information technology is "the most politicized issue of the modern organization" and that technical staff "need to get in the game." Refraining from

politics will lead to more serious problems and result in ineffective management of information technology.

Before the days of the World Wide Web and electronic government, managers and user departments often deferred computing decisions to technical staff because information management was not central to the organization (Lucas, 1984); generalist managers had little knowledge to contest decisions made by technicians. Now, since the information system has become a central concern, user departments often have their own technical staff, and generalist managers may become "technical junkies" (Molta, 1999, p. 24) who keep abreast of technological trends. The result is that information management is a much more prominent issue and the potential to become the source of disagreement. Consequently, technical skills themselves are not sufficient to be effective for information managers to achieve their goals. A study (Overton, Frolick, & Wilkes, 1996) of the implementation of executive information systems found that political concerns were perceived as the biggest obstacles to success. Many people felt threatened by the installation of such systems for a variety of reasons including fears of loss of their jobs and increased "executive scrutiny" (Overton et al., p. 50). Feldman (2002) also sees politics as one of the biggest challenges for technical managers. Feldman (2002, p. 46) observed that technicians often adopt a "bunker mentality" on important technology decisions and fail to take effective steps to achieve their goals. Peled (2000) also argues that information technology leaders need to bolster their politicking skills to boost the rate of their success. A survey (Anonymous, 1994) of over 500 British managers revealed that the majority believe that information flows were constrained by politics and that individuals use information politics for their own advancement. In short, the effective use of political skills is an important component of effective information management.

Over the past decade, computing has become much more important in governmental as well as private organizations. Major decisions about computing have always involved politics. Detailed studies of cities in the 1970s (Laudon, 1974) and 1980s (Danziger, Dutton, Kling, & Kraemer, 1982) demonstrate several cases involving computing and politics. However, computing was less central to public organizations then. Most employees had minimal contact with computing but now routinely employ computer technology in many of their day-to-day practices. They use e-mail, the Internet, and a variety of computer modules to accomplish their tasks. Computing is a central part of their jobs and they care about technology. The development of e-government and the Internet has greatly broadened the end users of governmental information systems so that now they include citizens and groups such as contractors. Information technology now is employed to provide greater forms of accountability to the public such as using computers to derive sophisticated assessments of performance and posting performance measures on the Internet. Many elected chief executives such as governors wanted to be associated with information technology. Coursey (in press) points out, for example, that Jeb Bush wants to be known as an "e-governor." As a result, information technology decisions are more complex and subject to the influence of external politics.

I analytically differentiate the politics of information management into two major categories: (a) internal organizational politics concerning issues involving organizational members and (b) external politics concerning how the governmental organization relates to its councils or boards, other organizations, external groups, and general citizenry. However, these two forms of politics frequently overlap and influence each other as they did in the California case. I will not be providing many prescriptions to managers on how to behave politically, not only because research about politics is sketchy but also due to the fact that politics is highly contextual. The course of action that should be pursued depends on the complex interplay of political resources of the actors involved, ethical concerns, and legal issues, as well as economic and technical factors. My purpose is to sensitize information managers and generalist administrators to major political issues that are likely to affect IT decisions. I outline examples of both successful and unsuccessful strategies that managers have employed to deal with information politics.

SOURCES

This chapter makes use of my own experiences as well as drawing on literature concerning public information management. I found very little formal research in recent years that explicitly focuses on the politics of internal information management. This aspect has not changed since I wrote earlier versions of this chapter. There is a rapidly growing literature on the use of external issues such as the use of the Internet to spur political involvement among citizens. However, my experience shows that internal political issues continue to be pervasive and important for IT managers; most of the major and rigorous academic studies concerning the politics of computing remain those from the mainframe era (e.g., Danziger, 1977; Dutton & Kraemer, 1985). Before IT became pervasive, these early studies by the "Irvine group" demonstrated that political and social factors generally affected how technology was structured and used (e.g., Northrop, Kraemer, Dunkle, & King, 1990). Due to its lack of coverage in traditional academic journals, I make use of periodicals such as computer magazines and newspaper articles concerning computing. Also, many of my examples are based on 25 years of experience in the IT field and also my study of public organizations at the municipal, state, and federal levels.

INFORMATION SYSTEMS AND INTERNAL ORGANIZATIONAL POLITICS

Although almost any decision about computing can become embroiled in politics, my experience is that the most prominent and important political issues involve questions of control and power over the following kinds of decisions.

1. **Information management structures:** How should information management be structured? Where should control over information be placed in the organizational structure? A related issue concerns what kind of background is most effective preparation for technology department heads—technological or political?

2. **Hardware and software acquisitions:** What should be the nature of the process? How centralized should it be? Who should be involved? Should outsourcing be used? Should open-source or other preferences be mandated?

3. **Information management, information sharing, and interdepartmental relations:** What process should be used to determine information sharing and exchange? How will computing influence and be influenced by other aspects of interdepartmental and inter-organizational IT issues? How can obstacles to sharing information be overcome?

4. **Managing personnel and communication flows:** How does computing influence employee relations and communication flows? What, if any, rules and procedures should be established? How do e-mail and other forms of CMC influence communication and organizational politics? How does information technology influence the careers of organizational members?

Although each of these issues has technical aspects, nontechnical issues such as concerns about autonomy and power often prevail. Below, I outline how each of these decision areas involves important political aspects. Many information managers prefer to avoid these political aspects. Likewise, generalist managers such as city managers have often ignored direct involvement in these decisions due to their lack of expertise concerning computers. As a consequence, it has been my experience that persons other than information system or generalist managers often dominate these decisions. Consequently, these issues are often decided without adequate attention from those with the most expertise or broadest perspective.

Information Management Structures

There is no consensus as to the best method of organizing computing. How centralized or decentralized should computing be? There are advantages and disadvantages to the centralization of computing: One major review of the centralization-decentralization debate (King, 1983) concluded that political factors are paramount in decisions on how to structure computing. Business organizations have encountered the same dilemma. Markus (1983) has described how business departments have resisted efforts toward the integration of information systems. Davenport, Eccles, and Prusak (1992) found several reasons behind information politics, including the following: (a) Units that share information fully may lose their reason for existence, and (b) weak divisions may be reluctant to share information when they are sensitive about their performance. Overall, in recent years, there has been an emphasis on the centralization of authority as organizations move toward an enterprise-wide approach in which databases are centrally organized and standards govern the hardware and software systems of organizations.

Where should computing be placed in the organizational structure of a public organization such as a city? Should it be a separate line department, a subunit of another department (e.g., budgeting and finance), or a staff unit to the manager or mayor? Should mayors or managers require that the head of computing report directly to them, or should they place a staff member in charge? Except for small organizations, the centrality of today's computing to all departments would suggest that information management should be in a separate unit and not be structurally placed under another department such as budget and finance. There has been a strong movement at the federal and state levels to establish a CIO to deal with problems of technological issues that cut cross-departmental boundaries and to head efforts at building corporate-wide e-government and intranet systems (Fabris, 1998). However, managers, both computing and generalist, need to think carefully about the implications of these different arrangements and which structure is most likely to meet the needs of the organization. Decisions concerning the structure will be based on a number of factors including the degree of interest of the generalist managers in computing as well as what goals managers have for IT.

Molta (1999, p. 23) defines politics as the "allocation of resources within an organization." Some departments will want to control their own computing as much as possible through hiring their own IT staff. Eiring (1999, p. 17) defines politics as the "art of negotiation, compromise, and satisfaction," and urges information management staff to form strategic alliances that are beneficial to the IT cause and to "nurture them as one would a good lasting friendship" (p. 19). Feldman (2002, p. 46) warns that "when departments are doing their own thing—namely hiring their own IT staff—a central IT department is in political trouble." He goes on to point out that hiring a staff implies unhappiness with the services of the central IT unit. However, in many organizations, it has been common and perhaps necessary for line departments to have staff dedicated to IT. For example, police departments often have their own dedicated systems and staff because of the early

development of police information systems, the centrality of computer searches to their function, and the need to have secure and easy exchange with other police departments. When non-IT-department IT staff exist, one political issue is how they should relate to the central IT staff. Feldman (p. 48) argues that the smart strategy is for the central IT staff to offer "to exchange information and support" with non-IT-department staff. By taking these steps, Feldman argues that they can at least establish "dotted line relationships." Feldman argues further that these non-IT-department technological staff are often isolated and appreciate the support from the central IT department. Anderson, Bikson, Lewis, Moini, and Strauss (2003) found examples of dotted-line relationships in states like Pennsylvania where the formal authority of the state IT head over state agencies was weak: "Additionally, all agency CIO's have a 'dotted line' relationship to the state CIO even though they formally report to their own agency heads; they meet quarterly with him" (p. 23). The only alternative is to try to control all computing from the central IT department, but this strategy can either work very well or turn out to be a disaster (Feldman).

A major rationale for the existence of a CIO (as opposed to a traditional data-processing manager) is that he or she will not be restricted to technical issues but act as a change agent, politician, proactivist, and integrator as well (Pitkin, 1993). The federal government (Koskinen, 1996; Pastore, 1995) has firmly established the use of CIOs in order to improve information management. Will it have a positive impact? Should the CIO model be followed in municipalities and other public organizations? Merely assigning the CIO title does not ensure that these functions will be performed. For example, a study (Pitkin) of CIOs in universities found that, despite their title, CIOs did not view themselves as executives and often do not perform nontechnical roles. Without a push from a CIO, public organizations may fail to make good use of information technology. For example, one study found that police regularly used their database systems for reports to external agencies but rarely for internal management purposes (Rocheleau, 1993). CIOs and centralized information structures help to fix responsibility and that can mean that they themselves become targets of unhappiness with technological decisions. There are many cases in which CIOs in the private sector have not been viewed favorably by their fellow managers (Freedman, 1994), and CIOs in both the public and private sector are blamed for failures (Cone, 1996; Newcombe, 1995).

With the growth and importance of IT, organizations of moderate to larger size now tend to have an independent IT department (Gurwitt, 1996) because IT is now viewed as infrastructure serving everyone and should not be under control of any single department. Also, because there is now a strong acceptance of the need to have as much standardization of hardware and software as possible, the IT unit is often vested with final approval over major purchasing decisions. However, the California case shows that this centralizing trend is not inevitable or necessarily linear. According to Peterson (2002), the structure recommended to replace the State Department of Information Technology was to decentralize, with the authority of the extinguished department being reassigned to the finance and general-services departments. By way of contrast, a study by Rand Institute researchers (Anderson et al., 2003) recommended a more powerful and centralized department to replace California's deposed DOIT. However, it is interesting to note that the Rand Institute researchers studied the governance structures of four other states and found that some of the states (e.g., Illinois) had IT structures that were weak in formal authority but nevertheless worked effectively due to the fact that the IT leadership worked through brokering relationships. Likewise, according to the Rand study, Pennsylvania's system does not vest strong authority in the state CIO, but it depends on successful dotted-line relationships.

Their conclusion is that there is no one best way to organize and that CIOs who have weak formal authority can use their negotiating and brokering skills to be successful. They also argue that management style is important. Successful state IT managers have a style that is "participative, collaborative," and emphasizes positive "carrots" rather than "sticks" in seeking change (Anderson et al., p. ix). In the California case, the politics of IT involved the legislature and also key vendors, so IT leaders have to practice their communication and political skills on key external as well as internal constituencies. Recently, the head of the National Association of State Chief Information Officers (NASCIO) reported that several state CIOs had told him that they preferred not to report directly to the governor because they wanted to focus on operational issues and avoid partisan politics (Towns, 2005).

In my experience, there is a wide variety in the amount of attention devoted by generalist managers to structural issues concerning computing. In one city, a city manager was very much focused on information management and devoted great attention to decisions made concerning computing by the city, in effect acting as the municipality's CIO. His focus on information technology enabled him to establish a positive reputation for innovation that helped to secure his next job. When this manager left for another city, he was replaced by another manager who was not especially interested in computing. Devoting great attention to computing can be both productive and counterproductive. The first manager who was heavily involved in computing decisions became embroiled in severe struggles with his new board and organization over IT issues that contributed to his resignation from his new job.

Although there is no single right way of organizing computing, each manager needs to ensure that the structure will provide relevant, timely, and reliable information. Kraemer and King (1976) argue that public executives spend too much of their time on decisions concerning the purchase of equipment and too little on other important information management issues that have less visibility but are equally important. Kraemer and King emphasize the need for generalist managers to take personal responsibility for computing and to be engaged in the following decisions: how to structure computing, the purposes to be served by computing, and implementation issues such as the goals of computing and the structures used to achieve them.

Some experts (e.g., Severin, 1993) argue that the chief executive officer (CEO) of an organization should also be the true CIO. The former mayor of Indianapolis, Stephen Goldsmith, is an example of a CEO who took charge of the information technology function and instituted a number of important policy changes such as privatizing many IT functions as well as encouraging e-mail from any employees directly to himself (Poulos, 1998). A related issue concerns the question of to what extent the head of IT needs to have a technical background. John Kost (1996) was appointed to be CIO of the state of Michigan by Governor Engler and instituted several policy goals of Engler's such as the consolidation of state data centers, the establishment of statewide standards, and the reengineering of IT including its procurement process. It is notable that Kost did not have any IT background at all (Kost). Kost maintains that it is more important that the CIO understand the business of government than have a strong technology background. Kost proceeded to do a major reengineering of IT in Michigan and claims that they successfully achieved many of the goals set by Engler. However, if the CIO does not possess strong technological skills as well as institutional knowledge about the IT system, he or she will need to have trusted and reliable staff who do have such skills in order to have the trust and respect of client agencies. One of the problems with the California DOIT was that it had little operational authority and was primarily an oversight agency. Thus, one of the recommendations of Anderson et al. (2003, p. 53) is to "transfer the majority of

people with technical skills" from the finance and other departments to the new IT department so that it would be "properly staffed and positioned to provide technical approval."

Paul Strassmann served as director of defense information at the defense department from 1991 to 1993 where he was in charge of a $10 billion annual budget for IT and instituted major changes in the procurement process. Strassmann (1995) subsequently published a book entitled *The Politics of Information Management* in which he argues that managing IT is "primarily a matter of politics and only secondarily a matter of technology" (p. xxv). Strassmann goes on to hold that only the technical aspects of information can be safely delegated to computer specialists. He supports a "federalist approach to information management, delegating maximum authority to those who actually need to use the information" (p. xxix). Strassmann (1995) believes that it is the duty of the CEO to establish general principles: "Without a general consensus about the principles and policies of who does what, when, and how, you cannot create a foundation on which to construct information superiority" (p. 10). He says that the CEO should never delegate the responsibility for information management to a CIO because it is the CEO who must decide how to apply information systems.

In a majority of organizations of large size, there tends to be one or more advisory committees or groups set to assist the IT head in making decisions. In my experience, these advisory groups tend to fall into three categories: (a) end-user groups involving end users who are especially engaged in IT, (b) representatives of departments served by the IT department, who may or may not be heavy end users, and (c) external people who have substantial experience in IT. In Anderson et al.'s (2003) study of four states that are regarded as having successful IT departments (New York, Pennsylvania, Virginia, and Illinois), the state IT units generally had both internal groups made up of the line departments who represent the end users of IT and an external group consisting of private-sector IT heads who provided their expertise. I have known municipalities to use the same approach, and one municipal IT head told me of how the private-sector committee saved their community money with their advice about telecommunications strategy to obtain low-cost services from vendors. A politically adept CIO can make good use of these committees to build her or his political base.

Comparison of Politically Appointed vs. Career Administrators

As I have documented above, political skills are a necessary component of IT management. This has been documented at the federal level in studies of the jobs of federal CIOs carried out by the United States General Accounting Office (U.S. GAO, 2004). Given the importance of politics, would we expect politically appointed or career administrators to be more effective? The GAO study has some support for both positions. The GAO publication outlined what most CIOs considered to be major challenges, and they all involve the use of political skills: (a) implementing effective IT management, (b) obtaining sufficient and relevant resources, (c) communicating and collaborating internally and externally, and (d) managing change.

According to the GAO (2004) report, many thought that politically appointed CIOs would be more successful because they have more clout and access. However, others thought that skilled career administrators would be more successful because "they would be more likely to understand the agency and its culture" (p. 23). Another variable is that politically appointed CIOs (in federal agencies) had a shorter tenure of 19 months vs. 33 months for the career administrator, and the career administrators thought that this gave them a significant advantage because it can take a good deal of time to accomplish major tasks. Concerning their communication and collaboration skills, the

GAO report concluded that it is critical for CIOs to employ these abilities to form alliances and build friendships with external organizations:

Our prior work has shown the importance of communication and collaboration, both within an agency and with its external partners. For example, one of the critical success factors we identified in our CIO guide focuses on the CIO's ability to establish his or her organization as a central player in the enterprise. Specifically, effective CIO's—and their supporting organizations—seek to bridge the gap between technology and business by networking informally, forming alliances, and building friendships that help ensure support for information and technology management. In addition, earlier this year we reported that to be a high-performing organization, a federal agency must effectively manage and influence relationships with organizations outside of its direct control. (p. 30)

Concerning the management of change, the GAO report (2004) found six CIOs (from the private sector) who said that dealing with government culture and bureaucracy was a major challenge and that they had to marshal resources to overcome resistance. A subsequent report by Lewis (2005) comparing political and career federal managers (this concerned all managers, not just CIOs) found that career managers were more successful based on the Bush administration's Program Assessment Rating Tools. A *Federal Computer Week* analysis found that only 16 out of 27 CIOs in office in 2004 remained in office in November of 2005 (Lunn, 2005). The most common reasons for leaving the job were to obtain better pay (19%) and a change in administration (16%).

The *Federal Computer Week* magazine (Hasson, 2004) conducted a survey that obtained responses from 129 CIOs concerning the career vs. political issue and found similar results. Two thirds of the CIOs agreed that the political appointee would have better access and one third agreed that they would be able to raise the profile of the IT department. One former CIO argued that the political appointee could be more aggressive while the career administrator "had to find a champion" to push projects through the legislature. However, two thirds also thought that the career CIO would have a bigger impact because of the longer tenure. In 2004, there was a number of prominent CIOs who left high-profile public positions, including the top IT officers of the states of Virginia and Florida (Towns, 2004). It is safe to say that in order to be effective, regardless of whether they are political appointees or career administrators, people in these positions will need to exercise effective political skills. Peled (2000) presents two case studies involving information technology leaders in Israel. In one case, a prestigious scientist with outstanding technical skills was called in to solve transportation problems by employing computing technology. This technologist viewed his job in technical terms and attempted to develop a project without communicating with and building support from other key actors. He refused to share information with other departments working on related projects and consequently encountered resistance leading to his resignation and the end of the project. His failure was largely due to deficiencies in communication and lack of knowledge of organizational politics such as the need to obtain support from others in order to develop a project. Peled provides a second case study in which a leader without any major technical skills was able to solve serious problems of building a land-registry database. He used a training system to develop a core of users and people committed to the new database and negotiated with unions about wage demands for using the new system. This leader viewed his project in political terms from the very beginning and this approach helped him to achieve success. The importance of political skills in managing e-government has been confirmed by a study by Corbitt (2000) of the eight factors associated with the failure of e-government projects—only one of these concerned technical problems. The others included the absence of a champion of change, lack of managerial support and attention, poor attitudes toward the IT department, lack of education and training, and a discrepancy between IT staff and the end users of the system. I am not saying that IT skills are not important. Indeed, in the numerous small governments that have only a tiny number of staff, they cannot afford to hire a nontechnical IT manager. Nevertheless, even in these small organizations, political skills are also an essential component to IT leadership.

Politics and the Purchasing Process

As we saw in the California DOIT case, the failure of a large IT system can often embroil an organization in politics, and it is crucial that generalist managers take measures to avoid such disasters. An underlying assumption of the current information resources management theory is that an organization's information system should be aligned with its business goals. A related assumption is that generalist managers must be involved in procurement and other important decisions. They need to specify what goals and functions should be achieved by purchasing new software and hardware. Sandlin (1996, p. 11) argues that managers need to be on guard for "technological infatuation." The author points out that generalist managers would never let the transportation departments buy a line of expensive cars, but they often allow equivalent purchases in the IT area.

The failure of expensive new computer systems is likely to expose governmental managers to political attacks. Even if knowledge of the failure remains internal, unsuccessful systems can undermine central management, IT, and other departments involved. The problem often begins with the failure of the internal management of the projects. For example, the Federal Retirement Thrift Investment Board fired and sued its contractor, American Management Systems (AMS) of Fairfax, Virginia (Friel, 2001), for breach of contract. The contractor defended itself by stating that the board had not determined system needs even 3 years after the beginning of the contract (Friel, 2000). The determination of system needs is primarily a managerial issue. The pervasiveness of contract failures has led to what some refer to as a "contract crisis" (Dizard, 2001) with political consequences: "Thanks to new project management techniques, improved oversight, employee training, and contract controls, several state CIO's reported that project failures are decreasing. But they agreed that the *political cost of bungled projects remains high* [italics added]."

The U.S. General Accounting Office (2002) studied the Department of Defense Standard Purchasing System and found that 60% of the user population surveyed were dissatisfied with its functionality and performance. If a failed project has high visibility, then often external political issues also develop, but even if not visible to outsiders, failed purchases weaken the credibility of IT staff and thus the purchasing process is one of the most critical areas for managers and IT staff to negotiate.

As end-user computing has grown, end users have enjoyed the freedom to innovate and strong centrifugal forces have resulted. Employees often have strong personal preferences and feelings concerning software and hardware purchases. Part of the ethos of end-user computing is the ability to make your own decisions about software and hardware. Allowing each end user (or end-user department) to make decisions about software is likely to lead to multiple hardware and software platforms.

A potentially major source of politics is developing due to the conflict between open-source software and proprietary software packages such as those of Microsoft. Recently, the CIO of the state of Massachusetts issued a policy that only open-source software would be used and that proprietary software would be phased out by 2007 (Towns, 2005). Other state agencies (e.g., secretary of state) questioned the authority of the CIO to mandate such policies for other agencies, and the state legislature considered a bill that would set up a state task force that would have to approve such mandates (Towns). Microsoft attacked the open-source policy labeling it as discriminatory. The Massachusetts CIO later resigned though the state maintained that it would continue its movement toward the open-source requirement (Butterfield, 2005). The movement to establish enterprise-wide standards as well as the move to open-source software promises to make the jobs of those involved in establishing IT standards politically sensitive in the future.

There are other trade-offs between allowing each department to use its preferred software and hardware vs. centralization. Multiple platforms complicate training, backup, and maintenance, too. The existence of "platform zealots" is not unusual and can lead to conflict (Hayes, 1996). In my experience, these problems with multiple platforms have led certain managers toward establishing a single platform and also centralized control over hardware and software acquisitions. Barrett and Greene (2001) make the point that leaders need to convince the end users of the strong advantages and rationale for the standardization of hardware and software. If they fail to take this step, they are likely to encounter directly or indirectly passive resistance to their policies. In some cases, formal control of IT purchases by the IT department is impossible if the funding source for hardware and software is from another level of government (e.g., state or federal funding). Regardless of what approach is taken, information management and generalist administrators need to provide the centripetal force needed to integrate information management in public organizations. If they do not do it, no one else will. However, this integrating role often runs into stiff resistance and it requires that the manager use powers of persuasion, negotiation, bargaining, and sometimes authority and threats.

Many generalist managers may want to establish standard policies that influence the purchasing choices of departments, such as the following: (a) Some governments take a position that data-processing functions should be privatized as much as possible, (b) many governments have instituted online purchasing and forms of purchasing pools that departments may be required to adhere to, and (c) some governments are establishing special arrangements with a small number of computer vendors with the idea of achieving advantageous pricing arrangements. Both the federal and many state governments have been revamping the purchasing process with more emphasis on speed and emphasizing value rather than lowest cost (Rocheleau, 2000). Kost (1996) believes that the CIO and CEO need to take charge of the purchasing process if they are to achieve goals such as privatization and "value purchasing": "For example, a policy advocating privatization is doomed unless the purchasing process allows privatization to occur... An intransigent purchasing director can often do more to thwart the direction of the administration than a policy-maker from the opposite political party" (p. 8).

At the federal level, Strassmann (1995) implemented a corporate information management (CIM) initiative that was aimed at streamlining the military's information system purchases such as the use of the same systems across the different services. Strassmann enunciated the following principle that the technicians were expected to follow: Enhance existing information systems rather than "opt for new systems development as the preferred choice" (p. 94). In one case, this CIM approach killed an $800 million Air Force system and replaced it with a similar one that was used by the Army (Caldwell, 1992). The Air Force had already spent $28 million on their system and resisted the move. Observers of the process noted that it was a "turf issue" and a GAO report concluded that CIM required centralization and a cultural change that were difficult for the defense department (Caldwell, pp. 12-13).

The acquisition and implementation of new systems often engender resistance. One of the basic principles of planning for new computer systems is to involve the people who will be using the system in its design, testing, and implementation phases. Indeed, there are entire books written concerning the principles of participatory design (Kello, 1996). An apparent example of user resistance occurred in Chicago when a new computer system was introduced to speed the building-permit process. After the system was implemented, lengthy delays drew widespread criticism (Washburn, 1998) and the delays caused a bottleneck during a time of booming construction. The new system tracked permit applications and allowed the scanning of plumbing, electrical, and other plans so that the plans could be viewed simultaneously on several screens. There were some technical problems acknowledged by city officials. For example, some staff had trouble seeing plan details on their screens and on-the-spot corrections were not possible due to the fact that applicants were not present when reviews were done. However, officials argue that many of the complaints were due to the fact that the system had changed the process of handling permits. Permits are now done on a first-in-first-out basis compared to the previous situation where expediters used to "butt into line," and, consequently, they feared loss of influence under the new system (Washburn). The contention was that the expediters deliberately spread false rumors about extensive delays in an attempt to "torpedo the new system."

The desire to standardize can create political resistance. For example, vendors who target their products to municipal governments begin with a basic general ledger and finance product and then expand to develop modules for other functions such as the permit and other processes. Managers see advantages to using the same vendor for all of their different modules such as ensuring interoperability among them as well as gaining favorable financial terms. However, in this author's experience, vendors who have strong financial modules often are weak in other areas and thus the desire to standardize on one vendor's software can lead to problems with end users who do not like these other modules of the vendor. In such cases, it is clear that generalist and information system managers will have to be sensitive to organizational politics and either accept the need for diversity in vendors or employ their personal and political resources to achieve change.

Computing, Sharing Information, and the Politics of Interdepartmental Relations

In addition to purchasing issues, there are many other interdepartmental issues that need to be dealt with by CIOs and generalist managers in order to establish an effective information system. For example, computing creates the possibility of free and easy exchange of information among governmental organizations. However, information is power and organizations tend to be sensitive about giving out information to outsiders, especially if it reflects on the quality of the organization's operations. Many agencies prefer to maintain autonomy over their data. For example, the author worked on a project with the job training agency of a state agency that was to employ databases drawn from several state agencies to evaluate the state's job training programs. However, despite obtaining verbal agreements from the top managers of the agency, the lower level programming staff delayed the sharing of data for months. It became clear that they saw our requests as an additional burden on them that would make their job more difficult if such requests were to become routinized.

Building e-commerce systems usually requires the cooperation and sharing of information among a number of different departments. Corbitt (2000, p. 128) conducted a case study of an organization that developed an e-commerce system and found that there were "important political and interest differences" among the departments as well as "differences in perceptions" that caused

problems. In particular, Corbitt found competition between the data division and the e-commerce group about what needed to be done and who should exert leadership over it. Corbitt (p. 128) concludes that power is a "very substantial issue affecting implementation success."

Some new technologies such as geographic information systems (GISs) are forcing changes in computing structures and procedures among departments. Generalist managers may need to act to ensure that appropriate new structures are established. For example, although many geographic information systems are initiated by a single department, the systems are expensive and the software is relevant to many different departments. When Kansas City decided to build a GIS (Murphy, 1995), they found it necessary to form a GIS committee (made up of representatives of four participating departments—public works, water, city development, and finance) to conduct an interdepartmental needs assessment and resolve problems such as how to resolve conflicts in databases and how to minimize database development costs. Although such developments do force structural changes, there is still wide latitude in regard to the nature of the structure. Sharing data can lead to conflict. In a study of the exchange of information between municipal departments such as fire and police, this author (Rocheleau, 1995) found that a large percentage of departments fail to exchange information despite overlaps in their job responsibilities concerning problems like arson and emergencies. I studied one city where the fire department, clerk's office, and building department all shared information responsibility for entering information about buildings, but each department tended to point their finger at others when mistakes in the data were discovered. A major task of generalist and information managers is to deal with departmental concern with autonomy over the databases. If they defer to the status quo, information management will be less effective. Bringing about the change required to achieve integration may aggravate such conflicts. Overcoming these obstacles requires negotiating, political, and organizational skills.

Top managers may force the exchange of information via command. However, employees often find ways to resist change. For example, they may provide poor-quality information that renders the exchange useless. Markus and Keil (1994) provide a case study of a new and improved decision-support system designed to help salespersons that failed because it worked counter to underlying organizational incentives. The system was aimed at producing more accurate price quotes, but it hampered the sales staff's ability to sell systems, their most important goal, so the new system was used little.

The relationship between technology and individual career ambitions can lead to political aspects of information management. Knights and Murray (1994) have conducted one of the few detailed studies of the politics of information technology. In their case study of IT in an insurance company, they concluded that the success and failure of the systems were closely tied to the careers of mangers. Consequently, these managers often attempted to control the perception of the success of these systems because perception is reality (Knights & Murray, 1994):

The secret of success lies in the fact that if enough people believe something is a success then it really is a success ... it was vital for the company and for managerial careers that the pensions project was a success. (p. 172)

One of the key points made by Knights and Murray (1994) is that computing decisions become inextricably entangled with career ambitions and fears of individual employees and become embroiled in a very personal form of politics. Another detailed case study (Brown, 1998) of the implementation of a new computer system in a hospital found that different groups (the hematology ward, hematology laboratory, and information

technology team) had very different perspectives on the reason for the failure of a new computer system. Moreover, each of the three groups used the common goal of patient care to legitimate their view of the system. Brown concludes that the study shows that participants were influenced by "attributional egotism" in which each person and group involved attributes favorable results to their own efforts and unfavorable results to external factors. Similar to Knights and Murray, Brown concludes that many of the actions are taken to protect individual autonomy and discretion.

Grover, Lederer, and Sabherwal (1988) borrowed from the work of Bardach (1977) and Keen (1981) to outline 12 different "games" that are played by those involved in developing new systems. They tested their framework by in-depth interviews with 18 IT professionals who confirmed that these games were played in their organizations. Most of their games involve inter-organizational or interpersonal struggles similar to those I discussed above. For example, they discuss how in the "up for grabs" game, control over a new IT system involves struggles between the IT and other departments. They illustrate what they call the reputational game with a story about an IT manager who projected "a rough exterior" (Grover, Lederer, & Sabherwal, p. 153) in order to reduce demands on the IT department, but this approach led to a coalition against him and the IT department and resulted in the eventual dismissal of the IT manager.

The lesson of the above cases is that, prior to implementing new systems, information managers need to assess the organizational context and determine how proposed systems will be affected by incentives, informal norms, resistance to change and sharing, as well as other forms of organizational politics. A broad stakeholder analysis needs to be done. Many of these factors may be addressed by including end users in the planning process. Managers will often have to be involved in exerting political influence and engage systems outside their direct control in order to assure a successful outcome. For example, Kost (1996) describes how the Michigan Department of Transportation decided to change from a mainframe to a client-server environment, and this change endangered the jobs of a dozen mainframe technicians. The logical step was to retrain the mainframe technicians to do the new tasks, but the civil-service rules and regulations required that the mainframe workers be laid off and new employees be recruited to fill the client-server positions. Thus, in order to have an effective information system, generalist and information managers will often have to seek to change rules, procedures, and structures and, at the same time, alleviate as much as possible any perceived negative impacts of change. Still, change may bring information managers inevitably into conflict with other departments.

Computing and Communication Patterns

Information technology such as e-mail can affect organizational communication patterns. Changes in communication flows can be extremely political. For example, if a subordinate communicates sensitive information to others without clearing it with her or his immediate supervisor, strife is likely to result. While he was mayor of Indianapolis, Stephen Goldsmith encouraged every police officer and other public employees to contact him directly via e-mail (Miller, 1995a). He claims to have read 400 e-mail messages a day. Should mayors or managers encourage such use of direct contact from employees? Although such communication can and does occur via phone and face-to-face communication, e-mail communications are different from face-to-face communications—there is less rich information and many people portray themselves differently in e-mail than they do in person.

E-mail has become the dominant form of communication in many organizations and it has implications for organizational politics

(Markus, 1994; Rocheleau, 2002b). Markus has shown that e-mail is routinely used as a device to protect employees in games in which they feel it is necessary to "cover your anatomy." E-mail now provides a digitized trail that can be used to support employees concerning their reasons for doing what they did. Employees often copy e-mail messages to their own or those of other superiors to let people know what they think is necessary, thus attempting to bring more pressure on the recipient of the e-mail (Phillips & Eisenberg, 1996). E-mail is now used for communicating bad news and even conducting negotiations. Many people (McKinnon & Bruns, 1992) are scornful of those who use e-mail for purposes such as reprimands and firings. However, some research now shows that e-mail may work better in communications that involve "dislike or intimidation" (Markus, p. 136).

The establishment of e-mail and other communication policies involves sensitive organizational issues. For example, if one employee sends a printed memo to an employee in another department concerning a matter of interest to his or her bosses, it is often expected that the sending employee will send a copy of the memo to the bosses. Should the same policy hold for e-mail exchanges? Is e-mail more like a formal memo where such a procedure is expected or more like an informal phone call where copying is not done? Such policies will likely lead to debate and perhaps conflict. Generalist and information managers need to be actively involved in making these decisions.

Technical leaders need to realize that keeping others informed in the organization is a crucial task, and devoting time to such communication often needs to take precedence over more technical issues as the following IT director for a local government described:

With the manager—I don't want any surprises and I don't want my manager to have any surprises. So if I see it [some problem] coming, I am up

there communicating with him. This morning before you got here, I went to give a heads up to purchasing and to the manager's office to let them know "hey, this is going to be coming to you" [an unexpected expenditure]. I spend a lot of time doing things like that. ... The complaints that I hear a lot about are that people send things in and the manager's office doesn't know what is about. ... So communicating those things to grease the skids, and letting people know that what I would like to have happen—I spend a lot of time on it. And I think it pays big dividends in getting things done.

In short, good political skills concern the ability to communicate effectively with all of the key actors in the IT process from the end users to the top managers.

THE EXTERNAL POLITICS OF INFORMATION MANAGEMENT

There are several ways in which computing can become involved with external politics. Here are some examples.

1. Information technology is being used to determine the performance of governmental organizations as well as the presentation of these performance measures on Web sites. These online evaluative reports (e.g., report cards for school systems) can have much greater visibility and accessibility than previous evaluations and thus e-government can lead to greater citizen involvement. Access of the public to information about the performance of governments and other organizations (e.g., hospitals, health professionals) can often lead to controversy.
2. Legislatures, councils, and boards of public agencies may contest the purchasing decisions of public organizations. Likewise, the

award of computer contracts may involve political rewards. In the California case (Anderson et al., 2003), the legislature stepped in to weaken the amount of authority given to the new Department of Information Technology created in 1995, thus ensuring that the General Services Administration and Department of Finance would continue to dominate IT decision making.

3. It is possible that public computer records could be used for political purposes. The information could be used to schedule campaigns or find information that brings candidates into disfavor.
4. Information systems often involve sharing amongst different levels of government as well as private organizations. Often there is conflict among these organizations over basic issues such as how the information system should be structured and what data they should gather.
5. The rise of the World Wide Web and e-government has created the potential for politics. Political issues have erupted over the use of Web sites and other forms of CMC. A wide range of issues have developed such as the use of Web sites to attack governmental officials or their use for advertising purposes.
6. Major computer disasters or failures can bring negative attention to public organizations. These failures both hurt organizational performance and also threaten the jobs of staff.
7. A variety of computing technologies are viewed as a way of increasing citizen participation in government. These include interactive Web sites that allow citizens to easily post comments on proposed rules and other public issues. Public-participation GIS (PPGIS) and Web logs could also be used to achieve enhanced participation but at the same time can lead to controversy and increased conflict.

Online Accountability

The development of computing technology has had an important impact on measuring accountability and presenting this information to the public. Many governmental organizations are now posting information such as report cards of their performance online. The hope and expectation is that using Web sites to make such performance information available will make organizations accountable and also lead to more trust in government. Indeed, Mossberger and Tolbert (2005) have found some limited evidence that use of governmental Web sites has positive effects on perceptions of governmental responsiveness.

The extent to which online information can improve accountability depends in part on the accessibility of information. The Mercatus report (McTigue, Wray, & Ellig, 2004) analyzes accountability information on Web sites by separating them into desirable characteristics, such as breaking the report into downloadable sections (and multiple formats) if it is large, as well as the inclusion of contact information if anyone has questions concerning the report. It is instructive to look at the Mercatus report's comments on specific government agencies concerning transparency to observe in more depth what kinds of actions the authors regard as providing for good transparency. The U.S. Department of Labor scored highly and the positive comments include the fact that the accountability report is linked to the home page and is downloadable in "multiple PDF documents" (McTigue et al., p. 30), and the authors praise the report for being "clearly written" and providing trend data since 2000, though it notes that more trend data concerning key problems would have improved it. By way of contrast, the report critiques the Department of Health and Human Services (DHHS) for the obscurity of its report, stating that they could only find the report on the department's Web site via a "circuitous trip." It also criticizes the report for not providing information about the quality of the data of any

of the 600 measures it uses. The Mercatus report acknowledges that an agency's actual performance may not be correlated directly with the Mercatus score. This brings up the issue of the quality of the data, and the Mercatus report states that the agency should indicate how confident it is in the quality of the data and, to ensure transparency, it should make the data available for independent verification.

The National Center on Educational Outcomes (NCEO) (Thurlow, Wiley, & Bielinski, 2003) assesses the reports done by state education agencies and has been assessing their Web sites for outcome information since 2001. Some of their evaluative criteria refer to the organization of the information on the Web site. Among the criteria they used to assess the state Web site were the following: (a) Are there clear words or links to get to the report on the agency Website, (b) how many clicks did it take to get from the agency's home page to the disaggregated results, and (c) what is the proximity of data on special education to the data for all students?

One of the major obstacles to the use of accountability efforts has been the argument that comparisons of performance are invalid—no two situations are the same. Consequently, organizations with poorer results have been able to point to factors that differentiate them from better performing organizations (Rocheleau, 2002a). The posting of information on the Internet makes this kind of information much more accessible than in the past when it would likely reside in obscure, hard-to-obtain governmental publications. These increased external forces often lead organizations to adopt strategies for resisting information or manipulating it so that negative information is not available to the public or oversight agencies (Rocheleau). For example, a U.S. General Accounting Office report (2002) found that abuse of nursing-home patients was rarely reported. Indeed, colleges, universities, health-maintenance organizations, and perhaps most organizations take steps to ensure that only positive information is reported via a number of strategies, especially if the information will affect high-stakes decisions (Bohte & Meier, 2001; Rocheleau). Information is power, and the demand for more external access to performance information makes the job of information management even more political. Now that this information is so accessible, organizations have to deal with demands for access to more information while other units may resist such demands and power struggles over information ensue. For example, the Tennessee teacher unions successfully resisted efforts to make public the scores of individual teachers based on a value-added system developed by the state (Gormely & Weiner, 1999). Other consequences include the likelihood that the data may be "cooked" in order to demonstrate high performance (Rocheleau) and the IT managers may face ethical issues concerning how to handle such situations.

The External Politics of Purchasing and Privatization

Many city managers attempt to defuse controversies over the purchasing process by involving council or board members in developing the proposals. Thus, decisions will not be brought up until strong council or board support exists. Achieving such a consensus may be more difficult these days because board members are more likely to be involved with computing in their own organizations (e.g., Pevtzow, 1989). When computing was restricted to mainframes and data-processing departments, council or board members were less likely to feel knowledgeable and able to challenge purchases. Rocheleau (1994) found that there could be conflicts over purchasing even if there is a consensus on what type of technology to use. Major contracts can be especially controversial during periods of budget strain, and expensive IT contracts may be viewed as taking away from services. For example, some state legislators argued that $52 million of a $90 million contract

that California State University had awarded to Peoplesoft should be redirected to educational programs to compensate for cutbacks made by Governor Gray Davis (Foster, 2004). There also may be tensions about whether to purchase from local vendors vs. outside vendors. We saw earlier (Peterson, 2002) that major failures of a large IT project led to the creation of a state IT department, but controversies over another contract (with the Oracle Corporation) led to the end of the department after only 7 years of existence. Major failures in procurement can turn a project that begins as primarily an internal matter into a political football and such failures have led several IT directors to lose their jobs.

The move to privatize information systems can create external conflicts with legislative bodies as well as unions. For example, the state of Connecticut's administration decided to change the state's entire system from mainframes to the desktop and hire an external vendor to handle every aspect of the information function (Daniels, 1997). Later, it decided against the outsourcing because of a number of factors such as disputes with the state legislature and the union representing the IT employees, as well as reappraisals of the proposed contracts. Several other states have considered privatization including Indiana, Iowa, and Tennessee. In order to implement such plans, the managers will have to negotiate with legislatures and unions in order to reach agreements. For example, the Connecticut administration (Daniels) moved to assure the jobs of the state IT workers for a period of 2 years at the same salary and benefits in order to have the privatization move approved. In more recent times, the cities of Memphis and San Diego have moved to outsource their entire information services function. The absence of unions has facilitated the privatization of the Memphis operation (Feldman, 2000). However, as we have seen above, effective communication and political skills are required for an effective IT system, and turning over the entire operation to a private vendor could disrupt the communication patterns and power relationships necessary for the system to work smoothly. That is why in many cases the selected vendor often is an organization consisting of former employees or, as in the Memphis case, the winning vendor is expected to hire employees of the former municipal IT department (Feldman). One of the principles that Anderson et al. (2003, p. 31) found in their study of state IT structures was that "states with successful IT initiatives demonstrate commitment to employees during major changes." In some recent cases (Kahaner, 2004), state governments (e.g., New Jersey and Massachusetts) have passed laws that have outlawed outsourcing of call centers for services such as answering questions concerning electronic benefits like food stamps. The outsourcing would have saved money directly in lower contract costs, but some point to unemployment and other benefits that would have to be paid to the workers who would lose their jobs. In 2004, Florida technology officials became embroiled in a controversial outsourcing (that includes e-government) in which losing bidders complained about the bidding process (Towns, 2004), leading later to the resignation of the Florida CIO. The era of budgetary shortfalls leads to demands that CIO cut budgets and save money (Hoffman, 2004). This situation can lead to failure and resignations when CIOs are unable to meet these cutback expectations as occurred with the CIO of New Hampshire who resigned (Hoffman). Dealing with the implications or even expectations of personnel cutbacks due to IT decisions is one of the most sensitive and important tasks for IT leaders and the generalist administrators of governmental organizations.

Although privatization may be used to achieve positive goals, it can also be used for political rewards and result in problems. One such example occurred when a computer vendor, Management Services of Illinois Inc. (MSI), was found guilty of fraud and bribery connected to the state of Illinois awarding a very favorable contract to them (Pearson & Parsons, 1997). MSI had legally donated

more than $270,000 in computer services and cash to Illinois Governor Edgar's campaign. The jury found that the revised contract had cheated taxpayers of more than $7 million. Campaign donations as well as the flow of governmental and political staff between government and private vendors can influence the awarding of contracts. More recently, there have been some suspicions that politics has been involved in the selection of no-bid contractors for "e-rate" contracts aimed at putting computers and other IT in Chicago's school system. Among the winners of no-bid contracts was SBC (then headed by Chicago Mayor Richard Daley's brother) and another company (JDL Technologies) headed by a friend of Reverend Jesse Jackson (Lighty & Rado, 2004).

At the same time that many states and municipalities are exploring the privatization of their information management function, there are several municipalities that are moving to become telecommunication owners and that leads to political controversy. For example, Tacoma's (Washington) municipal power company is aiming to build and provide cable services to homes and thus put it in competition with the local phone and cable companies (Healey, 1997). Many other cities including several small communities such as Fort Wright (Kentucky) are also planning to build telecommunication networks (Newcombe, 1997) in the United States and are providing telecommunication services for businesses and private homes in their communities. The rationale behind these moves is that the private cable and local phone companies have a poor record of providing up-to-date service (Healey). These moves have often been labeled as socialism and are opposed by the local cable and/or phone companies. However, in the Tacoma case, most local business leaders were backing the municipality because of the desire to have better technology (Healey). Some states (e.g., Texas, Arkansas, and Missouri) have prohibited municipal organizations from becoming telecommunication providers (Healey). The state of California is in the process of privatizing its state telecom system (Harris, 1998). In Iowa, many municipalities have been laying fiber to deliver cable in competition with cities, and the first suit brought by a phone company was found in favor of the municipality (Harris). More recently, the Supreme Court (Peterson, 2004, p. 27) "upheld the right of states to ban municipalities entering the broadband market." The Missouri Municipal League had argued that the Federal Telecommunications Act prevented states from passing laws to limit entry into providing services, but the court said that this provision of the law did not apply to governmental units. Thus, politics and the law are integrally related, but there are few fixed principles about law as it affects emerging computer technology.

When local governments decide to pursue broadband, they must be ready to be involved in a whole array of politics and will need to market their position to the public. One strategy of small local governments is to increase the viability of their position by collaboration with other municipalities. In Utah (Perlman, 2003), several municipalities joined together to form UTOPIA (Utah Telecommunications Open Infrastructure Agency) to provide high-speed fiber-optic networks to their communities. However, telephone and cable companies have allied with taxpayer groups to oppose the efforts. Eight of the 18 local governments that supported the initial feasibility study have withdrawn from UTOPIA, and the remainder has committed themselves to taxpayer-backed bonds to finance the required infrastructure. The feasibility issue depends heavily on assumptions about take-up rates: What percent of the targeted businesses and residents buy into the service, and will the project finance itself? According to Perlman, the take-up rate has averaged 40% in those local governments that have put "fiber to the home," and only a 30% take-up rate is required for the project to pay for itself.

A study by a conservative think-tank researcher (Lenard, 2004) found that none of the municipal entrants into the broadband market had been able to cover their costs and argues that they are not likely to do so in the future either. Defenders of municipal entry see it as a movement to bring services and competition to areas that telecommunication companies have poorly served or totally ignored and that broadband is now infrastructure needed to attract businesses to the community and is thus equivalent to building roads. Brookings researcher Charles Ferguson (2004) has labeled the broadband situation an example of "market failure" due to a lack of real competition. Defenders would argue that, by entering the market, municipalities will provide the competition to obtain the quality services that have been denied them. Lenard argues that the competitiveness of the telecom industry makes it likely that the private sector will meet these needs without governmental involvement. In short, the debate over local governmental provision of Internet services goes to the very heart of what government should be doing.

More recently, a similar controversy has erupted over the desire on the part of some local governments to provide "hotspots" or WI-FI (wireless fidelity) zones in downtown areas. These local governments view the provision of WI-FI capability as a service to their citizens as well as a way of assisting economic development. Opponents of municipal provision of hotspots view it as inappropriate public-sector competition with a service that is available from the private sector. For example, Philadelphia stated its intention to provide wireless service at very low prices (Peterson, 2005). A bill passed both houses of the legislature aimed at preventing other communities from taking similar steps (Peterson). In short, it is becoming clear that, although many information managers prefer to avoid controversy, telecommunications issues such as broadband and wireless may make it impossible for IT staff and governmental officials to avoid making politically sensitive decisions.

Computer Disasters and Information Management

It is likely that the majority of computer problems and disasters remain unknown to the public and even legislative bodies. However, certain disasters have so much impact on key operations that they do become public and create crises for generalist and information managers. For example, the delay in the opening of the new Denver Airport was due to software problems controlling the baggage system. Likewise, the state of Illinois' Medicaid program encountered many failures of the computer system with the system assigning patients to inappropriate health care providers (Krol, 1994).

Many disasters are beyond the control of managers and there is little they can do other than plan for emergencies. However, in many cases, disasters appear to result from overly high expectations for new computer systems and a lack of understanding on how difficult it is to implement a new system. This author has reviewed a large number of computer problems and failures (Rocheleau, 1997). Both the Federal Aviation Administration (FAA) and Internal Revenue Service (IRS) have experienced major failures that have led to threats from Congress to defund systems (Cone, 1998). Another example is the state of Florida's new human-services system that encountered much higher-than-projected costs and slower-than-expected implementation (Kidd, 1995). The perceived disaster led to the loss of the job of the state official in charge of the new system along with threatened legal action. However, over the long run, it appears that the system actually worked and has helped to reduce costs. Information management officials need to ensure that executives and the public have realistic expectations of system costs and performance. Computer problems and disasters are likely to occur more often as computing becomes central to governmental performance and communication with its constituents. In these situations,

managers cannot avoid dealing with computing even if they have removed themselves from any decisions concerning it.

In contrast to the disaster cases, some politicians and managers make use of notable achievements in computing to boost their reputation for innovation and effectiveness. However, it can be dangerous for politicians or managers to claim success for large-scale new systems until the systems have been fully implemented and tested. For example, a former state of Illinois comptroller introduced a powerful new computer system that was aimed at speeding the issuance of checks as well as improving access to online information during June of 1997 (Manier, 1997). Soon afterward, there were complaints that checks were arriving behind schedule and that matters had not improved (Ziegler, 1997). The agency stated that it was just taking time for workers to get used to the new system. This is one case where there does appear to be a clear prescriptive lesson for managers: New computer systems that are large scale and introduce major changes usually experience significant start-up problems and claims of success should be muted until success can be proven.

Information Management and Interorganizational Struggles

Many of our largest governmental programs involve complex arrangements where administration and funding are shared by federal, state, and local governments. These governments are often at odds over how they view information systems. For example, the welfare-reform legislation passed in 1996 led to needed changes in how state and local governments gathered and analyzed data. Since welfare recipients move from state to state, the new welfare time limits require states to share and redesign their systems so they can calculate time periods on welfare and whether a recipient has exceeded state or federal limits (5 years total and 2 years consecutively for federal limits).

Prior systems were oriented to yearly information and were concerned only with welfare activities in their own state. The federal government has established data-reporting requirements that many states view as burdensome and unnecessary (Newcombe, 1998). For example, they have to monitor the school attendance of teenage mothers and that requires sharing information with independent local school districts. The quality of the data submitted by the states is also an issue (Newcombe). The very purposes of the federal and state systems can be somewhat at odds. The federal government wants to use the system to determine the overall success of the program and to be able to compare the performance of states. The state governments often are opposed to the increase in the number of data elements required from 68 to 178 and the costs of gathering much new information (Newcombe). Similar disagreements can occur between state and local governments with the latter often feeling that states are too autocratic in how they implement information systems. The resolution of such disagreements will involve conflict and bargaining with creative solutions sought that meet the primary needs of all involved.

Schoech, Jensen, Fulks, and Smith (1998) provide a case study of a volunteer group in Arlington, Texas, who tried to create a data bank aimed at helping reduce alcohol and drug abuse. This volunteer group "discovered the politics of information." Hospitals opposed the identification of drug-affected births. When agency personnel changed, permission for access to the data had to be obtained over again. Changes in the structure of government and functions of office also led to the need to start again. They found that data gathering was not a high priority for other agencies involved and access to data was often delayed or not forthcoming.

The Center for Technology in Government (CTG) has conducted several case studies concerning the development of information systems that require the cooperation of several organiza-

tions. One case study involved the development of an information system for the homeless. First, several different actors needed to be involved in the development of the system including the New York State Office of Temporary and Disability Assistance, the Bureau of Shelter Assistance, the New York City Department of Homeless, the Office of Children and Family Services, the Department of Health, the Department of Labor, the Office of Alcohol and Substance Abuse Services, and the Division of Parole, and many independent nonprofit organizations contribute to and use information on the system. The huge number of actors meant that the development of the system had to be very deliberate and the first priority was to develop a sense of trust amongst them first before getting into technical design (CTG, 2000). The new information system was to be used to help set goals and thus affect evaluation. Consequently, there were issues that had to be settled about how ambitious to make goals. Consensus had to be forged on key definitions such as the "date of admittance" into the system because these definitions were important to funding of the end users of the system. Some agencies wanted a more detailed listing of ethnic options than others due to their federal funding requirements, so this detail needed to be negotiated, too. The basic points of this case study are that negotiation and trust are essential to the creation of interorganizational and intergovernmental systems. Organizations that believe that their financial interests and viability will be threatened by a new system will resist it regardless of how rational and sensible the policy looks on paper.

Another CTG (1999) study focused on attempts to build integrated criminal-justice systems. It found many conflicts over budgets, organizational relationships, and procedures. CTG concluded that these problems were not technical in nature but due to "conflicting visions" related to organizational and political interests. It also found that trust, participation, and understanding of the business were among those elements required for success.

To achieve buy-in, they had to pay much attention to "interests and incentives" and use marketing and selling techniques. Political pressures played an important role in some cases. The study found that "turf is the biggest killer of integration": "Protecting turf can be particularly important when the potential loss of autonomy or control could benefit other agencies that are political or institutional adversaries" (p. 11).

There was also a need for a champion of the system who had major organizational or political influence that allowed this person to overcome the political barriers to integration. Bellamy (2000) found very similar results in a review of attempts to create criminal-justice systems in England. Although technical skills are always useful and sometimes essential, the development of successful interorganizational systems necessitates major use of political skills and resources. The Anderson et al. (2003) study of four states found that it was important to have general executive leaders who are champions of IT:

States with exemplary IT practices have executive leadership (governor and state CIO) who are champions of IT initiatives. All four of the states we visited exemplify this characteristic. These leaders emphasize the value of IT for the state in performing its missions. They view IT as an investment, rather than a cost ... (p. 33)

These studies and other literature on IT have two important implications: (1) Generalist administrators who want to have successful IT programs need to be engaged in IT, and (2) IT heads need to cultivate support from generalist administrators.

One of the current trends in information technology management is to encourage the easy sharing of information and to bring an end to information silos. Thus, states such as Pennsylvania (Chabrow, 2005) have hired deputy chief information officers with one of the major goals of their jobs being to enhance IT effectiveness

by coordinating budgeting across agencies that share common functions (so-called communities of practice). For example, several agencies may have e-payment systems that could share a single application. Forcing agencies to share common applications is likely to lead to tension and political battles.

In some cases, the use of computing may help to reduce the amount of ad hominem politics and give more attention to the underlying facts of cases in development decisions (Dutton & Kraemer, 1985). They found that the computing models did not eliminate politics. Developers and antidevelopers employed competing models with different assumptions. However, the focus on the computer models helped to direct attention to facts of the case and away from personalities and unverifiable assumptions, thus facilitating compromise and agreement.

Information Management and the Politics of Databases

Most information managers prefer to avoid the release of information with political implications. However, often they cannot avoid releasing such information and need to have a defensible policy in this regard. The New York State Attorney General's Office (Yates, 2001) plan to track flows of donations to victims of the September 11th tragedy was resisted by organizations such as the Red Cross due to privacy and confidentiality issues. The Freedom of Information Act (FOIA) covers computer records in most states. Issues of privacy and public interest often collide and managers are often forced to make difficult choices. Although these problems existed prior to computers, the existence of computing has made it possible for outsiders to conduct very detailed critiques of the practices of public agencies with emphasis on pointing out their failures and questionable decisions. For example, the *Chicago Tribune* did a reanalysis of computerized information from the Illinois Department of Public Aid to do an exposé of fraud and waste in its Medicaid system (Brodt, Possley, & Jones, 1993). The extent, magnitude, and speed of their analysis would have been impossible without access to computerized records. Consequently, it is not surprising that many governmental agencies resist FOIA requests. A series of articles (e.g., Mitchell, 1999) by the *News-Gazette* newspaper in Illinois revealed that many resist FOIA using a variety of reasons such as the fact that they would have to create a new document. The existence of a good computerized system can serve to weaken the argument that the obtaining of records would pose too great a burden on the governmental agency.

Generalist and information managers picture technology as a way to better services, but they should be aware that the same technologies and databases can be employed for political purposes. For example, many municipal and state governments are now constructing powerful geographic information systems that are aimed at improving services to citizens through the mapping of integrated databases. However, GISs and their data are now being used for "cyber ward heeling" in the 1990s and facilitate such traditional functions like the mapping of volunteers, canvassing of voters, and location of rally sites (Novotny & Jacobs, 1997). Politicians are likely to seek data from these public information systems to conduct their political campaigns. For example, databases allow the targeting of campaigns so that candidates can use several different messages and conduct "stealth campaigns" without alerting their opponents. Thus, the more powerful and information rich local GISs become, the more attractive they will be as databases for political activities, which could lead to controversy.

Online Computer-Mediated Communication

The impact of the World Wide Web has especially important implications for politics. Researchers such as Robert Putnam (1995) point out a sub-

stantial decrease in some forms of civic participation on the part of the public. Many people are frightened to speak at public hearings. The Web offers a way of increasing public participation in community decisions (Alexander & Grubbs, 1998). Many people see us entering a new age of cyberdemocracy (Stahlman, 1995). Shy people and stutterers would be able to provide testimony electronically and their arguments would be judged based on content rather than their appearance or public speaking skills (Conte, 1995). Municipalities may help to develop useful networks such as senior-citizen discussions. Parents can use the system to update themselves on student homework assignments. However, as noted above, there are several drawbacks to teledemocracy and the development of interactive Internet applications.

- There is less inhibition in telecommunications than in in-person communications against intemperate statements. Consequently, electronic forums often degenerate into "flaming" wars. The originator of the Santa Monica (California) online discussion system argued that, if he were to do it over again, he would like to have a moderator for the system and charge user fees (Conte, 1995; Schuler, 1995).
- Some people lack the computing technology and/or skills to participate in these electronic discussions (Wilhelm, 1997).
- It is feared by some that easing access to public testimony and input to public officials may result in such a massive and discordant amount of input that democracy would be stymied and that gridlock would increase.
- The Internet raises fears about privacy. Efforts to improve access can often lead to resistance. For example, the Social Security Administration (SSA) made interactive benefits estimates available over the Internet but was forced to withdraw the service due to privacy issues (James, 1997; United States

General Accounting Office, 1997). Social Security numbers are not very private and all someone needed was the number plus the recipient's state of birth and mother's maiden name to gain access to earnings and benefits information.

- Public online systems may become campaign vehicles for certain politicians.

A detailed account (Schmitz, 1997) of a discussion group concerning homelessness on Santa Monica's PEN system made the following points about the successes and failures of online groups: (a) The discussion group was successful in bringing people who would never have engaged in face-to-face meetings together for discussion purposes on an equal basis, but (b) electronic media demand keyboarding and writing skills. Thus, there are many obstacles to the successful participation of the poor. One recent study by Gregson (1997) found that even politically active citizens were not able to transfer their activism to a community network without substantial training and experience. Hale (2004) did a study of the use of neighborhood Web pages, and his overall assessment was that the overall usage rates were low and that consequently these pages were not meeting the hope that they might help to "revitalize democracy."

Both generalists and information management staff need to give careful consideration to the possibilities and drawbacks of teledemocracy. If they decide to support electronic discussion groups, should they employ a moderator and, if so, who should act as a moderator? Would a moderator's censoring of input be a violation of the right to free speech? Fernback (1997) argues that most people accept moderation not as "prior restraint but as a concession" for the good of the collectivity. How can the argument that teledemocracy is elitist be handled? Is the provision of public places (e.g., in libraries) for electronic input sufficient to deal with this objection? In this author's experience, I have found strong resistance to the establishment of on-

line discussion groups. Many local governmental officials believe that such communication is likely to result in contentious and strident behavior. Some also feel that increased participation would make governmental decision making slower and more difficult. Thus, West's (2001) finding that few governmental agencies allowed interactivity such as the posting of online messages, much less online discussion groups, may not be merely the result of their lack of technological sophistication, but may also be due to a calculated reluctance to sponsor CMC.

The Politics of Web Sites and Other Online Information

The creation of Web sites has produced a whole new set of opportunities for politics to occur. What kinds of information should be online? Who should decide what information should be online? These are issues that have been highlighted by the Web. Before, most public information resided in reports that few had access to or even knew existed. The ease of online access has changed that situation and can lead to controversies that would not have existed when information was restricted to paper reports. As a result of the events of September 11th, some U.S. agencies have pulled from their Web sites information on hazardous waste sites. To many, these actions make good sense, but others have pointed out that the chemical industry has tried to keep such information private and that public access to this information can help to save lives ("Access to Government Information Post September 11th," 2002). The New York Attorney General's Office began to develop a database to track the distribution of money donated to victims of the attack, but the Red Cross raised privacy concerns (Yates, 2001). Placing some information on governmental Web sites can result in jeopardy for government officials. A U.S. Geological Survey contract employee was allegedly fired for posting a map on the U.S. government Web site that identified areas of the

Arctic national wildlife as moose calving areas that the Bush administration would like to open to oil exploration (Wiggins, 2001). Recently, the American Education Association and American Library Association (Monastersky, 2004) have accused the Bush administration of politics in deleting information from its Web site and cited an internal memo that it was policy to remove information that was outdated or did not "reflect the priorities of the Administration." Thus, putting up certain information or omitting information from Web sites can become a controversial and political issue.

A related issue is to what extent should Web sites of governments act as, in effect, a campaign Web site for the top elected officials? There is great variability in state and local governments, but some governmental home pages appear to be campaign sites with photos of the top-level officials and their personal positions, and accomplishments of the elected official dominating much of the page. Such activities can stimulate opposition to political uses, and Franzel and Coursey (2004) report that the state of Florida banned the placement of almost any information other than basic personal and legal information on their Web sites. Coursey (in press) cites an interesting example in which Governor Jeb Bush ordered an e-mail link be placed at the top of all of the state's Web pages, but that led to thousands of responses that could not be answered in a timely fashion and the policy was eventually reversed.

Should advertising by private businesses be allowed on governmental sites? Many governments are resisting advertising. Some of the most successful such as Honolulu (Peterson, 2000) have used advertising to fund advanced electronic governmental systems but few others have followed. Honolulu put out a banner for a bank on its Web site. Peterson cites other governments as either being interested in advertising or not depending on whether they see it as necessary for funding. Decisions about opening govern-ment sites to advertising will involve ethical and practical issues.

Even decisions about what links to have on Web sites can become involved in political and legal controversy. A court case was brought by an online newsletter (*The Putnam Pit*) against the city of Cookville, Tennessee, due to its failure to provide a link to the newsletter despite the fact that several other for-profit and nonprofit organizations were linked to from the city's Web site (Anonymous, 2001). Many governments avoid making such links. The consensus is that if governments do make links, they need to have a carefully thought-out (nonarbitrary) policy for doing so.

E-Governance Issues

There is a large and rapidly growing literature about how IT will affect and change the nature of political decision making as well as partisan politics. I will note some significant aspects of how e-governance can affect those who manage IT. E-governance is defined by Carlitz and Gunn (2002, p. 389) as the "use of computer networks to permit expanded public involvement in policy deliberations." One particular form of e-governance is to create an e-docket that is aimed at increasing participation in the creation of administrative rules so that they will be less likely to be challenged in courts. Coglianese (2004, p. 2) has defined e-rule-making as "the use of digital technologies in the development and implementation of regulations." He argues that IT may help streamline processes and allow agency staff to "retrieve and analyze vast quantities of information from diverse sources." He cites early examples of rule making such as the Bureau of Land Management's scanning of 30,000 comments concerning a proposed rangelands rule. Coglianese describes how the Department of Transportation and Environmental Protection Administration (EPA) created entire e-docket systems that provide "access to all comments, studies, and documents that are available to the public." Indeed, the EPA has been designated the managing partner in an interagency project to establish a common Internet site for all federal regulatory issues to help the public find and comment on proposed regulations. There is a governmental Web site that describes this initiative at http:// www.regulations.gov/images/eRuleFactSheet. pdf and has links to all of the federal-agency e-rule-making sites. Carlitz and Gunn (2002) have described how the e-rule-making process ideally would work:

An online dialogue takes place over a several week period. The dialogue is asynchronous, so participants can take part at their convenience, with ample time to reflect on background materials and the postings of other participants. Although in our experience a properly structured event is typically very civil, the dialogue is moderated to deal with the rare cases in which the discussion becomes too heated and to help keep the conversation focused. (p. 396)

However, the authors go on to acknowledge that there are many legal concerns about abridgement of First Amendment rights through attempts to moderate discussions and make them more civil. Carlitz and Gunn (2002, p. 398) said they were advised by the EPA's Office of General Counsel not to use their "usual prerogatives" as moderators because of these legal concerns, though they note that other departments have taken different positions.

A more recent study by Shulman (2005) raises serious questions about the ability of e-rule-making's ability to contribute useful input to the rule-making process. He studied randomly selected electronic contributions to e-rule-making and found that e-mail contributions give little deliberative input. The vast majority (more than 98%) of electronic contributions were exact or almost exact duplicates of form letters with little in the way of additions. Moreover, the process

used by the private outfits to analyze the electronic communications is likely to miss the few meaningful contributions according to Shulman. He concludes that the few thoughtful communications are likely to be drowned out by the huge electronic output.

Concerning the local-government level, Chen (2004) studied the involvement of local officials with e-mail and the Internet in the Silicon Valley area. She surveyed city and county officials. Her findings were somewhat surprising to me in that they found that these officials rated e-mail ahead of traditional "snail mail" in importance to their office, though the absolute differences were small. It is surprising to me because I would think that the act of writing and mailing a letter takes considerably more effort than sending an e-mail message so that letters would be assigned a higher priority by officials. However, Chen also found that only 9% of the officials checked their own e-mail, leaving this to their assistants. The burden of incoming e-mail was relatively small compared to the huge amount that goes to members of Congress—just over 50% said they got more than 50 e-mails per day (Chen). Although they used e-mail to communicate with the public, they were careful about using broadcast features of e-mail that would allow them to send mass mailings to the public because of the resentment that spam can cause in citizens. Many governmental sites now do provide the voluntary opportunity for residents to sign up for various forms of electronic communication. In Chen's study, some local officials had suffered from "spoofing" in which opponents sent offensive messages to the public that appeared to embarrass them. The overall assessment of e-mail contact by most local officials was that e-mail is useful once a good relationship had been established via in-person or phone contact.

A study by Ferber, Foltz, and Pugliese (2003) of state Web sites found few interactive political input opportunities such as public forums, chat rooms, or Listservs. Similar to my expectations, Ferber et al. put less weight on e-mail communications than traditional phone or snail-mail communications. One of the issues politicians have with e-mail is that it is difficult if not impossible to determine the location of the e-mailers and thus politicians do not know if the e-mailers live in their political districts. One approach to this problem is to require that the person fill out a Web form giving his or her address prior to accepting the electronic communication. However, as Ferber et al. note, the vision of computer-generated e-mails receiving computer-generated responses does not meet what constitute "increased democratic participation in the political process."

There are a number of other developments in which IT is being used to encourage greater participation on the part of the public. For example, public-participation GISs are now being designed to enhance citizen participation by allowing members of the public to be able to visualize consequences of development decisions by studying maps and accompanying images (Krygier, 1998). Likewise, blogs (logs of individual opinions on issues recorded on the Internet) are being employed by some managers and could be used by governments to provide an additional method for citizens to express their viewpoints about public issues. The use of blogs in government has been rare until now. The State of Utah CIO (Harris, 2005) offered blogs to employees in order to encourage more open communication. However, much of the material in such blogs appears to have high public-relations content, and if the blog becomes the subject of political controversy, the blog may be ended. For example, a blog established by a metropolitan transportation-planning agency in Orlando, Florida, ended its blog when the blog was used by opponents to attack the policies of the agency as well as the agency's officials (Crotty, Dyer, & Jacobs, 2005). Use of the Internet is now viewed by some as a way of reorganizing government according to the views of certain ideologies. For instance, some conservatives view the Internet and Web sites as

a way of increasing "choice-based policies" (Eggers, 2005) in areas such as education because, they argue, information would be presented about the efficacy of providers of education (both public and private schools) so that citizens could make an informed and voluntary choice.

CONCLUSION

Failure to become engaged and knowledgeable about internal politics can undermine the efficacy of information managers. I know of cases in which managers with good technical skills lost their jobs due to their failure to master organizational politics. Information managers need to negotiate, bargain, dicker, and haggle with other departments. They may need to form coalitions and engage in logrolling in order to achieve their goals. A good information manager needs good political skills to be effective. I have drawn from a number of resources to illustrate the politics of information management, but there exists little systematic research concerning the topic as Strassmann (1995) has pointed out. We need more research concerning the crucial issue—both in-depth qualitative case studies and surveys concerning how managers employ politics in their dealings with information technology.

The lessons of our review are clear. As Fountain (2001) has pointed out, generalist managers can no longer afford to ignore IT. Fountain sees the urgency for generalist-administrator involvement:

Public executives and managers in networked environments can no longer afford the luxury of relegating technology matters to technical staff. Many issues that appear to be exclusively technical are also deeply political and strategic in nature. In some cases, new use of technology furthers an existing agency or program mission. But in others, using the Internet can play a transformative role and lead to expansion or rethinking of mission and change in internal and external boundaries, accountability, and jurisdiction. (p. 249)

Likewise, IT managers can no longer afford to ignore politics. Internal political issues such as those I have discussed above (structures, purchasing, sharing information, and electronic communication) have become so central that managers will find that questions about these issues demand attention and decision. External political issues will continue to grow in number and importance as the Web and cyberpolitics become more prominent. For better or worse, information managers are going to have to possess effective political skills.

REFERENCES

Access to government information post September 11th. (2002, February 1). *OMB Watch*. Retrieved April 2, 2005, from http://www.ombwatch.org/article/articleview/213/1/104/

Alexander, J. H., & Grubbs, J. W. (1998). Wired government: Information technology, external public organizations, and cyberdemocracy. *Public Administration and Management: An Interactive Journal, 3*(1). Retrieved from http://www.hbg.psu.edu/Faculty/jxr11/alex.html

Anderson, R., Bikson, T. K., Lewis, R., Moini, J., & Strauss, S. (2003). *Effective use of information technology: Lessons about state governance structures and processes*. Rand Corporation. Retrieved July 30, 2004, from http://www.rand.org/publications/MR/MR1704/index.html

Anonymous. (1994). The politics of information. *Logistic information management, 7*(2), 42-44.

Anonymous. (2001). Court rules that Web publisher may contest denial of link to city's Website. *3CMA: News of the City-County Communications & Marketing Association*, p. 1.

Bardach, E. (1977). *The implementation game: What happens after a bill becomes a law*. Cambridge, MA: MIT Press.

Barrett, K., & Greene, R. (2001). *Powering up: How public managers can take control of information technology*. Washington, DC: CQ Press.

Bellamy, C. (2000). The politics of public information systems. In G. D. Garson (Ed.), *Handbook of public information systems* (pp. 85-98). New York: Marcel Dekker, Inc.

Bohte, J., & Meier, K. J. (2001). Goal displacement: Assessing the motivation for organizational cheating. *Public Administration Review, 60*(2), 173-182.

Brodt, B., Possley, M., & Jones, T. (1993, November 4). One step ahead of the computer. *Chicago Tribune*, pp. 6-7.

Brown, A. (1998). Narrative politics and legitimacy in an IT implementation. *Journal of Management Studies, 35*(1), 1-22.

Butterfield, E. (2005, December 28). Mass. CIO Peter Quinn resigns. *Washington Technology*. Retrieved December 28, 2005, from http://www.washingtontechnology.com/news/1_1/daily_news/27656-1.html

Caldwell, B. (1992, November 30). Battleground: An attempt to streamline the Pentagon's operations has triggered a fight for control. *InformationWeek*, pp. 12-13.

Carlitz, R. D., & Gunn, R. W. (2002). Online rule-making: A step toward e-governance. *Government Information Quarterly, 19*, 389-405.

Center for Technology in Government. (1999). *Reconnaissance study: Developing a business base for the integration of criminal justice systems*. Retrieved July 30, 2004, from http://www.ctg.albany.edu/resources/pdfrpwp/recon_studyrpt.pdf

Center for Technology in Government. (2000). *Building trust before building a system: The making of the homeless information management system.* Retrieved July 30, 2004, from http://www.ctg.albany.edu/guides/usinginfo/Cases/bss_case.htm

Chabrow, E. (2005, June 20). State CIO named governor's aide. *InformationWeek.* Retrieved June 23, 2005, from http://www.informationweek.com/story/showArticle.jhtml?articleID=164900717&tid=5979#

Chen, E. (2004, April). *You've got politics: E-mail and political communication in Silicon Valley.* Paper presented at the Annual Meeting of the Midwest Political Science Association, Chicago.

Coglianese, C. (2004). *E-rulemaking: Information technology and the regulatory process* (Faculty Research Working Paper Series No. RWP04-002). Cambridge, MA: Harvard University, John F. Kennedy School of Government. Retrieved January 18, 2006, from http://cbeji.com.br/br/downloads/secao/500122.pdf

Cone, E. (1996, August 12). Do you really want this job? *InformationWeek,* pp. 63-70.

Cone, E. (1998, January 12). Crash-landing ahead? *InformationWeek,* pp. 38-52.

Conte, C. R. (1995). Teledemocracy: For better or worse. *Governing,* 33-41.

Corbitt, B. (2000). Developing intraorganizational electronic commerce strategy: An ethnographic study. *Journal of Information Technology, 15,* 119-130.

Corbitt, B., & Thanasankit, T. (2002). Acceptance and leadership-hegemonies of e-commerce policy perspectives. *Journal of Information Technology, 1,* 39-57.

Coursey, D. (in press). Strategically managing information technology: Challenges in the e-gov era. In J. Rabin (Ed.), *Handbook of public administration* (3rd ed.). Marcel Dekker.

Crotty, R., Dyer, B., & Jacobs, T. (2005, September 25). MetroPlan drops blog after critics attack agency's plans. *Orlando Sentinel,* p. K2. Retrieved January 5, 2006, from http://pqasb.pqarchiver.com/orlandosentineal/

Daniels, A. (1997). The billion-dollar privatization gambit. *Governing,* 28-31.

Danziger, J. N. (1977, June). Computers and the frustrated chief executive. *MIS Quarterly, 1,* 43-53.

Danziger, J. N., Dutton, W. H., Kling, R., & Kraemer, K. L. (1982). *Computers and politics: High technology in American local governments.* New York: Columbia University Press.

Davenport, T., Eccles, R. G., & Prusak, L. (1992). Information politics. *Sloan Management Review,* 53-65.

Dickerson, C. (2002, November 4). The art of good politics. *Infoworld,* 52.

Dizard, W. P. (2001). CIOs labor over contracting crisis. *Government Computer News.* Retrieved November 21, 2004, from http://www.gcn.com

Dutton, W. H., & Kraemer, K. L. (1985). *Modeling as negotiating: The political dynamics of computer models in the policy process.* Norwood, NJ: Ablex Publishing Company.

Eggers, W. D. (2005). Made to order. *Government Technology.* Retrieved February 11, 2005, from http://www.govtech.net/magazine/story.php?id=92875

Eiring, H. L. (1999). Dynamic office politics: Powering up for program success. *The Information Management Journal,* pp. 17-25.

Fabris, P. (1998, November 15). Odd ducks no more. *CIO Magazine.* Retrieved April 13, 1999, from http://www.cio.com/archieve/111598_government_content.html

Feldman, J. (2002). Politics as usual. *Networking Computing, 13*(5).

Ferber, P., Foltz, F., & Pugliese, P. (2003). The politics of state legislature Web sites: Making e-government more participatory. *Bulletin of Science, Technology, & Society, 23*(3), 157-167. Retrieved January 7, 2006, from http://java.cs.vt.edu/public/projects/digitalgov/papers/Ferber.Statewebsite.pdf

Ferguson, C. (2004). *The broadband problem: Anatomy of a market failure and a policy dilemma.* Washington, DC: The Brookings Institution.

Fernback, J. (1997). The individual within the collective: Virtual ideology and the realization of collective principles. In S. G. Jones (Ed.), *Virtual culture: Identity and communication in cybersociety* (pp. 36-54). London: Sage Publications.

Foster, A. L. (2004, May 18). Faculty petition criticizes Cal Poly campus's plan to install People-Soft software. *Chronicle of Higher Education.* Retrieved May 18, 2004, from http://chronicle.com/daily/2004/05/2004051801n.htm

Fountain, J. E. (2001). *Building the virtual state.* Washington, DC: Brookings Institution Press.

Franzel, J. M., & Coursey, D. H. (2004). Government Web portals: Management issues and the approaches of five states. In A. Pavlichev & G. D. Garson (Eds.), *Digital government: Principles and best practices* (pp. 63-77). Hershey, PA: Idea Group Publishing.

Freedman, D. H. (1994, March 1). A difference of opinion. *CIO*, pp. 53-58.

Friel, B. (2001, July 18). TSP board fires, sues computer modernization firm. *GovExec.com.*

Gormely, W. T., Jr., & Weimer, D. L. (1999). *Organizational report cards.* Cambridge, MA: Harvard University Press.

Gregson, K. (1997). Community networks and political participation: Developing goals for system developers. In *Proceedings of the ASIS Annual Meeting* (Vol. 34, pp. 263-270).

Grover, V., Lederer, A. L., & Sabherwal, R. (1988). Recognizing the politics of MIS. *Information & Management, 14*, 145-156.

Gurwitt, R. (1996, December). CIOs: The new data czars. *Governing Magazine.* Retrieved February 3, 2003, from http:governing.com

Hale, M. (2004, April). *Neighborhoods on-line: A content analysis of neighborhood Web pages.* Paper presented at the Annual Meeting of the Midwest Political Science Association, Chicago.

Harris, B. (1998). Telcom wars. *Government Technology, 11*, 1, 38-40.

Harris, B. (2005). The coming of blog.gov. *Government Technology.* Retrieved February 25, 2005, from http://www.govtech.net/

Hasson, J. (2004, May 17). No easy answer to career vs. political standing. *Federal Computer Week.*

Hayes, M. (1996, August 19). Platform zealots. *InformationWeek*, pp. 44-52.

Healey, J. (1997). The people's wires. *Governing*, 34-38.

Hoffman, T. (2004, February 16). Turnover increase hits the ranks of state CIOs. *Computer World.* Retrieved January 10, 2006, from http://www.computerworld.com/governmenttopics/government/story/0,10801,90236,00.html

James, F. (1997, April 10). Social Security ends Web access to records. *Chicago Tribune*, pp. 1, 12.

Kahaner, L. (2004). A costly debate. *Government Enterprise*, 8-14.

Keen, P. G. W. (1981). Information systems and organizational change. *Communications of the ACM, 24*(1), 24-33.

Kello, C. T. (1996). Participatory design: A not so democratic treatment. *American Journal of Psychology, 109*(4), 630-635.

Kidd, R. (1995). How vendors influence the quality of human services systems. *Government Technology*, 42-43.

King, J. L. (1983). Centralized versus decentralized computing: Organizational considerations and management options. *Computing Survey, 15*(4), 319-349.

Knights, D., & Murray, F. (1994). *Managers divided: Organisation politics and information technology management*. Chichester, UK: John Wiley & Sons.

Koskinen, J. A. (1996, July 15). Koskinen: What CIO act means to you. *Government Computer News*, p. 22.

Kost, J. M. (1996). *New approaches to public management: The case of Michigan* (CPM Report No. 96-1). Washington, DC: The Brookings Institution.

Kraemer, K. L., & King, J. L. (1976). *Computers, power, and urban management: What every local executive should know*. Beverly Hills, CA: Sage Publications.

Krol, E. (1994, June 24). State's health plan for poor comes up short. *Chicago Tribune*, pp. 1, 15.

Krygier, J. B. (1998). *The praxis of public participation GIS and visualization*. Retrieved April 2, 2005, from http://www.ncgia.ucsb.edu/varenius/ppgis/papers/krygier.html

Laudon, K. C. (1974). *Computers and bureaucratic reform: The political functions of urban information systems*. New York: Wiley.

Lenard, T. M. (2004). *Government entry into the telecom business: Are the benefits commensurate with the costs* (Progress on Point 11.4)? The Progress Freedom Foundation. Retrieved July 24, 2004, from http://www.pff.org/publications/

Lewis, D. E. (2005). *Political appointments, bureau chiefs, and federal management performance*. Retrieved January 7, 2006, from http://www.wws.princeton.edu/research/papers/09_05_dl.pdf

Lighty, T., & Rado, D. (2004, September 12). Schools' Internet bungle. *Chicago Tribune*.

Lucas, H. C. (1984). Organizational power and the information services department. *Communications of the ACM, 127*, 58-65.

Lunn, F. E. (2005). *Survey by FCW Media Group confirms that frustration among public CIOs prompts short tenures despite long-term challenges*. Retrieved January 7, 2006, from http://www.fcw.com/article91325-11-07-05-Print

Manier, J. (1997, June 27). State endorses powerful machine. *Chicago Tribune*, pp. 1, 5.

Markus, M. L. (1983). Power, politics, and MIS implementation. *Communications of the ACM, 26*, 430-444.

Markus, M. L. (1994). Electronic mail as the medium of managerial choice. *Organizational Science, 5*(4), 502-527.

Markus, M. L., & Keil, M. (1994). If we build it, they will come: Designing information systems that people want to use. *Sloan Management Review, 35*, 11-25.

McKinnon, S. M., & Bruns, W. J., Jr. (1992). *The information mosaic*. Boston: Harvard Business School Press.

McTigue, M., Wray, H., & Ellig, J. (2004). *5th annual report scorecard: Which federal agencies best inform the public?* Mercatus Center, George

Mason University. Retrieved July 14, 2004, from http://www.mercatus.org/governmentaccountability/category.php/45.html

Miller, B. (1995a). Interview with Indianapolis mayor, Stephen Goldsmith. *Government Technology*, 24-25.

Miller, B. (1995b). Should agencies archive e-mail? *Government Technology*, 22.

Mitchell, T. (1999, July 26). Stiff-armed, but not by law. *The News Gazette*. Retrieved October 2, 2004, from http://news-gazette.com/OpenRecords/monmains.htm

Molta, D. (1999). The power of knowledge and information. *Network Computing, 33*(1), 23-24.

Monastersky, R. (2004, November 25). Research groups accuse education department of using ideology in decisions about data. *The Chronicle of Higher Education.*

Mossberger, K., & Tolbert, C. (2005). *The effects of e-government on trust and confidence in government.* Retrieved January 7, 2006, from http://www.digitalgovernment.org/dgrc/dgo2003/cdrom/PAPERS/citsgovt/tolbert.pdf

Murphy, S. (1995). Kansas city builds GIS to defray costs of clean water act. *Geo Info Systems,* 39-42.

Newcombe, T. (1995). The CIO: Lightning rod for IT troubles? *Government Technology*, 58.

Newcombe, T. (1997). Cities become telecomm owners. *Government Technology.* Retrieved from http://www.govtech.net/

Newcombe, T. (1998). Welfare's new burden: Feds tie down states with data reporting requirements. *Government Technology, 11*(4), 1, 14-15.

Northrop, A., Kraemer, K. L., Dunkle, D. E., & King, J. L. (1990). Payoffs from computerization: Lessons over time. *Public Administration Review, 50*(5), 505-514.

Novotny, P., & Jacobs, R. H. (1997). Geographical information systems and the new landscape of political technologies. *Social Science Computer Review, 15*(3), 264-285.

Overton, K., Frolick, M. N., & Wilkes, R. B. (1996). Politics of implementing EISs. *Information Systems Management, 13*(3), 50-57.

Pastore, R. (1995, December 1). CIO search and rescue. *CIO*, pp. 54-64.

Pearson, R., & Parsons, C. (1997, August 17). MSI verdicts jolt Springfield. *Chicago Tribune*, pp. 1, 12.

Peled, A. (2000). Politicking for success: The missing skill. *Leadership & Organization Development Journal, 21*, 20-29.

Perlman, E. (2000). Moving IT out. *Governing*, 58.

Perlman, E. (2003). Plug me in. *Governing Magazine.* Retrieved July 24, 2004, from http://www.governing.com/

Peterson, S. (2000). This space for rent. *Government Technology, 14*, 140-141.

Peterson, S. (2002). End of the line. *Government Technology.* Retrieved July 23, 2004, from http://www.govtech.net/magazine/story.php?id=25335&issue=10:2002

Peterson, S. (2004). Broadband battle. *Government Technology*, pp. 27-30.

Peterson, S. (2005, December 8). The golden egg. *Government Technology.* Retrieved December 10, 2005, from http://www.govtech.net/magazine/story.php?id=97502&issue=12:2005

Pevtzow, L. (1989, July 8). Bitterly divided Naperville leaders decide computer strategy. *Chicago Tribune*, p. 5.

Phillips, S. R., & Eisenberg, E. M. (1996). Strategic uses of electronic mail in organizations. *Javnost, 3*(4), 67-81.

Pitkin, G. M. (1993). Leadership and the changing role of the chief information officer in higher education. In *Proceedings of the 1993 CAUSE Annual Conference* (pp. 55-66).

Poulos, C. (1998). Mayor Stephen Goldsmith: Reinventing Indianapolis' local government. *Government Technology*, 31-33.

Putnam, R. D. (1995). Bowling alone revisited. *Responsive Community, 5*(2), 18-37.

Quindlen, T. H. (1993, June 7). When is e-mail an official record? Answers continue to elude feds. *Government Computer News*, pp. 1, 8.

Rickert, C. (2002, April 7). Web site look-alike causes concerns. *Daily Chronicle*, p. 1.

Rocheleau, B. (1993). Evaluating public sector information systems: Satisfaction versus impact. *Evaluation and Program Planning, 16*, 119-129.

Rocheleau, B. (1994). The software selection process in local governments. *The American Review of Public Administration, 24*(3), 317-330.

Rocheleau, B. (1995). Computers and horizontal information sharing in the public sector. In H. J. Onsrud & G. Rushton (Eds.), *Sharing geographic information* (pp. 207-229). New Brunswick, NJ: Rutgers University Press.

Rocheleau, B. (1997). Governmental information system problems and failures: A preliminary review. *Public Administration and Management: An Interactive Journal, 2*(3). Retrieved from http://www.pamij.com/roche.html

Rocheleau, B. (2000). Guidelines for public sector system acquisition. In G. D. Garson (Ed.), *Handbook of public information systems* (pp. 377-390). New York: Marcel Dekker, Inc.

Rocheleau, B. (2002a, March). *Accountability mechanisms, information systems, and responsiveness to external values.* Paper presented at the 2002 Meeting of the American Society for Public Administration, Phoenix, AZ.

Rocheleau, B. (2002b). E-mail: Does it need to be managed? Can it be managed? *Public Administration and Management: An Interactive Journal, 7*(2). Retrieved from http://pamij.com/7_2/v7n2_rocheleau.html

Ruppe, D. (2001). *Some US agencies pull data from Web.* Retrieved from http://dailynews.yahoo.colm/h/abc/20011005/pl/wtc_internetsecurity_011004_1.html

Sandlin, R. (1996). *Manager's guide to purchasing an information system.* Washington, DC: International City/County Management Association.

Schattschneider, E. E. (1983). *The semisovereign people: A realist's view of democracy in America.* Fort Worth, Texas: Holt, Rhinehart, and Winston.

Schmitz, J. (1997). Structural relations, electronic media, and social change: The public electronic network and the homeless. In S. G. Jones (Ed.), *Virtual culture: Identity and communication in cybersociety* (pp. 80-101). London: Sage Publications.

Schoech, D., Jensen, C., Fulks, J., & Smith, K. K. (1998). Developing and using a community databank. *Computers in Human Services, 15*(1), 35-53.

Schuler, D. (1995). Public space in cyberspace. *Internet World*, 89-95.

Severin, C. S. (1993, October 11). The CEO should be the CIO. *InformationWeek*, p. 76.

Shulman, S. (2005, September). *Stakeholder views on the future of electronic rulemaking.* Paper presented at the 2005 Annual Meeting of the American Political Science Association, Pittsburgh, PA. Retrieved October 16, 2005, from http://erulemaking.ucsur.pitt.edu

Stahlman, M. (1995, December 25). Internet democracy hoax. *InformationWeek*, 90.

Standing, C., & Standing, S. (1998). The politics and ethics of career progression in IS: A systems perspective. *Logistics Information Management, 11*(5), 309-316.

Strassmann, P. A. (1995). *The politics of information management.* New Canaan: The Information Economics Press.

Thurlow, M., Wiley, H. I., & Bielinski, J. (2003). *Going public: What 2000-2001 reports tell us about the performance of students with disabilities* (Tech. Rep. No. 35). Minneapolis, MN: University of Minnesota, National Center on Educational Outcomes. Retrieved July 15, 2004, from http://education.umn.edu/NCEO/OnlinePubs/Technical35.htm

Towns, S. (2004). Year in review: People. *Government Technology.* Retrieved December 15, 2005, from http://www.govtech.net/magazine.story.php?id=97500&issue=12:2005

Towns, S. (2005, December 7). The year in review: 2005. *Government Technology.* Retrieved December 10, 2005, from http://www.govtech.net/magazine/story.php?id=97500&issue=12:2005

United States General Accounting Office. (1997). *Social Security Administration: Internet access to personal earnings benefits information* (GAO/T-AIMD/HEHS-97-123).

United States General Accounting Office. (2002). *DOD's standard procurement system* (GAO-02-392T). Washington, DC.

United States General Accounting Office. (2004). *Federal chief information officers' responsibilities, reporting relationships, tenures, and challenges* (GAO-04-823).

Vittachi, I. (2005, March 25). Western Springs set to welcome wi-fi zone. *Chicago Tribune.*

Washburn, G. (1998, May 18). Building-permit delays spur city shakeup. *Chicago Tribune*, pp. 1, 10.

West, D. (2001, August-September). *E-government and the transformation of public sector service delivery.* Paper presented at the Meeting of the American Political Science Association, San Francisco.

Wiggins, L. (2001). Caribou and the census. *URISA News*, 5.

Wilhelm, A. G. (1997). A resource model of computer-mediated political life. *Policy Studies Journal, 25*(4), 519-534.

Yates, J. (2001, September 29). N.Y. plans to track flow of donations: Red Cross raises privacy concerns. *Chicago Tribune.*

Zeigler, N. (1997). Agencies say kinds worked out of new state computer system. *Daily Chronicle* (DeKalb, Illinois), p. 1.

Chapter XX
Knowledge Fusion:
A Framework for Extending the Rigor and Relevance of Knowledge Management

Peter Keen
Nanyang Technological University, Singapore

Margaret Tan
Nanyang Technological University, Singapore

ABSTRACT

The article proposes a simple framework termed 'knowledge fusion' to extend the rigor and relevance of knowledge management (KM). It points to some gaps in the current body of knowledge about KM, and provides a parsimonious set of 'partitions' that link to and from traditional knowledge management research and practice. It proposes that attention be paid to knowledge mobilization that reflects the demand side that is dominated by knowledge being part of individual identity and hence personal choice of whether, where, why and with whom to share knowledge and expertise as oppose to just understanding the traditional knowledge management that addresses only the supply side of information and the creation of environments for communication and collaboration, especially those "knowledge" largely being independent of the individual.

INTRODUCTION

The aim of this article is to point to some gaps in the current body of knowledge about knowledge management (KM) and in doing so to suggest extensions to its frameworks and to areas of investigation that build on its strengths. We propose a simple framework for what we term knowledge fusion, based on the following line of argument that captures what knowledge management is as a field, rather than what many of its critics feel it should *not* be as a domain of intellectual study and social action:

1. Knowledge management is axiomatically a mission-driven, corporatist field. Its focus is not on knowledge but on management processes that use information resources and related corporate "assets" to enhance innovation and collaboration: knowledge creation, knowledge sharing, and knowledge dissemination. There are many valid and powerful alternatives to the axioms of KM, explicated by Ekbia and Hara (2004), Ekbia and Kling (2003), Wilson (2002), and Fuller (2001), but they basically reject KM for its mission as much as its methods and intellectual base. To a large degree, "membership" in the KM field of both research and practice involves accepting the corporatist mission. We choose the word "corporatist" carefully, since it captures the view of knowledge as organizational assets, the aggressive goal of innovation, and the purposive intentions of generating a high return on investment that drives KM in both the private and public sectors. This view generates conflict for many thinkers who do not believe that knowledge is to be valued mainly for its contribution to organizational payoff.

2. KM as a corporatist practice is in many ways an announcement by the information systems community that it has positioned to move beyond information organization to information deployment; that shift is signaled by the choice of "knowledge" as the target of "management." A constant tension in the KM field is the difference between information and knowledge, but at its core KM has been information-centric. It aims at connecting innovation and growth, the core goals of the enterprise, back to information-based capabilities, one of the obvious means to that end, and to raise its own centrality as a strategic force in and of itself rather than as a support base for change management, process innovation, and business capability development. KM

is thus as much an organizational ambition as a domain of research and practice.

3. A major current limitation to progress in KM application and impact is that there is a very clear difference between the fundamental dynamics of knowledge management and of knowledge *mobilization*. Knowledge management addresses the supply side of information organization, creation of environments for communication and collaboration, leveraging of intellectual capital, and incentives for shifts in work practices, especially those that either impede or facilitate knowledge-sharing, with "knowledge" largely being independent of the individual; it is a corporate asset. Leonard's (1989) assertion is representative here: "Just as organizations are financial institutions, so they are knowledge institutions." Knowledge mobilization, by contrast, reflects the demand side that is dominated by knowledge being part of individual identity and hence personal choice of whether, where, why, and with whom to share knowledge and expertise (Keen, 2006; Qureshi & Keen 2005). Knowledge mobilization views information and knowledge in terms of situational needs—"what do *I* need to know *now*?"—while knowledge management tends to focus more on "what knowledge can we provide to our employees and what mechanisms can we put in place for them to make most effective use of it?" The push-pull tension between management and mobilization is captured in a comment by a manager that, "The organization does not understand how knowledge is shared here and I tend to ignore the knowledge management initiatives wherever I can" (Von Krogh, Roos, & Sloucm, 1994).

4. There can never be a universal "theory" of knowledge management, any more than there is any consensual agreement on what is knowledge in the mainstream of philosophy or any shared operational agreement as to its

nature across the arts, sciences, theological, and political fields. We highlight the word "never" here. KM relies on pragmatics to generate conceptions of knowledge that are actionable. There is a two-sided danger here: the pragmatics may be over-simplistic and also open to easy challenges from those who do not share the pragmatist perspective. Perhaps a larger and more damaging danger is that if the conception of "knowledge" remains a constant debating point and source of demurral, no one gains neither KM pragmatists, philosophical idealists, nor activists in the anticorporatist sphere. The discussion just gets cloudier instead of clearer.

5. KM thus should not get stuck in definitional debates, but it does need some shaping framework that encourages intellectual and pragmatic diversity and a balance between the thought leadership priorities of the pragmatists, often consultancy firms, and the research and scholarship excellence of the intellectual disciplines, mostly but not entirely in the academic communities. Our proposal is to "partition" the wider field of "knowledge" into four areas: knowledge *management*, the goal; knowledge *mobilization*, the enabler; knowledge *embodiment*, the study of what it means to "know"; and knowledge *regimes*, the organizational, political, and sociological factors that shape how knowledge is focused, authenticated, legitimized, and validated in the organizational and professional context. Each of these is a distinctive arena, in terms of its main fields of research and scholarship, axiomatic base, mode of investigation, and professional communities. Our knowledge fusion framework rests on the logic that contributions from these communities will come from how they link their specific body of theory and practice to the mission of knowledge management. We see three main links: (1) knowledge management and knowledge mobilization; (2) knowledge regimes and knowledge management; and (3) knowledge embodiment and knowledge mobilization.

6. As with total quality management (TQM) and business process reengineering (BPR), knowledge management is driven by two potentially conflicting traditions: thought leadership ambitions among leading consultants and consulting firms and research excellence priorities and practices in the academic community. TQM illustrates the fusion of these; consultants such as Deming, Juran, and Crosby led the field, drew on research by such figures as Ishikawa and on the management experience of many innovative companies, including Toyota and Motorola, to the benefit of all (Kruger, 2001). As BPR illustrates, thought leadership that is entirely detached from the scholarly and research communities lacks staying power, in that the gaps and contradictions in its claims and conceptions quickly erode its validity; it is more claims leadership than thought leadership. One of our aims in developing the knowledge fusion framework is to help KM be more like TQM than BPR. We suggest that just as academic research has formal criteria and standards that help define "excellence," thought leadership must be built around comparable criteria, which include its links to the intellectual traditions relevant to its claims and concerns.

We intend our framework to be common-sensical rather than controversial; we define a new commonsense as one that is obvious fifteen minutes after you hear it but that fifteen minutes beforehand you might never have thought of it.

THE GROUNDED THEORY DEVELOPMENT OF KNOWLEDGE FUSION

Our analysis of the KM field and formulation of the knowledge fusion framework is a grounded theory investigation that began from a wide-ranging scan of an almost unsurveyable field. Scholar Google lists 220,000 references to "knowledge management"; the fragmentation and breadth of the field is indicated by the fact that only a tiny fraction of these are cited in even twenty of the other close to a quarter of a million publications. A Google search on the term generates 57 million results. To put that in context, "business process reengineering" produces 1.3 million and "electronic commerce" produces 28 million (February 2006).

Such proliferation eliminates any practical possibility of a grand theory of knowledge management or a unified definition of "knowledge." Our approach to generating a grounded theory base for KM extension is to identify salient themes in knowledge management, such as communities of practice, knowledge sharing, knowledge creation, tacit knowledge, and intellectual property, and then to test how well conceptually and in practice they hold up. This process identified where we saw a need for new "codings." These are distinctions that we propose as part of a generic taxonomy of knowledge fusion and as researchable domains of investigation. For example, it became clear from our analysis that the widely-used distinction between explicit and tacit knowledge (Nonaka & Takeuchi, 1995) is not robust and has generated tautologies and challengeable conclusions, such as the claim that tacit knowledge is knowledge that cannot be made explicit and structured, followed by the statement that a goal for knowledge management is to make tacit knowledge structured and explicit (Gourlay, 2000; Haldin-Herrgard, 2000). Gray (2001) provides a succinct summary of the tacit-explicit knowledge distinction and states that "most organizations want to transfer tacit knowledge to explicit knowledge."

It is a substantive matter for the effectiveness of KM whether or not this transfer is possible and even conceptually meaningful. We propose, via Wilson (2002), a simple extension of the distinction to include implicit knowledge as the bridge between tacit and explicit. Implicit knowledge is what we take for granted, rarely think about, and are surprised to find that others do not share; many faux pas that we make when we travel abroad reflect the fact that a national culture has many areas of implicit knowledge concerning etiquette and social norms. The red-faced blunderer asks, "Why didn't you tell me about that?" One replies, "You didn't ask and it's obvious anyway." Our suggestion is that tacit knowledge be accepted as inherently tacit and that, using our coding distinctions, knowledge management should structure explicit knowledge, which is information-centric, explicate implicit knowledge through dialog, and leverage tacit knowledge through respectful collaboration.

Our grounded theory approach is more than taxonomic in its goals and less than ontological. It is a search for a parsimonious addition to the distinctions in the KM field which will help resolve conceptual contradictions and reported problems of application, such as the tacit-explicit contrast. This helps avoid getting caught in the definitional debate.

Clearly, new distinctions are needed for KM to achieve its targeted impacts. A review of the literature on disappointments and failures in knowledge management impacts (Lucier & Torsilieri, 1997), states that 84 percent of KM projects fail; Storey and Barnett (2000) and Barth (2000) thus pointed us to the needed distinction between knowledge management and knowledge mobilization that is at the core of our proposed framework. We did not "invent" knowledge mobilization nor redefine "knowledge" or "knowledge management" to incorporate it but instead added it as a new coding and then looked at where and how it contributes to the KM mission. That in turn pointed to the value of a new distinction in knowledge mobilization of three levels of personal knowledge identity in how individuals assess their own knowledge and how and when to share it: accountable, discretionary, and autonomous knowledge (Qureshi & Keen, 2005).

The final stage in the development of the knowledge fusion framework is to narrow down the very broad range of KM topics, distinctions, and concerns into a parsimonious set of "partitions" that link to and from traditional knowledge management research and practice. We propose that knowledge fusion has four main partitions:

- **Knowledge management:** The organizational mission for continuing the evolution of information management to become a core factor in business innovation; the supply and dissemination of knowledge-relevant information, communication and process capabilities, and the development of change management initiatives in order to build new knowledge-building and knowledge-sharing practices.

Given the mission, issues of technology options and methods are highly germane to this partition, whereas they are a distraction or even a red flag for commentators who largely oppose the main KM axioms. These critics stress that technology in and of itself is not relevant to knowledge. But it is highly relevant to knowledge management and there are many emerging developments in technology that are promising enablers of new knowledge work, especially in the library sciences, where exploration of and expertise in archiving the Semantic Web and library resource management are adding an often missing dimension to the mainstream information technology focus on data base management systems, data repositories, and Web portals (Khoo, Singh, & Chaudhry, 2006).

Technology is very much part of this partition of knowledge fusion.

- **Knowledge mobilization:** The dynamics of the processes by which individuals make their own personal choices about information seeking, knowledge creation, and knowledge sharing. This demand side must be synchronized with the supply side for effective joint benefit. The discretionary and personal nature of knowledge activation and identity leads to many gaps in practice between corporate supply and individual use, between push and pull. In addition, more and more elements of personal knowledge creation and sharing lie outside corporate ownership and control. Blogs, for instance, are becoming a significant force in professionals' knowledge-sharing and in the impact of blogs on a company's reputation and a number of companies are harnessing them to create two-way communication links with their constituencies, in effect mobilizing both company and stakeholder knowledge-sharing. In Microsoft and Sun Microsystems, over a thousand employees publish their own blogs about life in the company, technology, and industry trends. Both firms claim that these blogs have significantly improved their ability to reach, communicate with, influence, and even recruit from the development community; that is, to broaden the reach of their knowledge mobilization (Scoble & Israel, 2006). Blogging illustrates the potential value of the partitioning approach to knowledge fusion. It is as yet little studied in the context of corporate knowledge management, though there is a growing body of work on the role of blogs in e-knowledge and distributed knowledge creation in professional communities (Norris, Mason, & Lafrere, 2004). Given the rapid growth in blogging (around 60 million in early 2006) and its increasing corporate focus, this is a topic that merits study and certainly organizations should make them part of their knowledge mobilization if not part of their knowledge management.

One of the main conclusions from our initial scanning of the KM field that directly led to the identification of the need for a knowledge mobilization partition supports the often criticized "relabeling" of information management as knowledge management. It is that after around forty years of sustained effort to "manage" information, the state of good practice has solved most of the main historical problems of structuring, integration, standards, interoperability, data management, networking, scaling, and so forth. It has moved from information "systems" to information and communication platforms. These platforms are now positioned to enable a very wide range of new practices, processes, and relationships. A decade ago, many such uses of IT were impractical and the opportunities for knowledge mobilization highly constrained. At last, we have the knowledge management platforms; knowledge mobilization now becomes higher on the urgency list in terms of both research and practice. Mobile technology in particular transforms the very nature of on-demand access to and delivery of information and services. (e.g., Keen & Mackintosh, 2002.)

This is signaled by the larger number of studies on KM failures; most of these reflect successful technical designs and implementations but problems in mobilization. (See Keen [2006] for a brief review of the 9/11 Commission Report which shows that the information needed to first prevent and then respond to the terrorist conspiracies was almost all in place and available. The Report describes a knowledge management success but a knowledge mobilization disaster.)

- **Knowledge embodiment:** The deep processes of "knowing" in the widest sense of the term. The pragmatic and axiomatic KM

conception of knowledge as an organizational asset is obviously partial at best and many commentators claim that it is largely invalid and little more than a relabeling of information. (Wilson [2002] attacks the "nonsense" of knowledge management in this regard.) As we show later in the article, the KM conceptions are fully defensible in terms of its focus on knowledge as an organizational asset, and nonsensical only if the foundational organizational aims of KM are rejected.

That said, those aims do represent a selective and specialized view of the immensely wide world of knowledge creation, application, and use and will benefit from a complementary analysis, development, and application of theory from that wider world in order to extend and enrich knowledge mobilization. Many KM researchers are thus exploring reference disciplines, most obvious philosophy and epistemology, which address such topics as the social and political nature of knowing, speech act theory and the linguistic nature of knowledge, the nature of tacit knowledge, and ethical issues. Their goal is to enrich, not to attack KM.

Connecting such lines of investigation to the pragmatics of knowledge management concepts and applications is, in our view, best handled through viewing knowledge embodiment as a partition in and of itself, but one whose findings and frameworks can be brought into focus through being linked to the knowledge mobilization partition. The logic of this is that any effort to generate a consensual concept of knowledge will fail and that much of the research in this partition has had less impact on KM than it merits because it is positioned as a new approach to KM *as a whole*. We suggest that its power will come from rigorous scholarship and research made relevant by showing how and where it helps in increasing knowledge mobilization.

Knowledge fusion thus argues that the axioms, definitions, goals, and practices of KM form its chosen, deliberate, and selective bounding of the knowledge world and that rather than aim to impose competing, alternative, or conflicting views of knowledge embodiment on KM as counter theories, it is simpler and more pragmatic to map them into KM in a way that KM can absorb them. Anticorporatists and social theorists will reject this approach. And so they should. Our framework is not aimed at helping improve the rigor and relevance of the entire field of knowledge studies—that would be both absurdly pretentious and totally impractical—but only at helping the applied KM field to improve KM.

- **Knowledge regimes:** This term refers to the contextual rules, controls and processes that directly shape and constrain knowledge management. These include political, cultural, and sociological factors. Our identification of knowledge regimes as a partition of knowledge fusion was prompted by work in political science (Sowell, 1996), philosophy (Foucault, 1980), organizational decision making (Keen & Sol, in press), and the wide literature that links knowledge management to questions about capitalism and post-capitalism. The legitimacy, verification, use, and control of information are an integral part of what Foucault calls "Regimes of Truth" (Ebdia & Kling, 2003). Knowledge regimes are the sociopolitical forces that strongly affect the specific legitimacy, meaning, and effective rights of ownership of "knowledge." These include organizational design, information systems, professional associations, incentive systems, and "culture." Knowledge regimes vary widely between countries, with history, censorship, and social norms often creating bounds on knowledge embodiment, knowledge management, and knowledge mobilization.

Again, our proposal of knowledge regimes as a partition is intended to resolve the rigor-relevance tension in knowledge fusion. The mainstream of knowledge management is driven by relevance to business and organizational innovation and collaboration. It maintains that focus sometimes at the expense of rigor; the extreme instances of this are vendor claims that say document-management software is "knowledge," or the casual comment in a leading book on KM that begins, "Because of the human element in knowledge ……." (Davenport, De Long & Beers, 1997). Surely, any scholar in fields that address knowledge embodiment and knowledge mobilization would almost scream in reply that humans are not an element in knowledge but *are* knowledge. The remark makes more sense in its context of the conceptualization of knowledge as a corporate asset, much of which is embodied in information resources, not people. That said, this is certainly not a rigorous statement and it is typical of ones that critics of KM zero in on very quickly.

Conversely, discussions of knowledge regimes are often highly abstract and formalistic. They also often adopt very different axioms of "knowledge" than does KM. For example, Day's (2001) history of KM highlights "the European documentalist, critical modernist and Italian Autonomous Marxist influenced Post-Fordist traditions." Fuller's (2001) blandly titled *Knowledge Management Foundations* is anything but that; it is a resonant and complex exploration of "civic republicanism" and social epistemology. His KM manifesto includes discussion of "pseudo solutions" such as cyberplatonism, and academic bullionism (the "scourge of KM"). Both Day and Fuller offer a counterview to just about every assumption, goal, and application of knowledge management. An obvious question then is why they self-classify their work as KM, virtually guaranteeing that it will have no impact on the communities within the field? The logic of the knowledge fusion framework of partitions is that such work is a very valuable potential contribution to KM if, and only if, it can build linkages to the KM mainstream instead of trying to supersede it or bury it beneath a my-citations-are-more-obscure-than-yours bibliographic mountain.

Our proposal of partitions is aimed at helping improve both the rigor and relevance of the knowledge management field through appropriate use of reference disciplines. These are fields of scholarship and research—the two are not always equivalent—that offer insights, theories, and findings that are relevant to but not within the immediate academic and professional purview of KM. The knowledge management field as a whole will be enriched through such diverse and unconnected reference disciplines as epistemology, library sciences, and education (where there is an innovative stream of research and application on information-seeking, interface design, and learning behaviors directly relevant to knowledge mobilization) (Khoo et al., 2006), sociology (we are seeing a resurgence of references in KM articles to Berger and Luckman's [1966] work on the social construction of reality that is highly relevant to knowledge embodiment), political science (knowledge regimes), critical theory (e.g., Baudrillard, 1994), hermeneutics, economics, phenomenology, and computer science. Partitioning and linking to the core knowledge management plus knowledge mobilization fusion is a vehicle for making all this rigor relevant.

Figure 1 summarizes our knowledge fusion framework. To be of value, it must pass tests of parsimony (the knowledge management field does not need any increase in elaborate individual conceptual schema or in the vocabulary of terms floating across its many journals and topics), usefulness in helping provide a coherent and comprehensive high-level mapping of a very complex and fragmented field, and originality in pointing to new lines of investigation and lessons from existing research. That judgment will be made by our readers.

The recommended agenda for knowledge fusion is thus: (1) Maintain the mainstream focus in KM on harnessing organizational resources for the purpose of innovation, knowledge-creation, and collaboration; (2) Sharpen the focus on linking individual demand and use of peoples' own and others' knowledge (knowledge mobilization) to organizational supply and encouragement of new practices and processes (knowledge management); (3) Enrich the discussion of "knowledge" and

Figure 1. From knowledge management to mobilization to fusion

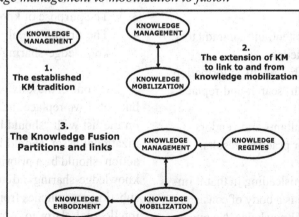

knowledge embodiment and thus of opportunities for knowledge mobilization; and (4) Investigate the impact of knowledge regimes on knowledge management assumptions and practices, including the role of dissent, and adapt those practices to meet the changing demands of other regimes, including those of customers, competitors, pressure groups, and social movements.

THE VALIDITY OF THE AXIOMATIC BASE OF KNOWLEDGE MANAGEMENT AS A MISSION-LED NOT TOPIC-DRIVEN FIELD

Our entire line of argument centers on one core conclusion from our analysis of the KM field: that the very criticisms made of it are at the same time valid but in many instances irrelevant. Most of the criticisms address weaknesses in the "knowledge" component of KM. But knowledge management is not about the topic of knowledge as such but the mission of management. Knowledge management is in fact part of a corporatist regime of truth, in Foucault's sense of the phrase. It is fully valid to attack that regime on social, political, or moral grounds—KM is very much a part of Big Business—but criticisms made on the same terms about the validity of KM itself largely miss their mark.

Here are some standard criticisms of knowledge management:

- It uses fuzzy, inconsistent, and contradictory definitions of knowledge.
- It is largely a relabeling of information management through "search-and-replace" marketing.
- It is driven by consultants and vendors.
- It has produced poor practical results.

The first criticism is misleading in that it implies that elsewhere there is a body of consistent and reliable definitions of knowledge. No one on this planet has successfully generated an accepted and universal theory of knowledge after 2,500 years of continuous effort. The irresolvable debate or more often conflict between science and religion is a difference of belief about what is knowledge and hence "truth." Just try and synthesize a definition of "knowledge" and "truth" from a sampling of the great philosophers, whose entire careers were devoted to answering the question of what is knowledge: Plato, Aristotle, Descartes, Kant, Locke, Kirkegaard, Nietzsche, Heidegger, Wittgenstein, Foucault, Habermas, and Searle, to name just a tiny few. These are titanic thinkers whose concerns were epistemological and ontological, with Heidegger's *Meaning and Being* an indicator of the scope and depth of their search.

Knowledge management is far, far less ambitious and basically adopts axiomatic views of knowledge. The test of the value of these axioms and their implications is the domains of effective action that they enable in organizations. Their limitations come not from any definition of knowledge but of gaps between axioms, actions, and impact. But the test is not one of "truth."

It must be recognized the axioms of KM do limit application and impact and thus merit investigation, including drawing on the field of philosophy as a reference discipline. There are four main elements in KM axioms:

1. Knowledge is an organizational asset.
2. It can be managed like other assets.
3. The purpose of knowledge is action.
4. The primary goal of KM is to encourage knowledge-sharing and collaboration.

Each one of these axioms is open to challenge, but not if we replace the word "is" in each item on the list with "should be"; should be an organizational asset, should be managed, should be action, should be a priority target, and should be knowledge-sharing and collaboration. That simple substitution switches from KM as a topic and an intellectual claim to a mission. It establishes a knowledge regime that excludes certain types of knowledge and knowledge embodiment.

One of the authors of this article, for instance, knows much more about Shakespeare than about information technology, his main field of study and application relevant to KM. If the purpose of knowledge is action (Alavi & Leidner, 1999), then he is a complete failure; the only actionable value of this knowledge is to read more Shakespeare. Similarly, he is an expert on antique Egyptian stamps; the only contribution to action here is to motivate him to spend a lot of money on eBay.

From a knowledge identity perspective, his knowledge of books and his philatelic hobby is core to his sense of self, his knowledge-seeking, and the communities in which he shares his knowledge. It is completely irrelevant to knowledge management in the business and academic communities he works in; unless he decides to become a stamp dealer. The axioms and mission of KM *exclude* many domains of knowledge embodiment on the basis of "should be" as the intention for the KM mission and "is" as the axiom that drives that mission.

Consider substituting "should not be" for "should be" on the KM list of axioms and a very different intellectual discourse emerges, one that many commentators on knowledge regimes and knowledge embodiment are really trying to build: knowledge should not be managed as a corporate asset, the purpose of knowledge should not be action, and so forth. "Should not" defines an alternative regime of truth, one that places civil society ahead of corporatist modernization, for instance. Ebdia and Kling (2003) dissect the degree to which the financial analyst, shareholder value, and business press regimes of truth explain how Enron so easily deceived the public and how complicit these regimes were in helping them do so. This is a powerful attack on the "recipe" that business has constructed as its social reality (Berger & Luckman, 1966). Such a view cogently states that that the problem with knowledge man-

agement is knowledge management. It stands outside the field of KM, looking in on it.

In our view, the entire field of KM will be improved in its intellectual focus by sharpening the being in and looking in distinction. Should KM be about the "shoulds?" That is an irrelevant question. It *is* about them. Should it move towards the "should not" extreme? Then it would not be knowledge management as a corporatist regime but something else. Knowledge fusion then means that the relevance test for linking research in reference disciplines in the partitions of knowledge embodiment, mobilization and regimes to knowledge management is to help turn "should" into "is." Epistemology, phenomenology, and post-Fordist social capital Italian Marxism may rigorously propose the "should not" viewpoint, but that is irrelevant to KM.

We do not intend in any way to make our analysis here a defense of knowledge management as a socially constructed reality and a corporate regime of truth. Indeed, our ongoing study of the impact of the Internet on corporate reputation, which alerted us to the growing impact of blogs, raises a complex question as to how organizations can avoid being so locked into their knowledge regimes that they exclude information and knowledge that may later turn out to be relevant to their success and even survival, and how they can include appropriate dissent and "whistle blowing." A cautionary tale here is the degree to which Wal-Mart's knowledge management strategies overlooked what was obvious to many observers who read *The Nation, Mother Jones,* and *Progressive* instead of *The Wall Street Journal*: the company was accumulating a reputation as an callous employer, union-buster, sexual discriminator, brutal exploiter of suppliers, ruthless outsourcer, and callous corporate machine indifferent to anything except its own growth. In 2005, Wal-Mart moved from being the darling of the business knowledge regimes to the Darth Vader of many of the political and social conscience knowledge regimes.

The issue here is not whether or not these accusations and the vivid adjectives we use in the above paragraph are "true"—they are certainly seen as truths in liberal democratic circles—but that Wal-Mart's knowledge regimes blocked out the information. Now, the company has installed a massive new knowledge mobilization capability, a "war room" (Barbaro, 2005) that monitors the entire Web, including blogs, to alert the company to positive and negative coverage, respond, communicate, and, perhaps most important of all, listen. In 2006, it began to reach out to the bloggers with offers of information and communication that, with their permission, Wal-Mart would provide for them to incorporate in their in their own knowledge mobilization: publishing, discussion, and community-building. Given that several surveys suggest that 2-8 percent of Wal-Mart's more affluent customers are beginning to boycott the company (Barbaro, 2005), Wal-Mart would have benefited from more and earlier attention to Web-enabled knowledge mobilization rather than just internal knowledge management.

This suggests that research in the knowledge regimes partition on the role of dissent, dialectics, and critical enquiry (Courtney, 2001) may offer valuable lessons for knowledge management and mobilization. It may well be that such research begins from rigorous obscurity and over time will establish its relevance.

THE CONSULTANTS' ROLE IN KM: THOUGHT LEADERSHIP VS.—OR WITH—RESEARCH EXCELLENCE

The second major criticism of KM as a field is that it is largely vendor- and consultant-driven. Wilson's (2002) excoriation of the nonsense of knowledge management states in its opening sentence that the growth of KM as "a strategy of consultancy companies is one of a series of such strategies dating from Taylor's (1911) 'scientific management'." The implied logic of this state-

ment is to suggest that the source of intellectual development matters as much as its nature, and that consultancy-driven work has some inherent built-in limitation, most obviously definitional weaknesses and biases ("in management consultancy it is, perhaps, not too serious to fail to distinguish between related concepts ….. the task of the academic researcher is to clarify the use of terms so that the field of investigation has a clearly defined vocabulary").

That certainly puts Taylor in his place (perhaps had he been an Assistant Professor at the Stevens Institute of Technology, to whom he left the bulk of his estate, scientific management would be legitimate), along with the other consultants who profoundly shaped management thought and stimulated a wide range of research that went a long way beyond clarifying terms: Deming, Juran and Crosby in TQM; Follett, the "prophet of management", whose work in the 1930-1950s on constructive conflict and "co-ordination" was immensely influential in its time and that has increasingly been recognized as foundational for organizational theory; and Beckhard, uniformly acknowledged by his colleagues at MIT as a core figure in the development of the modern human relations school. What makes them relevant to the development of the knowledge management field is that they are noted for what leading consulting firms routinely talk about as their goal for innovation: "thought leadership." A Google search on the term plus the name of any of the leading consulting companies produces between 20,000 and 200,000 results. "Knowledge management + thought leadership" generates 650,000.

There is some evidence that, contrary to the view that knowledge management was largely driven by consultancies in order to find a new revenue stream after the drying up of the largesse generated by Y2K and ERP implementation, the main factor was instead their own need to innovate. As many areas of their markets commoditized, including large scale information systems development, they needed to increase

Box 1.

	Google	Scholar Google
Total quality management	139 million	1.2 million
Business process reengineering	1.3 million	21 thousand

their internal productivity, which mainly meant improving collaboration and knowledge-sharing, particularly about projects, clients, and in-house expertise; in other words, they had to invent knowledge management. While the title of CIO (Chief Information Officer) originated in business, that of CKO (Chief Knowledge Officer) was very much the domain of the large consultancies. Much of the most influential work on KM has originated in the same firms, often written by individuals who have spanned the worlds of academia and consulting (such as Davenport, a professor at the University of Texas and Boston University and also director of KM research centers at Ernst and Young and Accenture.)

Thought leadership (TL), wherever it originates, plus research excellence (RE) would appear to be a powerful combination for a mission- rather than discipline-driven field. Our knowledge fusion framework implies that thought leadership will tend to center on the management-mobilization link, since that is where so many of the practical problems and disappointments of KM investments appear to be generated (Qureshi & Keen, 2005). Excellence in research will tend to focus on the regimes-management or embodiment-mobilization linkages.

Our line of argument obviously accepts the primacy of the corporatist view of the organizational purpose of KM for the evolution of the field, accepts that much of KM is really an extension of information management as a force for innovation and collaboration, and accepts the value of thought leadership being driven by consultants as well as

academics. That said, thought leadership based on weak thought will not create a sustainable forum for strong research and its momentum will inevitably evaporate as realism intrudes on assertion. The total quality management and business process management fields provide contrasting examples in this regard.

TQM was built on consultant evangelism (Juran, Crosby, Deming), supported by brilliant application by managers, most obviously Toyota's Ohno, and extended by a wealth of first-rate research (e.g., Ishikawa). The result is a field that continues to grow in terms of academic research outputs. Using Google plus Scholar Google as a rough comparative index for degree of interest plus degree of research activity respectively, commonsense would suggest that if the first is huge and the second tiny, then this is a field that is likely to be just a fad; the reverse would signal a specialist academic field. The contrast between TQM and BPR is shown in Box 1.

One might argue that the research/buzz ratio is higher for BPR than for TQM, but what these figures suggest is that few serious scholars now have any interest in BPR. Yet BPR certainly established a powerful thought leadership position for its best-known proponents, an MIT professor (Hammer) and the head of a leading IT consulting firm (Champy) that had a very distinguished record in the IT field in generating many of the most influential "big ideas" of the 1970-80s.

Unlike TQM, somehow BPR did not generate the creative tension and integration between thought leadership and research excellence that our formulation of knowledge fusion aims at encouraging. If KM is to be effective in generating a lasting impact on research and practice, it simply must ensure that the acronymic equation is KM = TL + RE. However, the pragmatics of KM as organizational mission opens the door to what might be termed intellectual sleight of hand: finessing problems by avoiding them. Hammer and Champy did this basically by not defining what a business process is and making almost casual assertions without a single citation to others' work. There is an aggressive anti-intellectualism in their work, illustrated by the command on the book jacket to "forget all you know about business; it's wrong."

Thought leadership demands intellectualism, in the form of the synthesis of experience and disciplined development of reliable methods that so marks the work of the TQM leaders, and scholarship-backed articulation of principles, exemplified by many writers who move between the worlds of academia and consultancy such as Hamel in corporate strategy and Davenport in knowledge management. Many of the critics of the KM field almost axiomatically assume that it does not need such thought leadership, and that good scholarship and applied research will generate momentum, credibility, implementation, and impact. We argue that thought leadership is integral to the very goals of KM, and that just as there are formal criteria for assessing research quality, there is a need for a comparable if less formal set of broad categories for intended though leadership. We suggest the following list:

- **A succinct and robust articulation of a "management lens."** A genuinely different perspective on some practical aspect of either the field as a whole or some specific area within it where the new lens opens up major opportunities for innovation and collaboration, the two basic reasons for investing in KM, however defined.

- **An explicit inclusion in the articulation and explication in the article or book of the axiomatic base underlying the new focus and of the limits of the domain of applicability**. This, rather than the much-debated issue of a definition of knowledge or knowledge management, appears to us to be key in moving KM forward. There can never be a universal grand schema for knowledge management. It should be perfectly acceptable for contributors to the field to state that, for instance, the purpose of knowledge is action but they need to recognize explicitly that that is an axiom not a truth and that it immediately limits the nature, domains, and methods the lens applies to. It also excludes many areas for investigation in the partition of knowledge embodiment in that it implies a narrow range of epistemological considerations (for instance, it implicitly defines what "expertise" means and how it should be leveraged).

Our knowledge fusion perspective argues for much more careful presentation of "here is one way of viewing XYZ" instead of "this is *the* way." How much richer and more dynamic a field might BPR have become had its leaders couched their message in such wording as, "Here is one perspective on business processes that emphasizes an industrial engineering approach...... it highlights as targets of opportunity..... it does not apply so well to processes that are less structured and that rest on negotiations and tacit knowledge......" Equally, we suggest that the quality of intellectual discussion in KM will be improved by critics and commentators getting away from attacks that basically begin, "ABC's paper claims that...... It is wrong and based on an incorrect definition... Here is the correct one."

- **An active search in the scholarly and research literature for grounded support**

for the conceptions and claims. The famous science fiction writer, Theodore Sturgeon, replied to a statement from the audience that "90 percent of sci-fi is crud"; "Madam, 90 percent of *everything* is crud." A responsibility of anyone staking a claim to thought leadership, whether through a consulting firm's "white paper," a business press article, a book, or an article in a research journal, is to know and build on the 10 percent. Fields such as TQM, BPR, and KM that are action- and mission-driven run the risk of becoming ahistorical. They look ahead at organizational "transformation" and stress the newness of their perspectives.

In passing, we note that in our view, Wilson's attack on KM as nonsense richly sampled the 90 percent of crud; many of the quotes and examples he provides are simply silly, vapid, ephemeral, consigned to the ashcan of dead trees, and unlikely (one hopes) ever to be cited again. For instance, Wilson ably garrotes a five line KM course description (whose Week 1 is a "collage overview"); written no doubt by a professor who had no idea that it would be selected as evidence of the flaws in the entire KM field. But his ability to mine the KM field and find so many nuggets of coal, not gold, is for us a warning signal that intellectual quality control must apply to white papers, MBA college curricula, trade press articles, guru interviews, and any other formal statement of a position on KM. Again, we hope that our partitioning of the field may contribute, if only a little, to sharpening its scholarly focus and perhaps to help highlight the 10 percent that matters. (In the spirit of knowledge mobilization, we have begun a program funded by Nanyang Technological University to build a blog/portal/literature repository/Semantic Web implementation that highlights the best of thought leadership and research excellence. Of course, "best" implies a particular knowledge regime and key general question for the Semantic Web: *whose* semantics, not which semantics).

One area of gold, not coal, for thought leadership is the scholarship of management theory. It is noteworthy that the leading books on knowledge management rarely investigate the literature of management and organizational theory. It is as if the knowledge worker somehow came into being around 1969 (when Drucker announced the coming of the knowledge economy) and that knowledge management as a discipline emerged in 1990 with Svelby's book that appears to be the first that explicitly uses the term. There is a wealth of earlier literature that addresses many of the core themes and concerns of KM but is rarely mentioned in the field. We referred to Follett's work on constructive conflict, to which should be added the Carnegie School's astonishing stream of thought leadership plus research excellence exemplified by March, Simon, and Cyert. Simon's *Sciences of the Artificial* and *Administrative Behavior*, for example, are directly about, not just relevant to, the goals and themes of KM and helped earn him a Nobel Prize. Other scholars whose work addresses knowledge regimes but that is relatively infrequently referenced by the KM thought leaders include Argyris, Schon, Galbraith, Churchman, Barnard, and Thompson, to name just a few.

In our articulation of knowledge fusion, we have largely emphasized how the partitions of knowledge mobilization, embodiment, and regimes can enhance that of the knowledge management partition. We suggest that as a partition within knowledge fusion, there is value for KM to link far more closely than it has to the resonant scholarship of management theory.

CONCLUSION

At the core of our framework is a single distinction that we view as fundamental to the effective development and impact of knowledge management as both a field and an area of management practice: knowledge mobilization. Initially, our investigation was targeted at arguing that knowledge management should incorporate and even convert to our viewpoint. Our work remains centered on knowledge mobilization but we quickly realized that unless we carefully maintained a respectful boundary between knowledge management and knowledge mobilization, we would merely add to the blur and multiplicity of KM and get caught up in the definitional debates. To establish our own axioms and distinctions, especially that of knowledge as identity with three levels of activation – accountable, discretionary, and autonomous knowledge – we would need to move into intellectual assault mode, attacking the axioms of knowledge as corporate asset and as independent of the individual. That made no sense at all; it would represent an intellectual arrogance, negativism, and waste of effort that impedes rather than contributes to a cumulative tradition of research and practice.

As we moved consciously to adopt a grounded theory approach to positioning our conceptions of knowledge mobilization, and activation, we increasingly acknowledged the extent to which knowledge management is axiomatic rather than definitional in its very varied domains of theory and practice and that in many ways the axioms drive the theory and practice. The heterogeneity of these domains is both the opportunity and the problem for knowledge management. They are an opportunity, for instance, in that the work of Habermas (1984), Rorty (1991) and Searle (1995) in the field of philosophy appears more and more as of direct practical relevance to our understanding of knowledge mobilization. They are a problem in that discussions of their work at the theoretical level and from the perspective of their own axioms do not connect well if at all to the mainstream of KM.

But it should do so. Partitioning the semi-infinite reference disciplines relevant to "knowledge" helps achieve this. The central test of the validity and value of our knowledge fusion framework is whether the proposed partitions parsimoniously but also comprehensively both capture the scope of the disciplines and focus them insights on knowledge management, rather than knowledge.

Our framework has a selfish purpose: to help us leverage our work. We hope that it helps others in the knowledge management field leverage their own. We have no interest in promoting knowledge fusion as a new theory or "model." We developed it to guide our own investigation and collaboration with colleagues. We offer it as a vehicle for knowledge mobilization in the knowledge management field. Every single one of the themes and viewpoints that we review in this article has been addressed by dozens and even hundreds of KM thinkers and practitioners and our bibliography does not do justice to the range and volume of work that we reviewed or the work we overlooked; it is largely illustrative. The diversity and quantity in many ways motivated our study; there is too much of it, it does not seem to be generating a cumulative tradition of study on which results build on each other, and at times KM is almost a haystack in which almost any needle can be found just by digging around. Something has to be done to frame KM, not to homogenize it, but to give it more shape. We hope that our framework offers a useful starting point.

Finally, we listed as one of the main criticisms of knowledge management as a field the claim that it so far has generated disappointing results. Compared to, say, the field of supply chain management (SCM), where the total costs of logistics have been reduced by 40 percent as a percent of gross domestic product (Earle & Keen, 2000) and commentators can point to companies such as Dell, Wal-Mart, UPS, and Li & Fung, whose growth and spectacular success were built on SCM. We have as yet no comparable large-scale successes in knowledge management, and the "learning organization" and "knowledge company" remain distant dreams. Binney (2001) states that we have many knowledge management *applications* but very few knowledge management *systems*. In the end, the validity of knowledge management as a field will be determined by its results. Knowledge fusion is aimed at helping mobilize critical enquiry, in the widest sense of the term, thought leadership and research excellence to influence and hopefully add value to the efforts of the managers who will build the KM equivalents of Dell and Toyota. That may be a long way off, but that is the reality test for the field of knowledge management.

REFERENCES

Alavi, M., & Leidner, D. (1999). Knowledge management systems: Emerging views and practices from the field. In *Proceedings of the 32nd HICCS Conference*, Hawaii.

Barbaro, M. (2005, November 1). A new weapon for Wal-Mart: A war room. *New York Times*, p. A1.

Barth, S. (2000, October). KM horror stories. *Knowledge Management Magazine*.

Baudrillard, J. (1994). *Simulacres et simulation, the body in theory* (S. Glaser, Trans). Ann Arbor: University of Michigan Press.

Baumand, P. (1999). *Tacit knowledge in organizations*. London: Sage Publications.

Berger, P., & Luckman, T. (1966). *The social construction of reality: A treatise on the sociology of knowledge*. Gardener City, New York: Anchor Books.

Binney, D. (2001). The knowledge spectrum: Understanding the KM landscape. *Journal of Knowledge Management, 5*(1), 33-42.

Courtney, J. (2001). Decision-making and knowledge management in inquiring organizations: Towards a new decision-making paradigm for DSS. *Decision Support Systems, 31*, 17-38.

Davenport, T., DeLong, D., & Beers, M. (1997). Building successful knowledge management projects (pp.1-16). *Center for business innovation working paper*. Ernst and Young.

Day, R. (2001). Totality and representation: A history of knowledge management through European documentation, critical modernity and post-Fordism. *Journal of the American Society for Information Science and Technology, 52*(9), 725-735.

Earle, M., & Keen, P. (2000). *From .com to .profit*. San Francisco: Jossey-Bass

Ekbia, H., & Hara, N. (2004). *The quality of evidence in the knowledge management literature: The guru version*.

Ekbia, H., & Kling, R. (2003). *The power of knowledge management in late modern times*.

Foucault, M. (1980). *Power/Knowledge: Selective interviews and other writings 1972-1977*. New York: Pantheon Books.

Fuller, S. (2001). *Knowledge management foundations*. New York: Elsevier.

Gourlay, S. (2000, September 13-15). On some cracks in the "engine" of knowledge-creation: A conceptual critique of Nonaka & Takeuchi's (1995) model. In *Proceedings of the British Academy of Management 2000 Conference (BAM2000)*, Edinburgh.

Gray, P. (2001). *Knowledge management overview*. University of California at Berkeley, Center for Research on Information Technology and Organization.

Habermas, J. (1984). *The theory of communicative action*. London: Polity Press.

Haldin-Herrgard, T. (2000). Difficulties in diffusion of tacit knowledge in organizations. *Journal of Intellectual Capital, 1*(4), 357-365.

Harvey, D. (1989). *The condition of postmodernity: An enquiry into the origins of cultural change.*

Heidegger, M. (1962). *Being and time* (J. Marquarie & E. Robinson, Trans.). Oxford: Blackwell.

Keen, P. (2006, April 3-6). Knowledge mobilization: The challenge for information professionals. In Khoo et al. (Eds.), *Proceedings of the Asia-Pacific Conference on Library & Information Education & Practice 2006.* Singapore.

Keen, P., & Sol, H. (in press). *Decision enhancement services: Improving decision agility.*

Keen, P., & Macintosh, R. (2002). *The freedom economy.* New York: McGraw-Hill.

Khoo, C., Singh, D., & Chaudhry, A.S. (Eds.). (2006, April 3-6). Preparing information professionals for leadership in the new age. In *Proceedings of the Asia-Pacific Conference on Library and Information Education and Practice,* Singapore.

Kruger, V. (2001). Main schools of TQM: "The big five." *The TQM Magazine, 13*(3), 146-155.

Leonard, D. (1989). *The wellsprings of knowledge: Building and sustaining the sources of innovation.* Cambridge, MA: Harvard Business School Press.

Lucier, C., & Torsilieri, J. D(1997a). Why knowledge programs fail. *Strategy and Business, 4,* 14-28

Lucier, C., & Torsilieri, J. D. (1997b). Why knowledge programs fail: A CEO's guide to managing learning. *Strategy & Business, 4,* 14-28.

Nonaka, I., & Takeuchi, H. (1995). *The knowledge-creating company: How Japanese companies create the dynamics of innovation.* New York: Oxford University Press.

Norris, Mason, & Lafrere. (2004, February) Transforming e-knowledge: A revolution in the sharing of knowledge, *i4d.* (book précis)

Polyani, M. (1958). *Personal knowledge: Towards a post-critical philosophy.* London: Rutledge.

Ponzi, L., & Koenig, M. (2002, October). Knowledge management: Another management fad? *Information Research, 8*(1).

Qureshi, S., & Keen, P. (2005). Activating knowledge through electronic collaboration: Vanquishing the knowledge paradox. In *Proceedings of the 40ᵗʰ HICCS Conference, Hawaii.*

Rorty, R. (1991). Objectivity, relativism and truth. *Cambridge: philosophical papers I.* Cambridge University Press.

Scoble, R., & Israel, S. (2006). *Naked conversations.* New York: Wiley.

Searle, J. (1995). *Rationality in action.* Cambridge, MA: MIT Press.

Sowell, T. (1996). *Knowledge and decisions.* New York: Harper Collins.

Storey, J., & Barnett, E. (2000). Knowledge management initiatives: Learning from failure. *Journal of Knowledge Management, 4*(2), 145-156.

Svelby, K. (1990). *The new organizational wealth: Managing and measuring knowledge-based assets.* San Francisco: Berrett-Koehler.

Von Krogh, G., Roos, J., & Sloucm, K. (1994). An essay on corporate epistemology. *Strategic Management Journal, 15.*

Wilson, T. (2002, October). The nonsense of knowledge management. *Information Research,* 8(1).

This work was previously published in International Journal of Knowledge Management, Vol. 3, Issue 4, edited by M. E. Jennex, pp. 1-17, copyright 2007 by IGI Publishing, formerly known as Idea Group Publishing (an imprint of IGI Global).

Chapter XXI
Pattern Management:
Practice and Challenges

Barbara Catania
University of Genoa, Italy

Anna Maddalena
University of Genoa, Italy

ABSTRACT

Knowledge intensive applications rely on the usage of knowledge artifacts, called patterns, to represent in a compact and semantically rich way huge quantities of heterogeneous raw data. Due to pattern characteristics of patterns, specific systems are required for pattern management in order to model, store, retrieve and manipulate patterns in an efficient and effective way. Several theoretical and industrial approaches (relying on standard proposals, metadata management and business intelligence solutions) have already been proposed for pattern management. However, no critical comparison of the existing approaches has been proposed so far. The aim of this chapter is to provide such a comparison. In particular, specific issues concerning pattern management systems, pattern models and pattern languages are discussed. Several parameters are also identified that will be used in evaluating the effectiveness of theoretical and industrial proposals. The chapter is concluded with a discussion concerning additional issues in the context of pattern management.

INTRODUCTION

The huge quantity of heterogeneous raw data that we collect from modern, data-intensive applicational environments does not constitute knowledge by itself. A knowledge extraction process and data management techniques are often required to extract from data concise and relevant information that can be interpreted, evaluated and manipulated by human users in order to drive and specialize business decision processing. Of course, since raw data may be heterogeneous, several kinds of knowledge artifacts exist that can represent hidden knowledge. Clusters, association rules, frequent itemsets and symptom-diagnosis correlations are common examples of such knowledge artifacts, generated by data mining applications. Equations or keyword frequencies are other examples of patterns, relevant, for example, in a multimedia context. All those knowledge artifacts are often called *patterns*. In a more concise and general way, patterns may be defined as compact and rich in semantics representation of raw data. The semantic richness of a pattern is due to the fact that it reveals new knowledge hidden in the huge quantity of data it represents. Patterns are also compact, since they represent interesting correlations among data providing, in many cases, a synthetic, high level description of some data characteristics. Patterns are therefore the knowledge units at the basis of any knowledge intensive application

Due to their specific characteristics, ad hoc systems are required for pattern management in order to model, store, retrieve, analyze and manipulate patterns in an efficient and effective way.

Many academic groups and industrial consortiums have devoted significant efforts towards solving this problem. Moreover, since patterns may be seen as a special type of metadata, pattern management has also some aspects in common with metadata management.

In general, scientific community efforts mainly deal with the definition of a pattern management framework providing a full support for heterogeneous pattern generation and management, thus providing back-end technologies for pattern management applications. Examples of these approaches are the 3W model (Johnson et al., 2000), the inductive databases approach — investigated in particular in the CINQ project (CINQ, 2001) and the PANDA framework (PANDA, 2001; Catania et al., 2004). In the context of inductive databases, several languages have also been proposed supporting the mining process over relational (or object-relational) data by extending the expressive power of existing data query languages with primitives supporting the mining process. Examples of such approaches are MSQL (Imielinski & Virmani, 1999), Mine-Rule (Meo et

al., 1998), DMQL (Han et al., 1996) and ODMQL (Elfeky et al., 2001). On the other hand, industrial proposals mainly deal with standard representation purposes for patterns resulting from data mining and data warehousing processes, in order to support their exchange between different architectures. Thus, they mainly provide the right front end for pattern management applications. Examples of such approaches are: the Predictive Model Markup Language (PMML, 2003), the common warehouse metamodel (CWM, 2001) and the Java Data Mining API (JDM, 2003).

In general, existing proposals can be classified according to the following aspects:

(a) The chosen architecture to manage patterns together with data.
(b) The pattern characteristics supported by the data model.
(c) The type of operations and queries supported by the proposed languages.

As far as we know, even if several proposals exist, no critical comparison of the existing approaches has been proposed so far. We believe that such a comparison would be very useful in order to determine whether the existing approaches are sufficient to cover all pattern requirements and to guide application developers in the choice of the best solution in developing knowledge discovery applications.

The aim of this chapter is to provide such a comparison. We first present a definition of patterns and pattern management. Then, specific issues concerning pattern management systems, pattern models and pattern languages are discussed, pointing out possible alternative solutions in the context of a given scenario. Several parameters relevant to the pattern management context will also be identified and then used to evaluate the effectiveness of various theoretical and industrial proposals. Moreover, relationships between pattern and general metadata management will also be identified, and some existing approaches for metadata representation discussed. Finally, we will briefly discuss solutions for pattern management, supported by some popular commercial DBMSs. The chapter concludes with a discussion of additional issues and possible future trends in the context of pattern management.

PATTERN MANAGEMENT: BACKGROUND

In many different modern contexts, a huge quantity of raw data is collected. A usual approach to analyze such data is to generate some compact knowledge artifacts (i.e., clusters, association rules, frequent itemsets, etc.) through data processing methods that reduce the number and size of data, to make them manageable for humans while preserving as much as possible their intrinsic information or discovering new interesting correlations. Those knowledge artifacts that constitute our knowledge unit are called *patterns*.

Definition 1: *A pattern is a compact and rich in semantics representation of raw data.*

Patterns may be regarded as knowledge units that effectively describe entire subsets of data (in this sense, they are compact). The quality of the representation achieved by a pattern can be quantified by using some statistical measures. Depending on their measures, patterns can describe relevant data properties (in this sense, they are rich in semantics).

Pattern management is an important issue in many different contexts and domains. The most important contexts in which pattern management is required are business intelligence and data mining. Business intelligence concerns a broad category of applications and technologies for gathering, storing, analyzing and providing access to data to help enterprises in business decisions. Data mining is one of the fundamental activities involved in business intelligence applications be-

sides querying and reporting, OLAP processing, statistical analysis and forecasting. The knowledge units resulting from the data mining tasks may be quite different.

As an example, in the context of the market-basket analysis, association rules involving sold items derived from a set of recorded transactions are often generated. In addition, in order to perform a market segmentation, the user may also be interested in identifying clusters of customers, based on their buying preferences, or clusters of products, based on customer buying habits. In financial brokerages, users cope with stock trends derived from trading records. In epidemiology, users are interested in symptom-diagnosis correlations mined from clinical observations.

Pattern management is a key issue also in many other domains not involved directly with a data mining process. For instance, in information retrieval, users are interested in extracting keyword frequencies and frequent sets of words appearing in the analyzed documents in order to specialize searching strategies and to perform similarity analysis. Content-based music retrieval is another domain in which patterns have to be managed in order to represent and query rhythm, melody and harmony (Conklin, 2002). In image processing, recurrent figures in shapes may be interpreted as specific types of patterns (Nakajima et al., 2000). In machine learning (Mitchell, 1997), predictions and forecasting activities are based on classifiers, which can be interpreted as specific types of patterns.

Recently, pattern management is becoming much more important, not only in centralized architectures but also in distributed ones. Indeed, the diffusion of the Web and the improvement of networking technologies speed up the requirement for distributed knowledge discovery and management systems. For instance, in the Web context, sequences of clicks collected by Web servers are important patterns for clickstream analysis. Moreover, knowledge representation and management, in terms of patterns, is a fundamental issue in the context of the Semantic Web and in agent-based intelligent systems where metadata have to be shared among different parties.

Depending on the specific domain, different processes may be used for pattern extraction, e.g., knowledge discovery processes for data mining patterns, feature extraction processes in multimedia applications or manual processes when patterns are not extracted but directly provided by the user or the application (for example, a classifier not automatically generated from a training set).

Patterns share some characteristics that make traditional DBMSs unable to represent and manage them. As discussed above, patterns may be generated from different application contexts resulting in very heterogeneous structures. Moreover, heterogeneous patterns often have to be managed together. For instance, in a Web context, in order to better understand e-commerce buying habits of a certain Web site's users, different patterns can be combined, for example:

(a) **Navigational patterns** (identified by click-stream analysis) describing their surfing and browsing behaviour.

(b) **Demographic and geographical clusters**, obtained with market segmentation analysis based on personal data and geographical features.

(c) **Frequencies of the searching keywords** specified by the user when using a search engine (typical information treated in information retrieval).

(d) **Metadata used by an intelligent agent-based crawling system** (typical of the artificial intelligence domain) the user may adopt.

Additionally, patterns can be generated from raw data by using some data mining tools (*a posteriori* patterns) but also known by the users and used, for example, to check how well a data source is represented by them (*a priori* patterns).

Since source data change with great frequency, another important issue consists in determining whether existing patterns, after a certain time, still represent the data source from which they have been generated, possibly being able to change pattern information when the quality of the representation changes. Finally, all types of patterns should be manipulated (e.g., extracted, synchronized, deleted) and queried through dedicated languages.

All of the previous reasons motivate the need for the design of ad hoc Pattern management systems (PBMSs), i.e., according to (Rizzi et al., 2003), systems for handling (storing/ processing/ retrieving) patterns defined over raw data.

Definition 2: *A* pattern base management system (PBMS) *is a system for handling (storing/processing/retrieving) patterns defined over raw data in order to efficiently support pattern matching and to exploit pattern-related operations generating intensional information. The set of patterns managed by a PBMS is called a* pattern base.

The pattern base management system is therefore not a simple repository for the extracted knowledge (patterns); rather it is an engine supporting pattern storage (according to a chosen logical model) and processing (involving also complex activities requiring computational efforts).

The design of a PBMS relies on solutions developed in several disciplines, such as: data mining and knowledge discovery for *a posteriori* pattern extraction; database management systems for pattern storage and retrieval; data warehousing for providing raw datasets; artificial intelligence and machine learning for pattern extraction and reasoning; and metadata management. Pattern management can therefore be seen as a relatively new discipline lying at the intersection of several well-known application contexts.

KEY FEATURES IN PBMS EVALUATION

In the following we first present a typical data mining scenario and then, based on it, we present useful parameters in comparing existing pattern management solutions. In particular, we consider three different aspects:

(a) Architecture for a pattern management system.
(b) Pattern models.
(c) Pattern languages.

The Scenario

The market-basket analysis is a typical data mining application concerning, in our example, the task of finding and handling *association rules* and *clusters* concerning customer's transactions. Given a domain D of values and a set of transactions, each corresponding to a subset of D, an association rule takes the form $B \Rightarrow H$, where $B \subseteq D$, $H \in D$ and $H \cap B = \emptyset$. H is often called the head of the rule, while B is its body. The informal meaning of the rule is that, given a transaction T, it often happens that when T contains B then it also contains H. This qualitative information can be quantified by using two measures: the *support* (i.e., the ratio between the number of transactions satisfying the body of the rule and the total number of transactions) and the *confidence* (i.e., the ratio between the number of transactions satisfying both rule body and head and the number of transactions satisfying just the body).

Suppose a commercial vendor traces shop transactions concerning milk, coffee, bread, butter and rice, and applies data mining techniques to determine how he can further increase his sales. The vendor deals with different kinds of patterns: association rules, representing correlations between sold items; clusters of association rules, grouping rules with respect to their similarity; and clusters of products, grouping products with respect to their type and price. Now, we suppose the vendor wants to execute the following operations, or steps:

1. **Modeling heterogeneous patterns.** Since the vendor deals with (at least) three different types of patterns, he would like to generate and manage those patterns together, in the same system, in order to be able to manipulate all this knowledge in an integrated way.

2. **Periodic pattern generation.** At the end of every month, the vendor mines from his transaction data association rules over sold products by filtering interesting results with respect to certain thresholds. He assumes the reliability of rules extracted from the instant in which they have been generated until the last day of the month. The vendor then groups the rules into clusters.

3. **Pattern querying.** The vendor may be interested in analyzing patterns stored in the system, i.e., to retrieve patterns satisfying certain conditions, to combine them in order to construct new patterns, to establish whether a pattern is similar to another and to correlate patterns and raw data. For instance, the vendor may be interested in retrieving all association rules mined during March 2005 involving "bread" or similar items, or in identifying all association rules extracted from a certain set of transactions with a reasonable level of detail (i.e., with quality measures higher than specified thresholds). In order to solve the last query, both the data management and the pattern management system have to be used.

4. **Promotion of a new product.** From April 2005, the vendor will start to sell a certain product P. To promote P in advance, he may promote some other products he already sells, for which there exists a correlation with P, in order to stimulate the demand for P. In this way, it is possible that customers

will start to buy P without the need for a dedicated advertising campaign. In order to know, for example, whether "bread" may stimulate the sale of P, he may insert in the system an association rule such as 'bread $\rightarrow$ P' (not automatically generated) and verify whether it holds or not with respect to the recorded transactions.

5. **Pattern update, synchronization and deletion.** Patterns may have to be updated. For instance, the user may know that the quality of the representation that a pattern achieves with respect to its data source has been changed because source data have been changed, thus the pattern quality measures (evaluated at insertion time) have to be updated, since the pattern may no longer be semantically valid, i.e., it may not correctly represent the updated source data. As an example, when on April 1, 2005, the vendor starts to sell a new product *P*, new raw data concerning sales are collected, new patterns are generated and, at the same time, patterns previously extracted may not correctly represent source data. Thus, a synchronization is required between data and patterns to reflect patterns changes occurring in raw data. In this case, the measures may change as well. Finally, there is the need for pattern deletion operations. For example, the vendor may be interested in deleting all patterns that are no longer semantically valid or in removing from the system all rules having "rice" as value in their head or its body.

Architecture for a Pattern Base Management System

The architecture of a PBMS may be integrated or separated. In an *integrated architecture*, raw data and patterns are stored together by using the same data model and managed in the same way. On the other side, in a *separated architecture*, raw data are stored and managed in a traditional way by a DBMS, whereas patterns are stored and managed by a dedicated PBMS.

Since in the integrated architecture a unique data model is used for both data and patterns, design of the pattern base is simplified. For example, an association rule can be represented in the relational model by using a set of relational tuples, each containing the head of the rule and one element in the body. However, traditional data models may not adequately represent all pattern characteristics, thus making manipulation operations more complex. Further, by storing patterns with data, we rely on traditional DBMS capabilities for what concerns query expressive power and query optimization. In particular, under an integrated architecture, the mining process is usually seen as a particular type of query. However, patterns may require sophisticated processing that, in traditional systems, can only be implemented through user-defined procedures.

Separated architectures manage data and patterns by using two distinct systems. Thus, two models and languages have to be used to deal with pattern-based applications. The usage of a specific pattern data model guarantees a higher and more tailored expressive power in pattern representation. Moreover, operations over data are activated by the PBMS only by demand, through the so-called *cross-over queries*. The PBMS can therefore support specific techniques for pattern management and retrieval. Mining operations are not part of the query language; rather, they are specific manipulation operators. Finally, specific query languages can be designed providing advanced capabilities, based on the chosen pattern representation.

Pattern Models

We can define a pattern model as a formalism by which patterns are described and manipulated inside the PBMS. In defining a pattern model, we believe that the following aspects should be taken into account.

User-defined pattern types support. The ability to model heterogeneous patterns is very important to make the PBMS flexible and usable in different contexts. Most of the systems allow the user to manipulate different types of patterns (see Step 1 of the scenario) that usually correspond to different data mining results, such as association rules, clusters, etc. However, in many cases they cannot be used "together" in a unified framework. Moreover, often it is not possible for the user to define new pattern types, which are therefore predefined.

Relation between raw data and patterns. Often patterns are generated from raw data through the application of some mining technique; it may be useful to store the relation between patterns and raw data in order to make the pattern richer in semantics and provide additional, significant information for pattern retrieval. Most of the systems recognize the importance of this aspect and provide a mechanism to trace the source data set from which a pattern has been generated. In the proposed scenario, this corresponds to maintain information concerning the dataset from which association rules have been extracted. Such information may then be used to solve some of the queries pointed out in Step 3 of the scenario. Besides the source dataset, it may be useful to exactly know the subset of the source dataset represented by the pattern. For example, to generate rule 'bread → milk', only transactions containing "bread" and "milk" are considered from the overall set of transactions in the source dataset. This subset can be represented in a precise way by listing its components, or in an approximate way by providing a formula satisfied by the elements of the source dataset from which the pattern probably has been generated. Most of the systems do not support the representation of this relationship or support it only in an approximated way.

Quality measures. It is important to be able to quantify how well a pattern represents a raw data set by associating each pattern with some quantitative measures. For example, in the identified scenario, each association rule mined from data is associated with confidence and support values. Most of the systems allow the user to express this quality information, which is generally computed during pattern generation and never modified.

Temporal features. Since source data change with high frequency, it is important to determine whether existing patterns, after a certain time, still represent the data source from which they have been generated. This happens when, given a pattern p extracted at time t, the same pattern p can be extracted at time $t' > t$ from the same raw dataset, with the same or better measure values. In this case, we say the pattern is semantically valid at time t'. When this happens and measures change, the system should be able to change pattern measures. In practice, it may be useful to assign each pattern a validity period, representing the interval of time in which it may be considered reliable with respect to its data source.

Hierarchies over types. Another important feature that a pattern management system should provide is the capability to define some kind of hierarchy over the existing pattern types in order to introduce relationships, such as specialization or composition, that increase expressivity, reusability and modularity. For instance, in the proposed scenario, the vendor deals with association rules and with more complex patterns that are clusters of association rules (see Step 1). Thus, a composition relationship is exploited.

Pattern Languages

Similar to a DBMS, a PBMS must provide at least two different types of languages: the *Pattern Manipulation Language* (PML), providing the basic operations by which patterns may be manipulated (e.g., extracted, synchronized and deleted), and the *Pattern Query Language* (PQL), supporting pattern retrieval. PQL queries take as input patterns and data sets and return patterns. On the other hand, PML operations take as input a pattern set and return a new pattern set, which replaces the input one in the pattern base. Aspects concerning both manipulation and query languages for patterns will be evaluated by means of several parameters introduced in the following.

Pattern Manipulation Language Parameters

Automatic extraction. This is the capability of a system to generate patterns starting from raw data using a mining function. It corresponds to the data mining step of a knowledge data discovery process and generates *a posteriori* patterns. In the proposed scenario, association rules generated in Step 2 of the scenario represent *a posteriori* patterns.

Direct insertion of patterns. There are patterns that the user knows *a priori* and wishes to verify over a certain data source. They are not extracted from raw data, but inserted directly from scratch in the system. Ad hoc primitives are therefore needed to perform this operation. In the proposed scenario, patterns described in Step 4 are examples of *a priori* patterns.

Modifications and deletions. Patterns can be modified or deleted. For example, users may be interested in updating information associated with patterns (such as their validity in time or the quality of raw data representation they achieve, represented in terms of measures) or in removing from the system patterns satisfying (or not satisfying) certain characteristics. For instance, in the proposed scenario (Step 5), the user is interested in removing an association rule when it does not correctly represent the source data set any longer. Not all the systems guarantee both deletion and update operations over patterns; in many cases, only pattern generation and querying are provided.

Synchronization over source data. Since modifications in raw data are very frequent, it may happen that a pattern extracted at a certain instant of time from a certain data source does not correctly represent the data source after

several modifications occur (Step 5). Thus, the need for a synchronization operation arises in order to align patterns with the data source they represent. This operation is a particular type of update operation for patterns. For instance, in the proposed scenario (Step 5), the user is interested in updating the measure values associated with a certain rule (such as 'bread → P') when the source data change. Synchronization may also be executed against a different dataset in order to check whether a pattern extracted from a certain data source holds also for another data source. In this case, we call it "recomputation." For example, suppose the vendor receives a data set DS concerning sales in the month of January 2005 in another supermarket. He may be interested in checking whether the association rules mined from his data set represent reasonable patterns for the new data set DS. Unfortunately, synchronization between raw data and patterns (Step 5) is rarely supported

Mining function. Patterns are obtained from raw data by applying some kind of mining function, e.g., the APriori (Agrawal & Srikant, 1994) algorithm may be used to generate association rules (Step 2). The presence of a library of mining functions and the possibility to define new functions if required makes pattern manipulation much more flexible.

Pattern Query Language Parameters

Queries against patterns. The PBMS has to provide a query language to retrieve patterns according to some specified conditions. For example, all association rules having "bread" in their body may need to be retrieved (Step 3). In general, pattern collections have to be supported by the system in order to be used as input for queries. Similar to the relational context where a relation contains tuples with the same schema, patterns in a collection must have the same type. Moreover, it is highly desirable for the language to be closed, i.e., each query over pattern must return a set of patterns of the same type over which other queries can be executed.

Pattern combination. Operations for combining patterns together should be provided as an advanced form of reasoning. Combination may be seen as a sort of "join" between patterns. For example, transitivity between association rules may be seen as a kind of pattern join.

Similarity. An important characteristic of a pattern language is the ability to check pattern similarity based on pattern structure and measures. Only a few general approaches for pattern similarity have been provided that can be homogeneously applied to different types of patterns. Moreover, few existing PQLs support such an operation.

Queries involving source data. According to the chosen architecture and the logical model, a system managing patterns has to provide operations not only for querying patterns but also data. Such queries are usually called *cross-over queries*. When the system adopts a separated architecture, cross-over operations require the combination of two different query processors in order to be executed. In our scenario, the second query of Step 3 is a cross-over query.

THEORETICAL PROPOSALS

As we have already stressed, the need for a unified framework supporting pattern management is widespread and covers many different contexts and domains. Thus, great effort has been put into the formalization of the overall principles under which a PBMS can be developed, providing the background for the development of back-end technologies to be used by pattern-based applications. In the following we briefly present and compare the following proposals by considering all the parameters previously introduced:

- **Inductive databases approach** (Imielinsky & Mannila, 1996; De Raedt, 2002; CINQ,

2001): an inductive framework where both data and patterns are stored at the same layer and treated in the same manner;

- **3-Worlds model** (Johnson et al., 2000): a unified framework for pattern management based on the definition of three distinct worlds: an intensional world (containing intensional descriptions of patterns), an extensional world (containing an explicit representation of patterns); and a world representing raw data; and

- **Panda Project** (PANDA, 2001): a unified framework for the representation of heterogeneous patterns, relying on a separated architecture.

Inductive Databases Approach

Inductive databases (Imielinsky & Mannila, 1996; De Raedt, 2002) rely on an integrated architecture. Thus, patterns are represented according to the underlying model for raw data. More precisely, the repository is assumed to contain both datasets and pattern sets. Within the framework of inductive databases, knowledge discovery is considered as an extended querying process (Meo et al., 2004; De Raedt et al., 2002). Thus, a language for an inductive database is an extension of a database language that allows one to:

(a) Select, manipulate and query data as in standard queries.
(b) Select, manipulate and query patterns.
(c) Execute cross-over queries over patterns.

Queries may then be stored in the repository as views, in this way datasets and pattern sets are intensionally described.

Inductive databases have been mainly investigated in the context of the CINQ project of the European Community (CINQ, 2001), which tries to face both theoretical and practical issues of inductive querying for the discovery of knowledge from transactional data. CINQ covers several different areas, spreading from data mining tasks to machine learning. The considered data mining patterns are itemsets, association rules, episodes, data dependencies, clusters, etc. In the machine learning context, interesting patterns considered by the project are equations describing quantitative laws, statistical trends and variations over data.

From a theoretical point of view, a formal theory is provided for each type of pattern, providing:

(a) A language for pattern description.
(b) Evaluation functions for computing measures and other significant data related to patterns.
(c) Primitive constraints for expressing basic pattern properties (e.g., minimal/maximal frequency and minimal accuracy).

By using primitive constraints, extraction and further queries (seen as postprocessing steps in the overall architecture) can be interpreted as constraints and executed by using techniques from constraint programming, using concepts from constraint-based mining. Other manipulation operations, such as the insertion of *a priori* patterns, are delegated to the underlying DBMS, since an integrated architecture is exploited. Note that since a theory is provided for each type of pattern, integration is not a project issue. Moreover, no support for temporal management and pattern hierarchies is provided.

From a more practical point of view, extension of existing standard query languages, such as SQL, have been provided in order to query specific types of patterns, mainly association rules. The combination of a data mining algorithm, usually some variation of the Apriori algorithm (Agrawal & Srikant, 1994), with a language such as SQL (or OQL) offers some interesting querying capabilities. Among the existing proposals, we recall the following:

- **DMQL (Data Mining Query Language)** (Han et al., 1996) is an SQL-based data mining language for generating patterns from relational data. An object-oriented extension of DMQL based on Object Query Language (OQL) (Cattell & Barry, 2000), has been presented in Elfeky et al. (2001). Discovered association rules can be stored in the system, but no post-processing (i.e., queries over the generated patterns) is provided. Indeed, they are simply presented to the user and a further iterative refining of mining results is possible only through graphical tools. The obtained rules can be specialized (generalized) by using concept hierarchies over source data. Besides association rules, other patterns can be generated, such as: data generalizations (a sort of aggregate), characteristic rules (assertions describing a property shared by most data in certain data set, for example the symptoms of a certain disease), discriminant rules (assertions describing characteristics that discriminate a dataset from another one) and data classification rules (patterns for data classification). For each type of pattern, a set of measures is provided (confidence and support for association rules) and conditions governing them can be used in order to generate only patterns with a certain quality level (Figure 1(a)).

- **MINE RULE** (Meo et al., 1998) extends SQL with a new operator, MINE RULE, for discovering association rules from data stored in relations. By using the MINE RULE operator, a new relation with schema (BODY, HEAD, SUPPORT, CONFIDENCE) is created, containing a tuple for each generated association rule. The body and head itemsets of the generated rules are stored in dedicated tables and referred to within the rule-base table by using foreign keys. The cardinality

Figure 1. Inductive languages: examples

```
                                  MINE RULE MarketAssRules      GetRules(Transactions)
                                  AS                            into MarketAssRules
                                  select distinct               where confidence > 0.9
                                            1..n item as Body,       and support > 0.3
  Find association rules                    1..n item as Head,             (c)
  from Transactions                         Support,
  with support                              Confidence          SelectRules(MarketAssRules)
   threshold=0.3                  from Transactions             where body has {(bread=yes)}
  with confidence                 group by tr#                            (d)
   threshold=0.9                  extracting rules with         select *
                                            Support:0.3,        from Transactions
          (a)                               Confidence:0.9      where VIOLATES ALL (
                                                                GetRules(Transactions)
                                            (b)                 where body has {(bread=yes)}
                                                                and confidence > 0.75 )
                                                                         (e)
```

of the rule body as well as minimum support and confidence values can be specified in the MINE RULE statement. MINE RULE is very flexible in specifying the subset of raw data from which patterns have to be extracted as well as conditions that extracted patterns must satisfy. However, no specific support for post-processing (queries) is provided, even if standard SQL can be used since rules are stored in tables. Similar to DMQL, hierarchies over raw data may be used to generalize the extracted association rules, or more specifically, to extract only association rules at a certain level of generalization. A similar operator called XMine, for extracting association rules from XML documents, has been presented in Braga et al. (2002).

- **Mine-SQL (MSQL)** (Imielinsky & Virmani, 1999) is another SQL-like language for generating and querying association rules. Similar to MINE RULE, only association rules are considered. Also, in this case input transactions and resulting rules are stored

in relations. With respect to MINE RULE, it supports different types of statements; one for rule extraction (*GetRules*), one for rule post-processing (*SelectRules*) and some predicates for cross-over queries (*Satisfy, Violate*). Concerning extraction, MSQL is less flexible in specifying the source data set; indeed, it must be an existing table or view. However, similarly to MINE RULE, constraints over the rules to be generated may be specified. Extracted queries can be queried using the *SelectRules* operator. Various conditions can be specified, depending on the body and the head of the rules. By using the *SelectRules* statement, it is also possible to recompute measures of already extracted rules over different datasets. In order to explicitly support cross-over queries, MSQL proposes the operators *Satisfy* and *Violate*. They determine whether a tuple satisfies or violates at least one or all the association rules in a given set, specified by using either *GetRules* or *SelectRules* commands.

Figure 1 presents a usage example of the just presented languages for extracting association rules from transactions stored in relation Transactions and storing them, when possible, in relation MarketAssRules.

Finally, we recall that results achieved in the context of the CINQ project have been experimented with in the context of machine learning in the implementation of a molecular fragment discovery demo system (MOLFEA, 2004). In the context of association rule mining, they have been experimentally used in the demo version of the Minerule Mining System (Minerule System, 2004).

3-Worlds Model

The 3-Worlds (3W) model (Johnson et al., 2000) is a unified framework for pattern management based on a separated architecture. Under this approach, the pattern model allows one to represent three different worlds: the intensional world (I-World), containing the intensional description of patterns; the extensional world (E-World), containing an extensional representation of patterns; and the data world (D-World), containing raw data. In the I-World, patterns correspond to (possibly overlapping) regions in a data space, described by means of linear constraints over the attributes of the analyzed data set. For example, a cluster of products based on their price in dollars can be described by the following constraint "10<=price<=20" (call this region "cheap_product"). More complex regions can be defined, composed of a set of constraints. In the E-World, each region is represented in its extensional form, i.e., by an explicit enumeration of the members of the source space satisfying the constraint characterizing the region. Thus, the extension corresponding to region "cheap_product" (contained in the I-world) contains all source data items with price between 10 and 20. Finally, the D-World corresponds to the source data set in the form of relations, from which regions and

dimensions can be created as result of a mining process. Note that regions in the I-World are not predefined, thus user-defined patterns are allowed. Each region can be associated with a number of attributes, including measures, which do not have a special treatment. Additionally, the framework does not support *a priori* patterns. Indeed, operations to directly insert patterns in the system are not supported. Moreover, no pattern temporal management is provided.

Query languages for all the worlds have been proposed. In particular, for the D-World and the E-World, traditional relational languages can be used (with some minor extensions for the E-World). On the other hand, dimension algebra has been defined over regions in the I-World, obtained by extending relational languages. The main operations of this language are described in the following:

- The **selection** operation allows pattern retrieval by invoking various spatial predicates such as overlap (∥), containment (⊂), etc. between regions.
- The **projection** operation corresponds to the elimination of some property attributes; this amounts to setting their value to *"true"* in every region.
- A **purge** operator, returning inconsistent regions, i.e., regions whose constraint cannot be satisfied by any data point (thus, with an empty extensional representation). For instance, a region with constraint "price>20 AND price<10" is clearly inconsistent, since the constraint is intrinsically unsatisfiable.
- Traditional relational operators (**cartesian product**, **union**, **minus** and **renaming**) have then been extended to cope with sets of regions.

The following cross-over operators are also provided, allowing the user to navigate among the three worlds:

- Automatic extraction of patterns (**mine**).
- The assignment of an extension to a region (**populate**), given a certain data source.
- The detection of the regions corresponding to a certain extension (**lookup**).
- A sort of synchronization, providing the computation of new extensions starting from combinations of regions and a given dataset (**refresh**).

Note that all the previous operators but mine can be interpreted as cross-over query operators. We remark that, even if no PML is explicitly provided, some of the proposed operators can be interpreted as PML operations when attempting to change the three worlds according to the query result. For example, the mine operator can be seen as a PML operator when the result of the mining is made persistent in the I-World.

PANDA Project

The purposes of the PANDA (PAtterns for Next-generation DAtabase systems) project of the European Community (PANDA, 2001) are:

1. To lay the foundations for pattern model-ing.
2. To investigate the main issues involved in managing and querying a pattern-base.
3. To outline the requirements for building a PBMS.

The PANDA approach relies on a separated architecture. The proposed model provides the representation of arbitrary and heterogeneous patterns by allowing the user to specify his or her own pattern types. It provides support for both *a priori* and *a posteriori* patterns and it allows the user to define ad-hoc mining functions to generate *a posteriori* patterns.

Under this modeling approach, pattern quality measures are explicitly represented, as well as relationships between patterns and raw data

that can be stored in an explicit or approximated way. For example, a cluster of products based on their price in dollars can be described in an approximate way by the following constraint: "10<=price<=20". However, not necessarily all products with a price between 10 and 20 belong to this cluster. Thus, an explicit representation of the relationship between patterns and raw data will list the exact set of products belonging to the cluster. Moreover, the definition of hierarchies involving pattern types has been taken into account in order to address extensibility and reusability issues. Three types of hierarchies between pattern types have been considered: specialization, composition and refinement. Specialization is a sort of inheritance between pattern types. On the other hand, composition is a sort of aggregation. Finally, refinement allows patterns to be used as source data. As an example, in the proposed scenario, clusters of association rules rely on a refinement relationship with association rules. If the representative of such clusters is an association rule, then there exists also a composition relation between them.

In this context, languages for pattern ma-nipulation and querying have also been defined. In particular, the pattern manipulation language supports the main manipulation operations in-volving patterns, such as pattern insertion and deletion. Both *a priori* and *a posteriori* patterns can be manipulated by using the language pro-posed. On the other hand, by using the proposed pattern query language patterns inserted in the system (directly or mined by applying a mining function) patterns can be retrieved and queried by specifying filtering conditions involving all pattern characteristics supported by the model. Additionally, it allows the user to combine differ-ent patterns and to correlate them with raw data, i.e., it supports cross-over operations. An approach for pattern similarity has also been provided by Bartolini et al. (2004).

Starting by the PANDA approach, an extended model for patterns has been proposed (Catania et al., 2004). Such a model addresses the need for temporal information management associated with patterns. In this way, it becomes possible to exploit and manage information concerning pattern semantics and temporal validity, including synchronization and recomputation. Furthermore, the previously proposed PML and PQL have been extended in order to cope with temporal features during pattern manipulation and querying.

Concluding Discussion

Table 1 summarizes the features of the frameworks presented above according to the previously introduced parameters. In the table, the PANDA approach refers to the extended temporal model (Catania et al., 2004).

Concerning the architecture, only inductive databases adopt an integrated approach. On the other hand, 3W and PANDA rely on a separated PBMS. For what concerns the model, the more general approach seems to be PANDA, where there is no limitation on the pattern types that can be represented. PANDA is also the only approach taking into account temporal aspects, hierarchies and providing both a precise and an approximated relationship of patterns with respect to source data. In particular, it can be shown that the approximated representation in PANDA is quite similar to the region representation in 3W.

Concerning the manipulation language, 3W and CINQ do not support direct insertion of patterns or deletion and update operations. On the other hand, all the proposals take into account synchronization (recomputation) issues. Concerning the query language, all the approaches propose either one (or more) calculus or algebraic languages, providing relational operators.

Specific characteristics of languages provided in the context of inductive databases are summarized in Table 2. Concerning extracted patterns, MINE RULE and MSQL deal only with association rules, whereas DMQL and ODMQL deal with many different types of patterns. When patterns

are stored, SQL can be used for manipulation and querying (including cross-over queries). Among the proposed languages, however, only MSQL proposes ad-hoc operators for pattern retrieval and post-processing.

As a final consideration, we observe that when dealing with applications managing different types of patterns (this is the case of advanced knowledge discovery applications), the 3W and PANDA theoretical frameworks are the best solutions, since they provide support for heterogeneous patterns in a unified way. On the other side, the inductive databases approach provides better solutions for specific data mining contexts, such as association rules management, with a low impact on existing SQL-based applications.

STANDARDS

The industrial community has proposed standards to support pattern representation and management in the context of existing programming languages and database (or data warehousing) environments in order to achieve interoperability and (data) knowledge sharing. Thus, they provide the right front-end for pattern management applications.

In general, they do not support generic patterns and, similar to the inductive database approach, specific representations are provided only for specific types of patterns. Moreover, they do not provide support for inter-pattern manipulation.

Some proposals, such as Predictive Model Markup Language (PMML, 2003) and common warehouse metamodel (CWM, 2001), mainly deal with data mining and data warehousing pattern representation, respectively, in order to support their exchange between different architectures. Others, such as Java Data Mining (JDM, 2003) and SQL/MM Data Mining (ISO SQL/MM part 6, 2001), provide standard representation and manipulation primitives in the context of Java and SQL, respectively. In the following, all these proposals will be briefly presented and

Table 1. Features comparison: theoretical proposals

		Inductive Databases	**3W Model**	**PANDA**
Model & Architecture	*Type of architecture*	Integrated	Separated. Three layers: source data, mined data and intermediate data.	Separated. Three levels: database, pattern base and intermediate data
	Predefined types	-Itemsets -Association Rules -Sequences -Clusters -Equations	Users can define their own types that must be represented as sets of constraints	Users can define their own types
	Link to source data	Yes. Datasource is part of the architecture	Yes. Datasource is one of the layers of the architecture. Relationship is precise	Yes. Datasource is one of the layers of the architecture. Relationship can be either precise or approximated
	Quality measures	Yes	Yes, but not explicit	Yes
	Mining function	Yes. The mining process is a querying process	Yes	Yes
	Temporal features	No	No	Yes
	Hierarchical types	No	Yes	Specialization, composition, and refinement
Manipulation Language	*Manipulation language*	Manipulation through constraint-based querying and SQL	Yes	Yes
	Automatic extraction	Yes. Constraint-based queries	Yes	Yes
	Direct insertion	No	No	Yes
	Modifications and deletions	Yes (SQL)	No	Yes
	Synchronization over source data	Yes, recomputation	Yes, recomputation	Yes, recomputation & synchronization
	Mining function	No	No	Yes
Query Language	*Queries against patterns*	Constraint-based calculus	Algebra	Algebra & Calculus
	Pattern combination	No	Yes, Cartesian product	Yes, join
	Similarity	No	No	Yes
	Queries involving source data	Yes	Yes	Yes

Table 2. Features comparison: theoretical proposals (query language)

		DMQL & ODMQL M	INE RULE M	SQL
Model	*Predefined types*	-Association rules -Data generalizations -Characteristic rules -Discriminant rules -Data classification rules	Association rules	Association rules
Manipulation Language	*Manipulation language*	Only e xtraction, b ut n o storage	Only extraction	Yes
	Automatic extraction	Yes	Yes	Yes
	Direct insertion	No	Using standard SQL	Using standard SQL
	Modifications and deletions	No	Using standard SQL	Using standard SQL
	Synchronization over source data	No	No Y	es, recomputation
Query Language	*Queries over patterns*	Only v isualization and browsing	Using standard SQL	SQL-like
	Pattern combination	No N	o	No
	Similarity	No N	o	No
	Queries involving source data	No U	sing standard SQL	Yes

compared with respect to the parameters previously introduced.

Predictive Model Markup Language

PMML (PMML, 2003) is a standardization effort of DMG (Data Mining Group) consisting of an XML–based language to describe data mining models (i.e., the mining algorithm, the mining parameters and mined data) and to share them between PMML compliant applications and visualization tools. Figure 2 shows an extract of a PMML association rule mining model. Since PMML is primary aimed at the exchange of data between different architectures, no assumptions about the underlying architecture are done.

PMML traces information concerning the data set from which a pattern has been extracted by allowing the user to specify the data dictionary, i.e., the collection of raw data used as input for the mining algorithm. Concerning the mining function, it is possible to express the fact that a certain pattern has been mined from a certain raw data set by using a specified mining algorithm. However, no assumption is made about the existence of a mining library. For instance, in the example shown in Figure 2, the represented association rule is the result of the application of the APriori algorithm (algorithmName = "Apriori").

Moreover, PMML does not allow the user to define its own types. Indeed, one can only define models of one of the predefined types that cover a very large area of the data mining context (see Table 3). It is also important to note that PMML allows the user to represent also information concerning quality measures associated with patterns.

Figure 2. PMML example

```
<PMML>
...
<!--items in input data for the mining of association rule #1 -->
  <Item id="1" value="milk"/>
  <Item id="2" value="coffe"/>
  <Item id="3" value="bread"/>
  ...
<!-- definition of the mining model used -->
<AssociationModel modelName="mba"
<!--mining algorithm used -->
       algorithmName="Apriori"
<!-- tuples in Transactions -->
       numberOfTransactions="10"
<!-- thresholds for support and confidence -->
       minimumSupport="0.3"
       minimumConfidence="0.9"
...
<!-- item sets involved in association rule #1 -->
  <!-- item set containing the item corresponding to 'coffee' -->
  <Itemset id="1" numberOfItems="1"> <ItemRef itemRef="2"/> </Itemset>
  <!-- item set containing the item corrsponding to 'bread' -->
  <Itemset id="2" numberOfItems="1"> <ItemRef itemRef="3"/> </Itemset>
...
<!-- association rules -->
<AssociationRule support="0.3" confidence="1.0" antecedent="1" consequent="2"/>
...
</AssociationModel>
</PMML>
```

Due to its nature, PMML does not provide temporal features. Even if no general support for pattern hierarchies is provided, PMML 3.0 supports refinement for decision trees and simple regression models. More general variants may be defined in future versions of PMML.

All major commercial products supporting data knowledge management and data mining attempt to be compliant with PMML standard. Among them we recall Oracle Data Mining tool in Oracle10g (Oracle DM), DB2 Intelligent Miner tools (DB2) and MS SQL Server 2005 Analysis Services (MS SQL).

Common Warehouse Metamodel

The common warehouse metamodel (CWM, 2001) is a standardization effort of the ODM (Object Management Group) and it enables easy interchange of warehouse and business intelligence metadata between warehouse tools, platforms and metadata repositories in distributed hetero-geneous environments. CWM is based on three standards:

(a) **UML (Unified Modeling Language)** (UML, 2003), an object oriented model-ing language used for representing object models.

(b) **MOF (Meta Object Facility)** (MOF, 2003), which defines an extensible framework for defining models for metadata and provides tools with programmatic interfaces to store and access metadata in a repository/

(c) **XMI (XML Metadata Interchange)** (XMI, 2003), which allows metadata compliant with the MOF meta-model to be interchanged as streams or files with a standard XML-based format.

CWM has been defined as a specific metamodel for generic warehouse architectures. Thus, it is compliant with the MOF metamodel and relies on UML for object representation and notation.

Table 3. Feature comparison: Industrial proposals

		PMML	JDM API	SQL/MM	CWM
Model & Architecture	*Type of architecture*	Only representation of patterns. No Architecture	Integrated	Integrated	Only representation of patterns. No architecture
	Predefined types	-Association Rules -Decision Trees -Center/ Distribution Based Clustering -(General) Regression -Neural Networks -Naive Bayes -Sequences	-Clustering -Association Rules -Classification -Approximation -Attribute Importance	-Clustering -Association Rules -Classification -Regression	-Clustering -Association Rules -Supervised -Classification -Approximation -Attribute Importance
	Link to source data	Yes	Yes	Yes	Yes
	Quality measures	Yes	Yes	Yes	Yes
	Temporal features	No	No	No	No
	Hierarchical types	Partial	No	No	No
Manipulation Language	*Manipulation language*	No	Java API	SQL	No
	Automatic extraction	No	Yes	Yes	No
	Direct insertions	No	Yes	Yes	No
	Modifications and deletions	No	Possible through direct access to objects via Java	Possible through direct access to objects via SQL	No
	Synchronization over source data	No	No	No	No
	Mining function	Yes	Yes	Yes	Yes
Query	*Query language*	No	Java-API	SQL	No

Since MOF is a metamodel for metadata, UML metamodels may also be represented in MOF. This means that both CWM metadata and UML models can be translated into XML documents by using XMI through the mapping with MOF.

CWM consists of various metamodels, including a metamodel for data mining (CWM-DM), by which mining models and parameters for pattern extraction can be specified.

Unfortunately, CWM has been designed to analyze large amounts of data, where the data mining process is just a small part. Only few pattern types can be represented: clustering, association rules, supervised classification, approximation and attribute importance. The user does not have the capability to define its own pattern types and no temporal and hierarchical information associated with patterns can be modeled.

Finally, no dedicated languages for query and manipulation are proposed, since it is assumed manipulation is provided by the environment importing CWM-DM metadata.

Due to the complexity of the model, CWM is supported to some extent by most commercial systems providing solutions for data warehousing, such as Oracle, IBM (within DB2), Genesis and Iona Technologies (providing e-datawarehouse solutions) and Unisys (providing backbone solutions for UML, XMI and MOF core tools for CWM development). However, CWM-DM is rarely integrated in specific solutions for data mining where often only import/export in PMML, providing a much more simple pattern representation, is supported.

SQL/MM — DM

The International Standard ISO/IEC 13249 (ISO SQL/MM part 6, 2001) "Information technology — Database languages — SQL Multimedia and Application Packages (ISO SQL/MM)" is a specification for supporting data management of common data types (text, spatial information, images and data mining results) relevant in multimedia and other knowledge intensive applications in SQL-99. It consists of several different parts. Part number 6 is devoted to data mining aspects. In particular, it attempts to provide a standardized interface to data mining algorithms that can be layered at the top of any object-relational database system and even deployed as middleware when required, by providing several SQL user-defined types (including methods on those types) to support pattern extraction and storage.

Differently from PMML and CWM, SQL/MM does not only address the issue of representation but also of manipulation. Thus, it can be used to

develop specific data mining applications on top of an object-relational DBMS (ORDBMS).

Four types of patterns are supported (thus, the set of pattern types is not extensible and no support for user-defined pattern types is provided): association rules, clusters, regression (predicting the ranking of new data based on an analysis of existing data) and classification (predicting which grouping or class new data will best fit based on its relationship to existing data). For each pattern type, a set of measures is provided. For each of those models, various activities are supported:

- **Training:** the mining task (also called the model) is specified by choosing a pattern type, setting some parameters concerning the chosen mining function, and then applying the just configured mining function over a given dataset.
- **Testing:** when classification or regression is used, a resulting pattern can be tested by applying it to known data and comparing the pattern predictions with that known data classification or ranking value.
- **Application:** when clustering, classification or regression are used, the model can then be applied to all the existing data for new classifications or cluster assignment.

All the previous activities are supported through a set of SQL user-defined types. For each pattern type, a type DM_*Model (where the "*" is replaced by a string identifying the chosen pattern type) is used to define the model to be used for data mining. The models are parameterized by using instances of the DM_*Settings type, which allows various parameters of a data mining model, such as the minimum support for an association rule, to be set. Models can be trained using instances of the DM_ClassificationData type and tested by building instances of the DM_MiningData type that holds test data and instances of the DM_MiningMapping type that specify the different columns in a relational table that are to be used as a data source. The result of testing a model is one or more instances of the DM_*TestResult type (only for classification and regression). When the model is run against real data, the obtained results are instances of the DM_*Result type. In most cases, instances of DM_*Task types are also used to control the actual testing and running of your models.

Since SQL/MM is primary aimed at enhancing SQL with functionalities supporting data mining, no specific support is provided for *a priori* patterns. Advanced modeling features, such as the definition of pattern hierarchies and temporal information management, are not taken into account. However, queries over both data and patterns can be expressed through SQL. In the same way, the specified mining model and patterns can be modified or deleted.

Java Data Mining API

The Java Data Mining (JDM) API (JDM, 2003) specification addresses the need for a pure Java API to facilitate the development of data mining applications. While SQL/MM deals with representation and manipulation purposes inside an ORDBMS, Java Data Mining is a pure Java API addressing the same issues. As any Java API, it provides a standardized access to data mining patterns that can be represented according to various formats, including PMML and CWM-DM. Thus, it provides interoperability between various data mining vendors by applying the most appropriate algorithm implementation to a given problem without having to invest resources in learning each vendor's API.

JDM supports common data mining operations, as well as the creation, storage, access and maintenance of metadata supporting mining activities under an integrated architecture, relying on three logical components:

(a) **Application programming interface (API)**, which allows end-users to access to services provided by the data mining engine (DME).

(b) **Data mining engine (DME)**, supporting all the services required by the mining process, including data analysis services.

(c) **Mining object repository (MOR)**, where data mining objects are made persistent together with source data.

Various technologies can be used to implement the MOR, such as a file-based environment or a relational/object database, possibly based on SQL/MM specifications. The MOR component constitutes the repository against which queries and manipulation operations are executed.

Through the supported services, *a posteriori* patterns of predefined types (see Table 3) can be generated by using several different mining functions. Similarly to SQL/MM, pattern extraction is executed through tasks, obtained by specifying information concerning the type of patterns to be extracted, the source dataset, the mining function and additional parameters. Each generated pattern is associated with some measures, representing the accuracy with respect to raw data. Patterns are then stored in the MOR and then used for mining activities. JDM supports various import and export formats, including PMML.

Concluding Discussion

Table 3 summarizes the features of the presented standards, according to the previously introduced parameters. From the previous discussion, it follows that all the proposals described above rely on an integrated architecture. Among them, PMML and CWM-DM simply address the problem of pattern representation. On the other hand, SQL/MM and JDM cope with both pattern representation and management.

All standards provide a support for the representation of common data mining patterns. Among them, PMML provides the largest set of built-in pattern types. No user-defined patterns can be modeled, i.e., the set of pattern types is not extensible.

All standards allow users to specify the mining function/algorithm they want to apply. However, in PMML it is just a string used only for user information purposes. Furthermore, all considered approaches support measure computation and description of the source dataset, which is used in SQL/MM and JDM for pattern extraction.

None of the standards supports advanced modeling features concerning patterns such as temporal information management associated with patterns and definition of hierarchies involving patterns. Moreover, no specific support for *a priori* patterns is provided by such approaches even if imported patterns in JDM may be seen as a sort of *a priori* patterns.

Concerning pattern management, no dedicated languages for pattern manipulation are supported. In ISO SQL/MM and JDM, since raw data and patterns are stored together, manipulation and querying are possible by using typical languages used for accessing data.

Finally, we outline that since PMML and CWM simply address the issue of pattern representation, they can be used in any PBMS architecture. As we will see later, most commercial systems support PMML, which guarantees a clear XML representation that can be easily integrated with other XML data; on the other hand, due to its complexity, CWM-DM is rarely supported. SQL/MM and JDM can be used to develop specific data mining applications on top of existing technologies. In particular, SQL/MM can be put on top of an ORDBMS environment, whereas JDM works in a JAVA-based environment, providing an implementation for the proposed API.

METADATA MANAGEMENT

Patterns may be interpreted as a kind of metadata. Indeed, metadata in general represent data over data and, since patterns represent knowledge over data, there is a strong relationship between metadata management and pattern management. However, as we have already stressed, pattern management is a more complex problem since patterns have some peculiar characteristics that general metadata do not have. Indeed, metadata are usually provided for maintaining process information, as in data warehousing, or for representing knowledge in order to guarantee interoperability, as in the Semantic Web and intelligent agent systems. Specific pattern characteristics, such as quantification of importance through quality measures, are not taken into account. Usually, metadata are not used to improve and drive decision processes. Since metadata management has nonetheless influenced pattern management, in the following we briefly describe some approaches defined in this context.

In the artificial intelligence area, many research efforts have been invested in the *Knowledge Sharing Effort* (KSE, 1997), a consortium working on solutions for sharing and reuse of knowledge bases and knowledge based systems. Standards proposals of such a consortium are computer-oriented, i.e., they are not dedicated to human users, even if in some cases they can take advantage of using the proposed standard languages. The most important contributions developed by the consortium are *Knowledge Interchange Format* (KIF) and *Knowledge Query and Manipulation Language* (KQML) specifications. The first is a declarative language to express knowledge about knowledge and is used to exchange knowledge units among computers. It does not provide support for internal knowledge representation, thus each computer receiving KIF data translate them into its internal logical model in order to be able to apply some computation process. The second contribution proposes a language and a protocol supporting interoperability and cooperation among collections of intelligent agents involved in distributed applications. KQML can be used as a language by an application to interact with an intelligent agent system or by two or more intelligent systems to interact cooperatively in problem solving.

Concerning the emerging Semantic Web research area, Web metadata management problems have been taken into account by the W3C and a framework for representing information in the Web, Resource Description Framework (RDF, 2004), has been proposed. One of the essential goals of *RDF* (and *RDF-schema*) is to allow — in a simple way — the description of Web metadata, i.e., information about Web resources and how such resources can be used by a third-party in order to make them available not only for human users but also for machines and automatic processes. RDF uses an XML-based syntax and it exploits the URI identification mechanism. Recently, an emerging research field coping with the integration of ontology management and Web data management has emerged. In this context, W3C proposes a recommendation for a dedicated language: the *Web Ontology Language* (OWL, 2004). OWL is primarily dedicated to applications that need to process the content of information instead of just presenting information to human users. OWL supports better machine interpretability of Web content than XML, RDF or RDF Schema (RDF-S) solutions since it provides an extended vocabulary along with a more precise semantics.

Issues concerning metadata management have also been extensively considered in the context of the *Dublin Core Metadata Initiative* (DCMI, 2005), "an organization dedicated to promoting the adoption of interoperable metadata standards and developing specialized metadata vocabularies for describing resources that enable more intelligent information discovery systems." The main aim of DCMI is to support Internet resources identification through the proposal of metadata standards for discovery across domains and frameworks (tools, services and infrastructure) and for metadata sharing.

PATTERN SUPPORT IN COMMERCIAL DBMSS

Since the ability to support business intelligence solutions enhances the market competiveness of a DBMS product, all the most important DBMS producers supply their products with solutions for business intelligence supporting data mining and knowledge management processes. Pattern management in commercial DBMSs is provided in the context of such environments. In the remainder of this section we will briefly discuss data mining solutions proposed by three leading companies in database technology: Oracle, Microsoft and IBM.

Oracle Data Mining Tool

Starting from release 9i, Oracle technology supports data mining processing (Oracle DM, 2005). In the Oracle Data Mining server, basic data mining features have been specialized and enhanced. Oracle Data Mining (ODM) is a tool tightly integrated with Oracle 10g DBMS, supporting basic data mining tasks such as classification, prediction and association, and also clustering and ranking attribute importance. By using ODM, the user can extract knowledge (in the form of different kinds of patterns) from corporate data in the underlying Oracle databases or data warehouses. Supported patterns include categorical classifiers (computed by applying naïve Bayes network or support vector machines), continuous/numerical classifiers relying on linear or non-linear regression models (obtained by Support Vector Machines), association rules and clusters (produced by the K-Means algorithm or a proprietary clustering algorithm).

Mining algorithms and machine learning methods are built into ODM, but the user may change some settings and/or define new parameters for the mining model through the ODM Java API. Statistical measures can be associated with classifiers and association rules.

In the latest release (i.e., ODM 10g-Release 1), ODM's functionalities can be accessed in two ways: through a Java-based API or through the PL/SQL interface. Up to now, Java API and PL/SQL API are not interoperable, i.e., a model created in Java cannot be used in PL/SQL and vice versa. To overcome this limitation, the next ODM release (10g-Release 2) will adhere to the JDM standard specification, a JDM API will be implemented as a layer on top of ODM PL/SQL API and the current Java API will be abandoned.

Concerning other data mining standards, ODM supports PMML import and export, but only for naïve Bayes and association rule models. Exchanges through PMML documents are fully supported between Oracle database instances, but the compatibility with PMML models produced by other vendors can be achieved only if they use core PMML standard.

Microsoft SQL Server 2005

The business solutions proposed by Microsoft SQL Server exploit OLAP, data mining and data warehousing tools (MS SQL, 2005). The pioneer data mining functionalities appeared in SQL Server 2000 (only two types of patterns were supported: decision trees and clusters), but they have been consolidated and extended in the recent SQL Server 2005 beta release. Within the SQL Server environment, there are tools supporting data transformation and loading, pattern extraction and analysis based on OLAP services.

SQL server 2005 allows the user to build different types of mining models dealing with traditional mining patterns (such as decision tree, clusters, naïve Bayes classifier, time series, association rules and neural networks) and to test, compare and manage them in order to drive the business decision processes. Seven mining algorithms are provided by SQL Server 2005. The entire knowledge management process is performed through a mining model editor to define, view, compare and apply models. Besides this editor, additional tools are provided to exploit other mining phases (for example, data preparation). Within the SQL Server 2005, through OLE DB for Data Mining (OLEDB, 2005), it is possible to mine knowledge from relational data sources or multi-relational repositories. OLE DB for Data Mining extends SQL to integrate data-mining capabilities in other database applications. Thus, it provides storage and manipulation features for mined patterns in an SQL style. Using OLE DB for Data Mining, extracted patterns are stored in a relational database. Thus, in order to create a mining model, a CREATE statement quite similar to the SQL CREATE TABLE statement can be used; to insert new patterns in your mining model, the INSERT INTO statement can be used; finally, patterns can be retrieved and predictions made by using the usual SQL SELECT statement. For the sake of interoperability and compatibility with standards, OLE DB for Data Mining specification incorporates PMML.

IBM DB2 Intelligent Miner

DB2 database management environment provides support for knowledge management by means of a suite of tools, DB2 Intelligent Miner (DB2, 2005), dedicated to the basic activities involved in the whole data mining process. Thus, users may use data mining functionalities as they use any other traditional relational function provided by the DBMS.

The interaction between DB2 Intelligent Miner's tools takes place through PMML standard.

In particular, an ad-hoc DB2 Extender for data mining allows the automatic construction of mining models within DB2/SQL applications and their update with respect to changes occurring in the underling raw data. The generated mining models are PMML models and are stored as binary large objects (BLOBs). The other DB2 tools supporting training, scoring (or prediction) and visualization of a model work on PMML models, thus they can manage third-party PMML models without additional overhead. It is quite important to note that the scoring tool has the ability to score a mining model over data recorded not only on DB2 databases but also on Oracle ones. This capability has a great impact in applications development since it may reduce design and building costs.

Since DB2 Intelligent Miner's tools are tightly integrated with the database environment and the mining results are stored as BLOBs, the user may interact with the system through an SQL API. In particular, by using SQL it is possible to perform association rules discovery, clustering and classifications techniques provided by the DB2 environment.

Moreover, through ODBC/JDBC or OLE DB, data mining results can be integrated within business applications developed using an external powerful programming language.

Concluding Discussion

As we have seen, commercial DBMSs do not provide a comprehensive framework for pattern management, yet. Rather they support business intelligence by providing an applicational layer offering data mining features in order to extract knowledge from data, and by integrating mining results with OLAP instruments in order to support advanced pattern analysis. For this reason, in general, they do not provide a dedicated logical model for pattern representation and querying, since these aspects are demanded to the applications using the mined results. An exception is represented by SQL Server 2005, where pattern storage, manipulation and querying are made through OLE DB for Data Mining, which can be considered an SQL-based language for pattern management.

None of the systems allow the user to define its pattern types. Moreover, mining functions are built into the system; however, the user can modify some settings, specializing the algorithm to the case he or she is interested in. Finally, none of

Table 4. Features comparison: commercial DBMSs

	Oracle D ata Mining (10g)	**Microsoft SQL Server 2005**	**IBM DB2**
Predefined types	-Association rules -Discrete and continuous classifier -Clusters -Attribute importance	-Association r ules a nd itemsets -Clusters -Decision trees -Naïve Bayes classifier -Time series -Neural Networks	-Association rules -Clusters -Classifiers
Quality measures	Yes Y	es	Yes
Mining function	Built-in (user-defined settings)	Built-in (user-defined settings)	Built-in (user-defined settings)
Temporal features	No N	o Y	es (scoring phase)
Hierarchical types	No N	o	No
Supported standards	PMML JDM (ODM 10g-Release2)	PMML P	MML

the DBMSs takes into account advanced modelling aspects involving patterns, such as temporal information management and the existence of hierarchical relationships between patterns. Only DB2 considers patterns-data synchronization issues, through a scoring mechanism that can be started up by some triggers monitoring raw data changes.

Table 4 summarizes the features of the described commercial DBMSs by considering a subset of the previously introduced parameters.

ADDITIONAL ISSUES

In order to make PBMSs a practical technology, besides issues concerning architectures, models, and languages, additional topics have to be taken into account when developing a PBMS. Among them, pattern reasoning, physical design, query optimizations and access control are fundamental issues that have only been partially taken into account by existing proposals. In the following, such topics will be discussed in more detail.

Pattern reasoning. Pattern reasoning is supported only in few theoretical proposals, in the form of similarity check (PANDA) or pattern combination (3W-model and PANDA). However, an overall approach for reasoning about possibly heterogeneous patterns needs more sophisticated techniques describing the semantics of pattern characteristics. As an example, consider measures. In general, various approaches exist for measure computation (general probabilities, Dempster-Schafer and Bayesian Networks — see, for example, Silberschatz and Tuzhillin, 1996). It is not clear how patterns, possibly having the same type but characterized by different measures, can be compared and managed together. Probably, measure ontologies could be used to support such quantitative pattern reasoning.

Physical design. Since patterns are assumed to be stored in a repository, specific physical design techniques must be developed. Unfortunately, up to now it is not clear what constitutes a reasonable physical layer for patterns. Most commercial DBMSs store patterns as BLOBs that are then manipulated using specific methods. However, in order to provide a more efficient access, specific physical representations, clustering, partitioning, caching and indexing techniques should be developed. Concerning theoretical proposals, as we have already seen in the context of the 3W model, patterns are represented as regions, thus techniques developed for spatial databases can be used for their physical management.

Query optimization. Query optimization for pattern queries has been only marginally investigated. Some preliminary work, concerning query rewriting, has been proposed in the context of the 3W framework. An overall query optimization approach, taking into account choices concerning physical design, has not been defined yet. Assuming the necessity of dealing with a separated architecture, the main issue is how to perform data and patterns computations in an efficient way. An important issue here is how it is possible to use patterns to reduce data access in data and cross-over queries and how data and pattern query processors can be combined. On the other side, under an integrated architecture, where extraction is a kind of query, the main issue is the optimization of pattern generation. Some work has been done in the context of inductive databases, where approaches to optimize pattern extraction, based on constraints over pattern properties (Ng et al., 1998), or refine the set of generated patterns (Baralis & Psaila, 1999), have been proposed. Techniques for reducing the size of the generated pattern sets by representing them using condensed representations have also been proposed for itemsets and association rules (CINQ, 2001).

Access control. Patterns represent highly-sensitive information. Their access has therefore to be adequately controlled. The problem is similar to that of access control in the presence of inference (Farkas & Jajodia, 2002). In general, assuming a user has access to some non-sensitive data, the inference problem arises when, through inference, sensitive data can be discovered from non-sensitive ones. In terms of patterns, this means that users may have the right to access some patterns, for example some association rules, and starting from them they may infer additional knowledge over data upon which they may not have the access right.

Techniques already proposed in the inference context should be adapted and extended to cope with the more general pattern management framework. Some of these approaches rely on pre-processing techniques and check through mining techniques whether it is possible to infer sensitive data; others can be applied at run-time (i.e., during the knowledge discovery phase), releasing patterns only when they do not represent sensitive information; finally, modifications over original data, such as perturbation and sample size restrictions, that do not disturb data mining results can be also applied in order to encrypt the original data and to prevent unauthorized user data access.

CONCLUSION

Patterns refer to knowledge artifacts used to represent in a concise and semantically rich way huge quantities of heterogeneous raw data or some of their characteristics. Patterns are relevant in any knowledge intensive application, such as data mining, information retrieval or image processing. In this chapter, after presenting a sample scenario of pattern usage, specific issues concerning pattern management have been pointed out in terms of the used architecture, models and languages. Several parameters have also been identified and used in comparing various pattern management proposals.

From the analysis proposed in this chapter, it follows that there is a gap between theoretical

proposals and standard/commercial ones that spans from a lack of modelling capabilities (such as no support for user-defined patterns, pattern hierarchies or temporal features management in standard/commercial proposals) to a lack of manipulation and processing operations and tools (no manipulation of heterogeneous patterns, no support for similarity, pattern combination and synchronization in standard/commercial proposals). More generally, the analysis has shown that, even if several proposals exist, an overall framework, in terms of the current standards, to represent and manipulate patterns is still missing. In particular, aspects related to the physical management of patterns have not been considered at all.

On the other hand, the diffusion of knowledge intensive applications that may benefit from pattern technology is increasing. A combined effort of the academic community with industries is therefore required for establishing the real need of such features and the extension of existing standards in these directions. We however remark that the support of pattern combination in the last PMML version seems to answer this question positively.

ACKNOWLEDGMENT

The authors would like to thank Maurizio Mazza for his valuable contribution to this chapter.

REFERENCES

Agrawal, R., & Srikant, R. (1994). Fast algorithms for mining association rules in large databases. In *Proceedings of VLDB'94* (pp. 487-499). Morgan Kaufmann.

Baralis, E., & Psaila, G. (1999). Incremental refinement of mining queries. In *Proceedings of DaWaK'99 (LNCS)* (Vol. 1676, pp. 173-182). Springer-Verlag.

Bartolini, I., Ciaccia, P., Ntoutsi, I., Patella, M., & Theodoridiss, Y. (2004) A unified and flexible framework for comparing simple and complex patterns. In *Proceedings of ECML-PKDD'04 (LNAI)* (Vol. 3202, pp. 496-499). Springer-Verlag.

Braga, D., Campi, A., Ceri, S., Klemettinen, M., & Lanzi, P. L. (2002). A tool for extracting XML association rules from XML documents. In *Proceedings of ICTAI '02* (p. 57). IEEE Computer Society.

Catania, B. et al. (2004). A framework for data mining pattern management. In *Proceedings of ECML-PKDD'04 (LNAI)* (Vol. 3202, pp. 87-98). Springer-Verlag.

Cattell, R. G. G., & Barry, D. K. (2000). *The object data standard:ODMG 3.0.* San Francisco: Morgan Kaufmann.

CINQ. (2001). *The CINQ project.* http://www.cinq-project.org

Conklin, D. (2002). Representation and discovery of vertical patterns in music. In *Proceedings of Second International Conference on Music and Artificial Intelligence'04 (LNAI)* (Vol. 2445, pp. 32-42). Springer-Verlag.

CWM. (2001). *Common warehouse metamodel.* Retrievable from http://www.omg.org/cwm

DB2. (2005). *DB2 intelligent miner.* Retrievable from http://www-306.ibm.com/software/data/iminer/

DCMI. (2005). *Dublin core metadata initiative.* Retrievable from http://dublincore.org/

De Raedt, L. (2002). A perspective on inductive databases. *ACM SIGKDD Explorations Newsletter, 4*(2), 69-77.

De Raedt, L. et al. (2002). A theory on inductive query answering. In *Proceedings of ICDM'02* (pp. 123-130). IEEE Computer Society.

Elfeky, M. G. et al. (2001). ODMQL: Object data mining query language. In *Proceedings of Objects and Databases: International Symposium (LNCS)* (Vol. 1944, pp. 128-140). Springer-Verlag.

Farkas, C., & Jajodia, S. (2002). The inference problem: A survey. *ACM SIGKDD Explorations, 4*(2), 6-11.

Han, J. et al. (1995). Knowledge mining in databases: An integration of machine learning methodologies with database technologies. *Canadian Artificial Intelligence.*

Han, J. et al. (1996). DMQL: A data mining query language for relational databases. In *Proceedings of SIGMOD'96 Workshop on Research Issues in Data Mining and Knowledge Discovery (DMKD'96).*

Imielinski, T., & Mannila, H. (1996). A database perspective on knowledge discovery. *Communications of the ACM, 39*(11), 58-64.

Imielinski, T., & Virmani, A. (1999). MSQL: A query language for database mining. *Data Mining and Knowledge Discovery, 2*(4), 373-408.

ISO SQL/MM Part 6. (2001). Retrievable from http://www.sql-99.org/SC32/WG4/Progression Documents/FCD/fcd-datamining-2001-05.pdf

JDM (2003). *Java data mining API.* Retrievable from http://www.jcp.org/jsr/detail/73.prt

Johnson, S. et al. (2000). The 3W model and algebra for unified data mining. In *Proceedings of VLDB'00* (pp. 21-32). Morgan Kauffman.

KSE (1997). *Knowledge sharing effort.* Retrievable from http://www.cs.umbc.edu/kse/

Meo, R., Lanzi, P. L., & Klemettinen, M. (2003). *Database support for data mining applications (LNCS)* (Vol. 2682). New York: Springer-Verlag.

Meo, R., Psaila, G., & Ceri, S. (1998). An extension to SQL for mining association rules. *Data Mining and Knowledge Discovery, 2*(2), 195-224.

Minerule System. (2004). *Minerule mining system* (demo version). Retrievable from http://kdd.di.unito.it/minerule2/demo.html

Mitchell, T. M. (1997). *Machine learning.* Mc-Graw Hill.

MOF. (2003). *Meta-object facility (MOF) specification, vers. 1.4.* Retrievable from http://www.omg.org/technology/documents/formal/mof.htm

MOLFEA. (2004). *The molecular feature miner based on the LVS algorithm* (demo version). Retrievable from http://www.predictive-toxicology.org/cgi-bin/molfea.cgi

MS SQL. (2005). *Microsoft SQL server analysis server.* Retrievable from http://www.microsoft.com/sql/evaluation/bi/bianalysis.asp

Nakajima, C. et al. (2000). People recognition and pose estimation in image sequences. In *Proceedings of IJCNN* (Vol. 4, pp. 189-194). IEEE Computer Society.

Ng, R. et al. (1998). Exploratory mining and pruning optimizations of constrained associations rules. In *Proceedings of SIGMOD'98* (pp. 13-24). ACM Press.

OLEDB. (2005). *OLE DB for data mining specification.* Retrievable from http://www.microsoft.com/data/oledb

Oracle DM. (2005). *Oracle data mining tools.* Retrievable from http://www.oracle.com/technology/products/bi/odm/

OWL. (2004). *Web ontology language.* Retrievable from http://www.w3.org/2001/sw/WebOnt

PANDA. (2001). *The PANDA project.* Retrievable from http://dke.cti.gr/panda/

PMML. (2003). *Predictive model markup language.* Retrievable from http://www.dmg.org/pmml-v2-0.html

RDF. (2004). *Resource description framework.* Retrievable from http://www.w3.org/RDF/

Rizzi, S. et al. (2003). Towards a logical model for patterns. In *Proceedings of ER'03 (LNCS)* (pp. 77-90). Springer-Verlag.

SIGKDD. (2002). *SIGKDD Explorations* - Special Issue on Constraint-Based Mining.

Silberschatz, A., & Tuzhilin, A. (1996). What makes patterns interesting in knowledge discovery systems. *IEEE Transactions on Knowledge and Data Engineering, 8*(6), 970-974.

UML. (2003). *UML specification, vers. 1.5.* Retrievable from http://www.omg.org/technology/documents/formal/uml.htm

XMI. (2003). *XML metadata interchange specifications vers. 2.0.* Retrievable from http://www.omg.org/technology/documents/formal/xmi.htm

Xquery. (2001). *Xquery 1.0: An XML query language* (W3C working draft). Retrievable from http://www.w3.org/TR/2001/WD-xquery-20011220

This work was previously published in Processing and Managing Complex Data for Decision Support Systems, edited by J. Darmont and O. Boussaid, pp. 280-317, copyright 2006 by IGI Publishing, formerly known as Idea Group Publishing (an imprint of IGI Global).

Section VI
Emerging Trends

Chapter XXII
Web Services Management:
Toward Efficient Web Data Access

Farhana H. Zulkernine
Queen's University, Canada

Pat Martin
Queen's University, Canada

ABSTRACT

The widespread use and expansion of the World Wide Web has revolutionized the discovery, access, and retrieval of information. The Internet has become the doorway to a vast information base and has leveraged the access to information through standard protocols and technologies like HyperText Markup Language (HTML), active server pages (ASP), Java server pages (JSP), Web databases, and Web services. Web services are software applications that are accessible over the World Wide Web through standard communication protocols. A Web service typically has a Web-accessible interface for its clients at the front end, and is connected to a database system and other related application suites at the back end. Thus, Web services can render efficient Web access to an information base in a secured and selective manner. The true success of this technology, however, largely depends on the efficient management of the various components forming the backbone of a Web service system. This chapter presents an overview and the state of the art of various management approaches, models, and architectures for Web services systems toward achieving quality of service (QoS) in Web data access. Finally, it discusses the importance of autonomic or self-managing systems and provides an outline of our current research on autonomic Web services.

INTRODUCTION

The Internet and the World Wide Web have gradually become the main source of information with regard to extent, versatility, and accessibility. Products and services are being traded over the Internet more than ever before. Due to the cost of building and maintaining functionality in a service, outsourcing and acquiring services from other service providers are becoming increasingly popular. Web services are a leading Internet-based technology and a perfect implementation of service-oriented computing (SOC; Casati, Shan, Dayal, & Shan, 2003; Curbera, Khalaf, Mukhi, Tai, & Weerawarana, 2003). It has great potential for being an effective gateway to information accessible on the Web. Web services follow specific standards to ensure interoperability and are accessible on the World Wide Web. In a service-based system, all applications are considered as services in a large distributed network. Web services, which have features like fine-grained functionality, interoperability, and Web accessibility, hold great potential for Web data access and business-to-business (B2B) communication (Hogg, Chilcott, Nolan, & Srinivasan, 2004; Seth, 2002) via cross-vendor service composition.

Efficient management is indispensable to provide good service quality, especially for complex Web service hosting systems that provide services around the clock over the Internet. Quality of service (QoS) is an increasingly important feature of Web data access. It is generally represented by a statistical metric of the system performance, such as the average response time for queries or the level of availability of a service that symbolizes a certain quality of system performance. In order to guarantee the QoS for business and legal aspects, the service provider and consumer should first agree upon a specific service level. This contractual agreement, which is called a service-level agreement (SLA), is a primary economic aspect of Web services management in a corporate environment.

Researchers are working on the architecture, policies, specifications, and enhancement of different standards to facilitate the development of Web services management systems (Farrell & Kreger, 2002). Some of the main management goals are ensuring QoS (Sheth, Cardoso, Miller, Kochut, & Kang, 2002), negotiating SLAs (Liu, Jha, & Ray, 2003), load balancing or resource provisioning (Chung & Hollingsworth, 2004),

dynamic reconfiguration (Anzböck, Dustdar, & Gall, 2002), error detection (Sahai, Machiraju, Ouyang, & Wurster, 2001), recovery from failure (Birman, Renesse, & Vogels, 2004), and security (Chou & Yurov, 2005). Most of the management-related research conducted by industry contributes to areas like the architecture and implementation of a management infrastructure for Web services (Catania, Kumar, Murray, Pourhedari, Vambenepe, & Wurster, 2003), the specification of event subscription and notification (*WS-Eventing*, 2004), security and trust relationships (WS-Trust, 2005) in a federated Web services architecture, and the automation of ensuring SLA negotiation (Dan et al., 2004) among coordinating Web services. There are yet many open problems in the area of Web services management that need to be addressed.

This chapter surveys the state of the art of Web services management to facilitate efficient Web data access. It specifically focuses on the importance of an effective management framework for providing reliable, efficient, and secure data access on the Web. The rest of the chapter is organized as follows. The next section provides background information about the architecture and basic standards of Web services. Then the chapter presents an overview and comparison of Web service management frameworks. It explains the criteria used to compare the frameworks, describes frameworks found in the research literature, and then gives a comparison of the frameworks. Finally, it discusses the open problems in Web service management, summarizes the chapter, and draws some conclusions.

BACKGROUND

Web Services

Web services are software applications that offer specific services to client applications and have Web-based interfaces to provide user access over the Internet through standard communication protocols. Information about accessibility, protocols, and the functionality of a Web service is advertised in standard-based registry services like Universal Description, Discovery, and Integration (UDDI; Organization for the Advancement of Structured Information Standards [OASIS] UDDI, 2005) hosted by well-known organizations. Client applications and users can look for required services in the UDDI. If a desired service is found, an SLA (Sahai, Machiraju, Sayal, Van Moorsel, & Casati, 2002) can be negotiated between the client and the Web service, if necessary, and then the service can be invoked (as shown in Figure 1). Client applications communicate with Web services by passing messages over the Internet using standard protocols.

Web services technology is based on standards and specifications in order to ensure interoperability. Two main consortiums, OASIS and the World Wide Web Consortium (W3C), work on standardizing various specifications for Web services. The eXtensible Markup Language (XML; W3C, 2004a) is the basis of all languages used for the communications or specifications of Web services. An XML schema describes data types used in an XML representation. The most frequently used message-passing protocol for Web services is the simple object access protocol (SOAP; W3C, 2003) over the hypertext transport protocol (HTTP). Web services are published in the UDDI using the Web Services Description

Language (WSDL; W3C, 2005), which is an XML-based specification language for service interfaces and accessibility. XML, SOAP, and WSDL are required for publishing, discovering, and invoking Web services. Numerous other standards and specifications have been published and are still being worked on for Web services in order to enable automated service discovery, composition, and management.

Several components are needed to host a Web service on the Internet. Management of the Web service system implies managing all these components to ensure satisfactory performance. The components are typically HTTP or the Web server, application server, SOAP engine, Web-service interfaces (WS1 and WS2 in Figure 2), and associated back-end applications. The back-end applications may in turn include database systems and legacy systems (as shown in Figure 2). These components can reside on the same server machine or be distributed among multiple interconnected servers.

SOAP messages to Web services are received by the Web server. There can be one or more instances of the application server acting as containers to host single or multiple Web services. Messages received by the Web server are forwarded to the application servers. These messages are basically XML data bounded by headers and footers containing the messaging protocol. In most cases, the protocol is SOAP and the interpreter used is called the SOAP engine. The engine

Figure 1. Web service life cycle

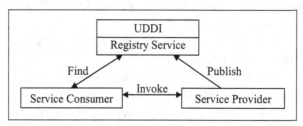

translates the envelope of the message and, after necessary preprocessing, passes the message to the appropriate Web service. Web services are applications built with technologies such as Java Servlets (Sun, 2004) that process the messages and compose replies to send back to the client. A more complex service can require connections to back-end applications, or legacy or database systems. These back-end applications may reside on separate servers connected to the HTTP server via a local area network (LAN).

In a more complex setup, the Web service may invoke other Web services provided by multiple enterprises and thus create a chain process constituting a large cross-vendor distributed, composite system. The client invoking a service may be a user using a Web browser, a client application, or another service. The services in a composite system can be selected and bound either before execution of the system (static composition) or on the fly (dynamic composition), in which case the system is built gradually with each service call. In either case, the structure is based on messages communicated over the Internet between the service requester and the service provider. A Web service can be a service requester and a service provider at the same time. The final

response can reach the root or initiator of the call through intermediate service providers or via direct messaging.

WEB SERVICE MANAGEMENT FRAMEWORKS

The management of Web services in its simplest form refers to monitoring, configuring, and maintaining Web services. Web service management is a specific case of network and systems management, which considers issues such as performance, configuration, accounting, fault detection and correction, and security (Cisco Systems, 2005). The various systems management tools and software perform monitoring, reconfiguration, updating, access control, error reporting, and repair. Web services have largely evolved during the last few years from standard-based, loosely coupled, cross-vendor compatible service components to an industry-wide technology having the potential for constructing complex, multivendor composite systems. It is important to the continued growth and acceptance of this technology that the service providers ensure the QoS desired by the customers. This calls for the specification of the desired

Figure 2. Components of a Web service hosting system

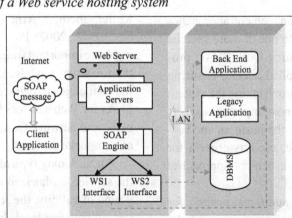

level of service through an SLA on the customer's side (Jin, Machiraju, & Sahai, 2002), and efficient management of the Web service system (Farrell & Kreger, 2002) to ensure the required service level on the service provider's side.

The unpredictable nature of the workloads of Web media and the need for high levels of interoperability and accessibility make the management of Web service systems a difficult and challenging task. Web services are also hosted and supported by a number of components, and these components must be managed harmoniously to render a desired service level. This obviously is far more challenging than managing a single application. Moreover, composite Web services can be created by a collaboration of multivendor Web services. The management of such systems, therefore, requires a collaborative service management framework (Lipton, 2004). For Web services, the management system particularly needs to address issues such as the Web media, varying workloads, distributed and heterogeneous clients and system components, and dynamic service composition.

In this section, we first discuss the criteria used to compare Web service management frameworks. A number of management frameworks are then described using a categorization based on their implementation infrastructure. The frameworks are then analyzed based on the given criteria.

Evaluation Criteria

Most of the proposed management approaches by the researchers focus on one or more specific aspects, such as maintaining QoS, SLAs, providing secure and controlled access, ensuring automatic recovery, and provisioning the system resources. These are the most important aspects as they directly influence the business and revenue. They are, therefore, used as criteria for analyzing the various management approaches discussed below.

We also identify two additional criteria for comparing the management frameworks, namely,

support for service composition and the implementation model used to develop the framework. The support for service composition can basically be classified as either static or dynamic, where static composition means that Web services are composed prior to run time, and dynamic composition means that Web services can be composed at run time. The implementation model is the main paradigm used to develop the framework, for example, agents, middleware, or reflective programming.

QoS and SLAs

The SLA specifies the required service properties as demanded by the service consumers, while QoS indicates how well a service is functioning. The most common QoS parameter is response time. Depending on the type of the system, other parameters such as memory usage, network delay, and queuing time can be monitored. A statistical QoS data set can also serve as a valuable guide for automatic service selection in a dynamic service composition (Zeng, Benatallah, Ngu, Dumas, Kalagnanam, & Chang, 2004). In most cases, the process of ensuring QoS is carried out by monitoring and analyzing performance data to build a predictive or reactive QoS model. The values of the configuration parameters are then determined to achieve a desired QoS based on the model, and those parameters are modified accordingly to reconfigure the system (Cardoso, Miller, Sheth, & Arnold, 2002; Liu et al., 2003; Sheth et al., 2002). Predictive models are becoming more important from the research perspective than reactive models. Ludwig (2003) discusses the challenges in delivering QoS as specified by SLAs for Web services because of the heterogeneity and network QoS, particularly in the case of composite services.

An SLA may typically define the purpose of the service, authorized parties or customers, the period of validity, the scope, restrictions, penalties, and service-level objectives like availability, performance, and reliability (Jin et al., 2002). The service provider is legally bound to provide the QoS as agreed through the SLA. Monitoring applications are deployed as part of the management application suite usually at both the customer's and service provider's ends to ensure the validity of the SLA throughout the service duration. Automating the process of creating and maintaining the SLA, especially for composite Web service systems, is one of the most challenging problems in the area of Web service management and dynamic service composition.

Recovery

An efficient management system should implement mechanisms to recover from minor and possibly major pitfalls in the least amount of time. Depending on the nature of the failure, the recovery can require a simple restart of the failed resource, or a complex error-tracking process (Sahai, Machiraju, Ouyang, et al., 2001) to identify and replace the failed resource. In a composite Web service system, the detection and replacement of a failed service with a similar service using automated service discovery and selection offers an interesting research problem. Resource provisioning also provides quick recovery from failure using replication with automatic resource replacement.

Security

Security is a major issue for Web services because of the nature of the network and interoperability (Chou & Yurov, 2005). However, currently, no standard security framework ensures all the security features such as authorized access, integrity, authenticity, and confidentiality of the information content. Some of the common approaches to implement security features are the use of access-control lists, security tokens, XML signatures, and message encryption and decryption techniques (Coetzee & Eloff, 2004; Wang, Huang, Qu, &

Xie, 2004). New standards to support Web service security are being worked on such as the Security Assertion Markup Language (SAML; OASIS SAML, 2005), eXtensible Access Control Markup Language (XACML; OASIS XACML, 2005), and Web services security (WSS; OASIS WSS, 2004). SAML leverages core Web services standards like XML, SOAP, transport layer security (TLS), XML signatures, and XML encryption. It enables the secure exchange of authentication, attribute, and authorization information between disparate security domains, making vendor-independent, single sign-on, secure e-business transactions possible within federated networks on the Web. XACML is an XML-based language for expressing well-established ideas in the field of access-control policy. It provides profiles for SAML 2.0, XML digital signatures, privacy policies, hierarchical or multiple resources, and role-based access control (RBAC). WS-Security provides an industry standard framework for secure Web service message exchanges.

Security policies may be defined and managed at a higher level as part of the management framework. Communicating parties can use these policies to establish and maintain a trust relationship. Furthermore, for specific business partners, a federation can be created and maintained (Wang et al., 2004) where members can share and distribute trust relationships.

Resource Provisioning

The typical "bursty" and varied nature of client requests to a Web service means that the optimum allocation of resources to a Web service is difficult to predict and will vary over time. As a result, without a resource sharing and provisioning strategy, resources can either remain underutilized or may be insufficient to handle user requests at the peak hours. The effective use of resource management techniques has been shown to improve performance in cluster-based Web service environments (Chung & Hollingsworth,

2004). Much research is going on about automatic resource management these days. The automatic replacement of failed resources can also contribute to efficient service recovery.

Management Frameworks

Researchers have proposed many different strategies and approaches to address the various management aspects. There is also considerable activity on Web management in consortiums and standards organizations such as OASIS and W3C. We categorize a number of management approaches based on the infrastructure used in the approach, that is, whether it is centralized, distributed, or autonomic, and describe their main features. Finally, we present self-managing or autonomic management approaches, and thereby describe our research on autonomic Web service systems. Most of the management frameworks have been implemented as models, and therefore the comparative analysis presented in the last section highlights the main features of the models against the evaluation criteria.

Centralized Management

Centralized management schemes employ a single central unit to carry out the management activities. Cibrán, Verheecke, Suvee, Vanderperren, and Jonckers (2004) present the Web service management layer (WSML), a middleware shown in Figure 3, which facilitates the development and management of integrated service applications. WSML supports client-side service management and criteria-based service selection for dynamic service composition. The rich run-time environment of JAsCo, an Aspect-Oriented Programming (AOP) Language, is used to modularize the implementation of the management functionality within WSML (Verheecke, Cibrán, Vanderperren, Suvee, & Jonckers, 2004). WSML lies between the client application and the Web services, and receives client requests for specific service types. A new JAsCo aspect bean is defined dynamically as required holding specific policies for each management aspect like service selection and binding, service swapping, automated billing, caching, and monitoring. JAsCo connectors are

Figure 3. General architecture of the WSML (Cibrán, Verheecke, Suvee et al., 2004)

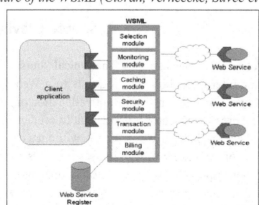

Figure 4. Web Services Management Network (WSMN; Sahai, Machiraju, Sayal et al, 2002)

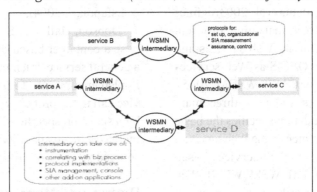

also created dynamically to bind the client application with a specific Web service based on the policies defined in the aspect bean. Client-side management is implemented using AOP in client applications. By isolating the management tasks in WSML, the replication and maintenance of similar management-related code in the applications is avoided.

Sahai, Machiraju, and Wurster (2001) suggested a management service provider (MSP) model for the remote or outsourced monitoring and controlling of e-services on the Internet. An automated and distributed SLA monitoring engine using the Web service management network (WSMN) agent, as shown in Figure 4 (Sahai et al., 2002), was proposed in a later publication. A specification language for SLAs was also proposed to be used with WSMN. The framework uses a network of cooperating intermediaries as proxy components in between a service and the outside world to enable message tracking. Each intermediary is attached to the SOAP tool kits at each Web service site of a composite process and communicates with each other through a set of protocols specifically defined for this purpose. WSMN agents monitor the process flow defined using WSFL (Web Service Flow Language) to ensure SLA compliance for managing service relationships.

The concept of workflow and process QoS is investigated by a group of researchers at the Large Scale Distributed Information Systems lab (LSDIS) at the University of Georgia. Typically, Web services are composed in a workflow, and it is necessary to manage the QoS metrics for all the services in the composition. Sheth et al. (2002) describe an agent-based service-oriented middleware (SoM) that provides an upper level middleware over Web services-based middleware and leverages the development of multiorganizational applications. SoM uses a process QoS model (Cardoso et al., 2002) that can be used to automatically compute the QoS of a composite Web service workflow process from the QoS metrics of the component Web services.

Fuente, Alonso, Martínez, and Aguilar (2004) propose the reflective and adaptable Web service (RAWS), which is a Web service design model that is based on the concept of reflective programming. It allows the administrators to dynamically modify the definition, behavior, and implementation structure of a Web service during its execution without requiring a shutdown of the service. Technically, the design implements behavioral and structural reflection in a two-level architecture, made of the base level and meta level, to allow the modification of one level to be reflected in the other level.

The Web-services management framework (WSMF) version 2.0 (Catania et al., 2003) defines a general framework for managing different types of resources including Web services and was later published by OASIS as Web-services distributed management (OASIS WSDM, 2005). The framework defines and uses three main concepts: WSMF-Foundation specifies the basic mechanisms for management using Web services, WS-Events introduces a Web-services-based event subsystem, and WSMF-WSM (WSMF-Web service management) describes the management of Web services using WSMF. However, it only allows generic security measures such as the use of HTTPS (secure HTTP), SSL (secure sockets layer) certificates, and access-control mechanisms at the API (application programming interface) level to be implemented.

Tosic, Pagurek, Patel, Esfandiari, and Ma (2004) define the Web Service Offering Language (WSOL) to allow the formal specification of important management information such as classes of service, functional and accessibility constraints, price, penalties, and other management responsibilities. The Web service offering infrastructure (WSOI), in turn, demonstrates the usability of WSOL in the management and composition of Web services (Tosic, Ma, Pagurek, & Esfandiari, 2004).

Dobson, Hall, and Sommerville (2005) propose a container-based fault-tolerant system for a general service-oriented architecture (SOA). It implements proxies to pass each incoming service call to the proper service replica as selected by a set of prespecified XML policies, and thus increases the availability and reliability for outsourced services of different types.

Distributed Management

Web service management systems with a distributed framework contain multiple, distributed management components that cooperate to perform the management functions. Researchers at IBM (Levy, Nagarajarao, Pacifici, Spreitzer, Tantawi, & Youssef, 2003) propose an architecture and prototype implementation of a performance-management system for cluster-based Web services as shown in Figure 5. The system supports SLA and performs dynamic resource allocation, load balancing, and server overload protection for multiple classes of Web services traffic. It uses inner level management for the queuing and scheduling of request messages. Outer level

Figure 5. Performance management system for cluster-based Web services (Levy et al., 2003)

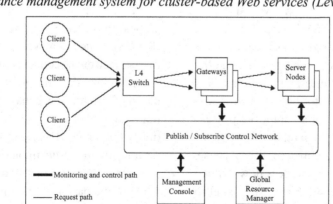

management implements a feedback control loop to periodically adjust the scheduling weights and server allocations of the inner level. The average response time is used as the performance metric for a given cluster utility function. The system supports multiple classes of Web-services traffic and allocates server resources dynamically to maximize the expected value of the utility function. However, it requires users to use a subscription interface to register with the system and subscribe to services.

Dan et al. (2004) define a framework that includes the Web Service Level Agreement (WSLA) Language, a system to provision resources based on SLAs, a workload-management system that prioritizes requests according to the associated SLAs, and a system to monitor compliance with the SLAs. The customers are billed differentially according to their agreed service levels.

Aggarwal, Verma, Miller, and Milnor (2004) present a Web service composition framework called METEOR-S (managing end-to-end operations for semantic Web services) to create and manage service composition. The framework allows automatic service selection, which facilitates the recovery and maintenance of composite Web service systems.

Coetzee and Eloff (2004) propose a logic-based access-control framework for single Web service-based systems. The framework implements authentication through identity verification and defines access-control policies to grant authorized access with the help of an authorization manager.

Autonomic Management

Manual management, especially the reconfiguration of numerous tunable system parameters of large heterogeneous complex systems, is becoming a nightmare for system administrators. Researchers are, therefore, seeking solutions to automate various tasks at different levels of system management. The autonomic-computing para-

digm promises a completely new era of systems management (Ganek & Corbi, 2003).

Autonomic systems are self-managing systems that are characterized by the following four properties.

- **Self-configuring:** Systems have the ability to define themselves on the fly to adapt to a dynamically changing environment.
- **Self-healing:** Systems have the ability to identify and fix failed components without introducing apparent disruption.
- **Self-optimizing:** Systems have the ability to provide optimal performance by automatically monitoring and tuning the resources.
- **Self-protecting:** Systems have the ability to protect themselves from attacks by managing user access, detecting intrusions, and providing recovery capabilities.

Autonomic systems are envisioned as imperative for next-generation highly distributed systems. Web services, in particular, can greatly benefit from autonomic computing because of their dynamic workloads and highly accessible communication media like the Internet (Birman et al., 2004). However, many problems need to be addressed in order to materialize the concept of autonomic Web services, rendering it as an interesting research topic. The approaches discussed below can also be categorized under centralized or distributed approaches according to their framework. However, for the self-management feature, they are described under this category.

The core part of an autonomic system is a *controller*, which is designed using either a performance feedback loop in a reactive manner or a feed-forward loop in predictive manner. Researchers propose different methodologies and frameworks to implement the controllers. Different search algorithms are proposed to search for the optimal values of the tunable configuration parameters. Various prediction logics are also followed by different approaches in case of

Figure 6. Active harmony automated tuning system (Chung & Hollingsworth, 2004)

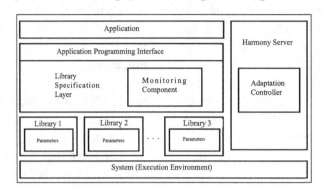

predictive controllers. Typically, a controller can dynamically manipulate the control switches, modify configuration parameters, or implement additional queues based on the performance data to provide optimal throughput.

An automated, cluster-based Web service performance-tuning infrastructure, which is shown in Figure 6, performs adaptive tuning with one or more active harmony servers using parameter replication and partitioning (Chung & Hollingsworth, 2004). The infrastructure contains a technique for resource sharing and distribution that allows active harmony to reconfigure the roles of specific nodes in the cluster during execution to further boost up the performance. In the active harmony framework, applications and services

reveal tunable sets of parameters through API that are dynamically tuned based on the workload, past performance history as recorded in a database, and the current performance level. The core part of the server is a controller that implements optimization algorithms for determining the proper value of the tuning parameters.

We also propose an architecture for an autonomic Web-services environment that supports automatic tuning and reconfiguration in order to ensure that the predefined SLAs are met in Tian, Zebedee, Zulkernine, Powley, and Martin (2005). Each component in the system is assumed to be an autonomic element, as shown in Figure 7, that is managed by an autonomic manager (AM). The framework is based on a hierarchy of autonomic

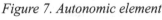

Figure 7. Autonomic element

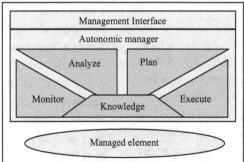

managers that coordinate with each other to provide an organized autonomic environment for Web services.

The autonomic manager consists of four functional modules that perform the following tasks: periodically monitor performance data; analyze the data based on past, current, and targeted performance; plan which parameters to tune in order to achieve the performance goal; and finally execute the action plan. We propose using reflection-based feedback controllers for our autonomic managers. A reflective system is one that can inspect and adapt its internal behavior in response to changing conditions. Typically, a reflective system maintains a model of self-representation, and changes to the self-representation are automatically reflected in the underlying system.

Control-theoretic approaches have been proposed by some researchers to implement the controllers. ControlWare is a middleware that embodies a control-theoretical methodology for QoS provisioning for software services (Abdelzaher, Stankovic, Lu, Zhang, & Lu, 2003). The feedback control mechanism guarantees QoS through the optimized allocation of system resources like various queues and cache sizes to different processes.

Bennani and Menascé (2004) create self-managing computer systems by incorporating mechanisms for self-adjusting the configuration parameters so that the QoS requirements of the system are constantly met. Their approach combines analytical performance models with combinatorial search techniques to develop controllers that run periodically to determine the best possible configuration for the system given its workload.

Birman et al. (2004) extend the general architecture of Web service systems to add high availability, fault tolerance, and autonomous behavior. The authors refer to the standards for Web services like WS-Events, WS-Transaction, and WS-Reliability while discussing failure protection, speedy recovery, and reliable messaging. The architecture includes server- and client-side monitoring, a consistent and reliable messaging system using information replication, a data-dissemination mechanism using multicasting, and an event notification system using WS-Events standards.

A framework for the deployment and subsequent autonomic management of component-based distributed applications is proposed by Dearle, Kirby, and McCarthy (2004). In their work, deployment goals are defined by specifying constraints over available resources, component mappings, and the interconnection topology. An autonomic deployment and management engine (ADME) is used to find a configuration that satisfies the goal, and the configuration is deployed automatically using the Cingal infrastructure (Dearle, Kirby, McCarthy, & Diaz y Carballo, 2004). If a deviation or change in the goal is detected, the configuration finder and deployment cycle is repeated automatically to generate a revised deployment. The proposed framework mainly addresses the self-configuration and self-healing aspects of autonomic management.

Comparative Analysis of the Management Approaches

The various approaches discussed above address one or more of the management aspects but not all of them. The QoS aspect has been addressed by several researchers in different ways. Sheth et al. (2002) introduce an additional agent-based middleware for computing the QoS of individual Web services and use the model proposed by Cardoso et al. (2002) to compute and thereby monitor the process QoS of a composite service system. Dan et al. (2004) present a more comprehensive distributed framework that contains a service-offering unit, WSLA-based QoS monitoring and differentiated service provisioning using a workload-management unit, and a resource-provisioning unit. Sahai et al. (2002) propose a

Table 1.

Reference	Type*	QoS/SLA	Security	Recovery	Service Composition	Resource Provisioning	Implementation Model
Cardoso et al., 2002	Cent.	Computes work-flow QoS	N/A	N/A	Static	N/A	Mathematical model
Sheth et al., 2002	Cent.	Computes QoS of composite service	N/A	N/A	Static	N/A	Agent-based middleware
Dan et al., 2004	Dist.	WSLA-based differentiated QoS provisioning	N/A	By component replacement	Static with service-offering unit	Separate unit for dynamic provisioning	Distributed-unit-based framework
Sahai et al., 2002	Cent.	WSFL-based monitoring for SLA compliance	N/A	N/A	Static	N/A	Agent-based network of intermediaries
Tosic et al., 2004	Cent.	WSOL for service offering and SLA	Usual security measures	N/A	Static or dynamic	N/A	WSOL for implementation of WSOL
Levy et al., 2003	Dist.	Differentiated reactive weighted message scheduling	N/A	Resource replacement and overload protection	Static	Dynamic server allocation & load balancing	Two-level management
Dobson et al., in press	Cent.	Higher availability & quick recovery	N/A	Service replication	Unsuitable for composite systems	Policy-based replica selection	Fault-tolerant system
Aggarwal et al., 2004	Cent.	Work-flow QoS	N/A	Dynamic service selection and replacement	Static or dynamic	N/A	METEOR-S framework

* Cent.- Centralized, Dist.- Distributed, Auto. – Autonomic

Table 1. Continued

Reference	Type*	QoS/SLA	Security	Recovery	Service Composition	Resource Provisioning	Implementation Model
Fuente et al., 2004	Cent.	Undisturbed during update	N/A	Source-code modification	Static or dynamic	N/A	Bi-level reflective programming
Verheecke et al., 2004	Cent.	Both client- and server-side management	Access control	Dynamic service selection and replacement	Static or dynamic	N/A	Middleware (WSML) using AOP
Coetzee & Eloff, 2004	Cent.	N/A	Policy-based access control	N/A	Not supported	N/A	Authentication and authorization verification
Abdelzaher et al., 2003	Auto.	Dynamic tuning using feedback control	N/A	Parameter tuning and reconfiguration	Static or dynamic	Message queuing and scheduling	Control-theory-based ControlWare
Bennani & Menascé, 2004	Auto.	Dynamic tuning using analytical model	N/A	Parameter tuning and reconfiguration	Static with service-offering unit	None	Uses a performance evaluation model
Chung & Hollingsworth, 2004	Dist. & auto.	Dynamic tuning of only registered parameters	N/A	Reconfiguration, resource sharing and distribution	Static or dynamic	Message queuing and scheduling, resource sharing	Active harmony for cluster-based systems
Tian et al., in press	Auto.	Management of SLA and QoS	N/A	Dynamic parameter tuning and reconfiguration	Static or dynamic	N/A	Reflective-programming-based hierarchy of AMs

* Cent. – Centralized, Dist. – Distributed, Auto. - Autonomic

less comprehensive agent-based WSMN using intermediaries as proxies that enables message tracking to monitor SLA compliance. However, it requires additional protocols for the intermediaries to communicate within themselves securely. WSOI mainly focuses on the application and manipulation of WSOL, a language for the formal specification of service offerings, and hence does not serve as a complete infrastructure for Web service management (Tosic, Pagurek, Patel et al., 2004). The framework by Levy et al. (2003) uses a feedback controller for weighted scheduling, message queuing, and server allocation in a cluster-based system. However, the clients need to subscribe to the service prior to using it.

The recovery aspect is addressed by Dobson et al. (2005), Aggarwal et al. (2004), and Fuente et al. (2004) in different ways. Dobson et al. designed a fault-tolerant system. However, it is difficult to apply rollback or other fault-tolerance mechanisms in case of Web services, especially in composite systems. Aggarwal et al. suggest dynamic service selection and composition in a workflow process using the METEOR-S framework to allow quick recovery. The bi-level architecture by Fuente et al. implements reflective programming to enable dynamic source-code update for Web services and thus facilitates deployment and recovery.

The WSML middleware implements each management aspect using separate aspect beans in AOP (Verheecke et al., 2004). It facilitates the modular implementation of various management aspects such as dynamic service selection, monitoring, and access control, and enables client-side management. Coetzee and Eloff (2004) propose a policy-based access-control framework for only single Web service based systems. Abdelzaher et al. (2003), Bennani and Menascé (2004), Chung and Hollingsworth (2004), and Tian et al. (2005) propose autonomic management approaches that perform parameter tuning and reconfigurations to maintain QoS. Abdelzaher et al. use control theory to design the feedback control framework augmented by elements of scheduling and queuing

theory for resource provisioning. Bennani and Menascé implement a performance evaluation model to search for the best configuration parameters to use with the controller, but the approach does not support resource provisioning. Chung and Hollingsworth use the active-harmony server to tune only the parameters that are registered with the server by the applications and services. In a cluster environment, it also performs resource sharing and distribution, and thereby supports quick recovery. Tian et al. use reflective programming with a hierarchy of autonomic managers to maintain QoS in a varying workload. However, none of the above approaches provide access control.

CONCLUSION

Open Problems

The above survey demonstrates that none of the proposed management frameworks addresses all the management aspects such as QoS, SLA negotiation, dynamic reconfiguration, security, recovery, and resource provisioning for dynamically composed systems. There has been considerable work done in the field of QoS and SLAs for Web services, but more research is needed to resolve the issues related to service dependency and providing differential services to different clients based on the SLA. The monitoring and maintenance of QoS and SLA for a composite service system is a challenging problem, especially when the QoS of the network is considered. The ranking of services based on specific service selection criteria is necessary to make automatic and run-time service selection. The publication and verification of QoS information that may be used as service selection criteria offer other interesting open problems.

Automatic service discovery and binding implemented by a management system can provide effective failure protection and recovery. However, this requires the use of well-defined semantics and specifications to enable automatic search and replacement of similar services.

Due to the nature and usage of Web media, they are vulnerable to malicious attacks. A good management framework should protect the system from such hazards. Standard specifications have been published for Web service security, but further research is needed to provide application-level security for Web services and to construct a secure management framework. End-user privacy is another important research area for Web services that is yet to be explored. The W3C is working on the Platform for Privacy Preferences Project (P3P) to provide a simple, automated way for users to gain more control over the use of personal information on Web sites they visit (W3C, 2004b). Privacy policies can be defined by service providers, which can be matched by service consumers before subscribing to a service. However, the monitoring of policy agreements at the provider's side is another problem.

Researchers are working on various policy specifications that may be incorporated into the management frameworks to implement policy-based management. The policies defined by service users need to be translated into system-usable formats. Further research is required to define strategies and implementation models to perform this translation effectively for different Web-services-based systems. SLA specification and QoS management for Web service systems have gained a lot of attention because of the wide range of user types and requirements. Resource provisioning for cluster-based Web services (Chung & Hollingsworth, 2004) is another important research problem.

With the rapid growth in the size and complexity of software systems, researchers are working toward designing autonomic systems featuring self-configuring, self-healing, self-optimizing, and self-protecting properties to reduce human intervention. Currently, fully autonomic systems do not exist. Researchers are now working on

achieving partial autonomic behavior through various control mechanisms. Regardless of the additional system components and increased management overhead, autonomic computing promises huge potential benefits as a systems-management solution. The existing solutions, in most cases, do not consider composite systems. New specifications and standards can be used to update the existing frameworks to provide enhanced management functionality.

SUMMARY

The World Wide Web is currently perceived as an indispensable resource of information. Different search engines and Web sites provide us with tools to search, select, and retrieve necessary information from the Internet. Most of these tools have an application at the back end that processes user requests and generates the responses to be sent back to the user. Web services are independent software applications that provide specific services to users or client applications on the Web through standard protocols and user interfaces. Thus, a Web service can be designed to effectively provide customized Web data management and powerful information-retrieval services over the Internet. Web services are also an effective implementation of SOC. The immense potential of composing Web services over multiple enterprises and building platform-independent, complex, interacting software systems has elevated the importance of Web services as a research area.

The management frameworks described are mostly research models and do not yet have any practical implementations. Some of the large companies are working together on standardizing various protocols like WS-Eventing, WS-Transfer, and WS-Management for Web-services management. WSMF by HP was later published as WSDM by OASIS. Currently, only a few Web service management software are available in the market. Managed Methods has released a Web service management software called JaxView to monitor availability, throughput, response time, faults, policies, and messages to assist service management. Mike Lehmann (2004), in an article in Oracle Magazine, presents new Web-services management capabilities in Oracle Application Server. AmberPoint Express is another management software that assists Web service developers to incrementally measure, debug, and fine-tune the performance and functionality of their Web services.

During the last few years, Web service technology has rapidly grown to become a part of our everyday lives. Many popular Web sites like Amazon.com are using Web services to serve customer enquiries. The success of this interactive Web technology largely depends on customer satisfaction. An efficient and reliable management framework is indispensable to ensure around-the-clock availability and service quality of Web service systems. This chapter provides an introduction and background on Web service management and outlines some of the challenging research problems in the area. It presents the state of the art of various management approaches for Web-services management. Newer and more interesting management problems will continue to arise from the growing complexity and expansion of this technology. The ongoing research on service management is focused toward achieving automated solutions requiring minimum human intervention. We envision autonomic computing as the most efficient technique for the continuous monitoring and management of large, heterogeneous, and complex systems such as composite Web service based systems.

REFERENCES

Abdelzaher, T. F., Stankovic, J. A., Lu, C., Zhang, R., & Lu, Y. (2003). Feedback performance control in software services. *IEEE Control Systems Magazine, 23*(3), 74-90.

Aggarwal, R., Verma, K., Miller, J., & Milnor, W. (2004). Constraint driven Web service composition in METEOR-S, services computing. *Proceedings of the IEEE International Conference on Services Computing SCC'04* (pp. 23-30).

Anzböck, R., Dustdar, S., & Gall, H. (2002). Software configuration, distribution, and deployment of Web-services. *ACM International Conference Proceeding Series: Vol. 27. Proceedings of the 14th International Conference on Software Engineering and Knowledge Engineering (SEKE'02): Web-Based Tools, Systems and Environments* (pp. 649-656).

Bennani, M., & Menascé, D. (2004). Assessing the robustness of self-managing computer systems under highly variable workloads. *Proceedings of the International Conference on Autonomic Computing (ICAC'04)*, 62-69.

Birman, K., Renesse, R. V., & Vogels, W. (2004). Adding high availability and autonomic behavior to Web services. *Proceedings of the 26th Annual International Conference on Software Engineering (ICSE'04)* (pp. 17-26).

Cardoso, J., Miller, J., Sheth, A., & Arnold, J. (2002). *Modeling quality of service for workflows and Web service processes* (Tech. Rep. No. 02-002 v2). University of Georgia, Department of Computer Science, LSDIS Lab, Athens.

Casati, F., Shan, E., Dayal, U., & Shan, M. (2003). Service-oriented computing: Business-oriented management of Web services. *Communications of the ACM, 46*(10), 55-60.

Catania, N., Kumar, P., Murray, B., Pourhedari, H., Vambenepe, W., & Wurster, K. (2003). *Overview: Web services management framework.* Hewlett-Packard Company. Retrieved June 20, 2006, from http://devresource.hp.com/drc/specifications/wsmf/WSMF-Overview.jsp

Chou, D. C., & Yurov, K. (2005). Security development in Web services environment. *Computer Standards & Interfaces, 27*(3), 233-240.

Chung, I., & Hollingsworth, J. K. (2004). Automated cluster-based Web service performance tuning. *Proceedings of IEEE Conference on High Performance Distributed Computing (HPDC'04),* (pp. 36-44).

Cibrán, M. A., Verheecke, B., Suvee, D., Vanderperren, W., & Jonckers, V. (2004). Automatic service discovery and integration using semantic descriptions in the Web services management layer. *Journal of Mathematical Modelling in Physics, Engineering and Cognitive Studies, 11,* 79-89.

Cisco Systems. (2005). Network management basics. In *Internetworking technologies handbook* (ch. VI). Retrieved June 20, 2006, from http://www.cisco.com/univercd/cc/td/doc/cisintwk/ito_doc/nmbasics.pdf

Coetzee, M., & Eloff, J. H. P. (2004). Towards Web service access control. *Computers & Security, 23*(7), 559-570.

Curbera, F., Khalaf, R., Mukhi, N., Tai, S., & Weerawarana, S. (2003). Service-oriented computing: The next step in Web services. *Communications of the ACM, 46*(10), 29-34.

Dan, A., Davis, D., Kearney, R., Keller, A., King, R., Kuebler, D., et al. (2004). Web services on demand: WSLA-driven automated management. *IBM Systems Journal, 43*(1), 136-158.

Dearle, A., Kirby, G., & McCarthy, A. (2004). A framework for constraint-based deployment and autonomic management of distributed applications. *International Conference on Autonomic Computing (ICAC'04),* 300-301.

Dearle, A., Kirby, G. N. C., McCarthy, A., & Diaz y Carballo, J. C. (*2004*). A flexible and secure deployment framework for distributed applications.

In W. Emmerich & A. L. Wolf (Eds.), *Proceedings of 2nd International Working Conference on Component Deployment (LNCS 3083, pp. 219-233). Edinburgh, UK*: Springer.

Dobson, G., Hall, S., & Sommerville, I. (2005, May). A container-based approach to fault tolerance in service-oriented architectures. *Proceedings of International Conference of Software Engineering (ICSE),* St. Louis, Missouri. Retrieved June 20, 2006, from http://digs.sourceforge.net/papers/2005-icse-paper.pdf

Farrell, J. A., & Kreger, H. (2002). Web services management approaches. *IBM Systems Journal, 41*(2), 212-227.

Fuente, J., Alonso, S., *Martínez*, O., & Aguilar, L. (**2004**). RAWS: Reflective engineering for Web services. *Proceedings of IEEE International Conference on Web Services (ICWS'04),* (p. 488).

Ganek, A. G., & Corbi, T. A. (2003). The dawning of the autonomic computing era. *IBM System Journal, 42*(1), 5-18.

Hogg, K., Chilcott, P., Nolan, M., & Srinivasan, B. (2004). An evaluation of Web services in the design of a B2B application. *Proceedings of the 27th Conference on Australasian Computer Science,* (**vol. 26,** pp. 331-340).

Jin, L., Machiraju, V., & Sahai, A. (2002). *Analysis on service level agreement of Web services.* Software Technology Laboratory, HP Laboratories. Retrieved June 20, 2006, from http://www.hpl.hp.com/techreports/2002/HPL-2002-180.pdf

Lehmann, M. (2004). Web services management arrives. *Oracle Magazine.* Retrieved June 20, 2006, from http://www.oracle.com/technology/oramag/oracle/04-nov/o64web.html

Levy, R., Nagarajarao, J., Pacifici, G., Spreitzer, M., Tantawi, A., & Youssef, A. (2003, March). *Performance management for cluster based Web services* (IBM Tech. Rep.). In *Proceedings of the IFIP/IEEE 8th International Symposium on*

Integrated Network Management (IM 2003), (pp. 247-261). Norwell, MA: Kluwer.

Lipton, P. (2004). Composition and management of Web services. In *Service-oriented architecture* (White paper). Retrieved June 20, 2006, from http://webservices.sys-con.com/read/43567.htm

Liu, B., Jha, S., & Ray, P. (2003). Mapping distributed application SLA to network QoS parameters. *Proceedings of ICT*, (pp. 1230-1235).

Ludwig, H. (2003). *Web services QoS: External SLAs and internal policies or: How do we deliver what we promise?* Proceedings of the 1st Web Services Quality Workshop, Rome.

Organization for the Advancement of Structured Information Standards Extensible Access Control Markup Language (OASIS XACML). **(2005).** *OASIS Extensible Access Control Markup Language (XACML) technical committee specification, v2.0.* Retrieved June 20, 2006, from http://www.oasis-open.org/committees/tc_home.php?wg_abbrev=xacml

Organization for the Advancement of Structured Information Standards Security Assertion Markup Language (OASIS SAML). (2005). *OASIS security services specification, v2.0, 2005.* Retrieved June 20, 2006, from http://www.oasis-open.org/committees/tc_home.php?wg_abbrev=security

Organization for the Advancement of Structured Information Standards Universal Description, Discovery and Integration (OASIS UDDI). (2005). *OASIS universal description, discovery and integration technical committee specification, v3.0.2.* Retrieved June 20, 2006, from http://www.uddi.org/specification.html

Organization for the Advancement of Structured Information Standards Web Services Distributed Management (OASIS WSDM). (2005). *Web services distributed management (WSDM), v1.0.* Retrieved June 20, 2006, from http://www. oasis-open.org/committees/tc_home.php?wg_abbrev=wsdm

Organization for the Advancement of Structured Information Standards Web Services Reliability (OASIS WS-Reliability). (2004). *OASIS Web services reliable messaging technical committee specification, v1.1.* Retrieved June 20, 2006, from http://www.oasis-open.org/committees/tc_home.php?wg_abbrev=wsrm

Organization for the Advancement of Structured Information Standards Web Services Security (OASIS WSS). (2004). *OASIS Web services security (WSS) technical committee specification, v1.0.* Retrieved June 20, 2006, from http://www.oasis-open.org/committees/tc_home.php?wg_abbrev=wss

Sahai, A., Machiraju, V., Ouyang, J., & Wurster, K. (2001). *Message tracking in SOAP-based Web services* (Tech. Rep.). HP Labs. Retrieved June 20, 2006, from http://www.hpl.hp.com/techreports/2001/HPL-2001-199.pdf

Sahai, A., Machiraju, V., Sayal, M., Van Moorsel, A., & Casati, F. (2002, October). Automated SLA monitoring for Web services. In *Proceedings of the 13th IFIP/IEEE International Workshop on Distributed Systems: Operations and Management (DSOM'02)* (LNCS 2506, pp. 28-41), Montreal, Canada. Springer-Verlag.

Sahai, A., Machiraju, V., & Wurster, K. (2001). Monitoring and controlling Internet based e-services. *Proceedings of the 2nd IEEE Workshop on Internet Applications (WIAPP'01)*, 41.

Seth, M. (2002). *Web services: A fit for EAI* (White paper). Retrieved June 20, 2006, from http://www.developer.com/tech/article.php/10923_1489501_2

Sheth, A., Cardoso, J., Miller, J., Kochut, K., & Kang, M. (2002). QoS for service-oriented middleware. *Proceedings of the 6th World Multiconfer-*

ence on Systemics, Cybernetics and Informatics (SCI'02), 528-534.

Sun. (2004). *J2EE, Java Servlet technology.* Retrieved June 20, 2006, from http://java.sun.com/products/servlet/

Tian, W., Zebedee, J., Zulkernine, F., Powley, W., & Martin, P. (2005, May). Architecture for an autonomic Web services environment. *Proceedings of 7th International Conference on Enterprise Information Systems (ICEIS'05)*, Miami, Florida, (pp. 54-66). Retrieved from http://www.cs.queensu.ca/home/cords/wsmdeis.pdf

Tosic, V., Ma, W., Pagurek, B., & Esfandiari, B. (2004, April). Web services offerings infrastructure (WSOI): A management infrastructure for XML Web services (Tech. Rep.). *Proceedings of IEEE/IFIP Network Operations and Management Symposium (NOMS)* (vol. 1, pp. 817-830), Seoul, South Korea. Retrieved from http://www.sce.carleton.ca/netmanage/papers/TosicEtAlResRepAug2003.pdf

Tosic, V., Pagurek, B., Patel, K., Esfandiari, B., & Ma, W. (in press). Management applications of the Web Service Offerings Language (WSOL). *Information Systems.*

Verheecke, B., Cibrán, M. A., Vanderperren, W., Suvee, D., & Jonckers, V. (2004). AOP for dynamic configuration and management of Web services in client-applications. *International Journal on Web Services Research (JWSR), 1*(3), 25-41.

Wang, H., Huang, J., Qu, Y., & Xie, J. (2004). Web services: Problems and future directions. *Journal of Web Semantics, 1*(3), 309-320.

Web services for management. (2005). Retrieved June 20, 2006, from http://developers.sun.com/techtopics/webservices/management/WS-Management.Feb.2005.pdf

Web service transfer. (2004). Retrieved June 20, 2006, from http://msdn.microsoft.com/library/en-us/dnglobspec/html/ws-transfer.pdf

WS-eventing. (2004). Retrieved June 20, 2006, from http://ftpna2.bea.com/pub/downloads/WS-Eventing.pdf

WE-Trust. (2005, February). *Web Service Trust Language (WS-Trust).* Retrieved from http://specs.xmlsoap.org/ws/2005/02/trust/WS-Trust.pdf

World Wide Web Consortium (W3C). (2003). *SOAP version 1.2 part 1: Messaging framework.* Retrieved June 20, 2006, from http://www.w3.org/TR/soap12-part1/

World Wide Web Consortium (W3C). (2004a). *Extensible Markup Language (XML).* Retrieved June 20, 2006, from http://www.w3.org/XML/

World Wide Web Consortium (W3C). (2004b). *The platform for privacy preferences project (P3P).* Retrieved from http://www.w3.org/P3P/

World Wide Web Consortium (W3C). (2005). *Web Services Description Language (WSDL) version 2.0* (Working draft). Retrieved June 20, 2006, from http://www.w3.org/2002/ws/desc/

Zeng, L., Benatallah, B., Ngu, A. H. H., Dumas, M., Kalagnanam, J., & Chang, H. (2004). QoS-aware middleware for Web services composition. *IEEE Transactions on Software Engineering, 30*(5), 311-327.

This work was previously published in Web Data Management Practices: Emerging Techniques and Technologies, edited by A. Vakali and G. Pallis, pp. 268-290, copyright 2007 by IGI Publishing, formerly known as Idea Group Publishing (an imprint of IGI Global).

Chapter XXIII
Electronic Risk Management

Tapen Sinha
Instituto Tecnológico Autónomo de México, Mexico
University of Nottingham, UK

Bradly Condon
Instituto Tecnológico Autónomo de México, Mexico
Bond University, Australia

ABSTRACT

Doing business on the Internet has many opportunities along with many risks. This chapter focuses on a series of risks of legal liability arising from e-mail and Internet activities that are a common part of many e-businesses. Some of the laws governing these electronic activities are new and especially designed for the electronic age, while others are more traditional laws whose application to electronic activities is the novelty. E-business not only exposes companies to new types of liability risk, but also increases the potential number of claims and the complexity of dealing with those claims. The international nature of the Internet, together with a lack of uniformity of laws governing the same activities in different countries, means that companies need to proceed with caution.

INTRODUCTION

Within 48 hours after Katrina came ashore, a number of Web sites cropped up claiming that they are for hurricane relief. At the click of a computer Web site, you could donate money for the victims. Some of them even allowed you to donate money through a Red Cross Web site. Unfortunately, many of them turned out to be fraudulent. When you thought you were going to the Red Cross Web site, you would be taken to a different one and your credit card information would be stolen and sold to the highest bidder. In the electronic parlance, this process is called "phishing" (see Appendix for terminologies).

Electronic information transfer has become the backbone of our information society. Therefore, it is not surprising that it has also increased the risks coming from electronic sources. The main risk comes from the Internet. For many businesses, and for many individuals, the benefits of being connected to the Internet have increased so much that not being connected to the Internet is no longer an option.

Companies who conduct transactions over electronic channels face a number of risks. Some of these risks, such as viruses, flow from the nature of modern technology. Others, such as theft, are age-old risks that have taken on new twists in the electronic age. For example, banks transfer huge amounts of money by wire, making them easy and lucrative targets for fraud, extortion, and theft. Other financial institutions, such as credit card companies, are prone to the same hazards. Software companies sell their products in electronic format. Copying files and programs is easy and cheap, making software companies particularly vulnerable to theft of their products. Electronic retailers that do all of their business online, such as Amazon.com, are subject to a wide array electronic risks associated with electronic money transfers and Web sites. However, even bricks and mortar companies face numerous risks emanating from (electronic) viruses, hackers, and the online activities of employees. These legal and technological risks associated with e-business—which may be referred to collectively as electronic or cyber risks—are the subject of this chapter.

The aim of this chapter is to survey a broad array of electronic risks that can cause their victims to lose money. It is beyond the scope of this chapter to provide advice on how to manage each and every one of these risks. Rather, this chapter seeks to raise awareness of a variety of risks so that readers will become conscious of the need to develop electronic risk management strategies. The best advice in this regard is to invest in expert advice. For example, where litigation risk exists, consult a lawyer early on regarding strategies to adopt that will avoid litigation or minimize the cost and risk of litigation should it become unavoidable. Where loose lips increase risks,

develop strategies for managing the content of correspondence, whether traditional or electronic, such as educating and monitoring employees. Where the problem is primarily a technical one, invest in the necessary technology and expertise. Finally, where insurance is available to manage the financial risks associated with doing business electronically, buy it.

A GLOBAL PROBLEM OF VIRUSES

Computer viruses have become synonymous with electronic risk on a global scale. The method of electronic infection has changed dramatically. In 1996, e-mail attachments were responsible for 9% of infections whereas 57% of infections came from floppy disks. In 2000, 87% infections came from e-mail attachments and only 6% came from floppy disks. By 2004, the rate of infections from e-mail attachments had topped 99% of total infections (Source: ICSA Labs Virus Prevalence Survey, various years). As a result, in 1997, only 30% of all institutions used virus protection for e-mails whereas by 2004, the use of virus protection had almost reached universality (ICSA Labs Virus Prevalence Survey 2004, Figure 15). However, the rise of the use of virus protection has not reduced the rate of infection. Figure 1 shows how the rate of infection has changed over a period of 9 years. Despite the near universal use of antivirus software, the rate of infection has increased more than eleven-fold. The biggest jump in infection came between 1998 and 1999. It has not decreased since (see Table 1).

The number of problems and the associated cost of computer viruses have gone up steadily over the past decade. DARPA created the Computer Emergency Response Team Coordination Center (CERT/CC) in November 1988 after the computer worm Morris worm struck. It is a major coordination center dealing with Internet security problems run by the Software Engineering Institute (SEI) at Carnegie Mellon University.

Table 1. Computer infection rates 1996-2004 (Source: ICSALabs.com)

Infection Rates	Per 1000 Computers
1996	10
1997	21
1998	32
1999	80
2000	90
2001	103
2002	105
2003	108
2004	116

Table 2. Number of incidents reported by CERT 1995-2003 (Source: http://www.cert.org)

Year	No. of Incidents
1995	2,412
1996	2,573
1997	2,134
1998	3,374
1999	9,859
2000	21,756
2001	52,658
2002	82,094
2003	137,529

Note: A CERT "incident" may involve one, hundreds, or thousands of sites. Some incidents may involve ongoing activity for long periods of time.

CERT/CC has compiled a comprehensive list of security "incidents" that have occurred since 1995 (see Table 2). The trend is showing an exponential rise of such incidents over time.

How much do such viruses cost the world? Estimates are available for 1995-2003. It shows that the cost went up quite rapidly between 1995 and 2000, but then there was no clear increase over time. One reason for such a recent slowdown is the widespread use of antivirus programs implemented by businesses as well as individuals.

The damage caused by computer viruses is not uniform across all viruses. A few viruses (and their variants) cause most of the damage. The undisputed world champion was a virus codenamed ILOVEU (see Table 4). It was created by a person in the Philippines. Yet, the most damage it caused was in the developed world. It propagated during the weekend of February 2000 around St. Valentine's Day. The biggest recent attack, in August 2005, was caused by a worm code named Zotob. It took out the computer system of CNN live. It spread through the entire Internet over the weekend. Within 2 weeks, the police in Morocco arrested an 18-year old as the main coder of the worm at the request of the Federal Bureau of Investigation. However, given that there is no extradition treaty in these matter between the United States

and Morocco, it is highly unlikely that the person would be extradited to the United States.

THE SPAM-VIRUS NEXUS

Being connected to the rest of the world through the Internet in general, and through e-mails in particular, has a cost. The cost comes in the form of spam. Spam is unsolicited e-mail. The problem of spam has become extremely large. In July 2004, spam accounted for more than 95% of all e-mails (see Figure 1). MessageLabs published a report in 2004 in which it noted that "more than 80% of global spam originates from fewer than 200 known spammers in the USA. Many are based in the small town of Boca Raton in Florida, one of three states in the U.S. which have no spam legislation in place" (Source: http://www.MessageLabs.com). In addition to being a nuisance, spam also represents a big source of electronic risk. Among the devastating viruses, SoBig.F (see Table 4) spread mainly through spam. Thus, spam can not only be a nuisance by itself, but can also carry a payload of viruses.

Figure 1 suggests that some electronic risks can be diminished with adequate legal protection.

Table 3. Annual financial impact of major virus attacks 1995-2003 (Source: http://www.computereconomics.com)

Year	Worldwide Economic Impact (US$)
2003	$13.5 Billion
2002	11.1 Billion
2001	13.2 Billion
2000	17.1 Billion
1999	12.1 Billion
1998	6.1 Billion
1997	3.3 Billion
1996	1.8 Billion
1995	500 Million

Table 4. Financial impact of major virus attacks since 1999 (Source: http://www.computereconomics.com)

Year	Code Name	Worldwide Financial Impact ($US)
2004	MyDoom	$4.0 Billion
2003	SoBig.F	2.5 Billion
2003	Slammer	1.5 Billion
2003	Blaster	750 Million
2003	Nachi	500 Million
2002	Klez	750 Million
2002	BugBear	500 Million
2002	Badtrans	400 Million
2001	CodeRed	2.75 Billion
2001	Nimda	1.5 Billion
2001	SirCam	1.25 Billion
2000	ILOVEU	8.75 Billion
1999	Melissa	1.5 Billion
1999	Explorer	1.1 Billion

However, there are limits to what can be achieved through the enactment of new criminal and civil laws to deal with illicit electronic activities, just as there are limits to what the law can achieve more generally. Civil litigation is an expensive and uncertain process. Judgments can be difficult to enforce against defendants that are determined to avoid payment. Criminal laws have not eliminated crime. The global nature of the Internet means that laws have to be coordinated and enforced across international borders, introducing further complications. As a result, managing electronic risk requires a blend of risk reduction and legal strategies.

Figure 1. Spam has become a huge segment of e-mails

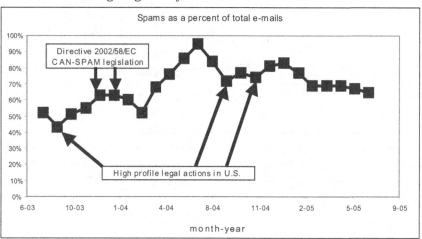

A Catalog of Risks and Legal Problems

The most common electronic risks are the following: (1) business interruptions caused by hackers, cybertheives, viruses, and internal saboteurs; (2) employer liability stemming from the inappropriate employee use of e-mail and Internet; (3) claims that products and services advertised on the Web fail to deliver; (4) Web-related copyright and trademark lawsuits; (5) patent infringement costs; (6) fraud-extortion hybrid.

General Legal Issues

Given the international scope cyberspace, several general legal issues arise. The first is how to address conflicts between the laws of different jurisdictions. Whose law governs when the parties involved live in different countries and the transaction occurs in cyberspace? Many Web sites now use online contracts that specifically provide whose law will govern the transaction. These online contracts generally require the user to click their agreement with the terms of the contract before they are allowed to proceed with the transaction.

A related issue is choice of forum. Where do you sue for breach of contract? Many online contracts also provide the answer to this question. However, where there is no contract involved, such as in cases of fraud or negligence, the issues of conflict of laws and choice of forum may not have clear answers. Moreover, the choice of forum that is of the most benefit to the party who is suing for damages will be the jurisdiction in which the assets are located that will serve to satisfy any award for damages. Alternatively, the plaintiff may prefer to sue in its own jurisdiction due to convenience or familiarity with the system.

If a plaintiff chooses to sue in a particular jurisdiction, that does not resolve the matter. In each jurisdiction, courts apply their own rules to determine whether to exercise jurisdiction over the defendant in a given case. For example, many U.S. courts base the decision to accept jurisdiction in Internet transactions on the nature and quality of the commercial activity. If a foreign defendant enters into contracts with residents in the jurisdiction that involve knowing and repeated transmission of computer files over the Internet, the court will accept jurisdiction. On the other hand, if the defendant merely operates a passive Web site that posts information that is accessible to users in other jurisdictions, the court will not exercise jurisdiction (Gasparini, 2001).

One crucial question is, who do you sue? In cases involving employees, it is generally wise to sue both the individual and the employer. In determining who to sue, several questions must be considered. Who has liability? Who has assets that can be seized to satisfy a judgment awarding damages? Where are the assets? What is the procedure to seize the assets in the jurisdiction in which they are located? Are the assets accessible? For example, are they held in the name of the responsible person and in a jurisdiction where the judgment can be enforced? In some jurisdictions, enforcing judgments may be problematic. For example, in Mexico, bank secrecy laws may prevent a determination of what assets are available to satisfy a judgment. In addition, enforcing the judgments of courts from one country in a second country can be problematic where the second country has no procedure for recognizing the awards of foreign courts.

Another important consideration is litigation risk. Litigation is costly and the outcome is uncertain. Even if the plaintiff secures judgment in his favor, enforcement may not be possible. If the party claiming damages is not able to collect from the guilty party, the cost of litigation is wasted. This leads to another important question. Is the guilty party insured? Does the insurance contract provide coverage for actions that generated legal liability? Should it?

BUSINESS INTERRUPTIONS

Any kind of business interruption is costly. It can increase cost of doing business or reduce revenue or both. It does not matter if it stems from strikes, fire, power failure, hackers or saboteurs. Electronic risk is increasingly becoming a bigger threat to business.

For example, a hacker overwhelmed several large Web sites through multiple distributed de-

nial-of-service (DDOS) attacks. The culprit hijacked various computers throughout the world to bombard target servers with seemingly legitimate requests for data. It is estimated that the DDOS attacks, which interrupted the sites' ability to efficiently conduct their business, caused over $1.2 billion in lost business income. (http://www.insurenewmedia.com/html/claimsexample.htm)

This raises several legal issues. The denial of service that occurs when the server fails could expose the business to claims for damages for breach of contract from clients. In the contract, the server agrees to provide the service. If the interruption of service causes financial loss, for example, due to lost business, the administrator of the server may be liable for the loss. Liability will depend on the terms of each contract. For example, if a *force majeure* clause excuses the server from performing the contract in the event of power outages or hacker attacks, there will be no liability.

The denial of service could also give rise to a claim for damages based on the negligence of the server administrator. Where the server can be protected against hacker attacks by readily available technology, the failure of administrator to employ the technology to protect client access to the service would be negligent.

Another issue is whether the server may sue the hacker for damages. However, this may be a moot point if the hacker cannot be located, lives in a jurisdiction where the law does not allow for such a legal claim to be filed, or has no assets with which to satisfy the claim for damages (for example, teenage hackers with poor parents).

INAPPROPRIATE USE OF E-MAIL AND INTERNET

Inappropriate use of e-mail and Internet can expose employers to claims for damages in three principal areas of law—human rights law, privacy legislation, and civil liability for damages caused by employees to fellow employees or third parties under negligence and libel laws.

In addition to the foregoing liability risks, e-mail communications are a rich source of evidence in any kind of legal dispute, which means that employees need to be careful about what they communicate electronically. Poorly managed written communications in e-mails and letters can come back to haunt any business that later finds itself enmeshed in litigation, accused of corporate fraud, or audited for SEC compliance. It is technically possible to recover e-mail messages that have been "deleted" in e-mail programs, making it difficult to destroy this type of evidence. As a result, these messages may be uncovered during a civil litigation procedure known as pretrial discovery in common-law jurisdictions such as Canada and the United States. This data needs to be managed well, both in terms of limiting its creation in the first place and in terms of reducing the cost of its retrieval should it need to be produced in pretrial discovery. (Just imagine the cost of teams of lawyers sorting through millions of e-mails.)

Many jurisdictions give employees the right to sue for sexual harassment under human rights legislation. A common inappropriate use of e-mail consists of sexual harassment of one employee by another. For example, a manager and his employer could be sued for communicating sexual messages via e-mail to a subordinate. The same act can create a cause of action for a civil suit against both the manager and the employer who allowed the act to take place. In litigation, reliable evidence that the harassment really took place becomes a central issue. When the means of communication is e-mail, that evidence is more readily available, increasing the risk of an award of damages against the employer.

Electronic communication raises the risks of violating general privacy legislation and professional rules regarding privileged information. One of largest health insurers in the United States inadvertently sent e-mail messages to 19 members containing confidential medical and personal information of 858 other members. Although the company immediately took steps to correct the problem, the company was exposed to lawsuits alleging invasion of privacy. Similarly, lawyers must take care not to violate solicitor-client privilege, which can expose them to both disciplinary proceedings in the profession and claims for damages from the client (Rest, 1998).

Internet telecommuting raises the risk that an employer's internal network will be exposed to "backdoor attacks" that exploit the telecommuter's connection and threaten confidential information belonging to a client or third party. In such cases, employer liability will probably depend on whether the employer provided adequate protection from such an attack (Maier, 2001).

Employee use of company e-mail to promote personal business is another source of legal problems. Where the actions of the employee can be considered part of the normal course of their employment duties, the employer may be held liable for the actions of the employee. For example, the employer may be liable for allowing its system to be used for the communication of the slanderous message. In the United States, however, the Communications Decency Act of 1996 has made Internet providers immune from liability for publishing a defamatory statement made by another party and for refusing to remove the statement from its service (King, 2003).

The employer may be held liable for failing to properly supervise employee use of e-mail and Internet. For example, an employee who uses e-mail to sexually harass a fellow employee can expose a company to lawsuits. Using the company's e-mail and Internet system to further criminal acts can also expose the company to liability. In such cases, traditional law regarding employer liability extends to e-risk cases.

Under the common law doctrine of *respondeat superior*, the employer is responsible for employee acts that are within the scope of employment or further the employer's interests. However, the employer cannot be held liable if the personal motives of the employee are unrelated to the employer's business. (Nowak, 1999) For example, in Haybeck vs. Prodigy Services Co., Prodigy Services was not held liable for the actions of a computer technical advisor when he used the company computer to enter Internet chat rooms and to lure his victim with offers of free time on Prodigy. The employee was HIV-positive and intentionally had unprotected sex without disclosing his infection. Where an employee's improper use of e-mail or Internet falls outside the scope of employment, the employer cannot be held liable under this doctrine.

However, the employer may still be found liable for negligently retaining or supervising an employee. Under the doctrine of negligent retention, an employer may be liable for hiring an unfit person in circumstances that involve an unreasonable risk of harm to others. The employer will be held liable for the acts of an employee where the employer knew or should have known about the employee's conduct or propensity to engage in such conduct. Moreover, the employer has a duty to set rules in the workplace and to properly supervise employees. (Nowak, 1999) Thus, there is a risk of liability if the employer has knowledge of facts that should lead the employer to investigate an employee or to implement preventive rules for all employees.

The key issue is whether the employer could have reasonably foreseen the actions of the employee. For example, in the Prodigy case, the court held that the employer was not liable for negligent retention because the plaintiff could not show that Prodigy had any knowledge of his activities. Nor was there an allegation that technical advisors commonly have sex with customers without revealing that they carry communicable diseases. However, in Moses vs. Diocese of Colorado, a church parishioner in Colorado successfully sued the Episcopal diocese and bishop for injuries she suffered having sex with a priest from whom she sought counseling. Sexual relationships between priests and parishioners had arisen seven times before and the diocese had been notified that greater supervision of the priests might be necessary. The court found the diocese negligent for not providing more supervision when it knew that such relationships were becoming more common.

Similarly, employers may be held liable for negligent supervision of employee use of e-mail and Internet if they know that their employees visit pornographic Internet sites and use e-mail for personal communications. In such circumstances, they have a duty to provide rules of conduct for employees and to monitor compliance. If they administer their own networks, they should monitor employee use of the system where incriminating communications may be stored. It would be difficult to argue that they are unaware of employee activities when contradictory evidence is stored on the company system. Employers should use software that blocks access to pornographic Internet sites and that screens e-mails for key words. However, they should also advise employees that their computer use is being monitored, to avoid liability for invasion of employee privacy.

A company's monitoring practices may be justified by the potential liabilities created by employees' misuse of e-mail and the Internet. However, the company's potential liability for invasion of employee privacy must also be considered. While employees in the United States have little privacy protection in this area, European employers must take reasonable precautions to protect their employees' privacy when they monitor their e-mail or Internet usage. (Rustad & Paulsson, 2005). Even in the United States, however, employers should take care not to violate labor laws by unduly restricting their employees' communications regarding labor rights (O'Brien, 2002).

Companies can reduce or eliminate the risk of liability for employees' use of electronic communication by implementing an effective Internet policy. Such a policy should (1) warn employees that their communications may be monitored; (2) require employees to sign consent forms for monitoring; (3) limit employee Internet access to work-related activities; (4) establish clear rules against conducting personal business on the company system; (5) define and prohibit communications that may be considered harassment of fellow employees and third parties or violate human rights laws; (6) forbid employees using another employee's system; (7) implement a policy on the length of time documents are retained on a backup system; and (8) ensure all employees understand and will follow the policy. (Nowak, 1999) To limit exposure to e-risk, insurers should insist that clients implement an effective Internet policy as a condition of coverage.

Sloan (2004) offers a series of practical suggestions for avoiding litigation problems. His advice includes the following recommendations: (1) Instead of using e-mails, it is preferable to use telephones when possible. (2) E-mails should not be sent immediately. Once sent, e-mails cannot be called back. If a cooling period is implemented, they can be recalled. (3) The distribution of e-mails should be limited. The default e-mail option should not include the possibility of sending it to a large group within a company all at once. (4) Within a company, sarcasm and criticism can do a lot of damage to the company's health. They should be avoided. (5) Swearing is a bad idea in an e-mail. This should be avoided at all cost.

FAILURE OF PRODUCT

Failure of a product to deliver can come from many different sources. For example, an antivirus software may fail to protect the customer from a particular virus leading to loss of mission-critical data for the company. Recently, a number of Web site development companies have been sued for being negligent with their design, which allowed hackers to enter and use computer portals for unauthorized use.

False claims regarding the characteristics of products and services can give rise to three types

of legal actions. If it is a case of fraud, criminal laws would govern. Criminal legal procedures differ from civil law suits in two important respects. The cost of filing a criminal complaint is negligible because the investigating police and the prosecutor are paid by the state. This provides a low financial threshold for the unhappy customer. However, defending a criminal charge is just as costly as defending a civil action for the business person who commits the fraud. However, a criminal case generally results in no damages award. Instead, the guilty party may be subject to fines and/or imprisonment. The customer thus has a low financial threshold for filing charges, but is likely to receive no financial reward at the conclusion of the proceedings, except in cases where courts order the defendant to pay restitution.

In many jurisdictions, consumer protection legislation gives customers the right to return a product for a refund where the product is not suitable for the purpose for which it is intended. As long as the business provides the refund, the cost to the business is relatively low because its liability ends with the refund. Should the business refuse to refund the purchase price, the customer may sue and be entitled to legal costs as well. However, where the value of the transaction is low, the cost of suing will exceed the amount owing, making it impractical to pursue.

In common law jurisdictions (such as Australia, Canada, England, and the United States), false claims regarding a product or service may give rise to a civil action for negligent misrepresentation. In a case of negligent misrepresentation, the customer could claim compensation for damages caused by the customer's reliance on the company's representation of what the product or service would do.

Traditional principles of agency may expose reputable companies to liability where they sponsor the Web sites of smaller firms. If the company creates the appearance of an agency relationship, and a consumer reasonably believes the companies are related, the consumer can sue the sponsor for the harm caused by the lack of care or skill of the apparent agent. This is so even where no formal agency relationship exists (Furnari, 1999).

FRAUD, EXTORTION, AND OTHER CYBERCRIMES

The Internet facilitates a wide range of international crimes, including forgery and counterfeiting, bank robbery, transmission of threats, fraud, extortion, copyright infringement, theft of trade secrets, transmission of child pornography, interception of communications, transmission of harassing communications and, more recently, cyberterrorism. However, the division of the world into separate legal jurisdictions complicates the investigation and prosecution of transnational cybercrimes (Goldstone & Shave, 1999).

There are numerous examples. In one case, eight banking Web sites in the United States, Canada, Great Britain, and Thailand were attacked, resulting in 23,000 stolen credit card numbers. The hackers proceeded to publish 6,500 of the cards online, causing third-party damages in excess of $3,000,000 (http://www.aignetadvantage.com/bp/servlet/unprotected/claims.examples). In another case, a computer hacker theft ring in Russia broke into a Citibank electronic money transfer system and tried to steal more than $10 million by making wire transfers to accounts in Finland, Russia, Germany, The Netherlands, and the United States. Citibank recovered all but $400,000 of these transfers. The leader of the theft ring was arrested in London, extradited to the United States 2 years later, sentenced to 3 years in jail, and ordered to pay $240,000 in restitution to Citibank. In yet another case, an Argentine hacker broke into several military, university, and private computer systems in the United States containing highly sensitive information. U.S. authorities tracked him to Argentina and Argentina investigated his intrusions into the Argentine telecommunications

system. However, Argentine law did not cover his attacks on computers in the United States, so only the United States could prosecute him for those crimes. However, there was no extradition treaty between Argentina and the United States. The U.S. persuaded him to come to the United States and to plead guilty, for which he received a fine of $5,000 and 3-years probation (Goldstone & Shave, 1999).

In these types of scenarios, the hackers could be subject to criminal prosecution in the victim's country but not in the perpetrator's home country. Even if subject to criminal prosecution in both countries, extradition may not be possible. Moreover, criminal proceedings would probably not fully compensate the banks for their losses or that of their customers. Indeed, the customers might be able to file claims against the banks for negligence if they failed to use the latest technology to protect their clients' information from the hackers.

A further complication arises when there are conflicts between the laws of different countries. For example, hate speech (promoting hatred against visible minorities) is illegal in countries such as Canada, but protected by the constitution in the United States. A court may order the production of banking records in one country that are protected by bank secrecy laws in another. For example, in United States vs. Bank of Nova Scotia, the Canadian Bank of Nova Scotia was held in contempt for failing to comply with an order that required the bank to violate a Bahamian bank secrecy rule.

The jurisdictional limits of the authorities in each country also complicate investigations. For example, a search warrant may be issued in one country or state to search computer data at a corporation inside the jurisdiction, but the information may actually be stored on a file server in a foreign country, raising issues regarding the legality of the search. International investigations are further complicated by the availability of experts in foreign countries, their willingness to cooperate, language barriers, and time differences (Goldstone & Shave, 1999).

Another cybercrime that is currently theoretical is cyberterrorism. While there have been no cases to date, there are likely to be in the future. A bill passed by the New York Senate defines the crime of cyberterrorism as any computer crime or denial of service attack with an intent to ... influence the policy of a unit of government by intimidation or coercion, or affect the conduct of a unit of government (Iqbal, 2004).

WEB-RELATED INTELLECTUAL PROPERTY RIGHTS INFRINGEMENT

Intellectual property infringements are a significant liability risk for Internet business and may lead to expensive litigation. For example, computer bulletin board companies have been sued for copyright infringement (in Religious Technology Center vS. Netcom Online Communication Services, Inc.) and for copyright infringement, trademark infringement, and unfair competition with respect to video games (in Sega Enterprises Ltd. vs. Maphia). (Richmond, 2002) In another case, an online insurance brokerage created a hyperlink that seemingly transferred its clients to additional pages on the site itself. It was later discovered that the brokerage "deep-linked" its users to the Web pages of various insurance companies, creating a seamless navigational experience. The insurance companies sued the online brokerage for copyright and trademark infringement (http://www.insurenewmedia.com/html/claimsexample.htm). With litigation of intellectual property claims against e-commerce ventures on the rise, the risk is increasing for insurance companies as well (General & Cologne Re, 1999).

Patent infringement claims are quite common. In the past, Microsoft had faced a whole slew of them (including the well-publicized ones from Xerox about the use of mouse as a computer interface). Computer software always builds on past programs. Therefore, the line between what is legal and what is not is not very clear (see, for example, http://www.borland.com/about/press/2001/webgainsuit.html for a recent lawsuit by Borland against WebGain).

Cybersquatters have led to the further development of trademark law. In the early days to the Web, cybersquatters registered Web sites using the names of well-known companies and celebrities. Many made substantial amounts of money later selling the name back to the company or individual. However, their joy ride ended with cases such as Madonna's, who successfully sued to claim the Web site name without paying the cybersquatter.

Intellectual property law protects legal rights such as those related to copyrights, patents, and trademarks. Intellectual property law has been globalized by several international agreements. Countries that are members of the North American Free Trade Agreement (NAFTA) (Canada, the U.S., and Mexico) and the World Trade Organization (WTO) (148 countries) are required to have laws providing both civil and criminal procedures for the enforcement of copyright and trademarks. In this regard, the requirements of NAFTA Chapter 17 and the WTO Agreement on Trade-Related Intellectual Property Rights (TRIPS) are virtually the same.

TRIPS requires members to make civil judicial procedures available to right holders, including minimum standards for legal procedures, evidence, injunctions, damages, and trial costs (TRIPS Articles 42-49). Rights holders may thus seek court injunctions to stop the illegal activity and have the perpetrator ordered to pay the costs of the legal action. The owners of intellectual property may sue producers and vendors of pirated goods for damages. While this is important, in many cases it is not a practical option for companies to pursue. Civil litigation is a costly and lengthy process, and seeking payment

Table 5. Pirated software in use and the losses due to piracy in 2003 and 2004 (Source: Second Annual BSA and IDC Global Software Piracy Study, 2005)

	% software pirated	% software pirated	Loss due to piracy in millions of $US	Loss due to piracy in millions of $US
Country	2004	2003	2004	2003
Australia	32%	31%	409	341
China	90%	92%	3,565	3,823
Hong Kong	52%	52%	116	102
India	74%	73%	519	367
Indonesia	87%	88%	183	158
Japan	28%	29%	1,787	1,633
Malaysia	61%	63%	134	129
New Zealand	23%	23%	25	21
Pakistan	82%	83%	26	16
Philippines	71%	72%	69	55
Singapore	42%	43%	96	90
South Korea	46%	48%	506	462
Taiwan	43%	43%	161	139
Thailand	79%	80%	183	141
Vietnam	92%	92%	55	41
Austria	25%	27%	128	109
Belgium	29%	29%	309	240
Cyprus	53%	55%	9	8
Czech Republic	41%	40%	132	106
Denmark	27%	26%	226	165
Estonia	55%	54%	17	14
Finland	29%	31%	177	148
France	45%	45%	2,928	2,311
Germany	29%	30%	2,286	1,899
Greece	62%	63%	106	87
Hungary	44%	42%	126	96
Ireland	38%	41%	89	71
Italy	50%	49%	1,500	1,127
Latvia	58%	57%	19	16
Lithuania	58%	58%	21	17
Malta	47%	46%	3	2
Netherlands	30%	33%	628	577
Poland	59%	58%	379	301
Portugal	40%	41%	82	66
Slovakia	48%	50%	48	40
Slovenia	51%	52%	37	32

continued on next page

Table 5. continued

Spain	43%	44%	634	512
Sweden	26%	27%	304	241
United Kingdom	27%	29%	1,963	1,601
Bulgaria	71%	71%	33	26
Croatia	58%	59%	50	45
Norway	31%	32%	184	155
Romania	74%	73%	62	49
Russia	87%	87%	1,362	1,104
Switzerland	28%	31%	309	293
Ukraine	91%	91%	107	92
Argentina	75%	71%	108	69
Bolivia	80%	78%	9	11
Brazil	64%	61%	659	519
Chile	64%	63%	87	68
Colombia	55%	53%	81	61
Costa Rica	67%	68%	16	17
Dominican Republic	77%	76%	4	5
Ecuador	70%	68%	13	11
El Salvador	80%	79%	5	4
Guatemala	78%	77%	10	9
Honduras	75%	73%	3	3
Mexico	65%	63%	407	369
Nicaragua	80%	79%	1	1
Panama	70%	69%	4	4
Paraguay	83%	83%	11	9
Peru	73%	68%	39	31
Uruguay	71%	67%	12	10
Venezuela	79%	72%	71	55
Algeria	83%	84%	67	59
Bahrain	62%	64%	19	18
Egypt	65%	69%	50	56
Israel	33%	35%	66	69
Jordan	64%	65%	16	15
Kenya	83%	80%	16	12
Kuwait	68%	68%	48	41
Lebanon	75%	74%	26	22
Mauritus	60%	61%	4	4
Morocco	72%	73%	65	57
Nigeria	84%	84%	54	47
Oman	64%	65%	13	11

continued on next page

Table 5. continued

Qatar	62%	63%	16	13
Reunion	40%	39%	1	1
Saudi Arabia	52%	54%	125	120
South Africa	37%	36%	196	147
Tunisia	84%	82%	38	29
Turkey	66%	66%	182	127
UAE	34%	34%	34	29
Zimbabwe	90%	87%	9	6
Canada	36%	35%	889	736
Puerto Rico	46%	46%	15	11
United States	21%	22%	6,645	6,496

of any damages that might be awarded can be problematic. Nevertheless, the global expansion of intellectual property law remedies, together with the global nature of the Internet, is sure to increase intellectual property litigation around the globe.

TRIPS also requires members to provide criminal procedures and penalties in cases of intentional trademark counterfeiting or copyright piracy on a commercial scale. Penalties must include imprisonment or fines sufficient to provide a deterrent, consistent with the level of penalties applied for crimes of a corresponding gravity. Where appropriate, remedies must also include the seizure, forfeiture, and destruction of the infringing goods (TRIPS Article 61).

As tough as this may sound, such criminal laws do not have a great impact on the enforcement of intellectual property laws in many developing countries. While authorities may occasionally conduct well-publicized raids on highly visible commercial operations, corruption and the lack of adequate human and financial resources means the vast majority of infractions still go unpunished. These practical and legal limitations inherent in intellectual property protection mean that producers of easily copied intellectual property, such as software, are likely to continue to experience worldwide problems with piracy, as the following table shows (Table 5). The amount of money at stake, together with the globalization of intellectual property laws, means that owners of intellectual property are likely to devote more of their own resources to the enforcement of their property rights in the coming years.

Insurance

In August 2000, St Paul insurance company commissioned a survey of 1,500 risk managers in the United States and Europe, along with 150 insurance agents and brokers. Only 25% of all U.S. companies and 30% of European companies had set up formal structures (such as a risk management committee) to identify and monitor technology risks.

Online attack insurance costs between $10,000 and $20,000 per million-dollar coverage. Main coverage takes the following forms: protection against third-party liability claims from the disclosure of confidential information when a hacker strikes or denial of service when a computer virus attacks. Another common coverage is electronic publishing liability, which can offer protection from third-party lawsuits for defamation, libel, slander, and other claims stemming from information posted on the company Web site.

While many of the legal sources of liability for online activity are not new (such as intellectual property infringements, defamation, and invasion of privacy), the accessibility of the Internet has increased the rapidity and scale of these actions and, thus, the potential liability. As a result, some believe that e-commerce will emerge as the single biggest insurance risk of the 21st century, for three reasons. First, the number of suits involving Internet-related claims will be exponentially greater than in pre-Internet days. Second, the complexity of international, multi-jurisdictional and technical disputes will increase the legal costs associated with these claims. Third, the activities giving rise to Internet-based claims will present new arguments for both insureds and insurers about whether they the liability is covered by the policy (Jerry & Mekel, 2002). For example, traditional first party insurance for physical events that damage tangible property may not help an Internet business whose most valuable property exists in cyberspace with no physical form (Beh, 2002). Even if a company has an insurance policy that covers its activities on the World Wide Web, there is a significant risk that it won't be covered outside the United States or Canada (Crane, 2001).

CONCLUSION

Like the more traditional marketplace, doing business on the Internet carries with it many opportunities along with many risks. This chapter has focused on a series of risks of legal liability arising from e-mail and Internet activities that are a common part of many e-businesses. Some of the laws governing these electronic activities are new and especially designed for the electronic age, while others are more traditional laws whose application to electronic activities is the novelty.

E-business not only exposes companies to new types of liability risk, but also increases the potential number of claims and the complexity of dealing with those claims. The international nature of the Internet, together with a lack of uniformity of laws governing the same activities in different countries, means that companies need to proceed with caution. That means managing risks in an intelligent fashion and seeking adequate insurance coverage. The first step is to familiarize themselves with electronic risks and then to set up management systems to minimize potential problems and liabilities.

ACKNOWLEDGMENT

We thank the Instituto Tecnológico Autónomo de México and the Asociación Mexicana de Cultura AC for their generous support of our research.

REFERENCES

Beh, H. G. (2002). Physical losses in cyberspace. *Connecticut Insurance Law Journal, 9*(2), 1-88.

Crane, M. (2001). International liability in cyberspace. *Duke Law and Technological Review, 23*(1), 455-465.

Furnari, N. R. (1999). Are traditional agency principles effective for Internet transactions, given the lack of personal interaction? *Albany Law Review, 63*(3), 544-567.

Gasparini, L. U. (2001). The Internet and personal jurisdiction: Traditional jurisprudence for the twenty-first century under the New York CPLR. *Albany Law Journal of Science & Technology, 12*(1), 191-244.

General, & Cologne Re. (1999). *Global casualty facultative loss & litigation report: A selection of Internet losses and litigation, 3*, 12-17.

Goldstone, D. & Shave, B. (1999). International dimensions of crimes in cyberspace. *Fordham International Law Journal, 22*(6), 1924-1945.

Iqbal, M. (2004). Defining cyberterrorism. *Marshall Journal of Computer & Information Law, 22*(1) 397-432.

Jerry, R. H. II, & Mekel, M. L. (2002). Cybercoverage for cyber-risks: An Overview of insurers' responses to the perils of e-commerce. *Connecticut Insurance Law Journal, 9*(3), 11-44.

King, R. W. (2003). Online defamation: Bringing the Communications Decency Act of 1996 in line with sound public policy. *Duke Law and Technology Review, 24*(3), 34-67.

Maier, M. J. (2001). Backdoor liability from Internet telecommuters. *Computer Law Review & Technology Journal, 6*(1), 27-41.

Marron, M. (2002). Discoverability of deleted e-mail: Time for a closer examination. *Seattle University Law Review, 25*(4), 895-922.

Nowak, J. S. (1999). Employer liability for employee online criminal acts. *Federal Communications Law Journal, 51*(3) 467-488.

O'Brien, C. N. (2002). The impact of employer e-mail policies on employee rights to engage in concerted. *Dickinson Law Review, 103*(5), 201-277.

Pederson, M., & Meyers, J. H. (2005). Something about technology: Electronic discovery considerations and methodology. *Maine Bar Journal, 12*(2), 23-56.

Rest, C. L. (1998). Electronic mail and confidential client/attorney communications: Risk management. *Case Western Reserve Law Journal, 48*(2), 309-378.

Richmond, D. R. (2002). A practical look at e-commerce and liability insurance. *Connecticut Insurance Law Journal, 8*(1), 87-104.

Rustad, M. L., & Paulsson, S. R. (2005). Monitoring employee e-mail and Internet usage: Avoiding the omniscient electronic sweatshop: Insights from Europe. *University of Pennsylvania Journal of Labor and Employment, 7*(4), 829-922.

Sloan, B. (2004, July). Avoiding litigation pitfalls: Practical tips for internal e-mail. *Risk Management Magazine*, 38-42.

APPENDIX: TERMINOLOGIES

Firewall: A firewall is a barrier that enforces a boundary between two or more computer networks. It is similar to the function of firewalls in building construction. A firewall controls traffic between different zones of trust. Two extreme zones of trust include the Internet (a zone with no trust) and an internal network (a zone with high trust). Setting up firewalls requires understanding of network protocols and of computer security. Small mistakes can render a firewall worthless as a security tool.

Hackers: In computer security, a hacker is a person able to exploit a system or gain unauthorized access through skill and tactics. This usually refers to a black-hat hacker. Two types of distinguished hackers exist. A Guru is one with a very broad degree of expertise, a Wizard is an expert in a very narrow field.

Malware: Malware is a software program that runs automatically against the interests of the person running it. Malware is normally classified based on how it is executed, how it spreads, and what it does.

Phishing: Phishing (also known as carding and spoofing) is an attempt to fraudulently acquire sensitive information, such as passwords and credit card details, by masquerading as a trustworthy person or business in an apparently official electronic communication, such as an e-mail. The term phishing alludes to to "fishing" for users' financial information and passwords.

Spam: Spam refers to unsolicited messages in bulk. It can refer to any commercially oriented, unsolicited bulk mailing perceived as being excessive and undesired. Most come in e-mail as a form of commercial advertising.

Spoofing: See *phishing.*

Spyware: Spyware is a malicious software intended to intercept or take control of a computer's operation without the user's knowledge or consent. It typically subverts the computer's operation for the benefit of a third party.

Virus: A virus is a self-replicating program that spreads by inserting copies of itself into other executable code or documents. A computer virus behaves in a way similar to a biological virus. The insertion of the virus into a program is called an infection, and the infected file (or executable code that is not part of a file) is called a host. A virus is a malware.

Worm: A computer worm is a self-replicating computer program. A virus needs to attach itself to, and becomes part of, another executable program. A worm is self-contained. It does not need to be part of another program to propagate itself.

This work was previously published in E-Business Process Management: Technologies and Solutions, edited by J. Sounder-pandian and T. Sinha, pp. 292-311, copyright 2007 by IGI Publishing, formerly known as Idea Group Publishing (an imprint of IGI Global).

Chapter XXIV
Organizational Culture for Knowledge Management Systems:
A Study of Corporate Users

Andrew P. Ciganek
Jacksonville State University, USA

En Mao
Nicholls State University, USA

Mark Srite
University of Wisconsin-Milwaukee, USA

ABSTRACT

Knowledge is increasingly being viewed as a critical component for organizations. It is largely people-based and the characteristics of groups of individuals, in the form of organizational cultures, may play a key role in the factors that lead to either the acceptance or rejection of knowledge management systems (KMS). The primary objective of this research is to explore how dimensions of organizational culture influence factors that lead to the acceptance of KMS. While researchers have agreed that culture plays an important role in KMS, the literature has only recently begun to examine organizational culture within this context. We examined the effects of three dimensions of organizational culture through a research model that was tested and analyzed utilizing a field survey of corporate knowledge management users. Our results indicated that both process-oriented and open communication system organizational cultures significantly influenced the factors that led to the acceptance of KMS.

INTRODUCTION

Organizational culture can either facilitate or be a major barrier to knowledge management system (KMS) acceptance (De Long & Fahey, 2000;

Grover & Davenport, 2001; Ruppel & Harrington, 2001). On February 1, 2003, the space shuttle Columbia was lost during its return to Earth. The Columbia Accident Investigation Board (CAIB) concluded that NASA's organizational culture as well as the piece of Columbia's foam insulation that fell off during launch shared equal blame for the tragedy (CAIB, 2003). According to the CAIB, the prevailing culture at NASA was of a mindset that accidents were inevitable, which led to the unnecessary acceptance of known and preventable risks. Although a KMS to assist with hazard identification and risk assessment was available at NASA (the Lessons Learned Information System), personnel only used that system on an *ad hoc* basis which limited its usefulness (CAIB, 2003). NASA's organizational culture consequently interfered with open communication, impeded the sharing of lessons learned, caused duplication and unnecessary expenditure of resources, and prompted resistance to external advice (CAIB, 2003).

The Columbia incident is an illustration of knowledge management system use failure. The acceptance of KMS, however, is a pressing issue in organizations (Kwan & Balasubramanian, 2003; Money & Turner, 2005). As knowledge is increasingly viewed as a critical activity for decision making (Markus, Majchrzak, & Gasser, 2002; Miranda & Saunders, 2003), organizations are becoming more receptive to using technologies to facilitate knowledge management (Schultze & Leidner, 2002). KMS are often employed to enhance organizational performance (De Long & Fahey, 2000) and are a reason why the KMS market has become one of the fastest growing areas in software development. While it is widely recognized that information technologies have the potential to facilitate knowledge management, the management of knowledge-based systems is an intricate process that involves a complex interplay of technical and social factors.

Recent studies have begun to investigate a variety of social factors and phenomena related to knowledge creation, sharing, and transfer. For example, Wasko and Faraj (2005) studied how individual motivations and social capital influence knowledge sharing in KMS. Ko, Kirsch, and King (2005) found that individual communication capabilities, motivations, and interpersonal relationships affected the transfer of complex enterprise software knowledge. Bock, Zmud, Kim, and Lee (2005) found that subjective norms and organizational climate had a significant impact on people's intention to share knowledge. Kankanhalli, Tan, and Wei (2005) similarly discovered that several social factors, including prosharing norms, influenced knowledge contribution. These studies provided strong empirical evidence of the social influences in knowledge management. Some of the factors that have been examined are conceptually similar to organizational culture dimensions that have been identified in the management literature. A more systematic study of organizational culture on KMS acceptance would provide theoretical congruence to this recent literature.

The primary objective of this research is to explore how dimensions of organizational culture influence the factors that lead to the acceptance of KMS (e.g., perceived usefulness, perceived ease-of-use, perceived behavioral control, subjective norms). In our investigation, organizational culture is postulated as a distal determinant for an employee's intention to use a KMS. In the next section, we present a literature review to support our hypotheses, followed by a discussion of our research methodology. We then empirically test our hypotheses with a field survey of corporate KMS users, discuss the results, and finish with some concluding remarks.

LITERATURE REVIEW

Knowledge Management Systems

Knowledge is information that exists in the mind of individuals (Alavi & Leidner, 2001; Berman-

Brown & Woodland, 1999; Grover & Davenport, 2001; Ruppel & Harrington, 2001). Given the nature of knowledge, which is created and applied in the minds of human beings, it is extremely difficult to manage and control (Alvesson & Karreman, 2001; Grover & Davenport, 2001). Indeed, an organization's efforts to facilitate knowledge sharing can be a "central competitive dimension" for a firm (Kogut & Zander, 1992, p. 384). Consequently, KMS are an organization's efforts to facilitate knowledge sharing through the use of information technology (IT) in order to obtain organizational benefits.

There are a variety of KMS that exist, such as knowledge repositories, corporate directories, and knowledge networks (Alavi & Leidner, 2001; Grover & Davenport, 2001). Knowledge repositories, the type of IT examined in this study, are the most common KMS in Western organizations (Grover & Davenport, 2001). These systems are typically used to capture knowledge from employees for subsequent and extensive use by others within the organization to assist in decision-making. Examples of knowledge that are contained in such systems may range from best practices and lessons learned to organizational strategies and recruitment efforts.

There have been a number of KMS reviews and meta-analyses done in the information systems (IS) domain. Alavi & Leidner (2001) provided a review of the knowledge management literature in different academic disciplines that identified some key areas of research, which included the concept of knowledge in organizations, knowledge management processes (i.e., knowledge creation, storage/retrieval, and transfer), and KMS. They indicated that while the design of a KMS is important, the extent of use by its intended users would also have a significant impact on KMS acceptance. Schultze & Leidner (2002) also examined knowledge management research in the IS area. They identified and classified knowledge management research into four theoretical streams, which are normative, interpretive, critical, and dialogic dis-

courses. Subsequent case-based research (Alavi, Kayworth, & Leidner, 2005-2006; Leidner, Alavi, & Kayworth, 2006) has found that differences in organizational cultural values leads to different uses of KMS. These research efforts demonstrated the importance and saliency of KMS in the IS context.

Organizational Culture

NASA's organizational culture had as much to do with this accident as foam did. Columbia Accident Investigation Report (CAIB, 2003)

As suggested in the quotation above, organizational culture is important and inextricably linked to KMS within organizations (Alavi & Leidner, 2001; Alvesson & Karreman, 2001; Cronin, 2001; De Long & Fahey, 2000; Grover & Davenport, 2001; McDermott, 1999; Tanriverdi, 2005). Organizational culture has been extensively studied in management research, and therefore, it is surprising that the relationship between KMS and an organization's culture has not been more thoroughly explored in the IS literature. Culture has historically been a factor that has received insufficient attention in the IS acceptance literature (Cooper, 1994; Robey, Wishart, & Rodriguez-Diaz, 1995a; Ruppel & Harrington, 2001), but is increasingly being viewed as a key ingredient for an organization's ability to embrace KMS (Cronin, 2001).

Organizational culture is widely believed to be a major barrier to KMS acceptance (De Long & Fahey, 2000; Grover & Davenport, 2001; Ruppel & Harrington, 2001). Without a match between an organization's culture and the cultural assumptions embedded within an IT innovation, costly implementation failures are likely to happen (Ruppel & Harrington, 2001). For example, in organizational cultures that are not suited to share and utilize knowledge (e.g., an organization where miscommunication is common and mistrust is prevalent), acceptance of a KMS can be problematic (Ruppel & Harrington, 2001). Without acknowledging cultural mismatches or modifying the organizational culture to better fit the IT, the impact on the organization could be disastrous, as evidenced in the Colombia tragedy.

Hofstede (1991) views culture as being collective, but often intangible and is what distinguishes one group, organization, or nation from another. There are two main elements of culture: the internal values of culture (invisible) and external elements of culture (visible), which are known as practices (Hofstede, 1991). Practices are particularly important to investigate because they are the most direct means for changing behaviors needed to support knowledge creation, sharing, and use (De Long & Fahey, 2000). Hofstede, Neuijen, Ohayv, and Sanders (1990) measured the perceived practices in employees' work situations in 20 organizational units and discovered six dimensions underlying organizational culture. Contrary to his dimensions of national culture (Hofstede, 1991), these organizational dimensions deal with key sociological issues. In favor of depicting a more manageable research model, we examine three dimensions of organizational culture, process-oriented vs. results-oriented, employee-oriented vs. job-oriented, and open communication systems vs. closed communication systems.

Technology Acceptance

Previous findings from the technology acceptance literature, which has been widely popular in the IS field for the past few years, suggest that for an advantage to be attained, the technology in question must be accepted and used (Venkatesh, Morris, Davis, & Davis, 2003). Organizations typically employ KMS to leverage their collective knowledge for competitive advantage (Alavi & Leidner, 2001). There has been relatively little research, however, that explicitly examines the influence that dimensions of organizational culture have on technology acceptance.

In the technology acceptance literature, a variety of psychological constructs have been examined with the goal of understanding how and why individuals adopt new information technologies. This has generated several competing models of technology acceptance, each with different sets of determinants for acceptance (Venkatesh et al., 2003). The following is a concise review of attributes that have been consistently shown to account for a significant amount of variance in the prediction of intentions and behaviors (Rogers, 2003; Tornatzky & Klein, 1982; Venkatesh et al., 2003).

Attributes of the Acceptance and Use of Technology

Based upon conceptual and empirical similarities across eight prominent models in the user acceptance literature, Venkatesh et al. (2003) developed a unified theory of individual acceptance of technology (the unified theory of acceptance and use of technology or UTAUT). The UTAUT theorizes four constructs having a significant role as direct determinants of acceptance and usage behavior: performance expectancy, effort expectancy, social influence, and facilitating conditions. Although we did not test the full UTAUT because the model was not published at the time of our data collection, each of the constructs that we did examine was conceptually similar. The four constructs that we utilized and their relationships to the constructs of the UTAUT model are discussed next.

The first construct examined in our model is perceived usefulness. Originally proposed in Davis' (1989) technology acceptance model (TAM), this is contained within the UTAUT construct of performance expectancy and is defined as "the degree to which an individual believes that using the system will help him or her to attain gains in job performance" (Venkatesh et al., 2003, p. 447). The second construct examined in our model is perceived ease of use. This construct, originally in Davis' (1989) TAM, is incorporated into UTAUT as part of effort expectancy which is defined as "the degree of ease associated with the use of the system" (Venkatesh et al., 2003, p. 450). Perceived ease of use has a significant direct effect on perceived usefulness (Davis, 1989).

The third construct examined, perceived behavioral control, indicates that a person's motivation is influenced by how difficult the behaviors are perceived to be, as well as the perception of how successfully the individual can, or cannot, perform the activity. Perceived behavioral control, originally in the theory of planned behavior (TPB) (Ajzen, 1985; Ajzen & Madden, 1986), is part of UTAUT's facilitating conditions construct which is defined as "the degree to which an individual believes that an organizational and technical infrastructure exists to support the use of the system" (Venkatesh et al., 2003, p. 453). Subjective norms, the fourth construct examined in this model, deals with the influence of important others, such as coworkers, supervisors, and top management. Subjective norms, originally in Fishbein & Ajzen's (1975) theory of reasoned action (TRA), are incorporated into UTAUT's construct of social influence, which is defined as "the degree to which an individual perceives that important others believe he or she should use the system" (Venkatesh et al., 2003, p. 451).

RESEARCH HYPOTHESES

Organizational Culture's Impact on Perceived Usefulness

An organization's attitude toward change, often elicited and reflected by the introduction of technology innovations, impacts the adoption of these technologies (Damanpour, 1991). Some organizations are relatively *process-oriented* and may have conservative attitudes toward innova-

tion and its associated risk, exerting minimal effort while preferring the use of existing or well-known methods (Hofstede et al., 1990). Such organizations innovate only when they are seriously challenged by their competition or by shifting consumer preferences (Miller & Friesen, 1982). In contrast, *results-oriented* organizations are risk-oriented and foster an environment that encourages and actively supports the use of innovative techniques for the survival and growth of the organization (Hofstede et al., 1990). As an organization's policies and practices are perceived by employees to encourage, cultivate, and reward their use of a technology (e.g., KMS) the stronger that culture will be for the implementation of that technology (Klein & Sorra, 1996). Organizations that promote innovativeness and a willingness to try new things among their employees have been found to have better success with a KMS implementation (Ruppel & Harrington, 2001). Such organizations and individuals usually try to obtain a competitive advantage by routinely making dramatic innovative changes and taking the inherent risks associated with those innovations. Consequently, employees in a results-oriented organization are likely to believe that using KMS would enhance their job performance. On the other hand, knowledge sharing is risky from an individual employees' perspective because their value depends largely on the knowledge they possess (Stenmark, 2000). A work environment that is more process-oriented, consequently, would view KMS as a threat and to be less useful for making decisions. This leads to the following hypothesis:

H1: *Employees who perceive their work environment to be more **results-oriented** will have higher levels of perceived usefulness than employees who perceive their work environment to be more **process-oriented**.*

Organizational Culture's Impact on Perceived Ease of Use

At one end of a continuum, job roles in an organizational environment are routine and similar from one day to the next (*process-oriented*) (Hofstede et al., 1990). Employees in this environment are resistant to change, new technology, and risk and will only exert minimal effort. At the opposite end of this continuum, job roles bring forth new challenges daily (*results-oriented*) (Hofstede et al., 1990). Employees in this results-oriented environment embrace risk, are comfortable in unknown situations, and are likely to more quickly exploit any opportunity that a technology may offer. These individuals are likely to have more experience using innovative or relatively complex technologies, and as a result, have a relatively high belief that using other complex technologies would not be difficult. In fact, complexity is the degree to which an innovation is perceived as being difficult to use and has the opposite meaning of ease of use (Davis, Bagozzi, & Warshaw, 1989; Moore & Benbasat, 1991; Thompson, Higgins, & Howell, 1991). Therefore, employees who work in an environment that is characterized as a results-oriented organization where using new or complex technologies in their daily tasks is common are more likely to believe that KMS are easy to use. Hence:

H2: *Employees who perceive their work environment to be more* **results-oriented** *will have higher levels of perceived ease of use than employees who perceive their work environment to be more* **process-oriented**.

Organizational Culture's Impact on Perceived Behavioral Control

When employees are asked to put what they know into a KMS, they tend to feel as if they have lost ownership of the knowledge that they alone had previously controlled (De Long & Fahey, 2000).

Individuals tend to resist such systems because when giving up control of their knowledge they may perceive their worth as an employee to be marginal, which is only propagated by the understandable fear that their job position has become interchangeable. In such circumstances an organization's culture is critical for the acceptance of KMS. As stated earlier, *results-oriented* organizations are risk-oriented, fostering an environment of daily challenges where employees feel comfortable in unknown situations (Hofstede et al., 1990). Although employees in results-oriented organizations may encounter more risky events, their capacity to tolerate risks is much stronger. Employees in this type of risk inclined environment would likely have strong beliefs in their ability to control outcomes (Delfabbro & Winefield, 2000) and hence, will be less worried about the potential negative issues associated with sharing knowledge. The more control an employee thinks they possess, the greater should be that person's perceived control over their behavior (Ajzen & Madden, 1986). Therefore, employees that work in an environment that is characterized as a results-oriented organization would believe that they can control the technology they use, which would make them more likely to use KMS. Hence:

H3: *Employees who perceive their work environment to be more* **results-oriented** *will have higher levels of perceived behavioral control than employees who perceive their work environment to be more* **process-oriented**.

Environments that typically do not favor KMS emphasize unilateral control, have high stakes for winning and losing, and attempt to minimize negative emotions (Ruppel & Harrington, 2001). Competition thrives in such environments and mistrust in others is high as sharing information or helping fellow employees is frowned upon because it creates a disadvantage for the employee being generous. A *job-oriented* environment exemplifies this scenario as it is an atmosphere where employees feel pressured to complete work (Hofstede et al., 1990).

On the other hand, an *employee-oriented* environment is one where individual personal problems are addressed and the organization has a genuine concern for the employee's welfare (Hofstede et al., 1990). This is critical particularly in the acceptance of KMS where employees must be able divulge, support, and trust the knowledge provided by other employees via the technology. The human relations management and job enrichment literatures (Hackman & Oldham, 1980) suggest that intrinsic rewards (e.g., employee of the month recognition) are at times more important than extrinsic rewards (e.g., salary raises, promotion). Resource-based theory also acknowledges the vital role that human assets/resources play in the contemporary hypercompetitive external environments where progressive organizations strive to keep their employees satisfied and thus retain top talent. Indeed, Ruppel & Harrington (2001) found that early adoption of KMS was most likely to occur in organizations where the culture was characterized as having a high concern for its employees and a setting of mutual confidence and trust. Consequently, employees who work in an environment that is characterized as an employee-oriented organization would be more likely to believe that they have access to greater opportunities and resources to perform a behavior than in a pressure-filled, job-oriented environment. Hence:

H4: *Employees who perceive their work environment to be more **employee-oriented** will have higher levels of perceived behavioral control than employees who perceive their work environment to be more **job-oriented**.*

Organizational Culture's Impact on Subjective Norms

An organizational culture that discourages open communication engenders a context that under-

mines knowledge sharing (De Long & Fahey, 2000). This is similar to a *closed communication system,* an environment that is secretive and reserved and also one in which it takes a relatively long time for employees to "fit in" (Hofstede et al., 1990). For KMS to be widely accepted within an organization, it should have a culture that supports knowledge sharing from a wide spectrum of coworkers, supervisors, and managers. Without this support, employees may not be willing to share and disseminate their knowledge and experiences, thus making the KMS essentially useless. Indeed, instilling a culture of sharing and maintaining information is critical for KMS acceptance.

An *open communication system*, alternatively, is an environment that is characterized as being open to newcomers and outsiders where it takes a relatively short time for employees to feel comfortable in the organization (Hofstede et al., 1990). Employees in this type of environment are likely to more willingly share their experiences and to support one another when attempting to make decisions on complex and unknown topic areas (e.g., relevance and mastery of new technologies). It is reasonable to expect that users of KMS would be more willing and prepared to assume any challenges posed by the new technology environment in view of the support that they can expect from their colleagues. Employees who work in an environment characterized by an open communication system, therefore, are more likely to be influenced by the opinions of important others and be more likely to use KMS. Hence:

H5: *Employees who perceive their work environment to be more **open** will have higher levels of subjective norms than employees who perceive their work environment to be more **closed**.*

Consistent with the TAM, the TRA, the TPB, and the UTAUT, perceived usefulness, perceived ease of use, perceived behavioral control, and subjective norms are expected to influence behavioral

Figure 1. Theoretical model

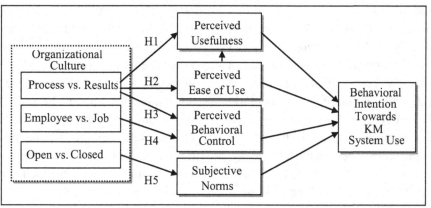

intentions. Following the technology acceptance model, perceived ease of use is expected to influence perceived usefulness. These relationships as well as our research hypotheses are depicted in the proposed theoretical model (Figure 1).

METHODOLOGY

This research utilized a questionnaire borrowing scales from prior literature. We adopted measures of organizational culture from Hofstede et al. (1990), perceived usefulness, perceived ease of use, and behavioral intention to use from Davis (1989), and perceived behavioral control from Ajzen & Madden (1986). The subjective norms construct contains two dimensions: normative beliefs (similar to the construct developed by Fishbein & Ajzen (1975) and motivation to comply from Bandura (1977). The subjective norms construct was formed by multiplying pairs of items (normative beliefs * motivation to comply). The order of the statements in the questionnaire was scrambled randomly to control for order effects. The dependent variable, behavioral intention was selected as it has been validated in prior literature as a reliable proxy for actual use in behavioral research (Magnus & Niclas, 2003).

The questionnaire employed a 7-point Likert-style scale, anchored from 1 (strongly disagree) to 7 (strongly agree).

Data Collection

The instrument was pilot tested using 24 MBA students who were familiar with KMS. The reliability and validity of all eight research constructs were found to be acceptable. A field survey was then administered via two procedures within a 1 week period. We first surveyed KMS users from a leading user group in a major Midwestern U.S. city. The KMS utilized by the users were repository-based and included applications for sharing corporate knowledge, best practices, and lessons learned, among others. We distributed paper-based surveys after briefly explaining our research agenda. There were 64 attendees that were solicited to participate with 41 completing the paper-based survey, yielding a response rate of 64%.

The initial participants in the study were subsequently asked to recruit additional KMS users within their firms via an online Web-based survey, which had the same questions in identical sequence as the paper-based version. The participants represented seven companies from a variety of industries, including manufacturing, finance, consulting, and education. The Web-based survey provided an additional 144 completed surveys from 7 companies, yielding an approximate response rate of 29% (144/500). This resulted in a total sample size of 185 (41 paper and 144 Web). With the exception of a single item, out of 31 total items, there were no significant differences between the paper-based and Web-based surveys after performing a series of t-tests at both the construct and item levels. The single item was not removed from the analysis because dropping it lowered the reliability of its construct. The mean age of the respondents was 38, and 60% of the participants were female and 40% were male. On average, the respondents had 15 years of work experience, 13 years of computing experience, and 2 years of KMS experience.

Consistent with the technology acceptance studies, gender (Venkatesh & Morris, 2000), age (Gist, Rosen, & Schwoerer, 1988; Igbaria, Parasuraman, & Baroudi, 1996), and experience (Venkatesh et al., 2003) were tested as control variables to see if they had a moderating effect on behavioral intention to use. Following Venkatesh et al. (2003), a hierarchical regression analysis was used to test the direct and moderating effects because sample size considerations prevented us from running the interaction terms in LISREL (our primary analysis tool). The moderating effects were modeled as interaction terms between the moderators and perceived usefulness (PU), perceived ease of use (PEOU), perceived behavioral control (PBC), and subjective norms (SN). With direct effects, PU, SN, and PBC were significant. With both direct and interaction effects, PU, PU x gender, PU x age, PU x gender x age, and PBC x experience were significant.

Psychometric Measures

The data were analyzed using the structural equation modeling (SEM) technique, which is suitable because our research model contains latent vari-ables. The model was tested using the two-step approach where the measurement model fit was first assessed followed by the structural model testing in which the path coefficients were estimated (Bollen, 1989). The reliability and validity of the data were tested before model assessment and the results demonstrated acceptable psychometric properties. The reliability coefficients of all eight constructs, with two exceptions, were above .70, which is an acceptable value as stated by Nunnally (1967). The employee-oriented vs. job-oriented and open communication system vs. closed communication system constructs were at .69. They were retained because they were close to the cutoff level1.

Construct validity was assessed by comparing the correlation coefficients within and between constructs. The average within construct correlation was .40, which is higher than the between constructs correlation of .19. The within construct correlations were higher than between constructs correlations, indicating construct validity. In addition, we examined convergent and divergent validity and tested the data for normality. Even though the maximum likelihood estimator performs relatively well under various conditions (Hoyle & Panter, 1995), it assumes the normality of the data. The mean skewness and kurtosis values were -.47 and .33 respectively, indicating that the variables approximate a normal distribution and were acceptable for LISREL analysis (Bollen, 1989; Byrne, 1998; West, Finch, & Curran, 1995).

Chi-square goodness-of-fit statistic, comparative fit index, and the root mean square error of approximation were also assessed. Chi-square (χ^2) goodness-of-fit statistic assesses the degree of departure of the sample covariance matrix from the fitted covariance matrix (Hu & Bentler, 1999) . A nonsignificant and small chi-square is desirable. Because the chi-square statistic is a direct product of sample size, when the sample size is large and models contain a large number of indicators, the statistic can often be significant

(Byrne, 1998). The comparative fit index (CFI) and root mean square error of approximation (RMSEA), however, are not sensitive to sample size. The comparative fit index is an incremental fit index that measures the improvement in fit by comparing a target model with a restricted, nested base model (Hu & Bentler, 1999). In addition, it is suggested as the best approximation of the population value for a single model (Medsker, Williams, & Holahan, 1994). The general accepted value is above .90. The root mean square error of approximation, a type of absolute fit index, assesses how well sample data are reproduced from an *a priori* model (Hu & Bentler, 1999). The general accepted cutoff is .10.

Using LISREL 8.54, we first tested the measurement model. Its fit statistics were χ^2 (406 df, N = 185) = 685.63, p < .001, CFI = .95, and RMSEA = .061. Overall, the statistics demonstrated good fit and the measures were acceptable for structural model assessment. Good model statistics are indicative of unidimensionality and convergent validity (Gefen, Karahanna, & Straub, 2003).

Divergent validity was assessed by comparing the original measurement model with an alterative model that includes all items as one construct (Segars, 1997). The χ^2 was significantly smaller in the original measurement model (χ^2 Alternative = 3234.07, χ^2 difference = 2548.44 with *df* change = 28, p = .00) establishing discriminant validity (Segars, 1997).

We assessed 10 paths in the structural model testing. The model fit statistics were χ^2 (421 df, N = 185) = 771.33, p < .001, CFI = .93, and RMSEA = .067. Overall, the statistics demonstrated a good fit of the model to the data. Figure 2 shows the estimated standardized path coefficients and their t-values in the structural model and the variance explained for each of the constructs. The asterisks on the path indicate the significance level and the variance explained are presented below the asterisks in parentheses. All links except those between an employee-oriented vs. job-oriented organizational culture and perceived behavioral control and between perceived ease of use and behavioral intention were significant. The model

Figure 2. Structural path coefficients

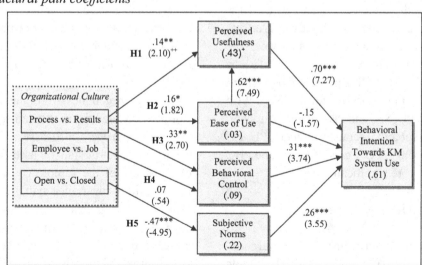

*P < .10, **p < .05, ***p < .001

had adequate predictive power for several constructs, including perceived usefulness (R^2_{PU} = .43), subjective norms (R^2_{SN} = .22), and behavioral intention (R^2_{BI} = .61). However, the predictive power was somewhat less for perceived ease of use (R^2_{PEOU} = .03) and perceived behavioral control (R^2_{PBC} = .09). In regard to the variance extracted in behavioral intention, our model exhibited better predictive power (.61) than that shown in the hierarchical regression with direct effects (.48), as well as direct effects and interaction effects (e.g., age, gender, experience) combined (.58).

The theoretical model was modified to add direct paths of the cultural dimensions influencing behavioral intention. None of the direct paths from the cultural dimensions to behavioral intention were significant. The change between the theoretical model and the modified model in χ^2 was 5.49 with 3 degrees of freedom (p = .1392). This suggested that the effects of the cultural dimensions on behavioral intention were mediated and, consequently, the theoretical model was utilized.

DISCUSSION

There was support for four out of the five research hypotheses. These results suggest that the organizational culture dimensions play a key role in the factors that lead to the acceptance of KMS. Our research also examined several prominent technology acceptance relationships and had similar findings to other research that has investigated the applicability of such relationships with the user acceptance of a KMS (Money & Turner, 2005). The relationships between perceived usefulness and behavioral intention to use a KMS, subjective norms, and behavioral intention to use a KMS, perceived behavioral control, and behavioral intention to use a KMS, and perceived ease of use and perceived usefulness were all significant. The relationship between perceived ease of use and behavioral intention to use a KMS, however, was

not significant although there was still a significant path through the model incorporating perceived usefulness. These findings are consistent with other studies of extended technology acceptance models (e.g., Adams, Nelson, & Todd, 1992; Hu, Chau, Sheng, & Tam, 1999).

In general, our model explained a reasonable amount of variation of the key variables. The variation in process-oriented vs. results-oriented organizational cultures (as well as the variation in perceptions of ease of use) explained 43% of the variation in perceptions of usefulness. Furthermore, the variability in process-oriented vs. results-oriented cultures explained 3% of the variance of perceived ease of use. Similarly, open communication systems vs. closed communication systems organizational cultures explained 22% of the variance in subjective norms and 9% of the variance in perceived behavioral control. The model accounted for 61% of the variability in behavioral intention to use. Most of the R^2 values are acceptable for technology acceptance research. The large amount of variance in behavioral intention to use is an indication that organizational culture, subjective norms, perceived behavior control, and technology acceptance together are strong factors to study with respect to KMS acceptance.

IMPLICATIONS AND CONCLUSION

In conclusion, our research found that organizational culture does significantly influence the factors that lead to the acceptance of KMS. Our research model was developed using commonly accepted measures from the technology acceptance and organizational culture literatures, tested by surveying corporate KMS users, and analyzed utilizing structural equation modeling. Our results indicated that both process-oriented and open communication organizational cultures significantly influenced factors that lead to the acceptance of KMS.

This research has relevance for both practitioners and researchers. In this article, we examine the influence that three dimensions of organizational culture have on KMS acceptance. It is necessary to examine organizational culture when investigating KMS because such systems are different from traditional information systems. Knowledge, which is information that exists in the minds of individuals, is inextricably linked to knowledge management systems. The emphasis on this human component may not be as prominent in other information systems, and suggests that we incorporate constructs, such as organizational culture, to match the nature of this technology.

This research builds upon the growing IS literature that examines organizational culture, which had historically received insufficient attention (Cooper, 1994; Robey, Wishart, & Rodriguez-Diaz, 1995b; Ruppel & Harrington, 2001). In this study, we have demonstrated that organizational cultural elements are important and should be considered in studies of technology acceptance. For researchers in the culture field, our study extends the importance of examining organizational culture with respect to information systems.

This research also offers several implications for practitioners. We identify different dimensions of organizational culture that lead to greater KMS acceptance. These organizational culture practices are particularly valuable because they are the most direct tools for changing behaviors needed to support knowledge creation, sharing, and use (De Long & Fahey, 2000). Although organizational culture is likely to be inherent in IS practitioner's day-to-day interactions with employees and IT, knowledge of more formally defined dimensions as investigated in this study could lead to better understanding and management of organizational cultural issues, such as office politics. In addition, it has been found that organizations that share common goals, principles, values, and language help facilitate IT relatedness, which can enhance knowledge management capability and ultimately,

firm performance (Tanriverdi, 2005). The findings in our research reveal specific dimensions of organizational culture that can influence the knowledge management capability of an organization. Consequently, managers should strive to foster a more results-oriented and open communication system environment in the workplace.

To develop a more results-oriented culture, managers need to encourage behaviors that are less risk averse, such as experimentation and exploration. Instead of a static technology with a limited adaptability, a KMS that has been experimented with by its users will generate new and novel uses of the system. Technologies are often not accepted due to a perceived misfit between the characteristics of the technology and the culture of the organization. Allowing employees the opportunity to adapt to the technology as an outcome of a results-oriented culture can generate a better fit. Consequently, managers should be required to focus more on the goals of job tasks instead of the processes of achieving the outcomes. The schemes for incentives and promotions of KMS users should be compatible with such strategies.

Allowing users time to experiment and explore the features of a new KMS could lead to increased perceptions of usefulness and ease of use, which were also found to influence KMS acceptance. As users experiment and find novel features of the system, they will find it to be more useful. Additionally, the increased time spent on the system would allow for greater perceptions of ease of use. Support for experimentation by management implies a tolerance for mistakes. With the understanding that a certain number of experiments will not have desirable outcomes, users would nevertheless still perceive a greater degree of control over the operation of the system.

Open communication plays a significant role in the acceptance of KMS. To develop a more open communication system culture, a number of strategies can be implemented. Users need to freely interact with their important others (such as coworkers, supervisors, and top management) as well as being included in the design, development, administration, and support of the system. Companies should encourage open communication through the use of forums and newsletters and can even design such features into a knowledge management system. Management can also reward users for openness, such as for voicing opinions regarding the system, and making suggestions for system improvements. These policies will cultivate the tendency to increase subjective norms among users and hence, increase KMS acceptance.

A limitation of our research is that it investigated only a few organizational culture dimensions. We believe that the dimensions most appropriate for KMS were captured in our study and that the germane features of other competing dimensions may be largely encapsulated in the dimensions that we investigated (Chatman & Jehn, 1994; Hofstede et al., 1990). Nonetheless, future research may wish to consider other cultural dimensions to examine the influence that they may have on KMS acceptance. Research can also pursue additional relationships among the cultural dimensions examined in this research, which may provide further insights into the influence that they have on the antecedents of KMS acceptance. The variance extracted for perceived ease of use and perceived behavioral control was less than 10%. It is important to recognize that due to limited variance extracted, the process/result-perceived ease of use and process/result-perceived behavioral control links need to be interpreted with caution and closely examined in future research (Falk & Miller, 1992). Another limitation is that the source of our data may be too limited to claim any universality for our research model. Certain industries, such as health and welfare, government, and retail were not represented in our sample. However, we believe that our research model is robust and will be suitable for testing in other environments and contexts.

REFERENCES

Adams, D. A., Nelson, R. R., & Todd, P. A. (1992). Perceived usefulness, ease of use, and usage of information technology: A replication. *MIS Quarterly, 16*(2), 227-247.

Ajzen, I. (1985). From intentions to actions: A theory of planned behavior. In J. K. A. J. Beckman (Ed.), *Action control: From cognition to behavior* (pp. 11-39). New York: Springer-Verlag.

Ajzen, I., & Madden, T. J. (1986). Prediction of goal-directed behavior: Attitudes, intentions, and perceived behavioral control. *Journal of experimental social psychology, 22*, 453-474.

Alavi, M., Kayworth, T., & Leidner, D. (2005-2006). An empirical examination of the influence of organizational culture on knowledge management practices. *Journal of Management Information Systems, 22*(3), 191-224.

Alavi, M., & Leidner, D. E. (2001). Review: Knowledge management and knowledge management systems: Conceptual foundations and research issues. *MIS Quarterly, 25*(1), 107-136.

Alvesson, M., & Karreman, D. (2001). Odd couple: Making sense of the curious concept of knowledge management. *Journal of Management Studies, 38*(7), 995-1018.

Bandura, A. (1977). Self-efficacy: Toward a unifying theory of behavioral change. *Psychological Review, 84*(2), 191-215.

Berman-Brown, R., & Woodland, M. J. (1999). Managing knowledge wisely: A case study in organisational behaviour. *Journal of Applied Management Studies, 8*(2), 175-198.

Bock, G.-W., Zmud, R. W., Kim, Y.-G., & Lee, J.-N. (2005). Behavioral intention formation in knowledge sharing: Examining the roles of extrinsic motivators, social-psychological forces, and organizational climate. *MIS Quarterly, 29*(1), 87-111.

Bollen, K. A. (1989). *Structural equations with latent variables*. New York: Wiley.

Byrne, B. M. (1998). *Structural equation modeling with LISREL, PRELIS, and SIMPLIS: Basic concepts, applications, and programming*. Mahwah, NJ: Lawrence Erlbaum Associates.

CAIB. (2003). The Columbia accident investigation report. Retrieved August 12, 2007, from http://www.caib.us/news/report/pdf/vol1/full/caib_report_volume1.pdf

Chatman, J. A., & Jehn, K. A. (1994). Assessing the relationship between industry characteristics and organizational culture: How different can you be? *Academy of Management Journal, 37*(3), 522-553.

Cooper, R. (1994). The inertial impact of culture on IT implementation. *Information Management, 27*(1), 17-31.

Cronin, B. (2001). Knowledge management, organizational culture and Anglo-American higher education. *Journal of Information Science, 27*(3), 129-137.

Damanpour, F. (1991). Organizational innovation: A meta-analysis of effects of determinants and moderators. *Academy of Management Journal, 34*, 555-590.

Davenport, T., & Prusak, L. (1998). *Working knowledge*. Harvard Business School Press.

Davis, F. (1989). Perceived usefulness, perceived ease of use, and user acceptance of information technology. *MIS Quarterly, 13*(3), 319-339.

Davis, F., Bagozzi, R., & Warshaw, P. (1989). User acceptance of computer technology: A comparison of two theoretical models. *Management Science, 35*(8), 982-1003.

De Long, D. W., & Fahey, L. (2000). Diagnosing cultural barriers to knowledge management. *Academy of Management Executive, 14*(4), 113-127.

Delfabbro, P., & Winefield, A. (2000). Predictors of irrational thinking in regular slot machine gamblers. *The Journal of Psychology, 134*, 117-128.

Dembla, P., & Mao, E. (2002). A research framework for knowledge management. In D. White (Ed.), *Knowledge mapping and management* (pp. 297-310). Hershey, PA: Idea Group Publishing.

Falk, R., & Miller, N. B. (1992). *A primer for soft modeling*. Akron, OH: University of Akron Press.

Fishbein, M., & Ajzen, I. (1975). *Belief, attitude, intention and behavior: An introduction to theory and research*. Reading, MA: Addison-Wesley.

Gefen, D., Karahanna, E., & Straub, D. (2003). Inexperience and experience with online stores: The importance of TAM and trust. *IEEE Transactions on Engineering Management, 50*(3), 307-321.

Gist, M., Rosen, B., & Schwoerer, C. (1988). The influence of training method and trainee age on the acquisition of computer skills. *Personnel Psychology, 41*(2), 255-265.

Grover, V., & Davenport, T. (2001). General perspectives on knowledge management: Fostering a research agenda. *Journal of Management Information Systems, 18*(1), 5.

Hackman, J. R., & Oldham, G. R. (1980). *Work redesign*. Reading, MA: Addison-Wesley.

Hofstede, G. (1991). *Cultures and organizations: Software of the mind*. New York: McGraw-Hill.

Hofstede, G., Neuijen, B., Ohayv, D. D., & Sanders, G. (1990). Measuring organizational cultures: A qualilative and quantitative study across twenty cases. *Administrative Science Quarterly, 35*(2), 286-316.

Hoyle, R. H., & Panter, A. T. (1995). Writing about structural equation modeling. In R. H. Hoyle (Ed.), *Structural equation modeling: Concepts, issues, and applications* (pp. 158-176). Thousand Oaks, CA: Sage Publications.

Hu, L.-T., & Bentler, P. M. (1999). Cutoff criteria for fit indexes in covariance structure analysis: Conventional criteria versus new alternatives. *Structural Equation Modeling, 6*(1), 1-55.

Hu, P. J., Chau, P. Y. K., Sheng, O. R. L., & Tam, K. Y. (1999). Examining the technology acceptance model using physician acceptance of telemedicine technology. *Journal of Management Information Systems, 16(2)*, 91-112.

Igbaria, M., Parasuraman, S., & Baroudi, J. J. (1996). A motivational model of microcomputer usage. *Journal of Management Information Systems, 13*(1), 127-143.

Kankanhalli, A., Tan, B. C. Y., & Wei, K.-K. (2005). Contributing knowledge to electronic knowledge repositories: An empirical investigation. *MIS Quarterly, 29*(1), 113-143.

Klein, K. J., & Sorra, J. S. (1996). The challenge of innovation implementation. *Academy of Management Review, 21*(4), 1055-1080.

Ko, D.-G., Kirsch, L. J., & King, W. R. (2005). Antecedents of knowledge transfer from consultants to clients in enterprise system implementations. *MIS Quarterly, 29*(1), 59-85.

Kogut, B., & Zander, U. (1992). Knowledge of the firm, combinative capabilities, and the replication of technology. *Organization Science, 3*(3), 383-397.

Kwan, M. M., & Balasubramanian, P. (2003). KnowledgeScope: Managing knowledge in context. *Decision Support Systems, 35*(4), 467-486.

Leidner, D., Alavi, M., & Kayworth, T. (2006). The role of culture in knowledge management: A case study of two global firms. *The International Journal of Electronic Collaboration, 2(1)*, 17-40.

Magnus, S., & Niclas, O. (2003). Behavioral intentions in satisfaction research revisited. *Journal of Consumer Satisfaction, Dissatisfaction and Complaining Behavior, 16*, 53-66.

Markus, M. L., Majchrzak, A., & Gasser, L. (2002). A design theory for systems that support emergent knowledge processes. *MIS Quarterly, 26*(3), 179-212.

McDermott, R. (1999). Why information technology inspired but cannot deliver: Knowledge management. *California Management Review, 41*(4), 103-117.

Medsker, G. J., Williams, L. J., & Holahan, P. J. (1994). A review of current practices for evaluating causal models in organizational behavior and human resources management research. *Journal of Management Information Systems, 20*(2), 439-464.

Miller, D., & Friesen, P. H. (1982). Innovation in conservative and entrepreneurial firms: Two modes of strategic momentum. *Strategic Management Journal, 3*, 1-25.

Miranda, S. M., & Saunders, C. S. (2003). The social construction of meaning: An alternative perspective on information sharing. *Information Systems Research, 14*(1), 87-106.

Money, W., & Turner, A. (2005). Assessing knowledge management system user acceptance with the technology acceptance model. *International Journal of Knowledge Management, 1*(1), 8-26.

Moore, G. C., & Benbasat, I. (1991). Development of an instrument to measure the perceptions of adopting an information technology innovation. *Information Systems Research, 2*(3), 192-222.

Nunnally, J. C. (1967). *Psychometric theory.* New York: McGraw-Hill.

O'Reilly, C. A., Chatman, J. A., & Caldwell, D. F. (1991). People and organizational culture: A profile comparison approach to assessing person-organization fit. *Academy of Management Journal, 14*(1), 487-516.

Polanyi, M. (1958). *Personal knowledge.* Chicago, IL: University of Chicago Press.

Robey, D., Wishart, N. A., & Rodriguez-Diaz, A. G. (1995a). Merging the metaphors for organizational improvement: Business process reengineering as a component of organizational learning. *Accounting, Management and Information Technologies, 5*(1), 23-39.

Robey, D., Wishart, N. A., & Rodriguez-Diaz, A. G. (1995b). Merging the metaphors for organizational improvement: Business process reengineering as a component of organizational learning. *Accounting, Management and Information Technologies, 5*(1), 23-39.

Rogers, E. M. (2003). *Diffusion of innovations* (5th ed.). New York: Free Press.

Ruggles, R. (1998). The state of the notion: Knowledge management in practice. *California Management Review, 40*(3), 80-89.

Ruppel, C. P., & Harrington, S. J. (2001). Sharing knowledge through intranets: A study of organizational culture and intranet implementation. *IEEE Transactions on Professional Communication, 44*(1), 37-52.

Sarvary, M. (1999). Knowledge management and competition in the consulting industry. *California Management Review, 41*(2), 95-107.

Schultze, U., & Leidner, D. E. (2002). Studying knowledge management in information systems research: Discourses and theoretical assumptions. *MIS Quarterly, 26*(3), 213-242.

Segars, A. H. (1997). Assessing the unidimensionality of measurement: A paradigm and illustration within the context of information systems research. *Omega, 25*(1), 107-121.

Stenmark, D. (2000). Leveraging tacit organization knowledge. *Journal of Management Information Systems, 17*(3), 9-24.

Tanriverdi, H. (2005). Information technology relatedness, knowledge management capability, and performance of multibusiness firms. *MIS Quarterly, 29*(2), 311-334.

Thompson, R. L., Higgins, C. A., & Howell, J. (1991). Personal computing: Toward a conceptual model of utilization. *MIS Quarterly, 15*(1), 124-143.

Tornatzky, L. G., & Klein, K. J. (1982). Innovation characteristics and innovation adoption-implementation: A meta-analysis of findings. *IEEE Transactions on Engineering Management, 29*(1), 28-45.

Venkatesh, V., & Morris, M. (2000). Why don't men ever stop to ask for directions? Gender, social influence, and their role in technology acceptance and usage behavior. *MIS Quarterly, 24*(1), 115-139.

Venkatesh, V., Morris, M. G., Davis, G. B., & Davis, F. D. (2003). User acceptance of information t technology: Toward a unified view. *MIS Quarterly, 27*(3), 425-478.

Wasko, M. M., & Faraj, S. (2005). Why should I share? Examining social capital and knowledge contribution in electronic networks of practice. *MIS Quarterly, 29*(1), 35-57.

West, S. G., Finch, J. F., & Curran, P. J. (1995). Structural equation models with nonnormal variables. In R. H. Hoyle (Ed.), *Structural equation modeling: Concepts, issues, and applications* (pp. 56-75). Thousand Oaks, CA: Sage Publications.

ENDNOTE

[1]   An exploratory factor analysis was performed, but not included in this article due to space limitations. These results are available from the third author.

This work was previously published in International Journal of Knowledge Management, Vol. 4, Issue 1, edited by M. E. Jennex, pp. 1-16, copyright 2008 by IGI Publishing, formerly known as Idea Group Publishing (an imprint of IGI Global).

Chapter XXV
IT Infrastructure Capabilities and Business Process Improvements:
Association with IT Governance Characteristics

Chuck C. H. Law
Chaoyang University of Technology, Taiwan

Eric W. T. Ngai
The Hong Kong Polytechnic University, China

ABSTRACT

It has been widely discussed in the management information systems (MIS) literature that the outcomes of information technologies (IT) and systems may be subject to the influence of the characteristics of the organization, including those of the IT and business leadership. This study was conducted to examine the relationships that may exist between IT infrastructure capabilities (ITC), business process improvements (BPI), and such IT governance-related constructs as the reporting relationship between the chief executive officer (CEO) and chief information officer (CIO), and senior management support of IT and BPI projects.

Using a sample of 243 multinational and Hong Kong-listed firms operating in Greater China, this study yielded empirical support for the perceived achievement of capabilities in some dimensions of the IT infrastructure in the companies under study. It was found that the BPI construct was related to the reporting relationship between the CEO and CIO (CEO-CIO distance), and to the levels of senior management support. The dimensions of the ITC construct were also investigated and identified by an exploratory factor analysis (EFA). Associations were found between the selected organizational constructs and the ITC dimensions, except in two hypothesized relationships. Those between CEO-CIO distance and the ITC dimensions of data integration and training were not supported at the significance level of 0.05.

INTRODUCTION

The last decades have seen generous investment in information technologies (IT) by companies around the world (Mitra, 2005; Strassman, 2002), and expenditures for IT infrastructure are estimated to account for almost 60% of a company's IT budget (Byrd & Turner, 2000). As IT has increasingly been perceived as a critical business enabler, companies are eager to take advantage of IT to support their operational and strategic objectives. Despite the huge investments made in IT in recent decades, the effects of such investment are less than satisfactory in terms of organizational benefits (Dasgupta, Sarkis & Talluri, 1999; Hu & Plant, 2001). One of the reasons for this paradox is the mismanagement of IT projects, as shown in a number of notorious examples of IT failures (Grossman, 2003; Spitze, 2001). Against this background, a series of sensible questions can be asked. What are the factors that would favorably affect the outcomes of such investments in IT initiatives? What are the proper types and amounts of IT investment a company should make? The first one points to many aspects of IT planning, implementation and management while the second relates to the proper investment decisions that need to be made, perhaps jointly, by the senior IT and business leadership (Ein-Dor & Segev, 1978; Ross & Weill, 2002).

The IT literature has presented many organizational factors relevant to the successful adoption of IT, ranging from project management issues to user involvement, and senior management support (Caldeira & Ward, 2002; Chatterjee, Grewal & Sambamurthy, 2002). Ignoring or mismanaging these factors may subject the projects to the risk of failure (Sumner, 2000). Among the many organizational issues that are said to affect the investment, deployment and use of IT,

are IT governance-related factors. As defined by Sambamurthy & Zmud (1999), "IT governance arrangements refers to the patterns of authority for key IT activities in business firms, including IT infrastructure, IT use, and project management" (p. 261). "The patterns of authority" could have many implications to the investment decisions, and running of the enterprise-wide IT initiatives. For instance, it may affect how much recognition and support an IT project could receive from the various levels of the organizations, and whether appropriate funding and resources would be allocated. In our article, the term "IT governance characteristics" focuses on the (a) reporting relationship between the chief executive and the IT leader, (b) the support and commitment of top management received by the IT projects, and (c) the support and commitment of top management on business process improvement. The former is used as a surrogate for the seniority of the IT leader as will be explained and discussed further in the next section. A review of the literature about enterprise IT and systems adoption indicates that many of the enterprise IT projects would not be successful unless the deployment of IT is accompanied by changes to business practices and processes (Davenport, 1998; Sumner, 2000; Wu, 2002). Thus, senior management's attitudes and commitment on business process changes would also be critical to the success of enterprise IT projects.

While many studies have discussed, and some empirically investigated the relationships among IT adoption, business process changes and such organizational factors as senior management support and the seniority of IT leadership, there is still a need for additional empirical evidence to support these concepts (Grover, Teng, Segars, & Fiedler, 1998). On the other hand, such studies mostly examined the relationships at a coarse level, and have not attempted to investigate what aspects of IT are affected by these IT governance factors and what aspects are not. It would be more interesting to investigate these associations with

IT at finer granularities, that is, considering the various dimensions of IT. Therefore, the primary goals of this study are (a) to conduct a thorough literature review on the selected IT governance factors in relation to enterprise IT and business process initiatives, (b) to explore more deeply the concept of IT infrastructure capabilities and define its constituent dimensions, (c) to produce a conceptual model highlighting the relationships between the IT governance-related constructs and these two types of initiatives, and (d) to conduct an empirical study to substantiate or disconfirm the relationships.

The remainder of this article is organized as follows. A review of the literature and the conceptual model are presented, the methodologies and guidelines of the study are discussed, the analysis and the findings are presented, and concluding remarks are made following a discussion of the findings and their implications.

LITERATURE REVIEW

IT Infrastructure Capabilities

IT infrastructure is important to an organization as it embodies many of the components necessary to support the organization's overall information architecture (Allen & Boynton, 1991; Mudie & Schafer, 1985). It has also been argued in the MIS literature that the enterprise architecture of an organization is composed of the technical, data, and application architectures; which jointly enable the processing, sharing and management of data resources across divisional and organizational boundaries (Spewak & Hill, 1993).

This broader view of IT infrastructure has earned the acceptance of many authors in IT or MIS (Mitchell & Zmud, 1999; Weill & Broadbent, 1999). Generally speaking, IT infrastructure capabilities (ITC) would consist of a wide spectrum of components, including the IT platforms, standards, and policies, and different types of service

arrangements that support the information-related activities of an organization. Included in this definition are corporate network infrastructure, hardware platforms, common business systems such as data management and project management systems, and IT management and support services. Among the latter is education and training (Weill & Broadbent, 1999). In fact, training has been considered an important issue by studies in IT investment and management (Brancheau, Janz & Wetherbe, 1996; Mahmood & Mann, 1993; Palvia & Wang, 1995; Sakaguchi & Dibrell, 1998). Many of these studies (Mahmood & Mann, 1993) put the focus on training IT staff, while some (Sakaguchi & Dibrell, 1998) considered IT training for users to be a key construct of the measurement model of the global use of information technology.

In summary, the construct of ITC is a multidimensional concept that may include many aspects of IT, ranging from the network infrastructure that enables communications within and across organizational boundaries, a portfolio of hardware and system software that supports transaction processing and information analysis, documentation that clearly defines the policies and procedures of IT management, expertise in managing the IT platforms and various stakeholders, and the training of IT staff and users.

In recognition of the contribution of IT to organizational performance, IT capabilities measures such as the monetary measures of IT investment and perceptual ratings have been used as surrogates in research on the business value of IT. Attempts have been made in such studies to explore the impact of IT capabilities on an organization. The studies of Bharadwaj (2000), and Santhanam and Hartono (2003) have confirmed the relationships between IT capability and the financial performance measures of profit- and cost-related ratios. In both studies, IT capability was defined using a dichotomous variable, by which a value of 1 denotes a firm that has been elected by InformationWeek as an "IT leader," and a value of 0 denotes a non-IT leader. In the study of Andersen and Segars (2001), the effects of IT on the decentralization of the decision structure and on the financial performance of firms in the apparel and textile industry were empirically investigated. The instrument for IT measured the extent to which electronic mail services, electronic data transmissions, the company-owned telecommunication network, and fiber distributed data interfaces are used in a company (Andersen & Segars, 2001). Other studies found that IT infrastructure such as electronic data interchange (EDI) and network infrastructure had a significant impact on improvements in business processes (Bhatt, 2000, 2001). In Bhatt (2000), two aspects of information system integration were measured: the degree of data integration, and the use of network communications. The use of EDI in Bhatt (2001) was measured using the following three items: (a) the extent to which the firm and its primary suppliers were linked by EDI, (b) the extent to which information on products and services could be distributed to suppliers by senior management using information systems, and (c) the extent to which information on products and services could be shared between the firm and its suppliers. Likewise, the relationships between IT diffusion and perceived productivity gain, and the mediating effects of the business process redesign construct for different types of information technologies such as electronic mail, relational database management systems, expert systems, imaging, and local area networks were examined and confirmed in the study of Grover et al. (1998).

The preceding literature review leads to two points that deserve further discussion. First, IT adoption or diffusion and business process changes are inter-related, according to the studies that have been discussed. Second, the instruments that were developed primarily measure the use of individual IT platforms, rather than multiple dimensions of the IT infrastructure. In fact, there is a paucity of studies on the development of standardized multi-dimensional instruments for

measuring the ITC of firms. The development of such an instrument would be conducive to IT studies in that it would assist with the repetitive and systematic measurements of ITC (Santhanam & Hartono, 2003).

Business Process Improvements and IT Adoption

Business process redesign refers to the revolutionary approach of process changes, which often requires "rethinking," and a drastic transformation of current business practices and processes. This approach is also called business process reengineering (BPR) (Earl & Khan, 1994; Hammer, 1990). Academic studies have also found that many firms have successfully made use of a "milder" evolutionary approach, which is referred to as business process improvements (BPI) (Harkness, Kettinger, & Segars, 1996; Stoddard & Jarvenpaa, 1995). This latter approach calls for less drastic changes to existing practice and processes.

Regardless of the approach adopted, changes in business process aim at the betterment and simplification of current practices and processes, and are considered critical for the deployment of IT systems in many circumstances. The inter-relationships between IT and BPR have been widely discussed in the academic studies on MIS and business process management (Wu, 2002). IT enables new practices that would have been impossible before the advent of the technologies or systems. A lack of, or poor, IT infrastructure will limit or jeopardize the success of business process changes. Conversely, deploying IT without proper changes to business processes could compromise the outcomes. Many have considered business process redesign to be an important organizational construct with the potential to affect the outcomes of IT adoption (Grover et al., 1998). While there is plenty of theoretical discussion of the relationship between IT and business process changes in the literature, many of the studies are qualitative in nature, each involving very few cases, and therefore lack of generalizability (Grover et al., 1998). On the other hand, some studies discussed the issues with very limited empirical support (Grover et al., 1998). This points to a need for further studies to gather empirical evidence across firms for the abovementioned relationship.

Organizational Factors for IT Adoption and Business Process Changes

The MIS literature is abundant in the discussion of organizational factors and how they may affect the outcomes of IT adoption and business process changes. These studies have explored a wide variety of organizational issues in different system contexts (Caldeira & Ward, 2002; Davenport, 1998; Chatterjee et al., 2002; Ein-Dor & Segev, 1978). To name a few as examples, organizational issues or factors discussed in these studies include the seniority of IT leaders (Ein-Dor & Segev, 1978), senior management support and attitudes (Caldeira & Ward, 2002; Counihan, Finnegan, & Sammon, 2002; Davenport, 1998; Wixom & Watson, 2001), IT governance and decisions (Ross & Weill, 2002), and many project management practices (Ahituv, Neumann, & Zviran, 2002; Kimberly & Evanisko, 1981; Wixom & Watson, 2001).

Support and Commitment of Top Management

Among the aforementioned organizational factors, those concerning the roles and behavior of top management may matter a great deal and probably be increasingly important since many IT initiatives nowadays are enterprise-wide projects, analogous to what is described as Type III IS Innovation in Swanson's (1994) taxonomy of IS innovations. This type of project would require a clear strategy and institutionalized efforts to mobilize the functions and its stakeholders across the organization to participate in the adoption process (Swanson,

1994). In many circumstances, the attitudes and actions of the company's leadership would help facilitate and shape the adoption process (Chatterjee et al., 2002; Swanson, 1994). Many IT initiatives such as ERP, are boundary-spanning efforts which often require a wide range of stakeholders to participate, and to accept changes to the business practices and processes. Unswerving support from the top management is necessary to resolve any conflict of interest among the various parties involved (Davenport, 1998; Grover, Jeong, Kettinger, & Teng, 1995; Ross & Weill, 2002). A lack of such support would likely pose a threat to the projects (Bingi, Sharman, & Godla, 1999; Sumner, 2000).

That said, the IT leadership may have an important role to play within an organization, for instance, in marketing an IT or business process initiative to the organization and to secure the support and resources for the initiative. The seniority of the IT leadership is one of the "IT governance characteristics" to be investigated in this study. The following subsections will explore into the concepts about the roles and the seniority of the IT leadership as found in the IT-related literature.

The Roles and Seniority of IT Leadership

The seniority of the IT leader within an organization is considered an important factor in the success of the abovementioned projects (Ein-Dor & Segev, 1978). The IT leader, called the IT manager, IT director, or CIO, is the most senior executive responsible for the IT function of an organization. In this study, we shall use the term CIO to refer to IT heads regardless of their formal job titles. A summary of relevant discussions about the ranks and roles of the IT leadership are provided in Table 1.

IT heads in some organizations are positioned under the finance function (Jones & Arnett, 1993). As reported by a survey conducted in 1990, 40% of the CIOs who participated in the survey re-

Table 1. Findings and discussions about the IT leadership

Findings and Discussions	References
Seniority–Hierarchical Position	
• Seniority of the IT executive is one of the factors affecting IT/IS adoption.	(Ein-Dor & Segev, 1978)
• The use of IT for competitive advantages must be supported by the rank and role of the IT leader.	(Karimi et al., 1996)
• "Proximity" between CEO and CIO would help to secure resources and support.	(Jain, 1997)
• Reporting relationship ("CEO-CIO distance") moderates outcomes of IT investment.	(Li & Ye, 1999)
• The position of IS affects IT/IS adoption.	(Marble, 2003)
• CIO's rank is conducive to business process reengineering	(Teng et al., 1998)
Seniority–Membership of TMT (Top Management Team)	
• CIO's participation in top management team enhances business knowledge.	(Armstrong & Sambamurthy, 1999)
• CIO's membership in TMT is more important than his reporting relationship.	(Earl & Feeney, 1994)
• CIO is a member of TMT and it is equally important to be perceived as senior executive.	(Rockart et al., 1982)
Responsibilities and Skill Requirements	
• CIO should possess competencies in four areas: business leadership, technology leadership, organizational leadership and functional leadership.	(Earl, 1989)
• CIO markets, and changes the perceptions about the IT function.	(Earl & Feeney, 1994; Lucas, 1999)
• CIO pro-actively communicates with and solicits support from the TMT.	(Lucas, 1999)
Problems Encountered	
• A junior IT leader finds it difficult to communicate with top management.	(Cash et al. 1992)
• Many IT leaders are not accepted by others in the TMT as senior executives.	(Rothfeder, 1990; Runyan, 1990; Strassmann, 1994)

ported to the COO, and a much smaller percentage reported to the CEO (Rothfeder, 1990). In other organizations, this leader is often a member of the senior management team, shares the responsibility of business planning, enjoys a senior status and, equally important, is perceived as a senior executive (Rockart, Bullen, & Ball, 1982). It was found in a survey conducted in 2002 that 51% of CIOs reported to the CEO (Field, 2002). This shows a trend that an increasing number of companies recognizes the strategic role of the IT leader and the IT organization, and places him or her higher in the corporate structure.

The CIO bears full responsibility for promoting the use of IT to improve or transform the current business practices of an organization, building relationships and soliciting support from the CEO and other executives (Lucas, 1999). In fact, one of the CIO's most challenging responsibilities is to manage the CEO's perceptions about IT—that is, to persuade the CEO to think that IT is an organizational asset, rather than a cost (Earl & Feeney, 1994; Lucas, 1999).

These responsibilities require quality bilateral communications with the chief executive and others in the top management team to achieve an appropriate degree of mutual understanding (or convergence) with each other (Johnson & Lederer, 2003). As the CIO does not possess authority over any of his or her peers in the senior management team, he or she must achieve these objectives through "influence behavior," rather than through authority. For instance, rational persuasion and personal appeal are the most effective forms of influence behavior in soliciting support from the senior management team (Enns, Huff, & Higgins, 2003).

However, many CIOs have reportedly failed to obtain the acceptance from their peers and are considered outsiders to the senior management team (Rothfeder, 1990; Runyan, 1990; Strassmann, 1994). This may create hurdles to their efforts in communicating with the senior executives, or participate effectively in strategic planning. One may find the communication problem more serious for a junior ranking CIO, or in firms with a culture of informal communications (Cash, McFarlan, Mckinney, & Applegate, 1992). Moreover, a low-ranking CIO may put his/her focus on handling daily operations, and managing his or her subordinates (Ives & Olson, 1981), likely at the expense of the more strategic responsibilities.

This problem has led to the view that a formal senior position in the organizational hierarchy would give the IT executive more authority and influence within the organization (Jain, 1997; Hambrick, 1981). Though some academics argue that a full membership in, and effective communication with the top management team are more important than a formal senior position, others believe that a formal place in the top management team would give the CIO many advantages in terms of closer bilateral communications, and enhanced understanding of business strategies (Feeny, Edwards & Simpson, 1992; Gupta, 1991; Raghunathan & Raghunathan, 1993; Watson, 1990). Some empirical studies seem to support the formal approach. Karimi, Gupta & Somers (1996) pointed out that successful competitive strategies must be supported by the rank and role of the CIO. Li and Ye (1999) also found that a closer reporting relationship between the CEO and CIO would be conducive to the productive use of IT. Accordingly, it is likely that a direct reporting relationship with the CEO may help a CIO execute his/her duties effectively.

Given these discussions, it would be interesting to determine how these IT governance characteristics would affect the achievement of IT infrastructure capabilities and business process improvements in the companies under study.

RESEARCH MODEL

To fulfill the objectives of this study, a research model is formulated to represent the key constructs and the conceptualized relationships, which will be discussed further in subsequent subsections. As depicted in Figure 1, the ITC dimensions and the extent of BPI are related, and these constructs are believed to be associated with the IT governance constructs of senior management support and CEO-CIO reporting relationship.

IT Infrastructure Capabilities

Following the broader definition presented in the last section (Weill & Broadbent, 1999), the construct of ITC is conceptualized to include items from five dimensions: network communications,

Figure 1. The conceptual model

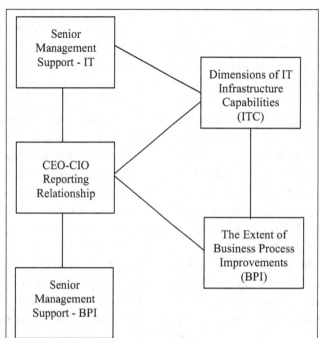

data integration, hardware and system software, IT management and support, and training. The items of the first two dimensions, network communications and data integration, are based on a subset of items in the studies of Bhatt (2000, 2001); while training is derived from the study of Sakaguchi and Dibrell (1998) with modifications. The items of the dimensions of hardware and software, and IT management and support were developed after a thorough search through the literature on the subject (Allen & Boynton, 1991; Sambamurthy & Zmud, 1999; Spewak & Hill, 1993; Weill & Broadbent, 1999).

It must be noted that this construct and its subordinate dimensions aim at measuring the perceived "realized" capabilities of IT infrastructure, rather than what is anticipated by the respondents.

The Extent of Business Process Improvements

The extent of BPI refers to the perceived degree to which changes in processes have been implemented to improve the efficiency and effectiveness of a company. The construct includes five items to measure process improvement in terms of error prevention, quality, ease of use, and intra- and inter-firm coordination. The first three items have been adopted from the study of Bhatt (2000), while the items concerning intra- and interfirm coordination have been added in recognition of the increasingly important concepts of cross-boundary coordination (Kogut, 1985; Stock, Greis, & Kasarda, 1998).

This study supports the assumption that a relationship may exist between IT deployment and process improvements. IT can be an enabler of changes to business processes, while the latter is necessary in many circumstances of IT deployment because automating inefficient processes would at best result in suboptimal outcomes (Hitt & Brynjolfsson, 1996; Stoddard & Jarvenpaa, 1995). Therefore, we put forward the following hypotheses:

$H_0 1$: *The perceived extent of a company's BPI and the perceived level of individual dimensions of ITC are positively related.*

Senior Management Support and CEO-CIO Reporting Relationship

In this study, we have placed our focus on three IT governance-related constructs, namely senior management support of IT, senior management support of BPI, and the CEO-CIO reporting relationship. Senior management support is considered by many to be an important organizational factor for enterprise-wide IT and BPI projects (Ein-Dor & Segev, 1978; Grover et al., 1995; Sumner, 2000). The success of enterprise-wide projects requires the involvement of the user communities and the proper investment of resources (Nah, Zuckweiler, & Lau, 2003). The political roles played by senior executives in mitigating resistance to change and resolving conflicts between various interest groups must be accorded unequivocal importance (Davenport, 1998). Moreover, a supportive senior management team may influence the rest of the organization to take actions in favor of enterprise-wide initiatives. Senior management support in this study is a perceptual assessment, by the respondents, of the degree of support that top management gives to projects involving IT and BPI.

As a measure of the reporting relationship, the variable of CEO-CIO distance reflects how close or far apart the CIO is from the chief executive in the organizational structure. It can, therefore, be regarded as a surrogate of the seniority of the CIO. It is supposed that a CIO who reports directly to the chief executive will have a closer working relationship with him or her, and enjoy a higher status within the organization, than one who reports to other senior executives such as the COO or CFO.

We speculate that a high-ranking CIO would very likely have more opportunities to engage in high-quality two-way communications with the CEO and other senior executives, and a better understanding of business strategies than his or her low-ranking counterparts because of frequent participation in top management activities (Cash et al., 1992; Ives & Olson, 1981). This would be very important to the CIO in terms of the alignment of business and IT strategies, and his or her relationship with the senior management team. In addition to issues concerning communication and convergence between the senior IT and business leadership, having an IT governance structure in which the CIO is closer to the CEO and other senior executives may make it easier to implement the appropriate measures to secure from the rest of the organization the support and cooperation necessary for the success of an enterprise-wide initiative. For instance, a project bonus or award may be presented to the top performers of a project, or the contribution to the project may be considered as one of the important factors in annual staff performance appraisal.

We therefore posit that a CIO who enjoys a more senior position will be able to solicit stronger support for initiatives on IT and BPI, leading to more satisfactory outcomes for both types of projects. As the CIO is the head of the IT function, the status or importance of the IT function within the company is implied by his or her status. The following hypotheses are formulated:

$H_0 2$: *CEO-CIO distance as a measure of the CEO-CIO reporting relationship is negatively associated with the perceived level of senior management support of IT projects.*

H_03: *CEO-CIO distance as a measure of the CEO-CIO reporting relationship is negatively associated with the perceived level of senior management support of BPI projects.*

H_04: *The perceived level of the individual IT infrastructure capabilities dimensions of a company is positively associated with senior management support for IT projects.*

H_05: *The perceived level of the individual dimensions of the IT infrastructure capabilities of a company is negatively associated with the CEO-CIO distance used as a measure of the CEO-CIO reporting relationship.*

H_06: *The perceived extent of the BPI of a company is positively associated with senior management support for BPI projects.*

H_07: *The perceived extent of the BPI of a company is negatively associated with the CEO-CIO distance used as a measure of the CEO-CIO reporting relationship.*

RESEARCH METHODOLOGY

Data Sources

Perceptual data were collected by a postal survey. A survey package, containing a cover letter, a questionnaire booklet, and a return envelope with prepaid postage was sent to companies operating in different business sectors, including manufacturing, finance, logistics, wholesaling and retailing, and services. The 3,377 firms in the mailing list included 852 firms listed in the Stock Exchange of Hong Kong, and 2,525 multinationals operating in Hong Kong and China.

The cover letters, addressed to the chief executives or managing directors, solicited their support by explaining the objective of the research

and the rules of confidentiality and anonymity, and asked them to forward the survey package, preferably to the IS executives, or to any officers nominated by them as appropriate to respond to the survey. A reminder postcard was sent to each nonresponding company at the end of the second week, and followed by telephone calls. These measures were taken to improve the response rate. In designing the study, serious consideration was given to the low response rates (around 10%) for social surveys conducted in Asian societies. This led to the decision to use a larger sampling frame for the survey.

Validity Guidelines and Research Procedures

Generally accepted guidelines in research (Churchill, 1979; Nunnally, 1978) were followed throughout the study, especially in the development of multi-item constructs. Items of individual constructs in this study were developed based on previously validated instruments and on a thorough review of the relevant literature. To ensure its face and content validity, the questionnaire was subject to a review and pretest, and then a pilot test.

An EFA was conducted for the sample, collected from the postal survey, on the ITC and the extent of BPI constructs to ascertain the convergent and divergent validity of the items under the dimensions (or subordinate constructs) in each construct. Items with factor loadings of 0.6 or above were retained for the constructs (Tracey, Vonderembse, & Lim, 1999), and those slightly below this cut-off point were reviewed for their importance and relevance to the objectives of the study following Dillon and Goldstein's (1984) guidelines. Internal consistencies were validated, and Cronbach's alpha coefficients equalling or exceeding 0.7 were considered acceptable (Kerlinger, 1973). In the purification process, items with corrected-item total correlations (CITC) of less than 0.5 were eliminated, or rephrased if they were important, following Churchill's (1979) recommendations.

This study followed a two-stage approach. An EFA was first performed to determine the dimensions of the high-level constructs, namely, the ITC and the extent of BPI constructs. Subsequent to the EFA, firm-level indices were calculated for individual ITC dimensions, and for the extent of BPI respectively. For example, the BPI index of a firm was derived by averaging the firm's perceptual inputs to the five BPI question items. The index for the training dimension of ITC was computed by taking the average of the firm's inputs to the three training items and so on. A data analysis was then conducted using a nonparametric correlation analysis (Spearman's rho) to test the relationships between the ITC dimensions, and the other constructs.

Instrument Development and Pilot Test

Instruments for soliciting perceptual ratings of ITC and the extent of BPI were developed based on a review of the literature, and on pretested instruments used in prior studies. The ITC instrument contains 16 items: four on network communications, three on data integration, three on hardware and system software, three on IT management and support, and three on training. The network communications and data integration items were based on the studies of Bhatt (2000, 2001) with adjustments to the wording. The training items included IT training for staff and users and were based on the study of Sakaguchi and Dibrell (1998). The items of hardware and software, and those of IT management and support measured the perceptual assessment of the capacities of the hardware and software facilities, administrative standards and procedures, and support services. These items were considered important to achieving a comprehensive ITC construct (Allen & Boynton, 1991; Mitchell & Zmud, 1999; Mudie

& Schafer, 1985; Spewak & Hill, 1993; Weill & Broadbent, 1999).

The extent of BPI consisted of five items to capture assessments of realized process changes in terms of error prevention, process quality, ease of use, and inter- and intra-firm coordination. The first three items were derived from Bhatt (2000), with adjustments to the wording, and the items of coordination were added to improve the comprehensiveness of the instrument.

The instrument items are based on a 5-point Likert scale, with 1 being equal to *strongly disagree,* 2 to *disagree,* 3 to *neutral,* 4 to *agree,* and 5 to *strongly agree.* As discussed previously, these instruments were reviewed and pretested by six MIS executives and two academics, followed by the pilot test involving 60 evening MBA students. Their comments concerning the comprehensiveness and wording of the questionnaire items led to improvements of the instruments. Cronbach's alpha coefficients were computed using the 51 usable cases collected from the pilot test. The ITC instrument demonstrated acceptable internal consistency (Kerlinger, 1973). The alpha coefficient of the BPI items was below the cut-off value of 0.7; these items were therefore rephrased.

Measures of the IT Governance Constructs

As discussed, this study used the reporting relationship between the CEO and CIO as a surrogate for the status of the CIO (and the IT function). The questionnaire included a question with four options. The question reads "The head of IT in your company reports to (1) the CEO, (2) the CFO, (3) the COO, and (4) others, please specify". The responses to option 4 were to be analyzed to determine the levels of the IT head and his or her supervisor within the structure of the organization. This question was recoded to form the CEO-CIO distance variable, whose values were 1 for a CIO who directly reported to the CEO, 2 for a CIO who reported to a senior officer other than the CEO, 3 for a CIO who reported to a manager on the next level downward in the organizational hierarchy, and so forth, to reflect the reporting distance of the IT head from the CEO. This coding method was adopted and expanded from that used in Li and Ye (1999).

Two questions were included to solicit perceptual ratings on senior management support: one for IT and the other for BPI projects. Both were 5-point Likert scale questions, with 1 indicating *strongly disagree,* 3 *not certain,* and 5 *strongly agree.*

To operationalize the nonparametric tests for the relationships between the IT governance constructs, ITC dimensions, and the extent of BPI construct, the BPI index (labeled BPI_I) and indices for the individual ITC dimensions (labeled ITC_IFC, ITC_DI, ITC_FM and ITC_TR) were

computed, after the EFA, for each firm based on its responses to the survey.

ANALYSIS AND FINDINGS

Profiles of the Respondents

Three hundred and six questionnaires were returned, giving a response rate of 9.1%. For the sake of data quality, returned questionnaires with missing data and those filled out by relatively junior staff such as programmers were dropped. Therefore, 243 usable cases were retained in the sample, yielding an effective rate of 7.1%. Among the 243 responding companies, 65 (26.7%) were listed in Hong Kong, 64 (26.3%) in Europe, 41 (16.97%) in North America, and 60 (24.7%) in

Table 2. Profiles of the respondents

Personal Attributes	Frequency	
Years of Age		
25–30	49	(20.2%)
31–40	109	(44.9%)
> 40	76	(31.3%)
Unknown	9	(3.7%)
Total	243	(100.0%)
Education Level		
Secondary	1	(0.4%)
Post-secondary certificate/ diploma	25	(10.3%)
Bachelor's degree	125	(51.4%)
Master's degree	85	(35.0%)
Doctoral degree	2	(0.8%)
Unknown	5	(2.1%)
Total	243	(100.0%)

Personal Attributes	Frequency	
Years in Present Profession		
Less than 3 years	13	(5.3%)
3 to 6 years	45	(18.5%)
7 to 10 years	59	(24.3%)
11 to 14 years	44	(18.1%)
More than 14 years	79	(32.9%)
Unknown	3	(1.2%)
Total	243	(100.0%)
Seniority Level		
Chief executive	22	(9.1%)
Senior management	44	(18.1%)
Middle management	111	(45.7%)
Front-line supervisors & project leaders	53	(21.8%)
Unknown	13	(5.3%)
Total	243	(100.0%)

Table 3. The four factors of the IT infrastructure capabilities construct

Item	Description	IFC	DI	FM	TR	Alpha
NC1	Networks link the firm and its main suppliers.	0.772				
NC2	Networks link the firm and its main customers.	0.795				0.8222
DI1	The same information in the database is shared across the firm.		0.761			
DI2	Duplication of data is eliminated.		0.769			0.8206
DI3	Definitions of data elements are standardized.		0.629			
HS1	Server platforms have sufficient capacity.			0.652		
HS2	Regular preventive maintenance minimizes down time.			0.684		
MS1	The firm has the expertise to manage IT facilities.			0.713		0.8848
MS2	Users are happy with the IT services.			0.663		
MS3	IT administration standards and procedures are well defined.			0.613		
TR1	The company has effective IT training pro-grammes.				0.752	
TR2	Training for users is sufficient.				0.799	0.8841
TR3	Training for IT personnel is sufficient.				0.771	

Note. IFC = interfirm communications, DI = data integration, FM = IT facilities and management, TR = training, Alpha = Cronbach's alpha (α).

Table 4. The extent of business process improvement construct and factor loadings

Item	Description	BPI	Alpha
BP1	Process changes help prevent defects and errors.	0.663	
BP2	Process standards are raised periodically.	0.728	0.8395
BP3	New processes are easier to work with.	0.738	
BP4	Work processes are improved to facilitate coordination within the firm.	0.814	
BP5	Work processes are improved to facilitate coordination with external parties.	0.644	

Note. BPI = the extent of business process improvement, Alpha = Cronbach's alpha (α).

other parts of Asia. The demographics of the respondents are presented in Table 2.

Exploratory Factor Analysis and Internal Consistency

Following the screening of returned question-naires, an EFA was performed separately on the ITC and the extent of BPI items. Maximum likelihood was used as the extraction method and Varimax as the rotation method in this study. Items with factor loadings of less than the cut-off value of 0.6 were dropped from the construct (Tracey et al., 1999). The dimensions and their items (indicators) that satisfied the criterion are shown in Tables 3 and 4.

Table 5. Reporting relationships of IT leadership

Title of Supervisor	Frequency	CEO-CIO Distance Encoded
CEO/Managing Director	128 (52.7%)	1
Chief Financial Officer (CFO)	68 (28.0%)	2
Chief Operating Officer (COO)	44 (18.1%)	2
Others[1]	3 (1.2%)	2
	243 (100.0%)	

Note. Three job titles entered by the respondents indicated positions that are one level below the CEO.

The EFA not only led to the elimination of some indicators from the ITC construct but also to the merger of two conceptualized dimensions. Two items concerning intra-firm communications under the "Network Communications" dimension ("NC3: Personnel can efficiently exchange information using e-mail systems," and "NC4: Company units can readily access data and applications on the network") were found to have insignificant factor loadings. One item, "HS3: Both hardware and system software are upgraded frequently," under the "Hardware and System Software" dimension was also dropped for low loading. The indicators initially conceptualized under the "Hardware and System Software" and "IT management and support" dimensions were identified as belonging to a single factor, renamed "IT Facilities and Management." Consequently, the ITC construct was found to be composed of four dimensions: "Interfirm Communications" (IFC), "Data Integration" (DI), "IT Facilities and Management" (FM), and "Training" (TR). An EFA found that the extent of BPI is unidimensional and that all five items loaded under a single factor.

The items under the extent of BPI, and those under individual dimensions of the ITC construct were analysed separately for internal consistency (refer to Tables 3 and 4). The Cronbach's alpha coefficients for the ITC dimensions exceeded the cut-off value of 0.7 (Kerlinger, 1973). The

Cronbach's alpha coefficient of the BPI construct was 0.8395, thus satisfying the threshold value of 0.7 (Kerlinger, 1973). In addition, the CITC (i.e. corrected-item total correlations) value of each item under these two constructs exceeded 0.5, meeting Churchill's (1979) guidelines.

Hypothesis Testing

Subsequent to the purification of measures and the EFA, the firm-level indices, namely BPI_I (for the extent of BPI construct), and ITC_IFC, ITC_DI, ITC_FM and ITC_TR (for the individual ITC dimensions) were calculated for each responding firm. The responses concerning the reporting relationship of the IT leadership were analyzed before recoding. In this sample, 128 (52.7%) IT leaders reported directly to the CEO or managing director, 68 (28.0%) to the chief financial officer (CFO), and 44 (18.1%) to the chief operating officer (COO). Three respondents indicated that their IT leaders reported to supervisors other than the CEO, CFO, and COO. Based on the job titles entered by respondents, we determined that these supervisors were one level below that of the CEO/Managing Director. Responses to this question item were then recoded to form the CEO-CIO distance variable (CC_DIST), which reflected how far the IT leader was from the CEO/Managing Director in the organization chart. As a result, 128 IT leaders in the sample were assigned a value of "1," and the rest were assigned a value of "2" in the CEO-CIO distance variable (refer to Table 5).

In addition, the descriptive statistics of variables used in this study were computed and presented in Table 6, showing that the data does not conform to the assumption of normal distribution.

This characteristic of data distribution and the fact that many variables are "ordered categories" justify the use of nonparametric statistical methods (Norusis, 2003).

Recall that the objectives of this study are to investigate whether the perceived level of ITC dimensions, and extent of BPI of a company

Table 6. Constructs, variables created, and descriptive statistics

Constructs	Variables Created	N	Mean	Std. Deviation
ITC Interfirm Communications	ITC_IFC	243	3.4486	0.91387
ITC Data Integration	ITC_DI	243	3.8299	0.75780
ITC IT Facilities and Management	ITC_FM	243	3.7407	0.74153
ITC Training	ITC_TR	243	3.1920	0.85960
The Extent of Business Process Improvement	BPI_I	243	3.4313	0.62272
Senior Management Support of IT Projects	MS_IT	242	3.8100	0.99200
Senior Management Support of BPI Projects	MS_BPI	242	3.8000	0.93500
CEO-CIO Reporting Relationship	CC_DIST	243	1.4733	0.50031

Note. ITC_IFC = Index of the ITC Interfirm Communication dimension, ITC_DI = Index of the ITC Data Integration dimension, ITC_FM = Index of the ITC IT Facilities and Management dimension, ITC_TR = Index of the ITC Training dimension, BPI_I = BPI Index, MS_IT = Management Support of IT, MS_BPI = Management Support of BPI, CC_DIST = CEO-CIO Distance.

Table 7. Correlation analysis (Spearman's rho)

Variables	ITC_IFC	ITC_DI	ITC_FM	ITC_TR	BPI_I	MS_IT	MS_BPI	CC_DIST
ITC_IFC	---	---	---	---				
ITC_DI	---	---	---	---				
ITC_FM	---	---	---	---				
ITC_TR	---	---	---	---				
BPI_I	0.333**	0.331**	0.548**	0.510**	---			
MS_IT	0.264**	0.298**	0.454**	0.355**	0.371**	---		
MS_BPI	0.279**	0.317**	0.424**	0.386**	0.445**	0.574**	---	
CC_DIST	-0.141*	-0.125	-0.187**	-0.114	-0.178**	-0.188**	-0.172**	---

Note. ITC_IFC = Index of the ITC Inter-firm Communication dimension, ITC_DI = Index of the ITC Data Integration dimension, ITC_FM = Index of the ITC IT Facilities and Management dimension, ITC_TR = Index of the ITC Training dimension, BPI_I = BPI Index, MS_IT = Management Support of IT, MS_BPI = Management Support of BPI, CC_DIST = CEO-CIO Distance.

* Correlation is significant at the 0.05 (2-tailed) level.

** Correlation is significant at the 0.01 (2-tailed) level.

Table 8. Summary of findings

	Hypothesis	Finding
$H_0$1a:	ITC_IFC and BPI_I positively related	S[a]
$H_0$1b:	ITC_DI and BPI_I positively related	S[a]
$H_0$1c:	ITC_FM and BPI_I positively related	S[a]
$H_0$1d:	ITC_TR and BPI_I positively related	S[a]
$H_0$2:	CC_Dist and MS_IT negatively related	S[a]
$H_0$3:	CC_Dist and MS_BPI negatively related	S[a]
$H_0$4a:	ITC_IFC and MS_IT positively related	S[a]
$H_0$4b:	ITC_DI and MS_IT positively related	S[a]
$H_0$4c:	ITC_FM and MS_IT positively related	S[a]
$H_0$4d:	ITC_TR and MS_IT positively related	S[a]
$H_0$5a:	ITC_IFC and CC_Dist negatively related	S[b]
$H_0$5b:	ITC_DI and CC_Dist negatively related	NS
$H_0$5c:	ITC_FM and CC_Dist negatively related	S[a]
$H_0$5d:	ITC_TR and CC_Dist negatively related	NS
$H_0$6:	BPI_I and MS_BPI positively related	S[a]
$H_0$7:	BPI_I and CC_Dist negatively related	S[a]

Note. ITC_IFC = Index of the ITC Interfirm Communication dimension, ITC_DI = Index of the ITC Data Integration dimension, ITC_FM = Index of the ITC IT Facilities and Management dimension, ITC_TR = Index of the ITC Training dimension, BPI_I = BPI Index; MS_IT = Management Support of IT, MS_BPI = Management Support of BPI, CC_DIST = CEO-CIO Distance, NS = Not Significant.
[a] *Significant at $p < 0.01$.* [b] *Significant at $p < 0.05$ (2-tailed).*

are interrelated, and whether associations exist between the former constructs and the IT governance-related constructs of senior management support, and the status of the IT leader within that organization (using CEO-CIO distance as proxy). To fulfill these objectives, nonparametric tests were conducted. The findings are presented in Tables 7 and 8.

Using a nonparametric correlation analysis (Spearman's rho), the associations between the indices of individual dimensions of the ITC construct and the variables representing other constructs were tested. The indices computed for the individual ITC dimensions (namely, ITC_IFC,

ITC_DI, ITC_FM, and ITC_TR) were first correlated to the BPI index (BPI_I), yielding statistical support for hypothesis 1 (refer to Tables 7 and 8 for the findings for $H_0$1a, $H_0$1b, $H_0$1c, $H_0$1d). The relationships between the individual indices of ITC dimensions and the variable of management support of IT projects (MS_IT) were tested, confirming hypothesis 4 (refer to Tables 7 and 8). Then, these indices for individual ITC dimensions were correlated to the variable of CEO-CIO distance (CC_DIST), and it was found that hypothesis 5 was only partially supported. While the negative associations between CC_DIST and ITC_IFC and ITC_FM were statistically supported, the ones between CC_DIST and ITC_DI and ITC_TR were not (Refer to $H_0$5a, $H_0$5b, $H_0$5c, and $H_0$5d in Tables 7 and 8).

Nonparametric correlation analyses were also performed respectively for the relationships between the variables of CEO-CIO distance (CC_Dist), and senior management support of IT projects (MS_IT); between the variables of CEO-CIO distance (CC_Dist), and senior management support of BPI projects (MS_BPI); between the variables of BPI index (BPI_I) and senior management support of BPI projects (MS_BPI); and between the variables of BPI index (BPI_I) and CEO-CIO distance (CC_Dist). The resulting correlation coefficients (Spearman's rho) were statistically significant, hence confirming hypotheses $H_0$2, $H_0$3, $H_0$6, and $H_0$7.

DISCUSSIONS AND IMPLICATIONS

Discussions of Findings

This study demonstrated the positive correlation between the capabilities of individual dimensions of IT infrastructure and the extent of BPI, reinforcing the symbiotic relationship widely discussed in the MIS literature. As an extrapolation from this finding, we would like to point out that the special relationship of these constructs needs to be given special attention. In IT deployment projects, business process issues need be properly managed, or vice versa. As is often discussed in the literature, IT deployment without process amelioration might be a waste of opportunities for efficiency gains and IT investment, as in the cases of implementing an ERP, or a document management/workflows system. On the other hand, IT would give business process redesign initiatives new possibilities in business practice and methods. For instance, the installation of networking and communications facilities (and the Internet) would give a firm the opportunities to reexamine how to organize its

project teams and work processes. Therefore, we incline towards the viewpoint that the role of each of these interacting constructs varies in different situations and according to enterprise objectives. It would be difficult to ascertain the cause–effect relationships between them. Given the mutual influence between IT and business process changes, success factors for both constructs need to be considered thoroughly and managed properly if improvements are to be made to IT and process management practices. Ignoring such factors will render the management model incomplete, thus exposing the project to the risk of failure.

Higher levels of management support and a closer reporting relationship between the CEO and CIO were found to be associated with better performance in BPI, and some dimensions of ITC, as perceived by the respondents. In parallel to these findings, a closer CEO-CIO reporting relationship was also associated with higher levels of senior management support. The statistical results appear to suggest that, regardless of company background, management support and the status of the IT leader (and that of the IT function) are among the key factors to successful outcomes in achieving the objectives of ITC and BPI. The reporting relationship of the CIO is initially dictated by the organizational structure of a company. A closer direct reporting relationship, indicating a senior ranking, might possibly put the CIO in a better position to communicate with and influence senior business executives in comparison to an indirect reporting relationship (Cash et al., 1992; Hambrick, 1981; Jain, 1997). As an executive has said in a survey of CIOs (Field, 2002), whom the CIO reports to does matter a great deal. A CIO who reports directly to the chief executive is perceived as being more important than one who does not, and what he says would therefore carry more weight among the audience (Field, 2002). The findings of this study have shed light on the general belief that positioning the CIO and his or her team prominently in the organization structure may help the organization achieve better performance in IT and BPI projects. The findings of this study are in alignment with the propositions of Ein-Dor and Segev (1978).

The finding that who a CIO reports to is important is also consistent with what has been discussed in the ERP literature (Davenport, 1998; Willcocks & Sykes, 2000). These studies emphasized the importance of the support from senior executives in enterprise-wide projects, which often require changes to boundary-spanning processes. Business leaders should play a key role in mediating between different divisions to defuse difficult political situations concerning the interests of various stakeholders in these cases (Davenport, 1998). It would be of interest to IT practitioners and academic researchers to explore this issue further. However, we need to take note of the other school of thought that considers communication quality and membership in top management team as more important than a formal senior job title (Earl & Feeney, 1994). Earl and Feeney's opinion may not be in conflict with that of the other academics espousing a formal senior hierarchical position for the IT leader. A formal senior position may mean a greater chance to participate in the top management team. Moreover, it must be reminded that a closer reporting relationship in the organizational structure works only if the CIO is in possession of the right attributes to effectively perform his/her job (such as the personality, skills and commitment necessary for building a good and trustful working relationship with the business leaders). Violating this assumption may render the CIO unfit for the organization.

Noteworthy is the attempt in this study to understand and pinpoint the dimensions of the ITC and the extent of BPI constructs. An EFA showed that the latter is unidimensional and the former consists of four dimensions, namely inter-firm communications, data integration, IT facilities and management, and training.

Subsequent to the EFA, this study demonstrated the associations of each dimension of the ITC construct with the BPI construct and

management support of IT projects. That is, the perceived levels in the extent of BPI, and senior management support are related to perceived levels of these individual aspects of IT. The CEO-CIO reporting relationship was found to relate significantly to the ITC dimensions of interfirm communications and IT facilities and management. These showed the associations between the organizational characteristics, particularly the chosen IT governance-related constructs, and enterprise IT capabilities. The reason for the insignificant relationships between the CEO-CIO reporting relationship and the ITC dimensions of data integration and training is unknown. Rather than contributing a speculative explanation, we would like to attribute these findings to data issues, and suggest that these relationships be retested using a different sample. As a consolation, the relationships were supported at the significance level of 0.10, indicating weak associations.

Academic and Professional Contributions

This study contributes to research by gathering empirical evidence on the associations between contextual constructs (such as senior management support and CEO-CIO reporting relationships), and the perceived levels of achievement in the various dimensions of ITC and BPI in Hong Kong-listed and multinational firms operating in Hong Kong and China. The influence of these constructs has been discussed in many studies, in some cases with limited empirical support, or in others with empirical findings that are weak in generalizability. The findings of this survey help fill the gaps that exist in the literature.

Executives and IT leaders are advised to learn to manage organizational constructs in conjunction with their enterprise-wide initiatives of IT adoption and BPI. Such organizational constructs as senior management support and CEO-CIO reporting relationship must be accorded paramount importance and managed cautiously. This also implies that firms that regard IT and business process management as important capabilities should place their CIOs and IT functions in prominent and influential positions (Karimi, Gupta, & Somers, 1996). Moreover, the CIO and CEO should work closely together to produce a synergistic effect on the strategic alignment of business and IT, and in securing support from other senior executives.

While this has important implications for business and IT executives, academic researchers in the disciplines of MIS and business management need to appreciate these findings and view them as pointers to more in-depth studies in the future.

Finally, in this study the concept of the ITC construct was empirically explored and those of its dimensions, comprising not only capabilities in communications and systems management but also those in data integration and training, were identified. An attempt was also made to investigate which of these ITC dimensions were associated with the organizational constructs under study.

Limitations

Although generally accepted guidelines and principles in research were followed in this study (Churchill, 1979; Nunnally, 1978), it has some potential limitations. First, this study relied on the perceptual inputs of the same respondents for the multiple variables in the research model; therefore, the likelihood of common method bias cannot be entirely ruled out. Second, this study is limited by its cross-sectional sample. The empirical findings, therefore, have substantiated correlational, but not necessarily causal relationships. For instance, while it is known that CEO-CIO distance and senior management support are negatively related, it cannot be determined whether higher levels of senior management support are the result of a closer CEO-CIO relationship, or vice versa.

Further Studies

Consequently, it must be added that a longitudinal study would help clarify and reinforce the relationships reported in this study. The findings of this study also point to many opportunities for further research. Practitioner reports have pointed to an upward trend over the last decade of placing the CIO directly under the chief executive (Field, 2002; Rothfeder, 1990). This practice may have hinted that more companies are treating IT as a strategic asset, rather than a cost to an organization. Studies should be conducted to examine whether there exists an association between the positioning of the CIO and the objective of using IT as an enabler of competitive capabilities in the business world as Karimi et al. (1996) suggested. Similarly, it would be of interest to ascertain whether the abovementioned trend in CIO positioning has actually contributed to the effective use of IT in supporting business strategies.

As a last note on the further advancement of MIS research, we would like to advise that academic researchers should continue to strengthen the theoretical explanations for the influence of the organizational constructs mentioned above. On the further development of the ITC construct, we would like to suggest that the ITC items and conceptualised dimensions be validated using another data sample as a further confirmation of its dimensionality. Additional efforts in this area would contribute to the development of a comprehensive standard instrument for measuring ITC that supports repetitive and systematic studies across contexts (Santhanam & Hartono, 2003).

Conclusion

This study has yielded empirical findings that demonstrate the associations between the perceived levels of achievement in some ITC dimensions and the organizational constructs, namely the BPI and IT governance constructs. Such associations may be regarded as hints that it is necessary for firms to properly manage these organizational factors, in the course of planning and executing any IT adoption and business process management initiatives. An in-depth understanding of the influence of various organizational factors may contribute to the further refinement of practice, and to better outcomes in IT adoption and business process management.

ACKNOWLEDGMENT

The authors are grateful to three anonymous referees and Professor Janice Sipior, Associate Editor, for their constructive comments on the earlier version of the manuscript. This research was supported in part by The Hong Kong Polytechnic University.

REFERENCES

Ahituv, N., Neumann, S., & Zviran, M. (2002). A system development methodology for ERP systems. *The Journal of Computer Information Systems, 42*(3), 56-67.

Allen, B. R., & Boynton, A. C. (1991, December). Information architecture: In search of efficient flexibility. *MIS Quarterly,* 435-445.

Anderson, T. J., & Segars, A. H. (2001). The impact of IT on decision structure and firm performance: Evidence from the textile and apparel industry. *Information &Management, 39,* 85-100.

Armstrong, C. P., & Sambamurthy, V. (1999). Information technology assimilation in firms: The influence of senior leadership and IT infrastructures. *Information Systems Research, 10*(4), 304-327.

Bhatt, G. D. (2000). Exploring the relationship between information technology, infrastructure and business process re-engineering. *Business Process Management Journal, 6*(2), 139-163.

Bhatt, G. D. (2001). Business process improvement through electronic data interchange (EDI) systems: An empirical study. *Supply Chain Management: An International Journal, 6* (2) , 60-73.

Bharadwaj, S. (2000). A resource-based perspective on information technology capability and firm performance: An empirical investigation. *MIS Quarterly, 24*(1), 169-196.

Bingi, P., Sharman, M. K., & Godla, J. K. (1999). Critical issues affecting an ERP implementation. *Information Systems Management, 16*(3), 7-14.

Brancheau, J., Janz, J., & Wetherbe, J. (1996). Key issues in information systems: 1994-95 SIM Delphi results. *MIS Quarterly, 20*(2), 225-242.

Byrd, T. A., & Turner, D. E. (2000). Measuring the flexibility of information technology infrastructure: Exploratory analysis of a construct. *Journal of Management Information Systems, 17*(1), 167-208.

Caldeira, M. M., & Ward, J. M. (2002). Understanding the successful adoption and use of IS/IT in SMEs: An explanation from Portuguese manufacturing industries. *Information Systems Journal, 12*(2), 121-152.

Cash, J. L., McFarlan, F. W., Mckinney, J. L., & Applegate, L. M. (1992). *Corporate information systems management text and cases* (3rd ed.), Homewood, IL: Richard D. Irwin.

Chatterjee, D., Grewal, R., & Sambamurthy, V. (2002). Shaping up for e-commerce: Institutional enablers of the organizational assimilation of Web technologies. *MIS Quarterly, 26*(2), 65-89.

Churchill, G. A., Jr. (1979). A paradigm for developing better measures of marketing constructs. *Journal of Marketing Research, 16,* 64-73.

Counihan, A., Finnegan, P., & Sammon, D. (2002). Towards a framework for evaluating investments in data warehousing. *Information Systems Journal, 12,* 321-338.

Dasgupta, S., Sarkis, J., & Talluri, S. (1999). Influence of information technology investment on firm productivity: A cross-sectional study. *Logistics Information Management, 12*(1/2), 120-129.

Davenport, T. H. (1998, July/August). Putting the enterprise into the enterprise systems. *Harvard Business Review,* 121-131.

Dillon, W. R., & Goldstein, M. (1984). *Multivariate analysis: Methods and applications.* New York: Wiley.

Earl, M. J. (1989). *Management strategies for information technology.* Englewood Cliffs, NJ: Prentice Hall.

Earl, M., & Khan, B. (1994). How new is business process redesign? *European Management Journal, 12*(1), 20-30.

Earl, M. J., & Feeney, D. F. (1994, Spring). Is your CIO adding value? *Sloan Management Review,* 11-20.

Ein-Dor, P., & Segev, E. (1978). Organizational context and the success of management information systems. *Management Science, 24*(10), 1064-1077.

Enns, H. G., Huff, S. L., & Higgins, C. A. (2003). CIO lateral influence behaviors: Gaining peers' commitment to strategic information systems. *MIS Quarterly, 27*(1), 155-176.

Feeny, D. F., Edwards, B., & Simpson, K. (1992). Understanding the CEO/CIO relationship. *MIS Quarterly, 16*(4), 435-447.

Field, T. (2002, March 1). The state of the CIO: Executive relationship. *CIO Magazine.* Retrieved August 28, 2004, from *http://www.cio.com/archive/030102/relationships.html*

Grossman, I. (2003, May). Why so many IT projects fail ... and how to find success. *Financial Executives,* 28-29.

Grover, V., Jeong, S. R., Kettinger, W. J., & Teng, J. T. C. (1995). The implementation of business process re-engineering. *Journal of Management Information Systems, 12*(1), 109-144.

Grover, V., Teng, J., Segars, A. H. & Fiedler, K. (1998). The influence of information technology diffusion and business process change on perceived productivity: The IS executive's perspective. *Information & Management, 27,* 141-159.

Gupta, Y. (1991). The chief executive officer and the chief information officer: The strategic partnership. *Journal of Information Technology, 6,* 128-139.

Hambrick, D. C. (1981). Environmental, strategy, and power within top management teams. *Administrative Science Quarterly, 26,* 253-276.

Hammer, M. (1990, July/August). Reengineering work: Don't automate, obliterate. *Harvard Business Review,* 104-112.

Harkness, W. L., Kettinger, W. J., & Segars, A. H. (1996, September). Sustaining process improvement and innovation in the information services function: Lessons learned at the Bose Corporation. *MIS Quarterly,* 349–368.

Hitt, L. M., & Brynjolfsson, E. (1996). Productivity, business profitability, and consumer surplus: Three different measures of information value. *MIS Quarterly, 20*(2), 121-142.

Hu, Q., & Plant, R. (2001). An empirical study of the causal relationship between IT investment and firm performance. *Information Resources Management Journal, 14*(3), 15-26.

Ives, B., & Olson, M. H. (1981). Manager or technician? The nature of the information systems manager's job. *MIS Quarterly, 5*(4), 49-63.

Jain, R. (1997). Key constructs in successful IS implementation: South-East Asian experience. *Omega, 25*(3), 267-284.

Johnson, A. M., & Lederer, A. L. (2003, April). Two predictors of CEO/CIO convergence. *Proceedings of SIGMIS Conference 2003*, 162-167.

Jones, M. C., & Arnett, K. P. (1993). Current practices in management information systems. *Information & Management, 24*(1), 61-69.

Karimi, J., Gupta, Y. P., & Somers, T. M. (1996). The congruence between a firm's competitive strategy and information technology leader's rank and role. *Journal of Management Information Systems, 13*(1), 63-88.

Kerlinger, F. (1973). *Foundations of behavioral research*. Ontario, Canada: Holt, Rinehart and Winston.

Kimberly, J. R., & Evanisko, M. J. (1981). Organizational innovation: The influence of individual organizational and contextual factors on hospital innovation of technological and administrative innovations. *Academy of Management Journal, 24*(4), 689-713.

Kogut, B. (1985, Fall). Designing global strategies: profiting from operational flexibility. *Sloan Management Review*, 27-38.

Li, M. F., & Ye, L. R. (1999). Information technology and firm performance: Linking with environmental, strategic and managerial contexts. *Information & Management, 35*, 43-51.

Lucas, H. C., Jr. (1999). *Information technology and the productivity paradox: Assessing the value of investing in IT*. New York: Oxford University Press.

Mahmood, M. A., & Mann, G. J. (1993). Measuring the organizational impact of information technology investment: An exploratory study. *Journal of Management Information Systems, 10*(1), 97-122.

Marble, R. P. (2003). A system implementation study: Management commitment to project management. *Information & Management, 41*, 111-123.

Mitchell, V. L., & Zmud, R. W. (1999). The effects of coupling IT and work process strategies in redesign projects. *Organization Science, 10*(4), 424-438.

Mitra, S. (2005). Information technology as an enabler of growth in firms: An empirical assessment. *Journal of Management Information Systems, 22*(2), 279-300.

Mudie, M. W., & Schafer, D. J. (1985). An information technology architecture for change. *IBM Systems Journal, 24*(3/4), 307-305.

Nah, F. F., Zuckweiler, K. M., & Lau, J. L. (2003). ERP implementation: Chief information officers' perceptions of critical success factors. *International Journal of Human-Computer Interaction, 16*, 5-22.

Norusis, M. J. (2003). *SPSS 12.0 Statistical Procedure Companion*. Upper Saddle River, NJ: Prentice Hall.

Nunnally, J. (1978). *Psychometric Theory*. New York, NY: McGraw-Hill.

Palvia, P., & Wang, P. (1995). An expanded global information technology issue model: An addition of newly industrialized countries. *The Journal of Information Technology Management, 6*(2), 29-39.

Raghunathan, B., & Raghunathan, T. S. (1993). Does the reporting level of the information systems executive make a difference? *Journal of Strategic Information Systems, 2*(1), 27-38.

Rockart, J. F., Bullen, C. V., & Ball, L. (1982). Future role of the information systems executives [Special issue]. *MIS Quarterly, 6,* 1-14.

Ross, J. W., & Weill, P. (2002, November). Six IT decisions your IT people shouldn't make. *Harvard Business Review*, 85-91.

Rothfeder, J. (1990, February 26). CIO is starting to stand for "career is over." *Business Week*, p. 78.

Runyan, L. (1990, April 1). Borderless banking draws IS interest. *Datamation*, pp. 98-100.

Sakaguchi, T., & Dibrell, C. C. (1998). Measurement of the intensity of global information technology usage: Quantitizing the value of a firm's information technology.*Industrial Management & Data Systems, 8,* 380-394.

Sambamurthy, V., & Zmud, R. W. (1999). Arrangements for information technology governance: A theory of multiple contingencies. *MIS Quarterly, 23*(2), 261-290.

Santhanam, R., & Hartono, E. (2003). Issues in linking information technology capability to firm performance. *MIS Quarterly, 27*(1), 125-143.

Spewak, S. H., & Hill, S. C. (1993). *Enterprise architecture planning*. Boston: QED.

Spitze, J. M. (2001, February 1). Inside a global system failure. *CIO Magazine.*

Stock, G. N., Greis, N. P., & Kasarda, J. D. (1998). Logistics, strategy and structure: A conceptual framework. *International Journal of Operations and Production Management, 18*(1), 37-52.

Stoddard, D. B., & Jarvenpaa, S. L. (1995). Business process redesign: Tactics for managing radical change. *Journal of Management Information Systems, 12*(1), 81-107.

Strassmann, P. A. (1994, September 15). CIOs should get back to basics. *Datamation*, 70-72.

Strassmann, P. A. (2002). *The persistence of the computer paradox: A critique of efforts to disprove the computer paradox*. New Canaan: Information Economic Press.

Sumner, M. (2000). Risk factors in enterprise-wide/ERP projects. *Journal of Information Technology, 15,* 317-327.

Swanson, E. B. (1994, September). Information systems innovation among organizations. *Management Science*, 1069-1093.

Teng, J. T. C., Fiedler, K. D., & Grover, V. (1998). An exploratory study of the influence of the IS function and organizational context on business process re-engineering project initiatives. *Omega, 26*(6), 679-698.

Tracey, M., Vonderembse, M. A., & Lim, J. S. (1999). Manufacturing technology and strategy formulation: Keys to enhancing competitiveness and improving performance. *Journal of Operations Management, 17,* 411-428.

Watson, R. (1990). Influences on the IS manager's perceptions of key issues: Information scanning and the relationship with the CEO. *MIS Quarterly, 14*(2), 217-232.

Weill, P., & Broadbent, M. (1999). Four views of IT infrastructure: Implications for IT investments. In L. P. Willcocks & S. Lester (Eds.), *Beyond the IT productivity paradox*. Chichester, UK: Wiley.

Willcocks, L. P., & Sykes, R. (2000). The role of the CIO and IT function in ERP. *Communications of the ACM, 43*(4), 32-38.

Wixom, B. H., & Watson, H. J. (2001). An empirical investigation of the factors affecting data warehousing success. *MIS Quarterly, 25*(1), 17-41.

Wu, I. L. (2002). A model for implementing BPR based on strategic perspectives: An empirical study. *Information & Management, 39,* 313-324.

This work was previously published in Information Resources Management Journal, Vol. 20, Issue 4, edited by M. Khosrow-Pour, pp. 25-47, copyright 2007 by IGI Publishing, formerly known as Idea Group Publishing (an imprint of IGI Global).

Chapter XXVI
Technology Trends in Knowledge Management Tools

Gilles Balmisse
KnowledgeConsult, France

Denis Meingan
KnowledgeConsult, France

Katia Passerini
New Jersey Institute of Technology, USA

ABSTRACT

A large number of tools are available in the software industry to support different aspects of knowledge management (KM). Some comprehensive applications and vendors try to offer global solutions to KM needs; other tools are highly specialized. In this paper, state-of-the-art KM tools grouped by specific classification areas and functionalities are described. Trends and integration efforts are detailed with a focus on identifying current and future software and market evolution.

BACKGROUND AND DEFINITIONS: A FOCUS ON PEOPLE AND CONTEXT

This paper focuses on presenting the variety of tools currently available to support KM initiatives and discusses trends in the vendors' arena. However, there are many definitions of knowledge (financial, human resources, information systems, organizational behavior, and strategic management-based definitions) (Alavi & Leidner, 1999) that have resulted in equally many definitions of KM (Davenport & Prusak, 1998; Jennex, 2005). There are many definitions of knowledge (financial, human resources, information systems,

Table 1. Knowledge and context relationships

Relationships		Definitions	Examples
K= I x U where	K= Knowledge I = Information U = Use	**Knowledge** *(Interiorized information put to action)* ⇑	I am in Paris today (*user context*) ⇓ I am going to wear a coat.
I = D x C where	I = Information D = Data C = Context	**Information** *(Data in context)* ⇑	The temperature is 10^0 Celsius today in Paris
		Data *(Raw facts)*	10^0 Celsius

organizational behavior, and strategic management-based definitions) (Alavi and Leidner, 1999) that have resulted in equally many definitions of knowledge management (KM) (Davenport and Prusak, 1998; Jennex, 2005). This paper focuses on presenting the variety of tools currently available to support KM initiatives and discusses trends in the vendors' arena. To place the discussion and classification of the tools within the specific framework and organizational view embraced by the authors, an operationa To place the discussion and classification of the tools within the specific framework and organizational view embraced by the authors, an operational definition of knowledge as *information accumulated and assimilated to implement a specific action* is used. Information is *data within a specific context* and data is the *raw facts, without context* (Binney, 2001; Cohen, 1998; Davenport & Harris, 2001). Table 1 summarizes the relationships among the definitions and provides a practical example to illustrate the link between data, information, and knowledge.

The example in Table 1 embeds a clear distinction: information is not transformed into knowledge unless it is accumulated, learned, and internalized by individuals. In addition, it needs to be translated into specific actions. The transformation of information into knowledge is

mediated by the "individual actor," who adds value to information by creating knowledge (Davenport & De Long, 1998; Kwan & Cheung, 2006). Thus, knowledge is strictly linked and connected to the individual (or group) who creates it, which may cast doubts on the ability of information systems tools to effectively support KM and perhaps explain some of the failures of the early tools (Biloslavo, 2005; Chua & Lam, 2005).

It follows that the "visible" part of knowledge—what the literature calls explicit as opposed to the tacit dimension of knowledge (Polanyi, 1966)—is only information regardless of the amount of other individual or project knowledge embedded into it. Therefore, the tools to collect, catalogue, organize, and share knowledge can only transfer information (the explicit knowledge) embedded in various forms and types of documents and media. When the transferred information is put back in the context of the individual recipient, its re-transformation occurs when the object of the transfer is put into action.

Figure 1 diagrams this distinction, giving to information systems a specific transfer or transportation role, rather than a substantial knowledge creation capability. Based on the definitions presented in Table 1, the roles of information management and KM are clearly distinct, even if

Figure 1. Information systems and knowledge transfer

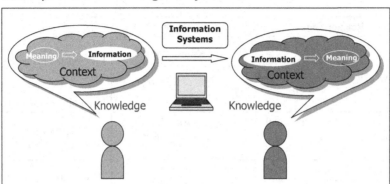

interconnected. The tools for information management are focused on data and information transfer; the tools for KM are focused on assimilation, comprehension, and learning of the information by individuals who will, then, transform data and information into knowledge.

The key difference between information and KM is the role played by the individual actors (Adamides & Karacapilidis, 2006; Davenport & Jarvenpaa, 1996; Frank & Gardoni, 2005). KM places people at the center, while information management focuses on the information infrastructure (Janev & Vranes, 2005; Ruiz-Mercader & Merono-Cerdan, 2006); KM focuses on people and their role in the organization. The first failed attempts at KM focused too heavily on tools (and the IT function often led the implementation of KM in organizations) (Davenport & Prusak, 1998). Finally, we have better understood the role played by people and brought back KM into human resources and strategic/leadership management realms (Biloslavo, 2005; Lyons, 2005).

Knowledge Management Tools Characteristics

Within the aforementioned premises, a KM tool will focus on facilitating individual continuous learning, use, and contextualization of organiza-

tional knowledge embedded in people and documents (Alavi & Leidner, 2001). This leads to at least four key functional requirements for KM tools: (1) facilitate information contextualization; (2) intelligently transfer information; (3) facilitate social interactions and networking; and (4) present a customized human-computer interface that meets user needs.

1. **Facilitate information contextualization.** Nonaka and Konno (1998) discuss the concept of "ba" or shared understanding and shared context. Individuals assimilate information much faster when presented in a familiar context. To facilitate *information contextualization*, metadata on its characteristics and integration within a specific environment must be attached to it before storing. This facilitates easier retrieval and management for the knowledge seeker. Past approaches to full text-based searches on documents yielded limited success, specifically when multiple media formats are stored. In addition, they yielded limited results as they decoupled the document from the context and taxonomy it belonged to. Better results are more often associated with access to the conceptual representa-

tion, structure, and links associated with the retrieved documents (Jarvenpaa & Staples, 2000; Turnbow & Kasianovitz, 2005). Sophisticated clustering and indexing search engines, like Vivisimo (www.vivisimo.com), are representative examples in this category.

2. **Intelligently transfer information.** The transfer of information needs to be aligned with its intended use (Bhatt & Gupta, 2005). Especially in liability issues that may emerge when the information is decoupled from the context where it is accumulated and transferred (Zhao & Bi, 2006), it is important to implement what we call *"intelligent transfer"* (Junghagen & Linderoth, 2003) Information transfer must occur by taking into account the user, the content, and the time of transfer. A tool that can optimize these three aspects can truly provide information according to the needs of the users, respecting one of the key functional foundations of KM (Argote & Ingram, 2000; Kwan & Cheung, 2006). More development is needed in this area, although upcoming location-aware applications are emerging.

3. **Facilitate social interactions and networking.** Direct communication and verbal knowledge transfer through *social interactions* among individuals is the most natural aspect of knowledge sharing (Huysman & Wulf, 2006). A KM tool must support this social aspect and facilitate exchanges. However, traditional group support tools designed to accomplish a specific objective or task (such as a project) may be ill suited to recreate the spontaneous milieu for the information and knowledge exchanges, which are important to knowledge creation. Digital socialization tools need to encourage spontaneous as well as casual meetings with multiple views and interactions. Research on ubiquitous social computing (Snowdon & Churchill, 2004) is trying to address these specific needs by creating ad hoc, location–aware, social interaction systems within university campuses. A KM tool that can informally and formally support social interactions needs to accommodate both individual and community synchronous and asynchronous discussions; enable peer reviewing and responses; discussions rankings; and support the management of social

Figure 2. KM tools framework

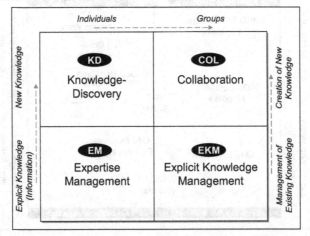

network representations and interactions (Van Der Aalst, Reijers et al., 2005).

4. **Present a customized human-computer interface.** The tools must also support *interface customization* and ease of use. The human-computer interface ease of use and usability will drive intention to use and reuse the tools (Jarvenpaa & Staples, 2000; Turnbow & Kasianovitz, 2005). The establishment of swift trust (Hiltz & Goldman, 2005), the error-free interface; the coherent structure and organization will also impact reuse. In addition, the application interface should also be supportive of ergonomics principles and be sociable. Finally, for the tools to support learning and utilization, they must also be geared to providing visual representations and maps linking taxonomies and documents.

Parallel to the aforementioned roles, which are meant to support individual use, a KM application needs to be designed to sustain KM implementations within the organization. This includes managing existing knowledge and sup-

porting the creation of new knowledge. This process is embedded and thrives on information that is transferred from individuals to groups with a continuous transformation of information into knowledge through contextualization and knowledge discovery.

Figure 2 presents roles and actors linked to KM tools in enterprises and highlights their functions. As described earlier, information is converted into knowledge by individuals and groups, who are the core of the information-to-knowledge transformation process (Rollett, 2003). These tools support KM and new knowledge creation by focusing on:

- *Management of explicit knowledge (EKM),* with specific focus on the compilation, organization, replenishment, and use of the knowledge base. Compilation and capture of knowledge includes facilitating the creation and publication of information in shared areas. Organization requires structuring information based on taxonomies and ontologies that facilitate document mapping. Replenishment and use (and re-use) can be

Figure 3. KM tools clusters

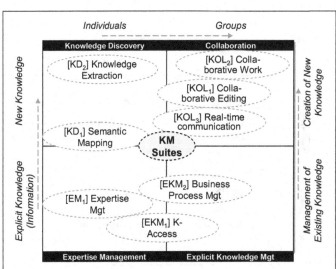

supported by providing users with tools to add comments on how the information was used and contribute to future uses. Case-based reasoning can be also implemented in repositories to support the resolution of future problems.

- *Knowledge discovery (KD)* through the uncovering of unexploited information stored in large databases. This includes text analysis and mining; knowledge extraction and automatic classification and visualization of patterns; and use of semantic mapping to link documents.

- *Expertise mapping (EM)* tools that link and facilitate knowledge exchanges within the enterprise. These tools go well beyond facilitating finding the right resources (as in employees' directories) because they dynamically ease contacts, follow ups, and communication.

- *Collaboration tools (COL)* for the production of knowledge, coordination, and communication. The production activities provide a static view of the results of team interactions and lessons learned after the exchange. The collaboration activities are more dynamic and support the definition of actors and roles, activities, and tasks throughout the duration of a project. Lastly, communication spaces facilitate direct exchanges among users and, therefore, are important new knowledge creation areas.

Table 1.

Tools for knowledge access		
Vendors	**Applications**	**Web Link**
Fast	Fast ESP	www.fastsearch.com
Convera	RetrievalWare 8	www.convera.com
Entopia	K-Bus	www.entopia.com
Exaled	Exaled Corporate	www.exalead.fr
Autonomy Verity	Idol K2	www.autonomy.com

Table 2.

Tools for semantic mapping		
Vendors	**Applications**	**Web Link**
Anacubis	Anacubis Connect	www.anacubis.com
Inxight	VizServer	www.inxight.com
Kartoo	KartooKM	www.kartoo.net
MapStan –Amoweba	mapStan	www.amoweba.com
Ontologies		
Cerebra	Cerebra suite	www.cerebra.com
Mondeca	ITM	www.mondeca.com
Ontopia	Knowledge suite (OKS 3.0)	www.ontopia.com
SchemaLogic	Enterprise suite	www.schemalogic.com

An Overview of KM Tools

A number of tools are currently available to support the functionalities and processes described. Some tools are highly specialized while others try to offer comprehensive solutions to the enterprise. This section briefly lists and describes the tools; the next section provides a brief synthesis of key market trends. Figure 3 presents a summary of the key categories of KM tools and functionalities. The tools are clustered based on the framework presented in Figure 2.

Tools to Access Knowledge [EKM$_1$]

These tools provide access to explicit knowledge that can be shared and transferred through the enterprise information systems. They rely on powerful indexing systems, including systems to classify expertise based on both content and collaboration dynamics and networks within the enterprise (e.g., Entopia K-Bus). Please see Table 1.

Tools for Semantic Mapping [KD$_1$]

Semantic mapping is emerging as a fundamental instrument to make sense out of the vast amount of data and information available in increasingly large repositories (Davies & Duke, 2005). Semantic mapping tools are meant to quickly support presentation of information, analysis, and decision making. The extent of interaction with the knowledge map varies by tools, with some tools being mostly static visualizations and others allowing continuous and dynamic interactivity by changing the data views. For example, KartooKM provides many different views from centric mapping; to clustering; topographical maps; interactive trees; closeness and social networks maps; circular maps; and animated charts. Ontology tools are also part of this category as they enable users to organize information and knowledge by groups and schemata that represent the organizational

knowledge base (e.g., Ontopia Knowledge Suite, OKS 3.0) (Parpola, 2005). Please see Table 2.

Tools for Knowledge Extraction [KD$_2$]

Tools for knowledge extraction support structured queries and replies. They help mining text by interpreting relationships among different elements and documents. Therefore, they help the knowledge seeker in identifying the exact document and the other documents related to his/her queries (e.g., vivisimo.com clustering), resulting in structured and more articulated answers. Some sophisticated data and text analysis tools also support the identification of relationships among concepts, using sound and rigorous statistical association rules (e.g., SPSS). Please see Table 3.

Tools for Expertise Localization [EM$_1$]

These tools enable quickly locating the knowledge holders in the enterprise and facilitating collaboration and knowledge exchanges (Huysman & Wulf, 2006). Therefore, they are focused on going beyond simple directories by enabling users to easily capture and organize the results of their project interactions (Coakes & Bradburn, 2005) by quickly locating project expertise and enabling re-use and innovation (e.g., Kankoon Skol). Please see Table 4.

Tools for Collaborative Editing and Publishing [COL$_1$]

Tools like Vignette and DocuShare enable collaborative editing of documents and the management of the entire document publication cycle. They include systems for document management within the enterprise, as well as more flexible systems such as Wikis and Blog creation tools (like the Movable Type software that enables users to share public spaces within company servers for discussion, comments, and knowledge exchanges) (Frumkin, 2005). Please see Table 5.

Table 3.

Tools for knowledge extraction		
Vendors	**Applications**	**Web Link**
ClearForest	ClearForest Text Analysis Suite	www.clearforest.com
Intelliseek	Enterprise Mining Suite	www.intellisik.com
Insight	InsightSmartDiscovery	www.inxight.com
Lingway	Lingway KM	www.lingway.com
Temis	Inxight Discovery Extractor	www.temis-group.com
Relationship discovery		
Grimmersoft	WordMapper	www.grimmersoft.com
SPSS	LexiQuest Mine	www.spss.com

Table 4.

Tools for expertise localization		
Vendors	**Applications**	**Web Link**
Agilence	Expertise Finder	www.agilence.com
Kankoon	Kankoon Skol	www.kankoon.com
Tacit	ActiveNet	www.tacit.com

Table 5.

Tools for collaborative editing		
Vendors	**Applications**	**Web Link**
Interwoven	TeamSite6	www.interwoven.com
Open Source	Drupal	www.drupal.org
Six Apart	Movable Type	www.movabletype.org
Vignette	Vignette V7 Content Services	www.vignette.com/fr/
Xerox	DocuShare4	http://docushare.xerox.com/

Table 6.

Tools for collaborative work		
Vendors	**Applications**	**Web Link**
EMC – Documentum	eRoom	www.documentum.com/eroom
IBM / Lotus	QuickPlace	www.lotus.com
Affinitiz	Affinitiz	www.affinitiz.com
Microsoft	SharePoint Services	www.microsoft.com
One2Team	One2Team Pro	www.one2team.com
Tomoye	Simplify 4.0	www.tomoye.com

Table 7.

Tools for real time collaboration		
Vendors	**Applications**	**Web Link**
Marratech	Marratech e-Meeting Portal	www.marratech.com
Microsoft	Live Communication 2003	www.microsoft.com
Microsoft	Windows Messenger	www.microsoft.com
WebEx	Meeting Center	www.webex.com
Yahoo	Yahoo Messenger	www.yahoo.com

Table 8.

Tools for business process management		
Vendors	**Applications**	**Web Link**
Boc	Adonis	www.boc-eu.com
IDS Sheer	Aris Process Platform	www.ids-scheer.com
Mega	Mega Process	www.mega.com
Workflows		
FileNet	Business Process Manager	www.filenet.com
TIBCO	Staffware Process Suite	www.tibco.com
W4	W4	www.w4.fr

Table 9.

Global Solutions and Suites		
Vendors	**Applications**	**Web Link**
Ardans	Knowledge Maker	www.ardans.fr
Thalès-Arisem	KM Server	www.arisem.com
Knowesis	Athanor	www.knowesis.fr
Knowings	Knowledge Manager	www.knowings.com
Sharing Knowledge	SK2	www.sharing.com
Portals		
Autonomy	Portal in a Box	www.autonomy.com
HummingBird	Humming Enterprise	www.hummingbird.com
IBM	Suite Lotus	www.ibm.fr
OpenText	LiveLink	www.opentext.com
Oracle	Enterprise Manager, Collaboration Suite, Data Hub	www.oracle.com
Plumtree	Enterprise Web Suite	www.plumtree.com
Vignette	Vignette V7	www.vignette.com

Tools for Collaborative Work [COL₂]

These tools enable teams to globally share dedicated spaces for managing the project lifecycle; editing and publishing materials; conducting live discussions and interactions; and maintaining a repository of materials associated with every step of the process (Frank & Gardoni, 2005). For example, using MS SharePoint servers, teams can quickly create password-managed and secure project areas and follow the lifecycle of document creation and exchanges. Other tools (e.g., Tomoye Simplify) are focused on bringing together and facilitating the work of communities of practice (Coulson-Thomas, 2005). Please see Table 6.

Tools for Real Time Communication [COL₃]

These tools overlap with some of the functionalities of the previous category. However, they are specifically focused on live communication exchanges, whiteboarding, and file sharing (e.g., Meeting Center, Yahoo Messenger). Please see Table 7.

Tools for Business Process Management [EKM₂]

These tools can be split into applications for process modeling and tools for workflow management. Process modeling tools focus on designing and optimizing processes (Gronau & Muller, 2005). They formalize and define the elements of the process, assign actors to roles, and identify data sources and flows within the processes (Hlupic, 2003). For example, the Aris Process Platform provides modules for the strategic, tactical, operational, and measurement tasks related to process management. Workflow specific tools, such as Staffware Process suite, are focused on the management of the rules and execution of enterprise processes. They also automate specific

operational and analytical steps around the process deployment. Please see Table 8.

Global Knowledge Management Solutions

Applications in this category are divided in software suites dedicated to KM, such as Knowledge Manager and SK2, and enterprise portal solutions that provide modular applications. For example, portal packages provide collaboration modules; content management; access to repositories and information; process management; text mining; and business intelligence (e.g., Lotus Suites; Plumtree Enterprise Web Suite). Please see Table 9.

Key Trends and Perspectives in KM Tools

Information systems have continued to evolve and change their role to better respond to the needs of organizations. Until recently, organizations have used information technology to support information management (Ruiz-Mercader & Merono-Cerdan, 2006; Schultze & Leidner, 2002). Therefore, organizational systems have been information bound and information centric. Today, we have a better understanding that for information to be effectively used by individuals, information systems need to be more people centric and support specific individual needs.

To better leverage the knowledge of individuals in organizations, firms need to understand that employees' daily activities are tightly interconnected to other people and processes in the organization. Therefore, firms need a support system for "the group," rather than an information system designed for individual and autonomous work. In few words, the paradigm needs to shift from an individualistic view of information systems to a collective and collaborative view. For this reason, ubiquitous social computing models (Snowdon & Churchill, 2004) are emerging in several organizations. Many KM tools have been traditionally used in an isolated interaction between the individual and the tool. The new KM logic implies that these tool be seamlessly integrated to manage group discussions, be used by groups, and foster a mix of face-to-face and distant collaboration. The boundaries of collaboration within the enterprise need to evolve. Three key trends are related to this transition.

First, starting from 2002, we have observed a convergence of KM tools (Edwards & Shaw, 2005) through mergers and acquisitions. Market share of pure communication players have become scarce and communication management has been complemented with content management solutions. Or, communication solutions have been integrated with other platforms to support existing tasks (for example, eBay acquisition of Skype to integrate VoIP in the auction transactions). These consolidations have attempted to provide an operational answer to firms faced with capturing the value of current communication interactions by quickly and clearly organizing, storing, and sorting the results of the exchanges through electronic document management solutions. Several vendors of document management solutions have added communication capabilities. Documentum (today part of EMC) bought e-Room; Interwoven acquired i-Manage; and Vignette acquired Intraspect. Following the same trends, actors in the collaboration arena have expanded into the document management realm. IBM/Lotus with Abtrix and Open Text with Ixos.

Second, the concepts of networked enterprises and collaboration have been augmented with the need for exchanges while multitasking. Users will not need to quit the applications they are currently using to augment their work with a synchronous communication component. These components will be easily integrated within the user workspace; will be highly interoperable; and information will be easily transferred across tools and applications. For example, Microsoft offers an integrated SharePoint solution that communi-

cates with office productivity tools (supported by .NET server solutions). IBM/Lotus is also moving quickly in this area with the Lotus Sametime integration of instant messaging, conferencing, and project spaces with Websphere Portal Server. These platforms are tightly integrated with the proprietary systems they interface with. However even if IBM and Microsoft hold a market advantage in this area, recent trends in the open source market are promoting standardization and alternative interoperable solutions that can be integrated across platforms.

Third, most of the emerging communication needs are focused on supporting individuals in managing communications and collaboration schedules, needs, and requirements. Tools need to integrate with personal information management systems (PIMs) and multiple hardware platforms (PDAs and Smartphone) in order to provide ubiquitous connectivity to an increasingly mobile workforce.

SUMMARY AND CONCLUSION

In this paper, we provided a summary overview of the types, functionalities, and clustering of KM solutions. Technical, organizational, and individual factors contribute to knowledge creation. From the technical standpoint, the KM tools need to demonstrate that they are beneficial to the organization, at least based on usage statistics. From the organizational standpoint, the tools must be supplemented with workplace changes that promote knowledge sharing and dissemination through the new platforms, for example, rewarding peer ranking and documents use as practiced by Infosys (Chatterjee & Watson, 2005; Kochikar & Suresh, 2004; Mehta & Mehta, 2005). Lastly, individuals must feel secure that participation and utilization of the tools is not targeted at personnel reduction; rather at personnel enhancement and long-term leadership and growth.

It is the mix of the aforementioned factors, coupled with a clear understanding of the market, the tools, and the drivers for a savvy selection of applications aligned with business needs, which may ultimately support successful KM initiatives.

ACKNOWLEDGMENT

An earlier version of this paper was presented at the 2006 University of Tunis-Carthage (UTC) Knowledge Management Forum. Sincere thanks to the UTC conference organizers and Dr. Murray Jennex for the opportunity expand this work for consideration in the *International Journal of Knowledge Management*.

REFERENCES[1]

Adamides, E. D., & Karacapilidis, N. (2006). Information technology support for the knowledge and social processes of innovation management. *Technovation, 26*(1), 50-59.

Alavi, M., & Leidner, D. E. (1999). Knowledge management systems: Issues, challenges and benefits. *Communications of AIS, 1,* 1-37.

Alavi, M., & Leidner, D. E. (2001). Review: Knowledge management and knowledge management systems: Conceptual foundations and research issues. *MIS Quarterly, 25*(1), 107-136.

Argote, L., & Ingram, P. (2000). Knowledge transfer: A basis for competitive advantage in firms. *Organizational Behavior and Human Decision Processes, 82*(1), 150-169.

Bhatt, G. D., & Gupta, J. N. D. (2005). Interactive patterns of knowledge management in organizations: Insight from a fashion company. *International Journal of Information Technology and Management, 4*(3), 231-243.

Biloslavo, R. (2005). Use of the knowledge management framework as a tool for innovation capability audit. *International Journal of Innovation and Learning, 2*(4), 402-424.

Binney, D. (2001). The knowledge management spectrum—Understanding the KM landscape. *Journal of Knowledge Management, 5*(1), 33-42.

Chatterjee, D., & Watson, R. (2005*)*. Infosys technologies limited. Unleashing CIMBA. *Journal of Cases on Information Technology, 7*(4), 127-142

Chua, A., & Lam, W. (2005). Why KM projects fail: A multi-case analysis. *Journal of Knowledge Management, 9*(3), 6-17.

Coakes, E., & Bradburn, A. (2005). *Knowledge management in a project climate.* Hershey, PA: Idea Group Publishing.

Cohen, D. (1998). Toward a knowledge context: Report on the first annual U.C. Berkeley forum on knowledge and the firm. *California Management Review, 40*(3), 22-39.

Coulson-Thomas, C. (2005). Using job support tools to increase workgroup performance. *International Journal of Productivity and Performance Management, 54*(3), 206-211.

Davenport, T. H., & De Long, D. W. (1998). Successful knowledge management projects. *Sloan Management Review, 39*(2), 43-57.

Davenport, T. H., & Harris, J. G. (2001). Data to knowledge to results: Building an analytic capability. *California Management Review, 43*(2), 117-138.

Davenport, T. H., & Jarvenpaa, S. L. (1996). Improving knowledge work processes. *Sloan Management Review, 37*(4), 53-65.

Davenport, T. H., & Prusak, L. (1998). *Working knowledge: How organizations manage what they know.* Boston: Harvard Business School.

Davies, J., & Duke, A. (2005). Next generation knowledge access. *Journal of Knowledge Management, 9*(5), 64-84.

Edwards, J. S., & Shaw, D. (2005). Knowledge management systems: Finding a way with technology. *Journal of Knowledge Management, 9*(1), 113-125.

Frank, C., & Gardoni, M. (2005). Information content management with shared ontologies—At corporate research centre of EADS. *International Journal of Information Management, 25*(1), 55-70.

Frumkin, J. (2005). The Wiki and the digital library. *OCLC Systems and Services, 21*(1), 18-22.

Gronau, N., & Muller, C. (2005). KMDL capturing, analyzing and improving knowledge-intensive business processes. *Journal of Universal Computer Science, 11*(4), 452-472.

Hiltz, S. R., & Goldman, R. (2005). *Learning together online. Research on asynchronous learning.* Mahwah, NJ: Lawrence Erlbaum Associates.

Hlupic, V. (2003). *Knowledge and business process management.* Hershey, PA: Idea Group Publishing.

Huysman, M., & Wulf, V. (2006). IT to support knowledge sharing in communities, towards a social capital analysis. *Journal of Information Technology, 21*(1), 40-51.

Janev, V., & Vranes, S. (2005). The role of knowledge management solutions in enterprise business processes. *Journal of Universal Computer Science, 11*(4), 526-545.

Jarvenpaa, S. L., & Staples, D. S. (2000). The use of collaborative electronic media for information sharing: An exploratory study of determinants. *Journal of Strategic Information Systems, 9*(2-3), 129-154.

Jennex, M. E. (2005). What is Knowledge Management? *International Journal of Knowledge Management, 1*(4), i-iv.

Junghagen, S., & Linderoth, H. C. J. (2003). *Intelligent management in the knowledge economy.* Cheltenham, UK; Northampton, MA: Edward Elgar.

Kochikar, V. P., & Suresh, J. K. (2004). *Towards a knowledge-sharing organization. Some challenges faced on the Infosys journey.* Hershey, PA: Idea Group Publishing.

Kwan, M. M., & Cheung, P.-K. (2006). The knowledge transfer process: From field studies to technology development. *Journal of Database Management, 17*(1), 16-32.

Lyons, P. (2005). A robust approach to employee skill and knowledge development. *Industrial and Commercial Training, 37*(1), 3-9.

Mehta, N., & Mehta, A. (2005). *Infosys technologies, limited.* Hershey, PA: Idea Group.

Nonaka, I., & Konno, N. (1998). The concept of "ba": Building a foundation for knowledge creation. *California Management Review, 40*(3), 40-54.

Parpola, P. (2005). Inference in the SOOKAT object-oriented knowledge acquisition tool. *Knowledge and Information Systems, 8*(3), 310-329.

Polanyi, M. (1966). *The tacit dimension.* London: Routledge and Kegan Paul.

Rollett, H. (2003). *Knowledge management: Processes and technologies.* Boston: Kluwer Academic.

Ruiz-Mercader, J., & Merono-Cerdan, A. L. (2006). Information technology and learning: Their relationship and impact on organizational performance in small businesses. *International Journal of Information Management, 26*(1), 16-29.

Schultze, U., & Leidner, D. E. (2002). Studying knowledge management in information systems research: Discourses and theoretical assumptions. *MIS Quarterly, 26*(3), 213-242.

Snowdon, D. N., & Churchill, E. F. (2004). *Inhabited information spaces: Living with your data.* London; New York: Springer.

Turnbow, D., & Kasianovitz, K. (2005). Usability testing for Web redesign: A UCLA case study. *OCLC Systems and Services, 21*(3), 226-234.

Van der Aalst, W. M. P., Reijers, H. A., Song. (2005). Discovering social networks from event logs. *Computer Supported Cooperative Work (CSCW) An International Journal, 14*(6), 549-593.

Zhao, J. L., & Bi, H. H. (2006). Process-driven collaboration support for intra-agency crime analysis. *Decision Support Systems, 41*(3), 616-633.

ENDNOTE

[1]   Please note all hyperlinks are valid as of January 2007

This work was previously published in International Journal of Knowledge Management, Vol. 3, Issue 2, edited by M. E. Jennex, pp. 118-131, copyright 2007 by IGI Publishing, formerly known as Idea Group Publishing (an imprint of IGI Global).

Index